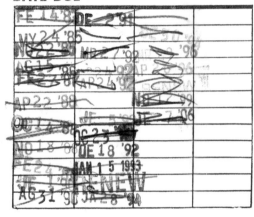

ARCHITECTURAL DRAFTING

FUNCTIONAL PLANNING AND CREATIVE DESIGN

SECOND EDITION

GEORGE K. STEGMAN
HARRY J. STEGMAN

american
technical
publishers, inc. alsip, illinois 60658

preface to the second edition

The new Second Edition of *Architectural Drafting: Functional Planning and Creative Design* has been completely updated in all chapters and the presentation of the material has been reorganized to better orient the coverage to professional needs. In addition, a wealth of new material has been added to cover the latest in architectural practices and building methods and materials, including photos illustrating pre-fabricated building sections, modular construction, and other modern building techniques.

A new chapter on *Sketching,* Chapter 2, has been added. Chapters on *Architectural Office Practice,* Chapter 17, and *Building Material Sizes,* Chapter 18, have been added and a new appendix has been included on *Metric Measurements in the Building Industry.* This appendix is much more than a mere explanation of metrics. It presents actual examples of designing and building to metric standards and to metric modules as now practiced in the United Kingdom. We believe this material is unique in architectural textbooks produced in the United States.

The Chapter on *Light Commercial Build-ing,* Chapter 20, has been greatly expanded to cover light and medium heavy construction in more depth and detail. The last chapter in the Second Edition, Chapter 21, *Sheet Check List* contains an entirely new and updated set of actual working drawings in contemporary style.

As in the First Edition, the student using this book will examine step-by-step procedures following the actual work of the practicing professional, and in so doing will gain a professional feel for the job. The illustrations and examples used throughout the book have been tested on students in the authors' classes, and many of these students have won top honors in state and national competition.

THE PUBLISHERS

contents

Lettering is an ancient art. This tablet from Ur, shown in obverse and reverse, is dated circa 2062 B.C.

Architectural Lettering

Lettering is thought to have been one of the earliest means of decoration used in architecture. The Romans, for example, adorned tombs, buildings, and arches with their style of lettering, the **Old Roman** alphabet. Our modern **Roman** alphabet is a direct outgrowth of the Old Roman alphabet. An example of today's use of the Old Roman style alphabet is shown in Fig. 1-1. The proper letter proportions and the relationships of curves to the height of the letters in the Roman alphabet is shown in Fig. 1-2.

Lettering

Frequently the question is asked: "Why does the lettering on an architectural drawing have to be so distinctive?" Architecture, by its nature, is one of the few creative areas where the designer thoroughly leaves his mark. Certainly there are many areas of creative endeavor in our technological world, where man is involved in design, but perhaps none as individual as the field of architecture. Generally in our day to day lives products that are mass-produced and mass-consumed bear few well-known marks of the designer.

Architecture by its very existence and philosophy is free, creative and individualistic. Great architects, such as Wright, Gropius, Stone, and Yamasaki, to mention only a few, have left their imprint on structures they have designed. As this is true of the great, to a lesser extent it is true as well of those architects and designers who have not achieved as high a degree of renown.

Because the architect is an individual originator of style, he takes license with his lettering to reflect the nature of his vocation. This may well be the reason why lettering on an architectural drawing does not adhere to the standard engineering single stroke gothic style. A distinctive style of lettering is adopted by each man on the board as he recreates the spirit of architecture. Architectural lettering is one means by which the architect or draftsman expresses his individuality. For this reason "lettering" has been placed at the beginning of this book since it is an introduction to an interesting and creative field.

The style of letter chosen for drawings

MINORU YAMASAKI AND ASSOCIATES, BIRMINGHAM, MICHIGAN.

Fig. 1-1. Architect Minoru Yamasaki used Old Roman lettering in the design of the McGregor Memorial building at Wayne State University.

McGREGOR MEMORIAL

WAYNE STATE UNIVERSITY, DETROIT, MICHIGAN.

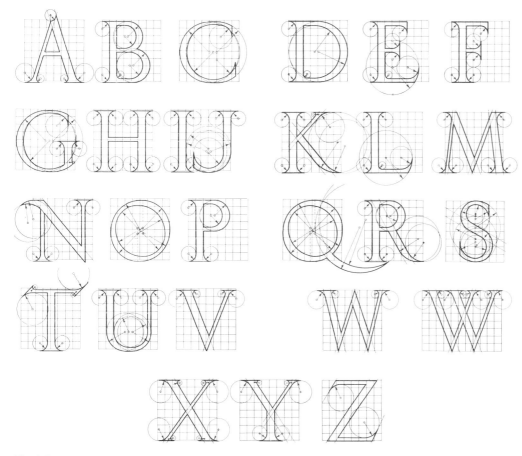

Fig. 1-2. The Dürer alphabet illustrates the careful attention to proportion and detail in the design of the Old Roman alphabet.

gives the feeling of skilled workmanship.

Since the early 1900's lettering used in all areas of drafting has been based on the single stroke Gothic letter. Prior to this time much of the lettering used on architectural, civil, and machine drawing was in a form of italic (inclined or vertical) shaded script lettering. (A shaded letter is one which has thick and thin elements.) Due to its ornate character, and the fact that it was inked, the shaded style of lettering was time-consuming. Industry soon realized that the beauty of a drawing did not contribute to the function of the drawing. Emphasis then began to be placed on simplification of the drafting procedures and practices.

As industry saw the distinct advantages of making the drawing less a thing of beauty and strictly functional, shaded lettering was simplified to what we now call the *single stroke Gothic alphabet*. Fig. 1-3 shows the vertical and inclined cap and lower case single stroke Gothic alphabet. Even the architectural style alphabet, as will be noted throughout this Chapter, is based on the single stroke alphabet. The term single stroke means that *each element* of the letter is a *single stroke*. It is not a shaded letter composed of thick and thin elements. The form of the letter may be altered to some degree, but each element is a single stroke.

In architectural lettering, alphabetical characters are formed with the six basic strokes illustrated in Fig. 1-4. These strokes can form every alphabet character,

should be simple and neat. Outstanding lettering on a drawing depends upon skill, simplicity and neatness. Without these elements the man on the board is unable to letter rapidly, effortlessly, and uniformly. Architectural drawings require more notes

(frequently referred to as "call-outs") and information than drawings from other fields of graphical representation. Good lettering, therefore, is essential on drawings and contributes to the overall impression created by an architectural firm. Quality lettering

U.S. STANDARD LETTERS & NUMBERS
(Vertical Style)

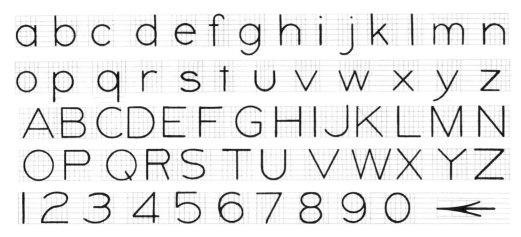

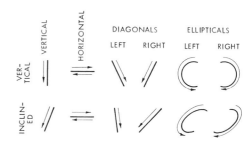

U.S. STANDARD LETTERS & NUMBERS
(Inclined Style)

Fig. 1-4. All architectural and engineering lettering may be analyzed into **Six Basic Strokes.**

Fig. 1-3. The Single Stroke Gothic Alphabet is the basis for all lettering on engineering and architectural drawings.

drawn either separately or in combination with each other. Quality lettering is based on the mastery of these six basic strokes.

Architectural lettering is not limited to a specific stroke style. Variation of form and mixing of lettering styles are permissible.

Students frequently remark, "I never could *print,* because my handwriting is poor.", or "I am left-handed and this causes my problems." Many of the finest draftsmen, architects, and engineers who are extremely deft in lettering have poor handwriting or are left-handed. Quality lettering is achieved through constant practice. One cannot study a given style of lettering, make several copying attempts, and then expect good results. Persistent practice, approximately 15 to 20 minutes a day, is necessary until the student has competency in the formation of all the letters, and until he has developed the coordinated finger and hand motions.

When learning to letter one's hand becomes tired and cramped. Even the experienced draftsman suffers from hand fatigue after a considerable amount of lettering. One of the secrets in avoiding hand fatigue is to move the hand when forming each element of the letter. Fatigue occurs essentially because the index finger and thumb are completely relied upon to move the pencil. As fatigue increases, the pencil is grasped tightly and the letters become shaky. As each letter character is formed, the fingers and hand should do an equal amount of work. When a draftsman learns to move his hand, as well as his fingers, his lettering will appear smoother.

To assist you in lettering, learn to hold the pencil with some degree of looseness. Allow the hand to move on the fleshy part of the palm to give the desired hand movement. Fig. 1-5 shows a photo of the hand forming a vertical element. The same kind of hand movement can be developed for horizontal, inclined or elliptical elements.

Once this technique has been mastered, the lettering will be smooth and have a tendency to be broader or expanded. When the pencil is held loosely, the muscles in the hand do not become tense. One of the reasons a pencil is held too tightly is that an excessive amount of pressure is applied to make the letter dark. Usually a draftsman will letter with an H, F or perhaps a 2-H pencil. Pencils used for lettering are normally softer than the pencil used for line work. A softer lead will produce a darker line. Therefore, the amount of pressure applied to the pencil point in forming a letter can be reduced by using a softer pencil.

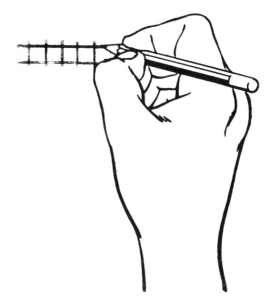

Fig. 1-5. When forming any element of a letter move the hand as well as the fingers.

Pressure Sensitive Lettering

Freehand lettering, however, is not always used on architectural drawings. In some cases (for display or presentation drawings) the designer or illustrator may use manufactured pressure sensitive lettering.

Dry Transfer Lettering. One of the latest innovations in the field of illustrating is the dry transfer method. These transfer letters are arranged on a transparent plastic sheet. Letters are transferred by rubbing over the desired letter with any smooth instrument, such as a ball point pen or a soft pencil. Fig. 1-6 illustrates the method of transfer-

Fig. 1-6. Dry Transfer lettering is easy to apply. Frequently it is used on presentation drawings and architectural models.

ring letters. The type sheet is then lifted away leaving the letter on the drawing surface. In circumstances where the illustrations may be handled, the letters may be "fixed" by the application of a clear *acrylic spray*.

An example of a title block that has been lettered with transfer letters is shown in

NEW JUNIOR HIGH SCHOOL
COOLEY DRIVE SITE
Portage Public Schools
Portage . . . . Michigan

ADRIAN R. NOORDHOEK / ASSOCIATES / AIA, KALAMAZOO, MICHIGAN.

Fig. 1-7. The title and other information in a title strip may be set in dry transfer lettering.

Fig. 1-7. Title layouts using transfer letters may use several different type faces, in addition to different point sizes of letters. The title block shown in Fig. 1-7 used 18, 16, and 14 point letters of the same type face. In graphic arts, the term *point,* a printer's term, is used to designate the height of a type face. A point is equal to .014".

Adhesive lettering is similar to the pressure sensitive type of lettering in appearance. The lettering rather than being directly transferred, however, is cut out, placed in the desired position, and rubbed with a smooth instrument. The plastic sheet has an adhesive material on the reverse side which holds the letter securely to the drawing surface.

Lettering Devices

In the architectural office the draftsman may use several different means of lettering a drawing, in addition to his own ability to letter. He should be familiar with, and understand, some of the basic lettering tools that he may be expected to use.

An architectural office may use a *mechanical lettering device* for specific kinds of drawings. For example the Leroy, Doric, or Wrico are some of the common types of mechanical lettering devices. Fig. 1-8 shows the Wrico and Doric lettering guides. All of these guides are similar in operation. Each guide uses a template which has grooved letters and numbers. A guide pin on the lettering instrument follows the groove which moves a tube pen (stylus) over the paper. The lettering instrument may be adjusted so the letters may be at the standard incline of 67½° or vertical. Different size templates and pens are available, as well as different styles that may be used for titles. The Leroy, Doric and Wrico lettering devices are best known for single stroke letters. Another commonly and widely used lettering device is the *Varigraph.* This instrument will produce a wide variety of built-up and single line style letters. Fig. 1-9 illustrates this instrument. A guide pen is moved in the depression on the lettering template. Through an adjustable mechanical linkage the pen (stylus) reproduces the form of the letter on the drawing sheet. The size of the letter (height and width) and angle of depression may be changed by adjusting the controls of the *Varigraph.*

Lettering templates are used for titles, as well as for sheet numbers. Fig. 1-10 shows one of several different types of single stroke templates that are used. As can be seen, the template has openings in which the pen is placed and moved. Most of the fill in Old Roman style lettering templates may be used with pencil or pen. These templates are usually used for titles on cover sheets and sheet numbers.

The *lettering typewriter* is a recent development in mechanical lettering devices used in drafting rooms. It is unique in the fact that it makes machine lettering available to the individual draftsman. Fig. 1-11 shows a Gritzner Lettering Typewriter being used on a drawing. Since the lettering typewriter may be moved to any position on the drawing, lettering may be placed at any space on the drawing. Because of this unique feature, the sheet does not have to be removed from the drawing board.

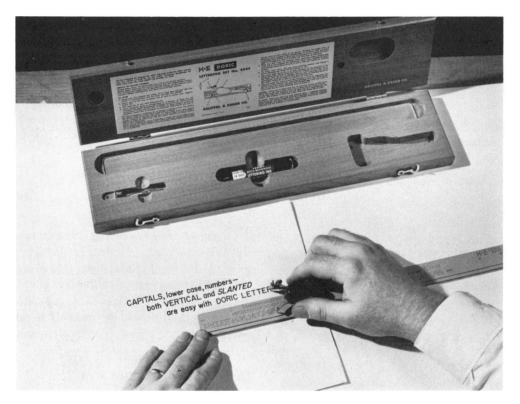

Fig. 1-8. The Doric (top) and Wrico (bottom) are two frequently used mechanical lettering devices used to produce single stroke letters.

Fig. 1-9. The Varigraph may be used to obtain a wide variety of character styles and sizes, from a single template.

The keyboard of the lettering typewriter is *not* the standard typewriter keyboard, but rather in alphabetical and numerical order. The lettering typewriter moves along an indexing rail that is used in place of the drafting machine straight edge or T-square. The index rail has its own spring-loaded drive which automatically moves the unit one space each time a letter is struck.

Some architectural offices use *standard typewriters* for placing notes and dimensions on drawings. These typewriters have long carriages, 24″ or 36″ in length, that will accommodate a C or D size sheet. Drafting room typewriters are not equipped with usual standard pica or elite type, but generally have large and small capital letters ⅛″ high.

If the draftsman is not responsible for

Fig. 1-10. Lettering templates are used for titles, sheet numbers, etc. to give variety and uniformity.

typing in dimensions and notes he will make a print of the tracing and quickly write in all of the information and give it to a typist who will then type the material as the draftsman has indicated. For better quality prints, the typist will place a piece of orange, yellow or sepia colored carbon paper, carbon side against the back of the tracing vellum. When the letter is struck, an impression will be on the front and back side of the vellum copy. Orange, yellow or sepia colored carbon paper blocks out more ultra-violet rays than does black carbon paper in the printing process.

Pencil Selection

A factor not to be overlooked in lettering is selecting the proper grade of pencil. Choosing the right pencil is dependent on several factors: (1) the pressure applied to the pencil, (2) the type of drafting medium used, and (3) the brand (manufacturer) of the pencil.

Pressure

Every person applies a different pressure or touch on his pencil. The grade of the pencil to be chosen depends upon the pressure applied on the pencil. One person may choose a 2H grade pencil, while another may prefer to use a pencil grade of H, T, or 3H on the same type of drawing medium to produce the desired dense, black line.

Drawing Medium

The kind and type of drawing medium, such as paper, vellum, cloth, or polyester film, plays an important part in pencil selection. Some mediums, because of their surface finish, are very receptive to hard lead pencil, while others may require a softer lead. Some vellums, pencil cloths, and polyester films are manufactured with a slightly rough surface. This type of surface media is very receptive to a pencil which produces a dense black line with a normal amount of pressure. Roughly surfaced media permits the use of a slightly harder lead pencil to produce the desired line quality.

Brands

Grades of hardness and softness of pencils vary from manufacturer to manufacturer. A 2H grade pencil from one manufacturer may be softer or harder than a 2H grade from another. One reputable brand of pencil should be used. It is not advisable to use mixed brands of pencils.

Lettering Over an Erased Area

When an area has been erased several times the "tooth" (roughness) of the paper is lost and becomes glazed. The glazing of the paper's surface causes difficulty in producing a dense black letter. Usually the draftsman will use a one degree softer pencil than he ordinarily uses for lettering over an erased area.

Humidity

When humidity rises, paper is not as receptive to pencil as it is on a low-humidity

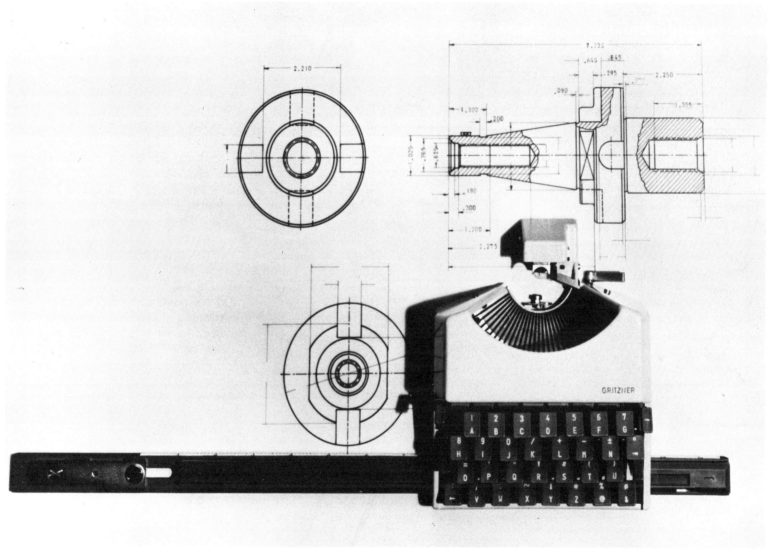

Fig. 1-11. The lettering typewriter is placed directly over the drafting medium on the drafting table, permitting the draftsman to type in all dimensions and notes.

day. As humidity increases, the draftsman will use a softer pencil; otherwise, lettering and line work will appear gray. Paper becomes softer when humidity is high, hence more prone to indentations. When the draftsman uses his regular grade of pencil on soft paper he must apply more pressure, thereby indenting the paper. If an erasure must be made, these indentations make it difficult to completely erase a line or letter. By using a softer pencil an excessive amount of pressure does not have to be applied.

Guide Lines

Height *guide lines* (very light gray lines) should be drawn for *all* lettering which appears on a drawing. The most accomplished draftsmen always use guide lines. There are numerous devices available on the market to aid the draftsman or student in drawing guide lines. Among the more popular lettering guide devices are the *Braddock Lettering Angle* and the *Ames Lettering Guide.* These are shown in Fig. 1-12.

Guide lines are drawn to help keep straight the outer edges of letters in a word or sentence. For most lettering, only two guide lines are needed: the base line and the cap (capital) line. However, when upper and lower case letters are used, two other guide lines, the waist and the drop lines, must also be included with the base and the cap lines, as shown in Fig. 1-13. Often, the

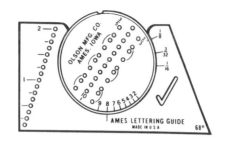

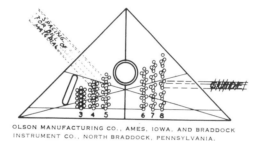

OLSON MANUFACTURING CO., AMES, IOWA, AND BRADDOCK INSTRUMENT CO., NORTH BRADDOCK, PENNSYLVANIA.

Fig. 1-12. The Ames (top) and Braddock (bottom) lettering guides aid the draftsman in drawing guide lines.

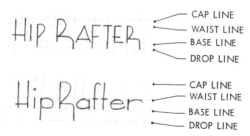

Fig. 1-13. Guide lines are used to maintain uniform character height for caps and lower case.

drop line is omitted. If large and small capital letters are to be made, the four guide lines are used. In addition to these horizontal guide lines, random vertical or inclined lines are also lightly drawn to insure uniform, parallel letters.

After many years on the board, draftsmen are able to draw a series of lines which appear to have been spaced by a divider or scale. In reality the draftsman has approximated them by "eye-balling" the distances. To save time in laying out guide lines the designer will "eye-ball" guide lines for dimensions and one, two or three line notes. It must be emphasized that only the *accomplished* and *experienced* use this trick!

Style

The style of lettering, in architectural drawing, is another important factor to be studied. As mentioned earlier, combining the six basic strokes in lettering will produce all the alphabet characters. However, there are some important points to consider when producing an architectural style of lettering. For example, attention must be given to: (1) the design of the letter characters, (2) the spacing of the letter characters within a word, (3) the spacing of words within a sentence or note, and (4) the size of the lettering.

Letter Design

Virtually all architectural lettering styles are now single stroke (i.e., all the lines and curves of the letter or character have the same line weight or thickness). This single stroke style is similar to the Gothic style lettering used on engineering drawings. Gothic style is similar to the lettering illustrated in Fig. 1-3. The only two probable exceptions are in the lettering of the title line on a presentation drawing or in the reference letters which indicate where a drawing section has been taken. These letters may be of the Old Roman style, or styled to be ornate to attract attention. In the past, architects or draftsmen have often used all caps (capitals or upper case letters)

for titles and subtitles, and upper and lower case letters for notes. Today, many architects and draftsmen in architectural firms are switching to all capital letters in the lettering of titles and notes.

In architectural lettering, the alphabet characters are not restricted to a mechanical form such as the lettering generally found in machine, electrical, civil, or other types of engineering drawings. The single stroke Gothic style is required for engineering work. In architectural lettering, the letters may have variations in their form, thus creating a pleasing style. The student is encouraged to study the lettering samples which are illustrated in Figs. 1-14 and 1-15.

The variations in form and design of each letter in architectural lettering are created by the artistic lettering skills of the architect or draftsman. He does not have to conform to any designated form or style of lettering. However, he must design his letters so that they demonstrate his lettering skills, while maintaining an identifiable form for each letter character. Fig. 1-16 shows characters modified to suit individual tastes. The architect or draftsman may

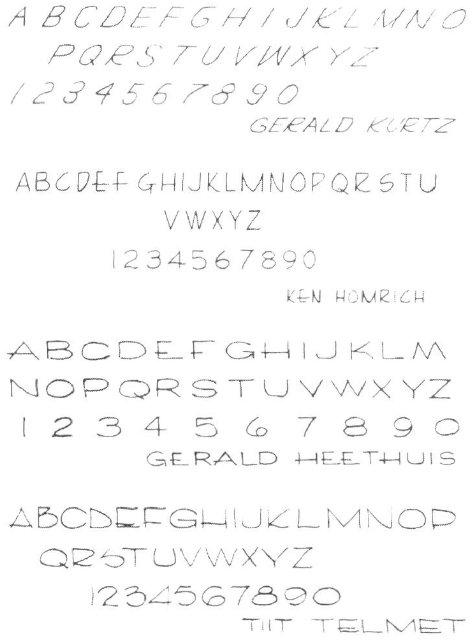

Fig. 1-14. Study these lettering samples. Notice how each draftsman has developed a style which is distinctive.

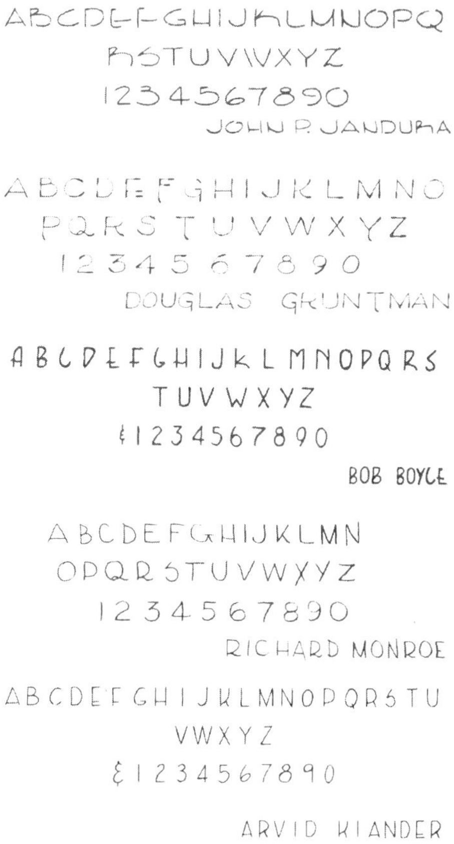

Fig. 1-15. Remember: All lettering must be simple and neat.

Fig. 1-16. Characters may be modified to suit the individual taste.

use *serifs* (short line strokes at the corners on the top and bottom of each letter) in the letters on his presentation drawings, but omits them when speed is more important than artistic lettering.

The variations in style and form are commonly found in the letters, E, F, H, P, R, and B. For example, the center horizontal line of the letter E may be located either above or below the center of this letter, and may be extended a short distance beyond the vertical line on the left and/or beyond the end of the upper or lower horizontal line.

Further attention may be focused on letters if the terminal points of each character are *pointed*. Fig. 1-17 shows several letters which have been pointed. Pointing emphasizes the terminal point of each letter with a slightly heavier pressure than is ordinarily exerted in forming the letter. The top and bottom of each letter that has been pointed is accurately aligned with the cap, waist, base, and drop line. This is a more accurate method than merely stroking the letters, and is usually performed after the character, word, line, or paragraph of lettering is completed.

In all cases, the design of the letters must be consistent with the design of all the other alphabet characters on a drawing. This will produce that artistic quality in architectural lettering which demonstrates the skills of the architect or draftsman.

Lettering for Microfilming

Drawings that are to be microfilmed (photographically reduced to an approximate frame size of $15\!/\!16''\times1\frac{3}{8}''$ on 35 mm film) must be lettered with care. If the letters are not properly formed, they will have a tendency to close or fill up when being reduced to such a great degree. To prevent filled-in characters, the style of lettering is changed and simplified. Fig. 1-18 shows a standardized style of lettering called *Microfont* that is used by draftsmen on drawings that will be microfilmed. Note how the letters C, G, and M appear more open than the typically formed character. Usually the capital letter I has no serifs, but in the Microfont style, serifs are added to the let-

ter so it will not be confused with the numeral 1 or lower case l. Numerals such as 2, 3, 4, 5, 6 and 9 are shaped distinctly different so they will not "close-up" in the photographic process and will not be mistaken for another numeral. Some architectural draftsmen have altered their style of lettering to conform to the basic appearance of Microfont.

Letter Spacing

Spacing the letter characters within a word is not difficult once the draftsman is completely familiar with the style of the alphabet. Spacing, or the proper placement of the blank area between the characters, is shown in Fig. 1-19. The spacing between these letters are uniform and are measured visually. However, there are some letter combinations, such as AT, VA, WA, and LT, where the spacing between them is not uniform with the spacing of the other letters. These letters are usually spaced closer together, because the sides of the letters, V,

Fig. 1-17. Lettering may be emphasized by pointing the terminal portions.

ABCDEFGHIJKLMN

OPQRSTUVWXYZ

1234567890

Fig. 1-18. The Microfont style of lettering is used on drawings that are to be microfilmed.

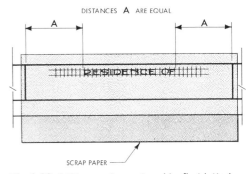

Fig. 1-19. The visual area between characters in a word should be approximately equal.

tered title. Perhaps the most fool-proof procedure is to first letter the title on a piece of scrap paper. By slipping the scrap paper beneath the velum sheet it may then be properly centered and lettered. Any succeeding lines are centered and then lettered in the same manner. Fig. 1-20 shows how this may be accomplished.

Fig. 1-20. A title may be centered by first lettering it on a piece of scrap paper and placing it beneath the vellum sheet.

A, and W are sloping, and thus produce a larger space when placed adjacent to such letters as L and T which have space either at the top or at the bottom. Visual judgment is exercised when spacing letters or characters within a word.

Word Spacing

In addition to good spacing of letters within a word, consideration must also be given to spacing words within a sentence, note, or title. Usually, one letter space or the width of the capital letter N or O is used between words. Each word should be a distinct unit spaced well enough apart so the words do not appear to be running together.

Composition of Titles

Titles are lettered in title strips or title boxes and placed beneath a detail, section, elevation or preliminary study. Several methods may be used in composing a cen-

Another method is to lightly sketch in letters (in their approximate width) above the guide lines. If the words appear too far to the right or left, begin lettering about one-half of that amount in the opposite direction. This method is used by draftsmen who have had many years of experience. Some may letter the title on a strip of paper and then place the paper above the guide lines. In this manner it can be determined where to begin lettering.

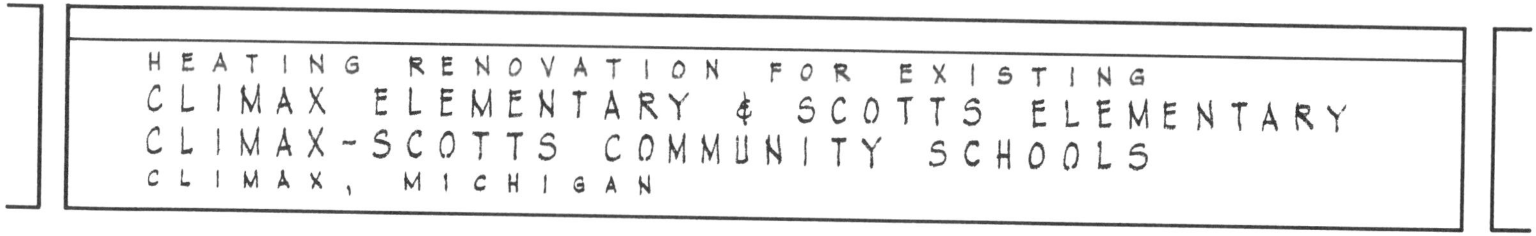

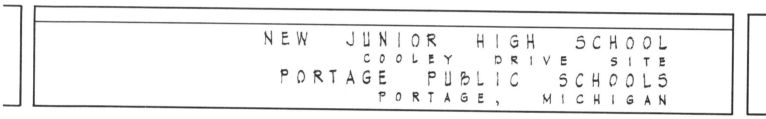

HEATING RENOVATION FOR EXISTING
CLIMAX ELEMENTARY & SCOTTS ELEMENTARY
CLIMAX-SCOTTS COMMUNITY SCHOOLS
CLIMAX, MICHIGAN

DESIGN BY JOHN STEELE

Fig. 1-21. A left-hand square format is being used in many architectural offices because it solves the problem of centering material.

NEW JUNIOR HIGH SCHOOL
COOLEY DRIVE SITE
PORTAGE PUBLIC SCHOOLS
PORTAGE, MICHIGAN

DESIGN BY JOHN STEELE

Fig. 1-22. For variety the draftsman may set up the title with a right-hand square format.

The square format title block layout is being accepted in many offices. Fig. 1-21 shows a left-hand square format title. A left-hand square format is one in which each line is aligned along the left edge. In addition, note in the figure how all of the letters in the title are aligned vertically. One of the reasons that the square format is gaining in popularity is that it saves in layout time. Another variation of the square format is shown in Fig. 1-22. Here is a right-hand square format. When this type of format is used, the draftsman may letter from right to left.

To achieve uniform space between letters the draftsman frequently scribes several lines parallel to the vertical edge of his lettering guide. These lines are spaced 1/8, 1/4, 3/8 and 1/2 inch, or any distance from the vertical edge. Fig. 1-23 shows these lines scribed on a new style Ames Lettering Guide. When drawing the guide lines for equal spaced lettering, the first vertical line is drawn and the lettering guide is moved so the desired scribe line is over the previously drawn line. The next line is drawn and the lettering guide is moved, etc.

Lettering Size

The size of lettering is dependent, many times, upon the size of the drawing. Lettering on a complete set of architectural working drawings is usually 3/32″ or 1/8″ high; titles are usually 3/16″ or 1/4″ high. Once the

OLSON MFG. CO.
AMES, IOWA
AMES LETTERING GUIDE
MADE IN U.S.A.
68°
1/8
1/4
3/8
1/2
5/8
3/4

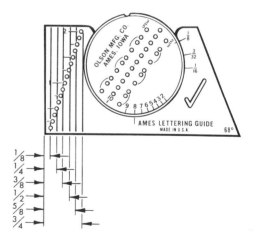

Fig. 1-23. To assist in laying out an expanded title, the draftsman will scribe lines on his lettering guide so vertical guide lines may be equally spaced.

TABLE 1-1
DRAWING SHEET SIZES

A – Size	8 1/2" x 11"	or	9" x 12"
B – Size	11" x 17"	or	12" x 18"
C – Size	17" x 22"	or	18" x 24"
D – Size	22" x 34"	or	24" x 36"
E – Size	34" x 44"	or	36" x 48"

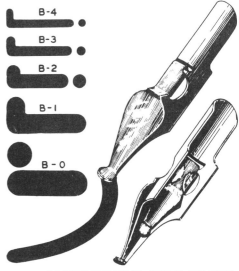

C HOWARD HUNT PEN CO., CAMDEN, NEW JERSEY.

Fig. 1-25. The drawlet pen is used for wide letters larger than one-half inch high.

size of the drawing, number of details on the sheet, and the sheet size have been determined, consideration may then be given to the height of the lettering.

Table 1-1 gives the standard sheet sizes. Most architectural drawings are executed on C or D sheets.

Lettering in Ink

Technical Fountain Pens. Occasionally a draftsman is required to letter in ink. When lettering is to be inked, one may use a technical fountain pen. These pens are primarily for ruling lines; however, they may be successfully used for letter if held vertically. Fig. 1-24 shows a photo of how the technical fountain pen is held for lettering with a template. Before lettering with a technical fountain pen, spend some time practicing.

Speedball. Speedball drawlet pens, see Fig. 1-25, are generally used for letters that are more than one-half inch high. They are used for sheet numbers and titles on large drawings. Several styles of Speedball

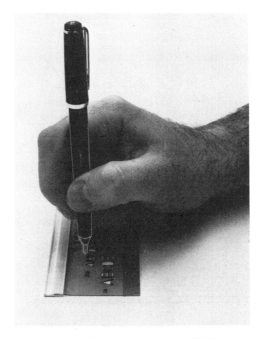

Fig. 1-24. A technical fountain pen is held vertically to the paper when lettering freehand.

pens are used for this type of lettering. These lettering pens are filled by using the drop-per or quill. Never dip the pen directly into the ink! By touching the dropper or quill between the ink reservoir and the pen, a small amount of ink will flow and load the pen sufficiently for lettering.

Title Blocks and Strips

Normally all drawings produced in an office have some type of identification to indicate firm, address, title, draftsman, checker, date, project number, and sheet number. This necessary identification is called a title block or title strip. In many cases the sheets are printed with or without border lines on a standard drawing size sheet. If a print becomes separated from a set it can be easily identified by the title or project number. The draftsman's or checker's name or initials appear in the title block so if questions arise the responsible person can be quickly located.

Titles blocks and strips take many different formats, as can be seen in Fig. 1-26, and are placed along the bottom or right hand edge of the sheet. Rather than being commercially printed, a title block can be applied by means of a *rubber stamp*. Some rubber stamps are so designed that they are stamped on the reverse side of the vellum sheet. By stamping the title block on the reverse side and lettering on the front side,

THE TITLE BLOCK SHOULD CONTAIN THE FOLLOWING INFORMATION:

1. NAME OF OWNER AND ADDRESS OF SITE (STREET NUMBER, CITY, AND STATE, OR LOT NUMBER, PLOT NAME, CITY AND STATE).
2. FIRM OR SCHOOL NAME, CITY AND STATE
3. TITLE OF SHEET
4. DRAWN BY (DESIGNER'S) OR DRAFTSMAN'S NAME)
5. APPROVED BY
6. CHECKED BY
7. SCALE
8. DATE
9. SHEET NUMBER

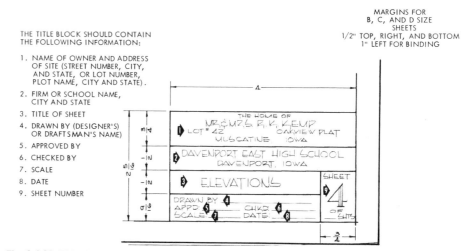

Fig. 1-26A. This title block may be used for architectural working drawings on B, C, or D size sheets.

Fig. 1-26B. A file strip may be used for architectural problems on a B size sheet.

G. E. DIEKEMA, AIA, KALAMAZOO, MICHIGAN.

Fig. 1-26C. A title block may be used without border lines. This title block is a plastic applique ' may be placed on any size sheet.

JOHNSON-HOWARD LUMBER CO., KALAMAZOO, MICHIGAN.

Fig. 1-26D. This title block is placed on the vellum sheet by a rubber stamp; border lines are then added. It may be used on any size sheet.

MILLER LUMBER CO., PLANNING SERVICE, KALAMAZOO, MICHIGAN.

Fig. 1-26E. This is a printed title block without border lines.

the possibility of smearing the imprint is eliminated. Some drafting rooms use title blocks that are printed on plastic film and applied to the drawing sheet. These *plastic appliques* have one side coated with a heat resistant adhesive which permits almost permanent bonding to the sheet.

Occasionally drafting rooms use 24, 34, or 36 inch width rolled stock for drawings. When rolled stock is used, separate title blocks are attached to the sheet. A standard format title block is used on which the title of the project and other necessary information is lettered either freehand, mechanically

or "stuck on" with transfer letters. The title blocks are then reproduced in the necessary quantity as *intermediate prints*. The

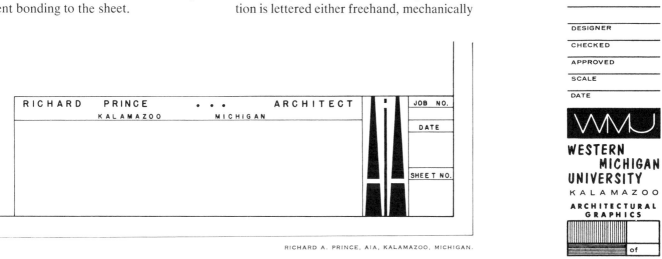

RICHARD A. PRINCE, AIA, KALAMAZOO, MICHIGAN.

Fig. 1-26F. This is a sample of a printed title block with border lines. Note the large space allotted for a description and location of the project.

Fig. 1-26G. This illustrates another style of unbalanced title blocks.

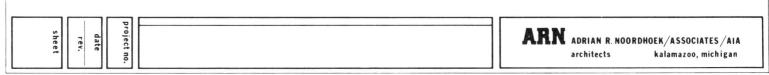

ADRIAN R. NOORDHOEK / ASSOCIATES / AIA, KALAMAZOO, MICHIGAN.

Fig. 1-26H. This title strip is placed along the right edge of a D size sheet.

Fig. 1-26I. This title strip is placed along the bottom edge of a C size sheet.

Fig. 1-27. An intermediate print of the title strip is attached to a drawing by ¼″ opaque cellophane tape.

intermediate print is attached to the roll stock with transparent or opaque cellophane tape. Fig. 1-27 shows an intermediate print ⟩ block being attached to a D size draw-ing sheet. Many sets of architectural plans range from 15 to 80 sheets. Obviously it would be too costly to letter the title, project number, date, etc., on each title block in a 40 sheet set. By using the method just described the title block must be filled in only once, thus saving the cost of the draftsman's valuable time.

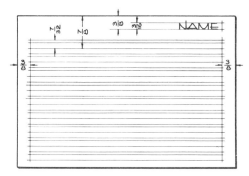

Fig. 1-28. A 4″ by 6″ card layout is used for lettering practice.

Problems

Obtain three 4″ × 6″ unruled filing cards, and prepare them with light horizontal guide lines in the same manner as that shown in Fig. 1-28. Select one of the sample sets of alphabets shown in Fig. 1-14 and 1-15. Complete the following on the three cards using all upper case lettering.

1. On the first card, lightly lay out the alphabet set which you have chosen. Modify the letters slightly to suit your taste, as shown in Fig. 1-16. When you have achieved a clear and legible set of letters, darken them on the card and show the card to your instructor for his approval.

2. On the second ruled file card, letter the following in the style you have developed in step no. 1.

ABCDEFGHIJKLM
NOPQRSTUVWXYZ
1 2 3 4 5 6 7 8 9 0 &
SIMPLICITY, LEGIBILITY,
SPEED, AND EASE OF
CHARACTER FORMATION
ARE PARAMOUNT FACTORS
IN CHARCTER DESIGN.

3. On the third card, use the same style of lettering as in steps nos. 1 and 2, and copy the following.

ABCDEFGHIJKLM
NOPQRSTUVWXYZ
1 2 3 4 5 6 7 8 9 0 &

Typical WALL SECTION
SCALE 1½″ = 1′-0″.
THE FIELD OF ARCHITEC-
TURE CHALLENGES MAN'S
URGE TO CREATE FOR
THE FUTURE IN A
FUNCTIONAL FORM.

4. Select a title block from those shown in Fig. 1-25. Lay out the chosen title block on another 4″x6″ unruled filing card. Letter very lightly, making sure that the alphabet characters are all in balance. Darken the letters on the card. This card will serve as a master title block template for all your future tracings. Trace the title block by placing the card under vellum or tracing paper.

5. Copy the first paragraph of this chapter in a clear legible style, and make all the letters about ⅛″ high. Keep the space between letters uniform, and the words about one letter space apart.

Sketching 2

Sketching is a thinking tool. It is quick, simple and easy. The value of sketching cannot be over-estimated. Many employers believe that an employee's ability to make a sketch is as important as his ability to make a finished drawing. Why is this? In any industry time is money. Frequently a finished drawing is not necessary, but the idea in the form of a sketch is important. Sketching is a quick and spontaneous means of expression; it is a thinking tool. A sketch is ready virtually the moment it is needed. No formal equipment is required—no drafting table, no parallel rule, no compass, just paper, pencil, and eraser.

Sketching Is a Tool

Sketches are hurriedly made on the corners of prints, scratch pads, backs of envelopes, etc. Of course, a sketch by itself usually is not a complete description. It may be the germ of an idea that has been hurriedly ~rded. It can be a complete drawing in the sense that all of the information is given. Sketching is a tool that is used from the beginning design stage through actual construction. It is a necessary part of technical training in many areas.

A hammer alone cannot be used to build a house; it is used along with many other tools. Frequently a sketch needs some words, either verbal or written, to go along as aids in understanding it. This is not unusual. A complete set of plans for any building always has a set of specifications. The formal plans do not give all the information that is needed. Written specifications must accompany these plans to call out the color, name, and manufacturer of the brick, the model number, color and manufacturer of the water closet; the kind, size, and maker of range top; the thickness, kind and color of the floor covering, etc. Sketching in architectural design and drawing is a working part of building construction.

Man's ability to symbolize graphically is not separate from his ability to speak or write. Communication in a graphic form is very similar to the processes of speaking or writing. Fig. 2-1 shows a comparison of the spoken or written form and the graphic form of communication. Through the years man has used sketching to record basic ideas or thoughts that would ultimately guide him in

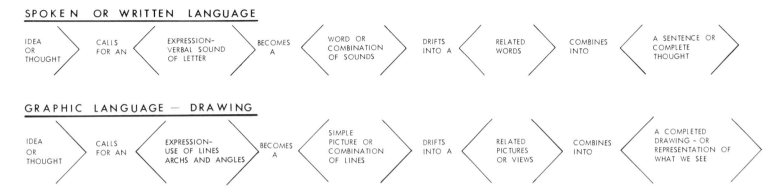

Fig. 2-1. The development of a sentence or thought is essentially the same as the development of a sketch or drawing.

the design and development of structures or devices for his use.

Perhaps one of the greatest engineers, inventors, draftsmen, artists, and creative talents the world has ever known was Leonardo da Vinci (1690-1730). His wide range of talents has never been equaled by any other person. Da Vinci recorded almost all of his ideas by sketching first, even though he was an exceptionally accomplished draftsman.

Most of da Vinci's idea sketches were composed of several pictorial views and occasionally a flat orthographic-like view. A search of his sketch books reveal some of his sketches to be rather crude while others exhibit a high degree of refinement. Leonardo used some shading in almost all of his sketches. It is interesting to note that most designers today employ some form of shading in their sketches.

Fig. 2-2 shows da Vinci's idea for an automatic spit. Here he used his knowledge of heat movement by convection to turn the spit. The action of the rising hot air turns a fan blade set in the flue of the chimney, driving the spit by a shaft.

Another example of da Vinci's inventive genius is shown in Fig. 2-3. This figure illustrates a problem that still vexes engineers—the movement of weight and how it may be most easily achieved. Leonardo spent much time studying and designing devices using the principles of the pulley, screw, and ratchet. Fig. 2-3 shows da Vinci's sketch of a pinion, gear and rack assembly used to lift a weight. Notice how this device is similar to the contemporary automobile jack. Notes da Vinci made on his sketches were written backwards. He developed this technique to discourage others from reading his explanatory material.

A further example of da Vinci's sketching ability is shown in Fig. 2-4, a design for a pile driver used to drive piling. Piles are large timbers that are driven into the ground to support a structure or a vertical load. By looking carefully at the sketch, it can be seen that a weight is raised by a hand-operated winch. As the weight reaches a certain height it is released automatically and drops to the wooden pile, thus driving it into the ground. This pile driver designed by Leonardo was a modification and refinement of the type in use during his life time.

Thomas Jefferson (1743-1826), third president of the United States, is perhaps best remembered as a Statesman, educator, and framer of the United States Constitution. Although Jefferson had many interests, he was absorbed in the field of architecture. Fig. 2-5 shows a preliminary sketch of how he envisioned the nation's capitol might appear in Washington, D.C. By looking closely at the sketch, one notices a strong influence of Renaissance architectural style. Here

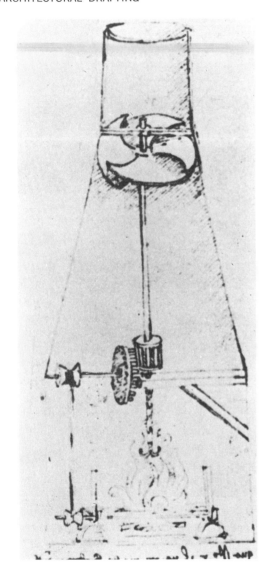

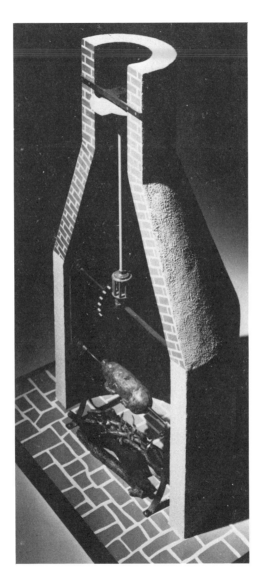

Fig. 2-2. An automatic spit turned by the upward flow of warm air. The sketch was made by Leonardo da Vinci. The model was made from the sketch.

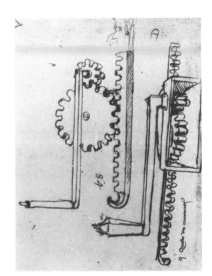

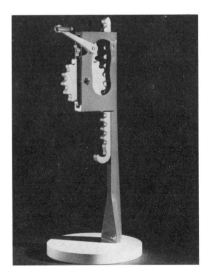

Fig. 2-3. A sketch by Leonardo da Vinci of a device for lifting a weight. Note how similar this object is to the modern automobile jack.

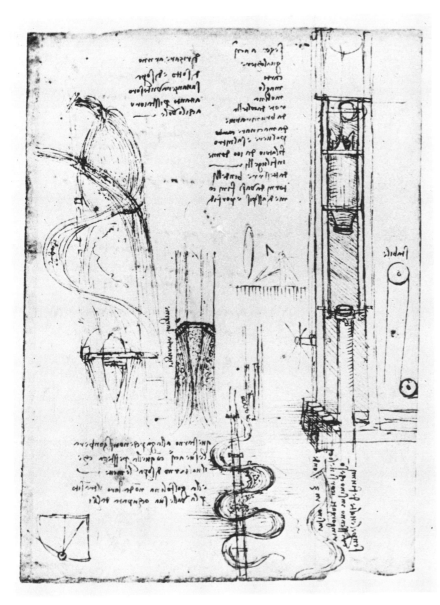

Fig. 2-4. A pile driver designed and sketched by da Vinci. The weight, raised by a hand-operated winch, was released automatically when it reached a certain height, dropping upon a wooden stake to drive it into the ground.

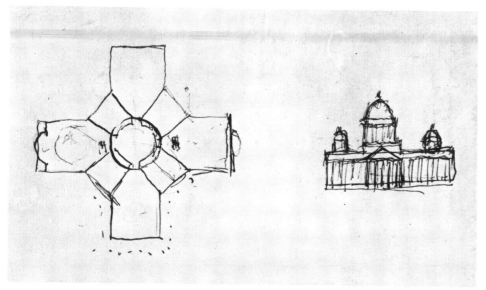

Fig. 2-5. Though Thomas Jefferson was mainly noted as a statesman and president, he had a deep interest in architecture. This is Jefferson's sketch for the Capitol of the United States drawn in 1792.

Jefferson was able to apply his classical education and knowledge of building design. Although Jefferson did not formally submit a design for the capitol, the design that was originally accepted and Jefferson's sketch are similar. Jefferson's estate home at Montecello is his best known piece of architectural design. It is looked upon by many as a classic work. As Jefferson's sketch of the capitol is studied, one can see a definite train of thought and a focus on a design by the means of a few lines. Too frequently a sketch is regarded as a finished masterpiece.

Frank Lloyd Wright (1869-1959), one of the greatest architects known, employed sketching in every facet of his work. Fig. ⁵ shows the first sketch of the Cheney

Fig. 2-6. Frank Lloyd Wright's initial sketch for the Cheney House, Oak Park, Ill.

Fig. 2-7. Frank Lloyd Wright's plan and perspective of the Cheney House, Oak Park, Ill.

Fig. 2-8. Photo of Frank Lloyd Wright's Cheney House, Oak Park, Illinois.

House, Oak Park, Illinois. The Cheney House, built in 1904, was designed in 1893 when Wright was still with Adler and Sullivan in Chicago. The sketch shows the recording of an idea and philosophy prior to drawing the plans. If the designer does not record his ideas rapidly, the general flavor or some small detail brought out in the sketch may be lost. Fig. 2-7 illustrates the plan of the Cheney House and a perspective. Here it can be seen how the plan has been modified from the sketch, but the basic design theme pervades the plan and rendering. A photograph of the Cheney House is shown in Fig. 2-8. Over the years a few changes have been made but the structure is still true to the rendering in Fig. 2-6.

Each example has shown how these outstanding men have used sketching to its truest and highest degree. Each man has not guilded or diluted the basic premise of sketching—that of simply recording an idea, a plan, a thought, or a philosophy. If your attempts at sketching, serve no other purpose than for the mere recording of an idea, then it has nobly served its purpose.

Where Is Sketching Used?

Sketching has many applications in the field of architectural drawing. The most ready application of sketching, of course, is by the designer as he plans a new structure. Before the architect begins to draw preliminary study plans, he will sketch many floor plans, as well as elevations, so that he can select the best for his client's needs. The architect will visit the building site and may make a rough topographic sketch of the area where the structure is to be located. A sketch is frequently made if a topographic study is not available.

The architectural draftsman uses sketching before he begins to lay out his sheet. By sketching he is able to determine where and how details will be placed. Draftsmen or delineators who make architectural renderings or presentation drawings usually have developed a high degree of sketching ability.

Building contractors or crew foremen frequently use sketching to interpret part of the plans to some of the staff and workmen. The designer or architect will use sketching to explain to the client how something will appear when the building is completed. Landscape architects rely on sketching to explain a new approach in land use planning to village councils or planning boards. The counter man in a lumber yard often employs sketching to explain a method of construction to the do-it-yourself handyman. The home owner who is planning to remodel his kitchen sees a sketch of the cabinets made by the salesman. Interior decorators depend heavily on sketching to illustrate an idea of how a new group of furnishings will appear in a living room. The floor covering salesman is often required to sketch as he estimates the amount of carpeting needed for rooms and hallways in a home.

Sketching plays an important role in every phase of building construction, from the initial stage of an idea for a structure, land development, construction, furnishings, and the sod, trees and bushes that are placed on the land.

Necessary Materials

Pencils. Either a wood-cased pencil or a mechanical lead holder is most ideally suited for architectural sketching. See Fig. 2-9. Some designers use a mechanical pencil with standard or very thin lead. Because of the lead's small diameter it does not require pointing. The most important factor in selecting a pencil is the softness of lead. Preferably for sketching an HB or H lead

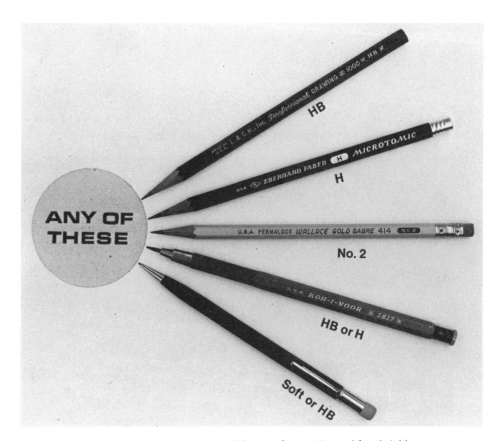

Fig. 2-9. A wood-cased pencil or a mechanical pencil is most frequently used for sketching. Never use a ball-point or fountain pen.

is used. In a pinch, a #2 common lead pencil may be used in place of an HB or H. Avoid any lead softer than HB because of its tendency to smudge. Harder leads, such as 2H or 3H are usually not used for architectural sketching. A hard lead produces a gray line and is difficult to use since it does not lend itself to a feeling of freedom.

Do not use a ballpoint pen or a fountain pen. A line made with any pen is final and difficult to erase. Pencil is easy to change.

Erasers. Anyone who is involved in drafting or designing and uses a pencil, knows the eraser is an essential tool. Any one of three types of erasers is recommended for sketching. See Fig. 2-10. A soft eraser, such as a Pink Pearl, is frequently used in sketching. This soft eraser will cleanly erase soft layout or preliminary sketch lines. Many designers prefer a pencil cap-type eraser. The rubber in many pencil cap erasers is generally slightly harder. Pencil cap erasers are placed over the end of a wood cased pencil

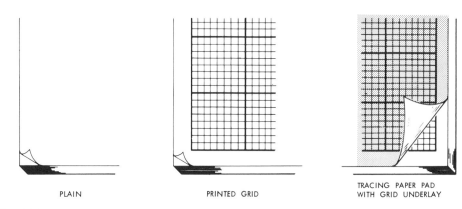

Fig. 2-11. Paper used for sketches may be either plain or gridded.

PLAIN   PRINTED GRID   TRACING PAPER PAD WITH GRID UNDERLAY

and some mechanical lead holders. One of the advantages of a pencil cap eraser is that it is never misplaced.

Another type of eraser which is finding favor among draftsmen is the vinyl eraser. The vinyl eraser was made specifically for erasing lines on polyester film. Draftsmen soon found that it was also ideally suited for

paper. One of the unique features of this eraser is that it will not smudge. Many draftsmen tend to favor this type of eraser because it will not "crumb" when erasing a line. The soft rubber and the vinyl erasers are available in both peel-off stick and block forms.

Paper. Designers are notorious for sketching on anything that is handy when an idea occurs. They may use old envelope backs, table cloths, napkins, or paper bags. Most preferable is a paper that has a slight "tooth." The "tooth" of the paper refers to its roughness. Ideally a paper best suited for sketching has a slight "tooth" that readily takes pencil. Hard, slick, shiny surface papers are not intended for sketching.

Paper may be either plain or gridded. Usually plain paper is preferred over paper with a grid. Fig. 2-11 shows three of the more popular sketch pads. Paper that is used for architectural sketching may either

Fig. 2-10. Erasers are necessary tools for the designer and draftsman.

be opaque or translucent. Translucent paper, such as tracing paper, has the advantage that white prints may be made from the original. Most plain opaque and translucent papers are made so that their surfaces have a slight 'tooth."

Some designers prefer a paper that has a printed grid. These gridded papers are available either on an opaque or translucent stock. Grid rulings may be 4, 5, 8, or 10 to the inch. These are referred to as 4 × 4, 5 × 5, etc. papers. Most grids that are printed on translucent papers are printed with an ink that will *not* block out the light when a print is made from the sketch. Grids that are printed with this special ink are called *fade-out* grids. Many persons who sketch feel that a grid restricts their freedom in sketching. This perhaps is a psychological factor.

Lines Used in Sketching

As with regular drafting practice, certain lines are used in sketching to indicate a specific meaning. Approximately the same lines are used in sketching as in engineering drawing. Fig. 2-12 shows the lines used in sketching.

Construction. One of the lines most often used in sketching is the construction line. It is a fine, *thin,* light gray line that is used for layout purposes. It is used to establish the placement of object, hidden, center, cutting plans, extension and dimension lines.

Object. This line is a *thick* bold, black, dense line that is used to define all visible aspects of an object. The object line represents an edge view of a surface or the intersection

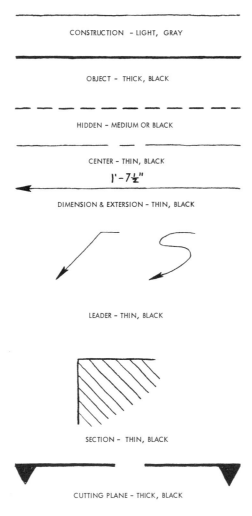

CONSTRUCTION - LIGHT, GRAY

OBJECT - THICK, BLACK

HIDDEN - MEDIUM OR BLACK

CENTER - THIN, BLACK

1'-7½"

DIMENSION & EXTENSION - THIN, BLACK

LEADER - THIN, BLACK

SECTION - THIN, BLACK

CUTTING PLANE - THICK, BLACK

Fig. 2-12. Typical lines used in sketching.

of any two surfaces that have a definite change in direction.

Hidden. A hidden line is a *thick or medium* dense bright black line that represents an outline on an edge view of a surface or the intersection of two surfaces that cannot be seen. As the name implies, it is hidden by another part of the object. The hidden line is made up of a series of dashes approximately ¼" in length with about ¹⁄₁₆" space between.

Center. A center line is a *thin* black dense line that is used to indicate the center of an object, a hole, a cylinder, or a cone. The center line is made up of a series of alternating long and short dashes. The length of the long dash is approximately ¾" to 1½" in length and the length of the short dash is approximately ⅛" to ¼". The space between each of these dashes is approximately ¹⁄₁₆". The length of the long and short dashes will vary, depending ultimately upon the size of the sketch.

Dimension. This line is a *thin,* dense, black line approximately the same width as the center line. The dimension line carries the dimensional value of the line to which it refers. An arrow head is placed at either end of the dimension line.

Extension. An extension line is used to refer the dimension line to the object. It too, like the center line and dimension line, is a *thin,* dense, black line.

Leader. Leaders are used to direct a note to a drawing. In architectural drawing practice a leader may be either curved or straight. It is a *thin,* black, dense line.

Section. Lines used to represent the cut surface of an object are called section lines. These lines are placed at an approximate angle of 30°, 45°, or 60°, spaced about ⅛″ apart and are the same weight and density as a center line, dimension line or extension line.

Cutting Plane. The cutting plane line shows where the structure or building component will be cut. A cutting plane line is a *heavy,* dense, black line made up of dashes, approximately ⅜″ long with an ⅛″ space between. The cutting plane line may also be a long dash, 1″ to 1½″ long, followed by two short dashes, each ⅛″ to ¼″ long, with ¹⁄₁₆″ space between. In either case the cutting plane line is wider than an object line so it will be noticeable and not confused with an object line.

An example of the lines used in sketching is shown in Fig. 2-13. This is a sketch that was made for a deck addition to an existing building. All of the lines previously described have been used in this sketch.

Sketching Techniques

Holding the Pencil for Sketching. When sketching, hold the pencil loosely. The pencil is not held as one ordinarily would when writing. Perhaps the most common mistake made by those who begin to sketch is to make a finished sketch with few lines. Always lay out a sketch with light construction lines. By using light lines your sketch will gain more freedom. After checking the preliminary layout, then darken the sketch.

Fig. 2-14. When sketching, the pencil is held so the point projects approximately 1¼″ to 1¾″ beyond the fingers.

When darkening in a sketch, the pencil is held more tightly so that pressure may be placed on the pencil point.

Fig. 2-14 illustrates how a pencil is normally held for sketching construction lines, as well as for darkening in the sketch. The point of the pencil is usually 1¼″ to 1¾″ away from the fingers.

Pencil Point. The shape of the pencil point has a bearing on how the finished sketch will look. The most ideal point for the pencil is one that is slightly rounded. Fig. 2-15 shows three different pencil points. When the pencil is shaped with a slightly rounded point, a sharp line will result. As each line is drawn on the sketch, rotate the pencil slightly. By constantly rotating the pencil, the point will wear evenly and require less sharpening.

A very long thin sharp point will give very thin, fine lines. When pressure is applied to this type of point, it is apt to break and

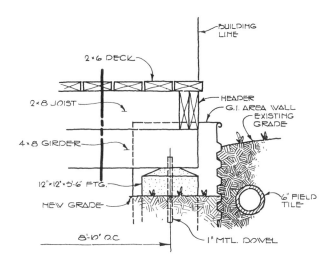

Fig. 2-13. This is an example of the different types of lines used in a sketch.

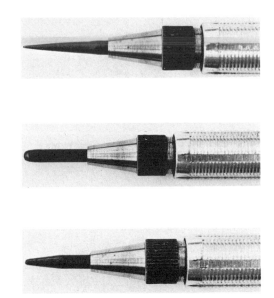

Fig. 2-15. The pencil point should be slightly rounded to produce a sharp-firm line.

require pointing again. By contrast, a blunt hemispheric (ball-shaped) point results in fuzzy lines. It is difficult to make a neat, sharp-looking sketch with a blunt point.

When sharpening the pencil use a pencil pointer, an ignition file, or a 6″ mill file. Some drafting rooms discourage abrasive paper for pencil pointing since it has a tendency to hold graphite particles. When a pencil is pointed with an ignition or a mill file, the particles can be easily knocked out on a wastepaper basket or on the leg of the stool. Though this practice is followed by some draftsmen it is not the most popular from the housekeeping standpoint.

Sketching Straight Lines

The old saying "I can't even draw a straight line with a ruler," is an easy "out" for those who don't practice. Sketching a straight line is really quite simple. All that is required is a little effort. Several methods can be used in sketching a straight line:

1. *Marking Gage Method:* When sketching a straight line with the marking gage method, hold the pencil as it would be normally held for writing or drawing. Fig. 2-16 shows how to hold the pencil. Note how the thumb, index and middle fingers are slightly extended. Move the pencil to its proper location on the sheet. Usually the middle finger is placed on the side of the sketch pad as shown in Fig. 2-16. The pen-

cil is then drawn from top to the bottom or bottom to top of the sheet. This will produce a relatively light line. If a single sheet of paper is used, place the sheet along the edge of any straight surface.

A series of parallel lines can be drawn using the marking gage method. Usually the pencil can be moved to the center of an 8½″ × 11″ sheet. If it is extended much beyond the center, some control of the pencil will be lost. If the lines are desired to be drawn on the other half of the sheet, simply turn the paper upside down. This method is generally limited to horizontal and vertical lines.

2. *Two-Spot Method:* This technique in sketching a straight line may be accomplished in several ways. For beginners, 2

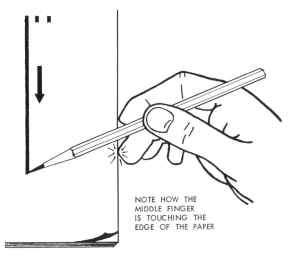

NOTE HOW THE MIDDLE FINGER IS TOUCHING THE EDGE OF THE PAPER

Fig. 2-16. A straight line may be sketched by using the pencil as a marking gage.

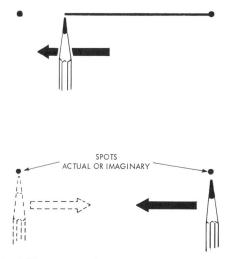

Fig. 2-17. A straight line may be sketched between two actual or imaginary spots.

movement as it reaches the midpoint of the arc. As the pencil travels the last half of its path, move the pencil outward. By practicing this slight finger movement, a relatively straight line will result.

3. *The Eye-Spot Method:* An *eye spot* is a visual spot or fixation at a particular location made with your eye. Try looking at a particular location on a plain piece of paper with your eyes. Now move your eyes away and then return them to the same spot. Easy, isn't it? With the eye-spot method, visually locate two spots on a plain piece of paper. Next move the pencil between these two locations. Lower the pencil and follow the same technique used with the two-spot method. A straight line will result with practice.

Any straight horizontal, vertical or inclined line may be drawn with these methods. Fig. 2-18 shows how an inclined line may be drawn by simply rotating the paper.

4. *Short-Stroke Method:* After perfecting sketching techniques, the short-stroke method of sketching straight lines can be used. Short strokes are shown in Fig. 2-19. Many designers and draftsmen who do a great deal of sketching use this method. The straight line may be sketched by using a series of short light strokes from ¾ ″ to 1¼ ″ long. These strokes are placed with a very small space between them, approximately $1/64$ ″ or shorter. Some designers connect these small strokes, thus giving the appearance of one long straight line. Don't try to draw a 6 ″ line in one stroke. Use four or five short strokes with a very small space

actual spots are placed on the paper. Fig. 2-17 illustrates how a line may be drawn using this method. These spots (points) represent the location through which the line will pass. Locate these spots about 4 ″ to 6 ″ apart. Hold the pencil so that the point is about ¼ ″ above the paper; then move the hand between the two spots. The movement of the pencil is controlled above the two spots as the point is gradually lowered to the paper. Then, without too much pressure, a line is drawn between the points. The resulting line will be relatively straight.

Control of the pencil is important. If attention is not given to the control of the pencil, it will have a tendency to describe an arc. To compensate for the arc, move the pencil toward your hand with a slight finger

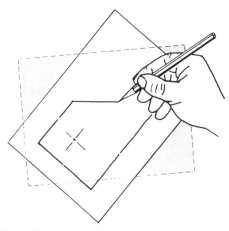

Fig. 2-18. An inclined line may be drawn by turning the paper and sketching a vertical or horizontal line.

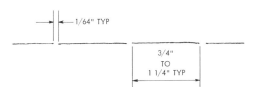

Fig. 2-19. A straight line may be drawn without a preliminary line by using a series of short strokes. Note the approximate length of strokes and the space between them.

between. Some beginners tend to shade or "play out" the line. See Fig. 2-20. This is not correct pencil technique. Always use light strokes that connect or have a slight gap.

Transferring Distances

The basic idea behind sketching is that it

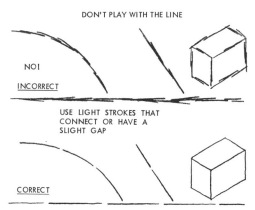

Fig. 2-20. Correct use of the pencil can save time and result in a neat appearing sketch.

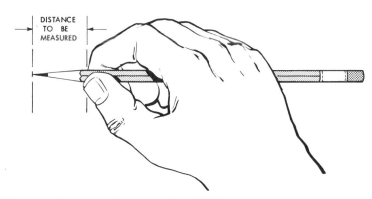

Fig. 2-21. A pencil is a useful measuring instrument in sketching.

is quick and easy. Beginners seem to think that using a straight edge and a rule helps make a better sketch. This is not true. When time is taken to use a straight edge and a ruler to transfer distances, the spontaneity and the freedom is lost. Distances may be transferred by using a pencil and the thumb as a measuring device. Fig. 2-21 shows the pencil being used to transfer distances.

Distances may be readily measured, transferred or compared by placing the thumb along the pencil. Place the pencil point at one end of the line and the thumb along the pencil at the other end. The measurements can then be transferred to its desired position. A slight movement of the pencil point will give a mark on the paper indicating the position.

Darkening In Sketched Lines

A frequent technique used in rendering

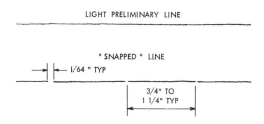

Fig. 2-22. When a sketched line is darkened in it is frequently "snapped." "Snapping" is a series of short, dark lines with approximately ⅟₆₄" space between.

the final sketch is that of "snapping." See Fig. 2-22. A "snap" is made up of a series of dark short lines ¾" to 1¼" in length with a small gap between. The space between these short lines should be less than $\frac{1}{64}$". This technique is almost identical with the short-stroke method of sketching a straight line, the only difference being the

amount of pressure applied to the point. If a line is darkened in without the technique of "snapping," the line will have a tendency to develop a slight bow or curve.

In some instances the gaps are completely omitted. After a short stroke, the pencil is lifted and slightly rotated and placed on or close to the end of the line previously drawn. The next short length is then drawn, the pencil raised and slightly rotated and placed at the end of the line previously drawn. Rotating the pencil will wear the point uniformly and require less sharpening. This is a particularly important feature since the lead used in sketching is a relatively soft lead and wears quickly.

Dividing the Area into Halves and Quarters

A necessary tool for those who sketch is the understanding of how an area may be easily divided into halves or quarters.

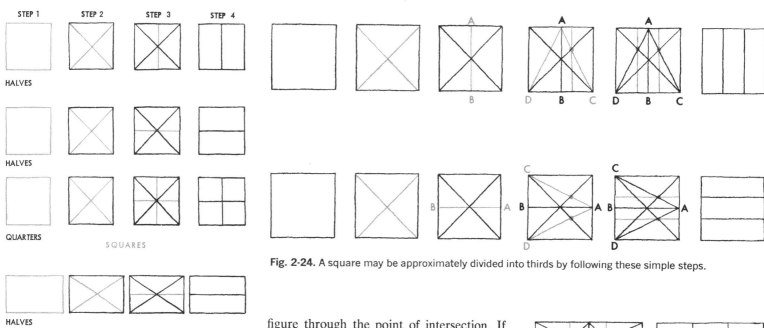

Fig. 2-24. A square may be approximately divided into thirds by following these simple steps.

Fig. 2-23. Squares and rectangles may be easily divided into halves and quarters.

figure through the point of intersection. If the area is to be divided into quarters, sketch another line parallel to the adjacent side to the point of intersection. The area is then divided into quarters.

Figs. 2-24 and 2-25 show how a square and a rectangle are divided into thirds. This is an approximate method. It cannot be proven geometrically but it is close enough for sketching purposes. Any square or rectangle may be divided into thirds by using the following procedure:

Step 1. Sketch 2 diagonals through the corners of the figure.

Step 2. Sketch line AB through the intersection of the two diagonals.

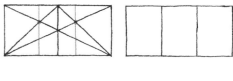

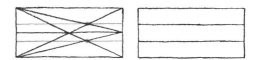

Fig. 2-25. Rectangles may be approximately divided into thirds by the same method as described for squares.

Line AB is parallel to one of the sides of the figure.

Step 3. Sketch a diagonal, line AC and AD, from point A on the figure.

Fig. 2-23 shows how a square or rectangle may be divided. Sketch two intersecting diagonals through the area to be divided. If the area is to be divided into halves, sketch a line parallel to one of the sides of the

Step 4. Where line AC and AD intersect the two diagonals, sketch two lines parallel to line AB. The figure is now divided approximately into thirds. If it is desired to divide the area into six equal parts, simply treat each as a rectangle and divide in half.

Basic Sketching Shapes

In learning to sketch successfully, there are some basic elements that serve as the footing and foundation of the structure which is to be built later. These basic shapes that are described in this section can be classed as the footings and foundation. Without a basic knowledge and the development of skill with each of these shapes, all efforts at sketching will be relatively futile. In order to sketch successfully, you must practice.

Square

There are a number of methods of drawing a square. However, the two that will be shown here are the easiest.

Fig. 2-26 shows the first of these two methods. To begin with, sketch two axes of the square. Next, use the pencil as a marking gauge, and tic off one-half of the length of the square on each position of the axis. Through each one of these tic marks, sketch a side of the square parallel to one of the axes. Inspect the square to make sure that it looks like a square, then darken it in.

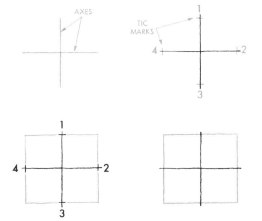

Fig. 2-26. A square may be sketched by first drawing two axes.

Note how the lines are "snapped" in the last portion of this figure.

The second method is simpler than the previous method, but it should be used only after gaining some experience in sketching. See Fig. 2-27. First, sketch two parallel lines. The distance between these lines should be equal to the length of the side of the square. Then rotate the paper 90° and sketch in two parallel lines, CD. The distance between CD should be equivalent to the distance between AD. To make sure that these lines are properly spaced, the distance between AD can be transferred by using the pencil as a marking gauge. Now check the square to see if it looks like a square rather than a parallelogram or rectangle, and darken the lines.

Rectangle

Rectangles may be sketched in the same manner as squares. The two methods that are illustrated here are identical with those described for the square.

Fig. 2-28 shows a step-by-step procedure for drawing a rectangle. First, sketch in two axes at right angles to each other. On one-half of the major axis, sketch in one-half of the length of the rectangle. Using

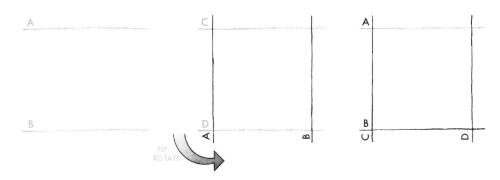

Fig. 2-27. Sketching a square by drawing two parallel lines and rotating the paper.

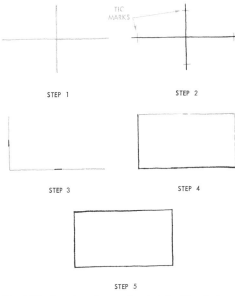

STEP 1   STEP 2

STEP 3   STEP 4

STEP 5

Fig. 2-28. A rectangle may be sketched by first laying out the axes.

your pencil as a marking gauge, tic off the same length on the other half of the major axis. Next take one-half of the height of the rectangle and tic it off on the upper half of the minor axis in a similar manner. Tic off the distance on the minor axis. From each of these tic marks, sketch in sides parallel to the axes. Once the rectangle has been checked to make sure that it has the proper shape, darken in the sides.

The second method of sketching rectangles requires simply drawing two parallel lines, AB, the correct distance apart. Fig. 2-29 illustrates how a rectangle may be sketched by using parallel lines. Next ro-

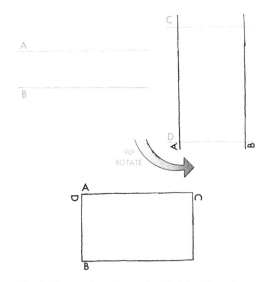

Fig. 2-29. A rectangle may be sketched by using parallel lines.

lel lines appropriately spaced. Once the accuracy of the figure has been determined, darken in by "snapping" the lines.

Circle

Perhaps one of the most difficult figures to sketch is a circle. Many persons have difficulty in sketching a circle because of two factors: (1) Not using the correct method and, (2) Insufficient practice. Again, there are a number of different ways of sketching a circle. The two methods shown here are tate the paper 90° and sketch in two parallel clearly the easiest for the beginner.

    a. Sketch a square, using two axes to divide the square into quarters. See Fig. 2-30.

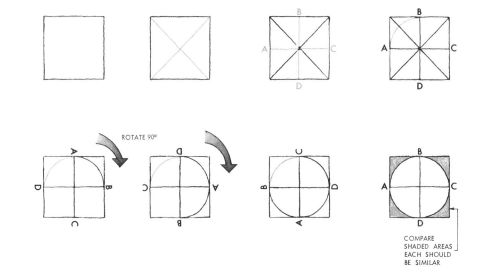

Fig. 2-30. This is one method of sketching a circle.

b. Sketch two diagonals through the square intersecting in the center.

c. In one quarter of the square, sketch in a 90° arc, AB. Each person will find that he will be able to sketch an arc more easily in one of these quarters than the other. Discover which quarter is easiest. Most right handed persons will find that the upper left hand quarter of the square is easier than the others.

d. After sketching arc AB, rotate the paper 90° clockwise or counter-clockwise. Sketch the next 90° arc, then rotate the paper again, sketch in the next arc, etc. until the circle is completed. Before darkening in the circle, check to see that it does not appear to be a 12″ ball squeezed into a 10″ box. The easiest way to compare each quarter of the circle is to look at the area between the circle and the square. See Fig. 2-31. Small areas may be more accurately compared than large areas. Note the shaded portions between the arcs and the square. If the circle has the proper shape, then darken it in by "snapping" the lines. As the circle is darkened in, rotate the paper with each movement of the hand.

Another method of sketching a circle is called the equidistance method. Fig. 2-32 shows the simple steps in sketching a circle by this method:

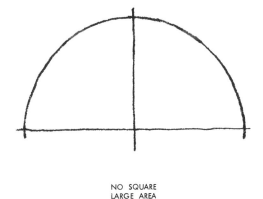

NO SQUARE
LARGE AREA

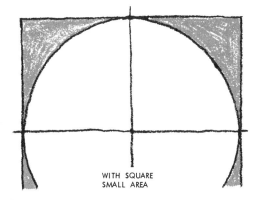

WITH SQUARE
SMALL AREA

Fig. 2-31. By placing the circle in a square, areas may be more easily compared by eye.

a. Sketch a square containing two axes that will divide it into quarters.

b. Inscribe a square within the larger square by sketching a diagonal through one of the small squares.

c. Draw two diagonals through the larger square so that they intersect at the center.

d. Locate points A, B, C, and D by eye. Each of these points is equi-distant from its adjacent side. These points will serve as a guide for sketching in the arcs.

e. Similar to the previous method, sketch in 90° arcs to form the circle.

f. After you are satisfied that the circle has proper shape, darken it in by "snapping" the lines.

Ellipse

An ellipse can be thought of as a circle viewed on an angle. Each of the objects shown in Fig. 2-33 is composed of either a cylindrical, spherical or conical shaped object. When each of the circular elements is viewed at an angle, other than 90°, it will appear as an ellipse. Ellipses are frequently used in architectural sketching.

Often an ellipse is incorrectly made to look like a parallelogram with rounded ends. See Fig. 2-34. An ellipse is a complete curved shape built on two axes that are called the major and minor axis. Fig. 2-35 illustrates the axes and the ellipse. The major axis is the long axis and the minor is the short axis. The major axis can be in any position, with the minor axis perpendicular to it. A number of methods may be used for sketching an ellipse. The two following methods have proven to be the easiest for those learning how to sketch.

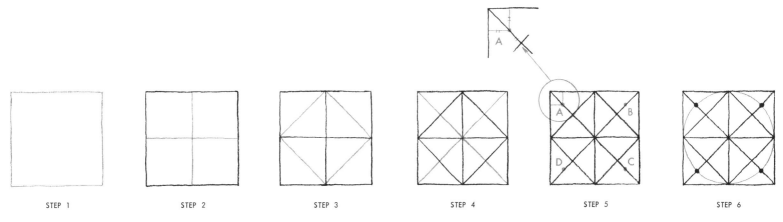

STEP 1   STEP 2   STEP 3   STEP 4   STEP 5   STEP 6

Fig. 2-32. This is another method of sketching a circle.

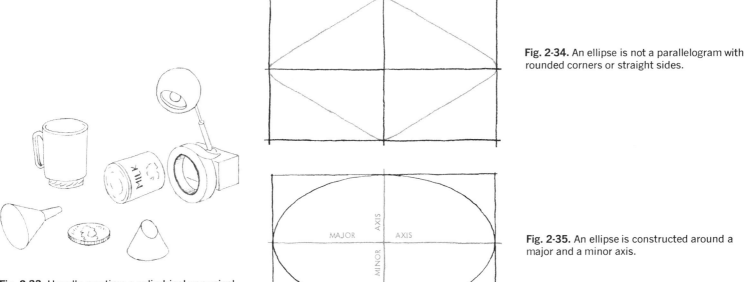

Fig. 2-34. An ellipse is not a parallelogram with rounded corners or straight sides.

Fig. 2-35. An ellipse is constructed around a major and a minor axis.

Fig. 2-33. Usually any time a cylindrical or conical object is viewed at an angle it will have an elliptical appearance.

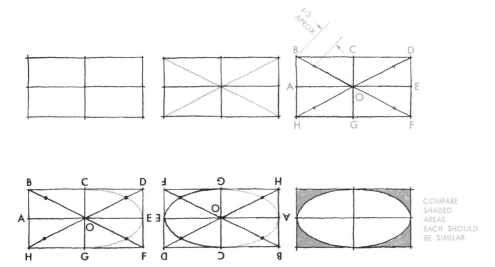

Fig. 2-36. Sketching an ellipse is easy if these steps are followed.

Method 1: The following step-by-step procedure, shown in Fig. 2-36, can be used to sketch an ellipse:

a. Sketch a rectangle whose sides are equal to the major and minor axes of the ellipse.

b. Sketch two diagonals through the rectangle intersecting at the center.

c. Place a tic mark on the diagonal approximately ⅓ of the distance from each corner of the rectangle. Note: This is ⅓ of ½ of the diagonal.

d. As with the circle, find one portion of the ellipse that is easiest to draw. Draw in that segment of the ellipse.

e. Rotate the paper and draw in the other portion(s) of the ellipse.

f. Compare the areas that lie between the ellipse and the rectangle. Compare each of these areas to see that they are similar in size and shape.

g. Darken in the ellipse by "snapping" the lines.

Method 2: This method of sketching an ellipse is much quicker than the previous one. It is used mainly by those who are very familiar with sketching and is illustrated in Fig. 2-37. Use this method only after you have gained experience with Method 1. The following step-by-step procedure is used in sketching an ellipse.

a. Sketch a rectangle.

b. Sketch two large arcs at both ends of the minor axis.

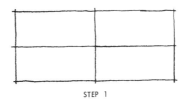

STEP 1

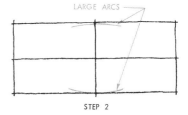

STEP 2

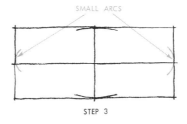

STEP 3

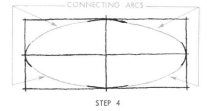

STEP 4

Fig. 2-37. An ellipse may be sketched by first sketching 4 arcs in a rectangle.

c. Sketch two small arms at the ends of the major axis.

d. Sketch in four connecting arcs.

e. Compare the areas that lie between the ellipse and the rectangle.

f. Darken in the ellipse by "snapping" the lines.

Angles

In some layouts the designer must sketch a 30°, 45°, or a 60° angle. To sketch a 45° angle, as shown in Fig. 2-38, simply sketch a right angle from the point of origin of the 45° line. Then sketch in any size arc with its center being at the point of origin of the 45° angle. Next divide the arc in half by eye. Then through this point draw in the 45° line. Another method, shown in Fig. 2-39, is to sketch in two right angle lines from the point of origin of the 45° angle. These two lines can represent two sides of a square. Then place a tic mark on each of these sides and sketch in two other lines representing a square. Next sketch a diagonal through the point of origin to the opposite corners of the square.

To sketch a 30° or 60° angle, as shown in Fig. 2-40, begin by sketching two right-angle lines through the point of origin, then sketch an arc with its center at the point of origin. Next divide the arc into three approximately equal parts. Each of these divisions represents a 30° angle. Draw a line through the appropriate division for a 30°, 45° or 60° angle.

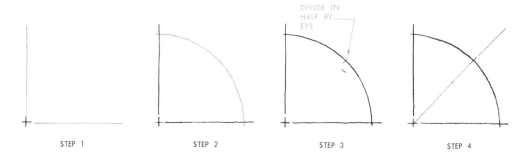

Fig. 2-38. Sketching a 45° angle is most easily done by first sketching an arc.

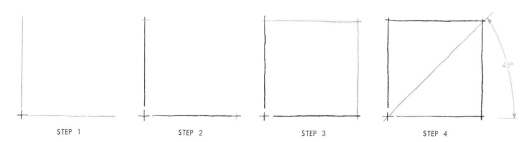

Fig. 2-39. A 45° angle may be sketched by first constructing a square.

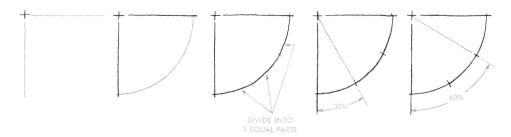

Fig. 2-40. Sketching a 30° or 60° angle is a matter of first sketching an arc and then dividing it into three equal parts by eye.

Irregular Curves

An irregular curve is normally sketched by first locating the path of the curve with a series of points. See Fig. 2-41. Once the points have been plotted, the curve is then drawn. Since an irregular curve is com-

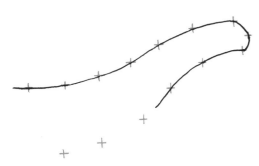

Fig. 2-41. An irregular curve is sketched by first laying out a series of points.

posed of a series of tangent arcs, many of these arcs can be drawn by adjusting the pencil and swinging the arc from the heel of the hand or finger resting on the paper.

Shading

Shading can be added to a sketch by using any of the methods described in Chapter 15, "Perspective." Many designers use these techniques in casting a shadow on the face of a building from a projected canopy or in a recessed area. Perhaps the most expedient is the "re-lining" method to give the appearance of depth.

Questions and Problems

1. Why is sketching important in the field of architecture?
2. Why is sketching called a "thinking tool?"
3. How can you use sketching in the courses in which you are presently enrolled?
4. Sketch the top, front, and side views of a drawing instrument case.
5. Use a 2 or 3 core stretcher concrete block, similar to the one shown in Fig. 9-93, Chapter 9, and sketch the necessary views.
6. Sketch the front and side view of the container used to hold pencil shavings of a pencil sharpener.
7. Sketch an elevation view of one of the windows in your drafting room.
8. Sketch an elevation view of two adjacent sections of the privacy screen shown in Fig. 5-11, Chapter 5.
9. Sketch the front and right elevation views of the movable room divider shown in Fig. 5-14, Chapter 5.
10. Redesign, by making a sketch, the floor plan shown on the left-hand side of Fig. 5-15, Chapter 5, by adding an attached double garage along the dining room and kitchen wall.
11. Sketch a section in elevation of the footing, foundation, and basement floor showing the membrane waterproofing and tile as in Fig. 9-22, Chapter 9.
12. Sketch a section in elevation of the box cornice. Include a portion of the roof and wall as shown in Fig. 10-11, Chapter 10.
13. Sketch a front and top view of the hammer head shown in Fig. 10-32, Chapter 10.
14. Make a front and right elevation sketch of the free-standing fireplace shown in the lower, right corner of Fig. 10-88, Chapter 10.
15. Sketch the front and right elevation view of the "Dutch Colonial" house shown in Fig. 8-2, Chapter 8.
16. Sketch the front and left elevation of the free-standing fireplace shown in the upper, left corner of Fig. 10-88, Chapter 10.

Architectural Office Practices

The architect's set of drawings for a residence or home is so small (approximately 1/48 actual size when drawn to a scale of ¼″ or ⅛″ = 1′-0″) in comparison with the actual building size, that some type of symbolic representation must be used. Each feature of a home cannot be represented on a set of architectural working drawings without the use of symbols or conventions. Almost all symbols and conventions for building materials, walls, floors, window and door openings, electrical and plumbing fixtures, heating and cooling facilities, and duct works have been standardized by the American National Standards Institute (ANSI).[1] Standardized symbols eliminate confusion and misunderstanding in architectural drawings.

In building construction, the general contractor and sub-contractors receive copies of the plans and specifications so they may bid on each specialized phase of work, such as plumbing, electrical wiring, sheet metal, heating, etc. Some general contractors are sufficiently large to employ tradesmen specializing in these various phases of work on a full time basis. Each of the specialized contractors necessarily reads and thoroughly understands the drawings and specifications. Thus all bids are predicated on the same basis. In part, this is accomplished through standardized symbols and office practice.

---

1. ANSI Y32.9, Y32.4, Z 32.2.3, and Z 32.2.4.

Symbols and Conventions

Because new materials are constantly being developed in the building industry, new symbols and conventions are also being devised or changed prior to their acceptance or recognition by the ANSI. If some material is not covered by ANSI conventions, the draftsman or architect devises the symbol and defines the material depicted by such symbol.

To the beginning student, the vast number of symbols may seem confusing. If a symbol is drawn in an area (e.g., kitchen, bathroom, or laundry) where it represents a fixture that is commonly found there, then it is not difficult to recognize. Many symbols resemble the object they represent.

Fig. 3-1 illustrates various types of doors in a floor plan view as they appear in common types of exterior walls. Note that in

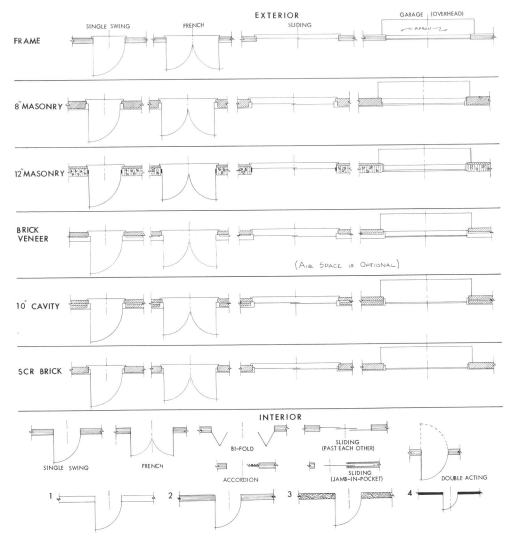

Fig. 3-1. Plan view symbols of several types of exterior doors in several kinds of walls are shown. The symbols for interior doors show the more common types. (Symbols 1 through 4 indicate a single swing door in a frame wall. The standard wall convention is shown by Symbol 1. Symbols 2 and 3 are occasionally used by architects. Symbol 4 would be used on plans drawn to a very small scale.)

the 8″ masonry, brick veneer, 10″ cavity, and SCR brick wall, the brick work is relieved (set back) around the door frames. The openings of all doors in masonry and frame walls shown in this illustration are the same, and only the brick work has been relieved.

Doors are usually identified by number or letter placed in a circle. The size of each door, its composition—whether wood or metal, its thickness, glazing, etc.—is given on the door schedule. The architect may give the dimension, width × height × thickness, along the door. Note how each door is shown in a 90° open position. By drawing the door open 90° one understands the amount of space required for the door swing.

In Fig. 3-1 (lower left) the symbols shown are used to represent different interior residential doors. Both interior and exterior doors are represented in the same manner. The only difference is that interior doors do not require a sill to be shown; the sill is shown for exterior doors. The four symbols shown in Fig. 3-1 (lower right) indicate a single swing door in a frame wall. Symbol 1 is the standard convention for a frame wall or partition. Symbols 2 and 3 are also used to designate a frame wall. Symbol 4, in which the wall is indicated by a single very heavy line, may be used on very small scale drawings.

Fig. 3-2 points out the symbols used for showing windows in a plan view. Note the representational similarity of the metal and wood windows. Each opening has a

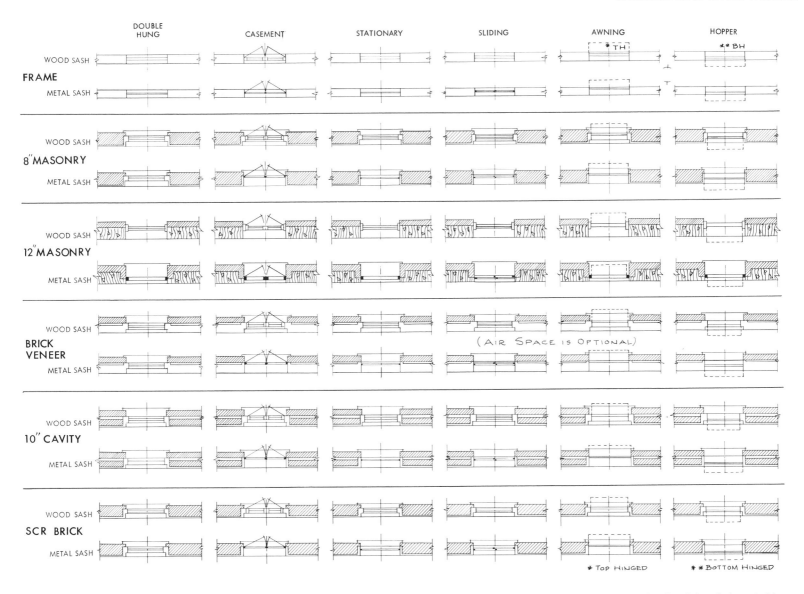

Fig. 3-2. Wood sash and metal sash window symbols in several types of walls are shown. The symbols are related to the actual details of the windows but have been greatly simplified so that they can be drawn at small scale.

different symbolic treatment, depending on the type of wall represented. Windows in all types of masonry walls, regardless of the sash material used (such as metal or wood) must be drawn with a sill. Representation

basic dimensions: (1) rough opening—the size which must be allowed by the builder to permit placement of the window in the wall (the distance between the inner faces of the *studs* and the distance between the

plan views. (It should be pointed out that each brick or roof shingle represented in elevation is not drawn completely; this would be too time-consuming).

Symbols play a more extensive role in

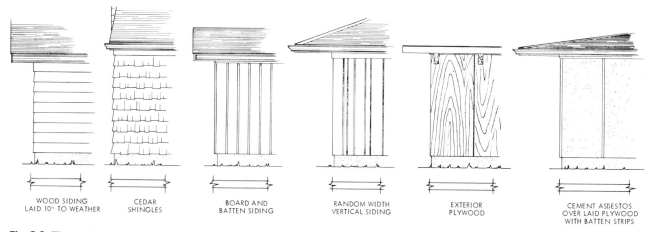

WOOD SIDING
LAID 10" TO WEATHER

CEDAR
SHINGLES

BOARD AND
BATTEN SIDING

RANDOM WIDTH
VERTICAL SIDING

EXTERIOR
PLYWOOD

CEMENT ASBESTOS
OVER LAID PLYWOOD
WITH BATTEN STRIPS

Fig. 3-3. These elevation and plan section symbols are used for various exterior wood building materials.

given to windows in masonry walls is the same as that given to exterior doors (i.e., the brick work is relieved around the window frames). The window opening, as it is drawn on the plan view, is the sash opening. Usually, all window sizes show three

header and the sill); (2) sash opening—the width and height of the sash; and (3) size of glass placed in the sash.

Numerous exterior building materials are shown in Figs. 3-3 and 3-4. These figures show the standard symbols in elevation and

the electrical area of the building trades than in other areas. This is because there are many different types of general, convenience, and switch outlets, as well as components of auxiliary electrical systems. Fig. 3-5 shows some general electrical symbols. The electrical plans that comprise a portion of the architect's set of plans frequently will include a key or legend on one of the sheets. The purpose in providing a key is to prevent any misunderstanding of

Some of the more common plumbing and heating fixtures are illustrated in Fig. 3-6. Depending upon the accepted practices in various localities, the *cold air returns* and *heat registers* may or may not be indicated

the symbols have been illustrated within this chapter. Any symbol not illustrated in the text will be found, in all probability, in *Architectural Graphic Standards.*[2]

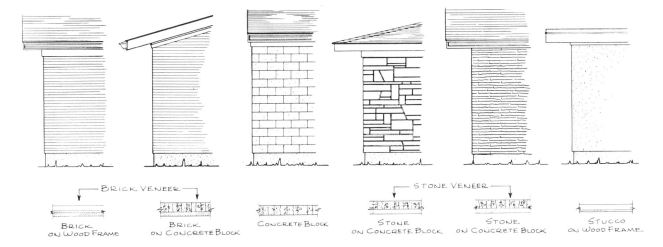

Fig. 3-4. These elevation and plan section symbols are used for various masonry building materials.

any switch, outlet, etc., because the symbol does not resemble the electrical device.

Plumbing and heating symbols have shapes similar to the objects they represent. Therefore, a key or legend *does not* appear on the mechanical sheets.

by the designer. The location of heating ducts and registers is often worked out with the advice of the heating contractor.

Fig. 3-7 gives the symbols for common building materials.

It should be pointed out that not all of

2. Charles G. Ramsey and Harold R. Sleeper (Joseph N. Boaz, Ed.) *Architectural Graphic Standards,* 6th ed. (John Wiley & Sons, Inc., 1970).

ELECTRICAL SYMBOLS

CEILING FIXTURE OUTLET	CEILING FIXTURE OUTLET
WALL FIXTURE OUTLET	WALL FIXTURE OUTLET
(B)	BLANKED CEILING OUTLET
(B)	BLANKED WALL OUTLET
(D)	DROP CORD
(F)	CEILING FAN OUTLET
(F)	WALL FAN OUTLET
(J)	CEILING JUNCTION BOX
(J)	WALL JUNCTION BOX
(L)	CEILING LAMP HOLDER
(L)	WALL LAMP HOLDER
(L) PS	CEILING LAMP HOLDER WITH PULL SWITCH
(L) PS	WALL LAMP HOLDER WITH PULL SWITCH
(S)	CEILING PULL SWITCH
(S)	WALL PULL SWITCH
(X)	WALL EXIT LIGHT OUTLET
o	SURFACE OR DROP INDIVIDUAL FLUORESCENT FIXTURE

OR	RECESSED INDIVIDUAL FLUORESENT FIXTURE
o	SURFACE OR DROP CONTINUOUS FLUORESCENT FIXTURE
OR	RECESSED CONTINUOUS FLUORESCENT FIXTURE
(C)	CLOCK HANGER OUTLET (SPECIFY VOLTAGE)
(C)	WALL CLOCK OUTLET (SPECIFY VOLTAGE)
DUPLEX CONVENIENCE OUTLET	DUPLEX CONVENIENCE OUTLET
1, 3	CONVENIENCE OUTLET OTHER THAN DUPLEX 1 = SINGLE, 3 = TRIPLE, ETC.
WP	WEATHER PROOF CONVENIENCE OUTLET
GR	GROUNDED OUTLET
	SPLIT WIRED OUTLET
R	RANGE OUTLET
AC	AIR CONDITIONER OUTLET
S	SWITCH AND CONVENIENCE OUTLET
R	RADIO AND CONVENIENCE OUTLET
▲	SPECIAL PURPOSE OUTLET (DESIGN IN SPECIFICATIONS)
●	FLOOR OUTLET
⊖	FLOOR SINGLE OUTLET
⊖	FLOOR DUPLEX OUTLET
△	FLOOR SPECIAL PURPOSE OUTLET

▬	LIGHTING PANEL
▨	POWER PANEL
—	BRANCH CIRCUIT; CONCEALED IN CEILING OR WALL
– – –	BRANCH CIRCUIT; CONCEALED IN FLOOR
- - - -	BRANCH CIRCUIT; EXPOSED
—►►	HOME RUN TO PANEL BOARD INDICATE NUMBER OF CIRCUITS BY NUMBER OF ARROWS
—	FEEDERS
[●]	PUSH BUTTON
[ ]	BUZZER
[ ]	BELL
◄	OUTSIDE TELEPHONE
◁	INTERCONNECTING TELEPHONE
◁|	TELEPHONE SWITCH BOARD
(T)	BELL RINGING TRANSFORMER
D	ELECTRIC DOOR OPENER
F	FIRE ALARM BELL
FS	AUTOMATIC FIRE ALARM DEVICE
W	WATCHMAN'S STATION
TV	TV OUTLET

ANY STANDARD SYMBOL GIVEN WITH THE ADDITION OF A LOWER CASE SUBSCRIPT MAY BE USED TO DESIGNATE SOME SPECIAL VARIATION OF STANDARD EQUIPMENT OF PARTICULAR INTEREST IN A SET OF ARCHITECTURAL PLANS. WHEN USED THEY MUST BE LISTED IN THE KEY OF SYMBOLS ON EACH DRAWING AND IF NECESSARY FURTHER DESCRIBED IN THE SPECIFICATIONS

S a,b,c	
S	SINGLE POLE SWITCH
S₂	DOUBLE POLE SWITCH
S₃	THREE WAY SWITCH
S₄	FOUR WAY SWITCH
S_D	AUTOMATIC DOOR SWITCH
S_P	SWITCH AND PILOT LAMP
S_K	KEY OPERATED SWITCH
S_CB	CIRCUIT BREAKER
S_WCB	WEATHER PROOF CIRCUIT BREAKER
S_RC	REMOTE CONTROL SWITCH
S_WP	WEATHER PROOF SWITCH
S_L	LOW VOLTAGE SWITCH
S_T	TIME SWITCH

Fig. 3-5. Standard electrical symbols simplify the work of the electrical contractor as he works out the details of wiring the house.

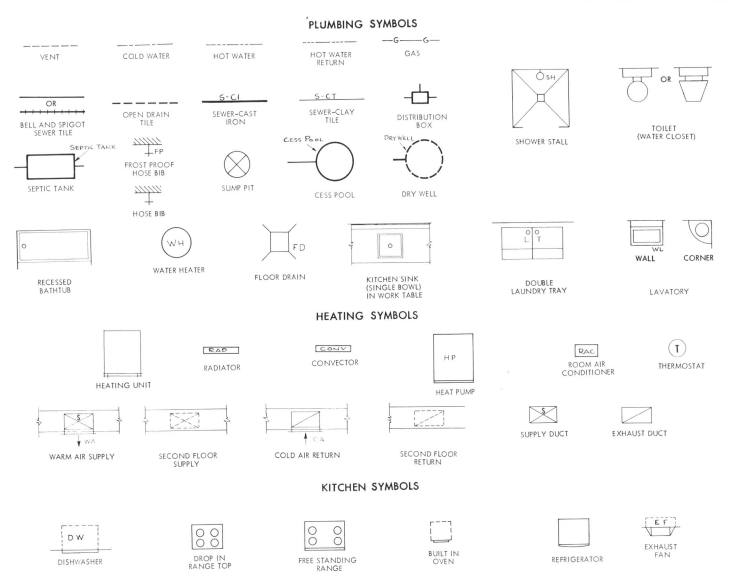

Fig. 3-6. Plumbing, heating, and kitchen symbols are essential to the designer as he plans the arrangement of facilities and leaves room for them. Some of the symbols are arbitrary in form, others resemble the objects they represent.

MATERIAL	PLAN	ELEVATION	SECTION
BRICK	COMMON / FACE / FIREBRICK	SAME AS COMMON BRICK / SAME AS ABOVE	SAME AS PLAN VIEW
STONE	CUT STONE / RUBBLE / CAST STONE (CONCRETE)	CUT STONE / RUBBLE	SAME AS PLAN VIEW
CONCRETE	CONCRETE / OR / CONCRETE BLOCK	CONCRETE / CONCRETE BLOCK	SAME AS PLAN VIEW
STRUCTURAL STEEL	OR / OR	NONE	I OR I
INTERIOR PARTITIONS	STUDS, LATH AND PLASTER / SOLID PLASTER WALL		SAME AS PLAN VIEW
GLASS	OR	OR	SMALL SCALE / LARGE SCALE
INSULATION	LOOSE FILL, OR BATTS / BOARD AND QUILT / SOLID AND CORK	NONE	SAME AS PLAN VIEW
WOOD	FLOOR AREAS LEFT BLANK NOTE INDICATES KIND OF WOOD USED	SIDING / PANEL	END OF BOARD (EXCEPT TRIM) / TRIM

MATERIAL	PLAN	ELEVATION	SECTION
SHEET METAL FLASHING	INDICATE BY NOTE		HEAVY LINE SHAPED TO CONFORM
EARTH	NONE	NONE	
ROCK	NONE	NONE	
SAND	NONE	NONE	
GRAVEL OR CINDERS	NONE	NONE	
FLOOR AND WALL TILE			
SOUNDPROOF WALL		NONE	NONE
PLASTERED ARCH		DESIGN VARIES	SAME AS ELEVATION VIEW
GLASS BLOCK IN BRICK WALL			SAME AS ELEVATION VIEW
BRICK VENEER	ON FRAME / ON CONCRETE BLOCK	SAME AS BRICK	SAME AS PLAN VIEW
CUT STONE VENEER	ON FRAME / ON BRICK / ON CONCRETE BLOCK	SAME AS CUT STONE	SAME AS PLAN VIEW
RUBBLE STONE VENEER	ON FRAME / ON BRICK / ON CONCRETE BLOCK	SAME AS RUBBLE	SAME AS PLAN VIEW

Fig. 3-7. The symbols for common materials help the designer to pass on information without having to designate every material used.

Abbreviations

Because of the multiplicity of items which must be represented on a single sheet of drawings, abbreviations for materials, construction procedures, equipment, etc., are necessary so the drawings will not appear too crowded. Many words have several abbreviations, and some words have the same abbreviation. Therefore care must be exercised in reading or lettering a note so there will be no misunderstanding.

When lettering or typing a room finish, door or window schedule, a list of the abbreviations is placed directly on the schedule or on another sheet in the set. *All* abbreviations appearing on the schedule, whether standard or not, are listed!

The following is a list of the more frequently used *standard* abbreviations found on architectural drawings.

Access Door	A D
Acoustic or Acoustical	ACST or AC
Aggregate	AGGR
Alarm	ALM
Alternating Current	A C or a-c
Altitude	ALT
Aluminum	AL
Anchor Bolt	A B
Angle	∠
Angle Iron	∟
Architect	ARCH
Area Drain	A D
Asbestos	ASB
Asphalt	ASPH or A

Asphalt Tile	A T
At	@
Avenue	AVE
Basement	BSMT
Bath Room	BATH
Bath Tub	B T
Beam	B M
Bed Room	B R
Bench Mark	B M
Better	BTR or Btr
Between	BET
Bidet	B
Block	BLK
Blocking	BLKG
Board	BD or bd
Boiler	BLR
Bolts	BT
British Thermal Units	B T U or Btu
Built Up Roof	B U R
By	×
Cabinet	CAB
Cast Concrete	C CONC
Cast Iron	C I
Cast Stone	C S
Catch Basin	C B
Ceiling	CLG or Clg
Cement	CEM
Cement Asbestos	CEM A
Cement Asbestos Board	CEM AB
Center	CTR
Center Line	₵ or CL
Center Matched	CM
Center to Center	C to C or c to c
Centimeter	cm
Ceramic	CER

Channel	C
Channel, Junior	M C
Channel, American Standard	C
Cinder Block	CIN BL
Circuit Breaker	CIR BKR
Cleanout	CO
Cleanout Door	CO D
Clear	CLR or Clr
Closet	C, CL, or CLO
Cold Rolled Steel	CRS
Cold Water	CW
Column	COL
Common	COM or Com
Concrete	CONC
Concrete Block	CONC B
Conductor	COND
Construction	CONST
Contractor	CONTR
Courses	C
Court	CT
Cubic	CU or cu
Cubic Yard	CU YD or cu yd
Damper	DMPR
Dampproofing	DP
Decimeter	dm
Detail	DET
Diameter	DIA
Dimension	DIM or dim
Dining Area	DA
Dining Room	DR
Dishwasher	DW
Ditto	DO, ", or do
Double Acting	D A
Double Hung	D H

Douglas Fir	DF	Flat Grain	F G	Hot Water	HW
Dovetail	DVTL	Floor	FL	Hot Water Heater	H WH or W H
Down	DN or D	Floor Drain	FD	House	HSE
Downspout	DS	Fluorescent	FLUOR		
Drain	D or DR	Flooring	FLG or Flg	I Beam	S
Dressed & Matched	D & M	Flush	FL	Inch	IN, in, or "
Drinking Fountain	DF	Foot	FT, ', or ft	Inside Diameter	I D
Dryer	D	Footing	FTG	Insulate or Insulation	INS
Dry Well	D W	Full Size	F S	Interior	INT
Duplex	DX			Invert	INV
Duplicate	DUP	Galvanized	GALV	Iron	I
		Galvanized Iron	G I		
Each	EA	Game Room	GR	Janitors Closet	J CL
East	E	Gage	GA	Joint	JT
Electric	ELEC	General Contractor	GEN CONT		
Elevation	EL or el	Glass	GL	Kiln Dried	K D
Enamel	E	Glass Block	GL BL	Kilo	K
Enclose	ENCL	Glaze	GL	Kilometer	KM
Entrance	ENT	Grade	GR	Kip (1000 lb)	K
Equal Leg Angle	∟	Grade Line	G L	Kilowatt Hour	KWH or kwhr
Estimate	EST	Granite	G	Kitchen	K
Excavate	EXC	Grating	GRTG	Knocked Down	K D or k d
Existing	EXIST	Grease Trap	G T		
Expansion Bolt	EXP BT	Grille	G	Ladder	LAD
Expansion Joint	EXP JT	Gravel Stop	G S	Landing	LDG
Exterior	EXT	Guard	GD	Lane	LN
Extra Heavy	X H or X	Gypsum	G	Lath	LTH
	HVY			Laundry	LAU
		Hardware	HDW	Laundry Trays	LT
Feet	FT, ', or ft	Hardwood	HDWD or	Laundry Chute	L C
Finish	FIN		Hdwd	Lavatory	LAV
Finish Floor	FIN FL	Head	HD	Lead	L
Firebrick	F BRK	Heater	HTR	Leader	L
Fire Extinguisher	F EXT	Height	HT, H, or	Leader Drain	L D
Fire Hose Cabinet	F HC		HGT	Left Hand	L H
Fireplace	FP	High Point	H PT	Length	LG, L, or lgth
Fixture	FIX	Horizontal	HOR	Library	LIB
Flashing	FL	Hose Faucet or Bib	H F or H B	Light	LT
				Light Weight Block	LWB

Light Weight Concrete	LWC	Outside Diameter	O D	Register, Ceiling	C R
Limestone	LS	Overall	OA	Register, Center	C R
Linen Closet	L CL	Overhead	OV HD	Register, Top	T R
Living Room	L R			Regulator	REG
Locker	LKR	Painted	PTD	Remove	REM
Louver	LV	Panel	PNL	Repair	REP
Louver Opening	LV O or L O	Pantry	PAN	Re-sawn	RES
Louvered Door	LV D	Partition	PTN	Return	RET
Low Point	L P	Passage	PASS	Revision	REV
Lumber	LBR or lbr	Penny (nail)	d	Revolutions Per Minute	R P M or rpm
		Per	/	Right Hand	R H
Manufacturing	MFG	Plaster	PL or PLAS	Riser	R
Marble	MR	Plastic	PLSTC	Rivet	RIV
Masonry Opening	M O	Plate	PL or P	Road	Rd
Material	MATL	Plate Glass	PL GL	Roof	RF
Mechanical	MECH	Plumbing	PLMB	Roof Drain	R D
Medicine Cabinet	M C	Plumbing Stack	ST	Roofing	RFG or Rfg
Metal	MET	Poly Vinyl Chloride	P V C	Rough	RGH
Meter (measure)	m	Portable	PORT	Round	RD or rnd
Mezzanine	MEZZ	Pound	LB, #, or lb	Round Bar	Bar ϕ
Millimeter	mm		LB/FT²,		
Minimum	MIN	Pounds Per Square Foot	#/□′, or	Scale	SC
Moulding	MLDG		PSF	Schedule	SCH
Movable Partition	M PART	Pull Chain	P C or P	Scupper	SCUP
Miscellaneous	MISC			Scuttle	SCUT
		Quantity	QTY	Section (drafting)	SECT
North	N	Quarry Tile	Q T	Section (land)	SEC
Nominal	NOM	Quarry Tile Base	Q T B	Service	SERV
Non-Slip	NS	Quarry Tile Floor	Q T F	Sewer	S
Not in Contract	N I C	Radius	R	Sheathing	SHTHG
Number	NO, #, or No	Random Length	R/L	Shelves	SH
		Range	R	Service Sink	SS
Office	OFF	Rectangular	RECT	Ship Lap	S/LAP
On Center	O C	Reflective	REFL	Shower	SH
1000 Board Feet	MBM	Refrigerator	REF	Siding	SDG or Sdg
Opening	OPNG	Register	REG	Sink	S or SK
Opposite	OPP	Register, Bottom	B R	Slate	SL
Outlet	OUT				

Socket	SOC	Suspend	SUSP	Vinyl Tile	V T
Softwood	SFTWD	Suspended Ceiling	SUSP CEIL	Vinyl Tile Base	V T B
Soil Pipe	S P	Switch	SW or S	Vinyl Tile Floor	V T F
South	S	Switch, Key Operated	SK	Viterous	VIT
Speaker	SPKR			Volume	VOL or V
Specifications	SPEC	Tangent	TAN		
Sprinkler	SPR	Tee	T		
Square	SQ	Tee, Structural		Wall	W
Square Bar	BAR □	See: Structural Tee		Wall Cabinet	W CAB
Square Foot	sq ft or □′	Telephone	TEL	Wall Vent	W V
Square Inch	sq in or □″	Temperature	TEMP	Washing Machine	WM
Stained	STN or stnd	Terrazzo	TER	Washroom	WR
Stainless Steel	S ST	Terra Cotta	T C	Water Closet	W C
Stairs	ST	Test Boring	TB	Water Heater	W H
Stairway	STWY	Thermostat	THERMO	Water Proofing	W P
Standard	STD	Thick or Thickness	THK or T	Watertight	WT
Stiffener	STIFF	Thousand	M	Watt	W
Stirrup	STIR	Toenail	TN	Weather Stripping	W S
Stock	STK	Toilet	T	Weatherproof	WP
Stone	STN	Tongue & Groove	T & G	Weephole	WH
Storage	STG	Transom	T or TR	Weight	WT or wt
Street	ST	Tread	T or TR	West	W
Structural	STR	Typical	TYP	White Pine	W P
Structural Tee from				Wide Flange	W
M Shape	MT	Unequal Leg Angle	∠	Width	W or Wth
Structural Tee from		Unfinished	UNFIN	Window	WDW
S Shape	ST	Up	U	Wire Glass	W GL
Structural Tee from		Urinal	UR	With	W/
W Shape	W T			Wood	WD
Structural Tubing	T S	Vapor Proof	VAP PRF	Wood Door	WD
Substitute	SUB	Varnish	VARN	Wood Frame	WF
Sump Pit	S P	Vent	V	Wrought Iron	WI
Supply	SUP	Vent Duct	V D	Water Table	W T
Surface	SUR	Vent Pipe	V P		
Surface Area	A or S	Vent Stack	V S		
Surface 1 Side 1 Edge	S1S1E	Ventilate	VENT	Yard	YD or yd
Surface 4 Sides	S4S	Ventilator	V	Yellow Pine	Y P
		Vertical	VERT		
		Vestibule	VEST	Zinc	Z

Standard Practices

Standards

The term "standards" is, as the name implies, a set of general standard practices established and used by an architectural office on all jobs. Architectural office standards basically cover drafting room procedure and engineering procedure. For the draftsman, such information as company approved and standard abbreviations, lettering heights and styles, accepted and preferred methods in dimensioning, call-out procedures, material specifications on drawings, preferred ways to indicate a section or detail, accepted wording of notes, heights of various pieces of equipment, design modules, etc. In offices employing large numbers of draftsmen, some type of standards are necessary. Fig. 3-8 shows an extract of a page of standards from a large architectural firm.

Project Numbers

Architectural offices assign a project or job number to any work undertaken. These numbers appear in the title block of each sheet. Project numbers normally consist of two or three series of digits. Generally the first set of numbers indicates the year the job was accepted by the firm. The second set of digits represents the consecutive number of projects for that year. A third digit may be included that would indicate the chief designer assigned to the project. In most cases the first two sets of numbers are used in project numbers. For example, the

Fig. 3-8. Many larger architectural firms institute their own standard practices so that notes, dimensioning, abbreviations are consistent.

number *7233* would identify that the proj. ect was begun in *1972*. The second set of digits in the number *7233*, indicates that this was the *33rd* commission by this particular architectural firm. No other project designed by this architectural firm can have the number 7233. If the chief designer's number is included it would follow preceded by a dash, such as 7233—2.

Detail Call-Outs

The most usual method of indicating a feature that will be detailed is to *circle the area,* called a *bubble* or *balloon,* and provide a means of identifying where the detail is to be located. Draftsmen may refer to a detail call-out as a *cherry.* Fig. 3-9 shows a portion of a plan that has been bubbled. Rather than drawing the bubble on the front face of the drawing sheet, many prefer to place it on the reverse side. If the bubble must be moved or some portion of the drawing changed in the bubble, it can be accomplished with a minimum amount of erasing.

The balloon and cherry are connected by a *common* radial line. The number in the top half of the balloon indicates the detail number on the sheet. The lower half contains the number of the sheet on which that particular detail will be located. As in the figure, the area detailed is number 7 on Sheet 28.

Usually the circle that encloses the area that is to be detailed does not exceed 1⅞″ or 2″ diameter. The bubble itself can be open or closed with a radial leader going

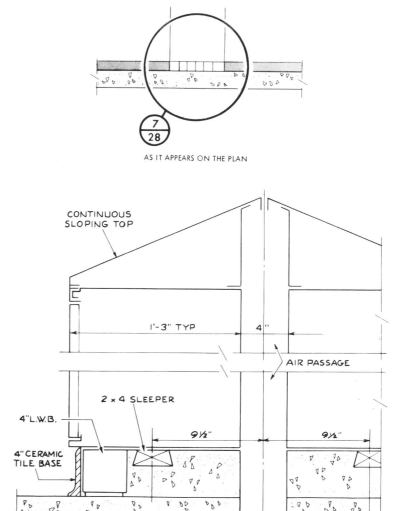

AS IT APPEARS ON THE PLAN

PHYSICAL EDUCATION LOCKER DETAIL
AS IT APPEARS ON THE DETAIL SHEET

Fig. 3-9. A portion that is to be detailed is "bubbled" and drawn to a larger scale on a detail sheet.

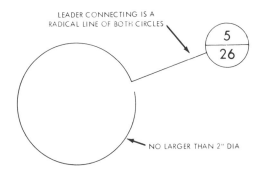

LEADER CONNECTING IS A
RADICAL LINE OF BOTH CIRCLES

NO LARGER THAN 2" DIA

Fig. 3-10. For most details a 2″ diameter bubble is sufficient.

to the cherry. Fig. 3-10 shows a typical bubble and balloon.

Portions of a drawing that are large or irregular in shape are enclosed by an oblong bubble. Fig. 3-11 shows this type of detail call-out.

Situations may arise where the detail of a feature is small and sufficient space is available in an adjacent portion of the sheet to connect the bubble and the detail with a line. An example of this technique is shown in Fig. 3-12. Depending upon the

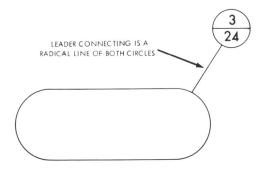

LEADER CONNECTING IS A
RADICAL LINE OF BOTH CIRCLES

Fig. 3-11. For long horizontal, vertical, or odd-shaped features an oblong bubble is used.

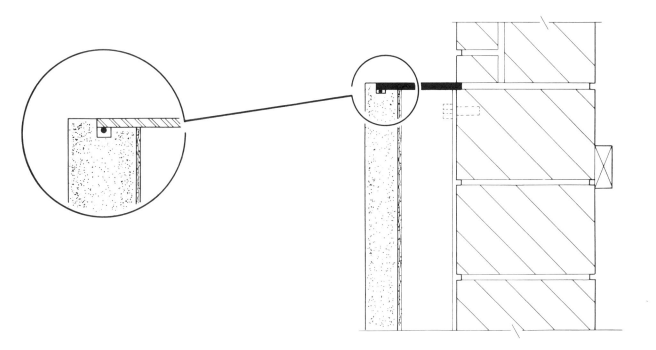

Fig. 3-12. Where space exists adjacent to the bubble, the detail is shown encircled and connected by a common radial line.

draftsman, he may treat a detail that appears on the same sheet by connecting the two with a line or with the conventional call-out procedure described above.

Fig. 3-9 illustrates a title lettered below the detail. A balloon is placed at the beginning or end of the title. Many offices prefer that the title be underlined with an indication of the scale placed immediately below. The height of the lettering for the title and for scale indication may be specified by the office as a standard or it may be determined by the designer draftsman. The number that is placed in the balloon adjacent to the title is the number of that detail, or section on the sheet. Details are not numbered consecutively from sheet to sheet. For example, if nine details and sections appear on Sheet 15, they are numbered 1 through 9. If on Sheet 16 there are seven details and sections, these would be numbered 1 through 7.

Section Call-Outs

In architectural practice the method of identifying where a section is to be taken is similar to that used in engineering drawing. Fig. 3-13 shows a typical application of a section. Fig. 3-14 shows three cutting planes that are commonly used on architectural drawings. For relatively small sections the cutting plane may be dashed or a continuous line and terminated by a shoulder with an arrow indicating the direction of sight. If it is not important to indicate the direction of sight, the shoulder and

AS IT APPEARS ON THE ELEVATION OR PLAN

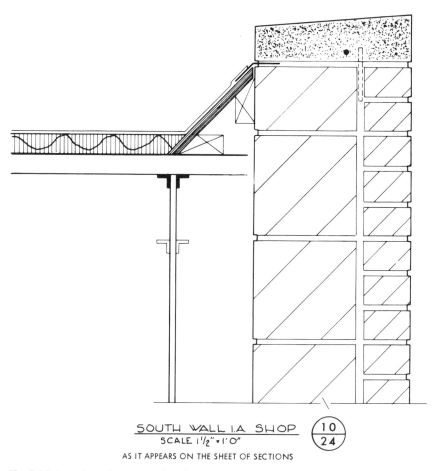

SOUTH WALL I.A. SHOP
SCALE 1½" = 1'0"
AS IT APPEARS ON THE SHEET OF SECTIONS

Fig. 3-13. A portion of a plan or elevation that is to be shown in section uses a cutting plane with a balloon and is drawn in section to a larger scale on a sheet of sections.

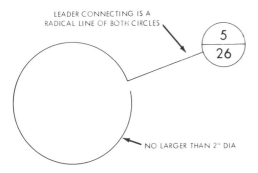

Fig. 3-10. For most details a 2″ diameter bubble is sufficient.

to the cherry. Fig. 3-10 shows a typical bubble and balloon.

Portions of a drawing that are large or irregular in shape are enclosed by an oblong bubble. Fig. 3-11 shows this type of detail call-out.

Situations may arise where the detail of a feature is small and sufficient space is available in an adjacent portion of the sheet to connect the bubble and the detail with a line. An example of this technique is shown in Fig. 3-12. Depending upon the

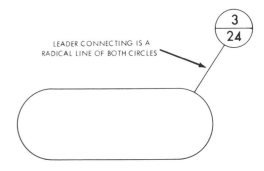

Fig. 3-11. For long horizontal, vertical, or odd-shaped features an oblong bubble is used.

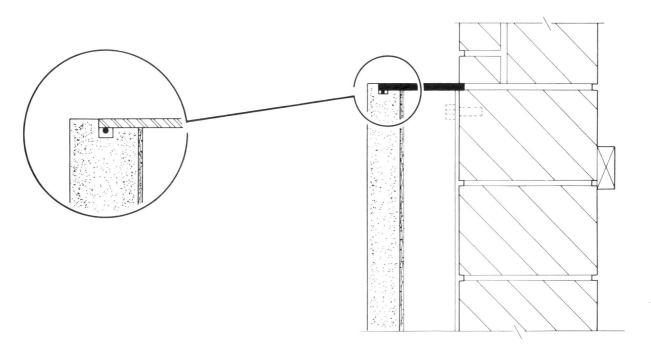

Fig. 3-12. Where space exists adjacent to the bubble, the detail is shown encircled and connected by a common radial line.

draftsman, he may treat a detail that appears on the same sheet by connecting the two with a line or with the conventional call-out procedure described above.

Fig. 3-9 illustrates a title lettered below the detail. A balloon is placed at the beginning or end of the title. Many offices prefer that the title be underlined with an indication of the scale placed immediately below. The height of the lettering for the title and for scale indication may be specified by the office as a standard or it may be determined by the designer draftsman. The number that is placed in the balloon adjacent to the title is the number of that detail, or section on the sheet. Details are not numbered consecutively from sheet to sheet. For example, if nine details and sections appear on Sheet 15, they are numbered 1 through 9. If on Sheet 16 there are seven details and sections, these would be numbered 1 through 7.

Section Call-Outs

In architectural practice the method of identifying where a section is to be taken is similar to that used in engineering drawing. Fig. 3-13 shows a typical application of a section. Fig. 3-14 shows three cutting planes that are commonly used on architectural drawings. For relatively small sections the cutting plane may be dashed or a continuous line and terminated by a shoulder with an arrow indicating the direction of sight. If it is not important to indicate the direction of sight, the shoulder and

AS IT APPEARS ON THE ELEVATION OR PLAN

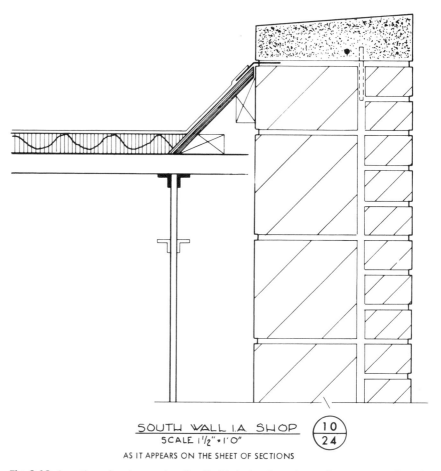

SOUTH WALL I.A. SHOP
SCALE 1 1/2" = 1' 0"

AS IT APPEARS ON THE SHEET OF SECTIONS

Fig. 3-13. A portion of a plan or elevation that is to be shown in section uses a cutting plane with a balloon and is drawn in section to a larger scale on a sheet of sections.

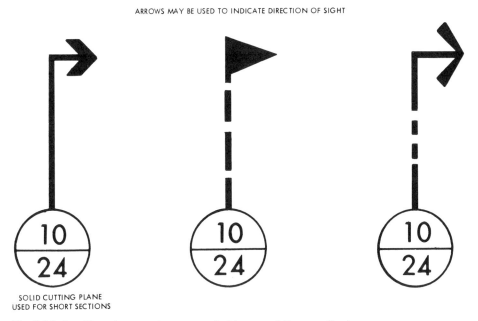

ARROWS MAY BE USED TO INDICATE DIRECTION OF SIGHT

SOLID CUTTING PLANE
USED FOR SHORT SECTIONS

Fig. **3-14.** A cutting plane can be represented by any of these methods.

Fig. **3-15.** When a cutting plane is extremely long, usually only the ends of the cutting plane and balloon are shown.

the cutting plane is a line *wider* than an object line so it is evident where the section is taken.

Since many sections are shown through walls, cornices, floors, foundation walls, footings, columns, etc., they usually do not appear on the same sheet as the cutting plane. The cutting plane, as in the case of a detail call-out, is connected to a balloon containing two numbers. The upper number indicates the number of the section on the sheet and the lower number refers to the sheet. In Fig. 3-13 the section will be found on Sheet 24 and is the 10th view on that sheet. The name and scale of each section is lettered below the sectional view. In order to identify the section more completely, a balloon is drawn preceding or following the title, and the numbers are repeated for identification.

Interior Elevation Call-Outs

In residential as well as in commercial architectural practice, it is necessary to *"elevate"* (draw an interior elevation of) different parts of the interior to show the design of cabinets, counters, tile heights and designs, drinking fountains, lavatories, etc. An interior elevation is typically identified by means of a balloon with an arrow drawn tangent to the arc. Fig. 3-16 shows one means of identifying an interior elevation. The upper half of the balloon indicates the interior elevation number and the lower half gives the sheet number. The

arrow are omitted. When a section through a structure is to be drawn, the cutting plane may be shown only at the extreme ends where the section is taken, as in Fig. 3-15, or it may be drawn completely through the structure. It will be noted that in any case

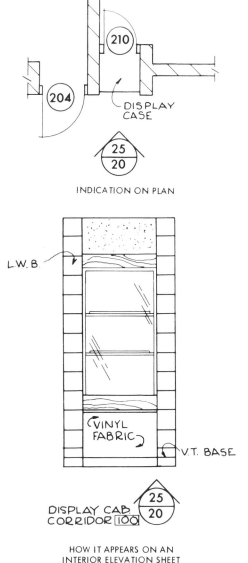

INDICATION ON PLAN

HOW IT APPEARS ON AN
INTERIOR ELEVATION SHEET

Fig. 3-16. Interior elevations are indicated by means of a balloon.

same means of identifying the interior elevation is given in the title below the elevation, as illustrated in Fig. 3-16.

Standard Details

Some architectural firms now use standard details in preparing a set of working drawings. The term "standard detail" usually includes sections, details and interior elevations. Structures, even though different in exterior and interior design, will employ many identical construction features such as structural connections, door heads and jambs, suspended ceilings, hand rail brackets, built-up roof, turned-under slab, etc.

An example of two standard details are shown in Fig. 3-17. Rather than re-drawing the same detail for each building project, a "standard detail" is pulled from a master catalog or file of details the architect has assembled. After all of the details have been selected for a project, they are then placed on the firm's sheet and photographed. The photographic negative is used ultimately to prepare a mylar-based print on which any additional call-out may be added by the architect.

Regardless of the scope or nature of the project (residential or commercial), standard details may be used to save drafting time. To save even more time in drawing details, many architectural firms are using freehand rather than mechanical delineation. Freehand methods are being used for standard details as well as new details.

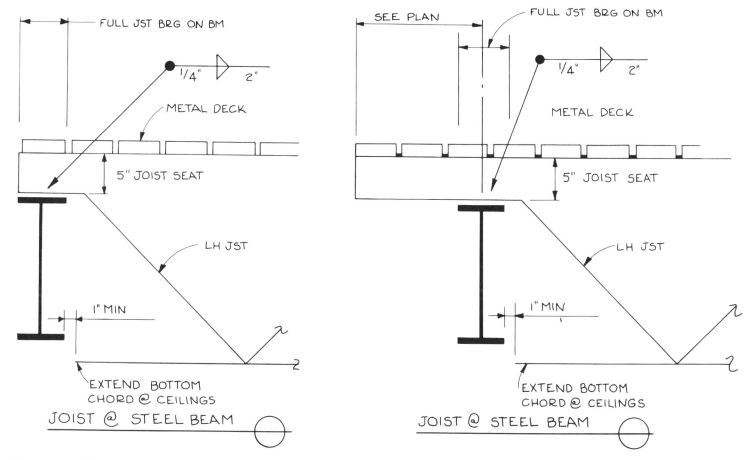

Fig. 3-17. Standard details are used to save time in preparing a set of working drawings. The details are placed on a sheet and are then photographed and printed.

Match Lines, Units and Key Plans

Match lines are used to match portions of a building that appear on several sheets. When a building is so large that it is placed on more than one sheet, some means of relating the various units must be established. Each portion of the building appearing on a separate sheet is referred to as a *unit*. Each side of a unit that abuts an adjoining unit is bounded by a *match line*. Each unit of the building is assigned a number called a *unit number*.

To assist the person reading the drawing, a *key plan* is placed on each sheet having a unit. The key plan is normally drawn to

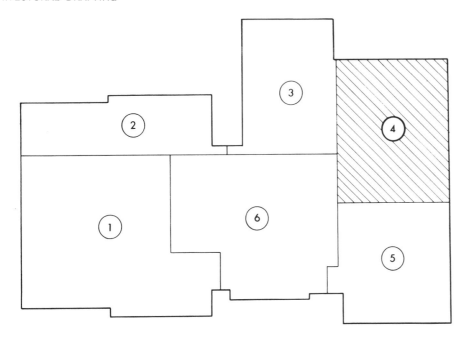

-KEY PLAN-

Fig. 3-18. A key plan identifies each unit of the building. The hatched unit indicates this is the unit which appears on this sheet.

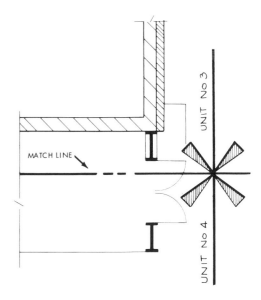

Fig. 3-19. A unit of a floor plan is bounded by a match line.

a *very small* scale such as $1'' = 50'$ and placed in the lower right or upper left corner of the sheet. Fig. 3-18 shows a key plan of a building divided into six units. The unit which appears on the sheet is generally *hatched* to facilitate quick orientation to the other units. A match line is a *wide* line, similar to a cutting plane line, but heavier than an object line. Units on both sides of the match line are identified by means of a wide filled-in arrow. Fig. 3-19 illustrates a typical set of match line arrows.

Notes

Architectural drawings contain many more notes naming materials than do machine, jig and fixture, marine, electrical, and other types of engineering drawings. For the most part, notes indicate the kinds of materials, usually not trade names, and procedures or operations. (The name of the product is given in the specifications. See Chapter 18.) All notes must be stated in the clearest possible terms so that no misunderstanding will occur. Standard abbreviations are always used. If the draftsman has any doubt regarding the correct abbreviation, he should consult a standard reference.

Two kinds of notes are placed on architectural drawings. These are *general* and *specific* notes. A *general* note is concerned with procedures or information for an entire set of drawings or a single sheet. Some examples of general notes are:

ALL INTERIOR ELEVATIONS ARE DRAWN TO THE SCALE

1/4" = 1'-0" UNLESS OTHERWISE NOTED

ALL DIMENSIONS ARE GIVEN FROM OUTSIDE OF

SHEATHING TO STUD FACE, TO STUD FACE, ETC.,

TO OUTSIDE OF SHEATHING

General notes are usually placed at the bottom of the sheet and may be underlined to attract attention.

Specific notes give the call-out of kinds of materials or operations. Even though identical materials are called out on other details, sections, or elevations—and on the same sheet—it is standard practice to identify all materials again. To some this practice may seem repetitious; however, this eliminates any question concerning the kind of materials or technique. Several specific notes are shown in the following examples:

12" DROP SIDING

BUILT UP ROOF ON 1-1/2" RIGID INSULATION

ON 1-1/2" STEEL DECK

6" DIA FIELD TILE LAID W/1-1/2" OPEN JOINTS

4" CERAMIC TILE

AL GRAVEL STOP

PLYWOOD GRAIN PERPENDICULAR TO JOIST DIRECTION

Leaders

All notes and call-outs of materials are lettered with guide lines. A leader is placed

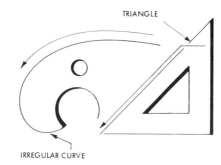

Fig. 3-20. Leaders are drawn with an irregular curve or triangle.

at the *beginning or end* of the note and terminates at the item with an arrowhead. Fig. 3-20 shows the proper method for drawing a leader. Leaders may be either straight or curved. Straight line leaders *always* have a horizontal shoulder that is centered at the *beginning* of the first or *end* of the last word. This is true, as well, with a curved leader. Fig. 3-21 illustrates the proper placement of a leader relative to the body of a note. The shoulder of the leader is *never* placed between the lines of a note, nor is a note underlined. Depending upon the "standard" of an office, curved leaders may either be drawn freehand or with an irregular curve.

To be sure a leader points to the proper location, it is terminated by an arrowhead. Normally the arrowhead of the leader touches the *edge* of the piece being identified. When the leader terminates on the surface rather than at the edge, a small

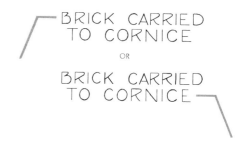

Fig. 3-21. A leader originates from the beginning or end of a note.

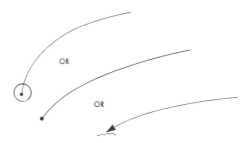

Fig. 3-22. A leader that refers a note to a surface is terminated with a small filled-in circle.

filled in circle is used in place of an arrowhead. An arrowhead may be used with wavy line to indicate a surface. Fig. 3-22 shows the terminal point of a leader which identifies a surface.

Laying-Out and Numbering of Details and Interior Elevations

Every building that is designed will ultimately require drawings of many sections, details and interior elevations. On large building projects there may be several sheets each of sections, details and interior elevations. The draftsman plans the sheet so it will appear to be balanced and with a minimum amount of open area. Fig. 3-23

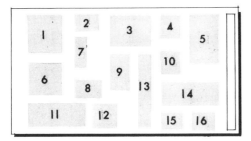

SECTION AND/OR DETAILS

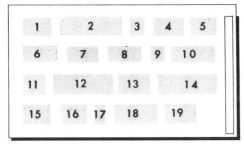

INTERIOR ELEVATIONS

Fig. 3-23. A sheet of details and/or sections or interior elevations are usually numbered from left to right.

shows how a well-planned detail and/or section sheet appears even though each detail or sectional view has a different size. Interior elevations are much easier to lay out because all elevations are normally of uniform height (floor to ceiling).

Numbering of the sections, details and elevation is from left to right, beginning in the upper left corner. When the end of the row is reached at the right side the numbers are continued on the row below at the left side. Fig. 3-23 illustrates how a sheet of sections, details and interior elevations is numbered.

Numbering of Sheets

There is no hard or fast rule about the order in which sheets are placed in a set of drawings. However, there are general guidelines that are followed in residential and commercial architectural design.

Residential. Usually the following order is established for residential plans. It must be understood that each office may have its own set standard to which it adheres. Generally, however, the order is as follows:

Sheet 1.   Site Plan and Sheet Index
Sheet 2.   First Floor Plan
Sheet 3.   Second Floor Plan
Sheet 4.   Basement or Foundation Plan
Sheet 5.   Elevations
Sheet 6.   Elevations
Sheet 7.   Electrical
Sheet 8.   Stair Detail
Sheet 9.   Fireplace Detail
Sheet 10. Joist Framing Plan
Sheet 11. Roof Framing Plan
Sheet 12. Structural Details and Sections
Sheet 13. Structural Details and Sections
Sheet 14. Door and Window Schedule
Sheet 15. Room Finish Schedule

Some contractors who build houses for speculation, that is, a house not built for a client but built and offered for sale by the contractor, may only have a floor plan and four elevations. Frequently the number of sheets in a set of plans depends upon the nature of the labor force and the amount of experience the workers have had with the contractor. In some instances the lending institution from whom the contractor obtains his construction loan will specify the type of drawings required. When a home is designed for a client, usually all the drawings listed above will be included. If a house is to have an FHA or GI insured mortgage, the insuring agency must be satisfied that the home is properly designed. The only way this can be determined is to have a full set of drawings and specifications or description of materials.

Commercial. As with residential plans, the number of sheets will vary according to the magnitude of the project. In commercial design, the order of sheets will vary slightly from residential plans as described above. In addition, the architectural designer and/or the architectural office may change the order of drawings from the usual procedure. The list of sheets given below is in typical order:

Sheet 1.   Site Plan and Sheet Index
Sheet 2.   Key Plan
Sheet 3.   Roof Plan
Sheet 4.   Foundation Plan
Sheet 5.   Floor Plan
Sheet 6.   Room Finish Schedule
Sheet 7.   Door Schedule
Sheet 8.   Frame Schedule
Sheet 9.   Exterior Elevations
Sheet 10.   Interior Elevations
Sheet 11.   Building Sections
Sheet 13.   Details and Sections
Sheet 14.   Casework Details
Sheet 15.   Special Equipment Plans
Sheet E-1   Electrical
Sheet M-1   Mechanical Plan (Plumbing
            & Heating)
Sheet S-1   Roof Framing Plan

If the building is sufficiently large to require breaking it into units, each unit is placed on a separate sheet while the foundation, floor and roof framing plan would be listed in multiple. For instance, a structure that is divided into three units would be numbered as follows:

Sheet 1.   Site Plan and Sheet Index
Sheet 2.   Key Plan
Sheet 3.   Roof Plan
Sheet 4.   Foundation Plan Unit 1
Sheet 5.   Floor Plan Unit 1
Sheet 6.   Foundation Plan Unit 2
Sheet 7.   Floor Plan Unit 2.
Sheet 8.   Foundation Plan Unit 3
Sheet 9.   Floor Plan Unit 3
Sheet 10.   Room Finish Schedule etc.

The electrical, mechanical and structural sheets *may not be* numbered in consecutive numbering of sheets. Each of these is prefixed by the letter of the area; that is, E, electrical, M, mechanical, and S, structural. If three sheets are in the electrical portion, 2 sheets in the mechanical, and 2 in the structural portions, the sheets would be numbered:

E-1.   Electrical
E-2.   Electrical
E-3.   Electrical
M-1.   Mechanical
M-2.   Mechanical
S-1.   Structural
S-2.   Structural

Schedules

Information such as door sizes, style and material; window size, type, and glazing; and materials and finishes on walls, floors and ceilings are almost impossible to place legibly on a plan, in addition to dimensions and notes. This task becomes extremely difficult when the plan is drawn to the scale of $\frac{1}{8}" = 1'0"$. For convenience and clarity the draftsman usually places this information in tabular form on a *window schedule, door schedule,* and *room finish schedule.* The aforementioned are the three essential types of schedules; however, some plans may include electrical and plumbing fixture schedules.

On small buildings window, door, and room finish schedules may be placed on the floor plan and elevation sheets. Most frequently the window and door schedules are together on a single sheet and the room finish schedule is on another sheet.

Window Schedules. A symbol is assigned to each type window or to each **window.** This symbol is placed on the floor plan at the centerline of each window. A residential window schedule will normally include the *symbol* (letter or number); *quantity* (number of units to be ordered); *size* (w″ x h″); *type* (casement, slider, fixed, etc.); *manufacturer and catalog number* (manufacturer's name and window number); *glazing* (double strength, pattern, welded insulating glass, etc.); *sash and frame* (wood, steel, or aluminum); *remarks* (any further information, such as bow window, middle sash, fixed, etc.). Fig. 3-24 shows the headings for a typical residential window schedule.

Door Schedules. Doors, like windows, are given a symbol (letter or number) and placed on the centerline of the door on the floor plan. If numbers are used for windows, then letters are used for doors or *vice-versa.* If there are more than 24 windows or doors, numbers are used on both schedules. A typical residential door schedule is shown in Fig. 3-25. The schedule will include a column for the *symbol* (letter or number); *quantity* (number of these units to be ordered); *size* (w″ x h″ x t″); *type* (flush panel, panel louvered, folding, sliding, etc.); *manufacturer and catalog number* (manufacturer's name and door number); *material* (wood—solid or hollow core, metal—steel or aluminum, plastic,

WINDOW SCHEDULE

SYM.	QUAN	SIZE	TYPE	MFG. & CAT. NO.	GLAZING	SASH & FRAME	REMARKS
A	3	4'-5" x 2'-3"	HORIZ. SLID.	RIMCO #4765	D.S.B.	WP	
B	3	3'-9" x 3'-3"	HORIZ. SLID.	RIMCO #3769	D.S.B.	WP	
C	1	2'-8 3/16" x 1'-6"	CASMT.	MALTA #1N30	D.S.B.	WP	PATTERN GLASS

Fig. 3-24. A window schedule is a standard method of tabulating the necessary information about each window.

DOOR SCHEDULE

NO.	QUAN	SIZE	TYPE	MFG. & CAT. NO.	MAT.	FRAME	REMARKS
1	2	2'-8" x 6'-8" x 1¾"	6 LITE	GRS #376	WP	WOOD	
2	1	6'-0" x 6'-8"	SLID	EDCO #415-C	AL	AL	¼" DBL. PL.
3	1	3'-0" x 6'-8" x 1¾"	2 PANEL	MS & D #23 DL	WP	WOOD	

Fig. 3-25. The residential door schedule contains all information for ordering doors.

etc.); *jamb or frame* (wood, metal, etc.); and *remarks* (any further information about the door).

A door schedule for a commercial, industrial, or institutional building varies slightly from a residential building in that additional information is included. A typical door schedule, see Fig. 3-26, includes a column for the *symbol* (letter or number); *size* (w″ x h″ x t″ and the letters PR if the doors are to be a pair of doors); *type* (referring to door elevations, showing placement of lite, louver, panel, etc.); *material* (hollow metal, wood, etc.); *glazing* (plate glass, wire glass, etc.); *undercut* (clearance between door and floor for ventilation or carpet); *hardware* (number refers to hardware specifications); *frame detail* (detail number on *frame sheet*); *frame material* (hollow metal, wood); *frame elevation* (frame elevation number); and *remarks* (any further information about the door—overhead, Dutch, fire rating, etc.).

Room Finish. Some type of information must be given about each room, corridor, entry, hall, and stairwell in respect to the type of material and finish used on the floors, walls and ceilings. The room finish schedule used for residential and commercial architecture is identical. Fig. 3-27 shows a Room Finish Schedule. The vast majority of offices use the following information: *symbol* (letter or number); *room name* (employment office, waiting room, kitchen, half bath, etc.); *floor* (material); *base* (material); *wall material* (block, plas-

DOOR SCHEDULE

NO	DOOR				FRAME				UNDER CUT	HDW	REMARKS
	SIZE	TYPE	MAT.	GLAZING	DET.	SHT.	MAT.	ELE.			
101	PR. 3'-0" × 7'-0" × 1¾"	A	H.M	¼"WIRE GL	9	29	HM	1		1	MULLION BETWEEN
102	PR. 3'-0" × 7'-0" × 1¾"	A	HM	¼"WIRE GL	9	29	HM	1		1	MULLION BETWEEN
103	PR. 3'-0" × 7'-0" × 1¾"	A	HM	¼"WIRE GL	9	29	H.M	3		1	MULLION BETWEEN
104	3'-0" × 7'-0" × 1¾"	B	WD	¼"WIRE GL	9,10	17	HM	4		10	
105	3'-0" × 7'-0" × 1¾"	B	WD	¼"WIRE GL	7,8	17	HM	5		10	

Fig. 3-26. A door schedule used for commercial, institutional, or industrial building lists additional information such as undercutting of doors, hardware, frame details, frame elevations, etc.

ROOM FINISH SCHEDULE

NO.	ROOM NAME	FLOOR	BASE	WALLS								WAINSCOT			CEILING		REMARKS
				NORTH		EAST		SOUTH		WEST							
				MAT.	FIN.	MAT.	FIN.	MAT.	FIN.	MAT.	FIN.	MAT.	FIN.	HGT.	MAT.	HGT.	
1	ENTRY	SLATE	W.P.	DW	WP	DW	WP	DW	P	DW	P				DW	8'-0"	
2	CORRIDOR	CAR.	WP	DW	FP	DW	FP	DW	FP	DW	FP				DW	8'-0"	
3	BED ROOM	H. WD.	W.P.	DW	WP	DW	FP	DW	FP	DW	FP				DW	8'-0"	
4	BED ROOM	H. WD.	WP	DW	WP	DW	FP	DW	FP	DW	FP				DW	8'-0"	
5	BED ROOM	H.WD.	WP	PAN		PAN		PAN		DW	FP				AT	8'-0"	
6	BATH	VT	VT	DW		DW		DW		DW					DW	8'-0"	

Fig. 3-27. A room finish schedule used for residential and commercial, industrialal, and institutional buildings is similar in that it gives information about the material and finishes for floors, walls, and ceilings throughout the structure.

ter, drywall, etc.); *wall finish* (paint, vinyl fabric, ceramic tile); *wainscot material* (ceramic tile, vinyl fabric); *wainscot finish* (paint, etc.); *wainscot height* (distance from floor to top of wainscot); *ceiling material* (plaster, drywall, acoustical tile, lay-in tile, exposed concrete, etc.); *ceiling height* (distance from finish floor to finish ceiling); and *remarks* (additional information regarding floor, walls, or ceiling).

Since the architect must specify the recommended quality of finishing materials, this information appears in the specifications. Some finish schedules will indicate the type of paint: flat, semi-gloss, gloss, epoxy, varnish, polyurethane, or sealer.

Reproduction of Drawings

Architectural drawings can be reproduced for use by clients, contractors, subcontractors, or suppliers by a number of different methods. Each of the following processes has its advantages and disadvantages. These methods are:

- A. Blueprinting
- B. Diazo
  1. Moist
  2. Dry
- C. Photographic
- D. Offset printing
- E. Electrostatic

Of these methods used in the architectural field, the diazo type print is the most widely used. The process of blueprinting is the oldest method of reproducing drawings. A blueprint (a negative print) derives its name from the blue background and white image. This process, developed in England by Sir John Herschel in 1837, is basically photographic, with the tracing acting as a film negative. Blueprinting remained for many years as the chief method of reproducing drawings.

Because of the time and cost required for 3 separate cumbersome steps in blueprinting, a faster means of reproducing prints was devised. This process is known as the *Diazo* type positive print. Diazo prints may be either *moist* (called a "B & W" or "black and white") and *dry* (called a "white print.") "Moist" and "dry" refer to the method of developing the exposed paper. Both of these diazo processes are based on the sensitive coatings placed on the paper and the type of developer used.

The *dry diazo* type of print is most frequently found in architectural offices because of its economy in terms of time and materials and the low maintenance factor. Because of these advantages, many architectural offices have a dry-diazo type ma-

GRAPHIC / ASSOCIATES
ARCHITECTS
KALAMAZOO, MICHIGAN

CLASSIFICATION S

CLASSIFICATION SYMOBOLS
P — PRELIMINARY
W— WORKING DRAWINGS
S — SPECIFICATIONS
J — SUPERVISION

TIME RECORD

PAY PERIOD: FROM 10/18 THRU 10/29 NAME: JOHN F. DOE

DESCRIPTION OF WORK	JOB NO.		10/18	10/19	10/20	10/21	10/22	10/25	10/26	10/27	10/28	10/29	TOTAL
ABC PLASTICS CO.	P	7013	6			2	5				4	6	23
G.L. BLDG	S	6931	2	3	5	3	1						14
P.P. SR. CITIZENS	J	6901		3				1					4
P.T. HS. ADDITION	W	7002		2	3		2	7	4	8	4	2	32
WOODWARD H.S.	J	6842				3							3
SICK									4				4
GENERAL													
GROSS TOTALS		8	8	8	8	8	8	8	8	8	8		80

Fig. 3-28. A time record sheet is used to identify the amount of time the architect, engineer, and draftsman spend on each project throughout a pay period.

chine. The dry diazo method of making a print is a two-step operation: (1) exposure and (2) development by ammonia vapors. This print paper is exposed to an ultra-violet light source that causes a chemical decomposition of the light sensitive coating when it has not been protected by a line on the tracing. The exposed print paper is developed by passing it through a chamber containing ammonia vapor. Even though the resulting print is a positive type print (dark image on a white background) the prints are still referred to as "blueprints." *Blueprint* properly refers to a specific process and kind of print.

Since the quality of the *white print* (dark blue or black lines on an off-white background) is important, it is essential that line work and lettering on the tracing is dense and opaque. If the pencil lines are weak, the light will filter through and partially destroy the light sensitive coating in the exposure process. The machine will reproduce the quality of the tracing. The beginning draftsman must attempt to have dense, dark, and vibrant line work.

Time Record Sheets

All architectural offices, whether a one-man or 35-man office, maintain some type of record showing the time that the architect and draftsman spends on each job. During a normal eight-hour working day a man may work on several different projects. All projects are usually divided roughly into four sequential phases: preliminary studies and drawings, working drawings, specifications, and supervision. At the end of each day the employee records his activities according to the name of the job, phase, job number and hours on a Time Record Sheet. Fig. 3-28 shows John F. Doe's time record sheet for a two-week period. At the end of a specified period—two weeks in this illustration—the hours are easily tallied for each job.

Questions and Problems

1. Copy a floor plan of a 5 or 6 room house, using a scale of ¼″ = 1 foot. Sketch in the symbols on the floor plan which will show the following:
   a. A masonry wall on the front of the house only; the sides and rear walls are frame covered with siding. The interior partitions are of frame construction.
   b. Casement windows in the kitchen, ribbon sliding windows in the bedrooms, and double-hung windows in the rest of the rooms of the plan.
   c. Front and rear entrance doors, a double acting door between the kitchen and dining room, bi-fold or accordion doors for the closets, and a plastered arch if the plan requires one.
   d. Draw plumbing fixtures on the plan.
   e. Locate electrical fixtures, outlets, and switches on the plan.
2. Identify the following symbols by a sketch:
   a. Electric range outlet (plan)
   b. Outside electric outlet (plan)
   c. 4-way switch (plan)
   d. Metal flashing (elevation)
   e. Stone (elevation)
   f. 2″ × 4″ dimensioned lumber (section)
   g. ¾″ × 3½″ casing (section)
   h. Sliding door (interior wall plan)
   i. Sliding door (exterior wall plan)
3. Study the first floor plan of a set of plans found in this text. List 20 to 25 items of information found on the plan which are shown by symbols.
4. Study the elevations of the set of plans found in problem 3 above, and list 15 or more items of information which are shown by symbols.
5. Why is there a need for symbols?
6. What organizations concern themselves with the standardization of symbols?
7. What are three distinct kinds of architectural drawings which use symbols?
8. Sketch a floor plan of a vacation cabin, using a scale of approximately ¼″ = 1 foot. Using symbols, show at least two doors, three different windows, a fireplace, an open porch, and a bath.
9. Copy a plan from a magazine, make the outside walls either frame or masonry, with the interior partitions of wood, using a scale of ¼″ = 1 foot. Indicate on this plan, by proper symbols, two different kinds of appropriate windows and doors, stairs, cabinets, plumbing fixtures, and chimney.

Building Site Considerations 4

The purpose of this chapter is to aid you in developing an understanding of the many factors that go into making up the ideal site, such as: schools, transportation, utilities, topography, physical features, zoning, ordinances, codes, tax rates, etc. While studying this chapter you will add some new terms to your vocabulary: *title search, easement, warranted deed, protective covenant, code,* and *zoning,* to name a few.

You will also find out how to develop a plot plan by locating the structure, landscaping and plantings and how to select a homesite by using the checklist.

Next to the building itself, there is no greater investment than the site. The site should not be viewed merely as an isolated plot of land, it must also be seen as part of the total community situation. A home site is more than a place upon which to build a house. It is a permanent location for the family residence. Great care, therefore, must be exercised to insure a site and neighborhood suited to the present and future needs of the family.

Neighborhood

Often, prospective site owners visit with the neighbors to gain a first-hand impression prior to purchasing. A tour of the surrounding neighborhood may reveal many features not discussed with the realtor. Look for factors which may detract from the neighborhood: below average housing, housing not in the same general price range, busy or noisy through streets, dumping areas, swamps, railroads, airports, factories, etc. Each of these undesirable features reduces the value of the site. The happiness of the new owner depends not only upon those who live nearby, but also upon the available facilities, the surrounding physical features of the neighborhood, and local ordinances.

Available Facilities

Schools. Closeness and quality of schools are particularly important to families with children. When choosing the site, investigate the location of all the nearest schools. Transportation to and from the schools may be a problem if they are not within walking distance. Information concerning nearby schools, such as enrollment, class size, school boundary lines, and school bus facilities or pick-up routes should be obtained from the local board of education.

Transportation facilities. The present trend in the design of residential areas is such that community facilities (schools, churches, theaters, etc.) and commercial areas are not located within walking distance. Distance is measured in terms of the time required for traveling, rather than in terms of mileage. *Time is the essential factor.* When selecting a site, investigate the public transportation facilities and major traffic arteries which go to commercial and community facility areas. Fig. 4-1 illustrates the recommended maximum distances between the home site to be chosen and the different community facilities. The distance between the home and the place of employment is shown in time measure rather than in terms of miles.

Utilities. It is considered essential today to have available such utilities as water, electricity, gas, municipal sewage disposal, storm sewer system, and telephone. In some fringe or suburban areas all such facilities are not available. A nominal fee may be charged for the extension of some or all of these utilities to the prospective site. It is sound business to investigate all these mat-

ters to determine who assumes the financial responsibility.

Physical Features

Topography is an important factor to consider when choosing a lot. Note the physical features of the site such as rocks, land slope, and soil condition. Excavations for the footings in rocky or steep sites may prove costly and exceedingly difficult. Lots which are too rocky eliminate the possibility of having a basement. Sloping land offers advantages as well as disadvantages. A slope is an aid to drainage, and a sloping lot lends itself to a partially or fully exposed walkout basement. However, lots having steep slopes generally require retaining walls and earth fill. *Be especially wary of lots which have been filled.* If a portion or all of the lot has been recently filled, or will require

filling prior to the construction of the building, it is possible that the building will settle and crack the foundation. Such damage may occur either during the building construction or at a later date depending upon how fast the fill below the structure settles. If the conditions of the earth are doubtful, it is always wise to have a soil engineer check the site before buying or starting building construction. If the site appears to be questionable, obtain all the necessary information, including excavation cost estimates, prior to any decision to purchase or to build.

Lot size. Some families enjoy spacious lawns, while others are interested in a minimal amount of yard work. Most experts recommend 50' wide by 100' deep as the minimum lot size unless neighborhood conditions, local customs, or land values dictate otherwise. Narrow lots may present difficulties in orientation of the major living areas and/or the placement of the building. Where building restrictions are such that an odd placement of the house is not permitted, a lot frontage of 60' is almost mandatory for sufficient light and ventilation. In many developments, lots vary from 80' to 130' in width and by 100' to 150' in depth.

Local Ordinances

Zoning is an important matter for the prospective site purchaser to investigate. Some zones permit only the erection of apartments and business structures. Other areas are solely residential. It is wise to investigate the zoning restrictions in the

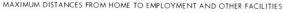

MAXIMUM DISTANCES FROM HOME TO EMPLOYMENT AND OTHER FACILITIES

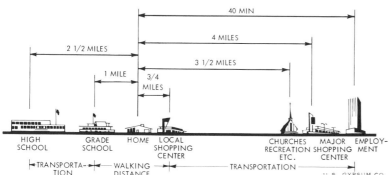

Fig. 4-1. Maximum distances from home to employment and other facilities are measured not only in miles but also in time.

immediate and adjoining neighborhoods. A multiple family dwelling or a business establishment may cause an appreciable loss in property values. Zoning restrictions, in part, determine the future of the neighboring area. A city concerned with its municipal pride permits very few amendments for *spot zoning* in single family residential areas.

Building codes vary from area to area. It is wise to investigate the building restrictions in the area prior to any lot commitment. Some restrictions are for the benefit of home builders; others outlaw many newly developed building materials and construction methods because they do not conform to extremely antiquated rules. Be very skeptical of areas which do not conform to contemporary practices as well as those which have no building codes.

Assessments and tax rates should be investigated before choosing a site. A quick check at the local, municipal, or county offices will reveal the amount of taxes and assessments (or impending assessments) which may be due on the lot in question.

Prospective buyers frequently have the opinion that taxes are lower in the suburban areas. This is often not actually true. Large cities and some large communities may have higher taxes because they offer as many as 300 services, while suburbs or fringe areas may offer as few as 20. Extra charges for water, refuse collection, or sewage disposal have considerable effect on the actual total costs of suburban living. Low taxes do not always indicate a desirable area in which to locate.

Title Search and Deed

Prior to purchase of the site, a *title search* should be instituted to determine if there are any claims (legal or monetary) against the property. This service is usually performed by an agency specializing in title searches. Reputable loan institutions will not lend money on a house or property unless the title has been searched and found to be satisfactory (no legal claims against the property). The deed to the site should be inspected for any restrictions and *easements*. Easements are rights given by the owner to the utility companies to cross the lot with gas, water, and power lines. This also includes a right for entry on the land for service and repair. Some easements may cause inconvenience or possible hazard after the building is constructed. The buyer should accept only a *warranted deed*. This is a guarantee, given by the seller, stating that there are no liens, encumbrances, easements, or claims against the property. With a warranted deed the seller will defend the title against all legal claims by other persons. The deed is valid when it has been (1) prepared in writing describing the property fully, (2) agreed upon by both the buyer and the seller, and (3) witnessed by a notary public.

Site Cost

It is impossible to project an average site cost because of the varying conditions in the different localities. A rule of the thumb states that approximately 12 to 20 per cent of the total cost of the house (materials and construction) should be expended for a lot. This percentage is not a hard-and-fast rule and will vary according to local land, material, and construction costs.

The site may require additional improvements and maintenance such as grading, additional top soil, or provisions for drainage. These expenses must also be considered in the total cost of the lot. Frequently, these are completely forgotten and come as an economic shock to the budget.

The initial cost of the lot is also dependent upon its location within a normal city block. A lot in the middle of a block is less expensive than one at a corner. Proportionally higher tax assessments are usually levied on a corner lot for streets, sewers, and other improvements.

Community Considerations

Some communities or neighborhoods are so poorly planned that neighborhood stability is almost non-existant. Those communities, having grown without a plan, eventually become transitional (i.e., deteriorate both economically and socially). Antiquated or inadequate zoning laws hinder the land developer in completing well planned community subdivisions. A properly planned community depends to a large degree on zoning. Zoning provides separation of land masses for basic use and restricts the size of lots and buildings.

Restrictions may be carried further by means of *protective covenants*. These are legal devices which allow a developer or a group of citizens within an area to establish and maintain minimum standards of quality. Covenants protect the home owner against impairment of home values by the addition of sub-standard buildings. Covenants also detail the standards of housing and provide for legal means of enforcement.

Much of today's building is in suburban or outlying areas, encompassing whole tracts of land which are subdivided by professional land developers. Many of these tracts are planned as virtually separate communities. These areas may include shopping centers, social centers, parks, recreational facilities, athletic fields, and churches. Fig. 4-2 illustrates such an area.

A recent trend in community planning, known as *clustering,* places houses closer together. Lot sizes are slightly reduced and houses are grouped around a *cul-de-sac* (a dead-end street often terminating in a circle)

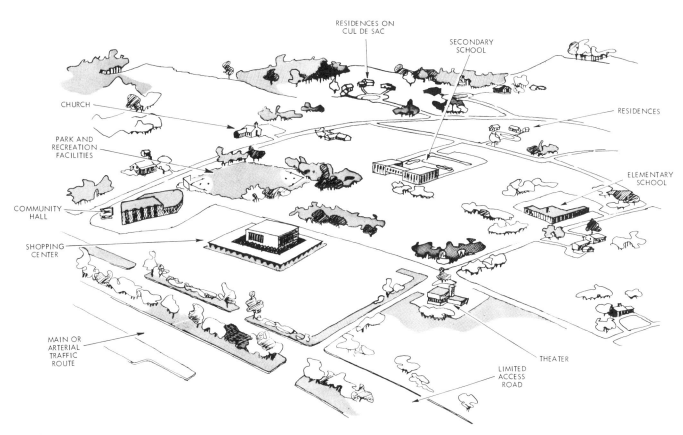

Fig. 4-2. Modern housing developments may be planned as virtually separate communities.

or *access court* (a cluster of houses without street access). The excess area, available from the reduced lot sizes, may then be made available as a common park area for all residents in the subdivision.

Street paving, sidewalks, and streetlights are assets to any well-planned community. This is true not only in terms of practicality and beautification, but also in terms of safety. Residential streets should be planned to eliminate through traffic. Small cul-de-sacs, courts, and minor residential streets discourage heavy traffic. Some communities use limited access roads which branch off into less direct, curved streets.

Site and House Relationship

Lot Shape and Topography

The shape and topographic features of the lot have an important influence on house planning. As suburban living becomes more popular, areas which offer a variety of lot shapes are being opened for development. The plan of many American communities is based on a rectangular grid system. This usually leads to a monotonous division of small land plots. In cities the lots are long and narrow so that a maximum number of sites per city block can be obtained. In the suburbs, however, the lots are often wide and deep and have irregular shapes (trapezoidal, triangular, etc.) which deviate from the basic rectangular grid. Fig. 4-3 graphically illustrates how the shape and topo-

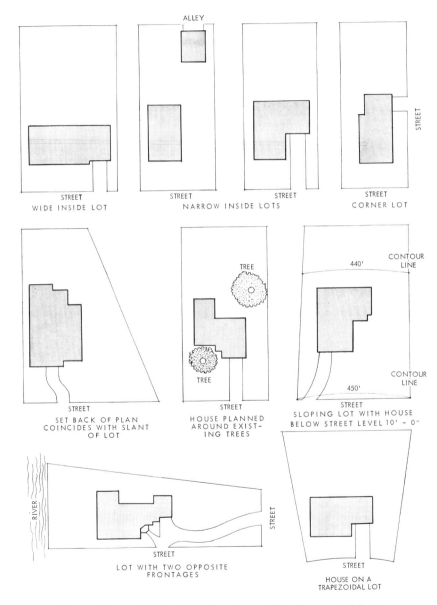

Fig. 4-3. The shape of the lot affects the plan and the placement of the house.

graphic features of the lot affect the planning and the orientation of a house.

There are several factors to consider when planning a house which conforms to the physical features of the lot. The following statements indicate the manner in which the shape and topography of the site affects the orientation plan of a house to be erected.

Shape. Frequently, the outline of a lot may determine the shape and orientation of the house. A triangular lot shape, for example, will probably have a house built with *set backs* (i.e., the face of the building is moved back) to coincide with the sides of the lot. See Fig. 4-3 (center left).

Size. A house which is excessively large for the lot is out of place. It is particularly so if the lots are small and the adjoining houses are well proportioned in size.

Topography. Irregular and sloping land, together with ledge rock, may offer an ideal situation for a multi-level type of a house. These physical features often produce very interesting plans provided excessive costs are not incurred.

Trees. The position and number of trees may control placement and room planning of the house on the site. Well developed trees may add as much as $1,000 or more to the value of a building site.

View. The length of lot frontage, or a desirable view in front of the house, may suggest a controlling position for the family room, dining room, or living room.

House Placement

Placement of the house on a site deserves much thoughtful consideration. The best approach is to study the particular conditions of the lot. Each building site, whether suburban or city, has individual characteristics such as size, location, topography, trees, bushes, direction of view, and number of improvements. Architects utilize these conditions in planning and designing, so that the site and the structure may complement each other.

When determining the proper placement of the house on a site, the lot may be divided into three functional areas. These areas are (1) *public,* that portion of the lot which is exposed to the public view, usually the front area; (2) *service,* that portion used for the kitchen entry, garage, laundry, delivery, and possibly the children's play area, the front, rear, or side; and (3) *private,* that area allotted for recreation, gardening, and outdoor living, usually at the rear or side. Location of the house relative to these three functional areas is also dependent upon the sun and the prevailing winds.

The house is best located forward on the lot unless prohibited by zoning restrictions. This permits the private area in the rear to be maximum in size. Houses placed in this manner eliminate long driveways and sidewalks which are expensive to construct. Privacy screens or plantings in the private area offer a further retreat from neighbors, provide shade, and serve as wind breakers. An attached garage may also provide privacy and act as a screen for the service area. Complete privacy in the living area may be obtained by making use of plantings and screenings, garage position, and the house placement.

Plot Plan

The first step after purchasing a site and before serious planning begins is drawing a plot plan. Plot plans present a graphic picture of existing topographic conditions and reveal, as well, any possible problems that may arise.

The designer usually lays out the plot plan as one of the initial steps in designing a building. A part of the architect's responsibility is to fit the proposed structure to the site. For this reason, he inspects the site and many times photographs it from various positions: from the road, sidewalk, drive, rear corner, etc. Prior to, or following the inspection, the architect will obtain a topographic map or topographic survey by a civil engineering firm. This map or survey will show contours of the area to be developed. The site plan is one of the primary drawings that is made. The shape of the building, as it blends with the surrounding area, must be determined and finalized. It is then placed on the plot plan and other features are added.

Whenever an extensive amount of land is consumed by a building project, ecological problems occur. As vast areas are paved for parking around an airport, shopping center, industrial or commercial building, church, nursing home, school, etc. or for the structure itself, the once grassy areas that are now occupied by the structure or parking area no longer can absorb water and support plant life. As our population continues to grow, man's needs for goods also increases; thus more and more land is used for mobility, production, distribution and retailing of goods, as well as dwellings.

Far sighted architects and urban planners are concerned with these problems. The topographic study and plot plan are necessary tools that aid in determining what will happen to the land surrounding the building, not only from the esthetic standpoint, but the ecological standpoint as well. As man changes the natural configuration of the land surface, he must then design and provide a more attractive scene that will, hopefully, complement the new structure and restore the ecological aspect. Essential to preliminary sketching and drawing the plot plan is an understanding of some basic features regarding land and its identification.

Land Identification

Much of the land in the United States and Canada is subdivided according to a system of land survey that was instituted in 1785 by the authority of the United States Congress. The areas affected by this survey system were the regions of the Great Lakes, Mississippi Valley, and Western States. Congress decreed that these new lands should be subdivided into Congressional Townships. Prior to that time land survey, as in the thirteen original Colonies and Southern States, had been irregular and unsystematic.

In order to establish a regular system for land identification, a series of north-south lines called *principal meridians* and east-west lines called *base lines,* were established. By using these north-south and east-west lines, the land was divided into *basically* square areas. There are now 36 principal meridians located in the United States. Each of these rectangular areas is identified by numbered townships and numbered ranges.

A column of townships running north and south is called a *range.* Townships are described at 2 townships north or south of a named base line and 3 ranges east or west of a named principal meridian. A township grid with the principal meridian and base line is shown in Fig. 4-4.

To identify Township "A," in Fig. 4-4,

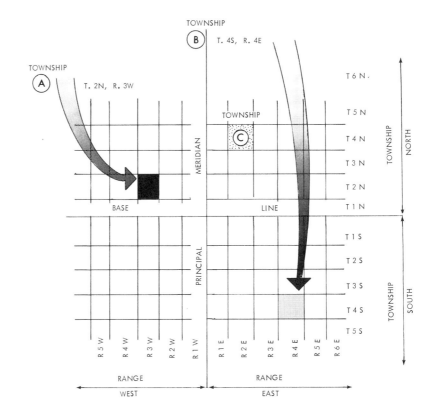

Fig. 4-4. The township grid is used to subdivide land and serves as a basis for land identification.

one must first look at the township and range identification. The township labeled as "A" would be referred to as Township 2 North, Range 3 West. It would be written at "T.2N, R.3W." Township "B" is Township 4 South and Range 4 East. Its identification would be "T.4S, R.4E." Townships are usually given names, such as Proviso Township, Texas Township, etc.

Each township is subdivided into 36 equal areas called *sections*. Township "A" (T.2N, R.3W) is shown divided into 36 sections in Fig. 4-5. Each section is essentially a square of approximately one mile per side, containing 640 acres. Each section in the township is numbered from 1 to 36, always beginning in the northeast corner with 1 and moving from right to left and then down left to right, etc. A specific section can be noted by its section number, township, and range.

The shaded section in Fig. 4-5 is identified as "Section 16, T.2N, R.3W." A section may be divided into a half section (320 acres), quarter section (160 acres), quarter-quarter section (80 acres), and quarter-quarter-quarter section (40 acres). The corner of every section and quarter section is permanently located on the earth's surface by a concrete conument. The exact location of the corner is stamped on a brass tablet on the top of the monument.

Any parcel of land may be identified by this system of survey. No other parcel may exist with the same description. To locate the parcel of land as shown as D in Fig. 4-5, the description would be: the southwest

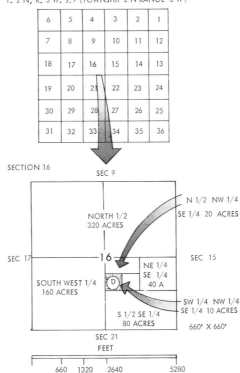

TOWNSHIP

T. 2 N, R. 3 W. S.9 (TOWNSHIP 2 N RANGE 3 W)

SECTION 16

Fig. 4-5. A township is divided into 36 sections, and each section is approximately 1 mile square.

quarter of the northwest quarter of the southeast quarter of Section 16 of Township 2 north, Range 3 west of the Michigan Meridian. This would be written as "SW ¼, NW¼, SE ¼, Sec. 16. T.2N, R.3W, Mich. M."

On land development plans, essential in-

formation is given in the following order:

1. Name of development
2. Section
3. Township, north or south
4. Range, east or west
5. Township name
6. County name
7. State

A portion of a land development plan is illustrated in Fig. 4-6, which shows the information in proper form. Note how the "Cascade Hills" development is identified in relation to the NE corner of Sec. 23. The point of beginning of "Cascade Hills" is 683.29′ from the northeast corner of Section 23.

The site or plot plan will usually have the same identification information as the land development plan. Since the designer or architect works from the land development plan, he must be more specific concerning the location of the structure. A site plan would include the following information:

1. Lot number
2. Name of development
3. Section
4. Township, north or south
5. Range, east or west
6. Township name
7. County
8. State

No mistake can be made in locating the land shown on a typical plot for a residence

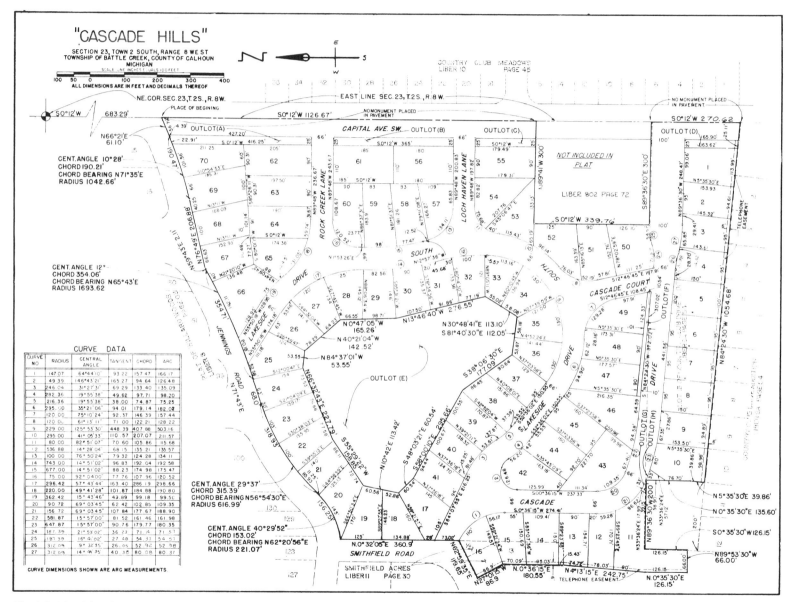

Fig. 4-6. A land development plan must show the location of the parcel being used for development purposes.

N. 89°-42'-45" W.   90.00'

+0.00

N. 28°-07'-30" E.   159.5'

HOUSE

NEW
GRADE LINES

EXISTING
GRADE

3'-0" WIDTH
SIDEWALK

POOL

STO.

CARPORT

PLANTER

NEW
TREES

CRUSHED STONE

BOLDERS

CONC.

SIDEWALK
WIDTH 4'-0"

NEW
TREES

EXISTING
TREES

N. 0°-02' E.   150.00'

41.50'

N. 76°-00' E.   191.30'

R-60.00'

ARCADIA NO. 2
SECTION 19, T. 2S., R. 11 W.
CITY OF KALAMAZOO, COUNTY OF KALAMAZOO, MICHIGAN
LOT NO. 167

NORTH

Fig. 4-7. The plot plan will give the exact location of the land on which the structure is to be built.

such as the one shown in Fig. 4-7. The brief description identifies the *lot* (167); *development* (Arcadia No. 2); *section* (19); *township and range* (T.2S, R.11W); *city* (Kalamazoo); *county* (County of Kalamazoo); and *state* (Michigan). No other descriptive material need be included. Usually Items 1 through 5 are stated on the plot plan; however, all may be included. Note that in Fig. 4-7, the location dimensions are given from the *rear* and *side* lot lines. This practice is sometimes followed when the lot is trapezoidal or odd-shaped.

Lot Lines. Each parcel of land that is identified today is bounded by a straight or curved line called a *lot line*. Every lot line has a specific direction, length, and if curved, a radius.

Direction of Lot Lines

The direction of any lot line is measured in relation to a north-south line. This relationship or direction is commonly called *bearing*. The bearing of a line is the horizontal angle between the line and a line pointing *true* north-south. The bearing is identified by the compass quadrant and degrees. The quadrant refers to the general compass direction, such as NE, SE, SW, or NW and limited to 90°. Fig. 4-8 shows the quadrants labeled according to compass direction.

Fig. 4-9 shows several lines and their bearing. For example, line AB has a bearing of N50°E. This means that line AB is measured from north in an easterly direction of 50°. Line CD in this figure has a

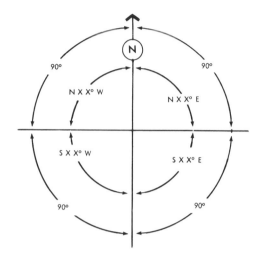

Fig. 4-8. The bearing of a line is identified by quadrants relating to compass directions and graduated into 90°.

EF has a bearing of S 26° E. It is measured from south in an easterly direction, 26° from the north-south line. Bearings of lines used for surveying, site planning or land development purposes are always measured from either north or south and never greater than 90°.

Lot line bearings are related to *true geographic north*. A compass needle will point to the true *magnetic north pole*. Magnetic north and geographic north are not the same. The difference between the two norths is called the *magnetic declination*. The magnetic declination is found on all U.S. Government maps and charts. A map declination symbol is shown in Fig. 4-10. Remember *true geographic north* is always used in site planning!

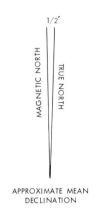

Fig. 4-10. All government maps show difference between magnetic north and true geographic north.

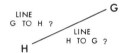

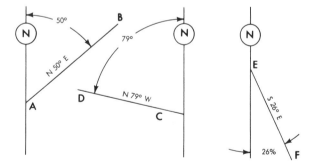

Fig. 4-9. The bearing of a line is first identified by north or south and its east or west direction.

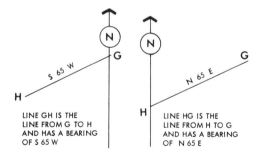

Fig. 4-11. The first letter of a line indicates the point of origin.

bearing of N 79° W. Line CD is measured from north in a westerly direction. Both of these lines, AB and CD, have been measured from north. On the other hand, line

Every line has a specific bearing. Fig. 4-11 shows a line; however, line GF is different from FG even though it appears the same. When referring to a line, some identi-

fication must be made. Letters are sometimes placed at the ends of a line. When discussing line GH, the first letter *G* means that this is the point or origin. The line begins at G and ends at H. When referring to line GH, it would have a bearing of 65° W. Using the same line, but identifying it as "line HG," H would be the point of origin. The line begins at H and terminates at G and has a bearing of N 65° E. The first letter always indicates the point of beginning.

Length of Lines

Straight Lines. Any straight line in a site, plot, or land development plan is identified by its bearing and length. The length of the line normally is carried to the hundredths of a foot (.xx′), such as 135.60′ or 78.69′. The bearing of the line may be placed before or after the length of the line, as N 02°-30′ E 156.50′ or 156.50′ N 02°-30′ E. If space is limited on a drawing, the bearing may be placed on one side of the line and its length on the other.

Fig. 4-12 shows two examples of indicating the length and bearing of the line.

Dimension lines are normally not used to give the length and bearing of a lot line. Length of lot lines, distances of setback, side setback, etc. are always given in feet and decimals of a foot. These measurements are usually *not* given in feet and inches. All measurements regarding the site are given in feet and decimals of a foot (xxx.xx′). Features such as driveway and sidewalk width, length and depth of house, out buildings, pool, or any other items directly related to the house are generally given in feet and inches, (xx′-x″).

Curved Lines. Lines which are curved on the plot or development plan are also measured. As with the straight line, the *length* of the curved line is given along the line in feet and hundredths of a foot (xxx.xx′). An example of the length of a curved line is illustrated in Fig. 4-*13*. For obvious reasons, the bearing cannot be given for a curved line.

For every curve that appears on the site plan, certain necessary information must be supplied. Curves which appear on plot or site plans are called *horizontal* circular curves. The designer, as well as the contractor, must have some information about the curve(s) forming part of the lot line. Fig. 4-14 shows the same curve that appeared in the preceding figure, but with some explanatory information. When describing a curve some basic terms must be understood. Some of these are:

1. PC denotes *Point of Curvature*. PC is called out where the curve begins. It is at this point where the curve is tangent to line AX.

2. PT means *Point of Tangency*. This is the terminal point of the curve and indicates where it is tangent to line XB.

3. T indicates *Tangent* lines. These are identified by the two straight lines marked T. The tangent lines join the curve. The curve is tangent to AX and XB and lines PCO and PTO are at right angles to AX

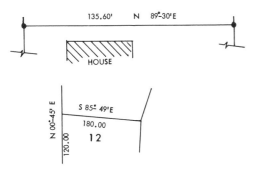

Fig. 4-12. The length and bearing of a line is placed adjacent to the line.

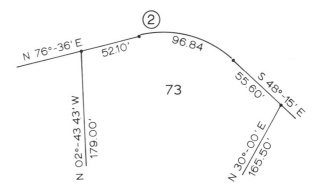

Fig. 4-13. The length of every curve is given on a land development and plot plan.

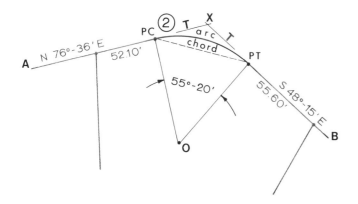

CURVE NO.	RADIUS	CENTRAL ANGLE	TANGENT	CHORD	CHORD BEARING	ARC
1	295.40'	27°-30'	72.74'	141.26'	N36°-45'-00"E	142.64'
2	90.00'	55°-20'	47.18'	83.58'	S 75°-49'-30"E	96.84'
3	120.00'	86°-00'	111.90'	163.68'	N13° 50'-00"W	180.12'

ALL CURVE DIMENSIONS SHOW ARC MEASUREMENT

Fig. 4-14. All land development plans give specific information about each curve. Some plot plans give this same information for each curve on a lot or parcel of land.

and XB. The intersection of lines from the PC and PT form the center point of the arc.

The angle formed by lines PCO and PTO is called the *central angle* or interior angle. Information about any curve is given in tabular form as in Fig. 4-14. Each curve is identified by a number or letter placed in a balloon or cherry. For example, the curve illustrated in Fig. 4-14 is curve number two (2). All necessary information about the curve is given in the table. Giving curve data in tabular form rather than placing it on the curve is the easiest and accepted standard. If each dimension for the tangent distance, chord length, bearing, etc., were to be given for each arc, the drawing would be cluttered and difficult to understand.

The distance from PC to X and X to PT is called the *tangent distance*. The tangent distance is calculated to aid in the proper layout of the lines tangent to the arc. Two other values given as curve data are the chordal distance and the bearing of the chord of a specific curve. These two values are used to locate the opposite point of tangency. The length of the arc is always placed above or below the curved line, as well as being placed in the curve data table.

Depending upon the original survey, all of the information (radius, central angle, tangent, chord, chord bearing, and arc) which is shown in the curve table in Fig. 4-14 may not necessarily be given. Three of the 6 pieces of data *must* be identified. These are: (1) Radius of the curve, (2) Central or interior angle, and (3) Length of the arc. Other information, such as tangent distance, chord, and chord bearing, are helpful for layout and checking purposes.

Certificate of Survey

Normally every piece of property which is purchased for the purpose of occupancy or construction must be surveyed and verified by a registered land surveyor who will prepare a Certificate of Survey. This document gives the exact written description locating the property. For example a Certificate of Survey will describe a piece of property thusly.

Lot 120, Plat of "Timber Brook #3," Section 5, Town 3 S, R 11 W, City of Portage, County of Kalamazoo, Michigan, as recorded in the office of Register of Deeds of said county.

Along with the written description is a graphic documentation of the property. A certificate will show the length of each lot line, and may give the bearing of each. If any structures exist on the property, these are shown along with their dimensions. Any easements that exist or are pending are also shown.

Contour Lines

Any plot plan, whether for a single family dwelling, office complex, or manufacturing plant, is based on a survey made of the site. The survey will identify existing features, such as trees, and the grade of the lot. The grade is shown by means of contour lines.

Contour lines are used to show changes in elevation on topographic maps, land developments, and plot plans. A contour line connects or passes through points of the same elevation along the surface of the earth. For example, the cone shown in Fig. 4-15 has a series of lines drawn on its surface at given uniform elevations. Perhaps contours can be better understood if they are thought of as being layers of the earth that are a specific thickness.

A schematic model of a building site is shown in Fig. 4-16 top. The changes in the

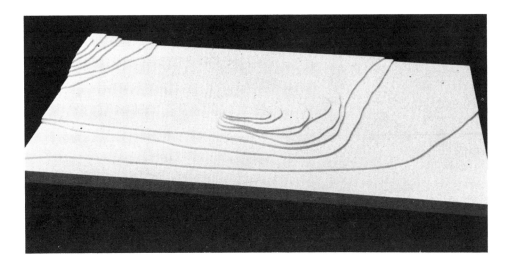

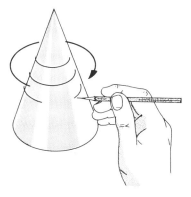

Fig. 4-15. A contour is an imaginary line that connects points of the same elevation.

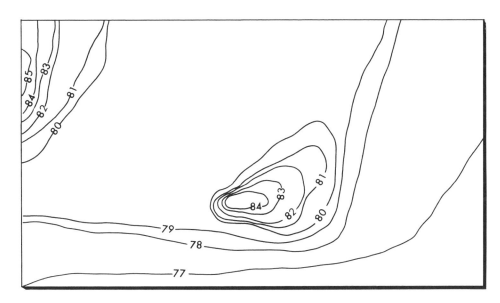

Fig. 4-16. Contour lines can be thought of as layers of earth as shown in this model.

earth's surface are shown as layers. The contour lines for this site model are shown in Fig. 4-16 bottom. It is evident that the contour lines match perfectly with the layers shown in the model. Topographic features, such as a mound will have a series of concentric contour lines drawn on its surface. It is easy to identify surface irregularities by noting the distance between the contour lines, as in Fig. 4-17. When the contours are far apart, the slope is gentle and when they are close together, the rise is steep. For most residential building sites, the contours would be spaced at intervals of 1′. Contour intervals are seldom less than 1′.

Contour lines are shown either as solid or broken. A solid contour line indicates an existing contour line and a broken contour line denotes a new or changed contour line. Fig. 4-18 illustrates a plot plan with existing contours (solid continuous lines) and

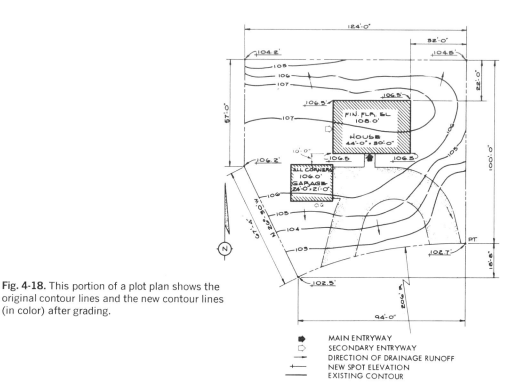

Fig. 4-18. This portion of a plot plan shows the original contour lines and the new contour lines (in color) after grading.

➡ MAIN ENTRYWAY
⇨ SECONDARY ENTRYWAY
→ DIRECTION OF DRAINAGE RUNOFF
┼ NEW SPOT ELEVATION
── EXISTING CONTOUR

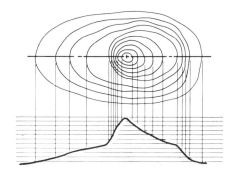

Fig. 4-17. When contour lines are close together the slope is steep and when they are far apart the slope is gentle. The profile gives an understandable expression of the slope along a certain line.

new contours (colored broken lines) after grading. Higher ground is graded down and may be used as fill for the low ground, thus making a more uniform site for the house.

Outline Sketch of the Plot Plan

Before drawing the plot or site plan, some type of preliminary planning is involved, usually in the form of sketches. The designer will place a piece of onion skin paper over the existing site plan or survey and sketch several schemes for the lot and proposed

structure. As he sketches he will take into account the following items:

Step 1. Make an outline sketch of the area surrounding the site, and indicate the following:

a. Compass direction
b. Direction of prevailing summer and winter winds
c. Location of neighboring buildings
d. Zoning and building restrictions which may affect the site

e. Location of pleasant views with respect to the site

Step 2. On the outline sketch, indicate the proposed areas for the following:

a. Play area for children (if applicable)
b. Garage or parking and driveway area
c. Refuse storage area
d. Outdoor living area (if applicable)
e. Flower garden area (if applicable)
f. Laundry drying area (if applicable)

Step 3. Next arrange the building in relation to public, service, and private areas. The shape of the structure should be approximately rectanglar. No detailed shape is necessary at this point. When planning the arrangement of the building, make the most advantageous use of the site conditions.

a. Observe the physical features of the site. Building placement on the higher area of a sloping lot is most desirable. (The site should be graded so there is a slight drop for ground water run-off.)
b. Observe the tentative location of the structure with respect to the neighbor's view. The house should be located for privacy.
c. Attractive views may determine the location of outdoor living areas.
d. Private areas should be properly screened from public and service areas.

Virtually all of the foregoing points are applicable in determining the placement of *any building* regardless if a single or multiple family dwelling, office building, or light manufacturing plant.

Drawing the Plot Plan

The plot plan shows where and how the structure is to be placed on the lot in relation to compass direction and the lot lines. In addition, the plot plan illustrates how the site will appear when the structure is completed. Elevations of the site are given at the corners of the building and site. If sufficient difference exists in the site contour, lines are used to show the change in topography. The plot plan is used to give the client a better idea of the site complete with the structure, existing and proposed plantings, sidewalks, driveways, parking areas, sidewalks, and other landscape features. Any other esthetic features the architect believes necessary to complement the natural beauty of the site or building are shown.

In large developments, building projects, and industrial parks, the services of a landscape architect are sometimes used to plan the site. When large acreages are developed, location of future buildings are identified and topographic features and plantings planned. This is referred to as a *land use plan*. Small projects and residences are frequently planned by the architect or designer.

Drawing the plot plan for a structure is not difficult if the following step-by-step procedure is followed:

1. Orient the lot so each street is located at the bottom and/or side of the sheet. If the lot is narrow and deep, place the longest dimension parallel to the long dimension of the sheet. North does not have to "point up" on the plot plan.

2. Draw the lot lines in their correct length and relationship to each other. Locate the street(s) with center line(s) the correct distance from each lot line.

3. Lightly draw contour lines. If less than 200′ difference exists in elevation, do not draw contour lines.

4. Locate and lightly draw existing plantings, such as trees and shrubs. The outline of foliage should be approximately the same as the foliage as it presently exists.

5. Locate and outline the structure according to the setbacks established by the prevailing ordinance and/or the developers covenant. Identify entryways with arrows.

6. Draw any outbuildings to be placed on the building site.

7. Locate and draw driveway, walkway, pool, garden area, display areas, etc.

8. Draw new contour lines if the topography is to be changed.

9. Locate and lightly draw proposed plantings. Foliage diameter of proposed plantings should be the approximate mature diameter. Indicate any existing plantings that must be removed or special treatment such as tree wells, etc., given to those planned to be preserved.

10. Dimension location of structure from lot lines. Use only two dimensions and give location in feet and decimals of a foot.

11. Identify earth elevations at corners of structure and at each corner of the lot.

12. Dimension all lot lines with bearing and length (xxx.xx') if straight, and radius and length if curved. Dimension distance (xx.xx) from center line of street(s) to lot line(s).

13. Darken in plantings and dimension the placement of new or future plantings.

14. Call out all features, such as street name(s), driveway, sidewalk, path, patio, decorative planting area, decorative materials, etc. Dimension widths of drives, walks, patios, and call out names of materials used: bituminous, crushed stone, marble chips, tan bark, etc. If any features are to be detailed, identify with proper symbol.

15. Draw north arrow.

16. Call out name of street(s) along center line and give elevation at center of street at each end of center line.

17. Identify lot number, subdivision or development name, city, section, township, township and range number, county and state.

18. Fill in title block.

Setbacks. One of the factors that have an influence on the shape of any structure on the building site is that of the setbacks. The minimum distances any building is placed from the lot lines are called *setbacks*. Each county, township or municipality governs the amount of setback. When a structure is built within the limits of a city or town, an ordinance will govern the minimum dis-tance from the front, sides and rear of a building may be placed from the lot lines. These distances may vary depending on whether the structure is a single or multiple family dwelling, commercial or industrial structure. In the event the building is not located within a municipality, the township or county will have an ordinance govern-ing the setbacks.

Some land developers establish protective covenants which in part state that all struc-tures located in the development will be a specified (not minimum) distance from the front lot line. Side setbacks are different for structures placed on corner lots than for in-terior lots. This is the reason why many cor-ner lots have wider frontages than interior lots.

Scale of the Plot Plan. The scale used to draw a plot plan will vary relative to the size of the site and drawing sheet size: B(11 × 17), C(17 × 22) or D(22 × 34). In almost every instance the site is laid out using a civil engineer's "chain" scale where $1'' = 10', 20', 30', 40'$, etc. Architect's scales are not normally used for plot plans. The civil engineer's chain scale is used because the length of the lot lines, curve radii, etc. are given in feet and decimals of a foot (xxxx.xx).

Occasionally only a small portion of a large parcel of land will be used for a build-ing. In this case, the entire parcel of land is drawn to a very small scale on the sheet. All bearings and lengths of lot lines, as well as the legal description of the complete par-cel are given on the small scale drawing. The land area of the large parcel to be developed is cross hatched. Some indication, either by standard detail call out or by note, is made for the portion to be developed. The por-tion of the parcel to be used for the structure is shown in larger scale on the sheet and is dimensioned with length and bearing of each lot line.

North Arrow. North arrows are some-times referred to as north points. North arrows belong on three of the drawings which go together to make a complete set of drawings. These are: the plot or site plan, the foundation or basement plan, and the first floor plan. The basic purpose of the north arrow is to give the orientation of the house on the lot. Perhaps of all the detail which the draftsman places on a plan, there is none more abused, from the standpoint of draftsmanship, than the north arrow. The biggest mistake the beginner makes is that the north arrow becomes reminiscent of the "wind rose" used by the ancient map mak-ers. Some typical north arrows used by draftsman are shown in Fig. 4-19. Each ar-row or point is fairly simple and not ornate.

Plantings on Plot Plans. Existing and proposed plantings are represented on the plot plan by stylized forms. Several designs used for trees and plantings are shown in Fig. 4-20. New or proposed plantings are identified by a letter or other symbol. Some plot plans, depending on the scale, may have all of the plantings identified by their common and/or Latin name.

To save time in drawing each planting, designers who prepare plans use entourage

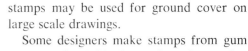

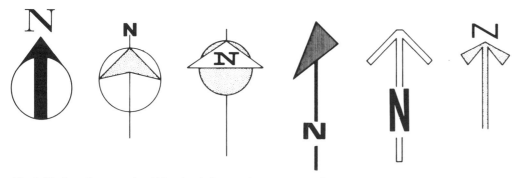

Fig. 4-19. A north arrow should be simple but yet have eye appeal.

stamps may be used for ground cover on large scale drawings.

Some designers make stamps from gum erasers. Fig. 4-23 shows three forms that have been made in this way. The outline of the design is laid out with a ballpoint pen and then cut with an X-Acto knife, using a No. 11 blade. Since the surface of the eraser is not smooth, the slight irregularities add to the texture of the image. Three or four sides of the eraser can be used for images.

A different method of printing the plot plan is used by some architectural offices

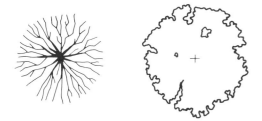

Fig. 4-20. Trees on a plot plan are basically circles that have a diameter equal to the mature size of the planting.

stamps. These stamps may either be purchased commercially or made from a gum eraser. Much more detail, variety of shape and scale may be obtained by using commercially available stamps. Some of the commercially available designs are shown in Fig. 4-21. Entourage stamps are inked with an ordinary stamp pad and pressed on the vellum or illustration board, as illustrated in Fig. 4-22. Some of the small scale

Fig. 4-21. Commercially made rubber stamps for plantings are available in a wide variety of styles and sizes. Stamps are shown actual size.

Fig. 4-22. Entourage planting stamps are used just as a regular rubber stamp.

Fig. 4-23. Entourage planting stamps may be cut from a gum type eraser.

and results in an eye-appealing sheet. The procedure is quite easy to follow. After the plot plan has been drawn with all necessary information, a plain piece of vellum, tracing paper, or onion skin the same size, is overlaid on the plot plan sheet. The outline of the structure and title block is then lightly drawn on the overlay sheet. Next, the overlay sheet is removed and the outline areas cut out with a razor blade or X-Acto knife. (Before cutting, be sure to place a heavy piece of cardboard beneath the overlay sheet to prevent cutting the table top.)

The overlay sheet is placed on the plot plan drawing and reproduced by the usual printing process. The openings in the overlay sheet must correspond with the outline of the structure and title block, otherwise the print will be out of register. The additional thickness of drafting medium partially blocks the light and results in an off-white background over the entire sheet with the exception of the cut-out areas. This method is particularly effective with blue or black line prints.

Landscaping

The final consideration is the landscaping. Landscaping lends a finished appearance to the building—it should not be omitted. A landscape plan is a long term investment in the property, not a luxury. Considerations given to grading, planting, and screening determine the success of landscaping.

Most local nurserymen or landscapers willingly supply a planning service for the owner. Frequently, the planting plan will extend over a period of several years. The plan consists of initially planting the necessary trees and shrubs and then adding more plantings each successive year. This method allows the owner to budget the cost of landscaping and to have a definite system for planting.

Top Soil

Fertile top soil is essential to the growth of any plant life. A valuable supply is available from areas where grading or excavating is required, such as the driveway, sidewalks, patio, and the house site. The top soil from these areas should be skinned or stripped (removed) from the surface and then piled separately prior to any construction. After the building is completed and the excavation is *backfilled,* a 4″ layer of top soil is usually spread over the site.

Caution must be exercised in checking for discarded scrap materials in the excavated area adjacent to the foundation. All scrap materials should be burned or hauled away and not disposed of in the excavated areas. Large voids and depressions will develop as the fill and top soil settles around these pieces of discarded materials. More dirt will be required as the fill continues to settle. Areas adjacent to the footing and foundation that are scrap filled may lead to water and termite problem at a later date.

Trees, Shrubs, and Evergreens

Nature has provided an abundance of plant sizes, shapes, and colors. Therefore, utmost consideration should be given to their efficient placement and combination. Fig. 4-24 illustrates, as an example, various plant shapes that may be employed. Individual creative ingenuity here may be allowed a wide range. It must be remembered, however, that adequate space must be left for growth. Home owners who have neglected this find that after several years their plantings have grown too close together and too near the house. Properly placed plantings, with allowance for spreading and growth, should result in a well planned landscaping. It is necessary, of course, to choose native plants, or plants that have demonstrated their growth ability under local soil and climatic conditions.

Trees are usually placed so they provide a maximum amount of shade from the afternoon sun, as shown in Fig. 4-25. Selection of trees should be based on their maximum mature height and spread, rapidity of growth, and color. For example, an American Elm will reach an adult height of 75′, develops a spread of about 50′, and grow at a medium rate. The Chinese Elm, on the other hand, reaches a height of about 50′, has a maximum spread of about 40′, and grows at a faster rate.

Small flowering trees may be used for accent; they usually provide a contrast to shrub plantings. The Redbud, for example, has a spread of approximately 18′, grows to a height of 25′, and has pink flowers early in the spring prior to its leafing. A Purple Leaf Plum provides colorful foliage through the season and attains a height of 25′ with a spread of about 15′.

Evergreens, shrubs and hedges are used to separate the plot from streets and neighbors, as well as to divide the driveway, garage, and rear entrance from other parts of the lot.

Plantings around the house, especially the front and sides, add beauty to the house and serve to conceal the concrete foundation. Slow-growing compact varieties of plantings should be chosen for this purpose. Higher growing specimens, such as Pfitzer Juniper which reaches a height between 6′ and 8′ or Cannarti Juniper which grows up to 15′, may be placed around corners or along large bare walls where there are no windows.

Low growing evergreens together with annually flowering shrubs are ideal for plantings near the foundation, for boundary plantings, and for providing color to the landscape. Low evergreens (4′ or less), such as Andora Juniper, Dwarf Japanese Quince, Spirea Frobelli, and Mugho Pine are ideal when mixed with low-growing shrubs and annual flowers (e.g., the Flowering Almond, Flowering Quince, and Virginal Mock Orange). Taller shrubs (8′ to 12′), such as the French Lilac, Nanking Cherry, and Viburnum, are generally used to bound the site, to screen the private and service areas, and to soften the lines of the building.

Japanese Spreading Yew

Japanese Upright Yew

Cannarti Juniper

Hatfield Yew

Douglas Fir

Andorra Juniper

Pfitzer Juniper

Fig. 4-24. Plantings have an almost infinite variety of shapes and sizes.

ILLUSTRATIONS: SWEENEY, KRIST & DIMM, HORTICULTURAL PRINTERS; PORTLAND, OREGON.

Fig. 4-25. Proper placement of trees is necessary to provide afternoon shade.

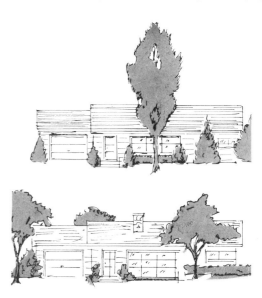

Fig. 4-26. Examples of improper and proper landscaping. *Improper* (top): Tall trees centrally located. High shrubs and evergreens obstruct view from windows. House is dwarfed by tall planting. *Proper* (bottom): Small trees for low house. Low shrubs and evergreens do not obstruct view. Proper planting accents entryway.

Plantings and House Relationship

A good relationship between the plantings and the structure is generally the product of a well planned landscaping. Fig. 4-26 demonstrates the difference between a poorly planned landscape and one that is ideally planned. For example, Fig. 4-26 (top) shows a tree planted in front of and towering over the house. Tall evergreens and shrubs surround the house in such a manner as to block the view from the windows. The building appears dwarfed by these plantings, so that the relationship between it and the surrounding landscape cannot be defined.

In Fig. 4-26 bottom, however, this is not the case. Here a few small shrubs at the corner are sufficient. Low shrubs and evergreens are located below the windows so as not to cover the view. Smaller trees, located off center and away from the picture window, give contrast between the landscape and the house. Small trees or shrubs at the sides of doorways or garage doors lend beauty to the general appearance of the house, especially at the main entryway.

Houses which are long and low, such as those shown in Figs. 4-25 and 4-26, look well with plantings at each end. This gives the appearance that the house is tied to the ground. Houses built on a slab generally need very little shrubbery or evergreens because they are built closer to the ground than those houses with a basement or crawl space.

Check List

When considering or investigating a site, it is always good practice to make a check list. The check list should call attention to important facts relating to the site and its surrounding areas, to the availability of public facilities, and to the home builder's needs and desires.

The following is a suggested check list based on the points covered in the preceding sections of this chapter.

Neighborhood or Community Characteristics:

	Yes	No
Residential	—	—
Below average housing	—	—
Developed areas	—	—
Far away from industrial or commercial areas	—	—
Far away from dumping areas, railroads, airports, factories, etc.	—	—
Excessive traffic and noises	—	—
Air pollution—unpleasant odors	—	—
Pleasant surrounding views	—	—
Good prevailing winds	—	—
Properly zoned areas	—	—
Well planned street layout	—	—

Community Facilities:

Quality schools nearby	—	—
School and public transportation facilities	—	—
Shopping centers nearby	—	—
Churches	—	—
Theaters	—	—
Playgrounds and athletic fields	—	—

Well paved streets with sidewalks	—	—
Good street drainage system	—	—

Availability of Public Utilities and Services:

Water, electricity, and gas	—	—
Sewerage: storm and sanitary	—	—
Telephone	—	—
Fire and police protection	—	—
Garbage and trash removal	—	—
Street lights	—	—

Building Protection and Limitations:

Good zoning laws	—	—
Proper restrictions on use of lot area	—	—
Proper type and use of structure indicated	—	—
Long duration of protection	—	—
Adequate building codes	—	—

Site and House Relationship:

House plan fits into site	—	—
House plan adequate for site conditions	—	—
Site and house conforms with general neighborhood character	—	—

Site and Landscaping Considerations:

Adequate size and shape	—	—
Good topographic features	—	—
Trees, shrubs, and evergreens	—	—

Firm soil	—	—
Little fill and grading required	—	—
Sufficient drainage	—	—

Purchasing Transaction:

Satisfactory appraisal	—	—
Satisfactory tax status	—	—
Adequate land contract terms	—	—
Satisfactory title search	—	—

The following is a list of items to consider and calculate when purchasing a lot for a building site.

Total price	$_____
Down payment	$_____
Balance of purchase price, plus interest	$_____
Possible special assessments (street, curb, sewer, etc.)	$_____
Assessed value	$_____
Tax rate per year	$_____

Questions and Problems

Each of the following questions is concerned with the important points in this chapter. Answer each question carefully.

1. Various factors have been explained as a basis for site selection. List six which may be considered as the most important.

Fig. 4-27. Housing Development.

2. List the requisites of a good building site.

3. What are the advantages and disadvantages of the placement of your present home? If you live in an apartment, imagine that its floor plan were moved to ground level. What are the advantages and disadvantages of its placement?

4. Select a lot near your home; sketch the lot and give the approximate size and compass direction. Evaluate the lot in terms of (a) size; (b) orientation; (c) wind and sun; (d) shape of plan best suited to the shape of the lot; (e) availability of transportation; and (f) general neighborhood.

5. What are some of the factors which may be used when evaluating a neighborhood?

6. Using your own observations, what items would you consider as essential in landscaping a new home?

7. Study the waterside housing development shown in Fig. 4-27. In what ways has the site determined the house placement? Under these conditions what landscaping improvements could you suggest?

8. What are the advantages in selecting a home in an area zoned for single family as opposed to multi-family dwellings?

Floor Plan Considerations 5

Floor plans are two-dimensional (length and width) drawings which show the location and relationship of the rooms or areas on a particular level of a building. The design characteristics of a floor plan should ideally demonstrate the **functional,** the **comfortable,** and the **livable** conditions of rooms in their basic relationships. When making floor plans, it is always good practice to come as close as possible to the ideal design.

The following characteristics of **good** floor plans should be studied in detail:

1. Adequate traffic circulation
2. Proper house and room orientation as well as good sun control
3. Adaptability to indoor-outdoor living
4. Open planning concept
5. Proper window location
6. Privacy in living areas
7. Adequate storage space
8. Well planned furniture arrangement
9. Flexibility for expansion

An understanding of these inter-related design qualities, which are studied in this chapter, will enable the student to evaluate and design good floor plans.

Many of the characteristics of a good floor plan are applicable in designing both residential and light commercial buildings. For example, the design of nursing homes, homes for the aged, retirement homes, office complexes, etc., can employ some of the guidelines found in this chapter. Other recommendations for light commercial design are listed in Chapter 20.

Adequate Traffic Circulation

The term *circulation,* when applied to floor planning, refers to the movement of traffic from room to room, floor to floor, or to the outside of the house. Hallways, stairways, and rooms, as well as interior and exterior doorways, are passageways for the circulation of traffic.

Good circulation, or ease of movement in and about the house, is one of the most desirable features of a good floor plan. This, however, is not always possible—particularly in the floor design of small houses. In any case, every route or path of circulation should be direct, well lighted, and have ample room for movement. Figs. 5-1 and 5-2 show paths of good traffic circulation in single and double level homes.

Privacy is an important factor in designing good circulation paths in floor plans. Notice in Figs. 5-1 and 5-2 that paths of circulation are designed to end where par-

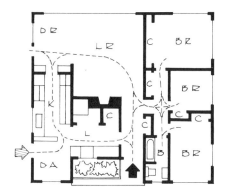

Fig. 5-1. Two examples of single-level homes showing well planned paths of traffic circulation.

LEGEND

- - - - -	CIRCULATION PATHWAY
	SECONDARY OR REAR ENTRYWAY
	PRIMARY OR MAIN ENTRYWAY

LR	LIVING ROOM
DR	DINING ROOM
K	KITCHEN
L	LAUNDRY ROOM
DA	DINING AREA
BR	BEDROOM
B	BATHROOM
C	CLOSET

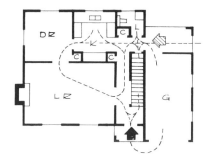

Fig. 5-2. An example of a bi-level home showing paths of traffic circulation.

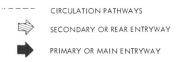

LEGEND

- - - - -	CIRCULATION PATHWAYS
	SECONDARY OR REAR ENTRYWAY
	PRIMARY OR MAIN ENTRYWAY

LR	LIVING ROOM
DR	DINING ROOM
K	KITCHEN
L	LAUNDRY
BR	BEDROOM
B	BATHROOM
C	CLOSET

ticular privacy is desired, such as in bedrooms or bathrooms. If possible, these rooms should not be used as circulation pathways or traffic lanes.

Passageways

Hallways, particularly in small houses where there may be only one, serve mainly to provide better circulation. A small family of two or three people requires very little space for traffic circulation. However, a large family has a greater need for space.

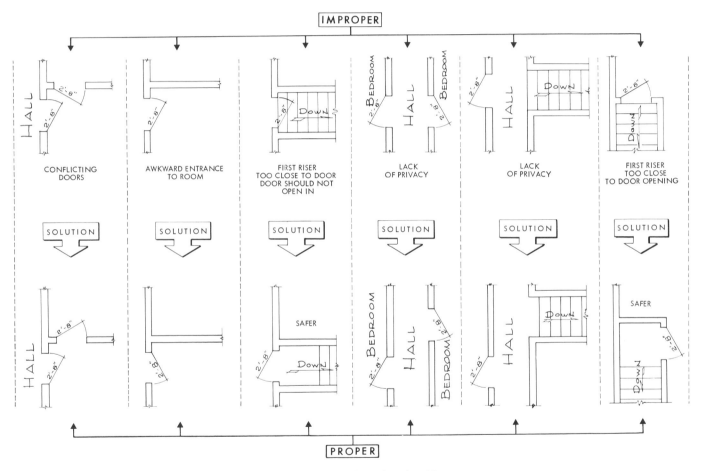

Fig. 5-3. Proper and Improper Placement of Doors: Improper method is shown in color at top; proper method is shown in black at bottom. Doors must be placed so that safety is the first consideration. They should not collide with other doors. As much floor space as possible should be saved.

In this case the hall is sometimes considered necessary.

The ease with which traffic can move through hallways is controlled by the width. In order to be practical, the hall should have a width ranging between 3'-0" and 3'-4", and should, ideally, be confined to within 10 per cent of the total floor area. Every effort should be made to keep hallways as short as possible.

When hallways are entirely eliminated from a floor plan, the circulation path must, of necessity, be through rooms having at least two doorways. Sometimes, for convenience, bedrooms, bathrooms, and other rooms designed for privacy have two doors. However, these rooms should never be considered as pathways for traffic. The rooms commonly used for circulation pathways are the living room, dining room, family room, recreation room, and kitchen. Furniture placement in these rooms should be such that they will not obstruct the traffic lanes.

In many cases, traffic circulation is not confined to one house level alone. Houses with more than one level, require stairways for traffic movement. The characteristics of good stairways are: (1) safety, (2) economy of space, (3) handrails, (4) landings (5) adequate lighting, and (6) a minimum width of 3'-0'. In most instances stairways are 3'-0" wide.

The size, placement, and swing of doors are of utmost importance in planning the home. To facilitate the movement of furniture, doors should be at least 2'-6" to 2'-10" wide. Depending upon the size and the extent of door swing (90° to 180°), between six and seven square feet of floor space may be eliminated from the room. Great care, therefore, should be taken to place doorways so they cause minimum interference with the living area. Doors located at the ends (or along the sides) of small hallways or stairwells should be placed so there is no conflicting swing. Fig. 5-3 shows the proper and improper placement of doorways, and also the proper and improper direction of door swing. Doors into structures and rooms *normally* open in. Hinged doors into closets usually open outward into the room or hallway.

Doorways for entrance to and exit from the house should be located for ease of movement. One of the entry doors should be planned to be 3'-0" wide. In most residential plans the main entry is a 3'-0" door or a double entry door. This simplifies movement of appliances, furniture, etc. in and out of the house. Activities such as carrying groceries into the house, disposing of refuse, or carrying wet laundry from the kitchen or basement to the rear yard or service area must be considered in planning doorway locations. Circulation paths between the house and the outside facility areas (such as garage, driveway, patio, rear yard, etc.) should be designed for maximum convenience.

Good Circulation Factors

The most important factors influencing good circulation are:

1. Direct routes between rooms
2. Each room as independent from another as possible
3. Rooms free from traffic lanes
4. Rooms designed for minimum interruption of social groups
5. No space wasted by unnecessary hallways
6. Traffic routed through "not too busy" areas to avoid unnecessary floor wear and extra cleaning

Check Points

To check any floor plan for adequate circulation, move from one area or zone within the floor plan. Each route should be as short and direct as possible. Where applicable, use the following check points in the two floor plans shown in Fig. 5-4.

Check the circulation path from:

1. Kitchen to front entrance
2. Kitchen to dining room
3. Kitchen to porch
4. Living room to kitchen
5. Living room to dining room
6. Front entrance to living room
7. Rear entrance to basement
8. Rear entrance to second floor rooms
9. Bedrooms to bathroom
10. Front or rear entrance to coat closets
11. Various areas of the first floor to any room on the upper level
12. Outside or basement to lavatories or bathrooms

LEGEND

LR	LIVING ROOM
DA	DINING AREA
K	KITCHEN
BR	BEDROOM
B	BATHROOM
C	CLOSET

⬈ PRIMARY OR MAIN ENTRYWAY

➡ SECONDARY OR REAR ENTRYWAY

Fig. 5-4. Check the paths of circulation on these two plans.

Proper Orientation

In floor planning, *orientation* refers to the house and room arrangement which takes into consideration the sun's rays, prevailing breezes, and scenic views.

Solar Orientation

Solar orientation, or house arrangement which obtains benefits from the sun, is an ancient concept. Even the earliest cave dwellers preferred a southern exposure. To efficiently apply solar orientation in floor planning, the position of the sun and the approximate latitude of the building site must be known.

Solar orientation of the home can best be achieved on a wide lot (between 75 and 100 feet), because the extra space allows more design freedom in floor planning. For example, a one-story house is feasible within a wide area. On a narrow lot, however, liberty in designing the single-level house is very limited because complete privacy from the public or neighbor's view may not be obtainable. This is generally true in areas where adjacent buildings are too close to the home site. In such areas, a two-story house design is more suitable.

Planning the house to take advantage of the benefits from the sun (in the northern hemisphere) almost always makes it necessary to place the most lived-in areas (living room, dining room, family room, or kitchen) on the southern part of the site. Placement and type of windows in these rooms usually depend upon (1) the activities for which the room will be used; (2) the surrounding views; and (3) the interior and exterior esthetic effects. However, in cases where solar orientation is of prime importance, some of these factors may be neglected. The areas of the house in which sunlighting is not of primary importance (garage, hallways, stairways, bathrooms, etc.) are usually located on the northern part of the site. (In the southern hemisphere or in warm or desert areas, the orientation of the house normally would be reversed.)

Orientation towards the sun may be applied to any house design. Generally, the *non-traditional* type of architectural design offers more liberty in planning and results in the best use of sunlight and solar heat. Non-traditional architecture includes styles such as the ranch type and contemporary, as opposed to the pure or true Cape Cod, Southern Colonial, New England Colonial, Dutch Colonial, etc.

The ranch and contemporary style house do not have any fixed or set locations for living areas, or any fixed size or style for the windows. Non-traditional designs, therefore, permit the use of large glass areas, such as picture windows, sliding glass doors, or window walls. This type of window allows more sunlight and radiant heat to come into the house during the winter months. To obtain utmost heat benefit from the sun without losing the interior heat of the house, window panes are double in thickness. Sealed dead air spaces between the panes allow radiant heat to enter and prevent the loss of internal heat. The size and angle of roof overhang on each window controls the amount of sunlight that enters the house (see Fig. 5-5, top).

Best sun advantage (in the northern hemisphere) is obtained when window walls face toward the south. During the winter months, maximum heat may be received from a southern exposure. During the summer, however, windows with southern exposure receive less heat than those oriented towards the east or west. This effect is due mainly to the elevated angle of the sun with respect to the house. During the summer months, the sun's angle of elevation is much higher than at any other time of the year. Fig. 5-5 (bottom) shows how the elevation angle of the sun changes during the four seasons of the year. The height of the sun at any particular time of day is dependent upon the time of year and the latitude of the site. The greatest change in the sun's angle occurs in the areas where the latitude of the building site is furthest from the equator.

The amount of roof overhang is dependent upon the angle of the sun line during varying times of the year. In some designs this is a critical factor because it may be

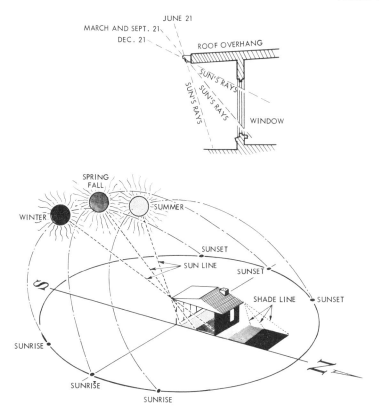

Fig. 5-5. The elevation angle of the sun with respect to a building changes during the four seasons of a year. The roof overhang is designed accordingly. (This building is set at 42° North latitude.)

necessary to screen the inside of the building from the sun's rays. For example, to determine the sun line for a home built in San Francisco, California (latitude 37°45′), for fall and spring, subtract the latitude of the building location from 90°.

Spring and Fall (March 21 and September 21)

$$90°00′ - \text{Latitude} = \text{Sun Line}$$
$$90°00′ - 37°45′ = 52°15′$$

On March 21 and September 21 the earth's axis is perpendicular to its orbit about the sun. See Fig. 5-6. During the summer and winter the earth's axis is inclined to its orbital path at an angle of 23°30′. Because of

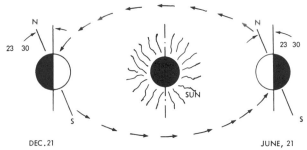

Fig. 5-6. The earth's axis is not perpendicular to its orbit about the sun on June 21 and December 21. The earth's axis is perpendicular on March 21 and September 21.

this fact the 23°30' value is used as a *constant* in the formula for determing the sun's angle in summer and winter. To find the sun line for summer, subtract the latitude from 90°00' and add 23°30'.

Summer (June 21)

90°00' — Latitude + 23°30' = Sun Line

90°00' — 37°45' + 23°30' = 75°45'

To obtain the sun line for winter, subtract the latitude and 23°30' from 90°00'.

Winter (December 21)

90°00' — Latitude — 23°30' = Sun Line

90°00' — 37°45' — 23°30' = 28°45'

If an atlas or map is not available to determine the latitude of a particular location, Table 13-2 in Chapter 13 gives these approximate figures.

The illustrations in Figs. 5-7 and 5-8 have been set at 40° North latitude to show the effects of the sun's high arc in summer and low arc in winter. In Fig. 5-7 the patio side faces west; in Fig. 5-8 the patio side faces south. The shadow on the east and north side is evident.

Wind and View Orientation

Orientation of large windows should not only be toward the sun, but also, if possible, toward the direction of prevailing breezes and scenic views. In areas where the winter season is very cold, however, large glass areas should not face towards the prevailing winter winds.

Orientation toward prevailing winds is important only if the breezes are able to aid in cooling the house during the summer season. Cooling or ventilating the house can be achieved by placing *louvered openings* (slatted openings) above and below the large glass walls or windows.

Prior to planning the orientation of major rooms, it is advisable to contact the nearest weather bureau office or local air-port for information regarding the direction of the prevailing breezes in the area. Breezes in Illinois, for example, are out of the southwesterly direction during the summer, and out of the northwesterly during the winter.

Existing trees and landscaping, as well as planned future landscaping, must be taken into account to ensure the most pleasing scenic view.

Room Orientation

Not all the rooms can be oriented toward the most desirable location. Some rooms may have to be placed in locations where their orientation with respect to sunlight, prevailing breezes, or scenic views is undesirable. When making the preliminary floor plan sketches of the house, major consideration should be given to its room orientation. The following paragraphs list the suggested orientation of major rooms.

The Living Room should face south and west (corner location is preferable) so it may receive an ample amount of sunshine at all times during the year. This room may view the garden or the patio.

Dining Room. It is generally agreed that the dining room should have an easterly exposure in order to receive the morning sunlight. Also, the dining room may be located in the southern part of the house.

Kitchen. Most architects suggest that the kitchen face north and/or east. Since most housewives do a considerable part of their work in the morning, sunlight is desirable.

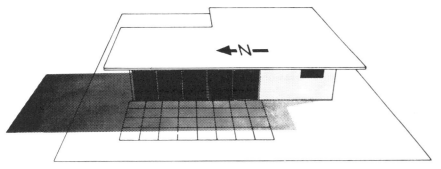

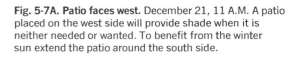

Fig. 5-7A. Patio faces west. December 21, 11 A.M. A patio placed on the west side will provide shade when it is neither needed or wanted. To benefit from the winter sun extend the patio around the south side.

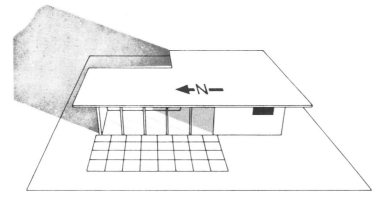

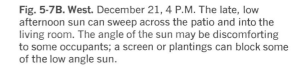

Fig. 5-7B. West. December 21, 4 P.M. The late, low afternoon sun can sweep across the patio and into the living room. The angle of the sun may be discomforting to some occupants; a screen or plantings can block some of the low angle sun.

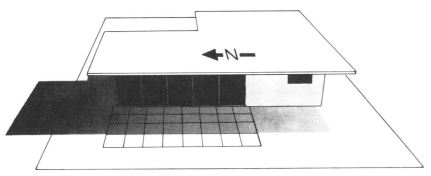

Fig. 5-7C. West. March 21-September 21, 11 A.M. A patio and living room oriented to the west offers no sun problem in the morning hours; however, no warmth can be derived from the sun on cool March mornings.

Fig. 5-7D. West. March 21-September 21, 4 P.M. During the warm season the western sun is at its most punishing angle. Vertical baffles and an extended overhang will help. A line of trees, tall shrubs, vertical screens, or louvers may provide the best solution.

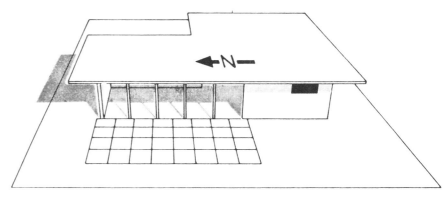

FROM: LANE PUBLICATIONS, MENLO PARK, CALIFORNIA.

Fig. 5-7E. West. June 21, 11 A.M. All during the year the west side of the house is in the morning shade. On the west side during the summer months temperatures vary more than in any other location.

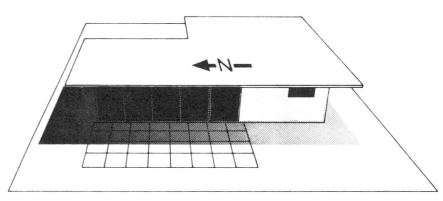

FROM: LANE PUBLICATIONS, MENLO PARK, CALIFORNIA.

Fig. 5-7F. West. June 21, 4 P.M. The sun's rays may be intercepted on the west side by vines, trees, or screens. This avoids the west wall's input or radiated heat long after sundown.

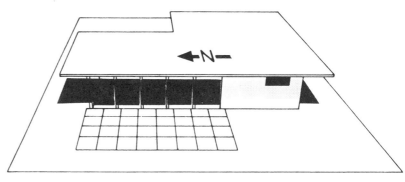

FROM: LANE PUBLICATIONS, MENLO PARK, CALIFORNIA.

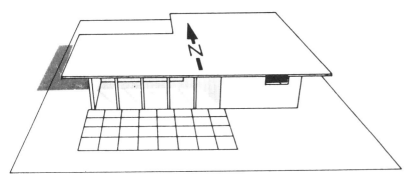

FROM: LANE PUBLICATIONS, MENLO PARK, CALIFORNIA.

Fig. 5-8A. Patio faces **south.** December 21, 11 A.M. The sun's arc is at it's lowest point on December 21 when the sun's rays stream across the patio and into the living area.

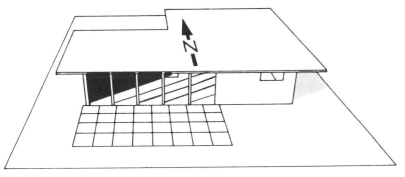

FROM: LANE PUBLICATIONS, MENLO PARK, CALIFORNIA.

Fig. 5-8B. South. December 21, 4 P.M. In Cold winter areas the sun should be allowed to enter unimpeded into the living areas. In milder winter areas this pattern can't be used without causing too much heat in October and November. A screening of trees will overcome this problem.

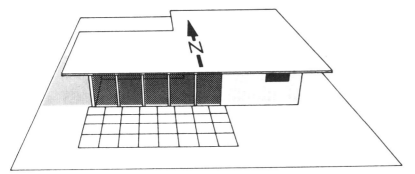

FROM: LANE PUBLICATIONS, MENLO PARK, CALIFORNIA.

Fig. 5-8C. South. March 21-September 21, 11 A.M. After September 21 the sun's arc becomes increasingly higher. After September 21 the arc becomes increasingly lower.

Fig. 5-8D. South. March 21-September 21, 4 P.M. Living areas oriented in this direction will obtain adequate protection during the late afternoon. To shade the patio in mild areas, a vertical screening must be built or grown on the west side of the house.

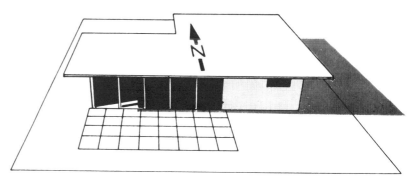

FROM: LANE PUBLICATIONS, MENLO PARK, CALIFORNIA.

Fig. 5-8E. South. June 21, 11 A.M. An adequate roof overhang will provide some protection for the patio at this time.

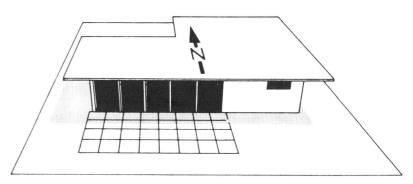

FROM LANE PUBLICATIONS, MENLO PARK, CALIFORNIA.

Fig. 5-8F. South June 21, 4 P.M. The late afternoon shade pattern leaves much of the patio in the sun while the living area is shaded. There will be less shade from this day on. Plantings can be utilized to add shade to the patio.

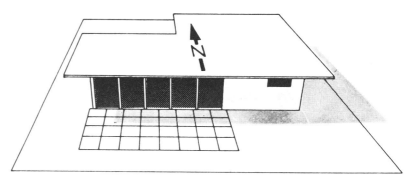

FROM: LANE PUBLICATIONS, MENLO PARK, CALIFORNIA.

A kitchen with a northern exposure remains cool during hot summer afternoons. The kitchen, for convenience, should be located as near as possible to the driveway.

Bedrooms. Usually, bedrooms are oriented according to personal preferences. If possible, however, it is better to have the master bedroom oriented towards the south, and the child's bedroom oriented towards the south or southwest.

Studios and Work Rooms. These rooms should be oriented towards the north because natural light is desirable for close work.

Porches and Terraces are generally used for relaxation in late afternoons. It is important, therefore, that these areas either face away from the late afternoon sun, or be protected with plantings, privacy screens, or awnings.

The Laundry and Utility Rooms should have direct access to the driveway. These rooms may be placed in the least desirable location on the site.

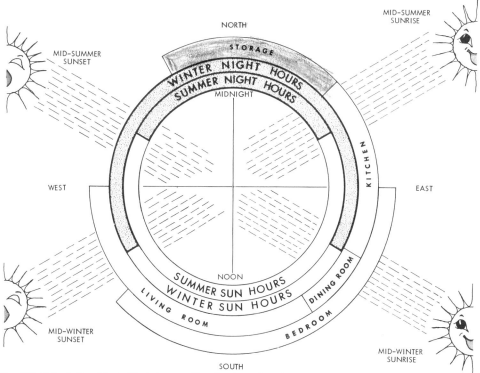

Fig. 5-9. Orientation Chart: Sketch a small scale plan, place it on the center of the chart, then revolve the plan to get the best position for maximum sunlight in the rooms.

Orientation Check List

Make a small sketch of a one story dwelling showing the basic living areas, and place it at the center of the orientation chart on Fig. 5-9. Revolve the sketch on the chart to get the best position for maximum sunlight in the rooms. Use the following check list for the ideal orientation of the rooms.

1. Principal living areas should face towards the south.
2. Living room should face south and/or west, and toward the prevailing breezes, if possible.
3. Kitchen should face either towards the north, the east, or the northeast.
4. Dining room should have either an eastern or southern exposure.

Adaptability to Indoor-Outdoor Living

The present trend in home building is toward back-yard outdoor living. Floor plans reflect this change by orienting the major living area to the rear, as shown in Fig. 5-10.

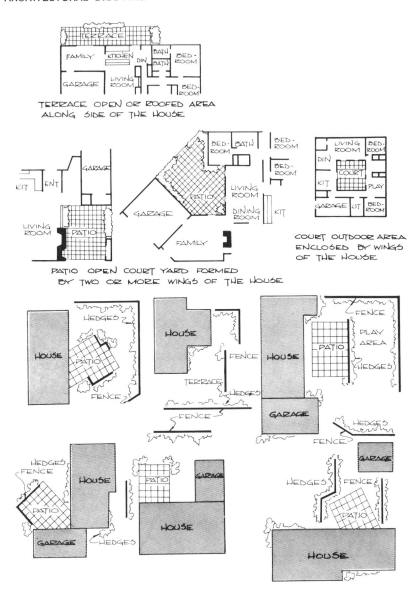

TERRACE OPEN OR ROOFED AREA
ALONG SIDE OF THE HOUSE

PATIO OPEN COURT YARD FORMED
BY TWO OR MORE WINGS OF THE HOUSE

COURT OUTDOOR AREA
ENCLOSED BY WINGS
OF THE HOUSE

Fig. 5-10. The outdoor living area may be extended by using screenings associated with patios, terraces, and courts.

Many new homes have the major rooms (living room, dining room, and/or family room) oriented away from the street. Living rooms (with large window areas) commonly face the rear of the lot. Orientation of the living areas in this manner allows a large amount of sunlight to enter the interior living area, and permits the possibility of future expansion of this area to the open space of the garden, the patio, or the terrace. Doors opening to the patio or terrace make the outdoor living area easily accessible from the living room, the dining room, and the other major rooms.

The house with a separate or an attached garage is usually placed well towards the front of the lot to provide the rear area with larger space for outdoor living. The proper orientation and placement of the house is always important in the consideration of an area for indoor-outdoor living activities. However, a house should not be arbitrarily placed merely to facilitate back yard living.

Lots which are small and extremely close to adjoining lots may have their outdoor-living area enclosed with either wall panels or fences as shown in Fig. 5-10. This form of enclosure is often considered temporary. In that event, shrubs, evergreens, or hedges may be planted close to the wall panels or fences. When the plantings reach their mature height, they may replace the temporary enclosure.

Figs. 5-11 and 5-12 show two types of privacy screens used for enclosures. Placement of such screens around the outdoor

Fig. 5-11. A privacy screen adds a decorative touch. Hardwood panels and clay tile fill the openings.

Fig. 5-12. Complete privacy is assured by using this type of screen made of plastic sheets.

living area provides a location blocked off from the neighbor's view. A barbeque fireplace, a good flooring, a ceiling made of open trellis work or corrugated plastic, or some built-in furniture may be included in the design of this area. Often, the outdoor living area is one of the most pleasant in the home.

The location of the patio has a direct bearing on the adaptability of an area to indoor-outdoor living. Fig. 5-13 shows the proper placement of patios at different locations on the lot. A patio located at the side of the house, for example, is ideally

suited to lots which are wide and shallow. A patio located at the rear of the house is generally best suited for narrow and deep lots, as the view from the street may be blocked or screened by the house itself. However, a patio located on the street side of the lot usually poses a design problem. This may be overcome by using esthetically designed screening which complements the landscape as well as the home. Most patios are oriented toward the eastern or southern side of the house for the best protection from the warm rays of the afternoon summer sun.

An outdoor living area which may be enclosed on all sides by the house (Fig. 5-13, bottom right) is ideal for a small lot. This type of house design permits every room to have a pleasant view of the patio or courtyard, while having maximum privacy from the neighbor's view. House designs of this form are best suited for areas where heating is not a problem and mild seasonal weather is predominant.

To determine the adaptability of floor plans to the indoor-outdoor living conditions, note the following questions.

1. Does the living area face the best outdoor area?
2. Is area oriented for best sunlight?
3. Are the indoor areas accessible from the outside by convenient openings (i.e., sliding or hinged doors)?
4. Does the indoor-outdoor area have privacy and is it shielded by house wings, fences, or plantings?

Open Planning Concept

To increase the livability of a small house, various design features may be employed to make some rooms appear larger. Open planning is one means by which this may be accomplished. When open planning is applied to a floor plan, the wall, which generally separates two adjoining rooms, is eliminated. Some examples of adjoining room combinations in which open planning may be applied are (1) kitchen and family room; (2) dining ell and living room; (3) dining room and kitchen; (4)

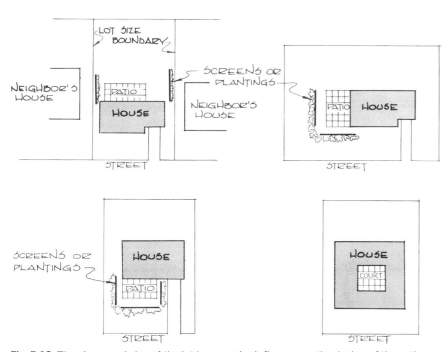

Fig. 5-13. The shape and size of the lot has a major influence on the design of the patio.

kitchen and laundry areas; (5) dining room and living room; and (6) kitchen, dining area, and living room.

In essence, open planning does not limit the view to the four walls of the room. The illusion of spaciousness is created by eliminating the partition wall between adjoining rooms and adding a large glass window which faces the back yard or a scenic view. Fig. 5-14 demonstrates the effect of spaciousness when special interior designing is incorporated in the plan of a room. The interior design of the living room area may create a spacious effect when the ceiling is of the *cathedral* type (ceiling which parallels the roof), and the partial partition between this room and the next does not extend all the way to the ceiling.

Room partitions or dividers separate one area from another and are usually not permanently placed within the room. Generally, dividers make area boundaries for ac-

Fig. 5-15. A movable room divider may add to the general decor as well as serve a functional purpose.

tivities less definite, thus allowing a more versatile use of the room. Examples of room partitions or dividers are: partial walls, draw drapes, screens, accordion-pleated or folding doors, pocket doors (doors sliding out of sight when not in use), dividers of translucent material, and furniture groups. An example of a room divider is shown in Fig. 5-15.

In open planning, walls often become functional because furniture or appliances are built into them. Generally, walls with built-in units (such as a bookcase, storage unit, desk, high fidelity-stereo system, television set, beverage cooler, washer, dryer, water heater, dishwasher, etc.) give more floor space to the room and add beauty to the interior design.

Open planning, because of the large open space involved, requires some form

Fig. 5-14. A cathedral ceiling, wide expanse of glass, and low partitions create a feeling of spaciousness.

of sound control. Examples of materials which aid in reducing sound within a room are: acoustical tile (generally for the ceiling), wood (for wall paneling), and rubber or asphalt tile (usually for the floors).

Floor plans with open planning deviate from the traditional concept of living areas as places for specific activities. Today's floor plan design permits flexible use of areas for different purposes. Fig. 5-16 shows examples of open planning as it is applied to floor plans. Note how different methods create the illusion of spaciousness and partial separation of activities.

Proper Window Location

In residential or commercial architecture, windows have long been the dominant element in the design of building exteriors and interiors. When windows are properly selected and located, they become functional, aesthetic parts of the home plan design. Today's millworks and window manufacturers offer a wide variety of windows which accent the character, the comfort, and the convenience of the home.

Window location should be planned so as to face the most pleasing view, while producing some degree of privacy in the room (see Fig. 5-17). Large windows give rooms the effect of spaciousness by "bor-

LEGEND	LR	LIVING ROOM
	DR	DINING ROOM
	K	KITCHEN
	BR	BEDROOM
	GBR	GUEST BEDROOM
	S	STUDY
	B	BATHROOM
	L	LAUNDRY
	WS	WORK SHOP
	LC	LINEN CLOSET
	C	CLOSET

PRIMARY OR MAIN ENTRYWAY

SECONDARY OR REAR ENTRYWAY

PRIMARY OR MAIN ENTRYWAY

SECONDARY OR REAR ENTRY

LEGEND		
	LR	LIVING ROOM
	K	KITCHEN
	BR	BEDROOM
	GBR	GUEST BEDROOM
	ST	STORAGE
	B	BATHROOM
	C	CLOSET
	CP	CAR PORT

Fig. 5-16. Open planning creates the illusion of spaciousness and adds flexibility when folding or sliding doors are used to create privacy when desired.

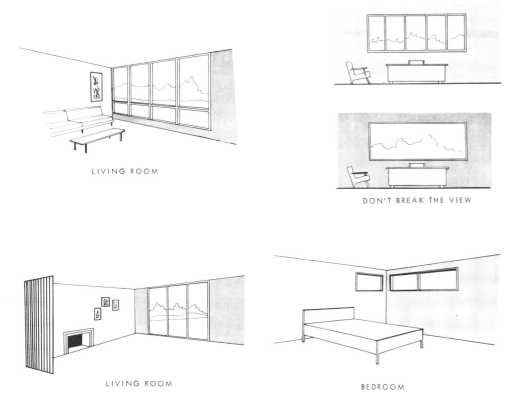

LIVING ROOM

DON'T BREAK THE VIEW

LIVING ROOM

BEDROOM

Fig. 5-17. Windows should be planned with regard to view and privacy.

Cape Cod or the *colonial* style of home design.

A room becomes very pleasant if the window sills are located below the eye level of a seated person. However, placing certain windows above the eye level, as in bed rooms, is sometimes desirable. Fig. 5-18 gives suggestions on sill heights for various types of rooms.

Cross ventilation within an individual room is directly related to the arrangement and proportioning of windows. This is sometimes called *fenestration*. Window arrangement, in this context, refers not only to the location of windows in elevation and plan, but also to their type (i.e., double-hung, casement, sliding, hopper, etc.). Fig. 5-19 shows the flow of air through a room with different window openings and arrangement.

Bedrooms located in the front or the rear area of a house should have their windows located near the *interior wall-partitions* to allow as much ventilation as possible. Fig. 5-20 illustrates the flow of

rowing" the outside light and view. Windows in all cases should be related to the exterior design. For example, a competent architect or designer would not consider specifying twelve pane *double-hung windows* for the living room of a home designed in the flat-roof *contemporary* style. A window of this type is better suited to the

DINING ROOM   LIVING ROOM

BEDROOM   KITCHEN

Fig. 5-18. Suggested Sill Heights: Sill heights should be in accordance with the use and purpose of the room.

Fig. 5-19. The window opening determines the air flow through a room.

LEGEND

LR	LIVING ROOM
DA	DINING AREA
FR	FAMILY ROOM
K	KITCHEN
BR	BEDROOM

Fig. 5-20. The location of the windows also determines the air flow. Correct window placement allows cross ventilation.

prevailing breezes through the house. Note that by placing the windows adjacent to the interior wall-partitions, the breezes will cross ventilate the room. Windows placed at a room corner would only ventilate that corner, with very little ventilating benefits for the rest of the room. Some windows cannot be placed directly adjacent to the interior wall partitions. Windows such as those in front of the house, for example, are often centered on the wall.

The absolute minimum window glass area, according to the Federal Housing Administration (FHA) standards, is 10 per cent of the floor area. About 4 per cent of the floor area is an adequate proportion for natural (window opening) ventilation. For example, according to minimum standards, a 10' x 13' bedroom must have 13 sq. ft. for window area; of the 13 sq. ft. approximately 5¼ sq. ft. must be given to natural ventilation. Conditions allowing, about 25 per cent of the floor space would be a more satisfactory window glass area. Excessive glass area, however, often contributes to cold rooms. Good insulation to a certain extent will decrease the heat loss. For adequate daytime illumination in the house, the window area should be equal to 17 per cent of the floor area.

Privacy in Living Areas

Sociologists have indicated that with increasing population, privacy of the individual, the family, or the group is becoming increasingly important. Many of our daily activities require an area where there is privacy. It is often difficult, however, to incorporate provisions for maximum privacy, especially in the plan of a small house. Small houses have some design limitations on the living areas.

Privacy in living areas is the result of careful planning. Activities requiring an area for privacy are sleeping, bathing, dressing, studying, etc. Generally, the rooms where these activities take place can be grouped into three areas: (1) living area, (2) quiet or sleeping area, and (3) service or work area.

The door location and swing direction generally adds to the privacy of an area. The bedroom door, for example, should not show the bed and dressing areas in full view of the other rooms or the hallway. The dining room and kitchen doors should not expose the working part of the kitchen. Similarly, the main entryway door should not offer an immediate view of the living room.

Privacy is possible in the outdoor living area with proper screening. The shape of the house, its orientation on the lot, or the slope and elevation of the lot may offer good screening for the outdoor living area. Other forms of screening used are: the garage or service sheds, wood fences, low masonry walls, hedges, low-growing fruit or ornamental trees, shrubs, and fast-growing vines on trellises.

Privacy should be thought of not only in terms of sight, but also in terms of sound. Extraneous sounds can be reduced by using good quality, close-fitted doors between adjoining rooms, and by using acoustical materials (rugs, drapery, acoustical tile, insulation, etc.). Sounds or noises from the living room, for example, may be isolated from the bedroom area by designing the floor plan with sound baffles such as hallways, closets, bathrooms, and quality doors.

Adequate Storage Space

Adequate storage space is a primary household need. In floor planning, closets should be functionally designed to meet all the requirements for storing or accommodating the family's accumulated possessions.

Closet Space

The closet space costs the same as almost any other space in the house. Houses in the medium price category must have their closets well planned so as to keep the total costs within reason.

In order to obtain maximum benefit from storage areas, the space should be specifically designed for the items to be stored. In addition, these storage spaces

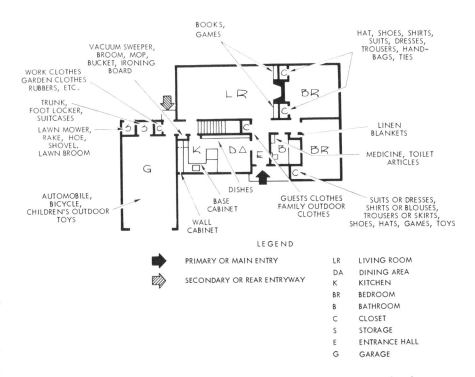

Fig. 5-21. Household articles are associated with particular storage areas. In planning, this should be taken into consideration.

should be located as near as possible to where the stored articles are to be used. Fig. 5-21 shows some of the more basic storage areas and associated articles. Unless closet spaces are planned carefully, considerable floor space will be wastefully consumed.

Although closet planning is often thought of as just making use of excess spaces in the floor plan, the size of these spaces are important in order to functionally utilize

them for storage purposes. Table 5-1 gives the *minimum* and the *suggested* closet space for a typical one story or multilevel home.

The place where closets are to be located, and the type of items to be stored, are the controlling factors in good closet designs. Bedroom closets, for example, should be conveniently located and designed for accessibility of stored items such as clothes, shoes, and other personal articles. The guest closet, located near the

TABLE 5-1

MINIMUM AND SUGGESTED SIZE OF CLOSETS

Closet Location	Minimum Size	Suggested Size
FIRST FLOOR: MAIN ENTRYWAY (Guest or Coat Closet)	2'-0" x 3'-0"	2'-0" x 3'-6"
HALLWAY OR KITCHEN (Cleaning or Broom Closet) (Pantry)	2'-0" x 1'-0" 2'-4" x 1'-0"	2'-6" x 3'-6" 2'-6" x 1'-0"
BACK ENTRYWAY (Utility or Sports Closet)		2'-6" x 3'-0"
LIVING ROOM (Living Room Closet)		2'-6" x 3'-0"
HALLWAY (Linen Closet)	1'-0" x 2'-0"	1'-0" x 4'-0"
MASTER BEDROOM (Bedroom Closets)	2'-0" x 3'-0" *	2'-6" x 4'-0" *
SINGLE BEDROOM (Bedroom Closet)	2'-0" x 3'-0"	2'-6" x 4'-0"
SINGLE BEDROOM (Bedroom Closet)	2'-0" x 2'-6"	2'-6" x 3'-0"

*Master bedroom generally requires two closet spaces.

main entrance, should be used for storing such articles as coats, rubbers, etc. The broom or cleaning closet, located near to or in the kitchen, should be used for storing such items as brooms, the vacuum cleaner, wet mops, dust mops, and other things generally used for cleaning. Fig. 5-22 shows various types of closet designs and arrangements for bedrooms and other areas. Closets used for storage of linens, if deeper than 1'-6", pose a problem not only

in seeing what is stored on the rear portion of the shelf, but also in reaching for the item after locating it.

Though not considered as a closet in the usual sense, the kitchen pantry is once again gaining popularity. The modern pantry is not a separate closet room as it once was, but it has taken the shape of a shallow closet. Most pantries are between 8″ and 10″ deep and are shelved from 2'-0″ above the floor to eye level (5'-2″) or slightly

above. Fig. 5-23 shows a typical kitchen "pantry closet" for the modern homemaker.

Storage Space Check List

In the following list storage space is associated with the items common to each type.

1. Master bedroom closets: suits, shirts, blouses, dresses, shoes, hats, neckties, etc.
2. Children's bedroom closet: clothes, shoes, toys, etc.
3. Guest bedroom closet: clothes, storage space, luggage, etc.
4. Guest closet: summer or winter outer garments, rain apparel, umbrellas, hats, rubbers, etc.
5. Linen closet: sheets, blankets, pillowcases, towels, bathroom supplies, table cloths, napkins, etc.
6. Cleaning closet: brooms, dust mops, cleaning supplies, vacuum cleaner, brushes, etc.
7. Game room or utility closets: sport equipment and games, tools, hobby supplies, etc.
8. Kitchen cabinets: food, staples, cooking utensils, kitchen utensils, etc.
9. Kitchen pantry: canned goods. (Storage shelves may be mounted on kitchen cleaning or broom closet door.)
10. Bathroom cabinet: medicines, etc.
11. Garage closet: lawn and garden equipment, garden clothes, car cleaning equipment, charcoal grill, etc.

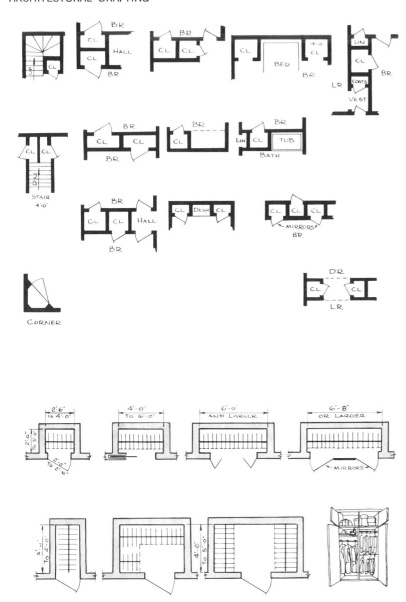

Fig. 5-22. Closets should be planned in relation to the available space.

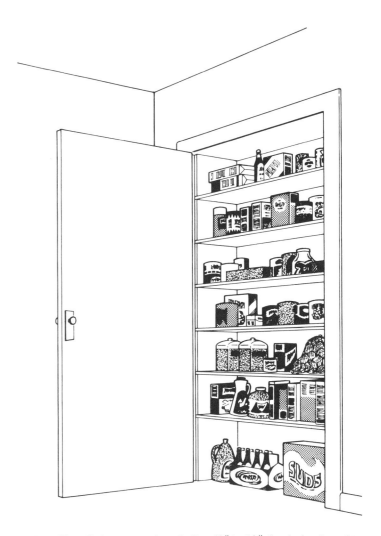

Fig. 5-23. A kitchen pantry is a shallow (8″ to 10″ deep) closet used to store canned goods and excess staple items.

Arrangement of Room Furnishings

Room size depends not only upon purpose, but also upon the number of pieces and the types of furniture the room must contain. Since most room furnishings are standardized, odd sized or odd shaped rooms are normally avoided. A 9′ by 12′ rug, for example, is the most common size. An odd sized room therefore may necessitate the purchase of non-standard and expensive rugs or carpeting.

Room furnishings should be arranged in accordance with traffic circulation. The fireplace and the furniture adjacent to it, for example, should always be out of the traffic path. When the height of the furniture is above the waist, single passage width between 2′-0″ and 2′-6″ is desirable. Space between low furniture, such as the coffee table and the sofa, should never be less than 12″.

Rooms should be planned so that more than one furniture arrangement is possible. The size and location of windows and their sill height — and consequently the amount of sunlight and the view—plays a major role in the possible furniture combinations. Furniture should not, for example, obstruct the view.

Fig. 5-24. Family changes can directly affect the floor plan of the home. With a flexible plan these changes may be made without great difficulty.

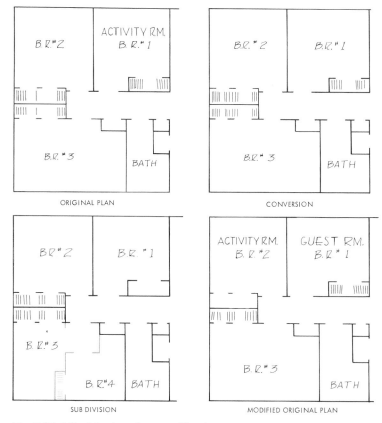

Fig. 5-25. A flexible plan allows modification.

In all cases, simplicity in furniture arrangement is better than complexity, which may result in overcrowding.

Flexibility of Expansion

In home planning, adequacy of space includes both the present and the future family needs. Provisions for later home expansion is always desirable, since most families normally change their manner of living and their activities. Possible family additions should also be taken into consideration. Future needs should not, however, dominate the main plan or the overall appearance of the floor plan. Fig. 5-24 shows how family changes affect the floor plan of a home.

With some consideration and forethought, designers can devise a plan that can be modified to accommodate the growing family. Fig. 5-25 illustrates one example of how an original plan has been changed by converting the activity room to an additional bedroom. As the family size increased, bedroom #3 was subdivided into two smaller bedrooms, #3 and #4. Though small in size, they offered the needed privacy that each occupant desired. As the family grew and left home, the plan could revert to its basic original design of three bedrooms. However, the function of two of the rooms was changed from the original intent. Use of trussed rafters eliminate the need for load bearing partitions. Partitions may be moved without structural considerations.

One of the most effortless and economical methods of expression is *conversion*. Conversion entails changing the purpose of a room or area to suit the changing family pattern. This may be accomplished by simply changing the nature of the furniture or by adding storage space and removing or adding a partition wall. Fig. 5-26 shows some methods of conversion.

Another method is expansion by *addi-*

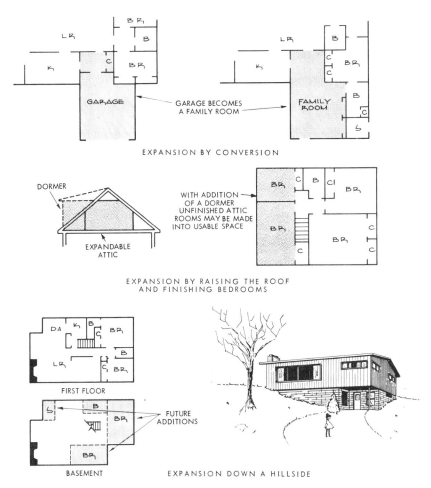

Fig. 5-26. Additional space may be gained by conversion, finishing, or expansion.

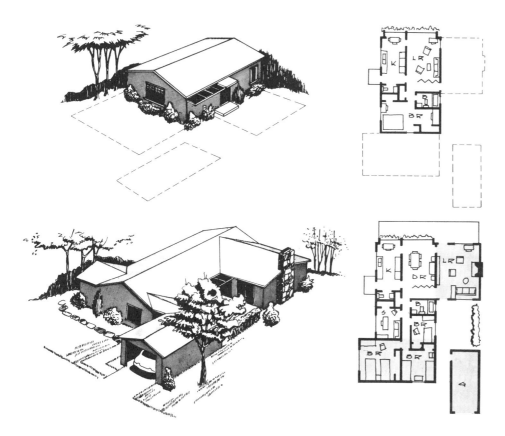

Fig. 5-27. A house may also be expanded by addition.

able floor space for family living is very important. When the available floor space is such that it becomes impossible to accommodate rooms having different functions, a room designed to serve a dual purpose is often incorporated into a small house plan. The following are examples of those rooms which serve dual or multipurposes.

1. Living room
   Used for a variety of family purposes and for entertaining guests or social groups.

2. Dining room
   Used for dining as well as for children's playing or studying.

3. Kitchen
   Used for cooking, dining, and/or laundering.

4. Bedroom
   Used for sleeping, studying, and radio or record listening.

5. Recreation room and den(s)
   Used for playing, sewing, or other recreational activities — may be used as a guest bedroom.

6. Garage extension
   Used for garage, hobby work, summer family room, photo darkroom, laundry facilities, laundry drying, and storage.

tion. This is illustrated in Figs. 5-27 and 5-28. Expansion by addition is dependent upon time, family requirements, and economic factors. Under this method, the complete house is built, then, as needed, extensions are added to the basic living areas. The sequence of additions to the basic unit should be determined and

planned with minimum waste of space and maximum convenience of traffic.

The house should be complete at each stage of expansion both in appearance and in function. The basic rooms must provide all the necessary facilities for the normal life of a family. In some cases, where the house is small, the utilization of all avail-

Fig. 5-28. Wings may be added to the basic structure.

Questions and Problems

The following questions are based on essential factors related to the characteristics of a good floor plan.

1. Sketch a floor plan or copy one from some floor plan source. Check this plan for indoor and outdoor privacy. What can be modified on this plan to increase the privacy factor?

2. What approximate percentage of floor area should be adequate for natural lighting and ventilation?

3. State the advantages and disadvantages of placing a garage near the front of a lot. Would the lot shape, either long and shallow, or narrow and deep, have an effect on your analysis?

4. Open planning is used in varying degrees in many plans. What are some factors which might influence a decision to use open planning?

5. What are the possible methods by which a house could be expanded?

6. Which are considered to be the essential rooms in a house?

7. A house is to be built on a lot near the street. How would this influence the room arrangement?

8. List the necessary storage facilities required by a family of four planning to build a three-bedroom home.

9. Quickly sketch a plan of your home, including the street, compass direction, adjacent topographic features, and neighboring houses. Check this sketch for all plan characteristics. How could this plan be improved?

10. Assume a proposed house plan has been developed with all the features presented in this chapter. However, the kitchen window faces west. What remedy can you suggest without changing the kitchen plan?

11. In the past, rooms were designed for a specific use. Today, rooms are designed for a number of uses. List the other uses for the following main rooms: living room, dining room, kitchen, bedroom, and garage.

12. What are the agencies of circulation in a house?

13. What criteria are used to check a plan for adequate circulation and orientation?

14. Select a lot from the plat shown in Fig. 5-29 and lay out a house that will illustrate the correct orientation for the following rooms:

   a. Living Room
   b. Dining Room
   c. Kitchen
   d. Family Room
   e. Three Bedrooms
   f. Attached Garage

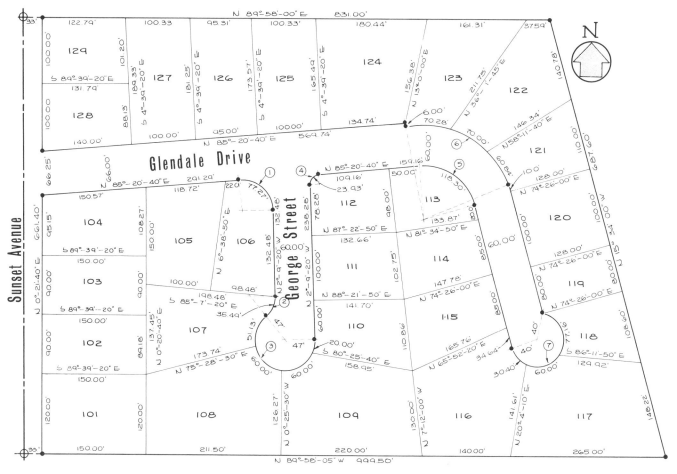

SPRINGFIELD PLAT

CURVE NO	ANGLE	RADIUS
1	92°-30'-00"	47.86'
2	53°-00'-00"	38.37'
3	233°-00'-00"	47.00'
4	87°-30'-00"	15.67'
5	79°-05'-20"	87.70'
6	79°-05'-20"	145.70'
7	240°-00'-00"	40.00'

Fig. 5-29. Springfield Plat.

Individual Room Plans 6

Planning the component areas of a home requires a knowledge of the family's social and recreational activities and number and ages of the family members. In general, each room or area should be planned with regard to (1) the different activities that may take place; (2) the frequency and degree of use; (3) the age, sex, and number of occupants; and (4) the furniture requirements. Ideally, a good house design would satisfy the prospective owner's needs and desires.

Regardless of the criteria used, the possibility of resale must be seriously considered. The mobility of our population has increased greatly over the past twenty-five years. It is wise, therefore, to plan a home that will be not only pleasing to the owner, but also to a future purchaser. The attractiveness which the potential home may have for others is an important economic factor in present planning.

This chapter is devoted to a study of component areas of the home. Room requirements, sizes, and shapes are shown in detail. By combining the material presented here with the information in the preceding chapter, the student should be ready to design the individual rooms of a home.

Planning individual rooms in light commerial buildings requires many of the same considerations that are used in residential design. Chapter 20 covers basic planning of light commercial facilities. However, state health department and fire regulations must be consulted for specific planning points.

One-Quarter Inch Furniture Cutouts

In planning the individual rooms, the student may find it difficult to visualize furniture dimensions, and clearances. Cutouts will aid in determining adequate room size. Individual pieces of furniture are shown in Fig. 6-1. These may be drawn to scale on *detail paper,* cut out, and placed on ⅛″ or ¼″ co-ordinate paper. The scale of the furniture cutouts depends on the grid size of the co-ordinate paper. By arranging the cutouts on the co-ordinate paper, various possibilities of furniture arrangement may be suggested. As these cutouts are being arranged, consideration must also be given to the possible window, door, and closet locations. These will invariably influence the furniture placement, and possibly the room size. Each component area or room in the

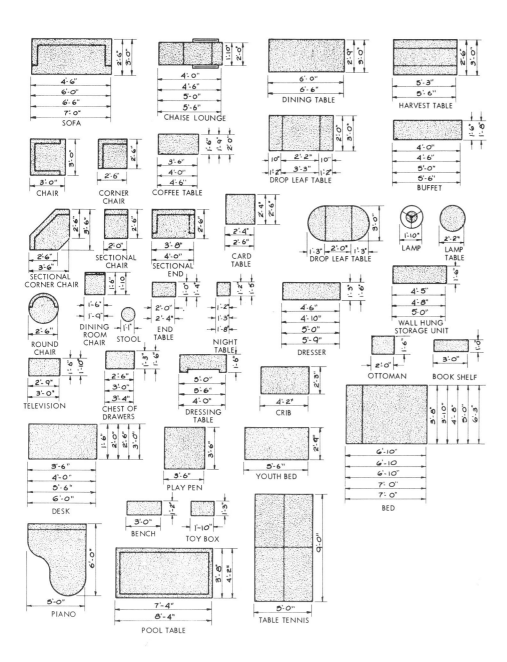

Fig. 6.1. Furniture Outlines: Furniture pieces may be copied to scale on coordinate paper.

Additional furniture sizes may be found in Architectural Graphics Standards or by writing for descriptive brochures from furniture manufacturers.

house must be studied to determine the proper clearances between the pieces of furniture.

Living Room

The living room, with its large floor area, is perhaps the most versatile room in the house. It may, for example, provide a place for receiving guests during the evening or afternoon hours. It may also be used as a place for listening to music, viewing television, or as a quiet place for reading a book or magazine. Sometimes, the living room is used as a rumpus room or as a supervised play area for the pre-school children in the home. Its interior design or plan is determined by the daily living requirements of the owner or family.

Size and Design Factors

The size and design of the living room will depend on several factors. The most important factors (exclusive of finance) are: (1) the frequency with which the owner or the family expects to entertain guests, (2) the number of people the room is expected to accommodate, (3) the expected requirement for furniture essential to comfort and relaxation, and (4) the possibility of using the design concept of open planning. For aid in designing the living room, minimum furniture clearances are given in Fig. 6-2.

Open Planning

The living room need not be limited by

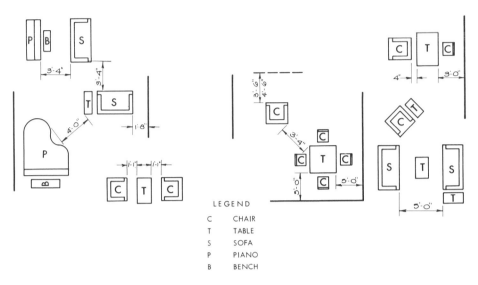

LEGEND

C	CHAIR
T	TABLE
S	SOFA
P	PIANO
B	BENCH

Fig. 6-2. Minimum Furniture Clearances: These may be used in designing the living room.

the enclosing walls—it may be extended in several ways. One way to create the illusion of spaciousness within the room is to use open planning. For instance, large windows and a sliding door oriented towards the patio or porch may extend the living room to the outside, as shown in Fig. 6-3. However, a living room that is extended to the outside in this manner may require exterior screening provisions for privacy. Orientation toward a pleasant view is also desirable. This adds to the charm and the beautiful appearance of the living room.

As explained in Chapter 5, open planning will extend the living room to the dining room, thus creating the effect of more space. The living room-dining room combination not only allows free and easy movement of traffic within the area, but also allows greater freedom for arranging the furniture. This combination is also very convenient for circulation from the kitchen for entertaining guests.

Window Type and Placement

The type and proper placement of windows in the living room are important factors to consider. Windows not only control the natural lighting of the room, but also the arrangement of furniture within the room. In general practice, for adequate natural lighting, the window area should be equal to about one-fourth the total floor space of the room. The windows should be selected so

ROLSCREEN CO.

Fig. 6-3. The appearance of spaciousness in a room may be increased by using sliding glass doors.

that a person who is either seated or standing in the living room has a view to the outside unobstructed by the window sills. Some window types, such as windows which extend from the floor to the ceiling, greatly limit the amount of free wall space for arranging furniture. Generally, living rooms with large glass areas have the furniture arranged away from the windows so as not to obstruct the view. Large windows should face toward the south or southwest (corner location) to receive as much natural light as possible.

Traffic Circulation

As mentioned in the previous chapter, traffic paths in and through a room (1) should be direct and short, (2) should have ample space for freedom of movement, and (3) should not disturb those areas requiring privacy. In some plans the living room is regarded as a type of hall carrying traffic from one part of the house to the other. This can be minimized by changing the door placement. Doors should be placed close together so one may pass through the living room without traveling the full length of the room. An ideal location for entrance and exit doorways is in the corner of the room. Doors and windows should be located so as to leave large unbroken spaces for location of major furniture pieces. When a fireplace is to be included in the design, its location should be either at the center of a living room wall or at a corner. Unless the room is wide, a fireplace located on the side will tend to make the room look narrow. On the other hand, if placed at the end of a room, seating space may be limited. In every case, the fireplace should be away from doors and windows.

Dining Room or Dining Area

Until the early 1940's the dining room was considered an essential part of most home plans. However, during the years which followed, surveys of prospective home owners indicated that a separate dining room was considered costly and unnecessary since it was not used more than three hours a day. In the 1960's, this trend reversed again. The dining room and dining ell have begun to appear with greater frequency in moderately priced homes.

The size of the dining area, whether separate or part of the living room, is partially determined by the dimensions of the table and the number of persons to be seated around it. For families who entertain informally, the dining area may be included as part of the living room, or as an extension of the kitchen. An effective dining-living room arrangement may be achieved by planning an "L" shaped room, the short leg of which may be the dining area. A room that is planned to have this shape will appear to be more spacious. Less floor area is required in an arrangement of this type than for a dining room which is separate from the living room. Generally, a minimum of 9'-6" and a maximum 12'-0" for the width of this area is ample. A smaller space may be used

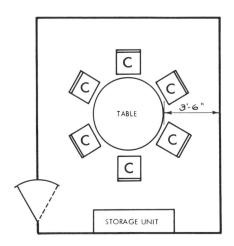
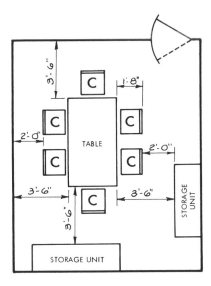

Fig. 6-4. Dining Room Furniture Clearances: When designing this room leave ample space for seating and serving.

by placing the table in a corner with built-in benches on two or three sides. If space is limited, the dining room may be converted to accommodate other activities or uses, such as children's study, after school gatherings, family room, supervised play area, etc.

Screens, draperies, or movable partitions, and sometimes furniture arrangements, may be used to separate the dining area from the living quarters. If the dining area is part of the kitchen, it is frequently separated by a partial partition or breakfast bar.

Dining rooms require a considerable amount of free wall space because the wall often accommodates a china closet, a hutch, a serving table, or a buffet. Ample clearance

should be allowed around the dining room table for seating space and serving. Minimum clearances for dining room furniture are shown in Fig. 6-4.

Multi-Purpose Rooms

Family Room

The family room is the first new room to be added to the home since the advent of the bathroom. During the early 1800's most families ate, socialized, and relaxed in the kitchen. Later the parlor, now generally called the living room, was added for these activities and a separate dining room assumed some of these functions. Over the past years, factors such as increased building costs, scarcity of household help, smaller families, and entertainment away from the home have influenced the living pattern of the family group. If a comparison of residential building plans were made between the 1900's and the present, it would be evident that the size of the living room has decreased. The changing structure of society and the demands made by various sociological and economic factors have created a number of new family needs. These demands influence the design of the family room.

Family life has been changed by the many technological developments in our time. Television, for example, has had a great influence on family living. Prior to its advent, spectator sports, movies, concerts, etc., attracted the family away from the home. Because these attractions are now being televised, this trend has been reversed. Today, many families are staying home.

Increased salaries and higher hourly wages have created a greater demand for conveniences. The work week of many blue and white collar workers is being shortened. This allows more time for hobbies, television viewing, and leisure activities with the family. Greater demands are being made upon the home to accommodate more possessions. Also, more people with a broader scope of activities stay at home for a longer period of time. A pattern of greater social-group informality in home living is being formed.

The family room, as the name implies, is the center of family activity. This major room may contain, or be adjacent to, cooking and dining facilities. The family room may contain such furnishings as lounge chairs, game or utility tables, hi-fi, stereo, and TV. Space should also be provided for hobbies and children's recreation. Many units (sewing machines, hi-fi, TV, washer, dryer, desk, etc.) may be concealed behind sliding or bi-fold doors. These units are usually placed along an inside wall. If a cooking area in the family room is to be included, it is often separated by a divider, base cabinets, or a fireplace. Sometimes the cooking area is planned as a cooking island.

The family room is often designed to open onto a terrace or patio through sliding doors. During mild weather, this arrangement greatly expands the group activities of the family.

Because a major portion of the family's time is spent in the family room, the tendency in planning has been to reduce the size of the living room. The living room in this case becomes a facility for formal entertainment.

Den, Study, or Guest Room

The extra room (called a den, study, or guest room) offers privacy for reading, studying, conversing, and working. It may also serve as sleeping quarters for guests.

Space should be provided for a hide-a-bed, lounge-type chair, desk, bookcase, closet, and possibly a lavatory. The minimum room area recommended is $9' \times 12'$. Its location should be near the living area. The closets should be designed to act as a baffle to reduce the noise which enters this room.

Bedrooms

In floor plans, the number of bedrooms is determined by the number of individuals in the family and the expected number of guests to be accommodated. The arrangement of bedrooms in a multi-level house is governed, to a great extent, by the first floor plan and the stair and window locations.

To permit the greatest freedom for furniture arrangement, consideration must be given to free wall space and window location. Regardless of the size or shape of the bedroom, the glass area of the wall should be equal to no less than 15 per cent of the floor area. In recent years, the trend has been to design windows which are wider and shorter, with sills located approximately $4'-6''$ to $5'-0''$ above the floor. Careful selection and placement of windows give a maximum range of free wall space, thus permitting various furniture arrangements.

Bedroom windows should be located where maximum cross ventilation may be achieved. A well planned bedroom has windows placed in such a manner as to allow fresh air to enter one window and stale air to escape through the others. Air movement should not, however, be directly across the bed.

A further consideration in planning the

bedroom is the number and size of the furniture pieces to be included. For example, the usual furnishings in a master bedroom include: one double bed, or a pair of twin beds; one dresser (single, double, or triple); one chest of drawers; one or two bedside tables; and one or two chairs. Children's or guest's bedrooms usually contain the same furniture with the exception of a dresser.

Passage space at both sides of the bed and at the foot should be at least 20″ wide. Adequate clearance between beds, beds and walls, and beds and other furnishings are shown in Fig. 6-5. The bathroom, closets, and the hall should be easily accessible without walking around the bed.

If two bedrooms are planned side by side, as in Fig. 6-6, the common wall should be utilized for closet space. The closet walls

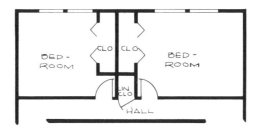

Fig. 6-6. The common wall between two bedrooms may be used for closet space.

shown in these figures compactly house a closet for each bedroom and a linen closet for the hall.

To provide maximum comfort, the following check points should be considered in the plan.

1. The bedrooms should be located as far away from the living area as possible.
2. The bedrooms should be located on the quiet side of the lot away from the street.
3. If the bedroom is expected to be used as a living area, it should have a southern or a south-eastern exposure.
4. Bedrooms should have direct access to the hall without passing through any other room.
5. The children's bedroom should be adjacent to or near the master bedroom.
6. Bedrooms should be provided with cross ventilation by planning the windows on two outside walls near the interior partitions. Avoid a room layout where the wind blows directly over the bed.
7. The plan should include one closet for each bedroom and two for the master bedroom.

Kitchen

Work Triangle

Kitchens planned for efficient operation depend upon the convenient location of

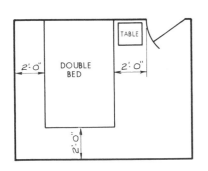
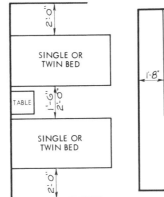
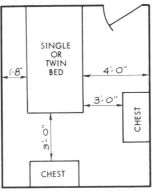

Fig. 6-5. Bedroom Furniture Clearances: Leave at least a 20″ clearance on both sides and at the foot of the bed.

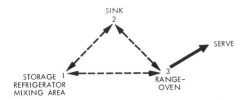

Fig. 6-7. The work triangle should have a perimeter of 12″ to 22″.

cabinets, appliances, and work centers. The relationship of the three basic work centers, containing the refrigerator, the sink, and the kitchen range, is called the *work triangle*. Fig. 6-7 illustrates this concept. For maximum efficiency, the perimeter or the total distance around the work triangle (refrigerator-sink-kitchen range) should be between 12′ and 22′. The preparation of food should move through the pattern of the work triangle directly to the dining area or living room where it is finally served. The kitchen should be near to and connected with the dining area.

The kitchen sink is the main corner of the work triangle. The sink area serves as a preparation and clean-up center. Counter space should be planned on both sides of the sink for food cleaning, draining, and for an auxiliary mixing area.

The kitchen range should be accommodated with a counter space on either side, and a cabinet above if possible. The oven, if separate from the stove, may be located in a less important area. As a fire precaution, the kitchen range should never be placed below a window. For convenience, a range

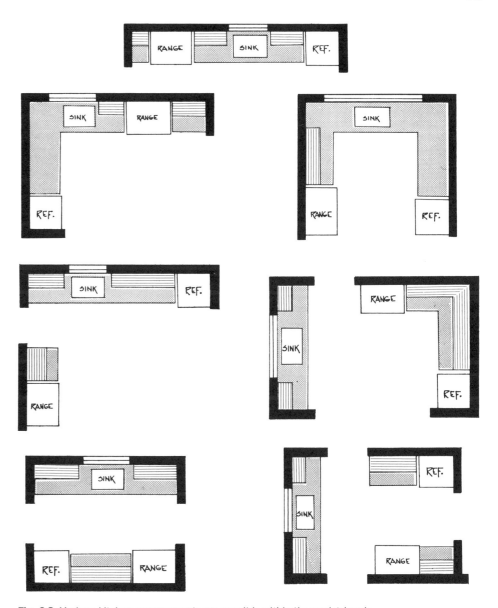

Fig. 6-8. Various kitchen arrangements are possible within the work triangle.

hood with an exhaust fan may be installed over the range.

Various kitchen arrangements are shown in Fig. 6-8. As with other areas of the house, the kitchen requires minimum clearances between cabinets, walls, doors, etc. Minimal clearances are shown in Fig. 6-9. Average cabinet sizes for both combined and individual work centers are illustrated in Fig. 6-10. (Views in Fig. 6-10 are shown from the front. The corner units are shown in both front and top, or plan, view.) Table 6-1 gives typical sizes of ranges, refrigerators, and sink bowls.

Storage

The amount of storage space is a prime

TABLE 6-1

TYPICAL DIMENSIONS OF RANGES, REFRIGERATORS AND SINK BOWLS

RANGES								
BUILT IN OVEN			BUILT IN RANGE TOP			CONVENTIONAL UNIT		
WIDTH	HEIGHT	DEPTH	WIDTH	HEIGHT	DEPTH	WIDTH	HEIGHT	DEPTH
20"- 24"	26" - 39"	21"- 24"	20"- 40"	6" - 11"	17" - 20"	30"- 43"	36"	23"- 31"
						36"- 48"	36"	30"

REFRIGERATORS			
CU FT	WIDTH	HEIGHT	DEPTH
3 - 4½	23½"- 24½"	44"- 54"	25½"-29"
5 - 6¾	25½"-29"	50½"-60"	25"- 29"
7 - 8¾	26"-31"	59"-65"	27"-31"
9 - 12	28"- 33"	62"-70"	27"-31"

SINK BOWLS		
Single Compartment		
24"x 21"		30" x 20"
Double Compartment		
32"x 20"	42"x 20"	36" x 21"

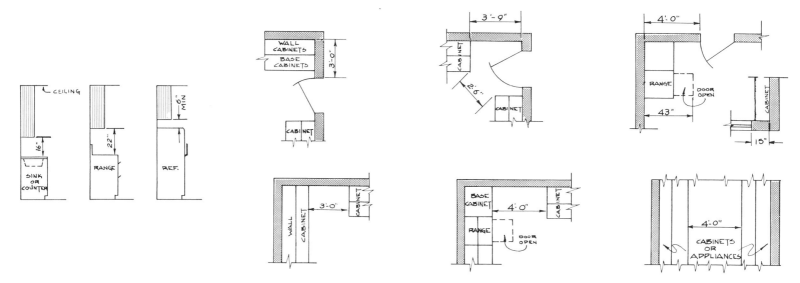

Fig. 6-9. Minimum Clearances for Kitchen Units.

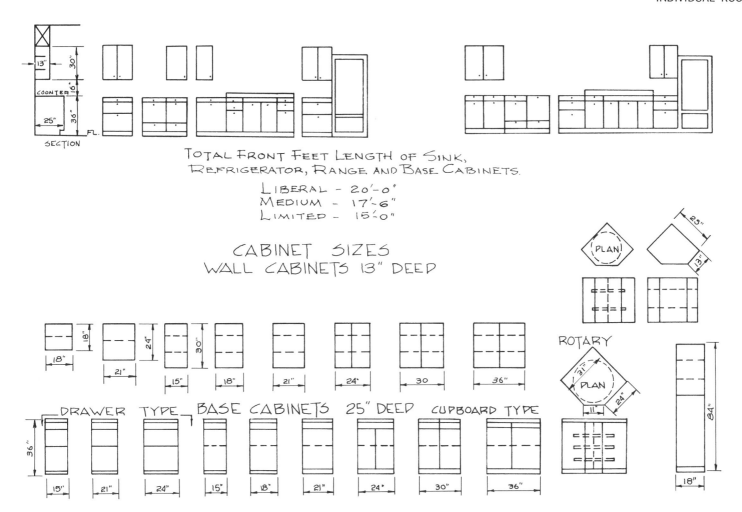

SECTION

TOTAL FRONT FEET LENGTH OF SINK,
REFRIGERATOR, RANGE AND BASE CABINETS.

LIBERAL - 20'-0"
MEDIUM - 17'-6"
LIMITED - 15'-0"

CABINET SIZES
WALL CABINETS 13" DEEP

DRAWER TYPE   BASE CABINETS   25" DEEP   CUPBOARD TYPE

PLAN

ROTARY

PLAN

Fig. 6-10. Standardized Cabinet Sizes: Various combinations and arrangements may be used.

consideration in kitchen planning. Food buying habits of the family and the amount of space required for dishes and utensils must be studied.

Supplies are usually stored where they are first used. For convenience, staple items should be stored adjacent to the mixing area. It is also convenient to store dormant vegetables (potatoes, onions, etc.) under or next to the sink where they are easily accessible for washing and peeling. Dishes should be placed near the serving area.

Windows, Ventilation, and Lighting

Adequate window area is usually considered to be about 15 to 20 per cent of the total floor area. However, cabinet space on a kitchen wall must not be sacrificed for excessive window space.

In addition to window ventilation, provision is usually made for an exhaust fan, or more preferably a range hood. For maximum efficiency, the exhaust fan must be located directly over the range center. A fan mounted on the wall behind the range is not as effective as a fan mounted on the ceiling.

Adequate lighting is a must in the kitchen since the homemaker spends a large portion of her day in this area. In addition to a central ceiling fixture, other lighting may be placed over each of the main work centers to assure sufficient illumination. For convenience, electrical outlets should also be placed near each work area.

Traffic Circulation

Ideally, the kitchen should have easy access to both the front entryway and the rear service entrance. However, the kitchen normally should not have more than two doors and should not be used as a traffic lane. Door swings should not interfere with the arrangement of equipment, appliances, or other doors. Many kitchen designs make use of sliding doors in lieu of conventional hinged doors.

Bathroom and Lavatory

The bathroom in today's home is viewed from a different standpoint than it was in the 1930's and 1940's. During and preceding this era, most moderately priced homes were planned with only one bathroom. Contrasting this with current planning practice, today's home buyer anticipates one and a half or two bathrooms for an average six room house. If conditions allow, the *ideal* plan would provide a bathroom for each bedroom. However, one bathroom will be sufficient for three people in a small home. In large homes a bathroom for every two additional bedrooms (after the first two) will insure adequate facilities.

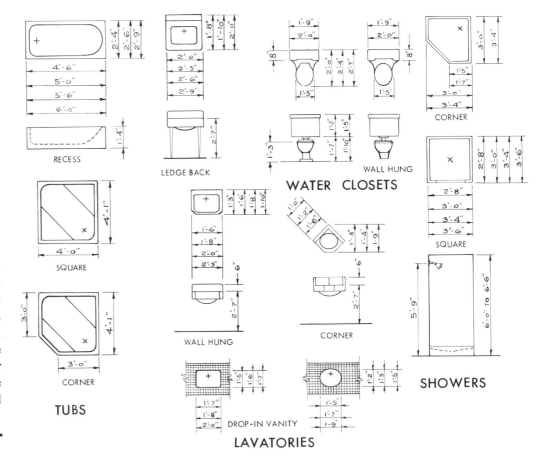

Fig. 6-11. Basic Bathroom Fixture Sizes.

The number and arrangement of fixtures, the number of persons these fixtures will serve, and the character of the dwelling will influence the bathroom size. Bathrooms are not difficult to plan. Fixtures are standardized and do not vary greatly in size. Fig. 6-11 shows some basic fixtures sizes. If the budget permits, the bathroom should be planned to be larger than the minimum sizes of 5' × 7' or 6' × 8'.

There are several methods of grouping bathroom fixtures around the walls. Plumbing fixtures may be arranged along one wall, on opposite walls, scattered along the walls, or divided by means of partitions. Many arrangement variations are possible by merely including extra fixtures, such as another water closet (with a partition) and another lavatory in the room. With the addition of extra fixtures, the design of two-bathroom efficiency is possible. The construction cost of this design is considerably less than that of the two separate bathrooms. Minimum clearances between fixtures and between adjacent or opposite walls are illustrated in Fig. 6-12.

If the home is to have only one bathroom, it should be accessible from the rear entryway as well as from the bedrooms. Traffic lanes must be well planned. Two doors entering into the bathroom may solve this problem. Another solution is to design an additional room, with a lavatory and water closet, near the rear of the house by the service entry or kitchen. This solution is advantageous when there are guests for it eliminates excessive traffic.

The greatest saving is gained in one-story or multi-level dwellings if the bathrooms are located over each other, adjacent to each other (especially if fixtures are backed up to each other in a common wall), or over the

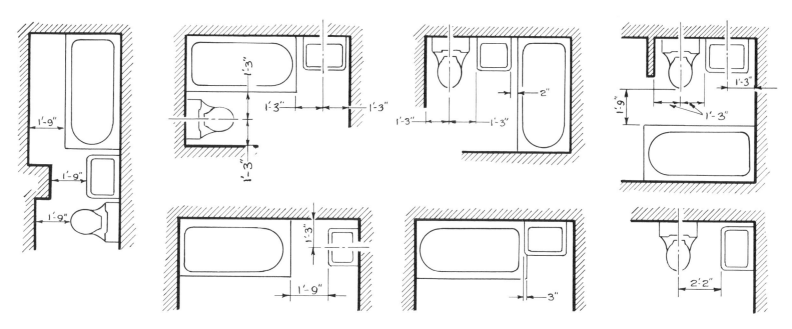

Fig. 6-12. Minimum Bathroom Clearances.

kitchen and laundry plumbing. It is false economy, however, to sacrifice convenience and utility for a savings in piping. Usually, good planning and piping economy are natural complements.

Some types of access should be provided for the bathtub or shower water supply pipes. Normally hot and cold water pipes are concealed in the wall. The designer should specify a small removable panel to be placed on the opposite side of the wall. The panel is flush-mounted and may be plain, as in the illustration, or "trimmed-out." Fig. 6-13 shows a portion of a bathroom with a plumbing access panel. The panel is symbolized by a heavy line and a note calling out: "PLUMBING ACCESS DOOR 1'4" W × 1'-0" H." An interior elevation would be necessary to describe the design of the plumbing access door.

In order to plan the bathroom for economy, efficiency, and convenience, the following points should be considered.

1. The bathroom should be located near the bedrooms.
2. It should be located near the head of the stairs or where it is accessible from the hall.
3. The entrance to the bathroom should be from the hall, near the head of the stairs in a two-story or split-level house.
4. When bedrooms are located on different floors additional bathrooms should be considered.
5. As a minimum, one additional bathroom should be planned for every two *additional* bedrooms after the first two.
6. Bathroom windows should be located where they may be easily approached for opening and closing. Window sills should be four feet above the floor.
7. Bathroom fixtures should be planned so they do not interfere with each other. (Place the lavatory between water closet and tub in a small bathroom.)
8. The water closet should be located as near to the vertical *soil stack* (waste pipe) as possible.

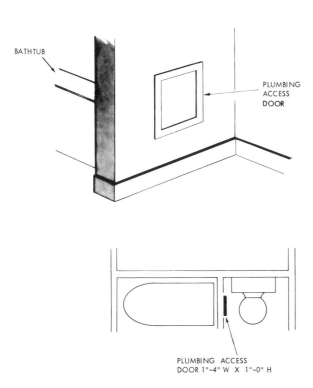

Fig. 6-13. Plumbing access doors are placed on the other side of the wall containing hot and cold water fixtures.

Laundry Area

In recent years the trend has been away from placing the laundry room area in the basement. Laundering is now generally done in a room specifically designed for this purpose. This room may be on the first floor in an area off the kitchen, recreation room, storage room, sewing room, or utility room. Where the climate is warm throughout the year, the laundry area may be located in the garage. In any case, it should be convenient to the service entry if the home maker desires to hang the wash outdoors.

In planning the laundry area, consideration must be given to pleasant lighting and step-saving. The laundry area should have space for work, storage, and equipment. Fig. 6-14 shows the general dimensions of laundry equipment and the necessary clearances.

The laundry-area plan is determined by the sequence of laundry operations. Equipment which is grouped according to the

following work cycle should result in an efficient plan.

1. Receiving and Preparation Center
   a. Sorting table or counter
   b. Supply cabinet or shelves

2. Washing Center
   a. Automatic washer or washing machine
   b. Stationary tub(s)

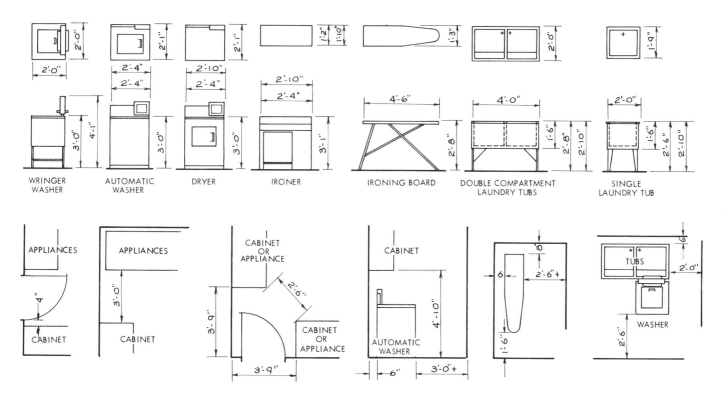

Fig. 6-14. Laundry Equipment and Clearances.

3. Drying Center
   a. Electric or gas dryer (should be adjacent to outside wall for venting)
   b. Drying lines
4. Ironing and Storage Center
   a. Counter for sprinkling and folding
   b. Ironer or mangle
   c. Ironing board
   d. Rack or counter (may be the same as the one above) for finished laundry
   e. Storage cabinet

Basement

Whether a basement will be built depends on the following factors: (1) slope of the lot, (2) climatic conditions, (3) desire or need for recreational facilities, and (4) available money.

Building a basement may double the home size. The cost for this addition is only about one-tenth of the total cost of the home. This may be the most inexpensive way to get additional space for living, recreation, and storage. Plumbing and drainage problems are easier to solve when a basement is included in the plan. Studies have shown that the basement is the most economical and efficient location for the furnace and water heater. In colder, northern climates where the foundation walls must be supported below the *frost line,* an additional few feet (usually two feet) below this line would be sufficient for placing a footing for the basement.

The following points should be considered in efficient basement planning: (1) Plan as much natural light in the basement as possible—use ribbonlike *hopper windows* for this purpose and for ventilation. (Hopper windows are long, narrow windows that open inward with hinges along the lower edge.) (2) make sure the basement construction is waterproof and that provisions are made for adequate exterior drainage. (3) The heating equipment and stairway should be located along one wall to make more space available in the basement. (4) If the house is built on a sloping lot, the basement may be planned with a large glass window located on the sloping side of the lot. If properly waterproofed, heated, and lighted, this type of basement may become the most used area in the home. (5) Whether the lot is sloping or level, it is desirable to have a basement with direct access to the outside.

To some home owners, the basement is not only an unnecessary space which must be cleaned and heated, but it is also an area where water problems may be encountered during rainy weather. When this situation exists, the basement may be regarded as unnecessary and costly. The money allotted for the basement could be utilized more efficiently for increasing the ground-level living area. In warm climates, the basement is usually omitted and a utility room is planned.

Utility Room

If the area for the basement is wet and water seepage would be an evident problem, a basement is not feasible. A substitute plan is to build a utility room above the grade level.

If the basement is dispensed with, such items as the furnace, hot water heater, automatic washer, and dryer are generally located in the utility room. The utility room should be near the kitchen and the service entry. It is also possible to eliminate the utility room by placing these items along one wall of the kitchen behind louvered, sliding doors.

Entrances and Hallways

The front entrance or main entryway should be located so that it leads to the central area of the house. In planning the entryway, the relationship of the entrance to the driveway and the street is a prime consideration. If possible, the front entrance should open into a hall rather than directly into the living room. If the area is limited, a small portion of the living room may be used as a hall or vestibule. This can be accomplished by designing a vertical louvered divider, a closet divider that is elevated from the floor, or a storage unit which will separate the entrance area from the living room. Fig. 6-15 illustrates several entrance areas.

In areas where severe weather prevails part of the year, an entrance hall in a home is almost a necessity. An entry hall serves as a barrier or shield against cold drafts and damp air which may enter the living areas. This hall may also serve as an ideal be sufficiently wide to allow free flow of traffic circulation. Hallways must also be wide enough to permit passage of furniture. In general, the width of a hallway should be no less than 3′-0″. Most hallways are 3′-0″ wide. Hallways wider than 4′-0″ are wasted space, unless designed for a specific purpose, such as a passageway for handicapped persons or invalids. The total floor area of a hallway should be kept to a minimum so as not to reduce the area allotted for family living.

Porches and Outdoor Living Areas

The porch may take many shapes and may serve many purposes. Common types of porches are: living porches, entrance stoops, sleeping porches, outdoor covered porches, and garden rooms. A porch often complements the indoor areas of the house and may be used for dining, playing, sleeping, or sitting. For greatest versatility and privacy, the porch is usually located at the rear or side of the house. If it is to accommodate table and chairs, etc., it should be at least 8′ wide.

Outdoor living may also be facilitated by building a patio, terrace, or deck. (Decks are made of wood planks laid down as a floor.) The total area of the house may be as much as doubled in this manner. Various paving materials may be used. The easiest and most economical are loose stone, asphalt, or concrete. Bricks, blocks, wood (planks, sawn tree trunks, etc.), stone, tile, adobe, etc., may also be used. One of the

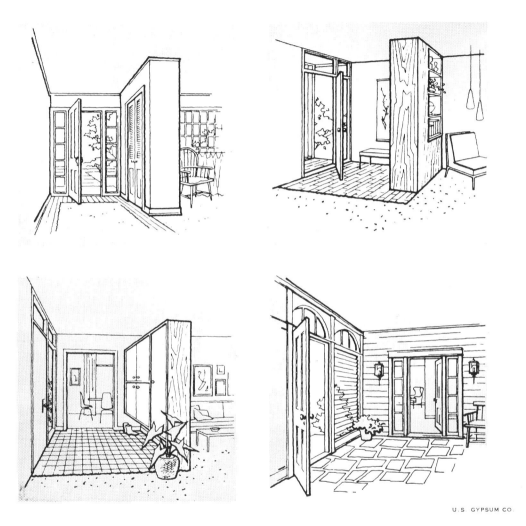

U.S. GYPSUM CO.

Fig. 6-15. Various layouts may be used to separate the entryway from the rest of living area.

location for a guest closet. Entry halls are usually 5′-0″ in width.

When planning the hallways of a house, the design should provide the most *direct routes* to the bathrooms, bedrooms, and other living areas. Also, hallways should

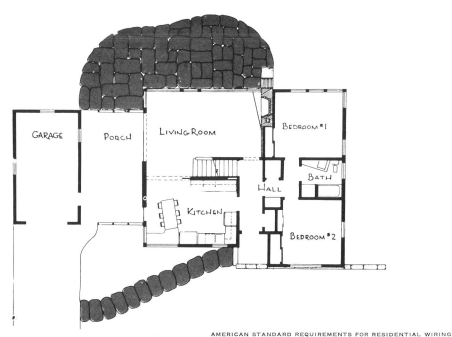

AMERICAN STANDARD REQUIREMENTS FOR RESIDENTIAL WIRING.

Fig. 6-16. Flagstones may be used to form an attractive terrace or walkway.

most popular materials, illustrated in Fig. 6-16, is flagstone. However, this is one of the most expensive paving materials. It is also one of the most permanent. Regardless of the material used, it should not be laid down haphazardly. Careful planning is necessary to create a pleasing esthetic effect. Both the shape and color must be considered. Existing features, such as trees and shrubs, must also be taken into account. A patio or deck may, for example, be built around trees.

Patios and decks may be joined to the house or they may be located away from the house in a garden area. They may, if desired, be wholly or partially covered. The house roof, for example, may be extended to provide a partial cover. Fig. 6-17 illustrates this possibility. If the surface does not drain easily, a slight grade should be provided. Locate south for the best sunlight, north for shade.

Lighting for night use should also be considered. Spot or flood lights may be used. Reflected light is the most comfortable and is recommended. In any case, light sources should not be located where they could shine in anyone's eyes.

Most patios and decks pose no serious construction problems. However, support is required for decks. Piers and footings will be required for a deck of any height. (Railings, depending on the height, may also be necessary.) With a simple low-level deck, however, little difficulty should be encoun-

AMERICAN BUILDER: LESLIE I. NICHOLS, ARCHITECT.

Fig. 6-17. A roof overhang is often used to shade the terrace area.

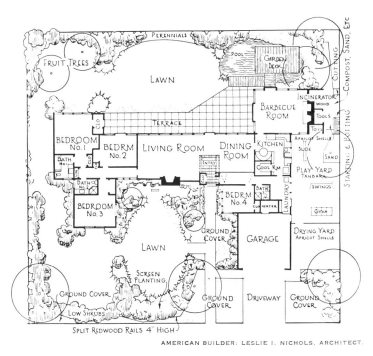

AMERICAN BUILDER: LESLIE I. NICHOLS, ARCHITECT.

Fig. 6-18. A terrace may be combined with a deck to form an attractive outdoor area.

tered. A simple footing may be used. In any event, local building codes should be consulted for requirements and restrictions. Fig. 6-18 illustrates a low-level deck. Here piers would be used. Note how the decking leads away from the terrace into the privacy of the pool area.

Garage or Carport

The garage today has developed from a simple shed-like structure to an all-purpose room or building. In some areas, however, a shed-like structure, known as a carport, has become very popular.

When the size of the lot permits, the garage is often designed as a separate building and combined with a porch, barbecue area, greenhouse, or work shop. However, today's garages or carports are usually attached to the house. This has the economy of using a common wall and the convenience of direct and semi-sheltered access to the house. A garage that opens directly into the kitchen is especially desirable since carrying groceries long distances is eliminated. Also, an attached garage with an open or closed breezeway (covered passage) gives the illusion that the building is long, and wide-

spread. A house with this design, however, is somewhat more expensive.

Since 1940, there has been an increasing tendency to locate the garage on the front portion of the lot near the street. Today most houses have the garage or carport attached to the house. In general, this not only locates the auto in the most convenient and practical place, but also frees the entire rear area of the lot for gardening and other development. In the northern areas where snow prevails during much of the winter season, this garage location eliminates excessive snow shoveling.

If a house is built without a basement, there may be a need for a garage with storage and work space. Although an allowance of $12' \times 22'$ is sufficient for any car, space for car door clearances, storage, and work areas should also be included in the total garage area. The garage may also provide space for storing such items as bicycles, wagons, baby carriages, screens, storm windows, fireplace wood, garden tools, hose, lawn mower, ladders, etc. In some cases the garage is designed to house laundry equipment and a clothes drying area. It may also be a convenient location for a porch-type play room where the children may play without disturbing the rest of the household.

In warm areas, where the winter season is not very severe, the need to house the auto in a completely enclosed building is not very important. The carport in most southwestern, southern, and southeastern seaboard states is used in place of a garage, since protection from cold and snow is not necessary. Recently, the use of carports has come into vogue, particularly in the southern and southwestern seaboard areas. Because of their simplicity, carports are very inexpensive. In design, carports are very much like a lean-to. One side of the roof is supported to the house, while the other is supported by columns. Carports may be open on two or three sides. In either case, the function is merely to provide a roofed shelter for the auto. The carport may be planned in such a manner as to allow conversion to a garage with a minimal amount of work.

The driveway should be designed simultaneously with the garage or carport. It should slope to the street and, if possible, conform to the level of the lawn. For safety, the view along the driveway should be unobstructed.

Questions and Problems

The following questions are designed as a self-checking device.

1. What are the most important factors to consider in making a plan for the living room? Assume the size has already been decided.
2. What are some other uses for main rooms such as the living room, dining room, kitchen, bedroom, and garage?
3. By what means can one be assured that certain pieces of furniture will fit into a specific room?
4. How much space is considered adequate between a wall and bed to allow sufficient clearance to make the bed?
5. What determines the size of a room?
6. What are the three activity centers or work areas in the kitchen?
7. What are some pros and cons for construction of a basement?
8. Make three thumbnail sketches of a kitchen and bathroom, using a common wall for plumbing and venting. Show the various items of equipment that would be necessary along each wall.
9. Draw or sketch the following rooms to scale ($\frac{1}{2}'' = 1'\text{-}0''$). Arrange all furniture with proper clearances; include doors, windows and closets.
   a. Living Room—Dining Room Combination—Size 16' × 22'. A 2' × 8' divider serves as a screen between the living and dining room. The divider contains a desk, bookcase, radio, stereo, TV, and games on living room side and shelves for linen and china on the dining room side. Other furniture to be included: 4 chairs, 2 arm chairs, dining room table, sectional sofa, end table, piano and bench, cocktail table, and an upholstered chair.
   b. Study or Den—Size 9' × 12'. Furniture to be included: a studio couch, low chest, table, 2 chairs, bookcase, desk, and storage closet.
   c. Master Bedroom — Size 12' × 16'. Furniture to be included: a double bed, bedside table, chest, double dresser, lounge chair, and closet(s).
   d. Girl's Bedroom—Size 10' × 12'. Furniture to be included: a single bed, night or bedside table, dressing table or bench, desk chair, boudoir chair, bookcase, and closet.
   e. Boy's Bedroom—Size 10' × 12'. Furniture to be included: a single bed; upholstered chair; cabinets (12″ deep attached to wall) for games, athletic equipment, and books; an 18″ deep workbench placed below cabinets; desk and chair; chest; and closet.
   f. Dining Room — Size 10' × 12'. Furniture to be included: a dining room table, 6 chairs, a hutch or china cabinet, and a buffet.
   g. Living Room—Size 18' × 21'. Furniture to be included: a 4 piece sectional sofa (including a corner section); 2 occasional chairs; 2 large lounge chairs; coffee table; piano and bench; fireplace; radio; stereo; TV; and storage facilities for records, music, games, card table, and guests' coats.
   h. Combination Kitchen and Laundry. Sketch a possible combination of these two areas, utilizing the following equipment and appliances: refrigerator, sink, separate range top and oven, washer dryer, furnace, and water heater.
10. Design a bedroom for two brothers age 8 and 12 years. Indicate on your sketch all the necessary furniture, and the appropriate dimensions.

Today's home is designed primarily for comfort and convenience. The livability of a house, regardless of size, depends upon good, sound planning. This involves **designing and placing rooms** in relation to family activities. Remember: Designing and planning should never be approached as separate entities.

Building materials, construction techniques, and methods of fabrication are changing constantly in the home construction field. In spite of research and development in housing, there is one problem which perpetually plagues the designer. This problem is determining the needs of the family. Because each family group has its own specific needs, pattern of living, and activities, it remains impossible for an outsider to generalize about the requirements of most families. It is evident that the requirements of an individual family should control the house plan. In order to find something that will suit the family needs, persons who seek to design a home usually search through numerous books and magazines on home planning, obtain ideas from existing floor plans, or visit homes which are for sale.

Searching For Ideas

Every designer has considered how he might change his present living quarters. Most "fresh" and "new" planning ideas generally originate from such contempla-

tion. In addition to this the designer seeks information on new materials and plans in architectural publications and buildings. By pinpointing planning ideas suited to the client's taste and combining them with his own ideas, a workable, satisfactory plan may be created.

The following procedure is useful in planning a house.

1. *Be a "Window Shopper."* Review houses on display at home shows, open houses, etc. Pick up brochures, plan sheets, and other home planning information which may be available. These are good sources for obtaining home planning ideas. It is advisable to look at all styles and types of homes. Usually, every house style and floor plan provides many different home planning principles. By shopping for ideas in this manner, the home designer is better able to devise a house which will meet the family requirements.

2. *Read Magazines.* Some of the better designed houses are no farther away than the public library or the corner news stand. Get in the habit of browsing through architectural and building magazines. Read books intended for the architect and builder. Check home magazines for new ideas and for house plans which may be featured periodically. Some publishers put out an annual or semi-annual home planning magazine which compiles all of the best plans of the preceding six months or year. Many local newspapers carry a weekly home planning section describing plans or aspects of planning which are valuable. When selecting publications, be sure to choose the best home planning sources available. The following is a list of some of the most reliable sources for good planning ideas: *American Builder, Architectural Forum, Architectural Record, House and Home, Interiors, House Beautiful, Professional Builder, Progressive Architecture, Architectural Record, AIA Journal,* and *Building Design and Construction.*

3. *Hold on to Your Ideas.* The purpose of "window shopping" and reading magazines is to obtain usable ideas. For easy reference, the collected information may be kept in a notebook or "idea file." The clippings and sketches should be classified according to rooms or areas in the house (i.e., family room, dining room, bedroom, floor plans, fireplaces, etc.). Save only those ideas which seem useful or interesting.

Planning Considerations

When planning a house, each room must be considered as a *vital part of the total plan.* Each room should be thoroughly examined for its use, location within the plan, and possible furniture arrangements. The formative planning stage should give primary consideration to (1) the family's space requirements, (2) the routing and implementation of household tasks, (3) the normal traffic circulation through the house, and (4) the proper room orientation. Remember, it is much easier to make changes in the formative planning stage than later, when building commitments have been made with the contractor.

To devise an intelligent plan, it is essential that the various rooms be studied individually to ascertain their *sizes, location, requirements,* and *uses.* Each room must be related to the whole plan.

Family Activities

A well-planned house should provide enough space for all living activities. Every room or area in the house should be designed for a limited number of activities. Rooms or areas which are designed to accommodate a large variety of activities should always be avoided. Such a design can never fully satisfy any of the planned activities. "Seldom used" rooms may be adapted to accommodate additional living activities. Multi-purpose rooms or areas are desirable only if their design provides maxi-mum functional conveniences with a minimum of wasted space.

The well-designed house plan must have: (1) all of the living space that the buyer can afford; (2) pleasing simplicity in its architectural treatment; and (3) utmost privacy from the neighbors. In home planning, the incorporation of these three home considerations may seem an impossible task with a limited budget, but clear thinking and a good evaluation of the family needs can produce excellent planning results.

Prior to designing the house, the requirements of the family must be analyzed and considered carefully. By gathering data about the family, it is possible to design the house plan according to their needs and desires. This gathered data, or inventory of the family, should provide: (1) the number, sex, and ages of the family members; (2) the number and type of family possessions, including those they expect to have in the future; (3) the family's design preferences in the home; and (4) the types of activities the family would ordinarily perform in certain areas of the home.

The test of the house plan is its ability to meet the requirements and needs of the family. Listed below are various family activities, both individual and group, and the rooms or areas involved.

Family Activities

Activities	Areas or Rooms Involved
Housework	
Food Preparing	Kitchen

Housekeeping	Cleaning cabinet, storage cabinet
Laundering	Utility room, kitchen, basement, garage
Serving	Dining room, family room, kitchen
Sewing	Utility, kitchen, laundry, dining room, den, bedroom
Gardening	Basement, utility, garage
House Upkeep	Basement, utility, garage

Family (Group)

Conversing	Dining room, kitchen, living room, family room, patio, outdoors
Dining	Dining room, family room, kitchen, living room, patio, outdoors
Relaxing	Living room, den, recreation room, family room, bedroom, basement, patio, outdoors
Entertaining	Living room, recreation room, family room, dining room, patio, outdoors
Playing (Recreation)	Recreation room, living room, family room, bedroom, basement, patio
Partying	Recreation room, living room, dining room, family room, patio, outdoors

| Storing | Closets, storage cabinet, storage room, basement, utility room, garage |
| Working | Den, study, bedroom, recreation room, family room, workshop, garage |

Family (Individual)

Dressing	Bedroom, bath
Bathing	Bath, laundry
Studying, writing, reading	Living room, family room, dining room, dining areas, bedroom, patio, den, study
Storing clothes	Clothes closets, chests, storage cabinets, storage room
Hobbying	Utility room, workshop, basement, garage, den, storage room, kitchen, living room, studio, workshop
Accommodating Guests	Extra bedroom, living room, den, recreation room, or other room

Room Sizes

In discussing room sizes, it is fallacious to arbitrarily specify the *best size* of a room. Before a room size can be considered, the planner should answer at least three main questions. (1) Has the inventory of the family shown the room size to be adequate for their activities? (2) Has consideration been given to existing and future furniture or equipment to be placed in the room? (3) Has the location of windows and doors been considered in relation to furniture and equipment?

Ideal room sizes are helpful as a starting point in planning, but strict adherence to the ideal sizes is not necessary. Table 7-1 lists the basic rooms and indicates the suggested area and dimensions for each room.

Room Combinations

An examination of plans for small homes will reveal fundamental relationships existing between rooms. This is a crucial factor in home planning! Various areas belong together for convenience and function. For example, the dining room is usually placed next to the kitchen. In some cases, the dining area is incorporated as part of the kitchen. The family room sometimes serves as the dining area, so this room also is commonly placed adjacent to the kitchen (see Fig. 7-1).

Many home plans frequently have the living room placed near the dining room or dining area. Often, the dining room is combined with the living room to form a dining area or a dining ell at one end of the room. The front entrance is located in or adjacent to the living room. The basement stairway is often near the kitchen, the rear of the house, or occasionally the front entryway.

On most plans, bedroom and bathroom arrangements can be broken into specific combinations. Fig. 7-2 shows a few of many

TABLE 7-1

ROOM SIZE ACCORDING TO SPACE AND SIZE ALLOCATION

Room	Minimum	Small	Medium	Large
KITCHEN	51 Sq Ft 6'-0" x 8'-6"	92 Sq Ft 8'-0" x 11'-6"	108 Sq Ft 9'-0" x 12"	168 Sq Ft 12'-0"- x 14'- 0"
DINING ROOM	100 Sq Ft 10'-0" x 10'-0"	117 Sq Ft 9'-0" x 13'-0"	140 Sq Ft 10'-0" x 14'-0"	160 Sq Ft 10'-0" x 16'-0"
DINING ALCOVE (Dinette)	25 Sq Ft 5'-0" x 5'-0"	49 Sq Ft 7'-0" x 7'-0"	566 Sq Ft 7'-6" x 7'-6"	76 Sq Ft 8'-9" x 8'-9"
LIVING ROOM	150 Sq Ft 10'-0" x 15'-0"	219 Sq Ft 12'-6"x 17'-6"	259 Sq Ft 14'-0"x 18'-6"	300 Sq Ft 15'-0"x 20'-0"
FAMILY ROOM	154 Sq Ft 11'-0"x14'-0"	192 Sq Ft 12'-0"x16'-0"	216 Sq Ft 12'-0"x18'-0"	273 Sq Ft 13'-0"x21'-0"
BEDROOM	90 Sq Ft 9'-0"x10'-0" (1 Bed)	120 Sq Ft 10'-0"x12'-0" (Twin Beds)	172 Sq Ft 12'-0"x14'-4" (Twin Beds)	219 Sq Ft 12'-0"x18'-4" (Twin Beds)
BATHROOM	35 Sq Ft 5'-0" 7'-0"	35 Sq Ft 5'-0" 7'-0"	40 Sq Ft 5'-0" 8'-0"	48 Sq Ft 6'-0" 8'-0"
GARAGE 1-Car*		193 Sq Ft 11'-0"x17'-6"	218 Sq Ft 11'-6"x19'-0"	258 Sq Ft 12'-0"x21'-6"
2-Car		288 Sq Ft 16'-6"x17'-6"	333 Sq Ft 17'-6"x19'-0"	410 Sq Ft 19'-0"x21'-6"

*Sizes shown indicate minimum width clearances.
Small, medium, and large refer to car sizes.
One-car garage for any car size is 11'-6" x 21'-6".
Two-car garage for any car size is 19'-0" x 21'-6".

standard combinations. These room combinations may be used in most plans regardless of the number of bedrooms and bathrooms.

Any of the standard arrangements may be doubled by reversing or "flipping" the plan. To reverse a plan, merely turn the paper over and view the image through the reverse side.

Closets play an important role in bedroom and bathroom combinations. By careful planning, space left between the end of the tub and a wall may be used as a closet for the adjoining bedroom. This and other suggestions are shown in Fig. 7-2. Closets also help to lessen noise travel from the bathroom to the bedroom.

A lavatory or half bath (that is, a room which contains a water closet and a sink only) may be placed adjacent to one of the bedrooms or located in close proximity to an entryway. Prior to World War II, the lavatory was located near the front entryway. Since that time, the trend has been to place a half-bath near the rear door or service entryway for greater convenience. With increasing frequency half-baths are being placed adjacent to a bedroom (or bedrooms) thereby freeing the main bath for others during congested times.

Room Layout

The rooms included in the plan should be arranged for maximum efficiency with a minimum of wasted space. A great amount of wasted space influences not only the cost of the house, but also its livability. Livability is the key to the layout of a house plan.

Often, the novice designer begins the house plan by designing the outside before the inside. In other words, the treatment of the exterior appearance is paramount. It is good practice to design the house interior first and let the exterior design be considered as the plan is being roughed in.

All plans have many possible variations. The planner should not crystallize his thinking with only one arrangement. Devise several alternate plans based on the same number of rooms, requirements, livability, etc.

A factor often overlooked on the preliminary house plan sketch is that a line drawn on the paper really has three dimen-

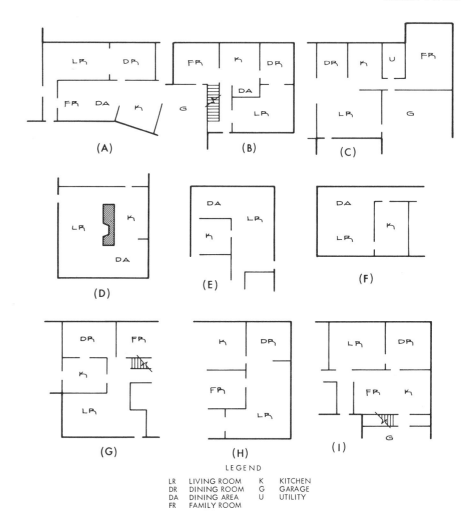

Fig. 7-1. Living, dining, and family room combinations go together for convenience and function.

LEGEND

LR	LIVING ROOM	K	KITCHEN
DR	DINING ROOM	G	GARAGE
DA	DINING AREA	U	UTILITY
FR	FAMILY ROOM		

sions. The hastily sketched line on the plan represents not only length and width, but also height which cannot be shown. The planner must visualize in three dimensions whenever he draws. A line on a rough layout of the plan may have many meanings as shown in Fig. 7-3.

Layout is a problem that is never simple; it always requires careful thought and imagination. Here the note book or file of newspaper and magazine photos, sketches, brochures, etc., may be very helpful. The

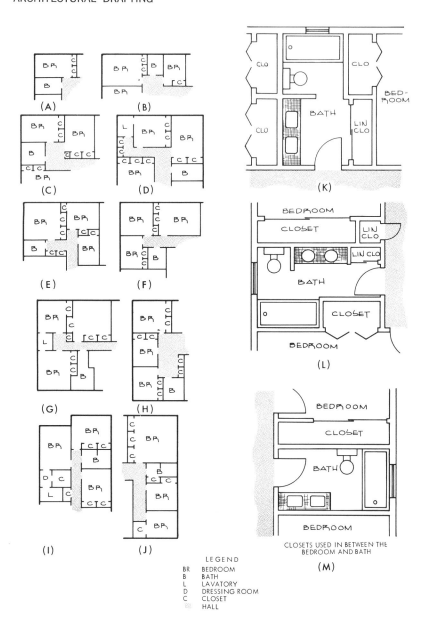

LEGEND
BR   BEDROOM
B   BATH
L   LAVATORY
D   DRESSING ROOM
C   CLOSET
      HALL

Fig. 7-2. Bedroom-bathroom combinations should be arranged for convenience.

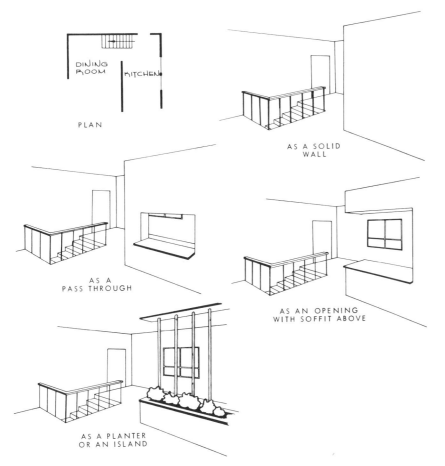

Fig. 7-3. A line on a rough preliminary sketch may have many interpretations.

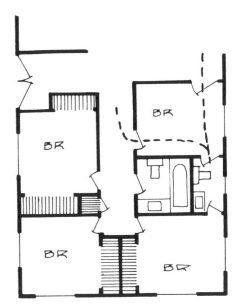

Fig. 7-4. A poorly placed traffic lane may make furniture placement impossible.

main purpose of the file is to help stimulate thinking—not to copy.

On the plan, each room should be designed to function basically as a room, and not as a passageway. If every room, with the exception of the living room and kitchen, can be designed as a *dead-end room,* traffic lanes which make furniture arrangements nearly impossible will be avoided. Fig. 7-4 is an example of traffic lanes which have cut a room to pieces and made furniture arrangement highly difficult. An ideal plan layout should first be developed, disregarding functionality. The plan layout should then be made functional and workable by eliminating or making compromises on problems such as multiple traffic lanes. Another helpful suggestion is to develop several different layouts based on the number of rooms, the sizes, and the groupings desired. In this manner various sections of one layout may be combined with another.

Planning by Templates or Room Cutouts

As mentioned in Chapter 6, the use of room cutouts or templates is perhaps the most flexible method of home planning. Each cutout is made from ⅛″ or ¼″ co-ordinate paper so the planner may quickly identify the size required and the area of the room that is used. For ease of size identification and arrangement, the cutouts may be placed on another co-ordinate paper that is of the same co-ordinate size. By trial and error, various area or room combinations may be tried and evaluated. The following steps illustrate the template or cutout method that is used in planning.

Step 1. Sketch rooms on ⅛″ or ¼″ co-ordinate paper, and cut each sketch out. See Figs. 7-5 and 7-6, Step 1.

Step 2. Sketch boundaries of lot on an-

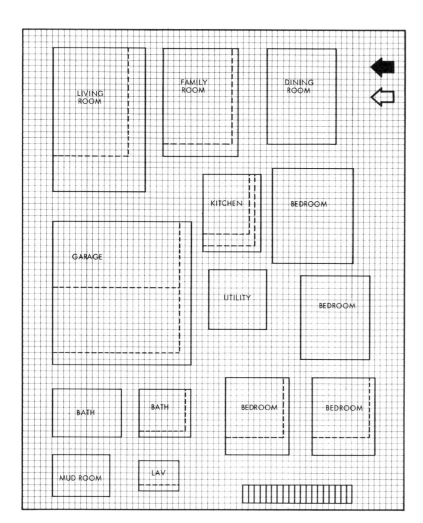

Fig. 7-5. Room templates may be drawn on coordinate paper and cut out.

Fig. 7-6. Step 1. Sketch rooms on coordinate paper and cut out.

other ⅛″ or ¼″ co-ordinate paper. (Draw lot plan on the same scale paper as used for cutouts.) On this sketch, indicate the topographical features such as existing trees, shrubs, nearby street(s), etc.; and also indicate north. See Fig. 7-7, Step 2.

Step 3. Arrange room templates on sketch of Step 2 by placing related rooms together to insure:

a. *Ease of service and control.* Related household activities are usually located in related rooms (i.e., kitchen and dining room, bedrooms and bath, living room and dining room, and laundry and utility room).

b. *Diversity of interests and activities.* Unrelated activities should be located at separate areas so activities in one area cannot disturb those in the others.

c. *Economy.* Greater economy may be afforded if plumbing fixtures in adjacent rooms are placed in proximity to each other. Hall space should also be reduced to a minimum.

d. *Full potential from each area.* The space allotted to each area must be justified in terms of need. Some activities, because of their nature, require more space. See Figs. 7-8 and 7-9, Step 3.

Step 4. Compare the characteristics of the floor plan in Figs 7-8 and 7-9 with a model plan in Fig. 7-10.

Step 5. Separate the rooms by allowing

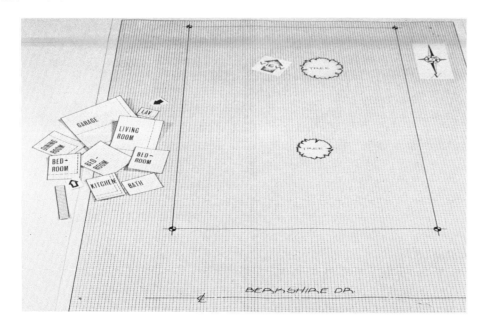

Fig. 7-7. Step 2. Sketch outline and indicate view, compass direction, streets, and existing trees.

Fig. 7-8. Step 3A. Arrange templates on sketch.

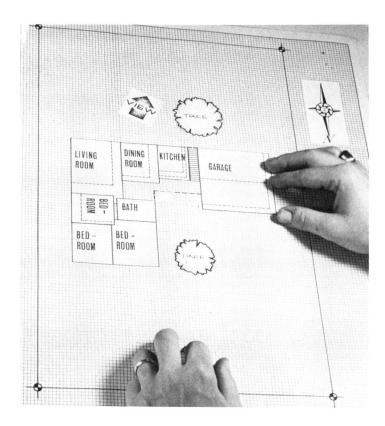

Fig. 7-9. Step 3B. Try for a better plan arrangement.

Fig. 7-10. Step 4. Adopt best plan.

roughly 6″ (in scale) for interior walls, 6″ for frame exterior walls, and 10″ for brick veneer exterior walls. Also allow spaces for closets, halls, stairs, storage, etc. Straighten the outside walls and check room sizes. Lightly pencil in the outline of the rooms.

Step 6. Create and study a tentative plan for window and door locations. See Fig. 7-11, Steps 5 and 6.

Step 7. Consider possible furniture locations and arrangements relative to window and door locations.

Step 8. Inspect the tentative plan as it is oriented on the lot and check to see that it answers the following questions:

a. Can the room positions be improved?

b. Is the house too compact?

c. Will the house be economical to build, heat, and maintain?

d. Is the front door accessible from the other rooms?

e. Are the "quiet" areas away from the "noisy" areas?

f. Are the rooms located where they can best be utilized?

g. Can better room and furniture arrangements be made if shape of the rooms are altered?

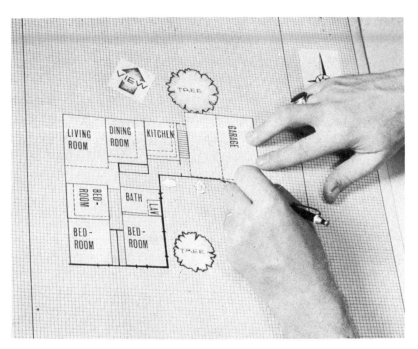

Fig. 7-11. **Step 5.** Allow room for closets, stairs, etc.; trace rooms. **Step 6.** Plan window and door locations.

h. Will "open planning" suit the layout better?

i. Does the room layout facilitate indoor-outdoor living?

j. Does the plan show adequate traffic circulation?

Step 9. Design the best plan, and darken the lines around rooms, halls, stairs, etc. Indicate room sizes, and entrance and window locations. See Fig. 7-12, Steps 7 to 9.

Planning by the Circle Method

Perhaps the simplest method of planning is called the *circle method*. This tentative planning develops strictly from the most desirable placement of rooms according to the physical features of the lot and the climatic conditions of the area. Once the "room-locating" circles have been suitably arranged, the room sizes and closets are roughly determined. The circle method may also be used as a preliminary step to using cutouts or templates.

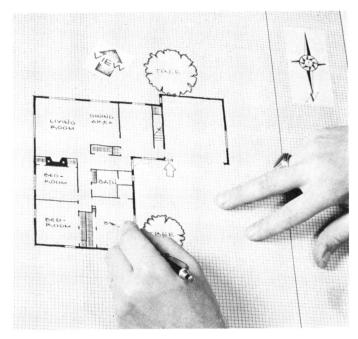

Fig. 7-12. Step 7. Consider furniture locations relative to windows and doors. **Step 8.** Inspect the plan. **Step 9.** Darken lines around rooms, halls, stairs, etc.

The following is the procedure for the circle method.

Step 1. Roughly sketch the lot, using any type of paper, and indicate the outstanding topographic features, views, streets, after-noon sun, prevailing seasonal winds, and direction. See Fig. 7-13, Step 1.

Step 2. Taking all lot conditions into consideration, draw a circle or

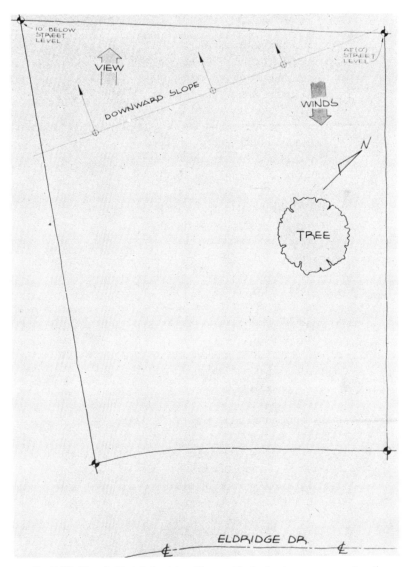

Fig. 7-13. Step 1. Sketch the lot outline and indicate view, compass direction, existing trees and bushes, prevailing winds, and any changes in elevation. Note: The changes in elevation need not be precisely indicated.

ellipse to represent the approximate size and shape of living room and family room.

Step 3. Locate kitchen and dining areas in relation to living room and other living areas. The kitchen should be located where it can receive benefit from the morning sun, and should face the patio. It should also be near the living room, dining area, and family room.

Step 4. Locate sleeping rooms in relation to the orientation of the lot.

a. Locate bedrooms facing away from direct sunlight and away from the **living** areas where noise may prevail. If possible, also locate all the bedrooms away from the street.

b. Locate bathroom adjacent to the bedrooms and near the living areas of the house. Locate lavatory near family room, rear entryway, or master bedroom.

Step 5. Locate garage, utility room (if needed), entrances, and halls.

a. Locate garage near kitchen and utility room.

b. Locate the entrances, drawing a filled-in arrow for the main entryway and open arrows for secondary entryways. See Fig. 7-14, Steps 2 to 5.

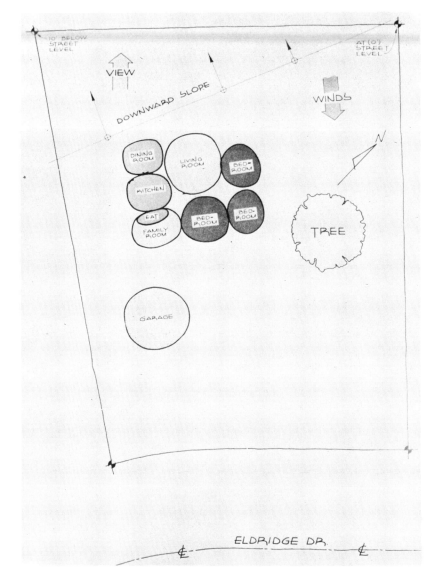

Fig. 7-14. **Step 2.** Draw circles or ellipses for the living room and family room. **Step 3.** Locate and draw a circle for the kitchen. **Step 4.** Locate and draw sleeping areas and bath rooms. **Step 5.** Locate and draw garage; locate entrances.

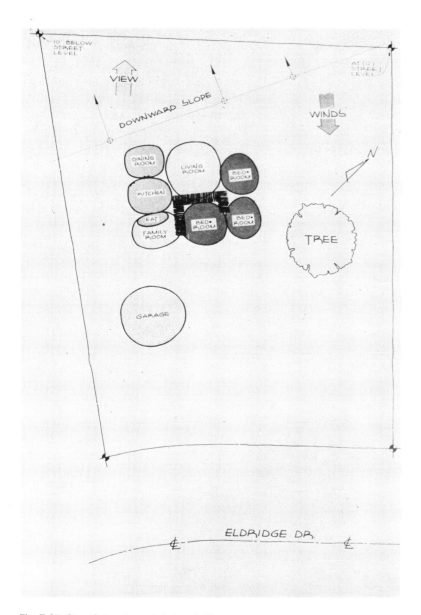

Fig. 7-15. Step 6. Locate and darken hall areas.

Step 6. Locate halls, and darken these areas on the sketch. See Fig. 7-15, Step 6.

Step 7. Redraw the plan sketched in Steps 1 through 6 on ⅛″ or ¼″ co-ordinate paper by sketching the actual outline of the over-all plan. See Fig. 7-16, Step 7.

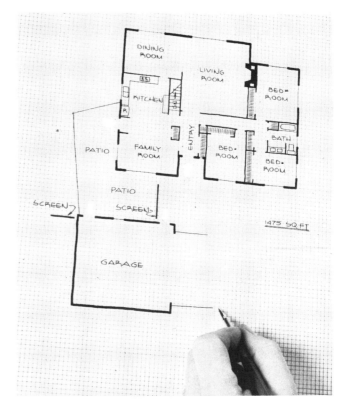

Fig. 7-16. Step 7. Redraw actual outline of overall plan.

Sketch Planning

Room arrangements can be studied most effectively by making a series of sketch plans. The ideas and plans that were developed from the arrangements of *room cutouts* or *templates* and from the *circle method* are best used in the beginning *sketch plan*. The component areas and rooms of the house *must* be in proportion to each other, otherwise little is gained in sketching. Hence, it is suggested that all plans be sketched freehand on co-ordinate paper. *Do not* use a straight edge or ruler to draw the lines. One is more reluctant to change a mechanically drawn line. A freehand sketched line is flexible, free, and psychologically easier to erase and change.

The following steps outline the approach to be used in planning.

Step 1. Draw the general outline of the house on co-ordinate paper. Use a single line to represent the exterior walls.

Step 2. Locate the partitions of the main rooms or areas. Check the room sizes to be sure they are sufficiently large to accommodate furniture, closets, etc. (Use the eraser freely; if the rooms or areas are too small, move out the walls.)

Step 3. Locate chimney and/or fireplace.

Step 4. Locate stairs.

Step 5. Locate secondary partitions such as closets, storage, etc.

Step 6. Locate openings.
   a. Indicate windows by erasing a portion of the wall line and drawing a center line across the opening.
   b. Indicate doors by erasing a portion of the wall line and sketch the doors opening inward 90°.

Step 7. Locate any other desired features.

If a basement or second floor of a multi-level house plan is to be drawn, simply place a sheet of tracing paper over the first floor plan. Trace the outside wall lines, stairs, fireplaces, and chimneys; then continue in general with the above procedure.

Elevation Planning

As the sketch floor plan develops, the designer must look to his "mind's eye" to determine what changes in the exterior are taking place as the room sizes and placement are altered. The planner should, after some experience, be able to perceive the roof line, exterior coverings, and the window style which will enhance the outside appearance.

After several floor plans have been sketched, select the best one and draw it to scale ($\frac{1}{4}'' = 1'-0''$ or $\frac{1}{8}'' = 1'-0''$). Draw only the outside walls, and include the primary and secondary interior partitions. Do not draw in the doors, windows, fireplaces, or other details at this stage of the sketch design.

When the house is in the preliminary stages of design, it is helpful to sketch the house elevations along with the floor sketch plans. As the floor and elevation sketch plans are being drawn at the same time, greater co-ordination is achieved between the interior and exterior designs. By *sketching* the elevations, changes may easily be made in the appearance of the structure, thereby offering more freedom in producing a pleasing design.

After the designer has determined the floor plan, he then begins to consider the elevation. How will the exterior appear? Each plan conceived by the designer has many different possibilities. Depending upon the desires of the client, the topography, nature of the surrounding structures, climate, weather conditions, and available materials, the designer will create an appropriate elevation.

Fig. 7-17 shows four different elevations for the same floor plan. In each elevation windows and doors have remained in the same position. By modifying the style of window, type of roof and building material, the appearance can change radically. As the designer modifies the exterior appearance through roof style, material and windows, construction cost as well as materials alter the final cost. One of the designer's duties in working with a client is to stay within the building budget. The four elevations in Fig. 7-17 were possible elevations for the plan shown in Chapter 21.

Another example of two similar but yet different treatments for the same floor plan

Fig. 7-17. Use of varying materials and roof lines alters the appearance of these elevations even though they are for the same floor plan.

GUNTIS VITUMS

GUNTIS VITUMS

Fig. 7-17   (Continued)

are shown in Fig. 7-18. Each of these elevations maintains the same window placement and a contemporary flavor. The appearance of each home is decidedly different because of the types of exterior building materials and the roof treatment.

For the development of the elevations, the following procedure is suggested.

Step 1. Place the sketch plan selected beneath a sheet of tracing paper.

Step 2. Draw vertical lines on the tracing paper locating the   of windows, doors, and the extremities of the outside walls for that elevation.

Step 3. Locate, by drawing a horizontal line, the finished grade (ground level) of the lot.

Step 4. Locate, with a light horizontal line, the finished floor approximately 1'-6" above the finished grade. This distance may be approximated or scaled using a corresponding piece of co-ordinate paper. See Fig. 7-19, Steps 1 to 4.

Step 5. "Block in" the elevation, using freehand straight lines. Draw the wall height as far as the *eave* or roof border, which is approximately 8' above the floor.

Step 6. Draw the roof type desired and also the chimney. See Fig. 7-20, Steps 5 and 6.

Step 7. Sketch the window and door openings; approximate the sizes, or scale them with a co-ordinate paper. See Fig. 7-21, Step 7.

Step 8. Complete the finished sketch, suggesting most of the details by light or dark markings. Do not erase the preliminary lines unless an actual mistake has occurred. The preliminary lines serve as background to soften and add coherence to the sketch. Study and compare the opening sizes, proportion of masses, and balance of areas. Any feature which seems awry may be adjusted easily with an eraser. See Fig. 7-22, Step 8.

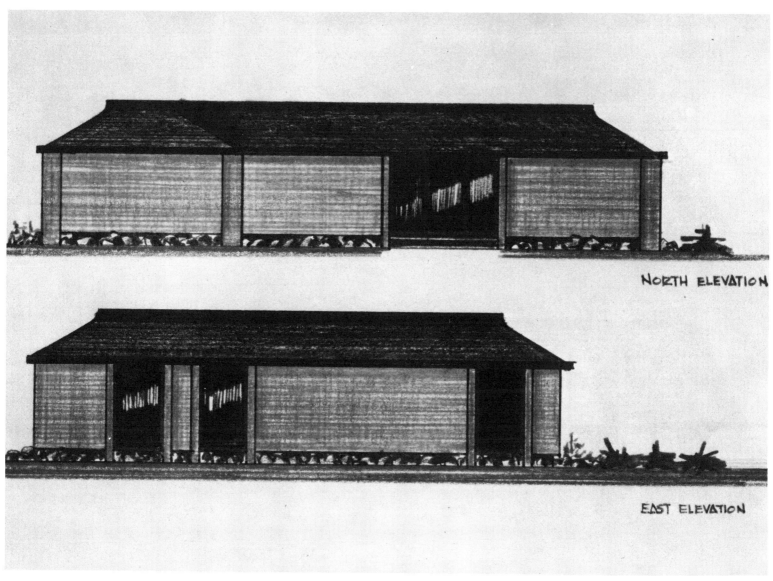

NORTH ELEVATION

EAST ELEVATION

ALAN LANT, JR.

Fig. 7-18. Similar shaped roofs but different building materials alter the exterior elevations for the same floor plan.

NORTH ELEVATION

EAST ELEVATION

ALAN LANT, JR.

Fig. 7-18 (Continued)

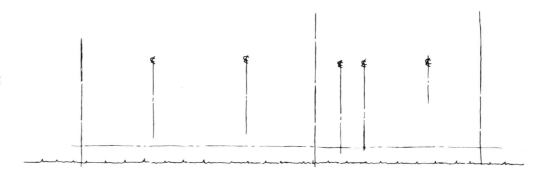

Fig. 7-19. Step 1. Place tracing paper over the floor plan. **Step 2.** Trace off center lines of opening and extremities of outside walls. **Step 3.** Draw in finished grade line. **Step 4.** Lightly draw in finished floor line (center line convention).

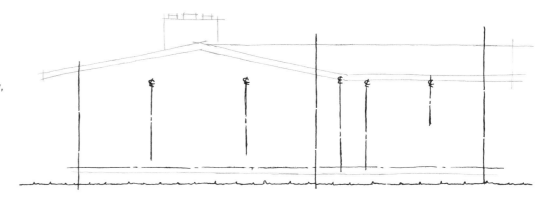

Fig. 7-20. Step 5. Block in elevation using sketchy, straight lines. **Step 6.** Sketch in roof type desired and chimney.

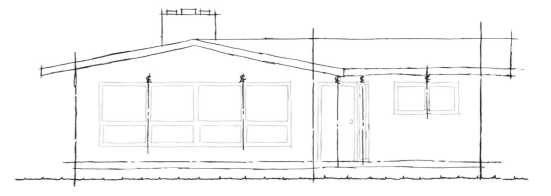

Fig. 7-21. Step 7. Sketch in the proper openings.

Fig. 7-22A. Step 8. Proceed to bring out the finished sketch. Study and compare openings, proportion, and balance of areas. Change any features which do not enhance design.

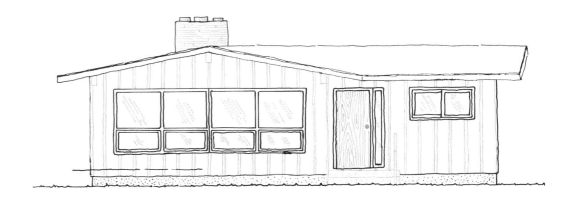

Fig. 7-22B. Finished Elevation Sketch.

Planning Points

Regardless of the methods used in home planning, the various aspects of the plan must be given careful consideration. Planning errors made by inexperienced planners are infinite and impossible to list. The following points, however, are those most frequently neglected or overlooked by students as they plan a house.

1. If the house has more than one floor, plan the chimney location first, because this may affect the upper levels or the basement arrangement.
2. Avoid using rooms as passageways, (i.e., going through a bedroom to get to another bed- or bathroom).
3. Plan halls within a minimum space and with some natural light. Hall space costs as much per square foot as sleeping, living, and eating areas.
4. Design the house to fit the lot. Do not neglect to consider the existing trees on the lot, as well as the shape, slope, and orientation.
5. Decide the location and the style of windows to be used and relate them to the street, adjoining lot, and the natural beauty.
6. Avoid an excessive number of windows and doors in the average size house design. Failure to consider this may cause problems in arranging furniture and will add to the cost of heating the house.
7. Avoid placing a bath room or lavatory over the living room.
8. If cost is a major factor, try to cover the tentative plan with a roof having as few breaks or *offsets* as possible. Every break in the roof line will increase the cost.
9. Allow roughly six inches for all interior partitions.
10. Plan all storage spaces so they are readily accessible and near to the area of their greatest use. The space must be large enough to contain items intended for storage.
11. Plan all bedrooms with windows which allow adequate ventilation.
12. Allow adequate space for a *stair run*. Do not end stairs against a blank wall.

Plan Types

In all aspects of life, advantages and disadvantages must be weighed prior to making a decision. The same is true in deciding whether to build a one-story, two-story, one-and-a-half story, or split-level dwelling. In many instances the choice of the number of levels is a matter of personal preference. However, building factors should be taken into consideration before any final choice is made. Each family, depending on their circumstances, should base their decision on such factors as cost, comfort, climate, convenience, beauty, upkeep, and lot size.

Single-Story Dwellings

Single-story houses have proven to be very popular. Quite possibly this may be due to the family experiences as apartment dwellers since many apartment dwellers desire the open spaciousness of a ranch-type house. The single-story dwelling saves the housewife and older persons many trips up and down the stairs. Cost analysis of single-level versus multi-level dwellings show little difference in small homes of 1000 to 1500 sq. ft.

The single-story house, as shown in Fig. 7-23 (top) may be built with a full basement, a crawl space, or on a slab. The basement is not classified as an additional house level. Without a stairway to an upper level, a more open floor plan may be designed giving the interior a larger appearance. Larger basements with more usable areas are possible in the single-level dwelling.

Families that plan a home for future expansion will encounter little or no difficulty expanding the single-level home, as compared to a two-level dwelling. Also, a greater variation of exterior design is possible with the single-level house.

The maintenance cost is often greater with a one-story house because the exterior walls and roof have larger areas. More heat loss occurs with the larger roof areas. Depending upon the interior plan, the one-story house may require more hall space than a multi-level house. In addition, the one-story house may require a larger lot area than a multi-level dwelling.

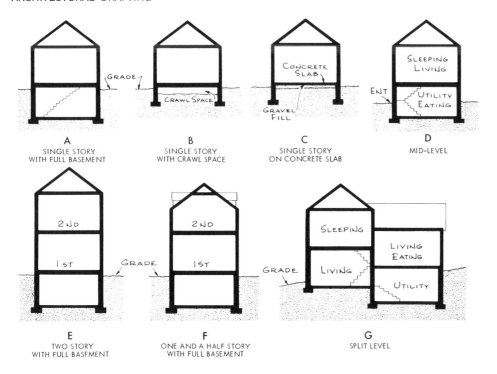

Fig. 7-23. Seven common house types.

Two-Story Dwelling

The two-story house (for the same volume) offers more living space and is more economical to heat because it has less roof and foundation area. The hall space in a two-story house can be greatly reduced. The two-story house does not usually lend itself to open planning because the rooms are enclosed and are not open to view from the outside. This type of home is commonly found in urban areas where the privacy of the family or individuals is important.

Often, the outside design appearance of a two-story dwelling is narrow and tall, giving a "box-like" appearance. This illusion is caused not only by the design, but also by the type of exterior covering materials which are used. Frequently, a garage may be planned at one end and a porch on the other to lower the height illusion.

It is unwise to plan a two-story house in an area populated with low, single-story dwellings. If the lots are extremely wide and the terrain is "rolling," however, a two-story house may be suitable. See Fig. 7-23 (lower left).

One-and-a-Half Story Dwellings

The one-and-a-half story house shown in Fig. 7-23 (lower middle) is essentially a single-story dwelling with a sufficiently high pitched roof to permit later expansion in the attic area. As indicated in the figure, a *dormer* (a raised roof and wall area to provide window space) may be added to increase the natural light and ventilation. Although the floor area of a one-and-a-half story house may be equivalent to the two-story house, it usually has the illusion of being lower. It has most of the advantages of the two-story with one possible exception. The upper floor areas of a one-and-a-half story house may be smaller, and a portion of its ceiling may slope. Because the upper rooms are immediately below the roof, these rooms are difficult to cool in the summer.

Split-Level Dwellings

The split-level house shown in Fig. 7-23 (lower right) is also referred to as a tri-level or bi-level. This type of plan has become very popular and has been widely adapted not only to sloping land terrain, but also to those areas where the terrain is level. The split-level house was originally intended for sloping or hilly land.

Split-level houses often present problems in design and construction. However, the construction cost per square foot, in relation to comparable materials and floor area, is often less than that of a single-level type.

The general arrangement of a split-level offers the basic functions, such as sleeping, eating, and living, on separate levels of the house. The eating and living areas are usually located on the ground level, so that they are easily integrated to the out-of-doors. The sleeping area is separated from the living area by a half or partial flight of stairs. The utility room, recreation or family room, and sometimes the garage may be located in a semi-basement. This is one of the economical attributes of the split-level because the foundation depth is a little more than that required for basementless construction. As with the two-story dwelling, split-level homes have more living space with less roof and foundation area, thus they are more economical to heat. Hall space may also be completely or greatly reduced. In addition to being economical, the split-level has other advantages. The raised sleeping area with a short flight of stairs gives a greater feeling of privacy, quietness, and security than does the conventional, single-level type of house plan.

Because of the frequent use of open planning, the heating system must be carefully planned to insure even heat in all the rooms. Frequently, *zoned heating* (a thermostat in every room or a group of rooms) is incorporated in the split-level home. Though the initial cost of heating equipment may be greater, savings introduced through heating economy, and the aditional comfort, may repay the investment in the long run.

Exposed Basement

Depending on the topographic features of the lot, additional living area may be added to any of the plan types discussed above (with the exception of basementless houses) by designing an exposed basement as shown in Fig. 7-24. The exposed basement offers added living area at a nominal cost. A portion of the basement may become a family or recreation room, home

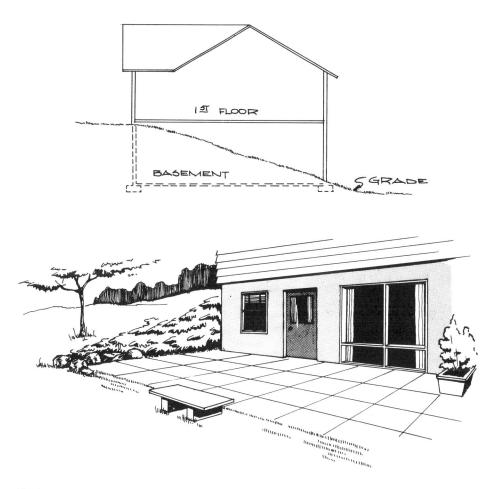

Fig. 7-24. An exposed basement adds living area to the home.

office, or a bedroom with direct access to the outside terrace, patio, or garden. Some builders construct the basement with its rear or side exposed to a lot which is level. This may create a drainage problem. If a correctly engineered retaining wall and adequate drainage are placed on the lot, this problem will not be encountered.

Plan Shapes

The outline or shape of a plan is determined by the arrangement and size of the rooms. Most house plans may be classified as one of the twelve shapes shown in Fig. 7-25. Each of these plan shapes has its own architectural possibilities, depending on room arrangements, location on the lot, ventilation, lighting, construction, and cost. The more a plan deviates from the basic square or rectangular shape, the more it becomes complicated and disjointed. The cost increases in proportion to the amount of wall surface, roof, number of offsets, etc. It is difficult, however, to estimate the additional cost of a projection on the basic square or rectangular house, even though the square footage may be the same. A comparison of square footage (total floor area) and a lineal-wall length (total perimeter length of the house) of four plan shapes is shown in Fig. 7-26. Although the general length and depth proportions of each plan may be similar, and the square footage may be equal, the lineal wall footage increases

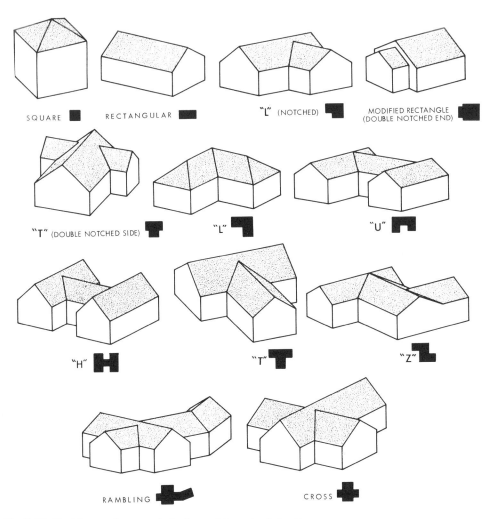

Fig. 7-25. Most house plans are derivations of these basic types.

with the number of offsets that are added.

The designer must decide the importance of deviation from the basic square or rectangular plan so that an interesting and attractive exterior design, as well as a functional floor plan, may be created.

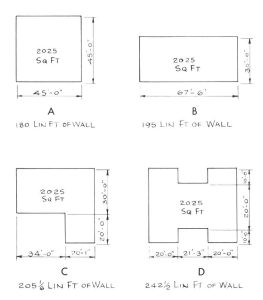

Fig. 7-26. As more offsets are introduced into the plan, more linear length is needed to give the same square footage. (Notice that a square plan has the smallest perimeter.)

Questions and Problems

These questions are based on significant factors of room arrangement in the home.

1. Visit several new homes. Sketch a floor plan based on observed ideas, and compare the livability, room arrangements, adequacy, etc.

2. Members of your family may have special interests and hobbies. What changes could be recommended in your home to accommodate their hobbies and interests?

3. Visit several real estate developments, and note the house and lot sizes, exterior designs, floor plans, proximity to shopping facilities, schools, and transportation. Based on your observations, are any of these homes a good investment?

4. List some of the building restrictions in your community. How do these affect the placement of the house on the lot?

5. Many communities have zoning restrictions; how do these affect a community?

6. What are some disadvantages that occur in sketching plans? Advantages?

7. Develop a floor plan, using any of the methods described in this chapter, for the following two houses.

   a. A basementless ranch-type house is tentatively designed having a combination living room and dining room, kitchen, three bedrooms, bathroom, half-bath, and utility room. The house is to be placed on a lot 70′ × 100′. The width of the lot is 70′ and is parallel to the center line of a street which runs in a NE direction. The front of the lot faces SE. The city code specifies a house must be set back a minimum of 35′ from the front lot line and a minimum of 8′ on the sides. The lot is level and a desirable view is due north.

   b. A summer cottage is planned with a combined living, dining, and kitchen area, 2 bedrooms, bathroom, and a large porch. The lot is 112′ × 250′, the short dimension parallels a lake and faces west. There are no restrictions as to placing the cottage on the lot. The rear ⅓ of the lot is heavily forested with pines and spruce trees, and slopes downward from the rear lot line at a 16 per cent slope.

8. Sketch two different sets of elevations (front and side) for each of the plans developed in problem 7a and 7b above.

Exterior House Design 8

In planning, the exterior appearance of a house is a major factor. The exterior design will emanate from and be dependent upon many previous decisions: choice of site, number of floors, style, available capital, future expansion, etc. The greatest determining influence on the exterior design, however, is exerted by the floor plan. This is particularly true in the pure forms of traditional and period styles. To design a preconceived exterior for some floor plans would be exceedingly difficult, if not impossible. A square plan, for example, does not lend itself to a ranch exterior, nor does a Cape Cod plan fit with a ranch elevation. However, a number of different exteriors **may usually** be developed for any one floor plan design.

Styles of residential architecture change just as women's fashions change. Architecturally (and this is particularly evident since the 1880's), home builders in any one area have tended to popularize particular types of architecture to the exclusion of others. Popularity of specific styles have become so great that in some areas styles are mixed. For example: the southern colonial ranch house, the Cape Cod ranch or the salt-box split level. This is not to say, however, that "mixtures" of this nature are bad.

Each of these styles may be identified by certain characteristics that "ear mark" them from other styles.

Period Architectural Styles

The architecture of the early colonists has survived for three centuries. The first dwellings were cabins made from the ready supply of timber. As the colonists were able to build better homes, the cabin developed into one-and-a-half and two-story dwellings. Eventually, regional differences began to evolve, not only in style but in building materials as well. Homes in the New England area were predominantly wood, those in Delaware and Pennsylvania were stone, while those farther south used bricks made from local clay.

Until the mid-1700's the architect was practically non-existent in the colonies. Many of the early colonial houses were designed by the "master of the house," with or without assistance from the master craftsman who would construct it later. The chief architectural references of the time were English and European books and periodicals. These publications showed perspectives, elevations, and details of English and European homes.

Basically, these colonial homes had a rectangular or square plan and were compact with the rooms grouped around a central stair hall or chimney. Fig. 8-1 illustrates two basic plans of many houses built during and following the colonial period. The plan built around the central chimney (Fig. 8-1, top) was common for a one-, one-and-a-half-, two-, or two-and-a-half-story house, one or two rooms deep. Fig. 8-1 (bottom) represents a plan built around the central hall. This type of plan was common to the Dutch style of architecture and was adapted to other styles as well.

Eventually these buildings were enriched, particularly along the eastern seaboard, by ships' carpenters who added delicate moldings, cornices, and ornate entrances. Many of these designs are still copied. Ships' carpenters were the first to introduce in the United States the double-hung sash, glass (oiled paper or parchment was previously used), *shakes* (hand split shingles) for exterior walls and roofing, and weather boards with rounded edges to combat the high winds. Large, efficient, and beautiful fireplaces were the focal points during the cold New England winters. The chimneys were masterpieces of design. The roof styles of these homes (whether gambrel, gable, shed,

CENTRAL CHIMNEY LOCATION

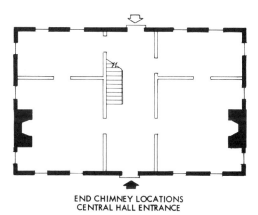

END CHIMNEY LOCATIONS
CENTRAL HALL ENTRANCE

Fig. 8-1. Two basic plans were used in building colonial homes.

or hip) are still much in evidence on houses today.

One reason colonial designs have survived is because they can be adapted to changing situations. These houses are found as one-, one-and-a-half-, two-, or two-and-a-half-story dwellings and for that reason can be made to fit almost any size lot. Due

to their extreme simplicity, the floor plan was easily expandable. For example, many of the one-and-a-half-, two-, and two-and-a-half-story buildings were expanded into saltbox style houses. This was accomplished by simply extending the rear of the house and continuing the rear half of the gable roof downward in the same plane. The profile or silhouette of this roof has the appearance of an inverted check mark.

Many designs were expanded, for example, into L, U, and T shapes. Because of the rugged, yet elegant, appearance of the colonial, Americans have continued making facsimiles—only improving the interiors with modern conveniences.

Structural Characteristics

The various styles of residential construction are the result of many conditions and influences. Some of the factors which may influence construction are availability of materials, climatic conditions, predominant religious beliefs, customs, living conditions, nationality, or ethnic origins.

Study houses and become familiar with good design. The ability to identify good and poor design requires experience in comparing various styles of buildings. Such publications as *Interiors, Architectural Record, House and Home, American Builder, Better Homes and Gardens,* and numerous other books dealing primarily with architecture, may serve as a basis for style values.

Fig. 8-2. This photograph shows an excellent example of a two-and-a-half story salt-box colonial home. This is the Major John Bradford house, located in Kingston, Massachusetts and built in 1674.

Fig. 8-3. This pen drawing illustrates a modern adaptation of the salt box. Note the overhang on the second floor.

Characteristics of Various Styles

Figs. 8-2 through 8-26 give a brief pictorial resume of the more popular styles of architecture in the United States. All photographs are of the original, historical structures. Each photograph was selected as representative of that particular type of architecture in an "unadulterated" state. Adjacent to each photo are perspective sketches which show modern applications of each style.

Salt-box Colonial—(Figs. 8-2 and 8-3.)

Roof	— Long slope on one side of the gable; no overhang. Dormers on the long sloping side. May have gambrel fronted roof. Long slope toward the direction of winter winds.
Walls	— Siding or shakes—little ornamentations. Double-hung windows and doors, symmetrical in appearance; shutters.
Height	— 1½ or 2 stories.
Chimney	— Large, centrally located in plan.
Plan	— Compact, rectangular.

Early American Colonial — (Figs. 8-4 and 8-5.)

Roof	— Steep gable, wood shingles.
Walls	— Siding, stained; small double-hung or casement windows, symmetrical; second floor overhangs; drops used.
Height	— 2½ stories.

HISTORIC AMERICAN BUILDING SURVEY, LIBRARY OF CONGRESS, WASHINGTON, D.C. PHOTO BY THOMAS T. WATERMAN.

Fig. 8-4. The early American Colonial is usually typified in part by the distinctive second floor overhang. Note the use of hand-carved drops or pendills at the corners and the use of brackets between stories. This is the Parson Capen house in Topsfield, Massachusetts; it was built in 1683.

Fig. 8-5. This drawing illustrates an adaptation of an early American Colonial L-shaped plan using a steep gambrel roof.

Fig. 8-6. The New England Colonial has very little overhang at the eaves or gable. Note the six-light transom above the door, and the decorative window cap. The Barnaby house, built in Freetown, Massachusetts before 1740 must have been an imposing structure.

HISTORIC AMERICAN BUILDING SURVEY, LIBRARY OF CONGRESS, WASHINGTON, D.C. PHOTO BY ARTHUR C. HASKELL.

Chimney — Large, centrally located in plan.

Plan — Compact, rectangular.

New England Colonial—(Figs. 8-6 and 8-7.)

    Roof — Gable, medium pitch, no overhang. Gambrel, no overhang on gable or eaves.

    Walls — Siding, shingles, brick. Double-hung windows and doors placed symmetrically; shutters.

        Only entrance ornamented.

    Height — 1, 1½, 2, and 2½ stories.

Fig. 8-7. This modern adaptation of the New England Colonial was designed with a breezeway and garage.

Fig. 8-8. The Cape Cod style is probably the simplest and smallest of all colonials. The Jonathan Kendrick house in South Orleans, Massachusetts was built in 1792 and is still occupied today.

Chimney — Large, centrally located in plan.

Plan — Square or rectangular, additions can be made.

Cape Cod Colonial—(Figs. 8-8 and 8-9.)

Roof — Medium pitch gable.
Small overhang on cornice.

Walls — Siding, painted.
Double-hung windows—symmetrically placed.

Height — 1½ stories.

Chimney — Large, centrally located in plan.

Fig. 8-9. The Cape Cod colonial may be enhanced by adding shutters and side lights on either side of the door and yet still retain an authentic colonial appearance.

Fig. 8-10. The Southern Colonial is earmarked by large, elaborate entrances using turned or paneled posts. The Dr. R. H. Richardson house built in 1835 at Athens, Alabama, is still used as a residence.

HISTORIC AMERICAN BUILDING SURVEY, LIBRARY OF CONGRESS, WASHINGTON, D.C. PHOTO BY ALEX BUSH.

Fig. 8-11. This modern example of the Southern Colonial uses an off-center entrance yet still maintains the dignity of the style.

Southern Colonial—(Figs. 8-10 and 8-11.)

Plan	— Compact, rectangular—wings may be added.
Roof	— Hip, gable, or flat. Slate or metal.
Walls	— Brick, stucco. Large double-hung windows and doors (symmetrical). Ornamentation of wood. Elaborate entrance, using turned or paneled posts.
Height	— 2 stories.
Chimney	— At each end projecting from or flush with gable end or short sides.

Fig. 8-12. The true Dutch Colonial is designed with a steep gable roof flared over the eaves. Though neglected, the Gerrit Haring house in Old Tappan, New Jersey is one of the few remaining Dutch Colonials. This house was built between 1751 and 1762.

HISTORIC AMERICAN BUILDING SURVEY, LIBRARY OF CONGRESS, WASHINGTON, D.C. PHOTO BY R. MERRITT LACEY.

Plan — Limited flexibility (not advisable for small lot).

Dutch Colonial[1]—(Figs. 8-12, 8-13, and 8-14.)

---

1. The true Dutch Colonial was typified by a steep gable roof. On some houses the coping on the gable walls extended several inches above the roof and the chimneys were flush with these walls. The Dutch builders were probably acquainted with the gambrel roof through the English and Flemish colonists. The gambrel roof was adopted during the 18th Century. A combination of the wide gambrel with the flared overhang was apparently developed by the Flemish but credited to the Dutch. The gambrel type roof, however, is synonymous with "Dutch Colonial."

Roof — Steep gable, gambrel, flush gable and eaves, or flush gable and flared eaves.

Walls — Brick, stone, wide siding, long shingles or combination.
Double-hung windows and doors symmetrically placed.

Height — 1½ to 2½ stories.

Chimney — Flush or projected on gable ends.

Plan — Rectangular, may have additions.

Ranch House—(Figs. 8-15 to 8-22.)

Roof — Gable—slightly pitched, flat or shed.
Wide overhangs, roof lower over garage and breezeway.

Walls — Wood or masonry or combinations of materials.
Large windows. Entrance without ornamentation.

Height — 1 story.

Chimney — Large, centrally located or projecting.

Fig. 8-13. The "Dutch Colonial" may also be designed with a New York or Flemish type gambrel roof. Note the Dutch door with the "bull's eye" lights in the upper half. This is the David Desmarest house located in New Milford, New Jersey, built about 1681.

Fig. 8-14. This modern Dutch Colonial is built on a sloping site and is designed with sufficient overhang to provide a comfortable porch.

Fig. 8-15. This early U-shaped ranch house, date unknown, was the residence of General Beale. (Tejon Ranch, Kern County, California.)

HISTORIC AMERICAN BUILDING SURVEY, LIBRARY OF CONGRESS, WASHINGTON, D.C.

Fig. 8-16. Many ranch-style houses are planned around a patio, court, or breezeway.

Fig. 8-17. La Casa del Rancho Aquaja de la Centinela, Ingleweed, California, was built in 1882 and originally had a flat roof. The central portion of the building is original adobe. A later addition was made at the left using board and batten.

Fig. 8-18. In many ranch-type houses a porch-like projection is added by extending the roof beyond the normal overhang.

HISTORIC AMERICAN BUILDING SURVEY, LIBRARY OF CONGRESS,
WASHINGTON, D.C. PHOTO BY LOUIS A. KONE.

Fig. 8-19. One of the original dwellings on the Sherwood Ranch, Monterey County, California, employs a continuous wide overhanging roof to afford protection from the sun and weather. This house was built in 1824.

Fig. 8-20. Frequently the contemporary ranch-type house has a rectangular floor plan and a wide overhang.

Fig. 8-21. The L-shaped ranch house is not new. La Casa del Rancho Guajome, San Luis Rey District, San Diego, California, was built in 1851.

HISTORIC AMERICAN BUILDING SURVEY, LIBRARY OF CONGRESS, WASHINGTON, D.C. PHOTO BY LOUIS A. KONE.

Plan   — Low, rambling for urban area.
Open planning.
Built-in furniture.

Split Level—(Fig. 8-23.)

Roof   — Flat, shed, or low or medium pitched gable.
Irregular roof lines.

Walls   — Masonry, wood, or combination.
Windows, may be large, and/or regular types.

Height   — Part 1 story, part 2 story.

Fig. 8-22. The ranch-type house may assume many plan shapes and may be designed to fit problem lots. The casual appearance of its design gives a feeling of openness.

Fig. 8-23. A split level designed for a sloping site uses mid-levels to the best advantage.

Fig. 8-24. The Robie House designed by Frank Lloyd Wright, though built in 1909, has the appearance of contemporary styling.

Plan — Compact, economical, space-saving.

Fits problem lots, sloping sites.

Contemporary—(Figs. 8-24, 8-25, and 8-26.)

Roof — Flat or low pitched, gable and shed.

Wide overhangs, low horizontal look.

Cantilevered roofs.

Walls — Masonry and wood, natural finish on both exterior and interior walls.

Large glass areas.

Height — Usually 1 story, may be 2.

Plan — Open or flexible plan, few interior walls.

Modern Adaptations

Period architectural styles that have survived are usually modern adaptations or borrowings in part or whole from the original designs.

The colonial-style homes that have been and are popular in New England are also prevalent, for example, in Kansas and Colorado, as well. Similarly, the rambling California ranch with its indoor-outdoor living is everywhere; the split level and contemporary are also located throughout the United States.

Cape Cod Colonial

The Cape Cod (Figs. 8-8 and 8-9) is the

ARCHITECT: NORMAN CARVER, JR. PHOTO BY ALLAN STAMBERG.

Fig. 8-25. This contemporary-style house shows Oriental influence. Note the use of horizontal and vertical lines to create a pleasing effect.

Fig. 8-26. The contemporary house fits the needs of the owner. It combines new methods of construction, new materials, and esthetic principles into a functional whole.

type of colonial that was originally native to the Cape Cod district of Massachusetts. Originally the plan was almost square, built close to the ground, and was one- or one-and-a-half-stories in height. This traditional style has regained its popularity over the country since 1930. Different window patterns are evident in the present day Cape Cods due to changes made in the basic arrangements of rooms. The modern plan is considerably narrower than its original models. This compact style is still one- or one-and-a-half-stories; the upper floor is often used for expansion.

Ranch Style

The ranch house (Figs. 8-15 to 8-22) is the result of a modern development over a long period of time. The ranch style was originated by Mexican and Spanish settlers in what is now Southern California. These dwellings were rambling, one-story houses with flat or low-pitched roofs. The rooms were planned around a patio or court. This type of home was extremely prevalent in the 1800's in Southern California and along the northern Pacific coast. Gradually the ranch house moved eastward into the prairie country.

The ranch home has undergone modifications, as have many of the other styles popular in the United States. The ranch style house of today is more compact and has smaller and fewer rooms than its western ancestor. The modern ranch-style home built in suburbia owes some of its salient features (such as open planning, floor to ceiling windows, corner windows, and built-in furniture) to Frank Lloyd Wright's early homes. Built-in furniture, coordinated and unified with the interior design gives the impressive decor.

Split Level

The split level (Fig. 8-23) evolved by placing a home on the side of a hill. Houses have long been placed on hilly terrain, but not until 1850, however, did the designer-craftsman elevate one portion midway between two others. Placing the split level on a flat site loses some of its effectiveness and exterior aesthetic value. Many of the split levels built in the 1950's, 60's and early 70's have plans that are ranch type in nature. The change of levels provides a saving in costs because of grouped plumbing, increased living space, greater privacy, and a new freedom in exterior design.

Contemporary

Any home that is built today is really called *contemporary*. In the architectural sense, however, contemporary has a specific connotation. Contemporary (Figs. 8-24, 8-25, and 8-26) is an imaginative and exciting style that has been developed during the 20th Century by architects. Again, Frank Lloyd Wright has appreciably influenced this style through some of his homes built as early as 1912.

The contemporary house is not a particular style, but a philosophical aspect of architectural design. This is reflected in the planning of space to conform to the needs of the modern family. The contemporary house strives to make maximum use of living space; areas are kept flexible, and a feeling of space and openness is achieved.

The feeling of additional space is not only given by removing partitions (yet still providing the sense of a separate area), but also by allowing the underside of the roof to serve as the ceiling. In the urban setting, the contemporary house is oriented towards rear-area living. Contemporary style incorporates the outdoors by using walls of glass, sliding doors, patios, and sun porches.

The contemporary home is characterized by flat or low-pitched roofs, wide overhangs, and cantilevered (projecting) roofs. Many contemporary homes are built on a slab. Attics are usually omitted. *Radiant heating* (see Chapter 13) has eliminated the necessity of using wall space for radiators and heat vents. Heating pipes are placed in the floor or ceiling. Larger expanses of glass, both in height and width, may be used. Large roof overhangs shield the window areas in the summer but are planned to allow entrance of the winter sun. Stone, brick, or concrete block masonry are allowed to remain in their natural state on both the interior and exterior. This allows the house to blend in with the surrounding areas. Wood is frequently left unstained and unpainted to enable the beauty of the material to blend with nature.

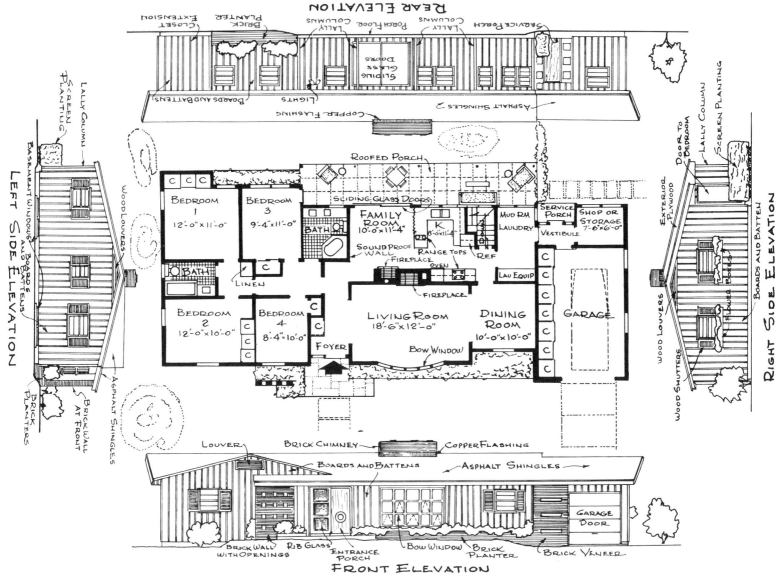

Fig. 8-27. Each elevation is drawn as if viewed from a point infinitely distant from each side.

Elevation Drawings

Drawings that indicate and show the exterior surfaces of the structure in their true proportions are called elevations. The elevations are designated *front, rear, left,* and *right side.* They are drawn as they would appear if viewed from a point directly in front of each side.[2] See Fig. 8-27. The basic purposes in drawing elevations are to graphically represent the exterior treatments and to give the builder (1) the height dimensions of windows and doors; (2) distances from finished grade to finished floor, floor to ceiling, and floor to floor; and (3) the ridge and chimney heights. In addition, by means of notes, the elevations indicate the type of exterior wall covering, roof material, and type of window and door openings. Elevations not only serve to give information, but also enable the designer to visually check, in part, the esthetic appeal. Floor plans show the placement and width of openings, but the elevations give the opportunity to "see" how a particular type of window, door, entrance, siding, stone, etc., will appear. Perspective sketches (such as Fig. 8-26, for example) are used to give a more easily visualized, realistic and picturelike representation. This makes an attractive illustration which may serve both as a visual aid and as an advertising medium.

2. The elevations may sometimes be referred to as the North, South, East and West elevation if the house is to be placed facing one of these principal directions.

Wall Section

Preparatory to drawing the elevations, a wall section (carried from the footing through the cornice) must be drawn in the same scale as the floor plan and proposed elevations. The wall section should show the footing, foundation, sill floor joists (or slab if applicable), floor (sub- and finish),

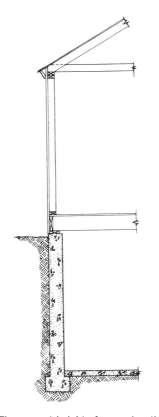

Fig. 8-28. The correct heights for an elevation are projected from the wall sections.

exterior wall, ceiling joints, cornice, and roof rafters or truss in approximately the correct pitch. Fig. 8-28 is an example of a wall section. It is necessary to have this section so the correct heights may be determined for the elevations.

In many instances, rather than placing the wall section adjacent to the elevation the designer will simply "pick-off" the heights with a divider or scale. This procedure saves time and board space particularly for long elevations.

Step-by-Step Drawing Procedure Elevations

There are a host of different methods used in drawing elevations. However, the method explained in the following step-by-step procedure has proved to be most expedient and systematic. Fasten four standard size sheets of vellum (size B or C) together at the top so they are free to be flipped over. See Fig. 8-29.

Elevations. See Fig. 8-30.

Step 1. Draw the wall section and fasten to the left of the sheets. See Fig. 8-30, Step 1.

Step 2. Flip the top three sheets (numbers, 4, and 2) over. With light lines project the footing, basement floor grade, and the joists (floor and ceiling) onto sheet No. 1. Flip over sheet No. 2 and trace these same features. Trace these same lines on sheets No. 3 and No. 4. See Fig. 8-30, Step 2.

Step 3. Transfer measurements with a *measurement strip* or *tick strip*[3] from the floor plan to the elevation. Indicate with a *tick mark* the exterior wall corners, window and door ℄'s, any wall offsets, and porch or stoop projections. These measurements are obtained by viewing the plan in the *same direction* as the elevation being drawn. See Fig. 8-30, Step 3.

Step 4. Transfer these locations to sheet No. 1 (side elevation). Draw vertical lines representing the outside wall corners and ℄'s representing window and door openings.

Step 5. Project roof and outside wall intersections (point X) from wall section to the outside corners on the elevation. If the ridge is needed on this elevation, draw its ℄. See Fig. 8-30, Step 5.

Step 6. Draw roof slope B-A through point X.

Draw other side of slope CA. If the slope doesn't appear satisfactory, erase original slope and revise. Check clearances, rafters,

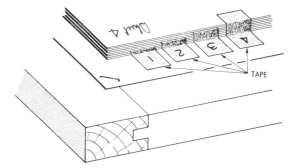

Fig. 8-29. Fasten four vellum sheets (B or C size) so they may be flipped over.

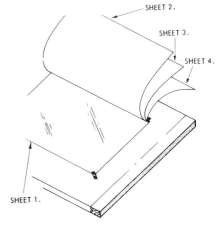

etc., of new slope. Revise wall section. See Fig. 8-30, Step 6.

Step 7. Tick off chimney location and size from the plan view and transfer to elevation. Draw in any unexcavated areas. See Fig. 8-30, Step 7.

Step 8. Drop sheet No. 2 over and tick measurements for front elevation from plan.

Draw vertical lines for exterior wall corners and for window and door locations.

Tick off chimney location and size from plan and transfer to elevation.

Trace window and door head heights.

Trace chimney height and intersection with roof (if shown in front elevation) from side elevation.

Trace ridge. See Fig. 8-30, Step 8.

Step 9. Complete cornice overhang, gutters, etc., on side elevation (sheet No. 1).

Trace line of cornice, gutter, etc., on front elevation (sheet No. 2).

Draw in windows,[4] doors, etc.

Draw in exterior wall covering,

---

3. The measurement strip or tick strip is used to transfer a series of measurements from one portion of a drawing to another. This is extremely useful when many distances must be duplicated and where a high degree of accuracy is not paramount. The tick strip used in this application is approximately 1″ × 5″. (See Fig. 8-30.)

4. Drawing windows may be simplified by using underlays available from window manufacturers, or by drawing the windows, at the same scale as elevations, on a piece of 8½″ × 11″ detail paper. Draw the casing and sill for each *different* type of window (see Chapter 10). *Note the catalog size,* and other pertinent data below each window.

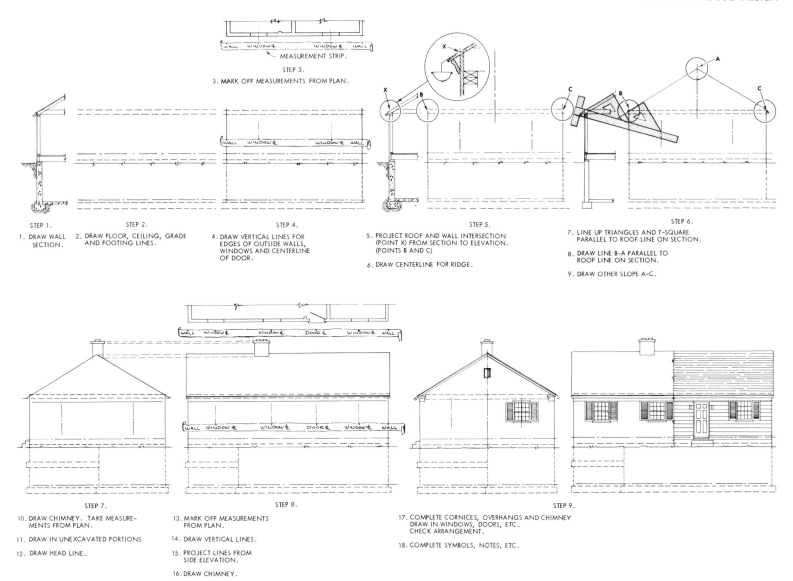

MEASUREMENT STRIP.

STEP 3.

3. MARK OFF MEASUREMENTS FROM PLAN.

WALL WINDOW ℄ WINDOW ℄ WALL

STEP 1.

1. DRAW WALL SECTION.

STEP 2.

2. DRAW FLOOR, CEILING, GRADE AND FOOTING LINES.

4. DRAW VERTICAL LINES FOR EDGES OF OUTSIDE WALLS, WINDOWS AND CENTERLINE OF DOOR.

6. DRAW CENTERLINE FOR RIDGE.

STEP 4.

STEP 5.

5. PROJECT ROOF AND WALL INTERSECTION (POINT X) FROM SECTION TO ELEVATION. (POINTS B AND C)

STEP 6.

7. LINE UP TRIANGLES AND T-SQUARE PARALLEL TO ROOF LINE ON SECTION.

8. DRAW LINE B-A PARALLEL TO ROOF LINE ON SECTION.

9. DRAW OTHER SLOPE A-C.

STEP 7.

10. DRAW CHIMNEY. TAKE MEASUREMENTS FROM PLAN.

11. DRAW IN UNEXCAVATED PORTIONS

12. DRAW HEAD LINE.

STEP 8.

13. MARK OFF MEASUREMENTS FROM PLAN.

14. DRAW VERTICAL LINES.

15. PROJECT LINES FROM SIDE ELEVATION.

16. DRAW CHIMNEY.

STEP 9.

17. COMPLETE CORNICES, OVERHANGS AND CHIMNEY DRAW IN WINDOWS, DOORS, ETC. CHECK ARRANGEMENT.

18. COMPLETE SYMBOLS, NOTES, ETC.

Fig. 8-30. Follow this step-by-step procedure in drawing elevations.

roofing and other ornamentation. Dimension finish grade to finish floor; finish floor to finish ceiling, ridge height, etc.

Note building materials (exterior wall covering, roofing material, chimney material, pitch triangle, ornamentation, finish grade, etc.). See Fig. 8-30, Step 9.

Step 10. Draw the other elevations on Sheets No. 3 and No. 4 in the same manner as has been outlined in the previous 9 steps.

Note: Do not trace the two remaining elevations directly from those elevations just drawn. All features will be reversed on opposite elevations, i.e., a porch attached to the front will appear on the left side of the right ele-

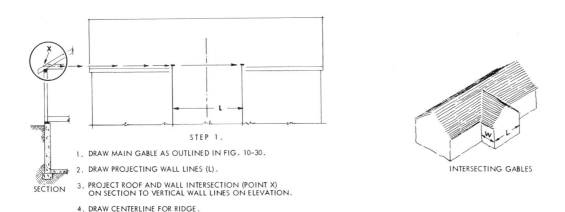

STEP 1.

1. DRAW MAIN GABLE AS OUTLINED IN FIG. 10-30.

2. DRAW PROJECTING WALL LINES (L).

3. PROJECT ROOF AND WALL INTERSECTION (POINT X) ON SECTION TO VERTICAL WALL LINES ON ELEVATION.

4. DRAW CENTERLINE FOR RIDGE.

SECTION

INTERSECTING GABLES

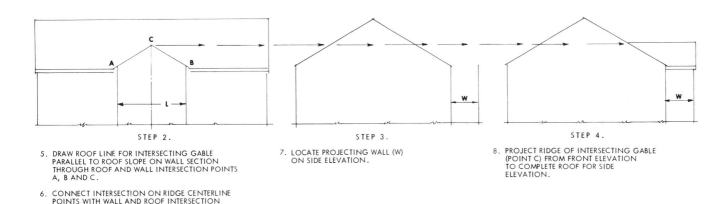

STEP 2.

STEP 3.

STEP 4.

5. DRAW ROOF LINE FOR INTERSECTING GABLE PARALLEL TO ROOF SLOPE ON WALL SECTION THROUGH ROOF AND WALL INTERSECTION POINTS A, B AND C.

6. CONNECT INTERSECTION ON RIDGE CENTERLINE POINTS WITH WALL AND ROOF INTERSECTION POINTS A AND B TO FORM SLOPE.

7. LOCATE PROJECTING WALL (W) ON SIDE ELEVATION.

8. PROJECT RIDGE OF INTERSECTING GABLE (POINT C) FROM FRONT ELEVATION TO COMPLETE ROOF FOR SIDE ELEVATION.

Fig. 8-31. Follow this step-by-step procedure in drawing an elevation with intersecting gables.

vation, and on the right of the left elevation.

After the elevations have been completed, transfer the window openings by ticking off the proper size and ℄'s to the plan. Draw in the proper symbols for the particular openings on the plan.

Step-by-Step Drawing Procedure: Roofs

Occasionally problems are encountered in drawing the roof—particularly in deciding exactly where to begin. The procedure for drawing the plain gable roof has been pointed out in Fig. 8-30. To eliminate any questions which may occur, step-by-step procedures are given for drawing three other types of roof.

Intersecting Gables. See Fig. 8-31.

Step 1. Draw the main gable as outlined in Fig. 8-31. Locate and draw the projecting wall lines (L). Project or transfer roof and wall intersection (X) from wall section to vertical wall lines on the elevation.

Locate and draw the ℄ for ridge. See Fig. 8-31, Step 1.

Step 2. Draw roof line for intersecting gable parallel to roof slope on the wall section through roof and wall intersecting points A, B, and C. (The roof slope of the projection is usually the same as that of the main roof.) Connect intersection of ridge ℄, C, with wall and B, to form slope. See Fig. and roof intersection points A

and B, to form slope. See Fig. 8-31, Step 2.

Step 3. Locate and draw projecting wall, W, on side elevation. See Fig. 8-31, Step 3.

Step 4. Project or transfer ridge height of intersecting gable (point C) from front elevation to side elevation to complete roof.

Complete cornice overhang, gutter, etc. See Fig. 8-31, Step 4.

Hip Roofs. In designing a roof for a residence, none offers more challenge for the designer than the hip roof. This need not be true if some basic steps are employed. A gable, mansard, flat, shed, folded, or butterfly roof may be designed with ease because they are formed by one or two intersecting planes. The hip roof, however, poses a problem because of different ridge heights, spans and valleys. Usually before the designer begins to draw a hip roof he will lay out the roof in plan. This is often accomplished by means of a sketch. Once the roof has been planned the designer can better envision the intersecting hips and proceed to draw the elevation.

The secret in designing a hip roof is to divide the plan into a series of rectangles. To begin with, first consider the simple rectangular plan in Fig. 8-32. In laying out a hip roof it is important to note that the horizontal length of the hip is equivalent to the *run* of the roof. (The *run* is equal to one-half of the span.) This will insure all pitches are equal. In Fig. 8-32 the pitch of the hip is equivalent to the pitch of the roof.

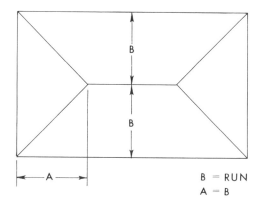

Fig. 8-32. A hip roof is designed so the horizontal length of the hip is equal to the run of the roof.

If these two angles are not equal, the framing of the roof will be more difficult for the builder. To illustrate this principle, Fig. 8-33 shows the step-by-step procedure in designing a simple hip roof by using the plan.

To draw a plain hip roof in elevation (see Fig. 8-34) follow this procedure:

Step 1. Project or transfer height of roof and wall intersection (X) from wall section to side elevation.

Draw ℄ for ridge. See Fig. 8-34, Step 1.

Step 2. Draw roof line extended to ridge ℄ parallel to roof slope on wall section.

Step 3. Project or transfer height of roof and wall intersection to front elevation.

Locate ℄ distance, ½ W, transferred from side elevation. See Fig. 8-34, Step 3.

TO LAYOUT A SIMPLE HIP

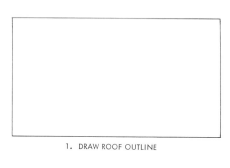

1. DRAW ROOF OUTLINE

2. DRAW IN RIDGE LINE

Fig. 8-33. Follow this step-by-step procedure in designing a simple hip roof.

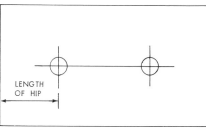

3. LAY OFF LENGTH OF HIP
EQUAL TO RUN OF SPAN

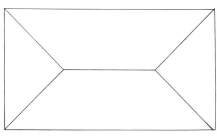

4. DRAW IN HIPS

Connect intersection of ridge ₵ with wall intersection to form other slope. See Fig. 8-34, Step 2.

Step 4. Project or transfer ridge height

from side elevation to vertical for hip.

Connect ridge intersections on ₵ with roof and wall intersections projected from wall section to form hip.

Complete cornice overhang, gutter, etc.
See Fig. 8-34, Step 4.

Since the majority of plans have some off-set or projection, next consider a basic "L"

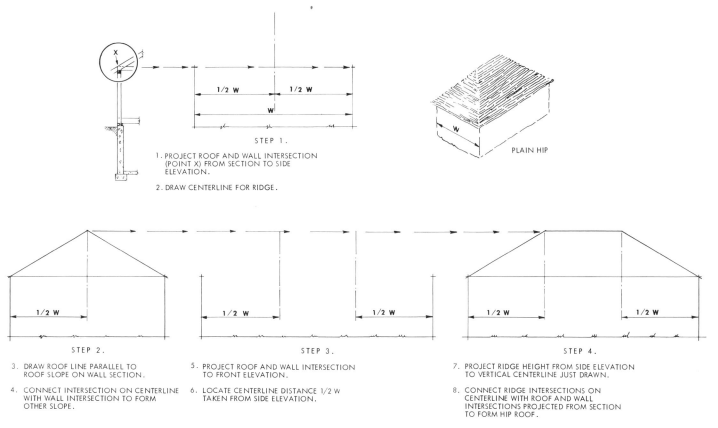

STEP 1.

1. PROJECT ROOF AND WALL INTERSECTION (POINT X) FROM SECTION TO SIDE ELEVATION.

2. DRAW CENTERLINE FOR RIDGE.

PLAIN HIP

STEP 2.

3. DRAW ROOF LINE PARALLEL TO ROOF SLOPE ON WALL SECTION.

4. CONNECT INTERSECTION ON CENTERLINE WITH WALL INTERSECTION TO FORM OTHER SLOPE.

STEP 3.

5. PROJECT ROOF AND WALL INTERSECTION TO FRONT ELEVATION.

6. LOCATE CENTERLINE DISTANCE 1/2 W TAKEN FROM SIDE ELEVATION.

STEP 4.

7. PROJECT RIDGE HEIGHT FROM SIDE ELEVATION TO VERTICAL CENTERLINE JUST DRAWN.

8. CONNECT RIDGE INTERSECTIONS ON CENTERLINE WITH ROOF AND WALL INTERSECTIONS PROJECTED FROM SECTION TO FORM HIP ROOF.

Fig. 8-34. Follow this step-by-step procedure in drawing an elevation with a plain hip roof.

shaped plan. In designing a hip roof for an offset plan, first divide the area into the largest possible rectangle and consider that shape first. Fig. 8-35 shows an "L" shaped plan and the step-by-step procedure used in designing the roof shape.

Step 1. Find the largest or main rectangular area of the plan. Draw a line in the center of the area representing the ridge of the roof.

Step 2. Lay off distance for the hip at the end of the roof equivalent to the run B. Draw in the hips.

Step 3. Draw the ridge in the smaller or secondary rectangular area of the L. Extend the ridge until it intersects the hip of the larger area at 1.

Step 4. Draw in the roof valley from 1 to 2. The valley represents the intersection of the roof's planes.

Step 5. Draw the hip on the smaller rectangular area. Lay off hip distance C equivalent to the run D.

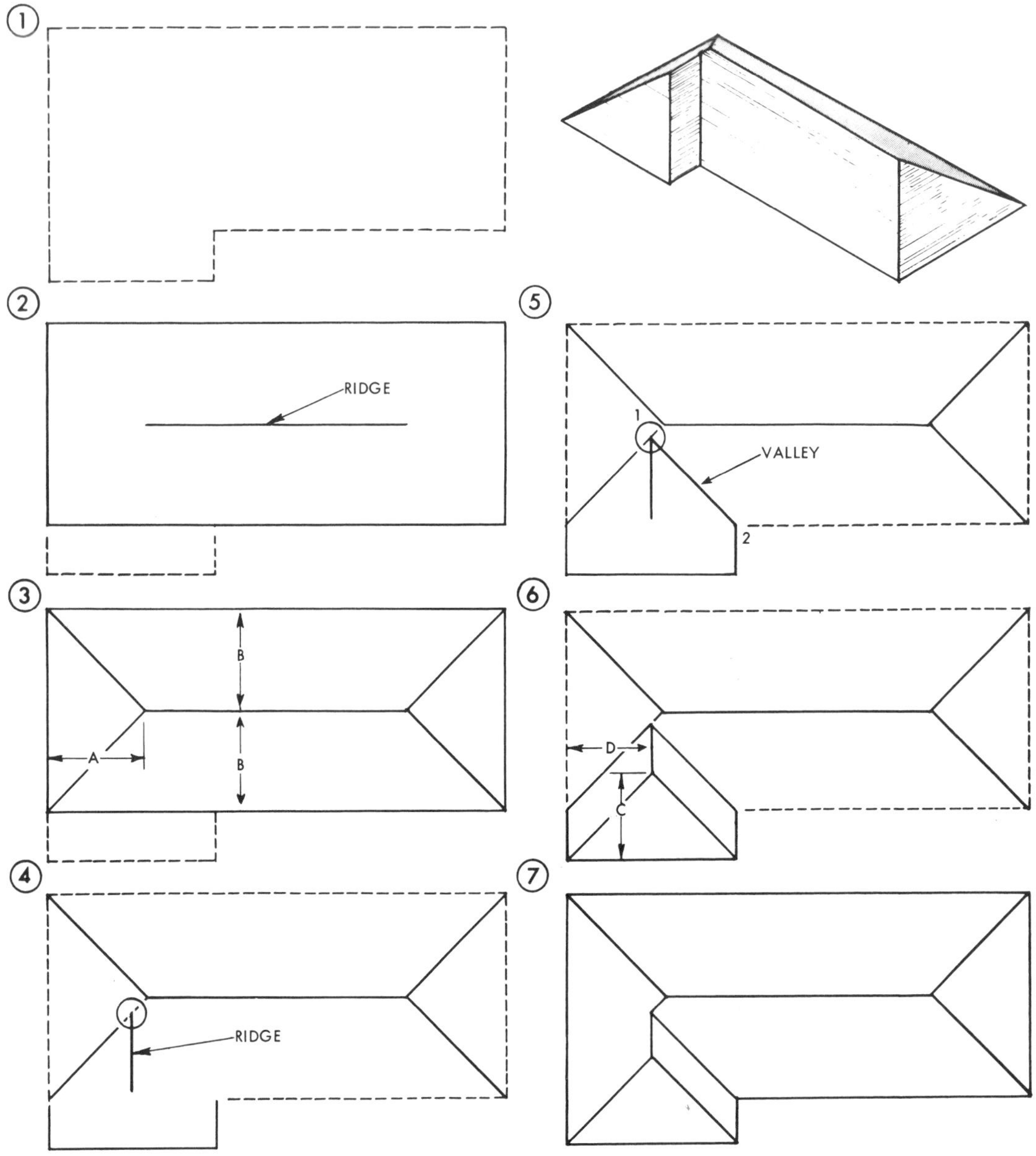

Fig. 8-35. Step-by-step procedure for planning a hip roof for an L-shaped plan by first dividing the roof into the largest rectangle.

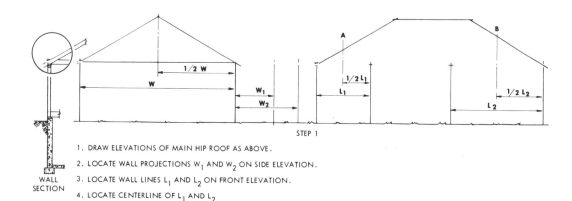

1. DRAW ELEVATIONS OF MAIN HIP ROOF AS ABOVE.

2. LOCATE WALL PROJECTIONS W_1 AND W_2 ON SIDE ELEVATION.

3. LOCATE WALL LINES L_1 AND L_2 ON FRONT ELEVATION.

4. LOCATE CENTERLINE OF L_1 AND L_2

WALL SECTION

STEP 1

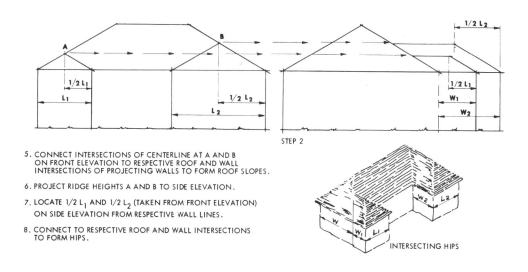

5. CONNECT INTERSECTIONS OF CENTERLINE AT A AND B ON FRONT ELEVATION TO RESPECTIVE ROOF AND WALL INTERSECTIONS OF PROJECTING WALLS TO FORM ROOF SLOPES.

6. PROJECT RIDGE HEIGHTS A AND B TO SIDE ELEVATION.

7. LOCATE $1/2 L_1$ AND $1/2 L_2$ (TAKEN FROM FRONT ELEVATION) ON SIDE ELEVATION FROM RESPECTIVE WALL LINES.

8. CONNECT TO RESPECTIVE ROOF AND WALL INTERSECTIONS TO FORM HIPS.

STEP 2

INTERSECTING HIPS

Fig. 8-36. Follow this step-by-step procedure in drawing an elevation with an intersecting hip roof.

Step 6. Darken in the ridge, valley, and hips of the roof for emphasis.

Step-by-Step Drawing Procedure: Hip Roof Elevations

Drawing an elevation of building roofed with intersecting hips (see Fig. 8-36) can be accomplished once an understanding of how much of the roof will appear.

Step 1. Draw elevation of main hip roof as described in the preceding section. See Fig. 8-36.

Locate and draw wall projections W_1, and W_2 on side elevations.

Locate and draw wall lines L_1, and L_2 on front elevation.

Locate and draw ₵ of L_1, and

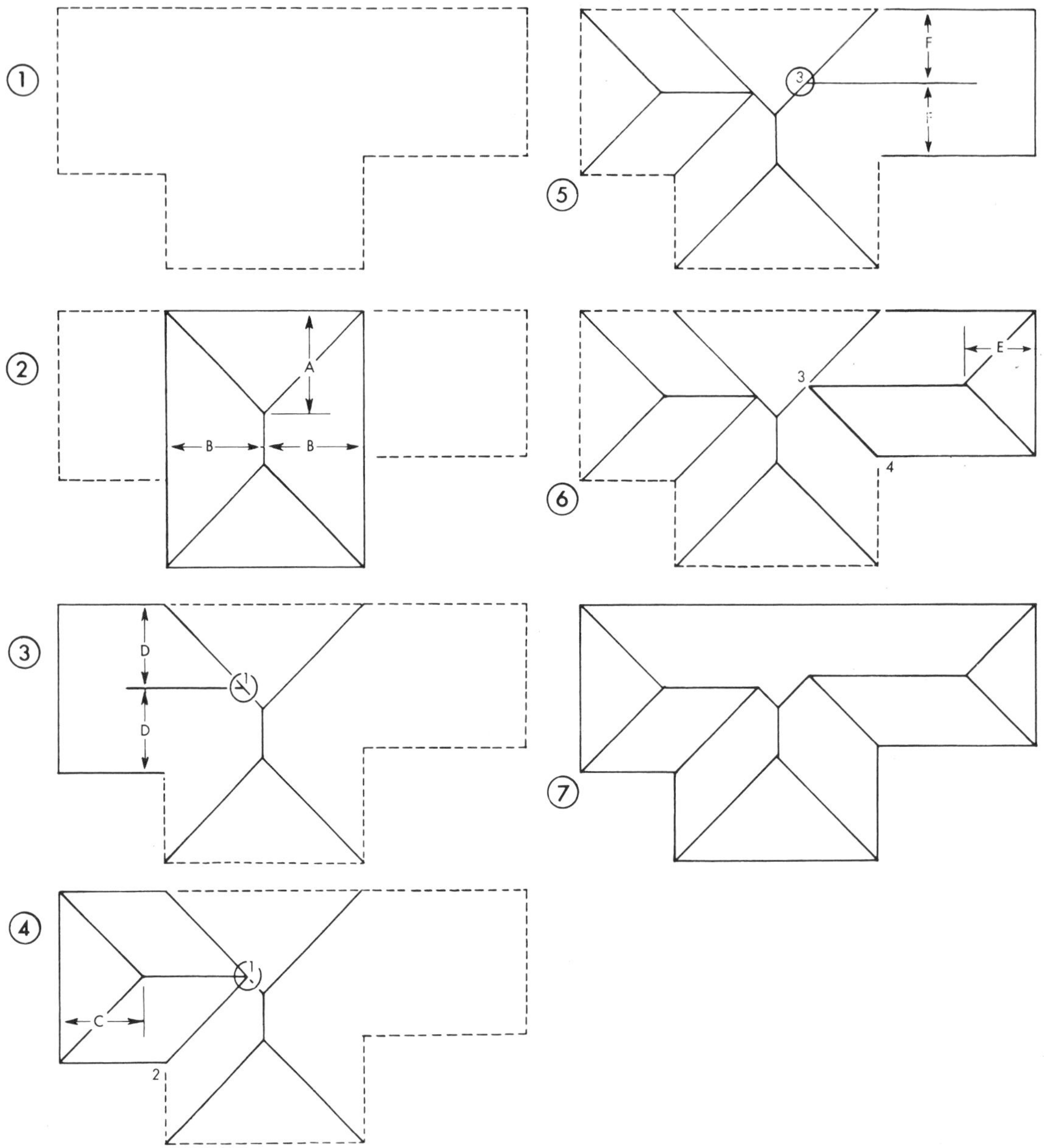

Fig. 8-37. Step-by-step procedure used in planning a hip roof for an odd-shaped plan. As in Fig. 8-35, the plan is first divided into rectangular areas.

L_2. Extend these ℄'s so they intersect the main hip at points A and B. See Fig. 8-36, Step 1.

Step 2. Connect intersections of ℄ at points A and B on front elevation to respective roof and wall intersection of projecting walls. Project or transfer ridge heights (points A and B) to side elevations.

Locate ½ L_1 and ½ L_2 (taken from front elevation) on side elevation from respective wall lines. Connect to respective roof and wall intersection to form hips. See Fig. 8-36, Step 2.

Step-by-Step Drawing Procedure: Hip Roof Outlines

Using the basic premise of dividing the plan into rectangular areas can be applied to more complicated roof outlines. Fig. 8-37 shows a plan where none of the component rectangles are equal in width or depth. The following step-by-step break-down explains how an apparently complicated plan may be easily roofed.

Step 1. Divide the plan into rectangular areas. In the largest of the three rectangular areas draw a ridge line parallel to the longest dimension. Lay off the length of the hip A equal to the run B of the span.

Step 2. Draw a ridge line in the second largest rectangular area. Next lay off the hip distance C equivalent to the run D.

Step 3. Draw in the valley from point 1 to the intersection of the two rectangular areas, point 2.

Step 4. Draw in a ridge line in the smallest rectangular area, extending it to the hip at point 3. Lay off the hip distance E equal to the run of the smaller span F.

Step 5. Draw in the valley between these two rectangular areas line 3-4. Darken in the hips, valleys, and outline of the roof for emphasis.

Several additional L-shaped plans with varying width "L's" are shown in Fig. 8-38.

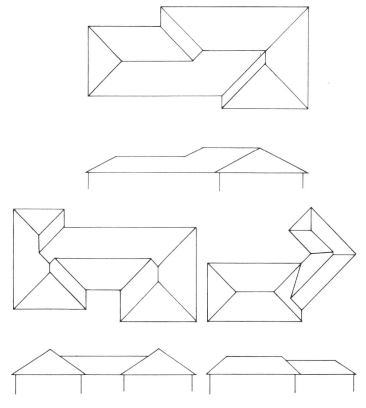

Fig. 8-38. Several plans that have been roofed with hips by the principle shown in Figs. 8-35 and 8-37.

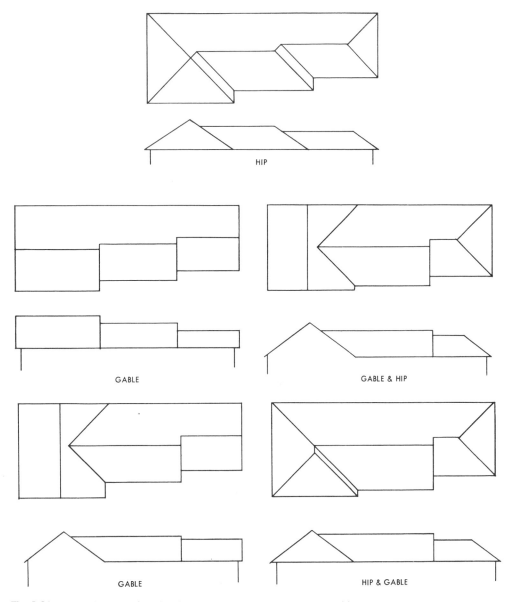

HIP

GABLE

GABLE & HIP

GABLE

HIP & GABLE

Fig. 8-39. A combination of roof styles lends a unique appearance and interest.

In each of these roof plans the main rectangle area is represented by a subordinate width line. The hip roof design has been dictated by the principle of first laying out the hips of the main area. It can be seen from the roof plan and elevation for each, how the appearances differ, though each has an L shape.

An additional plan is shown with five different combination roof styles in Fig. 8-39. Designers frequently use a combination of hip and gable to provide a pleasing appearance rather than a single roof style. How many other combinations of hip and gable can the designer create for this plan?

Questions and Problems

1. Select an architectural, building trades, or home-making magazine from your classroom library, school library, or home.

   Examine the photographs or drawings of houses and identify the styles.

2. Draw an exterior wall section of western frame construction with a concrete block foundation wall. Call out all materials with notes. Insulate outside walls and attic ceiling with either 4″ fill, or foil type insulation. Use 2″ × 4″s for studs, plates, soles, and girts; 2″ × 8″ joists for 1st and 2nd floors and header joists; 2″ × 6″s for attic floor joists and rafters; 2″ × 6″ sills; ¾″ × 16″ W.I. bolts, 6′-0″ O.C.; ¾″ fabricated fibre board; ½″ exterior

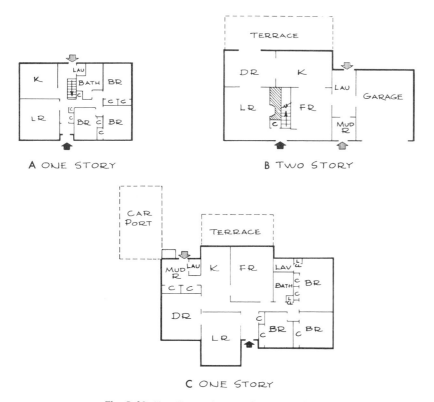

Fig. 8-40. Use these plans to draw elevations.

sheathing; ¾″ interior plywood for sub-flooring; and metal cross bridging or 2″ × 8″ solid bridging between joists. Scale 1½″ = 1′-0″.

4. Draw or sketch three different style elevations using the plans shown in Fig. 8-40. (Select the type of styles shown in this chapter. It may be desirable to slightly alter the plans shown in Fig. 8-40.

5. Is it possible that an elevation(s) may be completed before the plan? If so, state the circumstances where this may or may not be true.

6. Is a perspective sketch more important or valuable than a sketched elevation? Where may a perspective sketch be a significant aid?

7. Select 4 different *plans* and elevations from the home or real estate page of the daily newspaper, and sketch an elevation *different* from the one pictured. Do not change the floor plan.

grade plywood for roof sheathing; ¾″ interior plywood for sub-flooring; and 1″ × 2″ cross bridging between joists. Scale 1½″ = 1′-0″.

3. Draw an exterior wall section of balloon frame construction with a 10″ poured concrete foundation wall. Indicate all materials and notes. Insulate outside walls and attic ceiling with either 4″ fill, batt, or foil type insulation. Use 2″ × 4″ studs, plates, soles, and girts; 2″ × 8″ joists for 1st and 2nd floors and header joists; 2″ × 6″ joists for attic floor and rafters; 2″ × 6″ sills; 1″ × 6″ ledger or ribbon; 1″ × 4″ fire stop; ¾″ × 16″ W.I. bolts, 6′-0″ O.C.; ¾″ fabricated fibreboard; ½″ exterior grade plywood for roof

Construction Details: Foundations and Main Structure   9

Almost everyone who builds or buys a house is interested in obtaining the most for his dollar. Frequently, it is difficult to distinguish those items which are absolutely required from those which are desired but not necessary. Too often good construction is slighted for built-in conveniences which could have been added or installed later.

The best way to evaluate any home would be to examine the materials and workmanship during the actual construction. Usually, however, the buyer does not have this opportunity. Even if he saw the structure being erected, he might not recognize sound construction practices or honest use of materials. This chapter offers information essential to the basic understanding of building materials and construction.

A sound grasp of these basics is a prerequisite for good house design.

Footings and Foundations

The old adage, "A chain is no stronger than its weakest link," is particularly appropriate when discussing one of the most essential elements of any structure. An adequate foundation must be designed to support the building. Quality materials must be used for construction. By so doing, many settlement cracks will be eliminated, and the structure will better withstand the ravages of time.

Footings

A footing is an enlarged projection, either rectangular or triangular, at the base of the foundation wall. The primary purpose of the footing is to distribute the building's weight over a greater soil area. By using footings the building will have more resistance to settlement. Footings are used under every part of the structure which will support an appreciable amount of weight (e.g., foundation, porch, stoop, columns, fireplace, chimney, etc.).

The function of the footing may be easily visualized by the analogy shown in Fig. 9-1. In Fig. 9-1 (top) relatively little pressure would be required to push the *pointed* stake into dry sand. By comparison, however, if

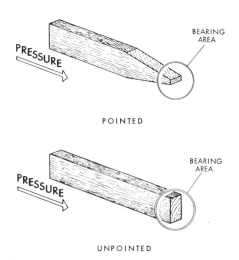

Fig. 9-1. A larger bearing area offers increased resistance to pressure.

an *unpointed* stake, Fig. 9-1 (bottom), were pushed into the same mound of dry sand, more pressure would be required to penetrate the sand. The unpointed stake has more bearing area, thereby offering more resistance. In the same manner, increased width at the lower portion of the foundation wall gives more bearing area and retards uneven settlement. Unequal settling causes cracks and other defects, not only in the footing and foundation, but in the walls as well.

Footing Design and Detail

Footings, in both type and size, should be suitable to the soil conditions and the type of structure. Poured concrete footings are more dependable than those made of other materials and are recommended for use in all residential foundations and footings. Building codes specify the footing size in relation to the structure type, height, and general soil conditions. In the absence of a code, however, the general practice is to design and construct residential footings with a depth equal to the thickness of the foundation wall (not less than 12″). The footings should project out on either side a distance of one-half the foundation wall thickness (not less than 6″). See Fig. 9-2.

Another formula for light residential footing design is shown in Fig. 9-3. The depth of this footing is equivalent to the thickness of the foundation wall. If a 60° line is drawn from the intersection of the foundation wall and footing to the depth of the footing, as in Fig. 9-3, it will graphically

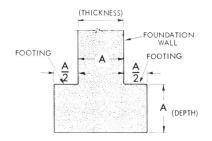

Fig. 9-2. The footings may have a depth equal to the thickness of the foundation wall.

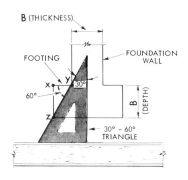

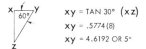

$$xy = TAN\ 30°\ (xz)$$
$$xy = .5774\,(8)$$
$$xy = 4.6192\ OR\ 5''$$

Fig. 9-3. A 60° angle drawn away from the base of the foundation wall (point Y) and extended to the depth of the footing (point Z) will give graphically the footing projection.

give the correct amount of footing projection. Apply the same amount to the other side of the foundation wall.

Reinforcing is frequently used to add strength and alleviate stresses in a residential footing. All footings for commercial or industrial buildings have reinforcing rods. Reinforcing rods or mesh are shown only in the detail sectional view of the footing, as in Fig. 9-4, and are listed in the written specifications as to their size, type, and spacing.

Stepped Footings. If the foundation is at two different depths (as in the case of a split-level dwelling), or if the house is to be built on sloping ground, the footings will of necessity be stepped as in Fig. 9-5. The purpose is to permit the slope of the footing to be composed of a number of horizontal surfaces. The horizontal surfaces should be as long as possible to derive the greatest benefit from the structural value of the concrete. This also prevents a sliding action by the footing and foundation.

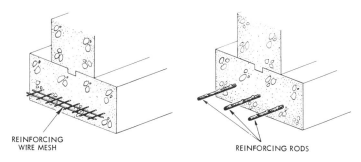

Fig. 9-4. Reinforcing rods or mesh may be placed in the footings for extra strength.

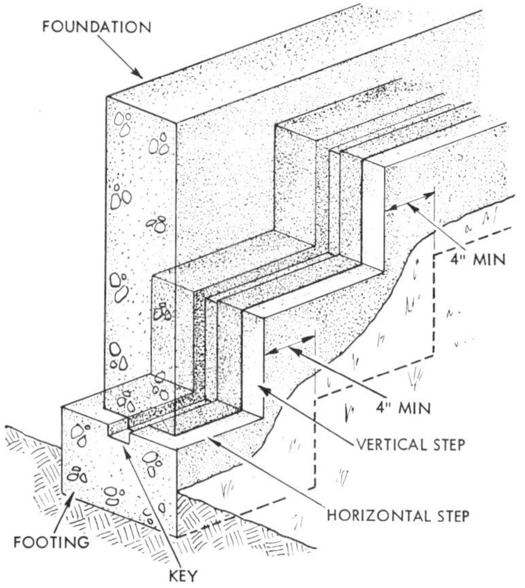

Frost Line

The effect of freezing and thawing is much greater upon soil than upon other materials, such as brick or concrete. Footings must be carried below the *frost line* (the depth that frost penetrates below the grade). Many building codes require the footing to be carried one foot below the frost line. If the footings are above the frost line they are likely to *heave* (move) as a result of soil pressures caused by extreme temperature change. It is evident from the map shown in Fig. 9-6 that the maximum frost penetration differs in various sections

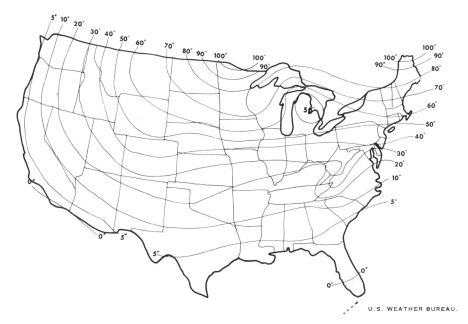

Fig. 9-5. Stepped footings are designed to give horizontal support when the ground is uneven or the house levels are not on the same plane.

Fig. 9-6. This map shows maximum frost penetration in United States.

TABLE 9-1
FOOTING DEPTHS AS REQUIRED BY REPRESENTATIVE CITY CODES

CITY		CITY	
MILWAUKEE, WISCONSIN	4'-6"	BALTIMORE, MARYLAND	3'-0"
CHICAGO, ILLINOIS	3'-6"	KANSAS CITY, MISSOURI	3'-0"
ST. PAUL, MINNESOTA	3'-6"	PHILADELPHIA, PA.	3'-0"
BOSTON, MASSACHUSETTS	4'-0"	LOUISVILLE, KENTUCKY	2'-6"
HALIFAX, NOVA SCOTIA	4'-0"	ST. LOUIS, MISSOURI	2'-6"
NEW YORK CITY, N.Y.	4'-0"	DENVER, COLORADO	1'-6"
DETROIT, MICHIGAN	3'-6"	SEATTLE, WASHINGTON	1'-6"
		JACKSONVILLE, FLORIDA	1'-0"

of the United States. Local building codes usually specify the footing depth. Depths below grade are determined by the general drainage conditions and extreme temperatures in a locality. Table 9-1 shows footing depths based on the frost line as required by building codes in representative cities in the United States.

Foundation Walls

In all structural work, proper support is essential to good construction. Foundation walls should be designed to provide adequate support to the main structure, and to prevent any moisture from entering the basement or crawl space. No building of any type or size will be sound unless it is built on a good, well designed foundation.

Foundation Thickness

Most cities publish building codes detail-

ing exact specifications for foundation design. In this case the architect indicates on the plans that the foundations are to be built in accordance with existing regulations. If a code does not exist, however, the architect must calculate the foundation thickness and height and show these dimensions.

Foundation thickness is primarily dependent upon the type of exterior walls and the height (number of floors) above grade. There are, however, no generally accepted rules for the design of concrete block, brick, or stone foundations. The type of block or brick must be taken into consideration,

TABLE 9-2
CONCRETE FOUNDATION THICKNESS

Construction	One Story	Two Story
WOOD FRAME (without basement)	**a** 6" Minimum	————
WOOD FRAME (with basement)	**a** 8" Minimum **b** 10" Minimum if longer than 20'-0".	**a** 10" if not more than 7'-0" below grade. **b** 12" if more than 7'-0" below grade.
SOLID MASONRY (with basement)	**a** As thick as the walls they support.	**a** As thick as walls they support if not more than 7'-0" below grade. **b** 12" if more than 7'-0" below grade
BRICK OR STONE VENEER (with frame backing)	**a** 8" if veneer does not extend beyond 1 1/4" of foundation. **b** Increase thickness so that veneer does not extend beyond 1 1/4".	**a** 10" if not more than 7'-0" below grade **b** 12" minimum if more than 7'-0" below grade

along with the quality of mortar. Generally, block and brick foundations should be at least as thick as the walls they support. Experience has shown stone foundations for residences should be 16″ or 18″ thick (if laid in Portland cement mortar).

Concrete foundation thickness may be roughly calculated by using Table 9-2. These "rules of thumb" are applicable to small home construction.

Some exterior house designs utilize a combination of brick and siding. The front elevation of the house may be brick or stone veneer, and the sides and rear may be *drop siding*. In such cases the thickness of the

foundation wall beneath the brick should be 10″, and the walls beneath the frame should be 8″. It would be an unnecessary expense for the home builder to have a 10″ foundation wall completely around the house.

Decorative effects can be created on the inside and outside of poured concrete walls by the use of form liners. One such form liner creating a brick pattern is shown in Fig. 9-7.

Small projection slips, for a stoop, etc. usually no greater than 3′-4′, can be supported by an integral part of the foundation wall. These supports are triangular in shape and are poured simultaneously with the

wall. Fig. 9-8 shows the forms stripped away from the foundation wall, having several stoop foundation supports. The same type of support can be obtained in a concrete block wall by corbelling block perpendicular to the face of the wall.

Basements

Poured concrete is usually used in forming a full basement. This has the advantage of being one solid piece of concrete, thus assuring a firm and continuous support of the house with less possibility of settlement. Fig. 9-9 illustrates a typical full basement constructed of concrete. Fig. 9-10 gives de-

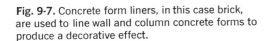

Fig. 9-7. Concrete form liners, in this case brick, are used to line wall and column concrete forms to produce a decorative effect.

SYMONS MANUFACTURING CO., DES PLAINES, ILLINOIS

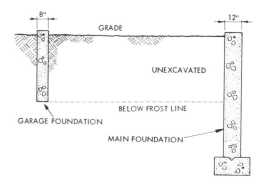

Fig. 9-10. Footings are not used for the garage foundation. (Section A-A of the foundation shown in Fig. 9-9.)

SYMONS MANUFACTURING CO., DES PLAINES, ILLINOIS

Fig. 9-8. A stoop foundation is poured as an integral part of the wall. Here the forms have just been stripped from the foundation wall.

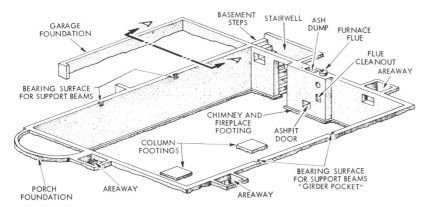

Fig. 9-9. Poured concrete forms a strong full basement without any breaks. Footings are required under the main wall and the stairwell wall.

tails of the garage and main foundations (Fig. 9-9, section A-A). Note that footings are not used for the garage foundations. This is true also of the porch and areaway foundations. The exterior stair well, however, does use a small footing to prevent possible settlement. Exterior stair wells and areaways are usually provided with a drain connected to the house sewer.

Concrete block or brick is also used for basement foundations. Care must be taken to form waterproof joints. Waterproof wall coatings should also be used.

Exposed Basement. If the entire length of a basement wall is exposed, a footing must be placed below and carried to the frost line. If the finished grading plan calls for the grade to slope upward from the rear of the exposed basement to the finished grade elevation at the front corner, the footing must be stepped to maintain its depth below the frost line. A stepped footing is

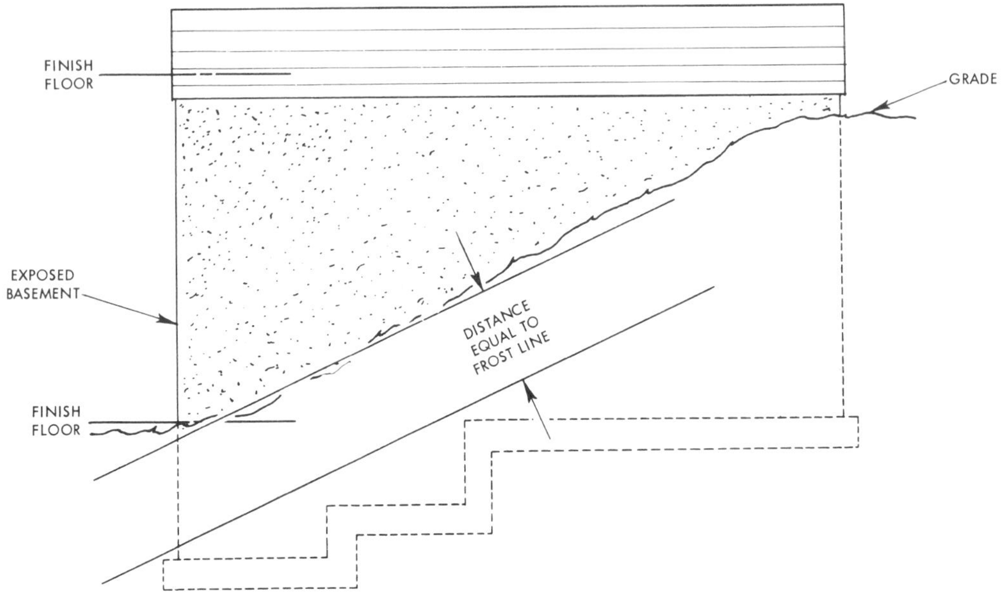

Fig. 9-11. Footing below the exposed portion of a basement wall must be placed below the frost line.

shown in Fig. 9-11. That portion of the foundation wall from the stepped footing to the under side of the basement floor must be 4″ wider. This increased width provides a ledge for the basement floor.

Basementless Houses

Foundations for basementless houses with the slabs on grade may be in either of two general classifications: (1) *perimeter wall foundations* or (2) *floating slab foundations*. Perimeter wall foundations derive their name from the fact that the foundation is carried to the frost line, thus creating a "wall" completely around the outside of the house. This type of foundation is sometimes

referred to as a *rim wall*. The floating slab foundation is just as its name indicates—it rests on the ground; there is no "wall" beneath the slab. This type of foundation is predominantly used in the warmer climates where no frost problem is encountered.

Perimeter Wall Foundation. A common perimeter wall foundation used in northern areas of the United States is shown in Fig. 9-12. Note the use of perimeter insulation extending 2′ or more under the floor. This prevents heat loss and moisture penetration. Fig. 9-13 shows the perimeter insulation and polyethylene film prior to pouring the concrete slab. Observe that in both figures

the upper surface of the foundation is a minimum of 6″ above finished grade.

Floating Slab Foundation. In the southern areas where frost penetration is not appreciable or common, and where the soil is predominantly hard and/or rocky, a floating slab foundation may be used successfully. Usually, when a concrete slab rests directly on the earth, there is an excellent chance for moisture and cold to penetrate the concrete. This is preevnted by using *membrane waterproofing* topped by 4″ of concrete and 4″ of *Zonolite concrete*. Since the foundation is not carried to any extensive depth, it is splayed inward to give additional bearing

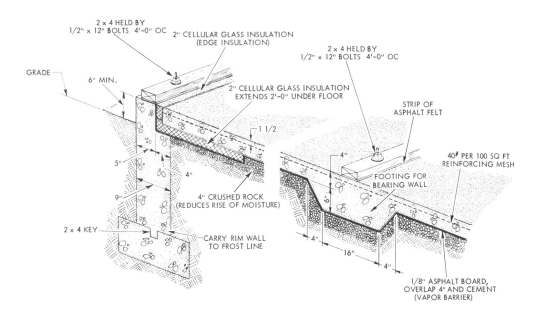

2 x 4 HELD BY
1/2" x 12" BOLTS 4'-0" OC
2" CELLULAR GLASS INSULATION
(EDGE INSULATION)

2 x 4 HELD BY
1/2" x 12" BOLTS 4'-0" OC

2" CELLULAR GLASS INSULATION
EXTENDS 2'-0" UNDER FLOOR

STRIP OF
ASPHALT FELT

GRADE

6" MIN.

1 1/2

4"

40# PER 100 SQ FT
REINFORCING MESH

FOOTING FOR
BEARING WALL

5"

4"

6"

9"

4" CRUSHED ROCK
(REDUCES RISE OF MOISTURE)

2 x 4 KEY

CARRY RIM WALL
TO FROST LINE

4"

16"

4"

1/8" ASPHALT BOARD,
OVERLAP 4" AND CEMENT
(VAPOR BARRIER)

Fig. 9-12. In northern areas the perimeter wall in a basementless house extends two feet under the floor to prevent heat loss and moisture penetration. Note the insulation at the perimeter of the slab.

NATIONAL GYPSUM CO., BUFFALO, NEW YORK.

Fig. 9-13. Perimeter cellular glass insulation and polyethylene film is used to prevent heat loss and moisture penetration in slab houses.

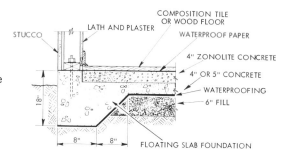

Fig. 9-14. In southern areas a floating slab foundation for a basementless house is used. Note how the foundation splays inward to give additional support.

surface, thereby distributing the weight over a wider area. See Fig. 9-14.

In slab houses space must be provided in the concrete for electrical conduit, water pipes, and heat ducts. If ordinary duct and register heating is not used, radiant heating may be desired. Radiant heating systems usually have pipe coils imbedded in the concrete.

Crawl Spaces. Fig. 9-15 illustrates a foundation used in many of the northern areas of the United States. This foundation is designed to have a crawl space of 18″ to 36″ to lessen the effects of moisture and cold on the floor framing materials. In addition, this crawl space provides an area for plumbing, electrical conduit, and heating ducts. Even though an air space is provided between the earth and floor joists, further insurance against heat loss and moisture penetration must be furnished. A means of preventing heat loss is vertical insulation board. This is nailed to the sill and carried down to the pre-molded membrane. Pre-molded membrane or polyethylene film may be installed as a moisture seal. See Fig. 9-15.

concrete block foundation wall is shown in Fig. 9-16. The length and width of a vent used in a masonry wall is equivalent to the size of the masonry unit.

Many mono-level and split level homes do not have basements under the entire area. The portion of the building that does not have a basement will in all probability have a crawl space. Usually a foundation wall

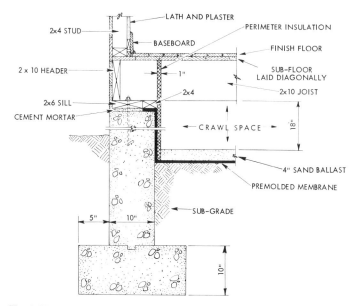

Fig. 9-15. Basementless houses are sometimes built with a crawl space.

All crawl spaces must have some means of ventilation to prevent damage to framing members by condensation. A wide variety of vents are available for concrete block or poured concrete walls. A typical vent for a

separates the crawl space area from the basement. To gain entry to the crawl space area, an access door is placed in the wall separating these two areas. Fig. 9-17 illustrates a typical crawl space access door.

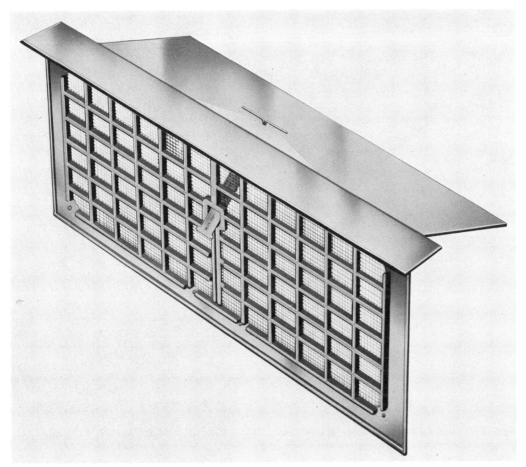

CLEVELAND STEEL SPECIALTY CO., CLEVELAND, OHIO

Fig. 9-16. All crawl spaces must be ventilated. This is a typical ventilator for concrete block walls.

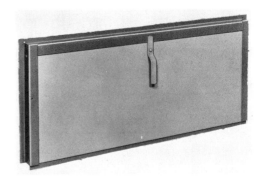

INLAND-RYERSON CONSTRUCTION
PRODUCTS CO., MILWAUKEE, WISC.

Fig. 9-17. Crawl space doors are used to gain entrance to the crawl space.

Pilasters are used in concrete-block foundation walls (Fig. 9-18) to provide increased rigidity in long runs of the wall. These, together with some type of horizontal joint reinforcement, provide extra wall strength. Pilasters are usually placed from 13′ to 14′ apart.

Horizontal Joint Reinforcement. When foundation wall is constructed with concrete block, some type of joint reinforcement must be used to prevent any shear forces from pushing in the wall. Two of the more common types of joint reinforcement are shown in Fig. 9-19. Horizontal joint reinforcement is usually spaced 20″ apart or every third course of block. If the blocks are carefully laid, they make a good foundation, and in some cases (dependent upon labor and material costs), are more economical than poured concrete.

Foundation Reinforcement

Pilasters. Poured concrete foundations seldom require any stiffening unless they are very high and over 20′ long. Exceptionally high concrete foundations are subject to considerable soil pressures. To resist this, *pilasters* are added for extra strength. Pilasters may also be added to support beams which are to carry extraordinarily heavy loads. This gives an increased bearing area.

Steel Rods. Steel rods (round or square) are sometimes placed in poured cement for extra strength. The rods provide a "bone structure" which gives strength to the concrete.

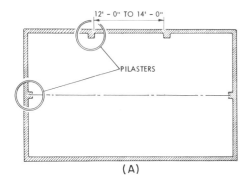

(A)

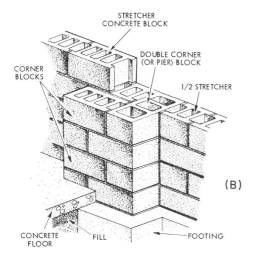

Fig. 9-18. Pilasters are added to basement walls to provide increased strength. When pilasters are used with concrete block they are tied into the wall by alternating the pattern on each level.

DUR-O-WAL PRODUCTS, INC., CEDAR RAPIDS, IOWA

Fig. 9-19. Horizontal joint reinforcement provides added lateral strength to a concrete block wall. Both rigid (top) and flexible (right) joint reinforcement provide the necessary strength.

KEYSTONE STEEL & WIRE CO., PEORIA, ILLINOIS

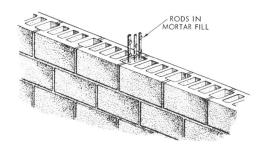

Fig. 9-20. Vertical wall stiffening is accomplished by "rodding" the cores. The rods extend through several block levels.

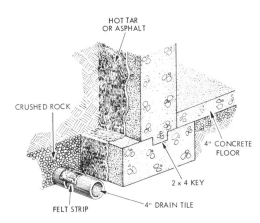

Fig. 9-21. Drain tile is laid around foundations to remove water. For waterproofing, tar or asphalt is applied to the foundation wall and footings. The felt strip prevents the open tile joints from filling up.

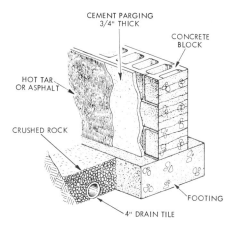

Fig. 9-22. Cement parging covered with tar or asphalt is applied to concrete block foundation walls on the outside.

Concrete block walls may also be strengthened by steel rods. Several ½″ diameter by 8′ long reinforcing rods are run vertically through the block cores of several courses. The cores are then filled with mortar. This is called "rodding the cores." *Rodded cores* are shown in Fig. 9-20.

Foundation Drainage

Drain Tile. Every foundation should be constructed with an adequate drainage system to remove any water which may accumulate. Drain tile is laid around the outside of the footing with open joints. This is covered with coarse stone or gravel to a depth of at least one foot. (The coarse stone or gravel allows the water to seep to the tile.) A piece of impregnated felt is laid on top of the open tile joints to prevent these spaces from becoming clogged with stone or soil. See Fig. 9-21. The tile is laid with a slight slope to drain the water away from the house.

Waterproofing. Foundations may also be protected by waterproofing. The method most generally used for residences with poured concrete foundations is to cover the wall and footings with several applications of asphalt or tar, sometimes called "black-jack." See Fig. 9-21. Concrete block foundation walls are usually covered (parged) with a rich cement grout, ¾″ thick, and several coats of asphalt or tar (Fig. 9-22).

Extremely damp soil conditions may require the foundation wall to be membrane waterproofed. Fig. 9-23 shows membrane waterproofing applied to the concrete wall and footings. This type of waterproofing employs several layers of fabric which are cemented together with asphalt. Often, the membrane waterproofing is covered with a

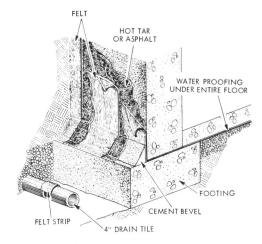

Fig. 9-23. Membrane waterproofing uses several layers of felt cemented together with tar or asphalt.

protective wall of brick or concrete. This adds protection against ground water damage and damage that may be incurred in backfilling.

Openings in Foundation Walls

Basement windows can be either set into the foundation wall after it has been erected, or they may be placed between the forms and the concrete poured around the frame. These are called self-forming windows. Fig. 9-24 shows two types of self-forming windows commonly used in poured walls. Normally the top of basement window frame is flush with the top of the foundation. Fig. 9-25 illustrates a typical method of floor framing over a basement window set flush with the top of the foundation wall. A ledger strip nailed to the header, as shown in Fig. 9-25, is used to give added support for the joists over the window. Some con-

SLIDE WINDOW
PARTIALLY OPEN

CENTER LOCKING
HOPPER WINDOW

Fig. 9-24. Metal basement windows eliminate the need for special window forms when pouring a foundation wall. These windows are also used for concrete block walls.

SIDE LOCKING
HOPPER WINDOW

SLIDE WINDOW
CLOSED

INLAND STEEL PRODUCTS CO., MILWAUKEE, WISC.

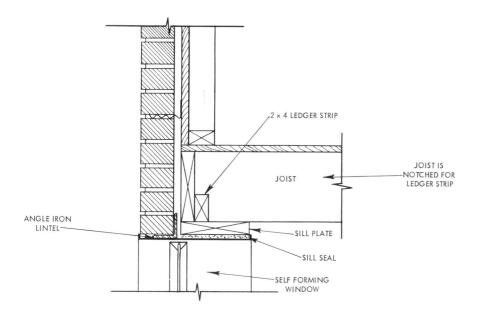

2 x 4 LEDGER STRIP

JOIST

JOIST IS
NOTCHED FOR
LEDGER STRIP

ANGLE IRON
LINTEL

SILL PLATE

SILL SEAL

SELF FORMING
WINDOW

Fig. 9-25. Conventional framing procedures are used over a basement window. The ledger strip extends 6″ beyond each side of the window.

tractors may omit the ledger strip. Basement windows set in concrete block walls are held in place by special metal sash blocks. These blocks are placed on both sides of the frame and have a 1⅜″ wide x 1″ deep vertical recess on their 7⅝″ x 7⅝″ face. As the wall is raised around the frame, mortar is placed in this recess, locking the frame in place. If mortar is not used, a wood key strip is placed in the recess in the block and frame. In either case, the mortar or key strip will prevent winds from penetrating.

Window and door openings in a poured foundation wall are formed by "boxing-out" the opening. Fig. 9-26 shows a worker boxing-out a door opening against one side of a concrete form. When all openings are

Fig. 9-26. Any opening in a poured concrete wall must have a form for the opening.

SYMONS MANUFACTURING CO., DES PLAINES, ILLINOIS

boxed, the other side of the form is positioned and held together with spreaders and tie strips. The concrete is then poured and the forms stripped from the wall. The boxing is then removed and window and door frames are positioned.

Area walls are used around openings in a foundation wall to allow light and air to enter through a window. Area walls are either round or rectangular shaped galvanized metal retaining walls that are nailed or bolted to the foundation wall. Fig. 9-27 shows two styles of metal area walls. When an area wall is adjacent to a walkway, a grate is placed over the area wall for safety purposes. See Fig. 9-28.

Grade Beam and Piers

The grade beam and pier system is a different approach to foundation support for single story basementless structures. It is used for residential as well as for light commercial buildings. The name "grade beam and pier" derives its name from the

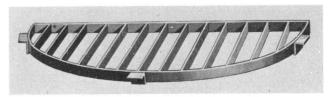

Fig. 9-28. Frequently a grate is placed over an area wall for safety reasons.

THE MAJESTIC CO., INC., HUNTINGTON, IND.

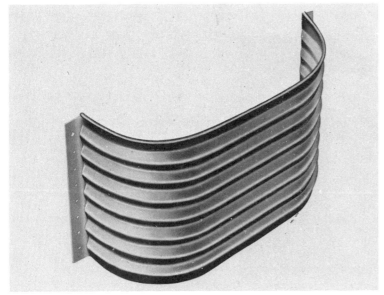

INLAND-RYERSON CONSTRUCTION PRODUCTS CO., MILWAUKEE, WISC.

THE MAJESTIC CO., INC., HUNTINGTON, INDIANA

Fig. 9-27. Area walls are used around basement windows.

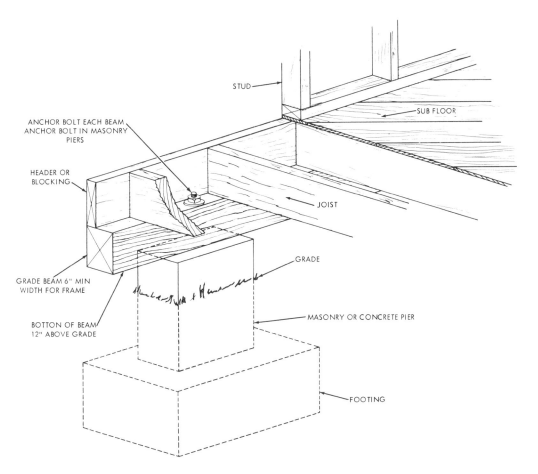

STUD

SUB FLOOR

ANCHOR BOLT EACH BEAM
ANCHOR BOLT IN MASONRY
PIERS

HEADER OR
BLOCKING

JOIST

GRADE BEAM 6" MIN
WIDTH FOR FRAME

GRADE

BOTTON OF BEAM
12" ABOVE GRADE

MASONRY OR CONCRETE PIER

FOOTING

Fig. 9-29. Typical free-standing pier supporting a grade beam.

fact that a concrete or wood beam placed at, or slightly above the grade, is used to support the structure. By comparison with the conventional foundation wall and spread footing design, the grade beam and pier is by far more economical. Essentially the saving results from a considerably smaller amount of concrete and a minimum of excavation and forming. The conventional foundation wall is replaced by a series of freestanding piers, exterior piers and curtain walls, or grade beams supported by piers or piles. See Fig. 9-29. Either combination will safely and adequately support a single story building.

A grade beam may be wood (6″ minimum width) when used for frame construction. The beam is supported by freestanding piers

TABLE 9-3
MINIMUM SIZES AND SPACING FOR PIERS AND FOOTINGS ‡

PIER MATERIAL	MINIMUM PIER SIZE	MINIMUM FOOTING SIZE	PIER SPACING	
			PERPENDICULAR TO JOISTS	PARALLEL TO JOISTS
SOLID OR GROUTED MASONRY	8" x 12"	16" x 24" x 8"	8'-0" o.c.	12'-0" o.c.
HOLLOW MASONRY*	8" x 16"	16" x 24" x 8"	8'-0" o.c.	12'-0" o.c.
PLAIN CONCRETE	12" DIA OR 10" x 10"	20" x 20" x 8"	8'-0" o.c.	12'-0" o.c.

*   INTERIOR PIER NOT SUBJECT TO WIND.
‡   TABLE BASED UPON PIERS SUPPORTING A ONE STORY BUILDING WITH AVERAGE SOIL CONDITIONS.

which are spaced according to the dimensions found in Table 9-3. The beam must be bolted to the masonry pier. The distance between the underside of the beam and the grade should be 12″ minimum. The underside of the floor framing system can be concealed by a masonry curtain wall between piers. The curtain wall is supported, see Fig. 9-30, by a continuous footing that is integral with the pier footing. Since the curtain wall is flush with the foundation side of the pier, it must be bonded or anchored to the pier.

Fig. 9-31 shows a reinforced concrete graded beam used to support a masonry wall. Concrete grade beams are also used where a concrete slab is ground supported as in Fig. 9-31. Concrete grade beams are cast in place and are anchored to the piers by the means of ⅝″ dia. steel dowels. Because of the ultimate load grade beams must carry, they must not only be reinforced, but also must have a minimum of 14″ depth, a minimum of 6″ width for frame, and a minimum of 8″ width for masonry walls. The base of each pier must be flared or belled and always carried to below the frost line. A grade beam used in conjunction with a ground supported slab requires the piers to be spaced no farther apart than 8′ o.c. A ⅝″ dia. steel dowel is used to pin the beam to the pier.

Grade beams do not necessarily have to be carried to the frost line. Damage to grade beams that do not extend below the frost line can be prevented in areas where the soil retains moisture by pouring the grade beam on a crushed rock base. See Fig. 9-32. Crushed rock or gravel is not susceptible to heaving caused by frost penetration. Since moisture is present in the soil, a drain tile should be connected to the trench containing the crushed rock or gravel, thereby removing any water that may collect. Areas that have unstable or expansive soil conditions require that creosote treated wood piles be used instead of concrete piers. Each pile is driven to a depth that will give a solid footing. The grade beams are secured to the piles by steel dowels. See Fig. 9-33. In portions of the country that are subjected to earth tremors or quakes, grade beams should be bolted to the piers. All piers should be reinforced to conform with FHA

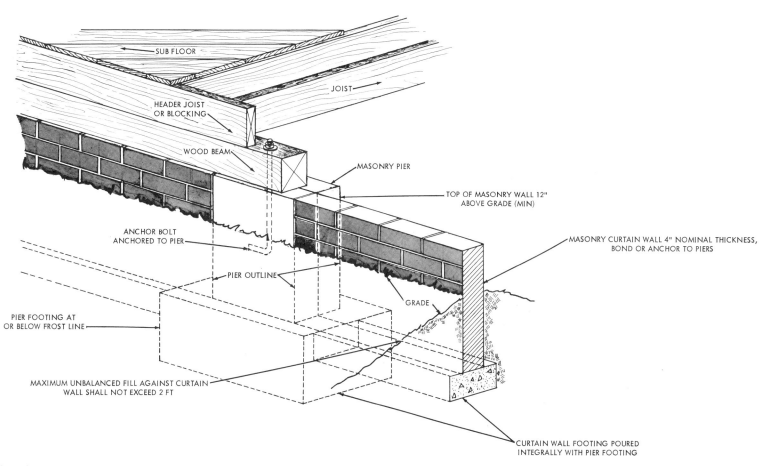

SUB FLOOR

JOIST

HEADER JOIST
OR BLOCKING

WOOD BEAM

MASONRY PIER

TOP OF MASONRY WALL 12"
ABOVE GRADE (MIN)

ANCHOR BOLT
ANCHORED TO PIER

MASONRY CURTAIN WALL 4" NOMINAL THICKNESS,
BOND OR ANCHOR TO PIERS

PIER OUTLINE

GRADE

PIER FOOTING AT
OR BELOW FROST LINE

MAXIMUM UNBALANCED FILL AGAINST CURTAIN
WALL SHALL NOT EXCEED 2 FT

CURTAIN WALL FOOTING POURED
INTEGRALLY WITH PIER FOOTING

Fig. 9-30. Typical exterior pier and curtain wall.

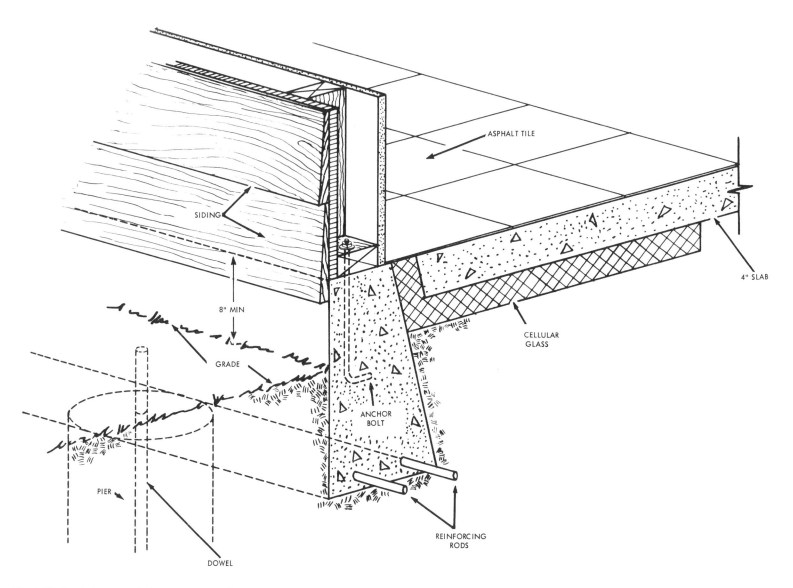

ASPHALT TILE

SIDING

4" SLAB

8" MIN

GRADE

CELLULAR GLASS

ANCHOR BOLT

PIER

DOWEL

REINFORCING RODS

Fig. 9-31. Grade beam and pier construction for frame superstructure on ground supported slab.

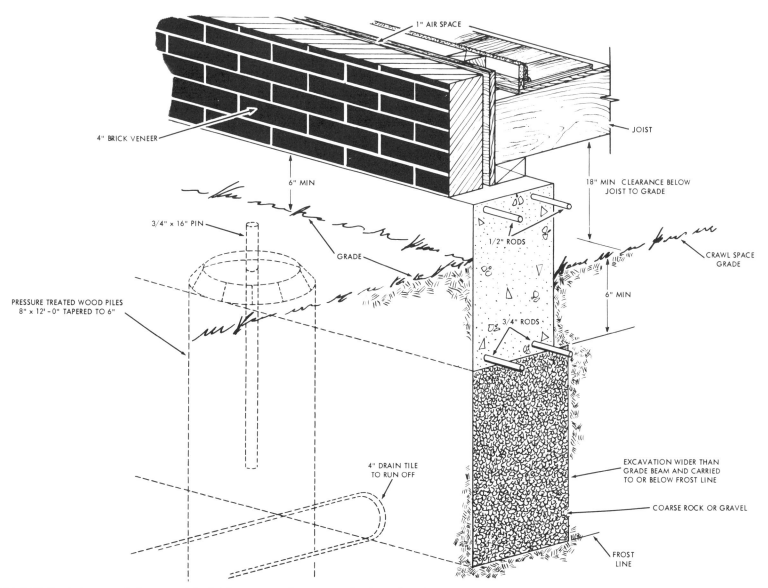

Fig. 9-32. Grade beam and pile support for brick veneer on frame superstructure where beam is not carried to frost line and soil retains ground moisture.

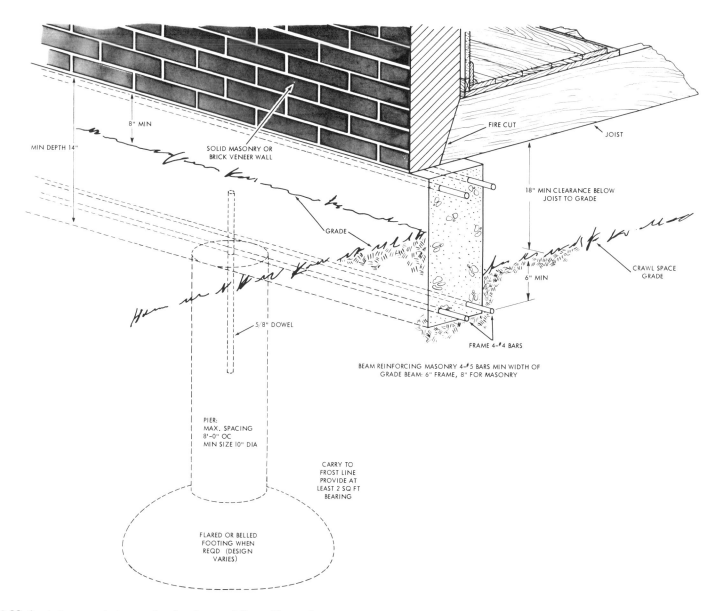

8" MIN

MIN DEPTH 14"

SOLID MASONRY OR
BRICK VENEER WALL

FIRE CUT

JOIST

18" MIN CLEARANCE BELOW
JOIST TO GRADE

GRADE

CRAWL SPACE
GRADE

6" MIN

5/8" DOWEL

FRAME 4-#4 BARS

BEAM REINFORCING MASONRY 4-#5 BARS MIN WIDTH OF
GRADE BEAM: 6" FRAME, 8" FOR MASONRY

PIER:
MAX. SPACING
8'-0" OC
MIN SIZE 10" DIA

CARRY TO
FROST LINE
PROVIDE AT
LEAST 2 SQ FT
BEARING

FLARED OR BELLED
FOOTING WHEN
REQD (DESIGN
VARIES)

Fig. 9-33. Grade beam and pier construction for wood floor with crawl space.

standards as required by that area's field office.

Secondary Foundations

Up to this point the discussion has centered around foundations and footings beneath the main building—no mention has been made of detached or semi-detached structures. Porches, garages, and other structures also require foundation planning.

Porches: A common concrete pier, in essence a footing, is used for porches which are exposed beneath the flooring, or for decks (floors) which extend from the house.

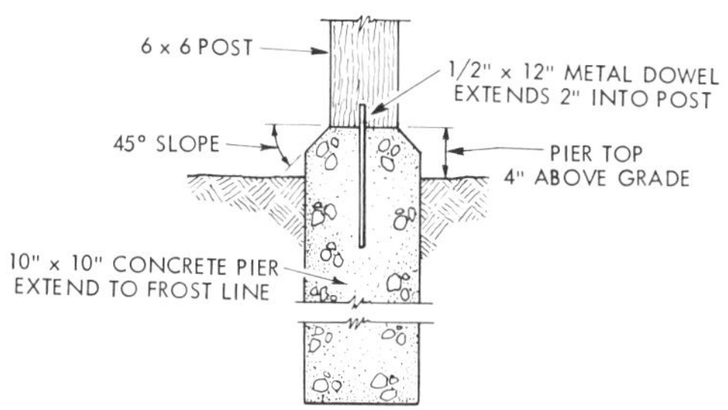

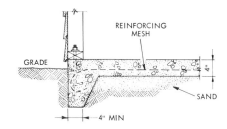

Fig. 9-34. A concrete pier is set into the ground to support a porch or decking column.

Fig. 9-34 shows a common concrete pier. If support for the porch or deck is made of wood, the top of the concrete pier should be sloped (preferably at a 45° angle) to shed

water. However, if a *lally column* (concrete-filled pipe) or a *pipe column* is used in place of a wood post, the top of the pier needs no slope. A metal *dowel,* similar to that shown in Fig. 9-34, should be imbedded in the pier and extended 2″ into the post to prevent movement.

Garages. The foundation wall for garages does not require footings to be carried to the frost line. Fig. 9-35 shows a common design for a detached garage foundation. Usually, the depth of the rim wall is between 12″ to 16″ below grade.

Fig. 9-35. A floating slab may be used for a detached garage foundation. The foundation is above the frost line.

Temporary Structures. Occasionally the home owner desires to erect a temporary structure such as a shed, small summer cottage, or cabin. A wooden post set on a flat rock for the footing is frequently used be-

cause of the economy and ease of construction (Fig. 9-36). The post should be thoroughly saturated with creosote or other preservative to retard deterioration and to guard against termites.

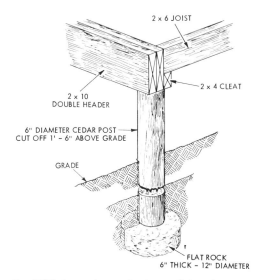

Fig. 9-36. A wooden post set on a flat rock may be used for temporary foundations. The posts must be treated to prevent termite damage and rot.

Step-By-Step Drawing Procedure: Footings and Foundation Walls

Drawing any footing and foundation wall is not complicated if the step-by-step procedure shown in Fig. 9-37 is followed.

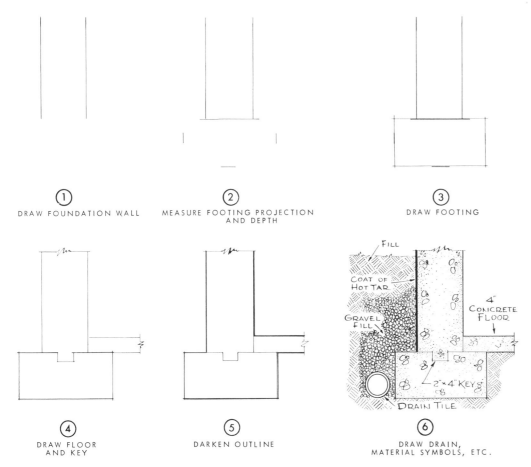

① DRAW FOUNDATION WALL

② MEASURE FOOTING PROJECTION AND DEPTH

③ DRAW FOOTING

④ DRAW FLOOR AND KEY

⑤ DARKEN OUTLINE

⑥ DRAW DRAIN, MATERIAL SYMBOLS, ETC.

FILL

COAT OF HOT TAR

GRAVEL FILL

4" CONCRETE FLOOR

2" x 4" KEY

DRAIN TILE

Fig. 9-37. Follow this step-by-step procedure in drawing a foundation wall.

Frame Construction

Nine out of ten homes built since 1940 in the United States may be categorized as *wood frame houses.* This statement may seem rash since every day we see houses made of brick, stucco, concrete asbestos shingle, stone, and imitation brick or stone. Regardless of the exterior covering, how-ever, these houses are in the general classification of wood frame construction if there is a wooden frame structure behind the covering.

Wood frame houses may be preferred **for** two basic reasons. First, frame construction is usually less expensive than solid masonry or steel. Secondly, wood frame construction, if properly designed and built, provides better insulation. A frame house is an extremely durable structure. Some of the oldest existing buildings in the United States (dating back to 1660) are of this type.

Framing may be placed in three categories: *balloon, western* or *platform,* and *braced.* The two framing systems which are most used are the balloon and western. The third type, the braced frame, has rarely been used in contemporary construction because of the size of many framing members and the cost of labor involved in erecting the structure.

Balloon Frame

The balloon frame (Fig. 9-38) is used in some areas for two-story houses. The exterior studs of this frame are continuous from sill to top plate. The second-floor joists rest on a $1'' \times 4''$ or $1'' \times 6''$ *ribbon* or *ledger board* recessed into the face of the studs. The advantage of balloon framing in a two-story structure is that a negligible amount of vertical shrinkage occurs between the sill and top plate. This makes it ideal for a masonry veneer.

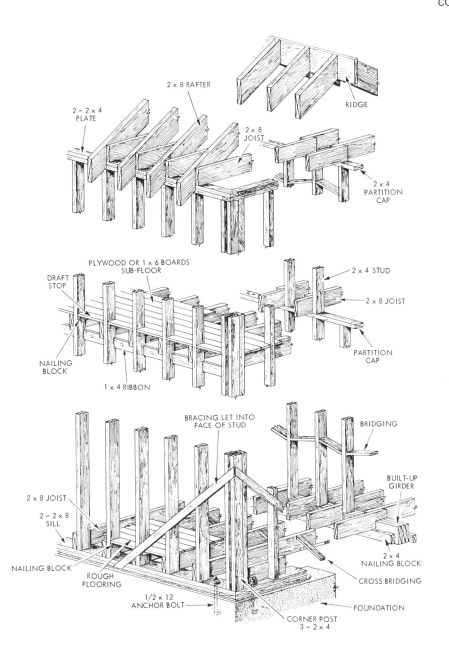

2 × 8 RAFTER

RIDGE

2 − 2 × 4
PLATE

2 × 8
JOIST

2 × 4
PARTITION
CAP

PLYWOOD OR 1 × 6 BOARDS
SUB-FLOOR

2 × 4 STUD

DRAFT
STOP

2 × 8 JOIST

NAILING
BLOCK

PARTITION
CAP

1 × 4 RIBBON

BRACING LET INTO
FACE OF STUD

BRIDGING

BUILT-UP
GIRDER

2 × 8 JOIST

2 − 2 × 8
SILL

NAILING BLOCK

ROUGH
FLOORING

2 × 4
NAILING BLOCK

CROSS BRIDGING

1/2 × 12
ANCHOR BOLT

FOUNDATION

CORNER POST
3 − 2 × 4

Fig. 9-38. Balloon Framing. Balloon framing is
sometimes used for two-story and masonry veneer
houses. Note that the studs are continuous between
floors: shrinkage is at a minimum.

Western or Platform Frame

The western or platform frame is comparable to a layer cake, where one layer or level is placed on the other. Each level is independent: studding is separate for each level or floor. This type of framing is preferred for one-story buildings, although it is also used for multilevel structures and is perhaps the most widely used for residential construction. The western frame permits uniform shrinkage and settlement on the outside and inside of the walls.

Fig. 9-39 shows a typical western framed house. Note that the studs extend through the height of one story *only,* and rest on the *sole* which is nailed to the top of the rough floor. The second floor joists are carried on a double $2'' \times 4''$ *girt* (sometimes called a *cap plate*) which is placed at the top of the first floor studding. On the second floor, a *header* (the same size as the second floor joists) is carried around the structure. At the first floor level the header rests on a sill which is fastened to the masonry foundation walls.

Braced Frame

Many of the oldest frame structures, dating back to colonial times, use braced frame construction. Originally, this type of construction was brought from Europe. The modern adaptation of the braced frame type of construction is shown in Fig. 9-40. The braced frame, as the name implies, is a very rigid construction. Stud walls extend only

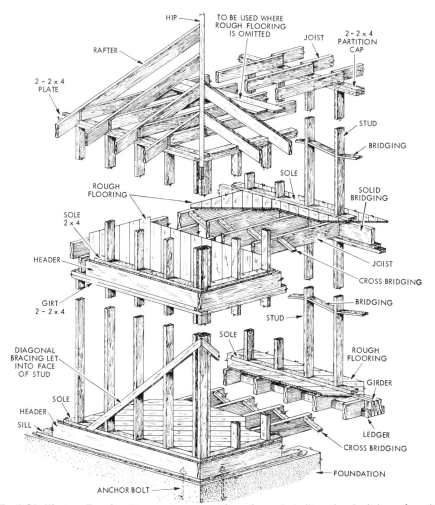

Fig. 9-39. Western Framing. The western or platform frame is built on levels; it is preferred for one-story buildings. Note that studs are **not** continuous between floors: shrinkage is equalized.

between floors and are topped by a $4'' \times 4''$ or a $4'' \times 6''$ girt (modern design uses a false girt of two $2'' \times 4\mathrm{s}''$). The girt forms a sill for the joists. Corner posts, girts, sills, and girders are heavier than those used in either the balloon or western type of fram-

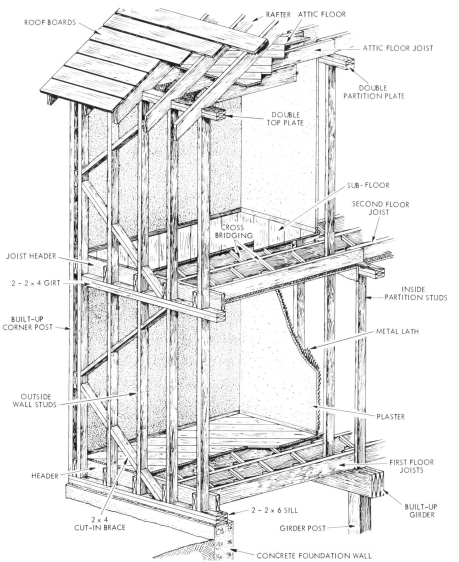

Fig. 9-40. Braced Framing. Braced frame construction is extremely rigid but it is seldom used because of the size of the framing members and the cost involved. This modified braced framing is very satisfactory where strong winds are encountered. Notice the girt at the second floor.

ing. Modern braced framing uses a **built-up post, sill,** and **girder.** These were solid in older designs.

24″ Spacing System

Residential builders are now using a framing system completely based on a 24″ module. By spacing wall studs, floor joists, ceiling joists, and roof rafters or trusses on 24″ centers, contractors are able to use less lumber and labor. Framing on 24″ centers is not new, because many aspects of this principle have been approved by major building codes throughout the years. The basic idea of the 24″ spacing system is the *alignment of all framing members:* trusses or rafters, studs and joists. Fig. 9-41 shows the in-line or aligned principle of framing. As each stud is placed in line with each joist, and each roof truss placed in line with each stud and then covered with a plywood facing, the framework becomes a rigid unit. By using the 24″ module, a more effective utilization of materials and more rapid erection can be accomplished over the traditional 16″ framing system or combination 16″ and 24″ systems.

Successful field tests have shown that the 24″ module in single wall construction can be used as efficiently and safely on two-story buildings as on single level structure. In the past, builders have traditionally used double wall construction in residential building. Single wall construction uses one layer of ½″ (minimum thickness) of exterior type plywood over the stud super-

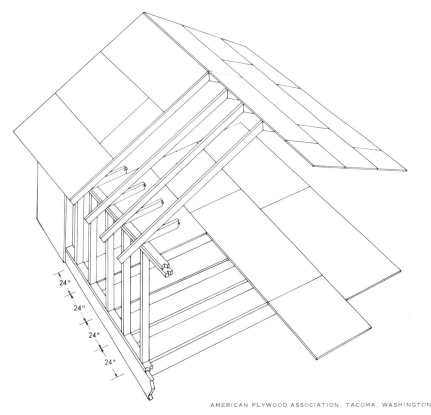

Fig. 9-41. The 24″ O.C. aligned framing system produces a series of in-line frames that use the framing members and plywood skin to the best advantage.

structure. The ½″ plywood serves as both sheathing and siding. Double wall construction uses a layer of sheathing applied to the stud superstructure and then a layer of plywood or wood siding.

The following paragraphs explain floor and wall construction using the aligned 24″ module.

Floors. A layer of ¾″ T&G (tongue and groove) plywood is placed over joists spaced on 24″ centers. The plywood floor is nail-glued to the joists. Using glue increases the stiffness of the floor system. Gluing the sub-floor to the joists eliminates the squeaky floor problem since no nails can become loose. The joists, rather than being lapped at the girder or bearing wall are placed in line. Placing the joists in line simplifies application of the plywood sub-floor.

Walls. Using 24″ O.C. stud spacing can result in a saving if windows and doors are placed on the module. Fig. 9-42 illustrates the location of a window on the module. When plywood is used as a covering material *without* sheathing, the thickness must be a minimum of ½″ and of exterior type. The ½″ plywood serves as both sheathing and siding.

By placing doors and windows on 24″ module, an average 17% can be saved on framing materials in a 6′ wall section containing a window.

Cantilever

The cantilever may be defined as a member that is not supported at one end. The principle of the cantilever is similar to a combination of the fulcrum and counterweight. Fig. 9-43 illustrates this concept. The weights on either side of the fulcrum are unequal, but the member is kept from moving since the load imposed on one side is heavier than the other. When the side of the member that carries the heavier load is firmly anchored, the projecting member may then be subjected to a change in forces without damage to the anchoring elements on the heavy side of the fulcrum. Heavy weights and/or extreme lengths that must be carried by the cantilevered member are difficult to calculate. However, the small

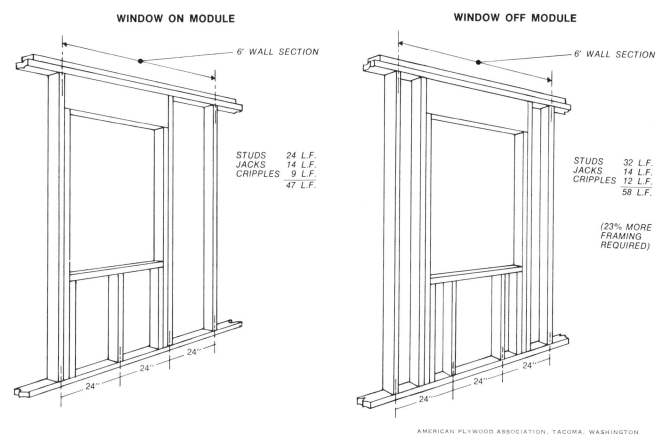

Fig. 9-42. Windows and doors placed on the module will reduce the need for cripples and double studs.

cantilevered overhang of a roof, bay window, or small balcony may be successfully designed by the student. For example, some buildings are constructed so the second floor or level projects over the first floor or level, as in the case of the split-level house.

If the second floor joists are parallel to the overhang dimension, the joists may be extended to the length of the projection. If, however, the joists are perpendicular to the overhang dimension, short joists may be cantilevered (see Fig. 9-44) from a double

joist. Note that the short joists must be notched for a $2'' \times 4''$ ledger strip nailed to the double joist. The same method of cantilevering is used for bay windows, as well as for the long overhang on gable ends of roofs.

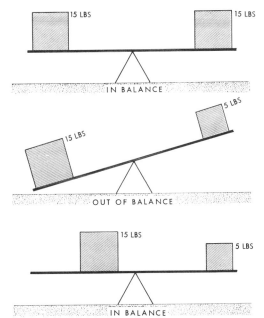

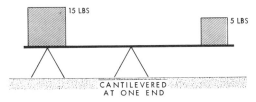

Fig. 9-43. The cantilever is a combination of the fulcrum and counter balance.

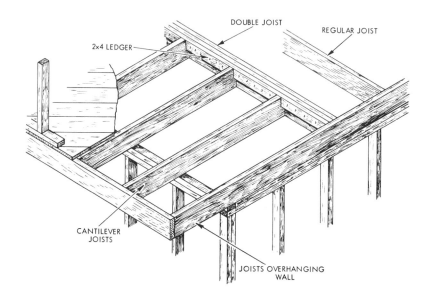

Fig. 9-44. Where regular joists do not extend over the wall, short cantilevered joists may be used. Cantilever joists rest on the wall plate and are fastened to a double joist and ledger.

Floor Support

Beams and Girders

Floor joists require some type of support to adequately carry the load created by the weight of the interior partitions, floors, and roof. Wide flange beams, S-beams, or wood girders are usually placed under the first floor joists for this purpose. The beam or wood girder is normally supported every 8′ to 12′ by a pipe column, wood post, or S-beam column. See Fig. 9-45.

Joists

Floors are supported by joists placed on edge and spaced 12″, 16″, or 24″ *on center* (abbreviated OC or O.C.). ("On center" is measured from the center of one member to the center of another.) The usual and most common joist spacing is 16″ O.C. The joists are supported at the outer ends by a sill bolted to a masonry wall. When openings are cut in the floor framing for a fireplace, chimney, stairs, etc., the joists must be doubled around these openings to maintain the structural value. Fig. 9-46 illustrates this practice. Those joists which are doubled and run parallel to the regular joists are commonly referred to as *double trimmers*. Those joists doubled and run perpendicular to the regular joists are usually called *headers*.

Joists when framed in the conventional manner are lapped over a girder, beam or

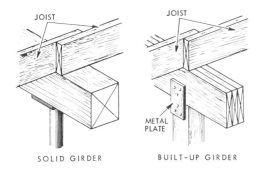

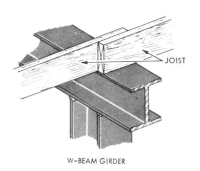

Fig. **9-46.** Floor joists should be doubled around openings.

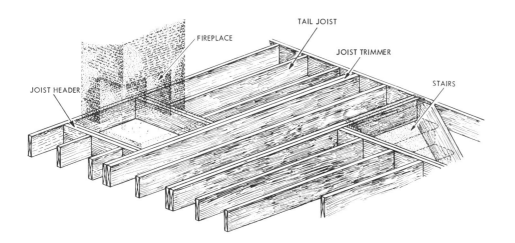

Fig. **9-45.** Various supports are used for the beams and girders under the floor joists.

load bearing wall. Some contractors cantilever joists rather than lapping. The cantilever principle offers a saving because less non-standard lengths of lumber is used. A house having a 30′ depth could be spanned by 2 joists 18′ and 12′ in length, rather than two 15′ lengths cut from a standard 16 footer. If a continuous joist were to span the 30′ depth with a girder located midway, less deflection would occur than with 2 joists lapped over the girder. Because of the principle of less deflection from a continuous member, in most cases a 2″ *smaller* joist could be used. For example, a 28′ span, 2″ × 8″s could be used, rather than 2″ × 10″s under the normal load with a girder placed in the middle. The principle of cantilevering is illustrated in Fig. 9-47. The joint must occur on either side of the support member. The angle joint is reinforced by the stressed skin action of the plywood sub-flooring.

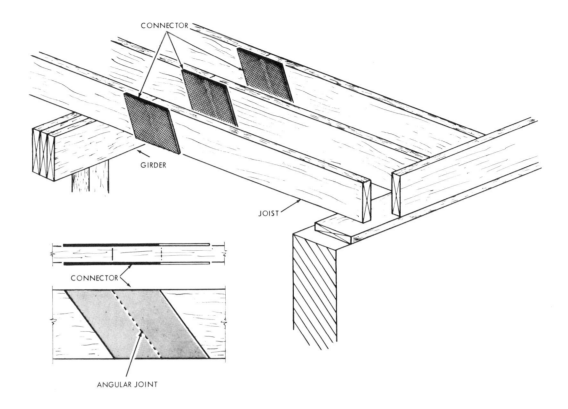

CONNECTOR

GIRDER

JOIST

CONNECTOR

ANGULAR JOINT

Fig. 9-47. Rather than lapping joists, they may be spliced with metal connectors.

Balconies whose framing members are parallel to the building's floor joists may be framed by using ledger strips. See Fig. 9-48. The 2″ × 4″ ledger strips (4′ long) are flush with the top of the floor joist. If 2″ × 12″ floor joists are used, the balcony framing is 2″ × 8″. If 2″ × 10″ floor joists, 2″ × 6″ balcony framing will be required. Solid bridging is placed between each of the cantilevered joists to prevent twisting.

Joist Bridging

All floor joists should be braced with bridging. (Refer to Fig. 9-39.) Bridging may take the form of: (1) cross bridging with 1″ × 2″, 2″ × 2″, or 2″ × 4″ pieces of wood (Fig. 9-49, top left); (2) solid bridging the same size as the joists (Fig. 9-49, top right); or (3) metal cross bridging (Fig. 9-49, bottom). Wood cross bridging is nailed *only* to the top edge of the joist prior to laying the sub-floor. After the sub-floor has been laid, the bottom may then be nailed to the opposite joist. Solid wood bridging and metal cross bridging is placed between the joists *after* the sub-floor has been laid. This prevents settlement strain.

Bridging helps maintain the joists in an upright position and stiffens the floor to eliminate movement. It also strengthens the floor by distributing the load over a large

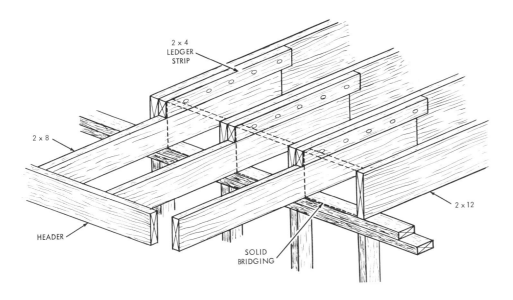

2 x 4
LEDGER
STRIP

2 x 8

HEADER

SOLID
BRIDGING

2 x 12

Fig. 9-48. A short balcony can be framed by cantilevering the balcony joists.

WOOD CROSS
BRIDGING IS LEFT FREE AT
THE BOTTOM UNTIL THE SUB-
FLOOR IS LAID.

SOLID WOOD
BRIDGING IS
ADDED AFTER THE
SUB-FLOOR IS LAID

METAL CROSS
BRIDGING IS
ADDED AFTER THE
SUB-FLOOR IS LAID.

Fig. 9-49. Various types of bridging are used to strengthen floors and distribute the load.

area. To be most effective, the rows of bridging should run in a straight line across the floor. If the joist span does not exceed 14′, one row of bridging is sufficient. Any span greater than 14′ necessitates two rows of bridging. The rows of bridging are normally placed 7′ apart.

Outside Walls

Outside or exterior walls are usually formed of 2″ × 4″ studs spaced 16″ O.C. Since the outside walls bear a large amount (sometimes all) of the weight of the house, care should be exercised in their design and construction. Outside walls are referred to as load bearing walls. As with the case with floors, all openings should be doubled.

Stud Bracing

Sometimes light wooden braces are *"let into"* (notched into) the outside wall studs of balloon and western type framing. (Refer to Figs. 9-38 and 9-39.) Frequently, however, metal cross bridging, as shown in Fig. 9-50, is used rather than *inlet* (recessed) bracing. This type of bracing is installed rapidly and eliminates all hand work that would ordinarily be involved. Metal cross bridging may be used as bracing in both the western and balloon type framing.

Many building codes permit the use of

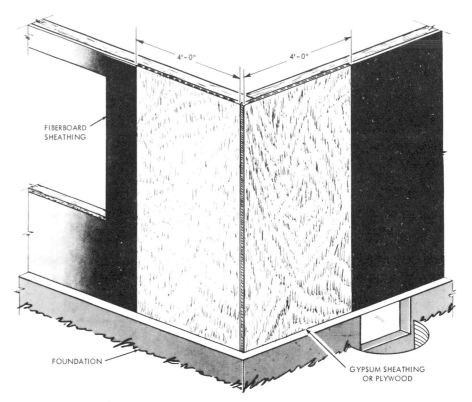

Fig. 9-51. Sheathing at the corners of a building is either gypsum or plywood when the corner studs are not braced.

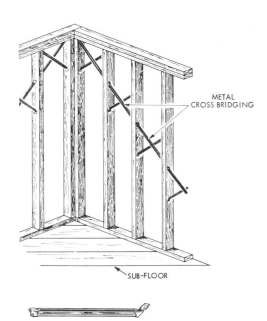

Fig. 9-50. Metal cross bridging may be used in place of bracing inlet into the face of the studs.

gypsum or plywood sheathing to be used at each corner of the structure. The use of plywood or gypsum sheathing replaces the necessity for bracing inlet into the face of the stud or metal cross bridging. Fig. 9-51 shows a corner braced with gypsum or plywood sheets. Because of the wood crossbands, plywood has greater shear strength than does fiber insulating board sheathing.

Sheathing

When a frame building is erected, it is customary to first cover the outside faces of the stud wall with wood sheathing, fabricated fiberboard, or plywood. Sheathing adds an extra protective surface; serves as an insulating material; strengthens the structure; and, when wood sheathing or plywood is used, forms a nailing base for ex-

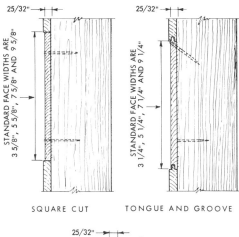

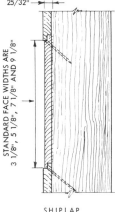

Fig. 9-52. Three basic types of sheathing edges are used for walls, sub-floors, and roofs.

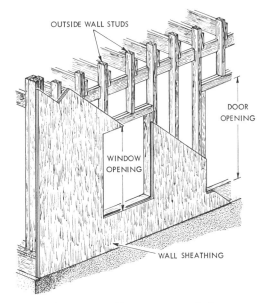

Fig. 9-53. Wall sheathing may be applied diagonally (45°) to increase the strength of the framing.

terior finishing materials. Wood sheathing may have edges that are square, tongue and grooved, or shiplapped. See Fig. 9-52. By placing wood sheathing at a 45° angle, as in Fig. 9-53, increased strength may be obtained in the framing.

Contractors in many areas do not use wood sheathing because of the increased expense for material and labor. To reduce the cost of erection, many now use fabricated fiberboard (composition board) or plywood sheathing. Fiberboard or plywood sheathing may be placed vertically or horizontally. The thickness of fiberboard is $25/32''$; width, 4'-0"; and lengths, 6'-0", 7'-0", 8'-0", and 9'-0". Any exterior siding materials placed over the fiberboard must be nailed to the studs or to special *furring strips* since this type of sheathing does not provide sufficient anchorage for nails. The

usual thickness of plywood sheathing is either ½" or ⅝"; width, 4'-0"; length, 8'-0". If the studs are 16 inches O.C., ½" plywood may be used; if the studs are 24" O.C., ⅝" may be used. Fiberboard and plywood are both more advantageous than wood sheathing because the wall units tend to be stronger and considerably more airtight.

The roof rafters and floor joists are covered in the same manner as the exterior walls, with *either* 1" × 6" wood sheathing or plywood.

Building Paper

Building paper is placed over the sheathing material to seal all joints and cracks from drafts. Building paper is not a vapor or moisture barrier. *If waterproof paper were used, this would prevent the escape of moisture on the inside of the wall in cold weather.*

The wall must breathe to prevent condensation. Polyethylene film or a similar type plastic film may be placed around window and door openings prior to setting the frames to insure a weather-tight seal.

Siding

The outside walls are finished with shingles, siding, plywood, stucco, etc. Shingles may be either wood (usually cedar) or cement asbestos. Wood shingles are often impregnated with creosote to prevent decay. The width of wood shingles vary, but they are usually 16" or 18" long. Depending

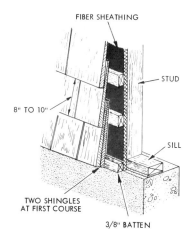

Fig. 9-54. Wood shingles on a frame wall are laid 8″ to 10″ to weather.

upon the desired effect, wood shingles or panels may be laid with either 8″ or 10″ *to the weather* (amount exposed). The overlap prevents wind, rain, or snow from entering. Fig. 9-54 shows a section through an exterior wall covered with wood shingles. The first course of shingles directly above the foundation is doubled and at the butt end is backed by a ⅜″ *batten*.

For greater economy in building construction, wood shingles are now available in panel form in 4′ or 8′ lengths. Fig. 9-55 illustrates three different types of shingle panels. These are put up just as siding is installed over a sheathed surface.

Siding is usually laid horizontally, but if a tight fit is possible (such as the tongue and groove joint) a vertical lay may be used. Board and batten or board on board, as in Fig. 9-56, is also used vertically. Alu-

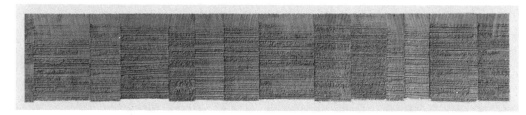

SHAKERTOWN CORP., CLEVELAND, OHIO

Fig. 9-55. Shingle panels in 4′ and 8′ lengths save time in applying an exterior shingle finish.

Fig. 9-56. Siding may be applied vertically with battens over joints or boards on boards.

BOARD AND BATTEN   BOARD ON BOARD

minum siding also comes in either horizontal or vertical panels.

Exterior type plywood panels with variously textured surfaces may be chosen in place of siding. The long dimension of these panels will be cut (routed) in a shiplap joint to create a continuous pattern. These plywood sheets come in standard 4′ widths, with either 8′ or 10′ lengths. They run both vertically and horizontally. Plywood panels may be joined with a special vinyl weatherproof paint.

Insulation

Insulation is used to retard or stop the flow of heat, from both inside and outside the building. In addition, insulation acts as a sound barrier within partitions and between floors. Regardless of the climate, insulation is an important factor for the ultimate comfort of the occupants. Most insulative materials are light in weight and easily installed during construction. All forms of insulation contain minute air spaces which provide resistance to the flow of heat lost or gained by conduction. Insulation in batt or blanket form frequently has one of its surfaces covered with a metallic foil which reflects radiant heat. Even though building materials offer some resistance to heat transmission, insulation must be added to prevent heat loss or heat gain.

All insulation, because of the air spaces it contains, resists the flow of heat. Its ability to resist heat flow is generally referred to as an "R" factor. The R factor for any

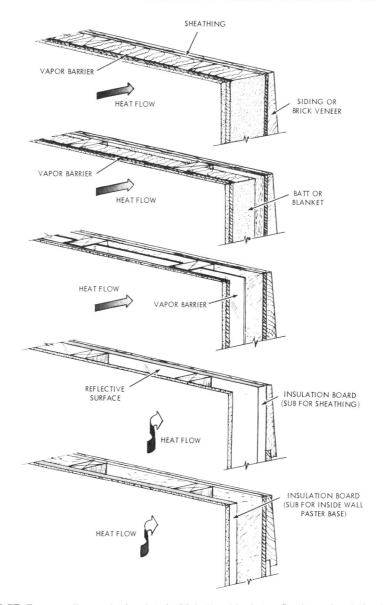

Fig. 9-57. Frame walls may be insulated with batt or blanket, reflective or insulation board.

insulative material depends upon: (1) thickness, (2) density, and (3) conductivity. When specifying insulation for walls, floors and ceilings, the designer must take into account the R factor, the thickness of insulation, and the outside temperature.

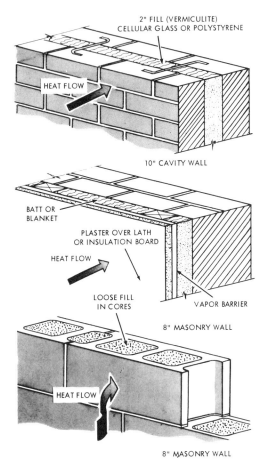

Fig. 9-58. Masonry walls may be insulated with loose fill and batt or blanket insulation.

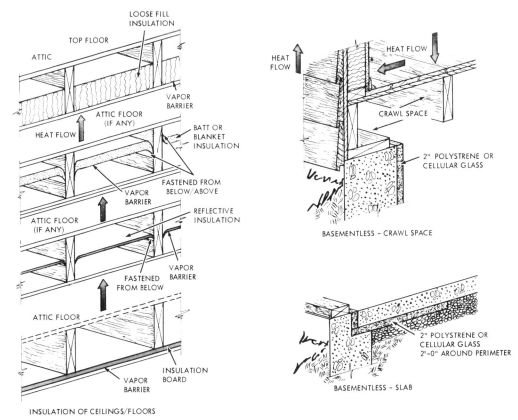

Fig. 9-59. Ceilings and floors may be insulated with loose fill, batts or blankets, reflective or insulation board, and basementless floor areas may be insulated with rigid foam insulation.

The more common types of insulation used are described below and are shown in Figs. 9-57, 9-58, and 9-59.

1. *Loose Fill.* Loose fill insulation can be divided into 2 categories: (1) fibrous and (2) granular, and is either poured directly from the bag, blown by machine, or packed by hand. Fibrous insulation is made from mineral wool (rock, glass, or slag) or vegetable fiber (wood). Granular insulation is usually mineral (perlite or vermiculite) or vegetable matter (cork).

2. *Batt or Blanket.* Blanket insulation is manufactured in rolls 15″ or 23″ wide and

in varying thicknesses. Usually blankets are made of mineral wool, processed vegetable or animal fibers (wood, cotton, marine plants and animal hair) and covered on one side with waterproof paper. The waterproof paper serves as a vapor barrier. Batts are similar to blankets only they are 48″ in length and are made for installation between studs. Normally one of the paper surfaces may be coated with aluminum foil. Blanket or batt insulation is nailed or stapled to the superstructure.

3. *Insulation Board.* Structural insulation board is generally made from wood or cane fibers formed into large sheets. It may be used as wall sheathing, insulating roof decking, roof insulation board, shingle backers, or as a plaster base.

4. *Reflective Insulation.* Reflective insulation is usually an aluminum foil surfaced material. To achieve its maximum effectiveness, this type of insulation depends on the thickness of air space and temperature differences. The foiled surface must be exposed to a ¾″ minimum air space. Some reflective insulation is designed to be used by itself, but most generally it is adhered to batts, blankets or insulating board. When used in conjunction with other insulative materials, it serves as a vapor barrier. The reflective surface is placed toward the warm side of the structure, thus preventing moisture from reaching the insulation.

5. *Foam.* "Foamed" insulation is a liquid resin that when mixed with a catalytic agent will foam, fill all spaces and ultimately harden. Because of its "foam" char-

acter, it has a closed cellular structure that results in an excellent insulating material.

6. *Sprayed-on.* This type of insulation is sprayed in hard-to-reach areas. Fibrous or mineral materials are mixed with adhesive and sprayed in place. The adhesive causes the particles to adhere to each other as well as the surface.

The following rules of thumb can be applied when specifying insulation:

1. 6″—attic ceilings
2. 3″—exterior walls (batt or blanket)
3. 4″—exterior walls (fill)
4. 4″-6″—attic floors (batt, blanket or loose fill)
5. 2″-3″—first floors if electirc heat is used.

To prevent moisture from condensing, some form of ventilation must be provided. In order that insulation may serve its intended purpose, attics, roofs and crawl spaces must be ventilated through the use of roof vents, ridge vents, gable louvers, and crawl space vents to remove surplus moisture. To prevent condensation, 4 sq. ft. of free area should be provided for each 1,000 sq. ft. of attic floor area and 1 sq. ft. of net free area for each 150 sq. ft. of crawl space.

Loose fill, batt or blanket, insulation board, and reflective insulation may be used in walls, ceilings and floors. The selection of one type of insulation as opposed to another is dependent upon the amount needed to achieve a specific R value, the cost of labor and material and the purpose for which the building is to be used.

Any insulation is of little value unless

the heat transmission through windows and doors is retarded. To achieve its maximum effectiveness, windows should be double glazed or equipped with a tight fitting storm sash. Doors should be weather stripped.

Partitions

Partitions (interior walls) within the structure are usually fabricated from 2″ × 4″ studs, with either lath and plaster or gypsum board (drywall) covering the framing members. These partitions may be either *bearing* or *non-bearing*. Bearing partitions, like the outside walls, carry the load of the joists and the wall of the floor above. A non-bearing partition forms the walls of a room but does not carry any load. The top and bottom (sole and top plate) of these walls have 2 × 4's spiked into them. When a partition runs parallel to a floor joist, those joists directly under the wall should be doubled to carry the increased load placed on that joist. This is also true in the case of heavy equipment or fixtures (such as the bathtub).

Bearing Partitions

Any openings designed in a bearing partition (or in a bearing wall) should (as in the case of floor joists) be doubled at the sides, top and bottom to increase the strength of the framing members which have been cut. (Fig. 9-60 shows an opening for a window and door in a bearing wall.)

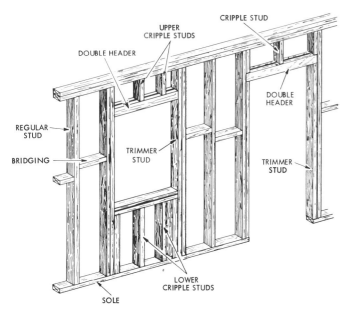

Fig. 9-60. Members around openings in frame walls are usually doubled.

In recent years emphasis has been placed on subdividing the basement into separate rooms. In this case, a bearing partition, usually masonry, may replace the post and girder and serve as the main dividing member. A bearing partition in the basement of either concrete block or 2″ × 6″ studs with solid bridging will adequately carry the imposed load. It is necessary that a footing be placed under this wall.

2″ × 12″ Header System

Savings in the cost of construction can be achieved by designing headers over openings in interior and exterior walls, using the 2″ × 12″ system. See Fig. 9-61. The conventional header over a standard 3′-0″ door uses two 2″ × 4″s placed on edge with a plywood spacer for the header and cripple studs between the header and the plate. Two 2″ × 12″s with a ½″ plywood filler can replace this conventional method of framing. Even though two 2″ × 12″s can span 13′-0″

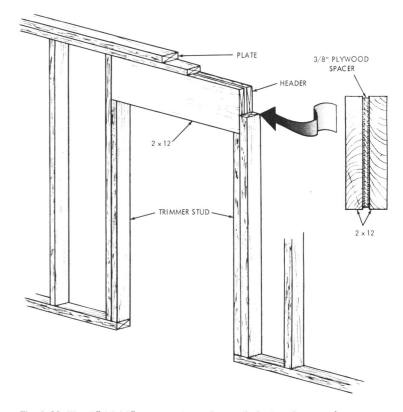

Fig. 9-61. The 2″ × 12″ system above doors eliminates the use of cripple studs above the door header.

TABLE 9-4
SPANS FOR HEADERS

HEADER SIZE (ON EDGE)	2 FLOORS CEILING ROOF	1 FLOOR CEILING ROOF	CEILING ROOF
2 - 2 × 4	2'	3'	4'
2 - 2 × 6	4'	5'	6'
2 - 2 × 8	6'	7'	8'
2 - 2 × 10	7'	8'	10'
2 - 2 × 12	8'	9'	12'

(see Table 9-4) when placed on edge, many contractors are using the 2″ × 12″ system for all openings because of the ultimate economy. Differences in lumber sizes may necessitate a filler strip between top of the header and the top of the plate. Ordinarily the bottom of the 2″ × 12″ header will give the proper door opening size for the standard 6′-8″ head height dimension for doors and windows.

Stack Walls

In many areas the local building code requires that walls housing the soil pipe (waste pipe) be constructed of 2″ × 6″ or 2″ × 8″ studs. This allows adequate space for the pipe. This wall is commonly referred to as a *stack wall* or *stack partition*. Before designing a stack wall check the local building code to determine the type and size soil pipe required.

Closet Walls

Closets which have a common wall may

be made of 2″ × 4′″ studs positioned so the 4″ dimension is parallel to the plaster or drywall rather than perpendicular. This will produce a thinner wall.

Interior Wall Finishes

In recent years interior wall finishes have become more diversified. Originally, plaster was considered as the main interior finishing material; however, drywall covering has been on a steady increase. Plaster is applied to a base of metal lath, rock lath, gypsum, or fiberboard. (Wood lath has all but been discontinued. This is due primarily to the fire hazard and time required for installation.) Fig. 9-62 illustrates two different types of lathing with plaster applications. *Sheet lath* is shown in Fig. 9-62 (top left) with a scratch coat (rough base) and a finish coat of plaster. Each piece of sheet lath has a series of holes so that when the scratch coat is applied, the plaster is forced into the holes, thereby bonding it to the lath. Sheet lath is either ⅜″ or ½″ thick. *Wire lath,* shown in Fig. 9-62 (bottom right), serves the same function as sheet lath, only the wire lath becomes an integral part of the plaster. The main disadvantage of plaster is that it requires a drying period which may halt construction. Drywall is easier and faster to work with. However, it is not considered to be as soundproof or as durable.

There are many different kinds of drywall construction materials, but the type most widely used is *gypsum board*. Gypsum board comes in standard 4′-0″ × 8′-0″

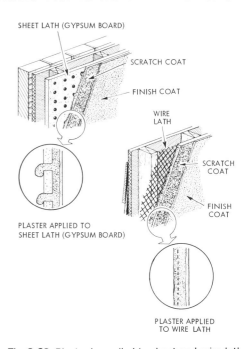

Fig. 9-62. Plaster is applied to sheet and wire lath.

sheets with thicknesses of ⅜″, ½″, or ⅝″ and is nailed directly to the studs. Gypsum board joints are cemented and covered with a paper tape. When the joints have thoroughly dried, they are sanded smooth and flush. Gypsum board has the appearance of a plastered wall, yet is less expensive.

Drywall construction may also use insulating board, manufactured in a wide variety of shapes and sizes, in place of plaster and sheetrock. Sometimes regular rigid insulation (wallboard) is used beneath the insulating board. Plywood, V-grooved boards, hardboard paneling, plastic laminates (these are available in wood grain and solid colors), planks, and other forms of wood are used for decorative effects.

Noise Control

As the population increases and conditions become more crowded, privacy in all forms becomes more important. Man is becoming more concerned with the state of his environment as technology advances. One of the five major pollution problems facing man today is that of noise pollution. Each person with normal hearing is subjected constantly to a volley of sounds in his home and at his place of work. It has been estimated that noise in the home is the source of 25 percent of the annoying sounds that Americans hear. Noise is recognized as a definite contributing factor to fatigue, irritation, and even to the impairment of an individual's hearing. Advancements in construction technology have attempted, in part, to control noise as it travels through the air and through solid materials.

Noise is caused by transmission or reverberation. For instance, sounds originating outside of a structure pass through windows, doors and walls and then are reflected from the wall or ceiling. The reflected sound added to the original, results in a sound of increased intensity. The reflected sounds reverberating from walls and floors contribute appreciably to audio discomfort. Reduction of sounds can be accomplished if there are sufficient barriers in the structure to block their transmission and absorbers to soak up the noise and prevent reverberation. Conventional building materials as concrete, glass, wood and hard plaster are poor acoustical materials.

In residential planning, noise control can be accomplished by locating the house as far from the street as possible. Trees, tall shrubbery, tight fences, and privacy screens (See Fig. 9-63) block much of the noise from outside the home. Floor plans having an L, U, or H shape are effective in reducing a portion of noise pollution. These types of plans can provide an aisle of outdoor privacy in the center of the house.

Areas within the house which lend themselves to noisy activities should be grouped together and separated from the quiet zones. This applies to the location of rooms in relation to the outside, as well as their proximity within the floor plan.

Noise leaks within a building can be sealed by the use of double glazing, storm sashes and tight fitting weather stripping around doors and windows. Heavier doors, such as solid core, retard sound transmission more efficiently than thin doors. Fixed sashes reduce unwanted sounds from the outside. Resilient flooring materials eliminate sounds at their source. Surfaces that are carpeted or have resilient floor coverings virtually eliminate sound. Quiet-acting plumbing, wrapped or insulated drain pipes,

Fig. 9-63. Unwanted outside noise may be stopped by different methods.

heating and cooling equipment, and electrical motors resting on sound-absorbing cushions do much to abate noise.

Noises may be absorbed within the room by the use of acoustical plaster, tile, or sound deadening boards. Most building materials are ineffective in their ability to absorb sound. Porous surfaces will absorb more noise than hard, dense surfaces.

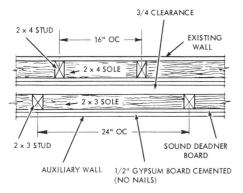

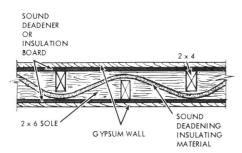

Fig. 9-64. These two methods may be used to soundproof walls.

Fireplaces, walls, storage walls, bookcases, closets, stairwells and bathrooms act as buffers against noise. Walls may be especially designed to absorb sound. This is accomplished by staggering studs within a wall or by having two independent walls with space and sound insulation between.

Fig. 9-64 shows how new and existing walls can be made sound resistant. Floors above noisy areas are excellent sound transmitters unless they are properly treated. Insulation between joists will retard the transmission of sound. Utilization of sound insulation between the finish and sub-floor, as well as between joists, will be more effective than batt insulation alone.

Fig. 9-65 shows two methods of sound proofing floors. Special patented metal and rubber spring clips are available that allow a ceiling or wall to be constructed away from framing members in order to make them resistant to sound transmission. Fig. 9-66 illustrates a ceiling clip holding the ceiling away from the joists. Any suspended ceiling will retard sound movement through a floor. Air passages left open because of poor wall closings at the floor and ceiling, pipe openings, or mounting of electrical fixtures back to back will have the same effect as a hole in the wall unless proper sound deadening precautions are taken.

Wood Trim

On plastered walls, wood trim, such as baseboards, window casings, door frames, and moldings, are fastened to a *nailing*

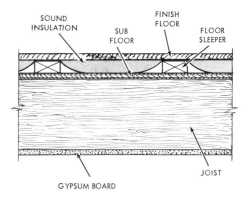

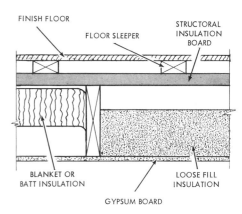

Fig. 9-65. Adequate insulation produces a sound barrier that impedes sound passage through floors.

ground (Fig. 9-67). The trim conceals the joint between the plaster and nailing ground to give a finished appearance. Mill work companies and building supply companies have catalogs showing various shapes of trim, base, shoe, etc. The nailing ground is the same thickness as the plaster and is

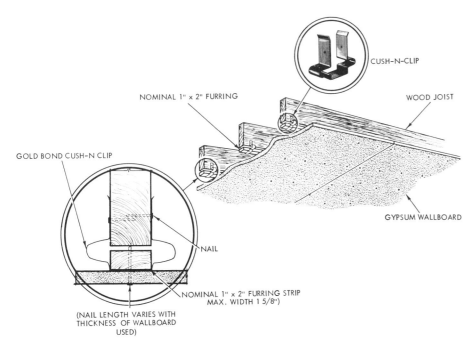

Fig. 9-66. Clips and furring strips are used in "floating" coiling construction. Floating wall construction is similar. The clips are made of spring steel which causes them to spring away from the joists after nailing. Drywall wood screws may also be used.

Fig. 9-67. A nailing ground serves as an anchor for the trim. (It also serves to indicate the desired thickness of the plaster.)

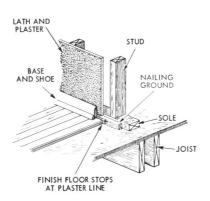

fastened to the framing member, i.e., a stud or joist. Drywall construction does not require the use of nailing grounds since there is relatively little danger of cracking.

Finish Floor

A wood *finish floor* is laid after the plaster is dry or the *taping* on the drywall has been sanded. To insure a soundproofing quality to floors and to prevent heat loss, sometimes the finished floor is nailed to *furring strips* placed 16″ O.C. over the sub-flooring which has been previously covered with building paper. See Fig. 9-68. This serves as a good base for the finish flooring. The finished flooring, however, is usually nailed directly to the sub-flooring that has been covered

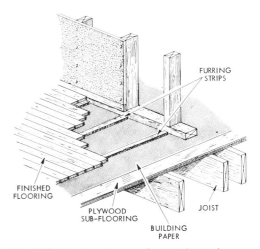

Fig. 9-68. Furring strips are frequently used beneath the finish floor.

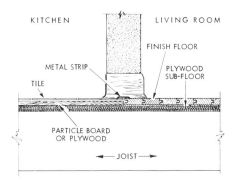

Fig. 9-69. Particle board or plywood is used beneath linoleum or tile floors to maintain the same level as a wood finished floor.

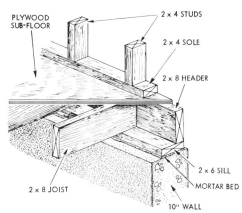

Fig. 9-70. Box sill construction is commonly used for western framing. Note: joists and headers are spiked to the sill; the flooring, sole, and studs are spiked to the joists and headers.

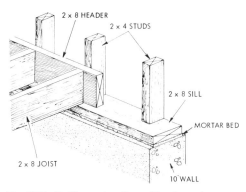

Fig. 9-71. T-sill construction without a sole beneath the studs is used for balloon framing. Note: joists and studs bear directly on the sill.

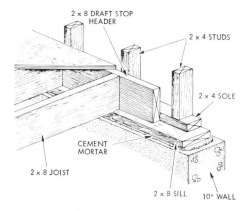

Fig. 9-72. T-sill construction with a sole beneath the studs is also used for balloon framing. Note: joists bear directly on the sill; studs on the sole.

with building paper. All finish flooring and floor boards are tongue and grooved and are *blind nailed* (nail diven diagonally in the upper angle formed by the tongue). Finish flooring varies in thickness from ⅜″ to 13⁄16″ and in width from 1¼″ to 3¼″.

Asphalt, rubber, or vinyl tile may be used in place of wood finish flooring. *Particle board* (or plywood) then must be placed over the sub-floor (see Fig. 9-69) to create the same thickness where tile is used (kitchen, bathroom, etc.), as where wood flooring is used (living room, halls, etc.).

Sills

It would seem logical to discuss sill construction immediately following footings and foundations since the sill is the first segment of framing to be constructed. The sill extends around the perimeter of the founda-tion and provides a base for framing members. Sills, however, cannot be intelligently discussed without some knowledge of basic types of framing and their specific purposes.

Box Sills

Western framing commonly uses the *box sill* (Fig. 9-70). This type of sill consists of a 2″ × 6″ sill plate anchored to the foundation to support the joists and headers. The joists and headers are then spiked to the sill. Some contractors may omit the header joist to reduce costs, but this is false economy from the standpoint of sound construction. The header provides better nailing ground for rough flooring and wall sheathing. It also helps as a fire stop (draft stop).

T-Sills

The T-sill is commonly used with the bal-loon framing. The studs and joists in the T-sill may bear directly on the sill plate as in Fig. 9-71, or may be spiked to a 2″ × 4″ sole nailed to the sill as in Fig. 9-72. Again, the header serves as a draft stop.

Eastern Sills

Another sill variation used for balloon construction is the *eastern sill* (Fig. 9-73). The structural qualities are comparative to the T-sill. Blocks equivalent to a header and serving as fire stops are cut to fit and are placed between the joists. Both the T-sill and the eastern sill have the advantage of less potential shrinkage, thus making them ideal for stucco, brick, and stone veneer residences.

Under most conditions, a 2″ × 6″ sill plate provides sufficient nail anchorage. A double or 4″ sill plate is desirable for the two-story home and for the home built in a locality subjected to high wind velocities.

Lowered Sill. To achieve certain architectural effects in designing a house to the topography of a given lot, it may be necessary to bring the level of the floor closer to the finished grade. In this case, the joists may be lowered completely or partly below the

Fig. 9-74. A recess along the top of the foundation wall allows the joists to be partly or completely below grade.

grade by providing a recess along the top of the foundation wall (Fig. 9-74). This type of construction is often not as strong as those previously discussed due to the decreased bearing area for the joists; however, it may be used for dropping the level of the floor for a sunken living room or stair landing.

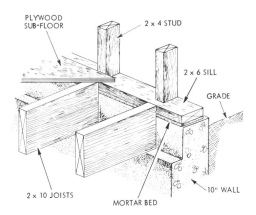

Another method of framing a landing is accomplished by end-notching the tail joists as shown in Fig. 9-75. A minimum of 4″ depth must remain on the joist for structural purposes after the notch is cut. One of the purposes in dropping a stair landing is to reduce the total run of the stair. An 8″ to 10″ stirrup or bridle iron may be used to support the tail joist if it is necessary to drop the landing more than 4″.

Building foundations covered with brick veneer up to the height of the foundation have typical sill framing. Fig. 9-76 shows an exposed basement wall covered with brick veneer with beveled siding starting at the top of the foundation. In the case where two walls would be exposed and covered with brick veneer, the sill plate, by necessity, will have to be increased in width. Because of the increased width of the foundation wall on the exposed side, the last

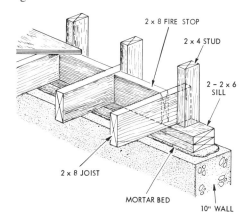

Fig. 9-73. The eastern sill offers an alternate type of sill construction for balloon framing. Note: the header is cut and placed between the joists; joists are nailed against the studs.

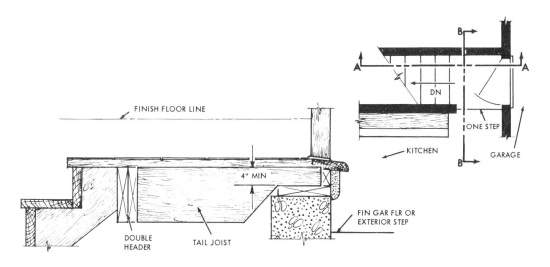

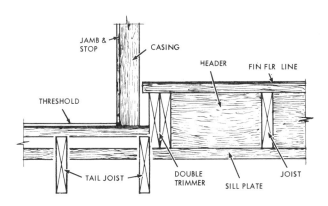

SEC **A–A**   SECTION THRU LANDING BELOW FINISH FLOOR LEVEL

SEC **B–B**   SECTION THRU LANDING BELOW FINISH FLOOR LEVEL

Fig. 9-75. Entryway landings can be dropped by notching the tail joists.

joist must be placed at the standard 16″ O.C. distance. If the on-center distance is not maintained and because of the increased total wall thickness, problems can arise for the heating contractor when he installs the heating ducts.

Sill Seal. In current building practice, the sill plate usually lies on a strip of sill seal. Fig. 9-77 shows a balsam wool sill seal be-

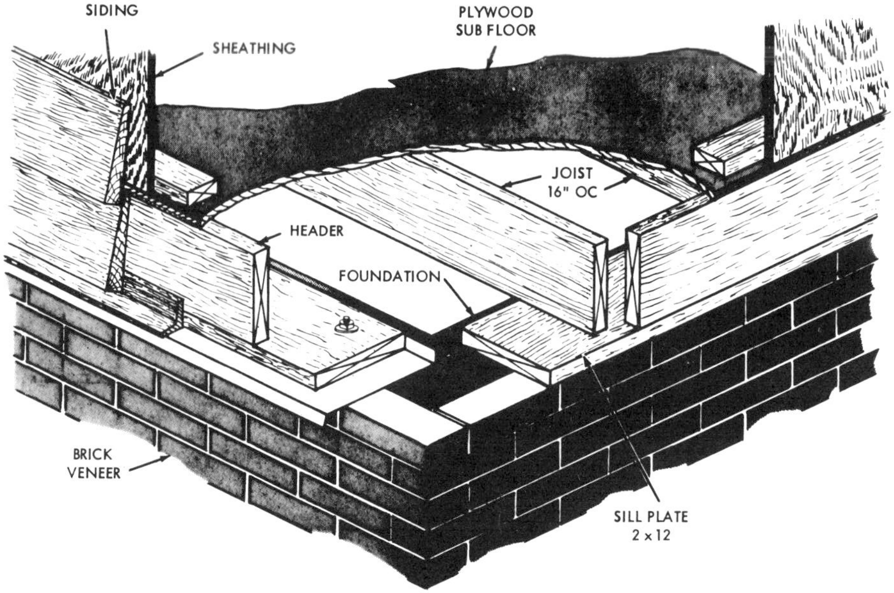

Fig. 9-76. Sill construction when foundation wall has brick veneer facing on two or three faces of an exposed basement.

SIDING

SHEATHING

PLYWOOD SUB FLOOR

JOIST 16" OC

HEADER

FOUNDATION

BRICK VENEER

SILL PLATE 2 x 12

Fig. 9-77. Balsam Wool sill seal fills in irregularities between the top of the foundation wall and sill.

CONWED CORP., ST. PAUL, MINNESOTA

ing installed along the top course of a concrete block foundation wall. Balsam wool is made with a moisture resistant binder and is placed between two layers of kraft paper, asphalted to each side of the seal blanket. Sill seal eliminates any irregularities that occur between the sill and the top of the foundation wall. Sill seal is also used on the top of masonry walls under the rafter plate and under the bottom wall plate where a floor slab is laid on the grade. The resilient nature of sill seal completely fills any irregularities and forms a tight gasket against the loss of heat and wind penetration. Depending upon the nature of construction, plates may be bedded in mortar. Figs. 9-70 through 9-74 illustrate this practice.

A ½″ to ¾″ layer of mortar is spread on top of the foundation and the sill is placed over this and leveled before the mortar has set. This provides an even bearing surface and prevents air leakage. Sometimes the sill is placed directly on the foundation and wood shingles are driven between the foundation and sill to fill any voids. Eventually these shingles may work loose, providing an opportunity for cracks to occur.

Anchor Bolts. It is imperative that the sill be fastened to the foundation wall. Anchor bolts, ½″ to ¾″ diameter by 16″ to 18″ long, are used for this purpose. Anchor bolts are set in the foundation every 6′-0″ O.C. and embedded at least in 6″ concrete or 15″ in masonry units. One bolt should be placed near each corner. Holes are drilled in the sill to fit the bolt spacing.

Sill Joints. When a single sill is joined

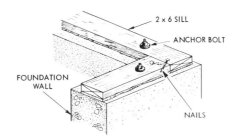

Fig. 9-78. Sill members are secured by anchor bolts and "toenailed" at corners.

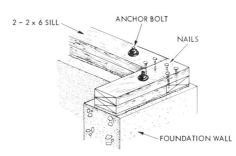

Fig. 9-79. Built-up sills are lapped at the corners and nailed.

at the corner of the building the ends are *toenailed* together as in Fig. 9-78. When a built-up or double sill, or sill with sole is required, the components are lapped and nailed at the corner as in Fig. 9-79.

Termite Protection. Protection against termites (subterranean, non-subterranean, or drywood types) should not be overlooked in sill design. The subterranean termite is found in almost every area of the United States. To eliminate the possibility of termites burrowing into lower framing mem-

bers, a termite shield may be used as shown in Fig. 9-80. These rustproof metal shields extend completely around the top of the foundation wall and are bedded in mortar. They should project on both sides of the wall. Creosote or other chemicals may be used to treat wood members so they will not be attacked by termites.

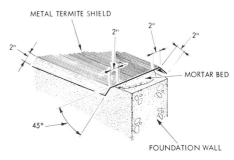

Fig. 9-80. A galvanized iron or copper termite shield extends without break around the top of the foundation wall.

Step-By-Step Drawing Procedure: Sills

Fig. 9-81 illustrates the step-by-step procedure for drawing any type of sill.

Stucco

Stucco is perhaps one of the oldest exterior finishes used in building construction. This finish is used especially in the southern and southwestern states. A stucco finish consists of three individual coats of Portland cement and sand mixture. The first

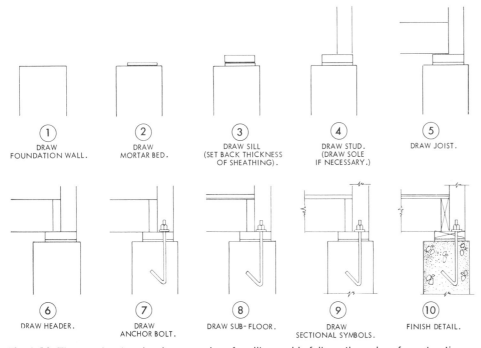

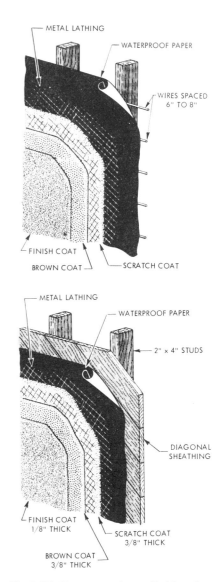

Fig. 9-81. The step-by-step drawing procedure for sills roughly follows the order of construction.

coat, about ⅜″ thick, is applied to metal lath. This first coat is scratched to provide a good mechanical key for the brown second coat, which is ⅜″ thick. The finish or final coat is ⅛″-¼″ thick, making the total thickness of the stucco about 1″. A stucco finish can be applied directly to masonry or to a frame building by one of the two methods. See Fig. 9-82.

The *open frame* method is one in which building paper is applied over 16 gage wire spaced 8″ O.C. perpendicular to studs. The wire acts as a backing for the sheathing paper. The expanded metal or stucco lath is held away from the building paper by furring nails. As the scratch coat is applied, the cement mixture penetrates the mesh and becomes an integral reinforced unit.

The second method of applying stucco to a frame superstructure is called *sheathed* frame construction. This is similar to the method previously described, except that ¾″ sheathing and building paper are placed between the wall framing members and the stucco lath. Regardless of the method of applying stucco, the metal lath

Fig. 9-82. Stucco may be applied to a frame superstructure by either the open or the sheathed frame method.

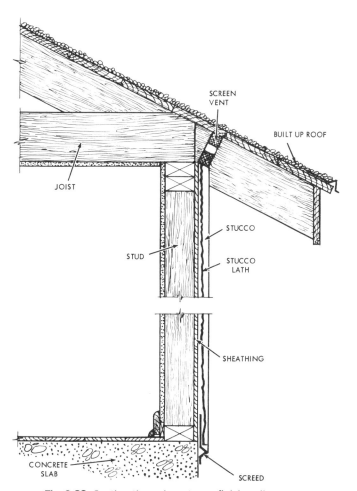

Fig. 9-83. Section through a stucco finish wall.

that metal lath be fastened to the wall before the scratch coat is applied. Even though an adobe wall is slightly rough, wire lath must be used.

The Manufactured House and Components

To keep pace with demands for quality and yet economical construction, builders each year are using some type of pre-built or manufactured unit. Depending upon the contractor, and the nature of the structure, these may range from a plumbing wall unit, truss, wall panel, to a complete modular house section. By using components the contractor can shorten construction time and thereby increase his dollar volume of business.

Some of the general public may question the quality of factory built components or homes. Perhaps the question is strictly psychological because the building is not "custom made at the site." Consider for a moment: if an automobile were designed and built on the same principle as a house, could you afford to drive a car? For most it would be economically impossible to own an auto, in addition to caring for its upkeep. Many families own at least one automobile because mass production techniques have placed its price within their reach. Housing can be viewed in the same perspective. Labor and material costs have continued to inch upward through the years, thereby denying many the opportunity of home ownership.

must be "furred-out" sufficiently from the building paper so that first coat will completely surround the lath. Fig. 9-83 shows a section through a stucco finish wall. To provide a watertight joint at the base of

the stucco coating, a galvanized iron screed is nailed to the sill plate. The screed is placed low enough to overlap the foundation wall. The screed acts as a drip cap.

Stucco applied to an adobe wall requires

Any manufactured component must meet building code requirements. Simply because a unit has been made in a factory does not mean that it is less than acceptable. Factory built components are equal to and in some instances superior to those constructed at the job site because of precise manufacturing techniques.

Perhaps the initial attempt to speed the building process was the *precutting* of materials. A precut structure is one where all materials are cut to specific lengths, delivered to the job site and assembled by conventional means. It is obvious that some time is saved if components are precut; however, the structure is still built by manual techniques. More time and money could be saved if the building were broken into small panels.

One of the major changes to affect the building industry has been the *panelization* of walls. Panelizing generally means dividing a wall into a series of manufacturable and transportable sections. Fig. 9-84 shows several completed wall panels. Windows, doors and sheathing are installed as the panel is being built on the jig table. Usually insulation and electrical wiring is not included in the wall panel. Interior walls, trusses, and gable ends are fabricated on the same principle. As each unit is removed from the truck it is positioned and fastened to the adjoining unit or member. The exterior and interior wall finishes, trim, mechanical and electrical work are completed at the building site.

A logical step from panelizing is *prefabrication*. A building that is prefabricated is one where the main components, such as exterior walls, trusses, floor panels, partitions are completely assembled at the factory, delivered to the job site, positioned and secured together. Fig. 9-85 shows a prefabricated panel being lowered into place by a crane. Note that the exterior wall is finished to the extent of siding, shutters and storm door, all completely installed at the factory. Following the erection of all members, the exterior and interior trim, mechanical and electrical work is completed.

A normal outgrowth of prefabrication would be the complete house assembled and delivered as a unit. This approach to building construction is called the *modular unit*. The basic concept of the modular unit began with the "house trailer" of the 1930's. Today they are called *mobile homes* (12' × 65'). The mobile home like its forerunner, the early trailer, was the first complete factory-built home. The modular unit can be thought of as a mobile home without wheels.

AMERICAN PLYWOOD ASSOCIATION, TACOMA, WASHINGTON

Fig. 9-84. Wall panels are built on a mass production basis.

AMERICAN PLYWOOD ASSOCIATION, TACOMA, WASHINGTON

Fig. 9-85. Prefabricated wall units are delivered complete to the construction site.

The term *modular* indicates a unit that is placed in combination with other units to form a completed structure. The units may be used singly or side by side. Fig. 9-86 shows a modular unit being placed adjacent to another unit.

Because of size restrictions for highway transport, some units are moved by helicopter to the building site. Once the units are in place, only electrical and mechanical hookups and fastening the units together need be completed.

Modular units may be single or multiple story buildings. Fig. 9-87 shows a small

Fig. 9-86. Modular units may be placed side by side to give maximum flexibility in space utilization.

AMERICAN PLYWOOD ASSOCIATION, TACOMA, WASHINGTON

Fig. 9-87. Modular units use the same type of construction as a conventional stick built structure.

Fig. 9-88A. Modular units may be stacked higher than one story.

Fig. 9-88B. Though the designer used a simple prism as a basis for design, the result is attractive.

modular unit being lowered into its location. Striking designs that depart from the traditional concept of shelter can be achieved with the modular concept. Figs. 9-88A and 9-88B show the unique appearance of a series of modular units. The modular unit mass produced in a factory may herald one of the new approaches to building construction.

Brick Masonry

Brick has been used as a building material for the last 6,000 years and ranks as one of man's greatest inventions. It is only one, however, of several kinds of materials used in masonry construction. Masonry building units include brick, stone, hollow tile, and concrete block.

Brick Sizes

Brick sizes are standardized just as lumber is standardized. In residential construction, standard brick, either face or common, is usually used. Fig. 9-89 shows the sizes of the most widely used types of brick.

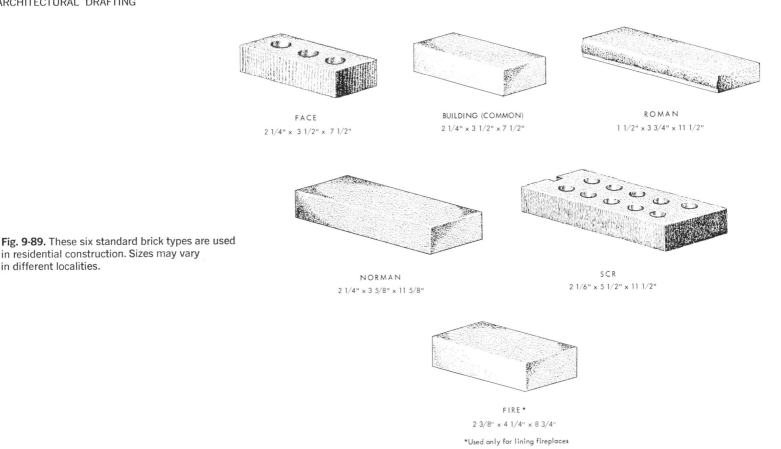

FACE
2 1/4" x 3 1/2" x 7 1/2"

BUILDING (COMMON)
2 1/4" x 3 1/2" x 7 1/2"

ROMAN
1 1/2" x 3 3/4" x 11 1/2"

NORMAN
2 1/4" x 3 5/8" x 11 5/8"

SCR
2 1/6" x 5 1/2" x 11 1/2"

FIRE *
2 3/8" x 4 1/4" x 8 3/4"

*Used only for lining fireplaces

Fig. 9-89. These six standard brick types are used in residential construction. Sizes may vary in different localities.

Mortar Joints

Sound, watertight joints are necessary for a strong wall. Mortar joints should not be less than ¼″ nor more than ½″ in thickness. Thicker joints are sometimes used for decoration but they are structurally weak. Joints are either left flush with the brick face, or formed with a *pointing tool*. See

Fig. 9-90. The concave or rodded joint is the most common shape used. The main purpose of treating the joints is to force the edges of the mortar into firm contact with the brick so water cannot penetrate. The shape of the joints may also play an esthetic role by giving different shadow effects to the wall.

Brick Bond

The strength of any masonry wall depends to a great extent upon the *bond* used in erecting the wall. A bond refers to the arrangement of brick or stone in the wall. The arrangements are designed to prevent the vertical joints between the masonry units from being directly above each other.

EXTRUDED

UNFINISHED

CONVEX   CONCAVE

RODDED   RAKED

WEATHERED   STRUCK

FLUSH   V-TOOLED

FINISHED

Fig. 9-90. The various types of finished mortar joints are designed to force the mortar into contact with the brick. Note the unfinished "buttered" joint.

There are many patterns for placing brick which will produce a structurally sound wall. The variation between bonds is brought about by the distribution of *stretchers* (the length of the brick laid parallel with the face of the wall) and *headers* (laid with the length at right angles to the face of the wall) laid in various *courses* (rows).

The following paragraphs list some of the basic bonds used in brick work.

Running or Stretcher Bond. (See Fig. 9-91A.) This bond uses stretcher courses with the joints breaking at the center of each brick immediately above and below. Face, common, Roman, or SCR brick is used for this bond.

Common Bond. (See Fig. 9-91B.) The common bond, or American bond as it is sometimes called, is a variation of the running bond, with a header course every 5th, 6th, or 7th course. This ties the wall to the backing masonry material. The header courses are centered on each other. Face or common brick is usually used in the common bond.

English Cross or Dutch Bond. (See Fig. 9-91C.) This bond uses alternate header and stretcher courses. The joints of the stretchers center on the stretchers two courses above and below; headers center on headers. This bond is usually common or face brick.

English Bond. (See Fig. 9-91D.) Alternate courses of headers and stretchers are laid so that the joints between stretchers are centered on the headers. Stretchers are cen-

HEADERS EVERY SIXTH COURSE

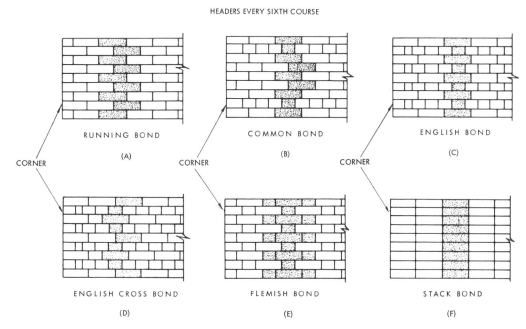

CORNER   RUNNING BOND   CORNER   COMMON BOND   CORNER   ENGLISH BOND
                     (A)   (B)   (C)

ENGLISH CROSS BOND   FLEMISH BOND   STACK BOND
        (D)   (E)   (F)

Fig. 9-91. The variations between brick bonds depend upon the distribution of stretchers and headers in various courses.

tered on stretchers; headers on headers. Face or common brick is usually used for the English bond.

Flemish Bond. (See Fig. 9-91E.) Alternate headers and stretchers are in each course. The headers in one course are centered above and below the stretchers in the other course. Face or common brick is used for this bond.

Stack Bond. (See Fig. 9-91F.) All courses are stretchers and all joints are in line. This is used primarily for esthetic purposes—it has relatively little structural value. The most effective brick for this type of bond is Roman.

Many of the more ornamental bonds have been excluded from this discussion — they are seldom used because of the cost.

Masonry Walls

Masonry walls are porous and after a driving rain or period of severe cold, moisture may condense on the inside of the wall. To prevent this, the inner wall covering (covered with lath and plaster or other finish) is separated from the back-up masonry by *furring* or *furring strips* as in Fig. 9-92. This air space will stop any moisture transfer.

Furring is adjusted to compensate for irregularities in the masonry wall and provides a nailing base for the wall covering. Furring may be either light steel channels or $1'' \times 2''$, $1'' \times 3''$, or $2'' \times 2''$ wood strips. These are positioned vertically and nailed to the inside face of the masonry unit. The spacing of the furring strips is determined by the

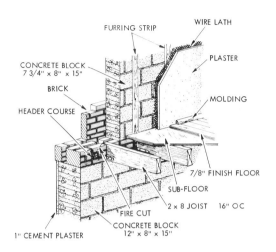

Fig. 9-92. A brick veneer is often used over concrete block. Note the furring strips.

type of interior wall covering. For example, if sheet rock is used, furring strips should be placed 16″ or 24″ O.C. to maintain the module of the standard size sheet (4′ × 8′). Placing the furring strips at a greater distance O.C. would cause too much flexibility when pressure was applied. The furring serves as a base for the interior finish: lath and plaster, drywall, gypsum board, paneling, plywood, etc.

Brick Walls. With mortar the standard brick width is roughly 4″. Therefore, brick walls are normally constructed in multiples of 4″: that is, in widths of 4″, 8″, 12″, and 16″.

A residential building less than 35′ high normally uses an 8″ wall. A 12″ wall is recommended if there are high winds or earthquakes. Usually the outside layer of brick is backed-up by an inside layer with a lesser grade of brick. Sometimes the outside brick wall is backed up by concrete blocks or hollow tiles. A brick veneer (one brick thick) may also be built over wood framing.

Concrete Block Walls. The most widely used size of concrete block is 7⅝″ × 7⅝″ × 15⅝″. If these are laid in a single wall thickness, they will produce roughly an 8″ thick wall. Block are also available in 4″, 10″, and 12″ widths, as well as other shapes, as shown in Fig. 9-93. The names given to each block are indicative of their use in construction.

The face of a concrete block wall will take on a new depth when laid with *textured blocks* (sometimes called shadow blocks).

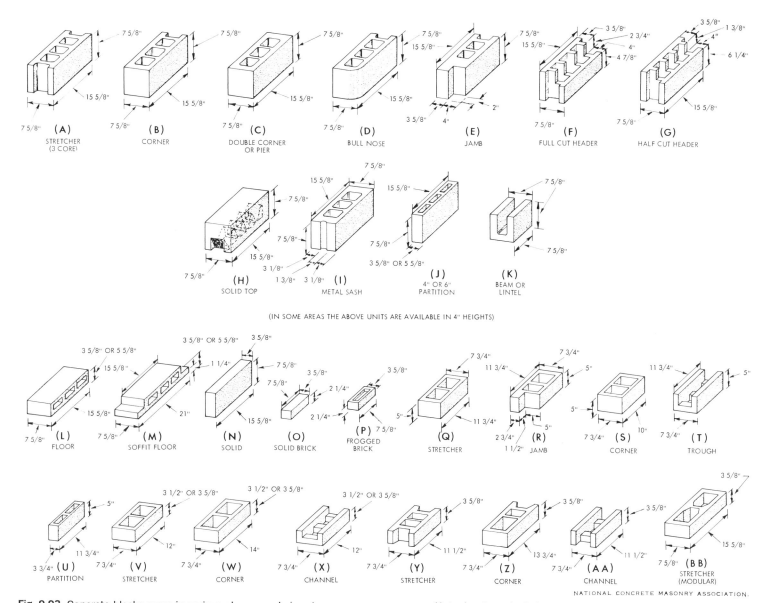

Fig. 9-93. Concrete blocks come in various shapes and sizes to serve many purposes. (Actual not nominal sizes are given.)

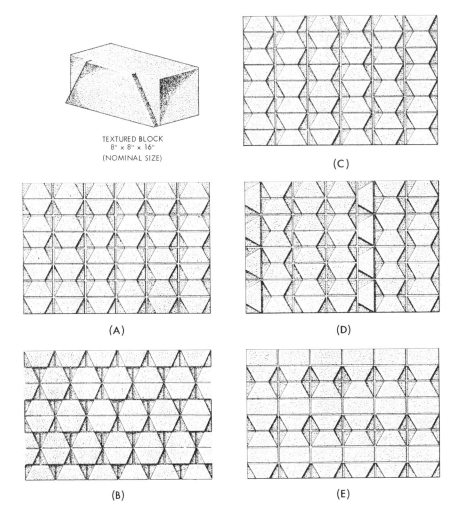

TEXTURED BLOCK
8" x 8" x 16"
(NOMINAL SIZE)

(C)

(A)

(D)

(B)

(E)

Fig. 9-94. Textured or shadow masonry block add beauty and variety to interior and exterior walls.

These may be randomly placed with plain blocks or used together to develop a pattern as in Fig. 9-94. Textured block may be used on both interior and exterior walls. A combination of blocks may produce an at-tractive interior wall as shown in Fig. 9-95.

Hollow Tile Walls. Hollow tile (sometimes called building tile) is composed of the same ingredients as brick. The thickness of the shell is ¾". Hollow tile are available in numerous sizes and shapes; selection is dependent upon its intended use (masonry wall backing unit, a wall, etc.).

SCR Brick Walls. In recent years the SCR (Structural Clay Products Research) brick

Fig. 9-95. An attractive interior partition has been produced with a combination of stretchers and core blocks.

PORTLAND CEMENT ASSOCIATION, CHICAGO, ILLINOIS

wall has been introduced into the masonry construction field. This wall was designed primarily to compete with the frame wall. It has met with success in many areas. Fig. 9-96 shows a typical SCR brick wall. The wall is one unit or brick thick. A jamb slot or notched cut is made into one end of every brick to accommodate metal or wood windows. It is necessary with the SCR brick wall to use furring strips to provide a cavity for the installation of wiring and insulation. Attachment of the 2″ × 2″ furring strip is made by a patented clip which fits into the masonry joint.

Brick Veneer Walls. Brick veneer is commonly considered as a skin of brick over a frame house. See Fig. 9-97. The foundation wall must be wide enough to accommodate a course of brick and also the sill for the frame wall. Allowance must be made for ¾″ sheathing on the frame wall and 1″ air space. Balloon frame construction lends itself to this type of wall because there is a minimum of vertical shrinkage. Corrugated galvanized metal strips or wires are used to tie the brick wall to the frame construction. One end is nailed to the sheathing and the other end is embedded in the mortar joint. See Fig. 9-98. The ties are placed every fifth course and spaced 2′-0″ O.C. horizontally. The masonry veneer of the wall usually is not load bearing. The roof, floor, and ceiling joists are supported by the frame wall.

Stone Walls. The oldest example of masonry houses in America are represented by the brick and stone buildings of colonial

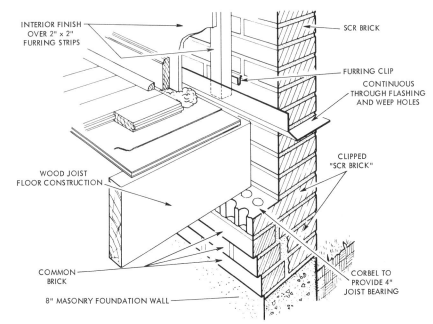

Fig. 9-96. SCR brick may be used to make a strong, durable wall with only one thickness of brick. Note the corbel used to provide joist bearing: the through wall flashing, and the furring strips fastened with clips to the wall.

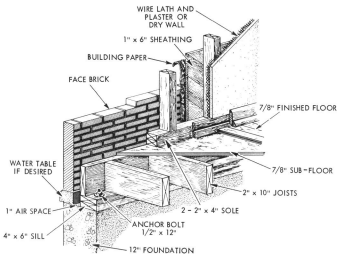

Fig. 9-97. Brick veneer construction is popular because it provides a brick exterior with the interior flexibilty of frame constructon.

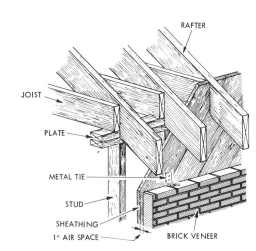

Fig. 9-98. Metal ties are used to hold the masonry wall to the frame superstructure.

days. Stones in a wall must overlap so that joints are not directly above each other. The size and shape of the stone used, in addition to the color and texture, will determine how it will be laid in the wall. Today, almost all stone homes are veneered. The wall section will be essentially the same as brick veneer. The only difference is that stone replaces the brick, and the numerous types and cuts of stone produce many patterns. A few of the more common stone-work combinations are illustrated in Fig. 9-99.

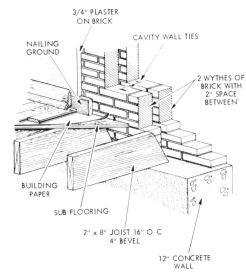

Fig. 9-100. A 10″ cavity wall is formed of two 4″ walls plus a 2″ cavity. Note the metal ties used for support.

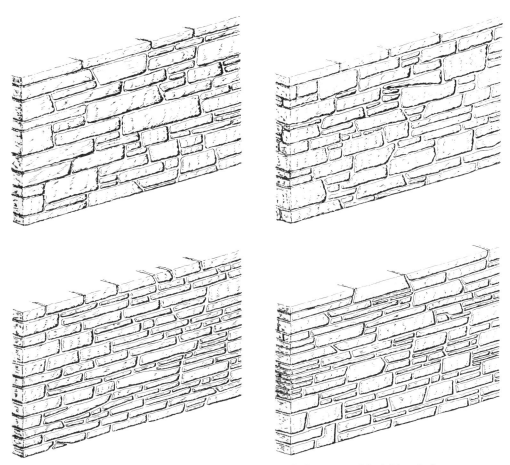

Fig. 9-99. Split stone may be used to form an attractive wall. Stones must be laid so that no vertical cracks can develop.

Cavity walls are used to produce a watertight wall with good thermal and sound insulation. These are made up of two 4″ walls normally separated by a 2″ air space. These are tied together by ¼″ metal ties placed in every 5th course and not more than 3′ apart horizontally. See Fig. 9-100. Cavity walls should not exceed 25′ in height. Since the cavity wall prevents the penetration of heat and cold, it is important that the air space be kept free of mortar drippings or other obstructions.

A cavity wall with an interior plaster finish would need no furring strips, since the void between the outside brick and the back-up brick serves the same purpose as furring strips. In other words, a dead air space is provided. Plaster, therefore, may be applied directly to the brick work, or the masonry may remain exposed for its esthetic value. Metal or wire lath is not necessary if plaster is to be used, since the rough surface will readily accept the scratch coat of plaster.

Flashing is placed wherever water may seep into a building, such as under windows and at the base of a wall. It is a continuous piece (usually metal) shaped to prevent moisture from entering the wall. See Fig. 9-101.

Wall Ventilation

Some type of ventilation must be sup-

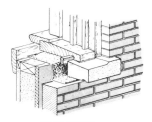

BRICK VENEER

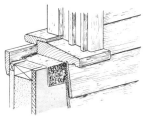

FRAME

Fig. 9-101. Flashing, either plastic or metal, is required wherever water may seep into the building.

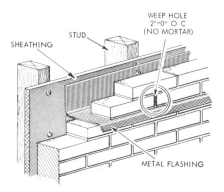

Fig. 9-102. Brick walls must be vented by weep holes or wall vents.

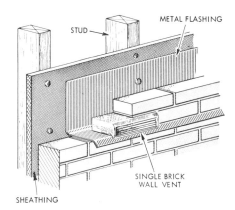

plied to the solid masonry or masonry veneer wall to drain off any moisture which may form. Ventilation in a solid or veneer masonry wall (Fig. 9-102) may be produced by either: (1) weepholes placed every 2′ O.C.; or (2) cavity ventilators spaced according to size and manufacturers specifications. Either method of ventilating should

be placed immediately above the flashing at the base of the wall, over flashing on the second story, and over openings.

Structural Details

Brick Ledge. Brick veneer over a frame or masonry backing is supported by the foundation wall. The first course of brick may rest on the top of the foundation wall or it may be dropped below the top as in Fig. 9-103. Brick may be dropped a maximum of 12″ below the top of a normal foundation wall. The decreased thickness of the foundation wall behind the brick veneer must be reinforced with rods placed 24″ O.C. In cases where the grade slopes along the foundation wall and the designer desires to carry the brick to the grade line, a different technique must be employed. For structural reasons, the foundation wall cannot be reduced in thickness as shown in Fig. 9-103. Instead, a brick ledge is formed by increasing the thickness of the foundation wall below the grade line. Normally this is done only in concrete block walls, where the thickness of the block may be readily changed. In the case of a poured concrete wall, support for the brick is achieved by using a concrete brick. Fig. 9-104 illustrates these two methods.

Gable End Construction. Siding or cedar shakes used to finish a gable end on a brick veneer building is backed by conventional 2″ × 4″ framing. The plate for the gable framing rests on the frame superstructure and the brick veneer. The 2″ × 8″ plate resting on the top brick course, as shown

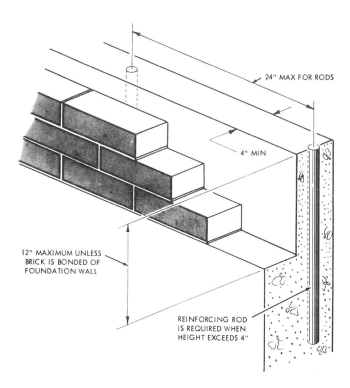

Fig. 9-103. Reducing the thickness of a foundation wall for brick veneer requires reinforcing rod in the foundation wall.

in Fig. 9-105, is nailed to the double 2″ × 4″ wall plate. Note the ceiling joist is placed adjacent to the top plate — not over the plate as in conventional framing. Care must be taken that the top course of bricks and sheathing are flush with the top of the double plate of the wall superstructure. The siding or shakes can be dropped several courses below the top of the brick veneer wall.

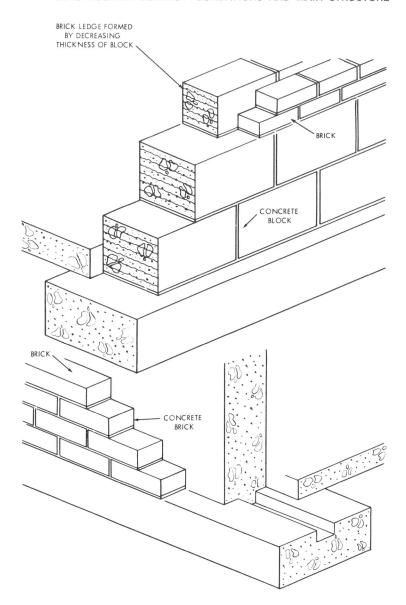

Fig. 9-104. These two methods may be used to produce a brick ledge.

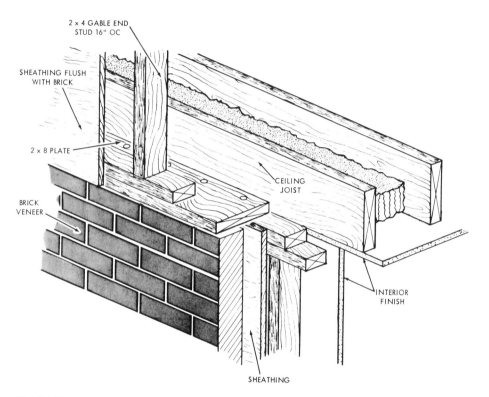

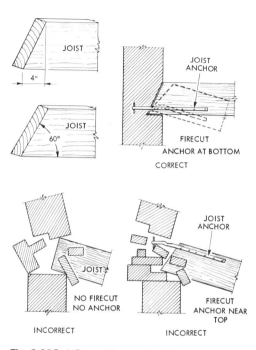

Fig. 9-105. The superstructure for a gable end rests on a 2″ × 8″ plate.

Fig. 9-106. A fire cut is used on joints in solid masonry walls. A joist anchor prevents the building from falling outward in the event of fire.

Joists that fit into masonry walls are cut on a 60° angle, or with a 4″ bevel (Fig. 9-106, top left). This angular cut is called a *fire cut*. In the event of fire, without a fire cut the falling joist could create a lever action causing the wall to topple outward (Fig. 9-106, bottom left) with hazard to life and property. In addition to the fire cut joist, anchors are usually required by city building codes. It is also necessary to anchor floors and roofs to walls because of possible high winds. Joists are secured to walls at the ends by metal anchors which are embedded in the masonry walls. These are fastened near the bottom of every 5th or 6th joist. See Fig. 9-106 (top right). Anchors are fastened to the bottom of the joists to prevent wall damage if the joist falls (Fig. 9-106, bottom right). Joists parallel to walls, as shown in Fig. 9-107, may be fastened by

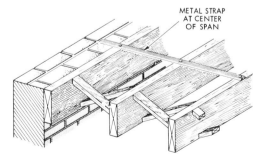

Fig. 9-107. Joists may be fastened to walls by a metal strip at the center of the span.

means of an anchor strip nailed across the top of 2 or 3 joists. The metal strip, for most small dwellings, is placed in the middle of the joist span and anchored to the masonry wall.

Anchor Bolts and Plates. To provide anchorage for roof rafters or trusses, a plate must be fastened to the top of the masonry wall. Bolts, ½″ to ¾″ in diameter, 12″ to 16″ long, are set in mortar every 5′ to 6′ O.C. A ¼″ diameter, 2″ × 6″ steel plate, is welded to the bottom of the bolt. See Fig. 9-108.

Stud partition ends are fastened in a similar manner.

Lintels. Masonry over the tops of windows and doors must be supported by *lintels.* Angle or channel iron is usually used in brick veneer; reinforced concrete is usually

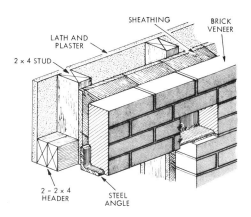

Fig. 9-109. An angle iron or steel angle is used as a lintel in brick veneer walls. Note the 2—2x4's used to support the frame.

used in concrete block walls. Wood is very seldom used as a lintel due to shrinkage which causes cracks in the masonry wall and eventual decay. The lintel in residential construction should have a 4″ bearing on each side of the opening. This is sufficient in most cases. If the opening is extremely wide, the size of the angle iron will have to be increased. Fig. 9-109 shows angle iron used as a lintel in brick veneer construction. Note the use of the laminated 4″ × 4″ header. Since the frame wall is not carrying the weight of the exterior wall, a 4″ × 4″ header is sufficient.

Fig. 9-110 illustrates a solid, reinforced, precast, concrete lintel in a brick veneer wall with concrete block backing. Greater strength is given to the lintel by placing the reinforcing rods close to the bottom edge of the lintel. Most "pure forms" of tradi-

tional or period residential architecture will use a precast or cut stone lintel in lieu of an angle or channel iron lintel. However, modern adaptations (of the colonial for example) will employ an angle iron lintel. A cast concrete, cut stone, or brick *rowlock* course sill (course of bricks laid on edge) is placed at a slight angle below *all* window and door openings to shed water.

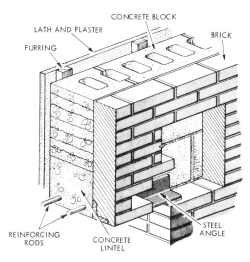

Fig. 9-110. A precast reinforced concrete lintel is used over the concrete block part of this brick veneer wall. Note the angle iron lintel used to support the bricks over the opening.

Chimneys and Fireplaces. Floor, roof, wall, or partition framing members must be kept free of the masonry chimney or fireplace. Figs. 9-111 and 9-112 show the

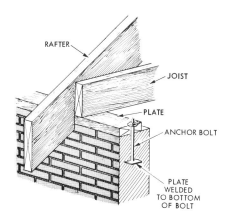

Fig. 9-108. Anchor bolts are used to secure the plate to the brick wall and to hold down the roof in the case of high winds.

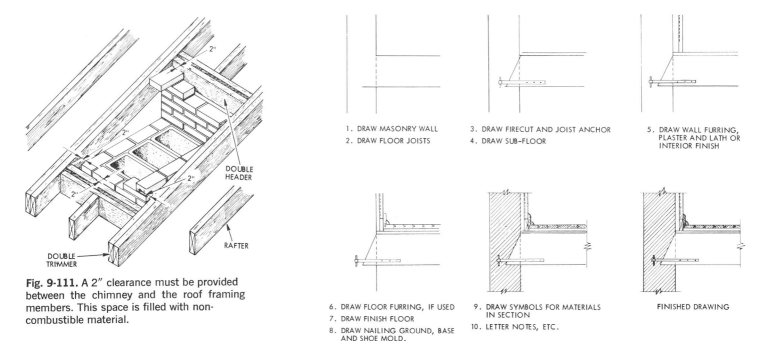

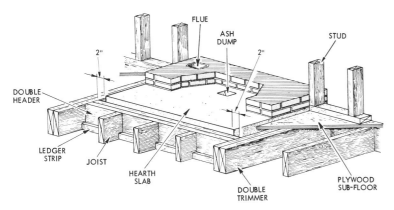

Fig. 9-111. A 2″ clearance must be provided between the chimney and the roof framing members. This space is filled with non-combustible material.

1. DRAW MASONRY WALL
2. DRAW FLOOR JOISTS
3. DRAW FIRECUT AND JOIST ANCHOR
4. DRAW SUB-FLOOR
5. DRAW WALL FURRING, PLASTER AND LATH OR INTERIOR FINISH

6. DRAW FLOOR FURRING, IF USED
7. DRAW FINISH FLOOR
8. DRAW NAILING GROUND, BASE AND SHOE MOLD.
9. DRAW SYMBOLS FOR MATERIALS IN SECTION
10. LETTER NOTES, ETC.

FINISHED DRAWING

Fig. 9-113. Follow this step-by-step procedure for drawing a masonry wall.

Fig. 9-112. A 2″ clearance must also be provided around the sides of the fireplace.

headers and trimmers around a chimney and fireplace at a minimum distance of 2″. This space between the masonry and structural members must be filled with non-combustible insulation. Mineral or glass wool is frequently used for this purpose.

Step-By-Step Drawing Procedure: Masonry Walls

Fig. 9-113 illustrates the step-by-step procedure used in drawing any masonry wall section.

Fig. 9-114 illustrates the step-by-step

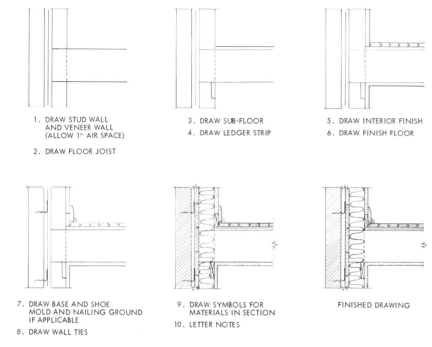

1. DRAW STUD WALL
AND VENEER WALL
(ALLOW 1" AIR SPACE)

2. DRAW FLOOR JOIST

3. DRAW SUB-FLOOR
4. DRAW LEDGER STRIP

5. DRAW INTERIOR FINISH
6. DRAW FINISH FLOOR

7. DRAW BASE AND SHOE
MOLD AND NAILING GROUND
IF APPLICABLE

8. DRAW WALL TIES

9. DRAW SYMBOLS FOR
MATERIALS IN SECTION

10. LETTER NOTES

FINISHED DRAWING

Fig. 9-114. Follow this step-by-step procedure for drawing a masonry veneer wall. (For simplicity the fire stops have been omitted.)

procedure in drawing a masonry veneer wall. A frame wall is similar to the masonry wall; however, siding is used in place of brick.

Questions and Problems

1. What is the basic purpose of a footing?
2. Does a difference exist between the local building code specification for a residential footing and the footing design shown in Fig. 9-2? Does the building code recommend different size footings for the varying types of soil that may be common in the area?
3. According to the map shown in Fig. 9-6 (maximum frost penetration), does a difference exist between that figure and the frost line in your community?
4. Is the bottommost portion of the footing placed at the frost line or slightly below?

5. Design a foundation wall and footing for a single-story frame, ranch-type dwelling on a flat site. Assume the site is located in your community.
6. What is the maximum frost penetration in the area in which you live? Does this differ from the depth used by most builders or specified by the local building code? If a difference does exist, is this an "error"?
7. Make a quick sketch of two sections taken through the foundation and footing of a single-story house. The house has brick veneer on the front and frame on the other three sides. Take one section through the front foundation wall and the other through the rear wall. Dimension each section.
8. What methods may be used to insure a dry basement?
9. Which type of frame superstructure is best suited for a masonry veneer exterior finish? How thick will the foundation wall be?
10. What purpose does bridging serve between (a) floor joists or (b) studs.
11. Why is it recommended that $1'' \times 6''$ wood sheathing be nailed diagonally on the studs of an exterior wall?
12. When an exterior wall is covered with shingles, why should the lowermost course of shingles be doubled and backed with a batten strip?
13. Take a section through a floor composed of $2'' \times 10''$ joists, ¾" plywood sub-floor, building paper, and ¾ (finish oak flooring. This is to be a detail

section. Scale $1\frac{1}{2}'' = 1'\text{-}0''$. Use the proper symbols in the section. Call out all materials and sizes. Draw another detail section through a kitchen floor that is covered with vinyl tile having a particle board underlayment.

14. Draw a detail section of four different types of sills as specified by the instructor. Place a different inside and outside wall covering on each sill. Carry each covering $1''$ below top of foundation wall. Use $\frac{1}{2}'' \times 12''$ anchor bolts, $8'\text{-}0''$ O.C. Place the finished grade line $6''$ to $8''$ below the top of the foundation wall. Draw all building materials *actual* size. Use a $\frac{1}{2}''$ mortar bed under all wood sills. Place a termite shield under all sills.

15. What purpose does the fire stop serve? Is it necessary in both the balloon and platform types of construction?

16. Must a termite shield be used on all sills?

17. What other type of material may be used for sill bedding other than mortar?

18. Relative to brick walls, what do the terms stretcher, header, and course mean?

19. Explain the purpose of weep holes in a masonry wall. How far apart and how far above the foundation wall are they placed?

20. Is it necessary to place vents in an exterior wall covered with wood siding?

21. How can an SCR brick wall be distinguished from a common or face brick wall?

22. What causes insulation to restrict the flow of heat?

23. Can the grade beam and pier construction (see Figs. 9-31 and 9-32) be used in an area where the frost penetrates $24''$ into the ground? Explain the reason for your answer.

Construction Details: Roofs 10 and Structural Openings

This chapter continues the examination of construction techniques begun in Chapter 9. The following sections give detailed information essential to understanding the construction and design of roofs and structural openings. Structural openings include windows, doors, fireplaces and chimneys, and stairs. Step-by-step drawing procedures are given for the main structural details.

Roofs

In quality construction a good roof is as essential as a properly designed and well-built foundation. The obvious primary purpose of the roof is to shed water and prevent leakage. The most common type of roof material is shingles. Shingles are lapped and their joints *broken* (staggered) to give as much protection as possible from the weather. Shingles may be of wood, cement asbestos, asphalt composition, slate, tile, or metal. Generally the first course or row of shingles is doubled to cover the joints of the under course and to give added protection. The portion of the shingle which is exposed is said to be *laid to the weather*.

Roofs with a slight slope or low pitch must have a tight, sealed covering. If sheet metal is used as a roofing material, the bonds are lapped and soldered. If asphalt composi-tion (rolled roofing) is used, the bonds must be made watertight by asphalt or other similar types of cement. On nearly all flat roofs, tar and gravel is applied over the surface of several *plies* (layers) of roofing felt. (The layers of roofing felt are bound to each other with tar or asphalt.) A more complete discussion of roof coverings is given in a later portion of this chapter.

The rafters are the structural framing members that support the roof and are covered by roof boards or plywood. This sheathing serves as a base for the roofing material.

Roof Types

There are many kinds of roofs—all having an almost infinite number of slopes. The most common types of roofs are depicted in Fig. 10-1.

Shed or lean-to roofs (Fig. 10-1A) are the simplest roof form and have a single pitch or slope. They are used on small temporary buildings, porches, and places where appearance may not be a primary factor.

Gable roofs (Fig. 10-B) are the most common roof type. Next to the shed roof, they are the simplest in design and construction. They have two slopes meeting at the *ridge* or center.

Hip roofs (Fig. 10-1C) consist of four slopes, all sloping in the same angle toward the center of the building.

A hip roof can be modified with a small gable at either end to change the appearance of the roof line. This treatment is called a "Scotch Gable" or "Dutch Hip". The gable end is used in most instances for ventilating purposes. See Fig. 10-1D.

Gambrel roofs (Fig. 10-1E) are formed by two slopes of unequal pitch on each side. This type of roof allows more space directly below the roof surface.

Mansard roofs (Fig. 10-1F) are a modification of the gambrel roof. The upper slope has considerably less slant than the lower. It slopes on *all four sides*. Both the gambrel and the mansard roof are beginning to regain popularity.

Flat roofs (Fig. 10-1G) are generally pitched just enough so that they will provide for adequate water run-off.

Butterfly roofs (Fig. 10-1H) have two roofs sloping inward—generally each has a slight pitch. The butterfly roof is the opposite of the gable roof.

Barrel vault roofs (Fig. 10-1I) are formed by a series of semi-cylindrical surfaces placed side by side. (The elements of the adjacent cylinders are parallel.) The inter-

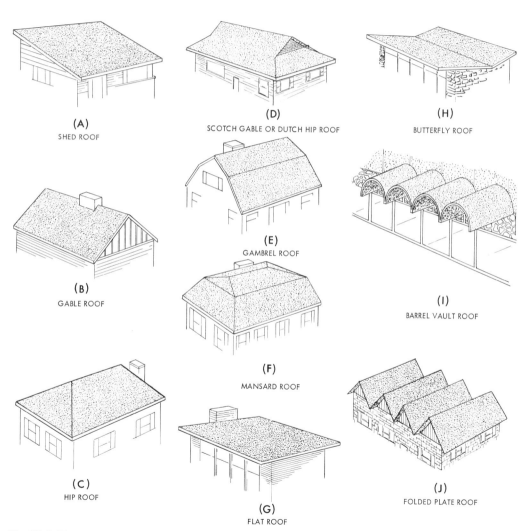

(A) SHED ROOF

(D) SCOTCH GABLE OR DUTCH HIP ROOF

(H) BUTTERFLY ROOF

(B) GABLE ROOF

(E) GAMBREL ROOF

(C) HIP ROOF

(F) MANSARD ROOF

(G) FLAT ROOF

(I) BARREL VAULT ROOF

(J) FOLDED PLATE ROOF

Fig. 10-1. These ten basic roof types are common to all types of construction.

section of each roof is pitched slightly to provide for water run-off.

Folded plate roofs (Fig. 10-1J) are similar to gable roofs that are placed adjacent to each other. The ridges of the folded plate roof are usually parallel, but in an octagonal or round building they may radiate from the center.

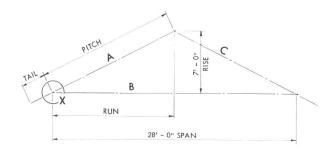

Roof Pitch

The angle of the roof is referred to as *pitch* or *slope* and may be expressed as x″ of *rise* in 12″ of *run*. This is denoted by a pitch triangle adjacent to the roof line (Fig. 10-2).

Pitch may also be referred to in fractional form, such as ⅓, ¼, ⅕, etc. To determine pitch by the fractional method, place the *rise* of the roof over the *span*. This fraction (rise over the span) is then reduced to its lowest terms.

Fig. 10-3 illustrates the various parts of the roof. *Rise* is the vertical distance measured from the top of the plate to the intersection of the "center" lines of the rafters. "Center" lines (sometimes called base lines or measuring lines) originate from the junc-

Fig. 10-3. This figure gives the basic rafter terminology.

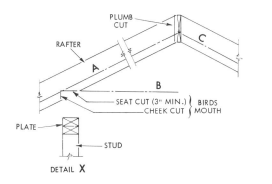

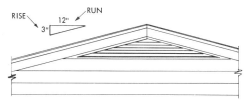

Fig. 10-2. The pitch triangle denotes the angle of the roof in terms of rise and run.

ture of the seat and cheek cut (see Fig. 10-3, detail) and run parallel to the rafter sides. This line (Fig. 10-3, A or C) is called "line of the bird's mouth." The *bird's mouth* (seat and cheek cut) provides a bearing surface for the rafter on the wall plate. *Span* is the horizontal distance from outside of one stud wall to the outside of the opposite stud wall. *Run* is one-half of the span.

Using the dimensions given in Fig. 10-3 (rise 7′ and span 28′), the fractional expression would be 7/28, or a ¼ pitch. Using the triangle method (x″ rise in 12″ of run), this roof would have a 6″ rise in 12″ of run.

This is found by converting the span (28′) to the run (one-half of the span, thus 14′). The rise to run is found by a simple proportion formula (X : 12 :: 7 : 14, thus X = 6).

Some of the more commonly used pitches are ¾, ⅝, ½, 5/12, ⅓, ¼, and ⅙. The design is not limited to these pitches — any pitch may be used which will enhance the appearance of the finished structure. In contemporary design the pitch is usually kept low.

Flat Roof. The flat roof is not only one of the easiest types of roof to design, but it is the most economical as well. The rafters in most flat roof designs act as ceiling joists. Comparable spans for flat and pitched roofs require that heavier rafters be used for flat roofs.

The live and dead loads of the roofing and ceiling material act differently on horizontal members than on those which are pitched. One of the difficulties of a flat roof is that little air space exists between the underside of the roofing material and the ceiling insulation. Because of the fact that there is comparatively little air circulation to remove the hot air, light colored aggregate is used as the surfacing materials to reflect the sun's rays. Fig. 10-4 shows the basic rafter terminology for a flat roof.

Roof Coverings

Pitched roofs on commercial or residential buildings can be covered with asphalt, wood or slate shingles. Flat roofs having a pitch of less than 2″ per foot are normally covered with built-up roofing. Most pitched roofs are covered with asphalt shingles be-

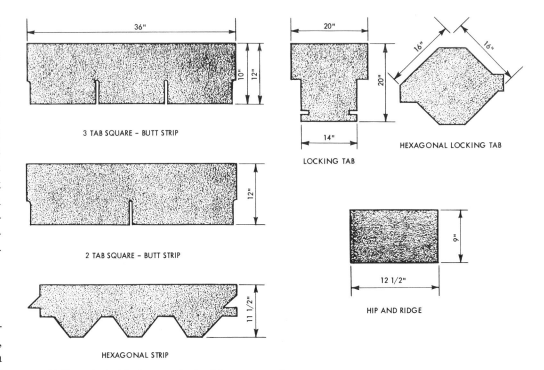

Fig. 10-5. Asphalt shingles may be in strips or separate.

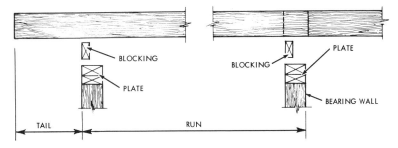

Fig. 10-4. This figure gives basic rafter terminology for flat roofs.

cause they are substantial and economical. Fig. 10-5 shows different types of shingle designs that are used in residential and commercial building construction. All asphalt shingles are manufactured from a felt base saturated with asphalt and surfaced with mineral granules. Fig. 10-6 illustrates a section through an asphalt shingle.

Many of the shingles used in residential construction are known as a "seal-down" shingle. A "seal-down" shingle has adhesive dots placed on the upper lengthwise

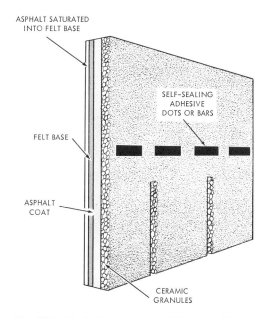

ASPHALT SATURATED INTO FELT BASE

SELF-SEALING ADHESIVE DOTS OR BARS

FELT BASE

ASPHALT COAT

CERAMIC GRANULES

Fig. 10-6. Most shingles have a felt base with an asphalt coat and protective ceramic granules.

BYRD & SON, EAST WALPOLE, MASSACHUSETTS.

Fig. 10-7. The left side of this roof has been shingled with seal-down shingles, while the right half has no adhesive material beneath each tab. Winds have devastating effects on roof coverings.

half of the shingle. As soon as the shingle is laid and the course above is nailed in place, the heat of the sun will melt the adhesive sealing the shingle above in place. The advantage of seal-down shingles is that they are wind-resistant. Fig. 10-7 shows a roof subjected to 120 mph winds. The left half of the roof has been shingled with "seal-down" shingles while the right half has been covered with conventional shingles. Shingles that do not have the self-adhesive feature, even when subjected to a 30 mph wind will raise and bend. Constant bending of the shingle will cause it to tear and blow off.

Shingles are laid in courses (rows) over

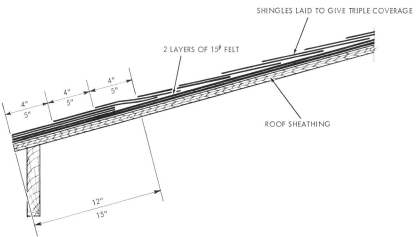

SHINGLES LAID TO GIVE TRIPLE COVERAGE

2 LAYERS OF 15# FELT

ROOF SHEATHING

4"
5"

4"
5"

4"
5"

4"
5"

12"
15"

Fig. 10-8. Roofs with a pitch as low as 2″ in 12″ may be shingled if they are laid with triple coverage.

an asphalt saturated felt (called roofing felt) underlayment. Roofing felt is used as an additional protection over the sheathing. The first course of shingles at the eave is doubled. A strip of metal roof edging is placed beneath the first course of shingles. Roof edging acts as a drip edge, preventing the water from backing up and damaging the sheathing. The amount of each shingle course laid to the weather is dependent upon the size of the shingle and the pitch of the roof. Roofs with pitches as low as 2″ in 12″ can be covered with asphalt shingles, provided the shingles are laid to give triple coverage. Usually two layers of building paper or felt are used between the shingles and sheathing. See Fig. 10-8.

Roofs may be covered with wood shingles. Cedar has proven to be the most durable wood shingle. Wood shingles may be either hand or machine split, with one end of the shingle being thicker than the other end. The thick end is called the butt end of the shingle. Cedar shingles are described as 4/2, 5/2-1/4 and 5/2. A 4/2 shingle indicates there are 4 shingles to 2″ of butt thickness. A 5/2-1/4 shingle means there are 5 shingles to 2¼″ of butt thickness, etc. Cedar shingles are usually 16″, 18″, or 24″ in length and are manufactured either in random widths or in specified dimensioned widths.

Slate. Where a high-quality, long-lasting prestigious roof covering is desired, slate blends well with any type of architectural style from Tudor to contemporary. Slate is a mineral substance that is quarried in the Eastern part of the United States. Generally slate is gray, black, or reddish brown. Slate coverings for roofs are not nailed or stapled in a conventional manner, but may be wired to the back or applied with special clips. Due to the total weight per square foot, rafters must be considerably heavier for slate than for asphalt shingles. Generally slate is not used in residential construction.

Built-up Roof. Roofs that are flat or with little pitch must be covered with a completely watertight surface. Shingles, even though they may be laid with 3 thicknesses, are designed only to shed water. Built-up roofing is made of separate layers of roofing felt bonded together by hot asphalt placed over a building paper underlayment on the decking. See Fig. 10-9. The top layer of

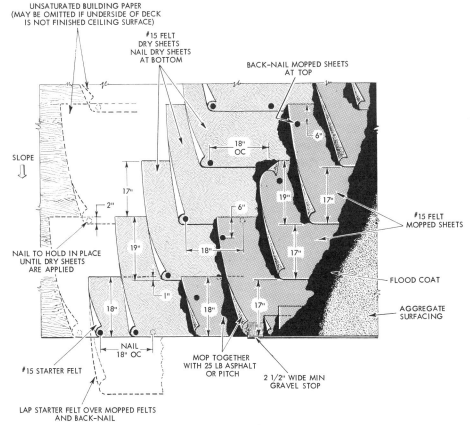

Fig. 10-9. Built-up roofs are made up of layers of roofing felt bonded by applications of hot asphalt.

roofing felt is coated with hot tar and covered with gravel, finely crushed slag, or marble chips.

Built-up roofing surfaces usually are used on roofs having no more pitch than 2″ rise per foot. A pitch greater than 2″/foot will cause the bond between the gravel and asphalt to loosen during heavy rain. Built-up roofing is used over wood or fiber roof decking. Industrial applications place the built-up roof directly over 1½″ rigid insulation that is laid over steel decking. Some applications of built-up roofing on industrial buildings omit the aggregate coating. The expected life of a built-up roof is called a "20 year bond" or "15 year bond" and is dependent upon the bonded number of layers of roofing felt.

Cornice

The cornice or overhang is used on the top exterior of the wall as protection and also as ornamentation. The amount of overhang designed for a cornice depends upon the style of the building and the designer. Houses having steep pitched roofs, such as a Cape Cod, require very little overhang. Houses with low pitched roofs, such as ranch homes, usually require wide overhang. The type or style cannot always be the guide in determining the amount of overhang. Houses designed and built on the ranch pattern, for example, may use a colonial exterior. The cornices in this instance could be either wide or narrow depending on the illusion desired by the designer.

If shading from the sun's rays (sun line) is a fact to be considered, the sun line can be calculated for spring (March 21), summer

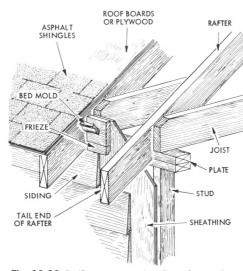

Fig. 10-10. In the open cornice the rafter ends are exposed. Note the frieze is cut to fit the space between rafters.

Fig. 10-11. Open cornices for low pitched roofs often have a taper cut on the rafter ends.

(June 21), fall (September 21), and winter (December 21). During these dates the earth's axis is at its extreme angular position in relation to its orbit about the sun. The method of calculating the sun line for cornice overhang is explained in Chapter 5.

Cornices may be categorized into two general types: the open cornice and the box cornice.

Open Cornice

The open cornice has visible rafter ends. The space between the rafters is closed by an upward extension of the *frieze*. See Fig. 10-10. Fig. 10-11 is another example of the open cornice which is used frequently in contemporary houses that require low pitched roofs with wide overhang. The tail portion of the rafter may be tapered to prevent an extremely heavy or bulky appearance.

An open cornice may be used on a flat

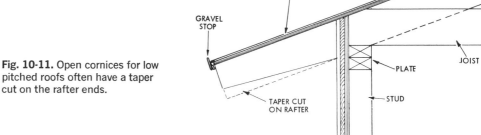

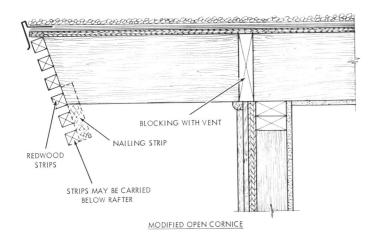

BLOCKING WITH VENT

NAILING STRIP

REDWOOD STRIPS

STRIPS MAY BE CARRIED BELOW RAFTER

MODIFIED OPEN CORNICE

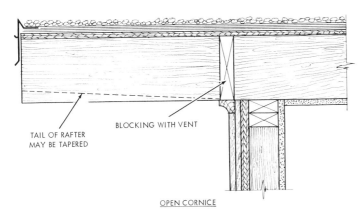

TAIL OF RAFTER MAY BE TAPERED

BLOCKING WITH VENT

OPEN CORNICE

Fig. 10-12. Flat roofs may have open cornices.

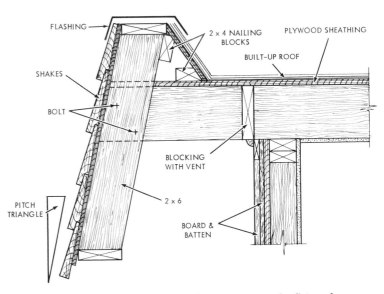

FLASHING

2 x 4 NAILING BLOCKS

PLYWOOD SHEATHING

SHAKES

BUILT-UP ROOF

BOLT

BLOCKING WITH VENT

PITCH TRIANGLE

2 x 6

BOARD & BATTEN

Fig. 10-13. A mansard facade adds to the appearance of a flat roof.

roof just as on a pitched roof. Fig. 10-12 shows two open cornice treatments for a flat roof. Note in these details how the blocking is vented to provide for air circulation. The upper portion of Fig. 10-13 is a modified open cornice for a flat roof with the use of redwood strips. The redwood strip placed on the angular cut of the end of the rafter provides a unique shadow line plus greater opportunity for air to enter the roof area. The tail end of the rafter, shown in Fig. 10-12, bottom, may be tapered to reduce the illusion of bulk.

With the renewed interest in the mansard roof in both residential and commercial designs, a mansard cornice can be applied to a flat roof. See Fig. 10-13. This cornice can be either open, as is shown in the figure, or it may be enclosed with a soffit and classed as a box cornice. Regardless if the mansard design is open or boxed, ventilation must be provided. Note how the flashing serves as a cap *over* the shakes and built-up roofing to make it weatherproof. The flashing is *not* "turned in" the built-up roofing as in Fig. 10-12.

Box Cornice

The box cornice has the tail portion and the underside of the rafters entirely closed with a *fascia* and *plancier* (Fig. 10-14). The plancier may be nailed directly to the underside of the rafter, extending from the wall plate to the fascia. Frequently the plancier is level rather than being nailed directly to the underside of the rafter. In this type of box cornice a *lookout* is nailed to the tail of the rafter and carried level to the wall. Note (Fig. 10-14) that the lookout is nailed to a $2'' \times 4''$ *nailing block* at the wall. An alternate method of attaching lookouts (Fig. 10-15) is by the means of plywood gusset

Fig. 10-15. A plywood gusset and $1'' \times 4''$ piece can be used in constructing the box cornice.

plates. In either case, the fascia is dropped $\frac{3}{8}''$ to $\frac{3}{4}''$ below the plancier to act as a drip mold and to prevent water from entering the cornice interior.

A box cornice treatment for a flat roof is shown in Fig. 10-16.

Gutters

To prohibit water from running directly off of the eaves, it is collected in gutters and

directed to an outlet. Gutters are pitched $1''$ to $1\frac{1}{4}''$ in every 20' to provide an even flowage. If this pitch is increased, the obvious angle of the gutter will detract from building design. Gutters may be either metal (galvanized iron, aluminum, or copper) or wood. Various types of gutters are available in standard sizes.

Half Round Hanging Gutters. The hanging gutter is semicircular in shape and is suspended from the roof by wire or strap hangers (Fig. 10-17). This is the simplest form of gutter; however, it is not used extensively on new construction.

OG metal gutters are probably the most common. This gutter has a molded face (Fig. 10-18) and is called the OG. The illustration shows two methods of hanging the gutter: either by a strap or by a fascia hanger. Regardless of the type of gutter or method of hanging, the gutter should be slightly below the roof line. On steep pitched roofs the outermost portion of the gutter should be approximately $\frac{1}{4}''$ below the roof line, on medium pitched roofs ($7''$ in $12''$)

Fig. 10-14. In the box or closed cornice the plancier and fascia conceal the rafter end. (Note the soffit screen in the plancier to ventilate the cornice and attic space.)

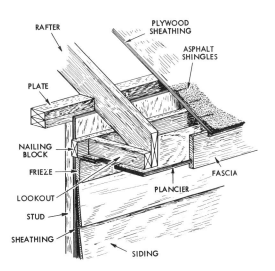

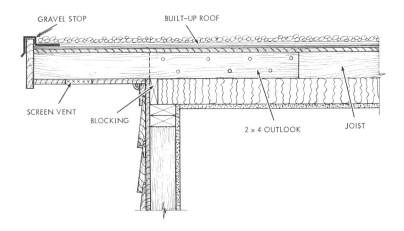

GRAVEL STOP — BUILT-UP ROOF — SCREEN VENT — BLOCKING — 2 x 4 OUTLOOK — JOIST

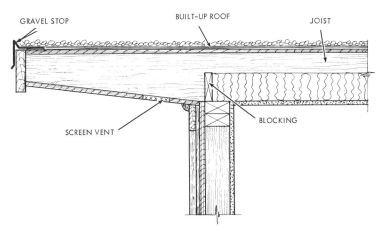

GRAVEL STOP — BUILT-UP ROOF — JOIST — SCREEN VENT — BLOCKING

Fig. 10-16. A flat roof may be extended by means of outlookers.

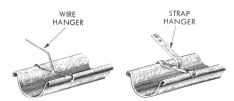

WIRE HANGER — STRAP HANGER

Fig. 10-17. The half-round hanging gutter is the simplest in construction.

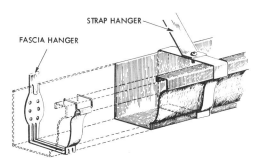

FASCIA HANGER — STRAP HANGER

Fig. 10-18. The OG metal gutter is probably the most common.

approximately ½″, and on low pitched roofs (5″ in 12″) approximately ¾″. This allows the snow to slide clear of the gutter.

Box gutters, illustrated in Fig. 10-19, are built up using a series of lookouts which are nailed together to form a framework for the built-up gutter. The metal lining extends from beneath the roof covering to the bed molding. The box gutter is generally used on traditional houses. It is relatively expensive and more difficult to waterproof than other types of gutters.

Wood gutters of straight grain fir, redwood, or cypress have long been noted for their durability. The face of the wood gutter is similar to that of the metal molded OG gutter. Fig. 10-20 shows a wooden gutter with various dimensions.

Various standard sizes and shapes of gutters are shown in Fig. 10-21.

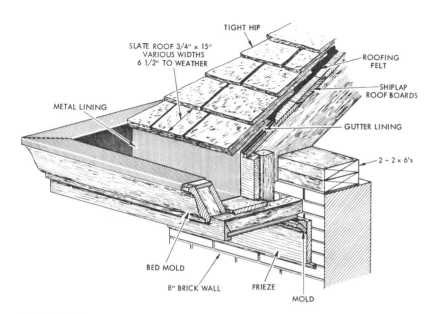

SLATE ROOF 3/4" x 15"
VARIOUS WIDTHS
6 1/2" TO WEATHER

TIGHT HIP

ROOFING FELT

SHIPLAP ROOF BOARDS

METAL LINING

GUTTER LINING

2 - 2 x 6's

BED MOLD

8" BRICK WALL

FRIEZE

MOLD

Fig. 10-19. The box gutter is used in traditional architecture. Special care must be taken to make the gutter lining waterproof.

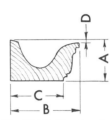

NOMINAL SIZE	A	B	C	D
3" x 5"	2 5/8"	4 5/8"	3 5/8"	1/8"
4" x 5"	3 5/8"	4 5/8"	3 1/4"	3/16"
4" x 6"	3 5/8"	5 5/8"	4 1/4"	3/16"
5" x 7"	4 5/8"	6 5/8"	4 3/4"	1/4"
6" x 8"	5 5/8"	7 5/8"	5 3/8"	3/8"

Fig. 10-20. Wood gutters (redwood or fir) come in various dimensions.

SINGLE BEAD	A
	3 1/2
	4
	5
	6
	7

DOUBLE BEAD	B
	3 1/2
	4
	5
	6
	7

METAL HALF ROUND GUTTERS

Fig. 10-21. Metal gutters come in various sizes and shapes.

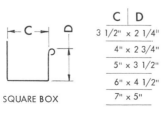

SQUARE BOX

C	D
3 1/2" x 2 1/4"	
4" x 2 3/4"	
5" x 3 1/2"	
6" x 4 1/2"	
7" x 5"	

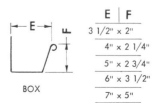

BOX

E	F
3 1/2" x 2"	
4" x 2 1/4"	
5" x 2 3/4"	
6" x 3 1/2"	
7" x 5"	

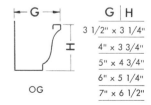

OG

G	H
3 1/2" x 3 1/4"	
4" x 3 3/4"	
5" x 4 3/4"	
6" x 5 1/4"	
7" x 6 1/2"	

METAL BOX GUTTERS

Leaders

Water is drained from the gutters by *leaders* or *conductor pipes* which are usually placed at the ends of the gutter and/or intersecting cornices. Leaders, just as gutters, may be galvanized iron, aluminum, or copper. They may be either round or rectangular, plain or corrugated. Round leaders, either plain or corrugated, range in size from 2″ to 6″ in diameter. Plain or corrugated rectangular leaders are available in the following standard nominal sizes: 1¾″ × 2¼″, 2″ × 3″, 2″ × 4″, and 3″ × 4″. The leader is fastened to the wall and may turn out at the bottom and discharge the water on a concrete splash block, or the leader may be connected by field tile to a dry well or storm sewer. (Note: many cities prohibit draining the run-off into the storm sewer.) One square inch of conductor pipe should be required for every 100 square feet of roof area to be drained.

Flashing

Where surfaces meet (as between chimney and roof or dormer and roof) the juncture must be made watertight. The most practical method is to use wide strips of rust-proof metal, such as galvanized iron, copper, and sometimes lead. These metal strips are called *flashing*. Unequal expansion of adjoining material, particularly when they are exposed to the elements, will cause shrinkage and leakage. For this reason the flashing must be worked in beneath the adjacent exterior covering materials. Flashing

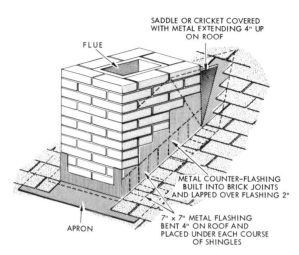

Fig. 10-22. Flashing around a chimney is turned into the mortar joints and carried under the shingles for 4″.

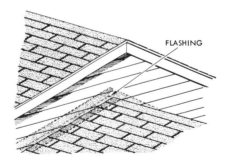

Fig. 10-23. Flashing must be installed at roof and wall junctures.

is required over the foundation and over and under all openings for windows and doors.

The flashing around a chimney is turned into the mortar joints, as in Fig. 10-22, and carried under the shingles for 4″. Frequently the garage roof butts against the main wall (Fig. 10-23). In this case, flashing must be carried over the siding and under the shingles to insure a watertight joint.

Step-by-Step Drawing Procedure:

Cornices

Fig. 10-24 points out the step-by-step procedures used in developing the cornice detail. These basic principles may also be applied to an open cornice just as they have been illustrated for a closed or box cornice.

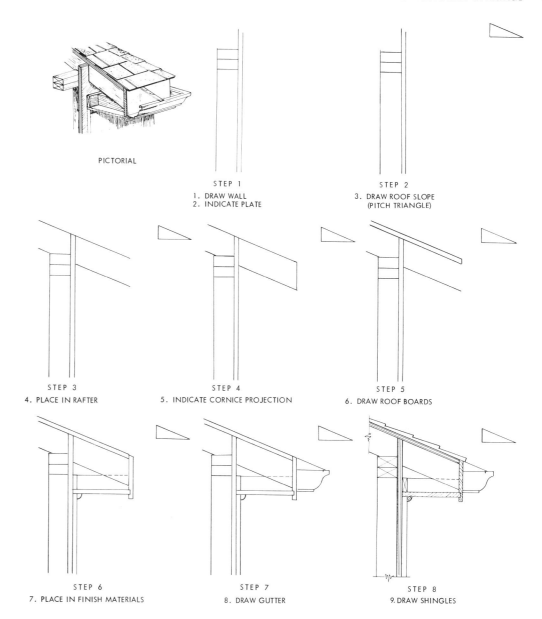

PICTORIAL

STEP 1
1. DRAW WALL
2. INDICATE PLATE

STEP 2
3. DRAW ROOF SLOPE
(PITCH TRIANGLE)

STEP 3
4. PLACE IN RAFTER

STEP 4
5. INDICATE CORNICE PROJECTION

STEP 5
6. DRAW ROOF BOARDS

STEP 6
7. PLACE IN FINISH MATERIALS

STEP 7
8. DRAW GUTTER

STEP 8
9. DRAW SHINGLES

Fig. 10-24. Follow this step-by-step procedure in drafting the cornice detail.

Wood Trussed Roofs

A roof can be more than a protection against the sun and rain. It can affect virtually every function of the rooms below. Few innovations have done more to change the orthodox pattern of home building than the wood trussed rafter. The trussed rafter (Fig. 10-25) is usually triangular in form and is supported internally by framing. The slanted sides of the triangle form the slopes of the roof. The chord or base of the triangle "clear spans" the entire width of the house and therefore requires no support. On the other hand, conventional roof framing requires a bearing wall approximately in the center of the structure to act as a support for the imposed load of the roof. The truss requires vertical support only at the outer walls. Load-bearing partitions are eliminated, thus permitting larger rooms and greater variations in planning. Fig. 10-26 graphically compares the trussed roof with the conventional framing method.

Trusses are usually spaced 24″ O.C. (16″ O.C. is common for conventional roof framing members). Interior finishing materials, such as lath and plaster, sheet rock, or fiberboard, are fastened directly to the underside of the bottom chord.

Trussed roofs, when properly designed, are stronger than conventionally framed roofs. Depending on the type of truss, a material savings up to 30 per cent may be realized. Both erection costs and lumber costs (smaller dimensioned lumber is used) are more economical.

To further the economies in building, construction trusses are designed and drawn with the aid of a computer. Figs. 10-27 and 10-28 show a truss being designed and drawn, augmented by a computer. The design parameter for the truss (pitch, span, load) is given to the computer. The computer will then calculate the size of the cords and webs and will print out this information in the form of a dimensioned drawing.

Trusses may be constructed in the shop or at the building site. For residential homes, they are usually fabricated in the contractor's shop or purchased commercially and delivered to the site. The trusses may be erected, fastened, and then sheathed rapidly. This permits the house to be "under roof" or "closed in" in a fraction of the

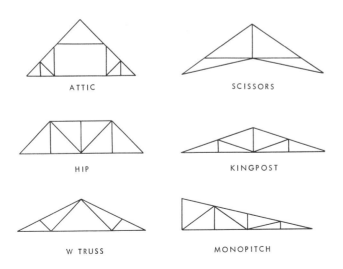

ATTIC

SCISSORS

HIP

KINGPOST

W TRUSS

MONOPITCH

Fig. 10-25. The trussed roof rafter has several basic shapes, each designed for a particular purpose.

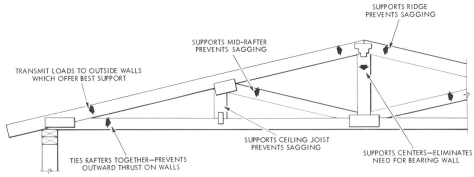

TRUSS ADVANTAGES
VS
CONVENTIONAL FRAMING HAZARDS

Fig. 10-26. This comparison of trussed and conventional roof framing illustrates the advantage of the truss.

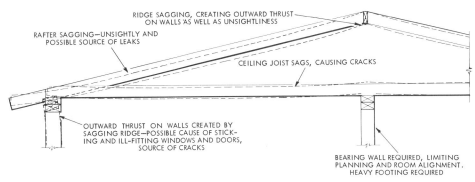

FROM: SANFORD TRUSS, INC., INDIANAPOLIS, INDIANA.

time required when using conventional framing methods. See Fig. 10-29.

Frequently it is assumed that the trussed roof is limited to those homes having a low pitched gable roof. This is not true. Trusses may be designed for any roof type.

Truss Connectors

Trussed rafters are usually assembled with either *split rings* or *truss plates (clip connectors)*.

Split rings (Fig. 10-30) may be used to as-

semble clear spans ranging from 20' to 250'. The split ring is placed in a specially cut groove in the overlapping members. Maximum strength is developed at the joint by distributing the stress over a greater area. The wedge shape of the split ring insures a

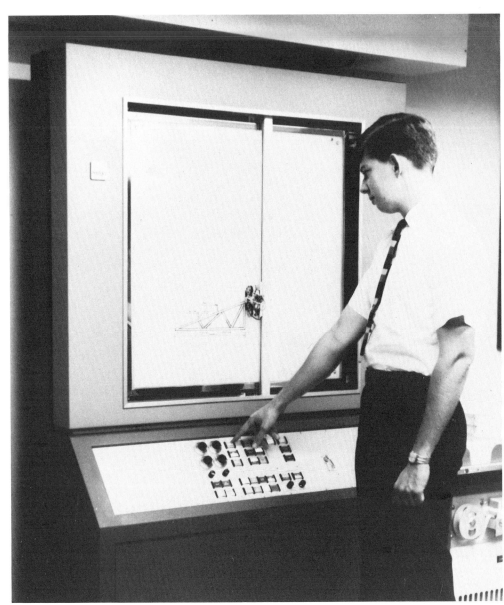

Fig. 10-27. A technician has given the computer the design parameter for a roof truss. All necessary calculations and delineations are made by the computer.

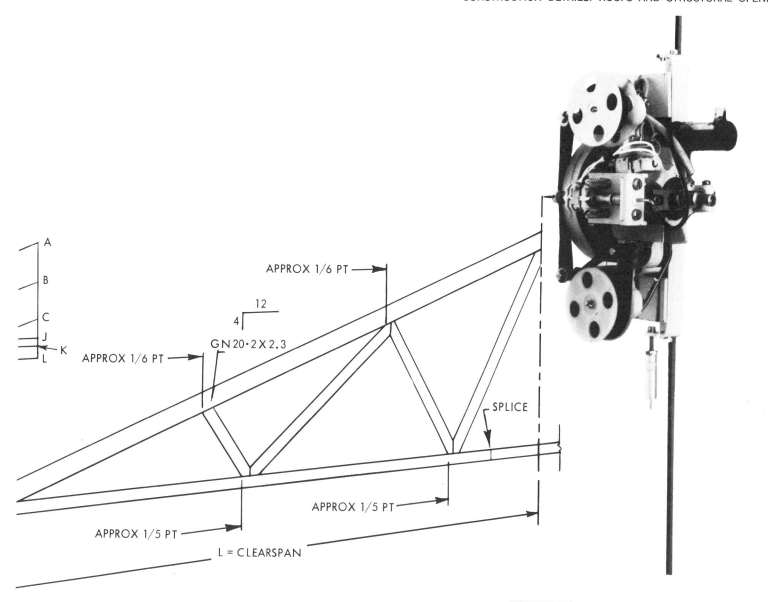

A
B
C
J
K
L

APPROX 1/6 PT →

12
4

GN 20·2 X 2.3

APPROX 1/6 PT →

SPLICE

APPROX 1/5 PT →

APPROX 1/5 PT →

L = CLEARSPAN

Fig. 10-28. The drawing created by the digitized head is ready to be reproduced.

AUTOMATED BUILDING COMPONENTS, INC., MIAMI, FLORIDA.

Fig. 10-29. In this photograph a kingpost trussed rafter roof is being erected. Note the hip trusses in the background.

Fig. 10-30. Split ring connectors give strength by distributing the stress over a greater area.

tight fitting joint when the ring is fully seated in the conforming groove. The 2½″ diameter ring which is used for residential trusses utilizes 2″ lumber.

Truss plates or **clip connections** (Fig. 10-31) have a strength comparable to the split ring connector. Depending upon the size of the connector, each clip has an effective holding power of 20 to 60 nails. One of the advantages in using a plate or clip connector (as compared with the split rings) is the constant thickness of the truss. The web members of a truss assembled with split

Plywood Connector Plates. Truss designs may *also* be fastened with plywood gussets (Fig. 10-32) glued and nailed or stapled to the chords and webs. Each plate must have a specific number of nails or staples depending upon the pitch and clear span of the truss as well as the imposed load. One of the problems, however, with the plywood gusset is that pressure must be applied if they are glued; also a specific amount of curing time is required for the glue to set. The plywood gusset is slowly being replaced by the clip type connector (Fig. 10-31).

Truss Anchors

Trussed rafters may be fastened to the plate by either a framing anchor (Fig. 10-33, top) or spacing blocks (Fig. 10-33, bottom). The framing anchor will produce a joint comparable to the usual toenail method. The framing anchor type of connection, however, is usually stronger and more efficient. All anchors are either galvanized or made from rust-proof material. The spacing block allows the rafter to be spiked to the block; the block, in turn, is toenailed to the plate.

W Truss

The W truss design is probably the most common design used in residential construction. Framing for a gable roof, assembled with split rings, is shown in Fig. 10-34. Web and chord dimensions are given for roofs having 4″, 5″, 6″, and 7″ rises in 12″

PANEL CLIP CO., FARMINGTON, MICHIGAN.

Fig. 10-31. Truss clips have an effective holding power of 20 to 60 nails.

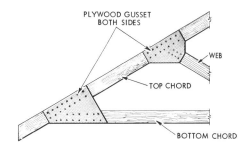

PLYWOOD GUSSET
BOTH SIDES

WEB

TOP CHORD

BOTTOM CHORD

Fig. 10-32. Plywood gussets glued and nailed in place serve to make strong, lightweight trusses.

rings must be bolted to the sides of the chord giving a thickness of 6½ ″, whereas the plate or clip connector method of fabrication produces a truss 1⅝ ″ thick (actual size of nom-inal 2″ lumber) plus the minimal thickness of the plates. Truss plates are either galvanized (zinc coated) to prevent rusting or they are made from a non-rusting material.

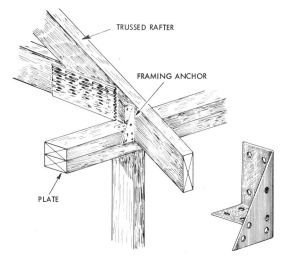

TRUSSED RAFTER

FRAMING ANCHOR

PLATE

Fig. 10-33. Either a framing anchor or blocking may be used to secure roof trusses.

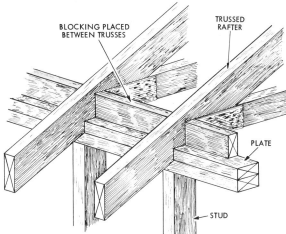

BLOCKING PLACED BETWEEN TRUSSES

TRUSSED RAFTER

PLATE

STUD

of run.[1] Note that dimensions are given for the maximum clear spans within each slope.

1. Design for other types of trusses for residential construction may be obtained from Timber Engineering Co., Washington, D.C.

As an example, assume that a W truss fabricated with split rings is to be used on a house having a clear span of 30'-0" and a $\frac{1}{6}$ slope roof (4" rise in 12" run). Using Fig. 10-34, the dimensions for the chords and webs may be determined. The lumber sizes and lengths are also given. For a 30'-0" span (4" in 12"), dimension A is 7'-10⅞", B is 7'-0½", C is 3'-6¹⁄₁₆". The lumber for the two top chords (E) will be 2" × 8" × 18'-0". The bottom chord (F) will require two 2" × 6" × 18'-0" lengths if the ceiling is to be plastered *or* two 2" × 4" × 18'-0" lengths if the ceiling is to be drywall. Two 2" × 4" × 12'-0" lumber lengths will be needed to construct the webs (G). Note that the measurements for chords are given *along* and *between* the centerline of the members and that the shorter of the webs is fastened to the top chord with a 1" × 4" scab.

W truss designs fabricated with Truss Clips (a patented clip connector) are shown in Fig. 10-35. The design of the W truss assembled with clip connectors is the same as that with split rings. If, for instance, a home is designed 42'-4" in length and 28'-11" deep and a W truss rafter having a ⅛ pitch is going to be used to support the roof, from the information given in Fig. 10-35 the top chords will be cut from 2" × 6" lumber and the bottom chord and webs will require 2" × 4" lumber. A "P" truss clip will be used at the intersection of top and bottom chord at joints 1 and 2; the "M" clip will be used to secure the juncture of the 2 webs and bottom chord; the "J" clip will be used at joints 5 and 6; the top chords will be joined with an "N" clip and a "D" clip placed on only one side of the truss; and, since the clear span of the house is *less than* 31'-5", an "M" clip will be used to splice the two bottom chords together.

Fig. 10-34. The W truss is probably the most common design in residential construction. Note that split rings are used. (The figures shown here will give a safe live and dead load of 35 lbs. per sq. ft. and a dead ceiling load of 10 lbs. per sq. ft. with trusses spaced 2'0" O.C.)

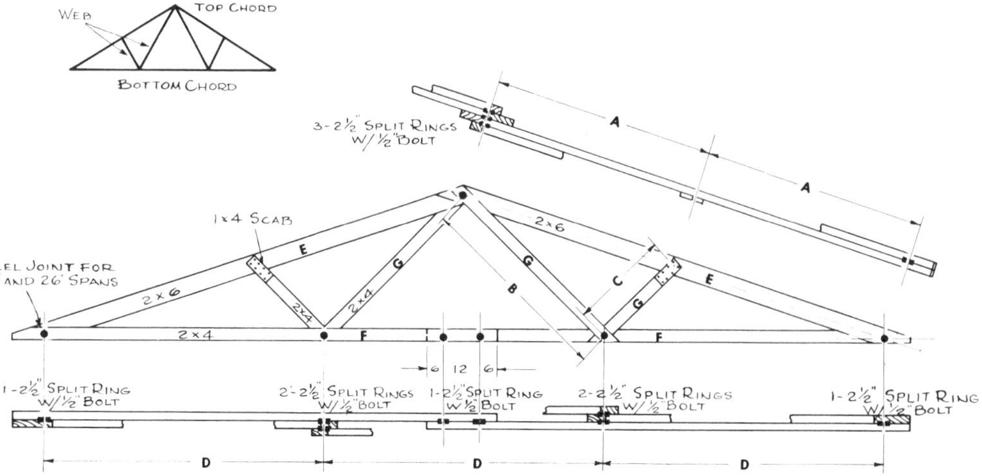

W TRUSS SIZING WITH DRYWALL CEILING

Slope	Length of Span	Dimensions A	B	C	D	Lumber Size (Two Lengths Needed) 2×8	2×6	2×4
4 in 12	20	5'-3 1/4"	4'-8 3/16"	2'-3 13/16"	6'-8"		E (12'-0")	F (12'-0") G (8'-0")
	22	5'-9 9/16"	5'-1 7/8"	2'-6 3/4"	7'-4"		E (14'-0")	F (14'-0") G (10'-0")
	24	6'-3 7/8"	5'-7 1/2"	2'-9 9/16"	8'-0"		E (14'-0")	F (14'-0") G (10'-0")
	26	6'-10 3/16"	6'-1 3/16"	3'-0 7/16"	8'-8"		E (16'-0")	F (16'-0") G (10'-0")
	28	7'-4 9/16"	6'-6 13/16"	3'-3 1/4"	9'-4"	E (16'-0")	F *(16'-0")	F (16'-0") G (12'-0")
	30	7'-10 7/8"	7'-0 1/2"	3'-6 1/16"	10'-0"	E (18'-0")	F *(18'-0")	F (18'-0") G (12'-0")
	32	8'-5 3/16"	7'-6 3/16"	3'-8 7/8"	10'-8"	E (18'-0")	F *(18'-0")	F (18'-0") G (12'-0")
5 in 12	20	5'-5"	5'-3 5/8"	2'-7 5/8"	6'-8"		E (12'-0")	F (12'-0") G (10'-0")
	22	5'-11 1/2"	5'-10 1/16"	2'-10 13/16"	7'-4"		E (14'-0")	F (14'-0") G (10'-0")
	24	6'-6"	6'-4 7/16"	3'-2"	8'-0"		E (14'-0")	F (14'-0") G (12'-0")
	26	7'-0 1/2"	6'-10 7/8"	3'-5 1/4"	8'-8"		E (16'-0")	F (16'-0") G (12'-0")
	28	7'-7"	7'-5 1/4"	3'-8 7/16"	9'-4"		E,F *(16'-0")	F (16'-0") G (12'-0")
	30	8'-1 1/2"	7'-11 11/16"	3'-11 5/8"	10'-0"		E,F *(18'-0")	F (18'-0") G (14'-0")
	32	8'-8"	8'-6 1/16"	4'-2 13/16"	10'-8"		E (20'-0") F *(18'-0")	F (18'-0") G (14'-0")
6 in 12	20	5'-7 1/16"	5'-11 11/16"	2'-11 5/8"	6'-8"		E (12'-0")	F (12'-0") G (10'-0")
	22	6'-1 13/16"	6'-6 7/8"	3'-3 1/4"	7'-4"		E (14'-0")	F (14'-0") G (12'-0")
	24	6'-8 1/2"	7'-2 1/8"	3'-6 7/8"	8'-0"		E (16'-0")	F (14'-0") G (12'-0")
	26	7'-3 3/16"	7'-9 5/16"	3'-10 7/16"	8'-8"		E (16'-0")	F (16'-0") G (12'-0")
	28	7'-9 15/16"	8'-4 9/16"	4'-2 1/16"	9'-4"		E (18'-0") F *(16'-0")	F (16'-0") G (14'-0")
	30	8'-4 5/8"	8'-11 3/4"	4'-5 11/16"	10'-0"		E,F *(18'-0")	F (18'-0") G (16'-0")
	32	8'-11 5/16"	9'-6 13/16"	4'-9 1/4"	10'-8"		E (20'-0") F *(18'-0")	F (18'-0") G (16'-0")
7 in 12	20	5'-9 7/16"	6'-8 3/16"	3'-3 7/8"	6'-8"		E (14'-0")	F,G (12'-0")
	22	6'-4 7/16"	7'-4 1/4"	3'-7 15/16"	7'-4"		E (14'-0")	F (14'-0") G (12'-0")
	24	6'-11 5/8"	8'-0 5/16"	3'-11 15/16"	8'-0"		E (16'-0")	F,G (14'-0")
	26	7'-6 5/16"	8'-8 3/8"	4'-4"	8'-8"		E (16'-0")	F (16'-0") G (14'-0")
	28	8'-1 1/4"	9'-4 7/16"	4'-8"	9'-4"		E (18'-0") F *(16'-0")	F,G (16'-0")
	30	8'-8 3/16"	10'-0 1/2"	5'-0 1/16"	10'-0"		E (20'-0") F *(18'-0")	F (18'-0") G (16'-0")
	32	9'-3 1/8"	10'-8 9/16"	5'-4 1/16"	10'-8"		E (20'-0") F *(18'-0")	F,G (18'-0")

* BOTTOM CHORD SIZES FOR PLASTER CEILING

LIVE LOAD, 35 LBS PER SQUARE FT; DEAD CEILING LOAD, 10 LBS PER SQUARE FT; SPACED 2'-0" OC

TIMBER ENGINEERING CO., WASHINGTON, D.C.

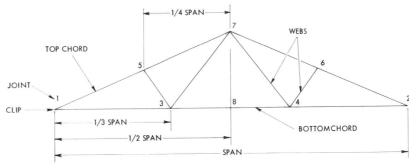

| PITCH | CLIPS FOR JOINTS* | | | | | CHORD SIZE | | WEB SIZE |
	1 and 2	3 and 4	5 and 6	7	8	TOP	BOTTOM	
4, 5 and 6 in 12 spans to 28' – 0"	M spans to 24' – 8" N spans 24' – 9" to 28' – 8"	K	D	L or M	K spans to 26' – 8" L spans 26' – 9" to 28' – 8"	2 x 4	2 x 4	2 x 4
4 in 12 spans to 36' – 0"	N spans to 32' – 8" O spans 32' – 9" to 36' – 8"	L	J	M	L	2 x 6	2 x 4	2 x 4
3 in 12 spans to 28' – 0"	N spans to 24' – 8" O spans 24' – 9" to 28' – 8"	L	J	N	L spans to 24' – 8" M spans 24' – 9" to 28' – 8"	2 x 4	2 x 4	2 x 4
3 in 12 spans to 34' – 0"	P	M	J	D** and N	M spans to 31' – 5" N spans 31' – 9" to 34' – 8"	2 x 6	2 x 4	2 x 4
7 in 12 Spans to 27' – 0"	P	M	J	O	M spans to 22' – 8" N spans 22' – 9" to 27' – 8"	2 x 4	2 x 4	2 x 4

* ALL CLIPS PLACED ON BOTH SIDES TO TRUSS   ** CLIP PLACED ON ONE SIDE OF TRUSS

CLIP SIZES

LETTER	SIZE	LETTER	SIZE
D	1 7/16 x 4 5/8	M	3 5/8 x 9 27/32
J	3 5/8 x 3 15/16	N	3 5/8 x 11 15/16
K	3 5/8 x 5 29/32	O	5 5/8 x 13 25/32
L	3 5/8 x 7 7/8	P	3 5/8 x 19 11/16

Fig. 10-35. Truss clips may also be used with the W. truss.

Trussed Roof Cornice

The cornice for the trussed roof, just as with a conventionally framed roof, may be either open or closed. The same principles of design for cornice construction apply to both kinds of roofs.

Roof Ventilating

An attic that is improperly vented is the most frequent cause of waterspots on the ceiling, frost at the junction of the wall and ceiling, and ice dams in the gutters. To eliminate damp areas and frost, fresh **air in** sufficient quantities must circulate through the attic. Areas in the attic that are not directly vented usually do not have circulating air. For example, if the roof is vented only with louvers on the gable ends, the areas at the extremities of the attic will have little or no circulating air. When the air has an opportunity to circulate, the warm moist air that leaks into the attic will not have sufficient time to condense and form water. Adequate circulation will eliminate the condensation problem during the winter months. It will also eliminate heat build-up during the summer months, thus making the house much cooler.

Attics

Until recently little regard was given to attic ventilation. Houses were extremely hot in summer and condensation formed during

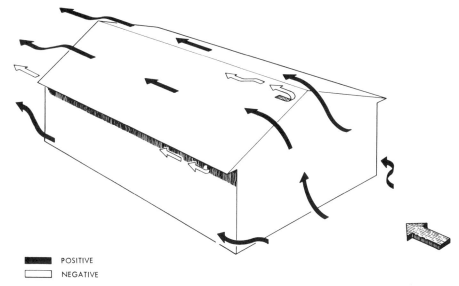

Fig. 10-36. External air flow creates negative pressures (vacuums) and positive pressures on the roof, sides, and ends of a building.

the winter. As more information was obtained about home insulation and new and more economical insulative materials were available, heat loss was no longer a problem. Vents were placed in the roof or gable ends to provide ventilation.

The direction and velocity of the wind will definitely affect the movement of air in the attic. As the air flows around a residence (Fig. 10-36), areas of negative pressure and positive pressure are created on various parts of the sides and roof. The areas of positive and negative pressure will vary with the direction and velocity of the wind. The variations of pressure will affect the air movement within the attic.

An adequately ventilated attic must have a reasonably uniform flow of air through *all parts of the attic* under all ranges of wind velocity and direction.

Gutters

In some areas ice dams along gutters pose maintenance problems. Ice dams are caused by appreciable differences in attic and outside temperatures. By maintaining an attic temperature similar to the outside, snow melting from the roof will not refreeze on the overhang and gutters. By maintaining an adequate air flow *through all parts of the attic*, this problem can be eliminated.

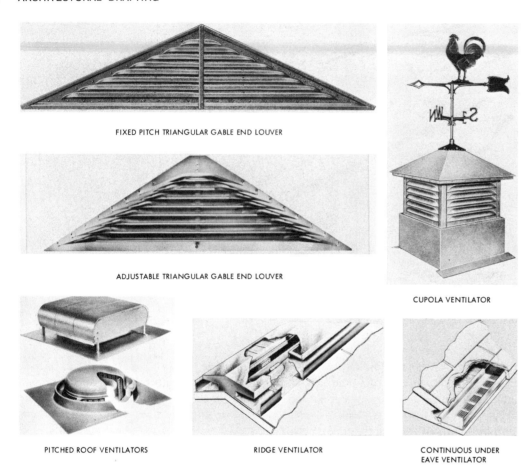

FIXED PITCH TRIANGULAR GABLE END LOUVER

ADJUSTABLE TRIANGULAR GABLE END LOUVER

CUPOLA VENTILATOR

PITCHED ROOF VENTILATORS

RIDGE VENTILATOR

CONTINUOUS UNDER
EAVE VENTILATOR

H. C. PRODUCTS CO., PRINCEVILLE, ILLINOIS.

Fig. 10-37. Various devices are used to vent the attic.

vent is dependent on the *placement* and the *total free ventilating area* relative to the positive and negative pressure areas. Winds frequently shift direction as much as 30° and occasionally as much as 90° in a short period of time. These changes in wind direction will affect the air flow within the attic. Recent research has shown that the total volume of air flowing through an attic is not sufficient basis to indicate the quality of ventilation. In certain circumstances, most of the air may flow through one portion of the attic leaving other portions with a minor amount of air movement.

Rather than depending upon normal circulation to cause air movement, a power attic ventilator will do the job more effectively. Power attic ventilators are controlled by a preset thermostat and humidostat. See Fig. 10-38. Power ventilators may be mounted on pitched or flat roofs, on gable ends, walls, or concealed in a decorative cupola. Manufacturer's recommendations should be followed regarding size and the number of square feet to be vented.

Vent System Requirements

H. C. Product's research has brought out several ventilating factors:[2]

    1. Roof louvers, either when used alone or in combination with soffit vents, contribute very little to effective air flow through the attic.

2. H. S. Hinrichs. *Comparative Study of the Effectiveness of Fixed Ventilating Louvers* (Princeville, Illinois: H. C. Products Co., 1961).

Venting Devices

Obviously the amount of air permitted to enter and leave the attic is dependent upon the number, size, and type of venting devices. Fig. 10-37 shows six different types of venting devices. Frequently two of these are used in combination, such as the ridge ventilator and the continuous under-the-eave (soffit) ventilator. The air flow through any

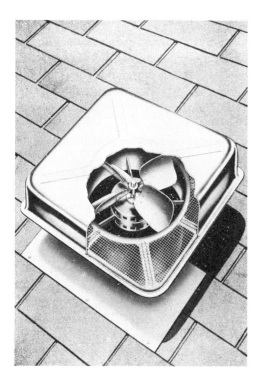

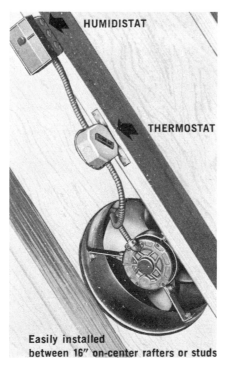

KOOL-O-MATIC CORP., NILES, MICHIGAN.

Fig. 10-38. Power ventilators aid in removing excessive heat from attic areas. Both interior and exterior fans are used.

as at 10 m.p.h. This type of vent provides air flow due to temperature differences.

4. Continuous soffit vents produce substantial air flow proportional to wind velocity regardless of wind direction. The major portion of the air flow remains near the attic floor with the result that effective air flow is approximately $\frac{1}{5}$ of the total air movement.

5. Combination of continuous ridge and soffit vents provide a steady flow of air through the attic regardless of wind direction and velocity. Utilizing both a soffit and ridge vent will provide an *effective* air flow 3 to 5 times as great as any other combination of fixed venting equipment, i.e., roof and soffit vent, gable end louvers and roof vent, ridge and roof vent, etc.

6. Prevailing wind direction has a limited value as a basis for the design of an attic ventilating system.

7. Control of moisture condensation requires a minimum effective *air flow of 0.8 cubic feet per minute per square foot of ceiling area* during winter.

Various figures may be located which enable the designer to *approximately* calculate proper attic ventilation. Most existing tables have proven to be *too low to adequately control* condensation during the winter and reduce attic temperatures in summer. The figures shown in Table 10-1 give the correct net free areas in square inches for a non-mechanical venting systems per square foot

2. Gable end louvers are dependent upon favorable winds, either perpendicular or diagonal to the louver face. With such favorable winds the effective air flow is approximately $\frac{1}{6}$ of the total air flow through the louver. This fractional air flow is not appreciably increased when the gable end louver is combined with continuous soffit vents. Gable end louvers provide very lim-

ited attic ventilation when the winds are perpendicular to the ridge (parallel to the louver face). Under *these* conditions, the addition of a continuous soffit vent will increase the effective air flow by 50 per cent.

3. Continuous ridge vent when used alone has the important characteristic that effective air flow remains approximately the same at zero wind velocity

TABLE 10-1

VENT SYSTEM REQUIREMENTS FOR ADEQUATE

Air Flow in the Attic (5 mph winds)

VENTING DEVICE(S)	Square Inches of Net Free Area Needed per Square Foot of Ceiling Area
ROOF LOUVERS ONLY	11.0
GABLE END LOUVERS ONLY	8.2
CONTINUOUS RIDGE VENT ONLY	7.3
ROOF LOUVERS AND CONTINUOUS SOFFIT VENT	6.9
CONTINUOUS SOFFIT VENT ONLY	6.4
GABLE END LOUVERS AND CONTINUOUS SOFFIT VENTS	5.5
CONTINUOUS RIDGE AND SOFFIT VENTS	1.2

From: H. C. Hinrichs, Comparative Study of the Effectiveness of Fixed Ventilating Louvers (Princeville, Illinois: H. C. Products Co., 1961).

of ceiling area. This will give a system which will provide an air flow of 0.8 cubic feet per square foot of ceiling area at 5 m.p.h. winds. (Free net areas for venting systems are given in manufacturers specifications.)

For example, given a total ceiling area of 1200 sq. ft., a venting system using only a continuous ridge vent would need a net free area of 8760 sq. in. (7.3 × 1200). If a continuous ridge *and* soffit vents were used, only 1440 sq. in. (1.2 × 1200) would be needed in the system.

Windows

The first window was also a door. The cave dweller had one all-purpose door-window for access, light, and air. As man's abode increased in complexity, separate openings for light and ventilation were inserted into the exterior walls. The Egyptians, as early as 5000 B.C., used simple windows with sculptured frames. At that period in history, the window was elevated from its location near the floor and placed higher in the wall for light and ventilation; the sill was placed below the opening. Later, transparent material was inserted in the openings to afford protection from the weather. Better control of ventilation was instituted by the hinged casement window. Other forms of protection were developed: shutters (for winter warmth, summer coolness, and protection against intruders), curtains, blinds, insect screens, awnings, and jalousie windows. In France, during the 18th Century, an improved type of window, having a vertically sliding sash, was developed. This was nicknamed *Fenetre Guillotine*. Today it is known as the common double-hung window.

Fig. 10-39 (top) graphically depicts the relationship between the rough opening, frame, sash, and window panes. The vertical sides of the sash are called *stiles*. The horizontal members of the sash (top and bottom) are called *rails*. The two vertical sides of the frame and the top piece are called the *jamb*. The exposed vertical pieces on the outside are called the *trim* and the piece at the top is called the *drip cap*. The bottom of the frame is called the *sill*. Glass panes are called *lights*. Dimensions of the glass panes or lights are given in inches. The width is given first, the height second: 26″ × 14″ or $26/_{14}$. Fig. 10-39 (bottom) illustrates the correct manner of showing the direction of swing.

Window Styles

The home designer is no longer limited to a few styles of windows. There is now a wide selection from which to choose. Fig. 10-40 illustrates windows which are currently used in small home construction.

Double-hung windows (Fig. 10-40A) are one of the most popular types of windows since they provide excellent ventilation.

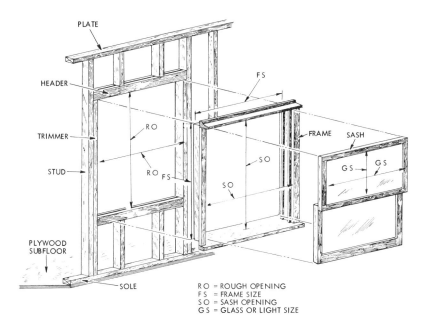

R O = ROUGH OPENING
F S = FRAME SIZE
S O = SASH OPENING
G S = GLASS OR LIGHT SIZE

This is facilitated by raising the lower sash and lowering the upper sash to permit continual air circulation; however, only 50 per cent of the window may be opened. The double-hung window was originally held in its open position by spring-loaded pins in the sash. Later, the sashes were counterbalanced by cords, pulleys, and weights. Virtually all double-hung windows now are fitted with spring loaded balances or friction holding devices. Very little maintenance is required for the new models of double-hung windows. They are easy to clean since many manufacturers are now building windows so that each sash may be removed from the frame. The double-hung window placed in a frame wall is essentially the same as the double-hung placed in a masonry wall. The

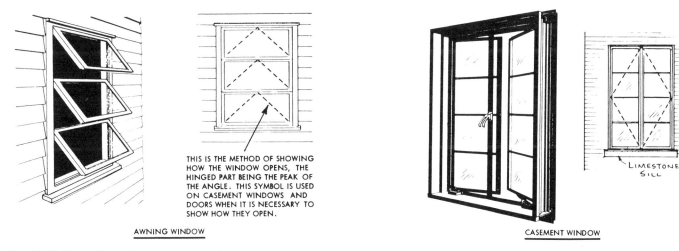

THIS IS THE METHOD OF SHOWING HOW THE WINDOW OPENS, THE HINGED PART BEING THE PEAK OF THE ANGLE. THIS SYMBOL IS USED ON CASEMENT WINDOWS AND DOORS WHEN IT IS NECESSARY TO SHOW HOW THEY OPEN.

AWNING WINDOW

CASEMENT WINDOW

Fig. 10-39. These illustrations give window framing details and show the manner of depicting the hinge swing.

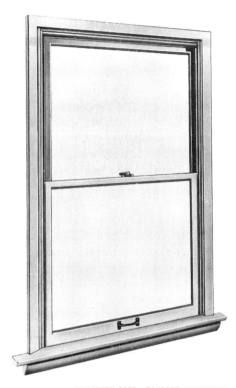

A. Double-Hung Window.

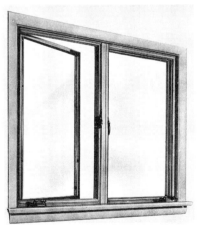

B. Horizontal Sliding Window or "Slider"

C. Awning Window.

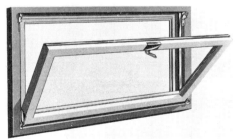

D. Hopper Window.

Fig. 10-40. Various window styles are used in home construction.

E. Casement Window.

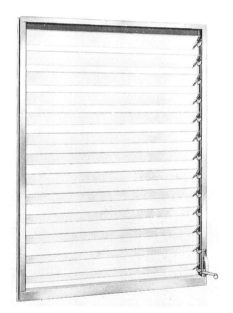

F. Jalousie Window.

difference in wall construction will require different details in the opening.

"Sliders" or horizontal sliding windows (Fig. 10-40B) operate just as double-hung windows only they are placed on their side. Sliders were designed primarily for the modern ranch style home. There are a minimum number of working parts — usually only nylon rollers since no counter-balancing or holding device is needed. Sliding windows are made so that either both sashes slide or only one sash slides with the other fixed. Some manufacturers have designed the movable sash with a spring tension device to allow removal of the sash for painting and cleaning. This type of window is placed 3'-6" to 4'-6" above the floor and creates extra wall space that would otherwise be used by a double hung window.

Awning windows (Fig. 10-40C) are top hinged and open to the outside. This type of window may be used either as a single unit or as a multiple unit with several windows placed in a vertical or horizontal line. They may be used in combination with fixed sash units, that is, those that do not open. When awning windows are placed together, side by side, they are called *ribbon* windows. When fully opened, the awning window gives 100 percent ventilation. Most units are operated by a geared crank, thus making opening, closing, and locking easier. The top hinging feature of the awning window permits opening for ventilation during rain.

Hopper windows (Fig. 10-40D) are a variation of the awning window. The difference is that they are hinged at the bottom and open to the inside. Frequently, single hopper units are used as basement windows. These, similar to the awning window, may also be used in combination with fixed sash units. Either singly or in combination with fixed glass units they are often used high on the wall for bedroom windows. The hopper-type window provides draft-free ventilation since it deflects the incoming air upwards.

Casement windows (Fig. 10-40E) are hinged to the frame on either side and swing outward for ventilation. The projecting sashes act as scoops to bring in any available breezes. It is difficult, however, to make the casement window completely weathertight. To overcome this situation a drip molding is placed along the bottom rail to prevent water from entering at the sill. Metal casements may be set in a mastic (bituminous) cement to insure a complete seal around the frame. These windows may be used singly, in multiple units, or in combination with a fixed window unit. When open, the casement window provides 100 percent ventilation.

Jalousie windows (Fig. 10-40F) are a comparatively recent development in the window manufacturing field. They operate on the principle of a venetian blind. The jalousie is similar to a series of glass louvers, each louver being 2' to 6' wide. They also provide 100 percent ventilation when open. These louvers are activated by means of a geared crank. Generally, jalousies are located in living areas which are used in mild, seasonal weather.

Picture windows are large, stationary windows which provide no ventilation since the sash is fixed. These windows are usually installed with welded insulating glass (two layers of glass separated by a sealed air space) which requires a thicker sash. Fig. 10-41 shows insulating glass in a sash. This type of *glazing* (i.e., glass installed in the sash) allows for a large glass area with a small amount of heat loss. Picture windows are ventilated by double hung, casement, hopper, or awning windows at either side. Louvered openings or hopper windows are used at the bottom. Some designers, however, use picture windows which are carried to the floor.

Lights

The glass in the sashes of the double hung and casement windows may be divided into *lights*. These are small squares or horizontal sections of glass separated by *muntins* (thin bars of wood or metal). Small lights are used primarily in traditional Cape Cod, colonial, and early American style houses. Windows using small lights or divided sash are not limited to the special architectural types just mentioned — they may also be used in the contemporary ranch-type home.

Two or more windows may be placed together in a common frame to form a multiple window. The vertical member separating the windows is called a *mullion*. (Note: do not confuse *mullions* with *muntins,* defined above.)

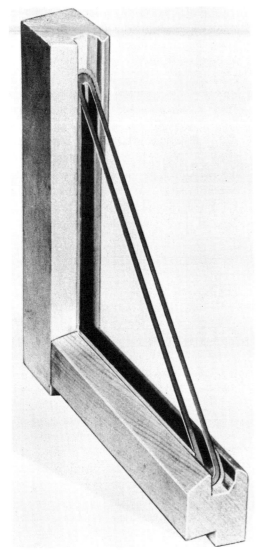

ANDERSEN CORP., BAYPORT, MINNESOTA.

Fig. 10-41. Insulating glass (two layers of sealed glass) is one of the most efficient methods of insulating a window.

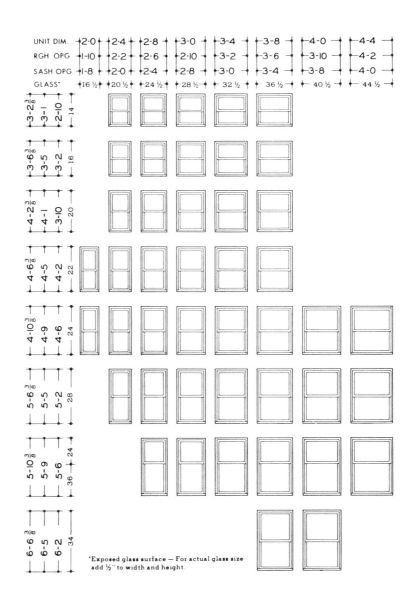

ANDERSEN CORP., BAYPORT, MINNESOTA.

Fig. 10-42. Standard Double-Hung Window Sizes.

Metal Windows

Windows have traditionally been constructed with a wood frame and sash. Many windows are now made of steel or aluminum structural components or a combination of metal and wood. As an insulator, however, wood remains the most efficient.

Window Samples

The great majority of windows are completely assembled at the factory or mill with hardware, glazing, weather stripping, and screens. The architectural designer or architectural draftsman does not design the windows as was the practice years ago. Today he selects the windows from a wide range of styles and sizes listed in catalogs. Figs. 10-42, 10-43, 10-44, and 10-45 are samples from manufacturers' catalogs. The sash opening or light size must always be specified on the drawing.

Almost all window manufacturers' catalogs indicate the rough opening size, sash size, and light size. Some, however, list only the rough opening and frame size. The size of the rough opening is slightly larger than the actual window frame. This extra space provides sufficient room between the frame and opening for leveling and blocking in the window.

Window Schedules

For convenience and clarity the draftsman usually puts important information concerning windows in a table. This table,

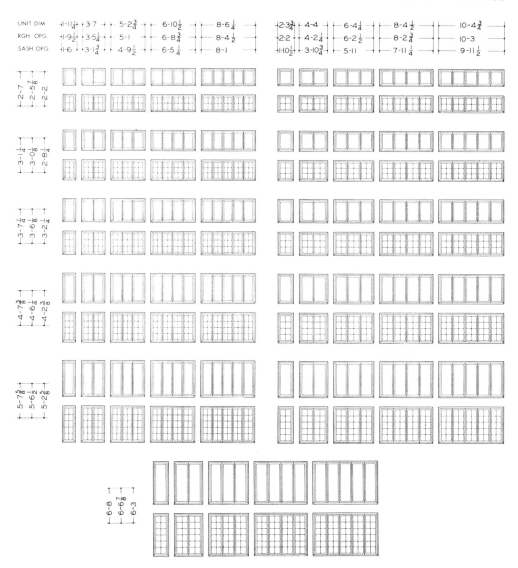

ANDERSEN CORP., BAYPORT, MINNESOTA.

Fig. 10-43. Standard Single and Combination Casement Window Sizes.

UNIT DIM.	3'-0"	3'-4"	3'-9½"	4'-8"	5'-4"	6'-0"
ROUGH OPG.	2'-10"	3'-2"	3'-7½"	4'-6"	5'-2"	5'-10"
SASH OPG.	2'-8"	3'-0"	3'-5½"	4'-4"	5'-0"	5'-8"
GLASS SIZE (Ea. Sa.)	14"	16"	18¾"	24"	28"	32"

Scale: ¼" = 1' 0"

ROCK ISLAND MILLWORK CO., ROCK ISLAND, ILLINOIS.

Fig. 10-44. Standard Horizontal Sliding Window Sizes.

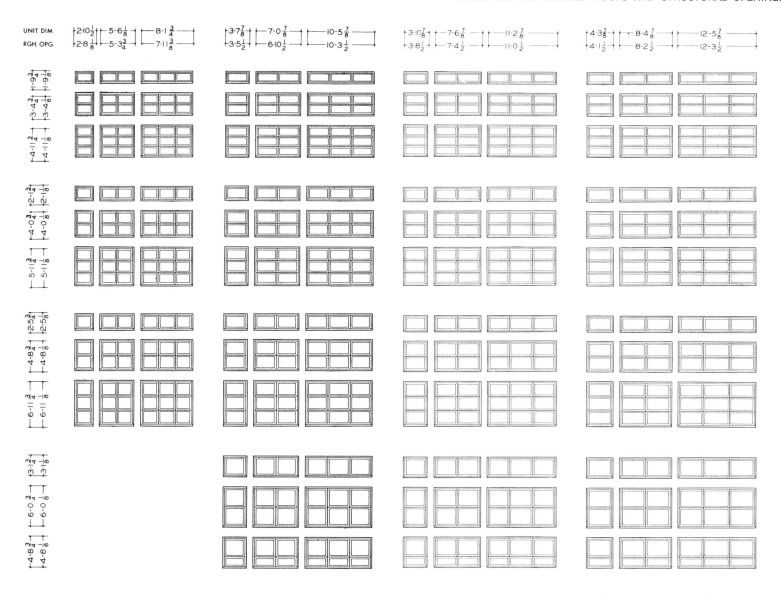

ANDERSEN CORP., BAYPORT, MINNESOTA.

Fig. 10-45. Standard Awning and Hopper Window Sizes. (Note that any of the compound units may be designated as awning, hopper, or fixed).

WINDOW SCHEDULE

SYMBOL	QUANTITY	TYPE	ROUGH OPENING	SASH SIZE	MFG No	REMARKS
1	3	AWNING, 1 LT	$3'-1\frac{1}{2}'' \times 2'-0\frac{1}{4}''$	$3'-0'' \times 1'-8''$	1-36-20	OBSCURE GL IN ONE SASH
2	2	CASEMENT, 4 LTS	$5'-2'' \times 4'-6\frac{3}{8}''$	$1'-6'' \times 4-2\frac{3}{8}''$	6434	MIDDLE SASH FIXED
3	1	" "	$6'-9\frac{3}{4}'' \times 4'-6\frac{3}{8}''$	$1'-6 \& 3'-3'' \times 4-2\frac{3}{8}''$	342	" " "
4	3	" 3 LTS	$3'-6\frac{1}{4}'' \times 4'-6\frac{3}{8}''$	$1'-6'' \times 3'-6\frac{1}{4}''$	4323	—
5	2	FIXED SASH, 3 LTS	$3'-10\frac{1}{2}'' \times 6'-10\frac{1}{2}''$	$3'-8'' \times 6'-8''$	—	CENTER SASH IN SPACE SHOWN
6	3	" " 1 LT	$4'-3\frac{3}{8}'' \times 7'-3\frac{3}{8}''$	SEE REMARKS	—	$4'-0'' \times 7'-0'' \times \frac{1}{4}''$ PLATE GLASS
7	4	" " "	$5'-0\frac{3}{8}'' \times 7'-3\frac{3}{8}''$	" "	—	$4'-9'' \times 7'-0'' \times \frac{1}{4}''$ PLATE GLASS
8	1	CASEMENT, 3 LTS	$1'-10\frac{1}{2}'' \times 3'-0\frac{1}{4}''$	$1'-6'' \times 2-8\frac{3}{16}''$	23103	OBSCURE GLASS
9	1	" 4 LTS	$3'-6\frac{1}{4}'' \times 4'-6\frac{3}{8}''$	$1'-6'' \times 4-2\frac{3}{8}''$	4424	—

Schedule A.

referred to as a *window schedule,* is usually located on the elevation drawings. Window schedules (as well as door and room finish schedules) may also be placed on the first or second floor drawings. Sometimes a single sheet is used for all the schedules. A symbol (number or letter) is given to each type of window. This code symbol is placed on the work drawing by each particular window. The quantity, type, rough opening dimensions, sash size, and the manufacturer's number are also placed in the schedule. A remarks column gives information unique to each type, such as the kind of glass, etc. Schedule A gives an example of a typical window schedule.

Window Detail

It is not necessary on the elevation draw-ings to completely draw each window. One window of each type may be detailed (with schedule symbol indicated); others of the same type are indicated by the symbol only. An elevation detail shows the sill, stiles, rails, trim, lintel or dripcap, muntins, and mullions. Many designers do not detail windows since it is a time consuming process. Special windows must, of course, be detailed for special manufacture. In addition to the normal window details which may be drawn on an elevation, the direction of window swing should also be shown. This is done by dashed lines converging to the hinge side of the window. Fig. 10-39 (bottom) illustrates how window swing is shown.

Sometimes, to show detailed construction, sectional details are drawn.

Window-section details will show (1) *a section through the head* (a vertical cut taken through the top of the frame and adjacent header); (2) *a section through the sill* (a vertical cut taken through the bottom of the frame and adjacent header); and (3) *a section through the jamb* (a horizontal cut taken through the side of the frame and adjacent studs). These three sections are shown pictorially (outside and inside) in Fig. 10-46. Two typical details of a double-hung window showing sections through the head, jamb, and sill are illustrated in Fig. 10-47. Fig. 10-47 (left) shows a detail of a window in a frame wall. Fig. 10-47 (right) shows a detail of a window in a frame wall with brick veneer. The framing around the window, in either frame or brick veneer construction, would be the same for *any* type of window.

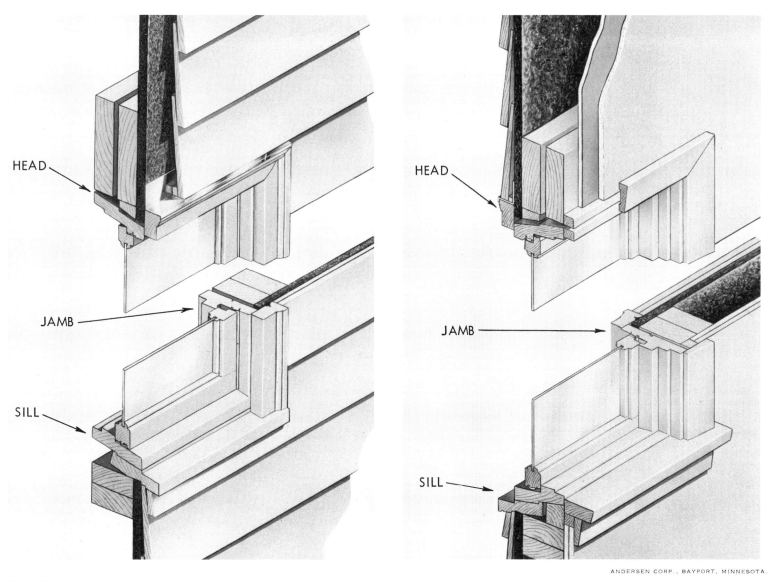

HEAD

JAMB

SILL

HEAD

JAMB

SILL

ANDERSEN CORP., BAYPORT, MINNESOTA.

Fig. 10-46. These pictorial views, one taken from the inside and one from the outside, show where the cuts are taken when drawing a section through a window. This is an awning type window.

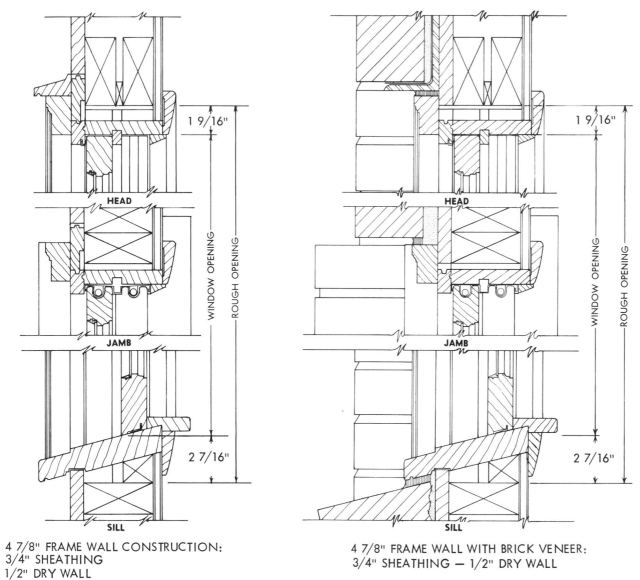

1 9/16"

WINDOW OPENING

ROUGH OPENING

HEAD

JAMB

SILL

2 7/16"

4 7/8" FRAME WALL CONSTRUCTION:
3/4" SHEATHING
1/2" DRY WALL

1 9/16"

WINDOW OPENING

ROUGH OPENING

HEAD

JAMB

SILL

2 7/16"

4 7/8" FRAME WALL WITH BRICK VENEER:
3/4" SHEATHING — 1/2" DRY WALL

ROCK ISLAND MILLWORK CO.,
ROCK ISLAND, ILLINOIS.

Fig. 10-47. This typical window detail drawing shows sections through the head and sill and a section through the jamb turned into position so that sash, trim, etc. line up.

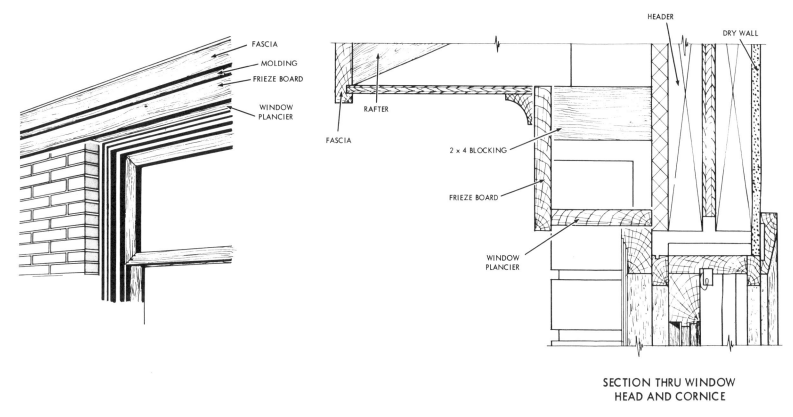

FASCIA
MOLDING
FRIEZE BOARD
WINDOW PLANCIER

HEADER
DRY WALL

RAFTER
FASCIA
2 x 4 BLOCKING
FRIEZE BOARD
WINDOW PLANCIER

SECTION THRU WINDOW HEAD AND CORNICE

Fig. 10-48. A frieze board lowers the apperance of the cornice as well as eliminates brick and a lintel over a window.

Frieze Board

A lower appearance can be created in a single story brick structure by placing a frieze board above the windows. A frieze in classical architecture is the portion immediately below the cornice. In building construction today, the name and applica- tion are identical. The frieze board elimi- nates the necessity for a brick and angle iron lintel above the window. The number of brick courses eliminated would, of course, depend upon the roof pitch and amount of cornice projection. Fig. 10-48 shows a sec- tion through the head of a double hung window and the frieze board. A window plancier is nailed to the brick mold and in turn the frieze board is nailed to the window plancier.

Step-by-Step Drawing Procedure: Windows

Fig. 10-49 shows the step-by-step proce- dure for drawing the window in section.

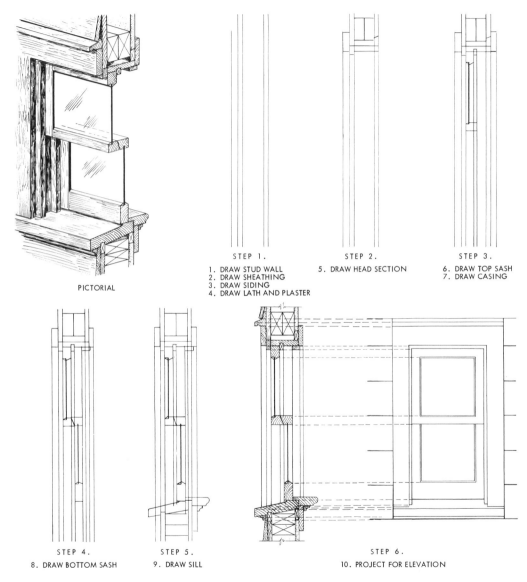

PICTORIAL

STEP 1.
1. DRAW STUD WALL
2. DRAW SHEATHING
3. DRAW SIDING
4. DRAW LATH AND PLASTER

STEP 2.
5. DRAW HEAD SECTION

STEP 3.
6. DRAW TOP SASH
7. DRAW CASING

STEP 4.
8. DRAW BOTTOM SASH

STEP 5.
9. DRAW SILL

STEP 6.
10. PROJECT FOR ELEVATION

Fig. 10-49. Follow this step-by-step procedure in drawing a window section.

With slight modifications this same sequence of steps may be used for drawing the jamb section.

Doors

Doors are one of the most critical aspects in the exterior appearance of the house. Doors (along with windows) are major focal points that influence the opinion of the design. The design of the main entry door should blend well with the architectural style.

Doors are no longer designed by the architect but are selected from standard designs offered in millwork catalogs. Doors, like windows, have many designs and sizes for various styles of dwellings.

Door Types

Doors may be classified according to appearance, use, or construction. The two basic types are panel and flush doors used for both interior and exterior applications. Louver, accordion, French, double acting, sliding (pocket and bi-pass), and folding doors have special construction features or use. They are used as interior doors.

Panel doors (Fig. 10-50) consist of *stiles* (vertical members) and *rails* (horizontal members) which are generally *mortised and tenoned* together: grooves on the inside edge of the stiles and rails accommodate the panels (thin boards). Glazing may replace the upper panels. The rails and stiles may be made of solid pieces of wood or they may have a built-up core of small pieces of soft wood covered with an oak, birch, mahogany, etc., veneer.

Flush doors (sometimes called slab doors) are perfectly flat, i.e., the surface is unbroken by panels or moldings. There are two types of flush doors. The *solid core door* (Fig. 10-51) consists of small pieces of wood in varied combinations which are covered on both sides with veneer. The *hollow core door* (Fig. 10-52) is similar in appearance to the solid core flush door, but it is constructed with built-up rails, stiles, and lock block. The space between the door members in the hollow core door is filled with a grid of crossed struts; the exterior is covered with two-ply veneer. This makes a door that is light, serviceable, and strong.

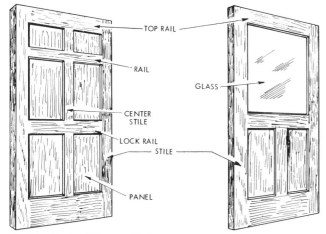

Fig. 10-50. Panel Doors—Six Panel and Two Panel Glazed.

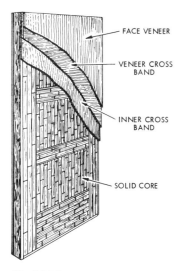

Fig. 10-52. Hollow Core Flush Door.

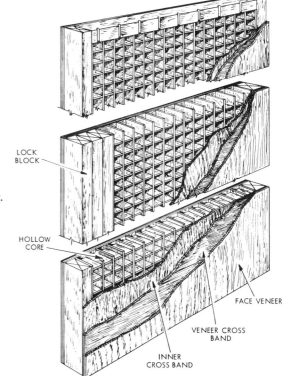

Fig. 10-51. Solid Core Flush Door.

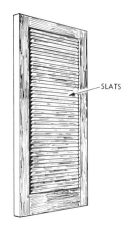

Fig. 10-53. Louvered or Slatted Door.

Louvered or slat doors (Fig. 10-53) have an outside frame of rails and stiles holding a series of horizontal slats set at an angle to provide ventilation.

Accordion doors are a relatively recent development in the building field. The folding portion of the door is made of narrow strips of wood (4″ to 8″ wide) hinged or fastened with fabric or plastic material. Other types are made from vinyl plastic hung from a track and hanging device. The folding portion may use either an accordion fold or a scissors linkage—both permit the "door" to "fold flat" or "stack" against the jamb. Fig. 10-54 shows a cloth or plastic accordion door with a scissors linkage.

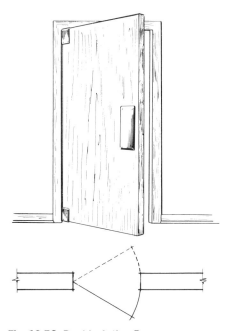

Fig. 10-56. Double Acting Door.

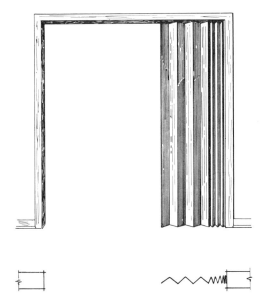

Fig. 10-54. Accordion Door.

Fig. 10-55. French Door.

French style doors (Fig. 10-55) are similar to panel doors except that they have glass from top to bottom rails and from stile to stile. The glass is usually divided by muntins. These may be used between rooms or where the room opens onto a terrace.

Double acting doors may be panelled, flush, or louvered. The door is hinged in such a manner that it will swing in either direction (Fig. 10-56). This is an ideal door when there is a great deal of travel between rooms, and it is desirable to have the door closed most of the time.

Sliding doors may be either *bi-pass* or

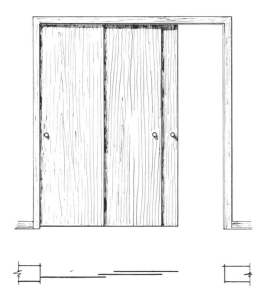

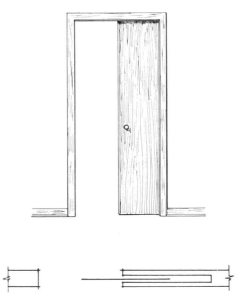

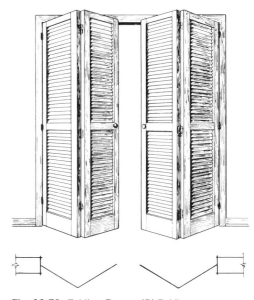

Fig. 10-57. Bi-Pass Sliding Door.

Fig. 10-58. Pocket Sliding Door.

Fig. 10-59. Folding Doors. (Bi-Fold)

pocket. Sliding doors are hung from a track mounted on the head of the door and either slide past each other, as bi-pass doors (Fig. 10-57), or slide into a wall pocket (Fig. 10-58). Bi-pass doors are used almost exclusively on closets; the pocket door finds its greatest use as a door between rooms, particularly between the kitchen and dining or living areas. Unless sliding doors are properly sealed and finished they may warp and scrape the adjacent door or pocket. The flush door is usually used for the sliding or pocket door. If it is desired, however, a panel door may be specified. Sliding doors do not require a swing radius and do not interfere with furniture or other doors.

Folding doors (Fig. 10-59) may be flush, louvered, or a combination of both; they are hinged in the center of each section so they may be folded back against the jamb. Folding doors are ideal for wide closet entrances. This type of door may also be fabricated of metal. (Some home owners object to the folding door since it does not have a "solid" sound when opened or closed.)

Door Size

The inside opening dimension of the door frame is normally ¼″ larger than the door; the rough opening in the framing is made a total of 1″ to 1½″ larger than the outside dimension of the frame.

Exterior doors are usually 1¾″ thick; sometimes they are only 1⅜″ thick. The width of the main exterior door is usually 3′-0″, while other exterior doors, such as rear and service doors, are 2′-10″ or 2′-8″. Manufacturers' catalogs list stock doors in heights of 6′-6″, 6′-8″, and 7′-0″.

Interior doors are more simply constructed than exterior doors. The common thickness for an interior door is 1⅜″; sometimes closet doors or narrow doors may be only 1⅛″ thick. Stock door sizes vary in height between 6′-6″ and 7′-0″ but are usually 6′-8″. Most interior doors are 2′-4″, 2′-6″, and 2′-8″ wide. Small closet doors may be as narrow as 1′-4″.

TABLE 10-2
STANDARD SIZES OF INTERIOR AND EXTERIOR PANEL (P) AND FLUSH (F) DOORS

Width	EXTERIOR						INTERIOR			
	Thickness 1 3/8"		Thickness 1 3/4"				Thickness 1 3/8"			
	Height		Height				Height			
	6'-8"	7'-0"	6'-0"	6'-6"	6'-8"	7'-0"	6'-0"	6'-6"	6'-8"	7'-0"
1'-6"				F	F			P, F	P, F	
2'-0"			F	F	F	F	F	F	P, F	
2'-4"			F	F	F	F	P	P, F	P, F	P
2'-6"	P		F	F	P, F	F	F		P, F	
2'-8"	P	P	F	F	P, F	P, F			P, F	P
3'-0"	P				P, F	P, F			P, F	P
3'-4"					P, F	P, F				

Table 10-2 gives basic standard sizes for interior and exterior panel and flush doors. Doors with other than stock sizes are usually available on special order. It is advisable to follow standard sizes as much as possible to eliminate extra cost.

Package Units

Emphasis is now being placed on labor saving methods, new materials, etc. This, of course, helps to reduce building and maintenance costs. Many mills and manufacturers now "package" the door and frame as a unit, with the door "pre-hung" (i.e., the door is fitted and hinged to the frame). The entire unit is placed in the rough opening, eliminating the steps of fitting the frame, hanging the door, etc. Packaged units are available for both interior and exterior doors.

Metal Doors

Due to warpage of exterior doors, many designers are now specifying metal clad doors. Most metal clad doors are filled with expanded resin foam that prevents heat loss and retards sound transmission. The advantage of a metal clad door is that it will not warp or twist. Because of the metal sheath these doors offer a good seal when magnetic weather stripping is applied. Some building codes require that the door opening into the garage from the dwelling be covered on the garage side with galvanized iron, tin plate or cement asbestos board for fire protection.

Glass Doors

Complete glass doors are rarely used in the main entryway in residential construction. Sliding glass doors, however, are fre-

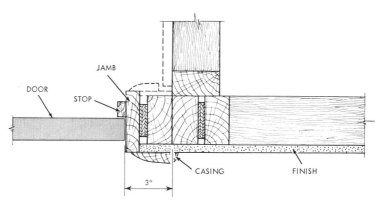

Fig. 10-60. When an interior door is located adjacent to 2 intersecting walls it is placed 3" from the intersecting wall.

quently used in living areas opening onto a patio, terrace, or garden area. These glass doors have a wood frame, aluminum frame, or steel reinforced wood frame and are not, in the true sense, a glass door.

Door Placement in the Plan

When locating a door adjacent to a wall, floor space utilized by the swing can be minimized by placing the door 3″ from the intersecting wall. Fig. 10-60 illustrates a section through a door and two intersection walls. In most instances locating a door more than 3″ away from a wall is poor planning. When drawing the door in the plan, place one side of the opening 3″ from the stud face of the intersecting wall. Placing the door in this position minimizes framing costs (labor and materials). Additionally, the location of the door will not have to be dimensioned because it is understood by the carpenter that the door stile is 3″ from the stud face of the adjacent wall. This principle does not apply for sliding glass doors because these are usually covered with a drape. Consideration must be given to the stack dimension of the drape as it is opened to allow sufficient passage through the door.

Door Schedules

Door schedules, like window schedules, are usually located on elevation drawings. They may also be located on the first or second floor plans, or on a separate sheet with window and room finish schedules. As with window schedules, door schedule code symbols are placed on the plans and elevations by each particular door. The door schedule also gives the quantity, type, rough opening dimensions, door size, manufacturer's number, and information unique to each door, such as type of wood, etc. Schedule B gives an example of a typical door schedule.

Door Sections

Fig. 10-61 shows the standard section taken through the door frame to detail the construction. Sections A, B, and C through the *head* (top member), *jamb* (vertical member at the side), and *threshold* or *saddle* (lower member) respectively show the door frame in a frame wall. Sections D, E, and F show the same detail-section treatment in a brick veneer wall.

An interior door frame has *only* a jamb and head. It is framed in an identical manner to the exterior door. Fig. 10-62 shows pictorial sections through the head and jamb. Note the use of a metal plaster casing around the head and jamb, and the use of wood casing over drywall finish.

Step-by-Shep Drawing Procedure: Doors

Fig. 10-63 shows the step-by-step procedure for drawing all doors.

Schedule B.

		DOOR SCHEDULE				
SYMBOL	QUANTITY	TYPE	ROUGH OPENING	DOOR SIZE	MFG No	REMARKS
Ⓐ	2	STANDARD	3′- 2½″ × 6′-9¼″	3′-0″× 6′-8″	—	BIRCH, FLUSH
Ⓑ	1	"	2′-10½″ × 6′-9¼″	2′-8″× 6′-8″	—	" "
Ⓒ	2	"	2′- 8½″ × 6′-9¼″	2′-6″× 6′-8″	—	" "
Ⓓ	1	FOLDING	— —	6′-0″× 6′-8″	—	—
Ⓔ	4	SLIDING	2′-10½″× 6′-9¼″	2′-8″× 6′-8″	52A	BIRCH, FLUSH
Ⓕ	1	CANOPY	SEE MFG INSTRUC	16′-0″× 7′-0″	1670	STEEL (PRIMED)

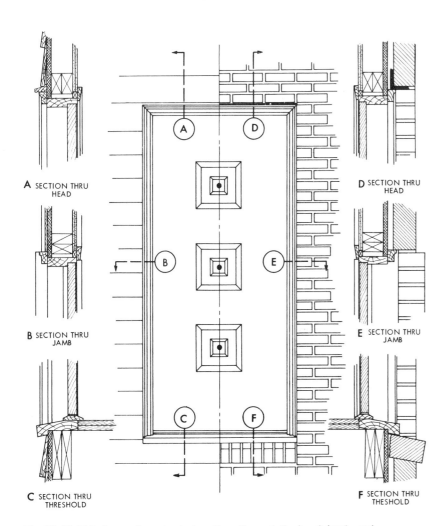

A SECTION THRU HEAD

B SECTION THRU JAMB

C SECTION THRU THRESHOLD

D SECTION THRU HEAD

E SECTION THRU JAMB

F SECTION THRU THESHOLD

Fig. 10-61. This figure shows typical sections through the head, jamb, and threshold of an exterior door in a frame and in a brick veneer wall.

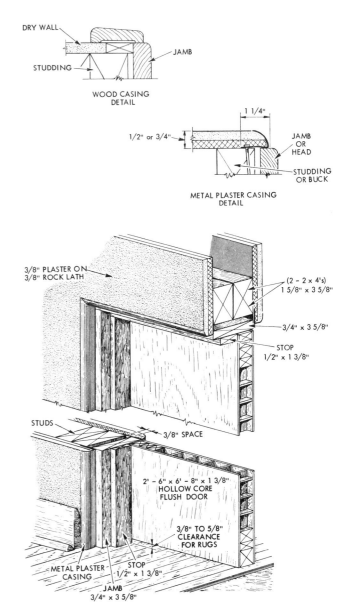

DRY WALL

JAMB

STUDDING

WOOD CASING DETAIL

1 1/4"

1/2" or 3/4"

JAMB OR HEAD

STUDDING OR BUCK

METAL PLASTER CASING DETAIL

3/8" PLASTER ON 3/8" ROCK LATH

(2 - 2 x 4's) 1 5/8" x 3 5/8"

3/4" x 3 5/8"

STOP 1/2" x 1 3/8"

STUDS

3/8" SPACE

2' - 6" x 6' - 8" x 1 3/8" HOLLOW CORE FLUSH DOOR

3/8" TO 5/8" CLEARANCE FOR RUGS

METAL PLASTER CASING

STOP 1/2" x 1 3/8"

JAMB 3/4" x 3 5/8"

Fig. 10-62. This figure shows details for an interior door.

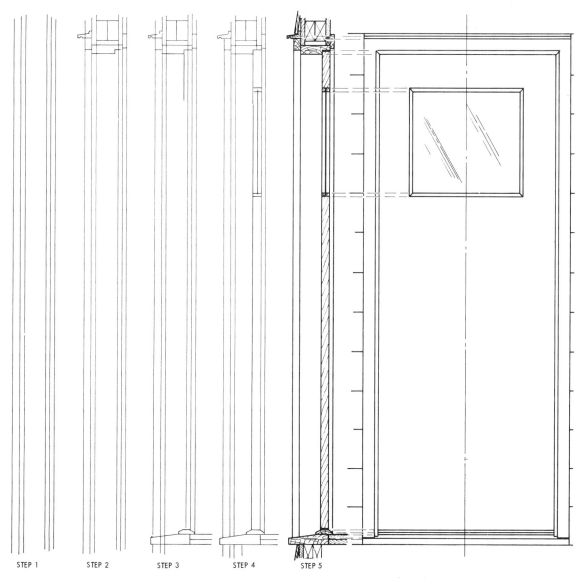

STEP 1   STEP 2   STEP 3   STEP 4   STEP 5

Fig. 10-63. Follow this step-by-step procedure in drawing exterior door framing and door in elevation. **Step 1.** Draw vertical lines representing stud wall, sheathing, plaster and lath, inside casing, and outside casing. **Step 2.** Draw head section. **Step 3.** Measure height of door; draw sill section. **Step 4.** Draw door. **Step 5.** Erase surplus lines and project for elevation.

Fig. 10-64A. Skylight in living room ceiling brings outside light to an ordinarily dark area.

BELL SKYLIGHTS DIVISION, RICHARD GRANT CO., HOUSTON, TEXAS.

Fig. 10-64B. Multiple skylights are frequently used to help illuminate large areas in industrial buildings.

BELL SKYLIGHTS DIVISION, RICHARD GRANT CO., HOUSTON, TEXAS.

Skylights

Skylights are generally thought of in terms of commercial or industrial applications. They are, however, used in residential architecture as well. Regardless of the application, the purpose of a skylight is to bring outside light into an ordinarily unnatural lighted enclosure. Note in Figs. 10-64A and 10-64B the amount of light added by the skylights.

BELL SKYLIGHTS DIVISION, RICHARD GRANT CO., HOUSTON, TEXAS.

Fig. 10-66. In residential applications, interior skylight openings may be finished with translucent light.

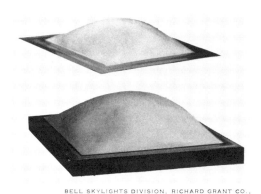

BELL SKYLIGHTS DIVISION, RICHARD GRANT CO., HOUSTON, TEXAS.

Fig. 10-65. Depending on the application, the skylight may be flush or project above the roof surface.

Skylights may be used on either flat or pitched roofs. Two types of skylights are shown in Fig. 10-65. The bubble shaped light may be either translucent or clear plastic. In residential designs the skylight ceiling opening may be finished with translucent plastic mounted in a frame as in Fig. 10-66. The framing around a skylight opening in the ceiling and roof is identical to that for an interior chimney.

Fireplaces

A fireplace may be considered a luxury when compared with the cost of the house and the *total number of hours the fireplace is used per year*. Tradition, however, makes the fireplace a desired feature. Pre-historic man met around the fire for warmth and fellowship; in the rush of today's society we still derive solace and cheer from a warm glowing fire.

New locations and designs for fireplaces have evolved with recent innovations in contemporary architecture. The fireplace is no longer necessarily thought of as a brick covered enclosure with a mantel above the opening. Creative design may turn the fire-place into a piece of dynamic furniture. Modern fireplaces may be free standing and have three dimensional geometric shapes, such as those in Figs. 10-67 and 10-68.

Correct fireplace design is based on three principles. First, the proper proportional relationship of width, height, and depth for the fire chamber must be maintained. Second, the flue must be sized in relation to the fireplace opening. Third, the chimney must be carried 2'-6" above the roof ridge

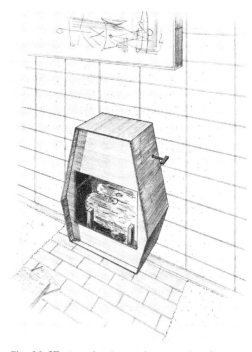

Fig. 10-67. A prefabricated free-standing fireplace may add interest in the contemporary home.

Fig. 10-68. A spherical free-standing fireplace is ideal for a family room, cottage, or weekend lodge.

or above the highest point to eliminate a smoky fireplace.

Hearth and Fire Chamber

The front hearth serves as a floor protection against sparks. This area may be shortened to 6" if a fireplace screen is installed. The hearth rests on a hearth slab which is supported by a 2" × 4" cleat attached to the double trimmer and header. Fig. 10-69 shows the hearth in relationship to the rest of the fireplace. The hearth may be elevated above or recessed in the floor.

The back hearth, the surface on which the fire is built, is lined with firebrick using fire clay joints. (Fire clay is a mortar-like material used to bond the firebrick.) Also note that the sides and back of the opening are *laid up* with firebrick and fire clay. Common brick and mortar is not used because

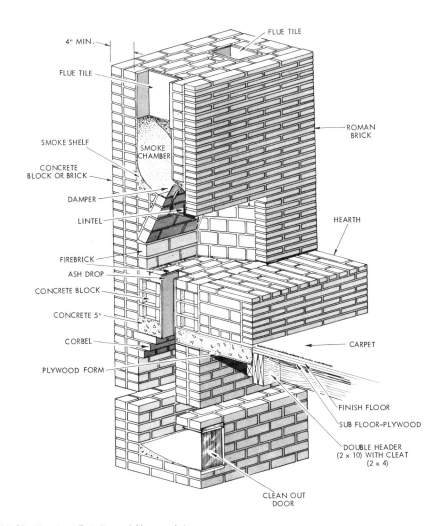

Fig. 10-69. Fireplace Details and Nomenclature.

they will not withstand heat. Frequently, an ash dump is installed in the center of the back hearth. This leads to an ash pit below. The interior walls of the fire chamber (Fig.

10-70) are inclined to reflect the heat into the room. (Note: wood trim should be placed no closer than 6" around the sides and top of the fireplace opening.)

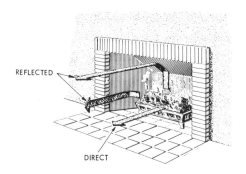

Fig. 10-70. Proper design of the fire chamber increases the reflected heat.

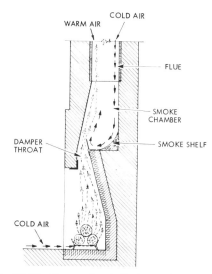

Fig. 10-71. The smoke shelf directs the cold air toward the warm, rising air.

WALKER SALES & MANUFACTURING CORP., ST. JOSEPH, MISSOURI.

Fig. 10-72. A fireplace draft fan pushes the gasses up the chimney.

Damper and Smoke Chamber

A cast iron or sheet steel damper is located in the *throat* (between the fire area and smoke shelf) to regulate the draft. The damper is the same length as the fireplace opening and is adjustable so the down drafts are deflected up the chimney. (The square inch area of the damper *should not* be less than that of the flue.) The smoke chamber is pyramidal in shape, connecting the damper with the flue. The curved surface of the smoke shelf, in addition to the angle of the damper prevents the downrushing air currents from forcing the smoke into the room. See Fig. 10-71. If the draft should be shut off temporarily by the wind, the smoke chamber will hold any accumulated gases. The damper is closed to prevent cold air flow when the fireplace is not in use.

To create a draft and prevent smoke from entering the room, fireplace draft fans can be installed directly above the smoke chamber. See Fig. 10-72. The fan and the motor shaft project inside the chimney, pushing the air upward within the chimney. This air movement creates a draft suction at the fireplace opening, pulling the gases up and out the chimney.

Flue

The chimney flue begins at the top of the smoke chamber and extends up the chimney. Clay flue linings are almost universally used to satisfy building codes and the recommendations of the National Fire Underwriters. The flue tile lining, for safety reasons, should be backed up with a minimum 4″ of brick. If the flue tile lining is omitted in a chimney, the thickness of brick around the opening should be 8″.

Chimney

Chimneys should project above the highest point on the roof to provide for an adequate draft. If the chimney is *on* the sloping portion of the roof and not at the ridge, the chimney is extended 2′-6″ above the ridge. A chimney *at* the ridge is projected 2′-0″ above the ridge. In the case of a flat roof, the chimney extends 3′-0″ above the roof line. The flue lining projects 2″ above the concrete cap. Fig. 10-73 gives details of concrete cap. If a single chimney houses several flues, these flues should be carried to different heights above the cap. If the flue linings project above the cap equally, a down draft from interior suction may pull the smoke from the top of one flue down into an adjoining flue.

When the flue openings are exceedingly large, they may be covered with a metal or cast concrete cap. This cap prevents excessive rain from running down the flue and

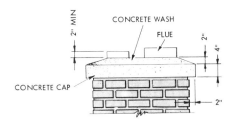

Fig. 10-73. The flue lining projects 2″ above the concrete cap.

dripping into the fire chamber. A clearance of 6″ to 8″ exists between cap and the top of the flue tile. Fig. 10-74 illustrates a metal cap over a flue tile. Some building codes require spark arrestors to be placed on fireplace chimneys. Spark arrestors are a woven wire extension placed on the top of the flue tile. See Fig. 10-75. If trees are adjacent to a chimney a spark arrestor prevents birds or squirrels from falling down the flue.

Greater fireplace efficiency may be obtained if the chimney is placed within the structure rather than on an outside wall as in Fig. 10-76. Frequently however, due to space limitations, the fireplace must be placed on an outside wall.

A single chimney is used to house several flues. *Separate* flues are needed to al-

EXPOSED AND COLD

IN CENTER

Fig. 10-76. Location of the chimney on an interior wall promotes greater efficiency.

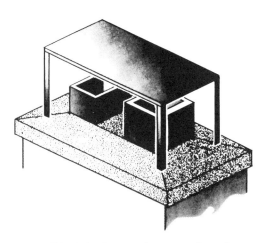

Fig. 10-74. If the flue openings are extremely large, a metal cast concrete cap is placed over the chimney to prevent excessive rain from entering.

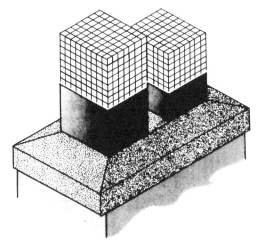

Fig. 10-75. A spark arrester is placed on the chimney outlet to prevent flying sparks.

WALKER SALES & MANUFACTURING CORP., ST. JOSEPH. MISSOURI.

Fig. 10-77. Commercial chimney caps increase draft suction and prevent down-drafts.

low for proper draft. A chimney would have three separate flues to accommodate, as an example, a fireplace, a furnace, and an incinerator. Fig. 10-69 shows an example of a two flue chimney.

Single chimneys or flues for a space heater may be covered with a commercial chimney cap. See Fig. 10-77. These chimney caps are designed to increase draft suction while preventing the occurrence of down-drafts. Additionally, they prevent rain, snow and moisture from entering the chimney.

Heating devices for single family residential dwellings should have a minimum effective flue area as follows:

FLUE AREAS FOR HEATING DEVICES
SMALL SPECIAL STOVES AND HEATERS
28 sq. in.
COAL OR WOOD STOVES, RANGES AND ROOM HEATERS
40 sq. in. (RECTANGULAR FLUE) 6" DIA. (INSIDE) (ROUND FLUE)
FIREPLACES
AT LEAST 1/12 MINIMJM (1/10 RECOMMENDED) OF THE FIREPLACE OPENING 70 sq. in.
WARM AIR FURNACES, STEAM AND HOT WATER BOILERS (GAS, OIL, OR COAL FIRED)
70 sq. in.

Fireplace Framing

Framing members, flooring, roof members, and walls must be free of the chimney. A minimum space of 2″ must always be provided. Non-combustible insulation is inserted between the framing members and the chimney masonry. The fireplace itself always has a 2″ clearance with insulation on both sides and the back. If the exterior covering of the dwelling is wood siding, shingles, etc., the junction of the wood and brick must be caulked.

Framing around the chimney placed on an exterior wall is accomplished by two double trimmers resting on the wall plate (Fig. 10-78). A double header is spiked between the trimmers to carry the regular floor joists. A 2″ clearance with insulation is provided only on the sides of an exterior fireplace.

The opening in the roof is framed in a similar manner with double rafters and trimmers.

Fireplace Proportions

Few experiences can be more disappointing to the home owner than an ill-functioning fireplace. Mistakes in fireplace construction are inexcusable considering the amount invested in this home feature. The successfully operating fireplace is based on simple principles of design. Standard proportions for the conventional single opening fireplace are shown in Fig. 10-79. Probably the most important construction features of the single opening fireplace are: (1) the relation of the width, height, and depth dimensions of the fire chamber to the inclined faces in the rear of the chamber, and (2) the proper flue, damper,

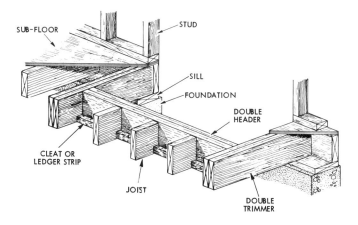

Fig. 10-78. Framing is doubled around a chimney placed on an outside wall.

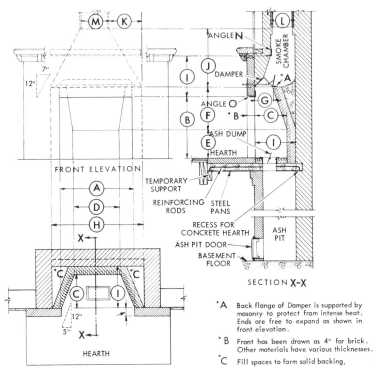

*A Back flange of Damper is supported by masonry to protect from intense heat. Ends are free to expand as shown in front elevation.

*B Front has been drawn as 4" for brick. Other materials have various thicknesses.

*C Fill spaces to form solid backing.

Fig. 10-79. With these standard dimensions the student may design a conventional, opening fireplace.

TABLE OF FIREPLACE DIMENSIONS

Finished Fireplace Opening										Rough Brick Work and Flue Size						Equipment	
										New Flue Sizes**		Round	Old Flue Sizes		Ash Pit Door	Steel Angles*	
A	B	C	D	E	F	G	H	I	J	K · L M			K · L M			N	O
24	24	16	11	14	15	8¾	32	20	19	10	8x12	8	11¾	8½x 8½	12x8	A-36	A-36
26	24	16	13	14	15	8¾	34	20	21	11	8x12	8	12¾	8½x 8½	12x8	A-36	A-36
28	24	16	15	14	15	8¾	36	20	21	12	8x12	10	11½	8½x13	12x8	A-36	A-36
30	29	16	17	14	21	8¾	38	20	24	13	12x12	10	12½	8½x13	12x8	A-42	A-36
32	29	16	19	14	21	8¾	40	20	24	14	12x12	10	13½	8½x13	12x8	A-42	A-42
36	29	16	23	14	21	8¾	44	20	27	16	12x12	12	15½	13 x13	12x8	A-48	A-42
40	29	16	27	14	21	8¾	48	20	29	16	12x16	12	17½	13 x13	12x8	A-48	A-48
42	32	16	29	14	23	8¾	50	20	32	17	16x16	12	18½	13 x13	12x8	B-54	A-48
48	32	18	33	14	23	8¾	56	22	37	20	16x16	15	21½	13 x13	12x8	B-60	B-54
54	37	20	37	16	27	13	68	24	45	26	16x16	15	25	13 x18	12x8	B-72	B-60
60	37	22	42	16	27	13	72	27	45	26	16x20	15	27	13 x18	12x8	B-72	B-66
60	40	22	42	16	29	13	72	27	45	26	16x20	18	27	18 x18	12x8	B-72	B-66
72	40	22	54	16	29	13	84	27	56	32	20x20	18	33	18 x18	12x8	C-84	C-84
84	40	24	64	20	26	13	96	29	61	36	20x24	20	36	20 x20	12x8	C-96	C-96
96	40	24	76	20	26	13	108	29	75	42	20x24	22	42	24 x24	12x8	C-108	C-108

*ANGLE SIZES: A-3 x 3 x 3/16, B-3 1/2 x 3 x 1/4, C-5 x 3 1/2 x 5/16.

**NEW FLUE SIZES—CONFORM TO NEW MODULAR DIMENSIONAL SYSTEM. SIZES SHOWN ARE NOMINAL. ACTUAL SIZE IS 1/2 IN. LESS EACH DIMENSION.

DONLEY BROS. CO., CLEVELAND, OHIO.

and smoke chamber size in relation to the fireplace opening. An attractive, well sized, single-opening fireplace made from split 4" concrete block is shown in Fig. 10-80.

Two- and Three-Way Fireplaces

Fireplaces are no longer limited to a one-way opening. In recent years novel variations in basic fireplace design have taken place. This change is in part due to the popularity of large living areas. Sometimes the fireplace design assumes the role of a room divider. The projecting corner fireplace (Fig. 10-81) has the opening visible on the side and front. Where a partition separates two rooms, a two-way fireplace (Fig. 10-82) will serve both areas. A three-way fireplace (Fig. 10-83) may project a sufficient distance into the room to form a semi-partition between two living areas.

A three-way fireplace offers many advantages over one that has a conventional opening. Fig. 10-84 shows a three-way fireplace with a hinged grill which drops over the fire chamber. The grill may be used for brazier foods. A typical flue for two and three way fireplaces is shown in Fig. 10-85.

Metal Circulating Fireplaces

The heating capacity of a fireplace can be increased considerably by using metal built-in circulating units, such as shown in Fig. 10-86. These units are efficient and easily installed. Firebrick lining is not necessary in the fire chamber since the entire unit is fabricated of heavy sheet metal. A double wall surrounds the fire chamber so

Fig. 10-80. A fire adds warmth and beauty to a room.

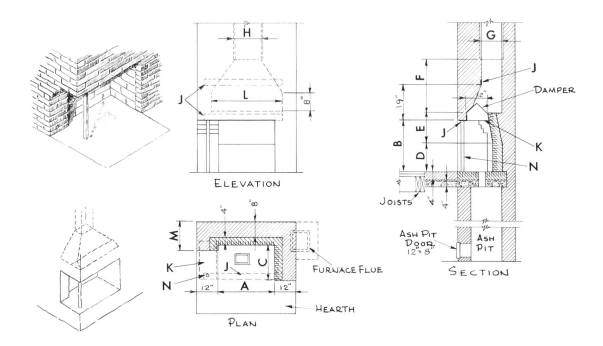

ELEVATION

PLAN

SECTION

Fig. 10-81. A projecting fireplace may be designed using these dimensions.

TABLE OF DIMENSIONS AND EQUIPMENT (IN INCHES)

A	B	C	D	E	F	OLD FLUE SIZES				NEW FLUE SIZES				L	M	STEEL ANGLE J *	PLATE LINTEL K	CORNER POST N
						IN G OUT		IN H OUT		IN G OUT		IN H OUT						
28	26½	20	14	20	29¼	11¼	13	11¼	13	10¼	12	10¼	12	36	16	*A-36	11×16	3φ×26½
32	26½	20	14	20	32	11¼	13	11¼	13	10¼	12	13½	16	40	16	*A-42	11×16	3φ×26½
36	26½	20	14	20	35	11¼	13	11¼	13	10¼	12	13½	16	44	16	*A-48	11×16	3φ×26½
40	29	20	14	20	35	11¼	13	15¾	18	13½	16	13½	16	48	16	*B-54	11×16	3φ×29
48	29	24	14	24	43	11¼	13	15¾	18	13½	16	13½	16	56	20	*B-60	11×16	3φ×29

* ANGLE SIZES   *A 3×3×3/16   *B 3½×3½×¼

DONLEY BROS. CO., CLEVELAND, OHIO.

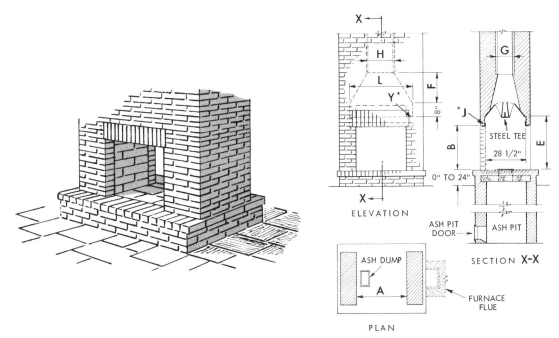

Fig. 10-82. A two-way or double fireplace may be designed using these dimensions.

TABLE OF DIMENSIONS AND EQUIPMENT (IN INCHES)

Width of Opening	Height of Opening	Damper Height	Smoke Chamber	Old Flue Size		New Flue Size		Angle 2 req'd		Tee	Ash Dump	Ash-Pit Door
A	B	E	F	G	H	G	H	*J	L			
28	24	30	19	13	13	12	16	A-36	36	35	58	12 x 8
32	29	35	21	13	18	16	16	A-40	40	39	58	12 x 8
36	29	35	21	13	18	16	20	A-42	44	43	58	12 x 8
40	29	35	27	18	18	16	20	A-48	48	47	58	12 x 8
48	32	37	32	18	18	20	20	B-54	56	55	58	12 x 8

*ANGLE SIZES: A-3 x 3 x 3/16"; B-3 - 1/2 x 3 1/4".

NOTE Y—THE DAMPER AND THE STEEL T SHOULD NOT BE
     BUILT IN SOLID AT THE ENDS BUT GIVEN FREE-
     DOM TO EXPAND WITH HEAT.

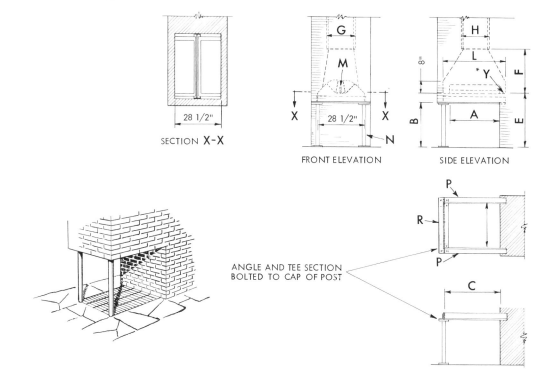

SECTION X-X

FRONT ELEVATION

SIDE ELEVATION

ANGLE AND TEE SECTION
BOLTED TO CAP OF POST

TABLE OF DIMENSIONS AND EQUIPMENT (IN INCHES)

A	B	C	E	F	Old Flue Size		New Flue Size		L	Steel Tee	Post Height 2 req'd	Drilled Angle 2 req'd	Special Welded Tee
					G	H	G	H		M	N	P	R
28	26½	32	32	24	18	18	16	20	36	35	26½	36	34
32	26½	36	32	27	18	18	20	20	40	39	26½	40	34
36	26½	40	32	32	18	18	20	20	44	43	26½	44	34
40	26½	44	32	35	18	18	20	20	48	47	26½	48	34
48	26½	52	32	35	20	20	20	24	56	55	26½	56	34

*Y—DAMPER AND STEEL T SHOULD NOT BE BUILT IN SOLID
AT THE ENDS BUT GIVEN FREEDOM TO EXPAND WITH HEAT

Fig. 10-83. Using these dimensions, three-way fireplaces may be designed.

WILLIAM WALLACE DIVISION, WALLACE-MURRY CORP., BELMONT, CALIFORNIA.

Fig. 10-84. If a fireplace must project into a room, a three-way fireplace is the most functional.

THE MAJESTIC CO., INC., HUNTINGTON, INDIANA.

Fig. 10-85. Two and three-way fireplace damper.

that cold air entering near the bottom (through ducts) is warmed by passing over the hot sides. The heated air then rises and is discharged into the room through outlet ducts. These pre-formed units include the firebox, heat chamber, damper, smoke shelf, throat, and smoke chamber. All that needs to be provided is a hearth slab, brick work to cover the unit, flue tile, and the chimney. Most manufacturers of circulating fireplaces have units designed similar to the conventional fireplaces discussed above.

Free Standing Prefabricated Fireplaces

Small, free-standing prefabricated fireplaces are becoming more popular. These units are complete in themselves: the hood, damper, chimney pipe, hearth, base, grate, and screen are included.

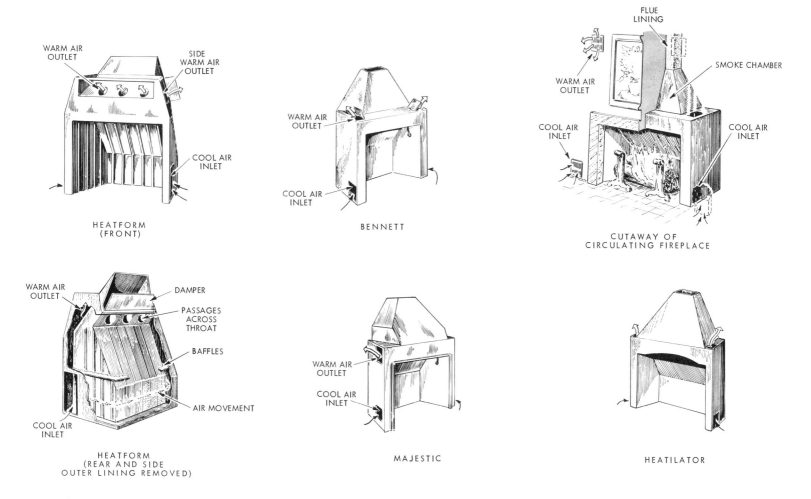

WARM AIR OUTLET
SIDE WARM AIR OUTLET
COOL AIR INLET

HEATFORM (FRONT)

WARM AIR OUTLET
COOL AIR INLET

BENNETT

FLUE LINING
WARM AIR OUTLET
SMOKE CHAMBER
COOL AIR INLET
COOL AIR INLET

CUTAWAY OF CIRCULATING FIREPLACE

WARM AIR OUTLET
DAMPER
PASSAGES ACROSS THROAT
BAFFLES
AIR MOVEMENT
COOL AIR INLET

HEATFORM (REAR AND SIDE OUTER LINING REMOVED)

WARM AIR OUTLET
COOL AIR INLET

MAJESTIC

HEATILATOR

Fig. 10-86. Metal, built-in circulating fireplaces increase the heating efficiency by permitting air to circulate around the fire chamber.

The fire chamber of the free standing fireplace is lined with refractory material. No exterior masonry work is required since these fireplaces are attached to the wall or stand free. Local building codes should be checked for the distance that a free standing fireplace should be placed from the wall and if a non-combustible base is required beneath the fireplace. Fig. 10-87 illustrates a few of the many different types of free standing fireplaces. For many who have small summer cottages where central heat-

THE MAJESTIC CO., INC., HUNTINGTON, INDIANA.

MALM FIREPLACES, SANTA ROSA, CALIFORNIA.

MALM FIREPLACES, SANTA ROSA, CALIFORNIA.

MALM FIREPLACES, SANTA ROSA, CALIFORNIA.

THE MAJESTIC CO., INC., HUNTINGTON, INDIANA.

VEGA INDUSTRIES, INC., SYRACUSE, NEW YORK.

Fig. 10-87. Free-standing fireplaces are designed to fit different room decors. They are simple to install as well as being functional and economical.

ing would be a needless expense, a small fireplace can provide the necessary warmth for a chilly evening or morning.

Pre-Fab Chimneys

Pre-fab, light-weight chimneys are frequently used in areas where building codes permit. Their cost is low and they are easy to install. Brick walls and footings are not required with this type of chimney. Fig. 10-88 shows an exploded view of a factory-built chimney.

Prefab metal chimneys are sometimes used in place of an exterior masonry chimney. Fig. 10-89 shows a prefab chimney placed on the exterior of a structure. Many of these chimneys blend well with the exterior design of the building.

Fireplace Drawing Details

Fireplace details usually consist of three drawings. First, an *elevation* of the fire-

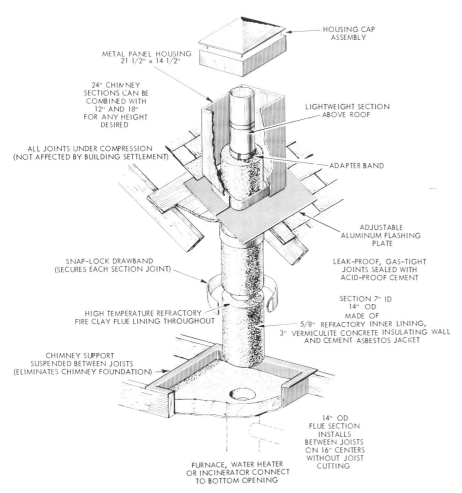

HOUSING CAP ASSEMBLY

METAL PANEL HOUSING 21 1/2" x 14 1/2"

24" CHIMNEY SECTIONS CAN BE COMBINED WITH 12" AND 18" FOR ANY HEIGHT DESIRED

LIGHTWEIGHT SECTION ABOVE ROOF

ALL JOINTS UNDER COMPRESSION (NOT AFFECTED BY BUILDING SETTLEMENT)

ADAPTER BAND

ADJUSTABLE ALUMINUM FLASHING PLATE

SNAP-LOCK DRAWBAND (SECURES EACH SECTION JOINT)

LEAK-PROOF, GAS-TIGHT JOINTS SEALED WITH ACID-PROOF CEMENT

SECTION 7" ID 14" OD MADE OF 5/8" REFRACTORY INNER LINING, 3" VERMICULITE CONCRETE INSULATING WALL AND CEMENT ASBESTOS JACKET

HIGH TEMPERATURE REFRACTORY FIRE CLAY FLUE LINING THROUGHOUT

CHIMNEY SUPPORT SUSPENDED BETWEEN JOISTS (ELIMINATES CHIMNEY FOUNDATION)

14" OD FLUE SECTION INSTALLS BETWEEN JOISTS ON 16" CENTERS WITHOUT JOIST CUTTING

FURNACE, WATER HEATER OR INCINERATOR CONNECT TO BOTTOM OPENING

THE FLINTKOTE COMPANY, NEW YORK, NEW YORK.

Fig. 10-88. Metal chimneys (used where local building codes permit) eliminate the chimney foundation and allow greater freedom in floor planning.

WILLIAM WALLACE DIVISION, WALLACE-MURRY CORP., BELMONT, CALIFORNIA.

Fig. 10-89. Some prefabricated metal chimneys are used in place of exterior masonry chimneys for fireplaces.

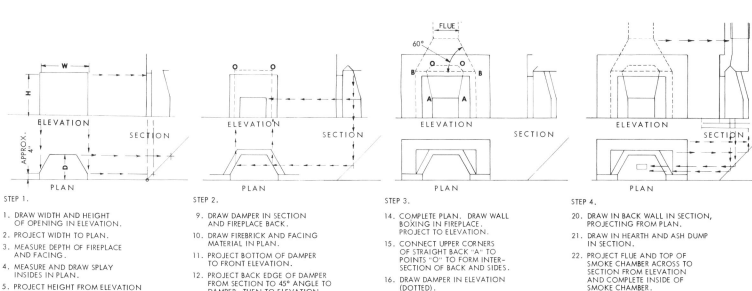

STEP 1.

1. DRAW WIDTH AND HEIGHT OF OPENING IN ELEVATION.

2. PROJECT WIDTH TO PLAN.

3. MEASURE DEPTH OF FIREPLACE AND FACING.

4. MEASURE AND DRAW SPLAY INSIDES IN PLAN.

5. PROJECT HEIGHT FROM ELEVATION TO SECTION.

6. DRAW 45° ANGLE WHERE FACES OF ELEVATION AND PLAN INTERSECT.

7. PROJECT DEPTHS OF FACING AND FIREPLACE FROM PLAN TO SECTION.

8. DRAW IN SLANTING BACK AND SMOKE SHELF.

STEP 2.

9. DRAW DAMPER IN SECTION AND FIREPLACE BACK.

10. DRAW FIREBRICK AND FACING MATERIAL IN PLAN.

11. PROJECT BOTTOM OF DAMPER TO FRONT ELEVATION.

12. PROJECT BACK EDGE OF DAMPER FROM SECTION TO 45° ANGLE TO DAMPER, THEN TO ELEVATION TO POINTS "O" INTERSECTION.

13. PROJECT STRAIGHT BACK TO ELEVATION FROM PLAN AND SECTION.

STEP 3.

14. COMPLETE PLAN. DRAW WALL BOXING IN FIREPLACE. PROJECT TO ELEVATION.

15. CONNECT UPPER CORNERS OF STRAIGHT BACK "A" TO POINTS "O" TO FORM INTER-SECTION OF BACK AND SIDES.

16. DRAW DAMPER IN ELEVATION (DOTTED).

17. AT INTERSECTION OF POINTS "B" DRAW LINES AT 60° ANGLE TO FORM SMOKE CHAMBER

18. DRAW IN FLUE.

19. DETERMINE AND DRAW IN MANTEL HEIGHT.

STEP 4.

20. DRAW IN BACK WALL IN SECTION, PROJECTING FROM PLAN.

21. DRAW IN HEARTH AND ASH DUMP IN SECTION.

22. PROJECT FLUE AND TOP OF SMOKE CHAMBER ACROSS TO SECTION FROM ELEVATION AND COMPLETE INSIDE OF SMOKE CHAMBER.

23. DRAW WALL ADJOINING FIREPLACE IN PLAN.

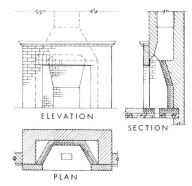

STEP 5.

24. COMPLETE ELEVATION, SECTION AND PLAN. SHOW MATERIALS IN SECTION BY SYMBOLS. SHOW MATERIAL IN ELEVATION BY SYMBOLS.

Fig. 10-90. Follow this step-by-step drawing procedure in drawing fireplace details.

place from the finished floor to the beginning of the flue tile. Second, a *plan view* in section where the cutting plane has been placed midway through the elevation. And third, a *vertical section* taken midway through the fireplace opening. (These three views were shown in Figs. 10-79 and 10-81.)

The *elevation view* shows the fireplace opening, general exterior design and materials, smoke chamber, and the lower portion of the flue (usually shown in hidden lines). The *plan view* shows the flue for the space heating facilities (if the same chimney is used), ash dump (if this is included), firebrick, and depth and angle (given in offset dimensions not degrees) of fire chamber sides and the hearth. The *vertical section* shows the placement of the ash dump, flue, damper, and the construction of the hearth. All these drawings give the dimensions necessary for the construction of the fireplace. The mason should be able to complete the job without any question.

The overall dimensions of the fireplace should be closely calculated. The brick size should be checked and ⅜″ should be allowed for each mortar joint. With this information, it is then possible to calculate the width and depth of the fireplace.

Step-by-Step Drawing Procedure: Fireplaces

Fig. 10-90 outlines the step-by-step procedure for detailing a fireplace. These general instructions may be used for a masonry fireplace, as well as for a metal built-in unit.

Stairs

Stair construction is a specialized area within the home construction field. Many builders have found that stairs constructed by manufacturers or mills are more economical and just as efficient as those cut and built on the site. The designer should have knowledge of stair construction so he can provide the correct design and stair space. Care should be taken to assure that the stair construction is in keeping with the general house design.

A well-designed stairway should be based

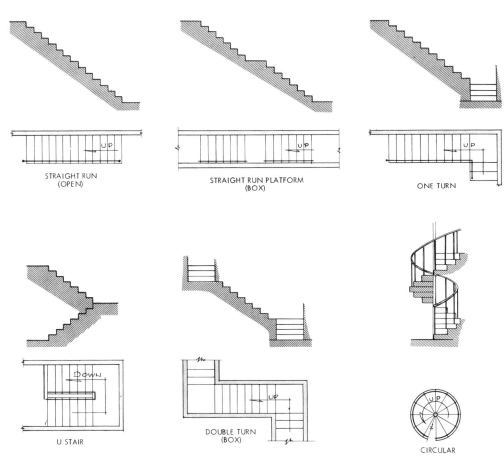

Fig. 10-91. Six basic types of stair flights are commonly used in residential housing.

on three tenets: (1) the stair should be easy to ascend; (2) all stair treads and risers should be uniform; and (3) the stairs should have ample artificial and/or natural light.

Stair Types

Stairs are generally classified as "open" or "closed." A stair that has no wall on either side is an *open stair.* If the stair has a wall on one side, it is referred to as a *semi-housed stair;* if it is between two walls, it is then a *closed, housed,* or *box stair.*

It may be necessary to place a *platform* or *landing* in a *straight flight* of stairs; this is known as a *straight run* platform, Fig. 10-91 (top center). If the stair turns 90° with the landing, it is called *one turn* stair, Fig. 10-91 (top right). If a stair turn 180° at the landing, it is known as a *U-stair,* Fig. 10-91 (bottom left). A *double turn* stair turns 90° at each landing, Fig. 10-91 (bottom center). Circular or spiral stairs are also being used in some contemporary homes, Fig. 10-91 (bottom right) and Fig. 10-92.

Folding stairs are often used to reach attics and storage areas (such as the garage storage area). Fig. 10-93 illustrates the common design for a folding stair. These stairs are manufactured in various lengths suitable for residential ceiling heights. Tread widths are commonly 2'-0", 2'-2", or 2'-6".

Basic Stair Parts

Stairs consist of three basic parts: *tread, riser,* and *stringer.* See Fig. 10-94. The *tread*

WOODBRIDGE ORNAMENTAL IRON CO., CHICAGO, ILLINOIS.

Fig. 10-92. The spiral stair is being used with increasing frequency.

is the horizontal member of the stair; the *riser* is the vertical member between any two treads or between a tread and the floor or landing. The portion of the tread extending beyond the face of the riser is

Fig. 10-93. A folding stair may be used for reaching seldom-used spaces.

called the nosing. *Stringers* carry the treads and risers through the stairwell opening.

The depth of the tread (exclusive of the nosing) is called the *run* and the height of the riser is referred to as the *rise.*

Staircase Layout

Headroom is the clearance (*measured vertically*) from the top of the tread at the front edge of the riser to the headroom line (*a line drawn from the underside of the stairwell opening header or trimmer and*

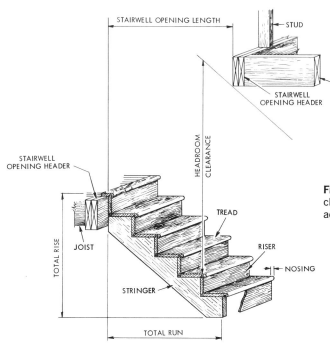

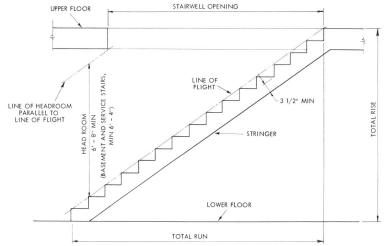

Fig. 10-94. Stair Details and Nomenclature. Stairs must be designed in accordance with the stairwell opening.

length is important because it is during the floor framing stage of construction that this opening must be located and framed. Length of the stairwell opening, depending upon the amount of headroom clearance, is measured from header to header, or trimmer to trimmer.

Railing. The *newel* (Fig. 10-96) is the main post, either at the top or the bottom of the stair, which receives the *handrail*. Small upright members called *balusters* are placed at the outer end of the stairs to support the handrail. The height of the handrail is usually 2'-6" from the top of the tread on a line with the face of the riser. On a

parallel to the line of flight.) See Fig. 10-95 for headroom clearance and stairwell opening. Building codes specify a minimum headroom clearance of 6'-8". Stairs between the first and second floors usually have a headroom clearance of 7'-0". Tri-level homes require a stair headroom clearance of 7'-0" for all stairs since each run of stairs receives approximately the same amount of traffic. The headroom for basement and attic stairs is a minimum of 6'-4". In all cases local codes and FHA Standards should be consulted.

Opening length. The stair well opening

Fig. 10-95. Headroom is very important in stair design. The stairwell or the line of flight must be adjusted until the required headroom is obtained.

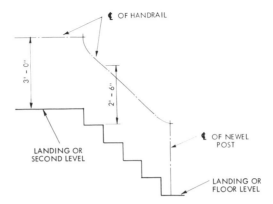

Fig. 10-96. This unusual stair adds a contemporary touch. Stair and rail parts are designated. Note the 2'6" height for the rail on the slope and the 3'0" height on the landing.

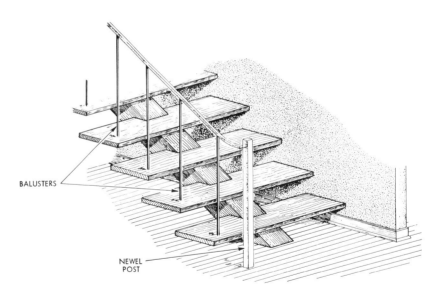

landing, balcony, or main level the height of the handrail is increased to 2'-8" or 3'-0". The increase in height is necessary to afford the maximum protection at landings, balconies, and levels. To compensate for this increased height, the upper end of the handrail is curved upward at the top of the stairs. (This is called *ramping*.) The lower end of the handrail is finished similarly with an *easement* at the newel post. The easement prevents an abrupt change of direction. Fig. 10-96 illustrates the relationship of the newel, balusters, and railing.

Stringers. The treads and risers are supported by stringers (sometimes called car-

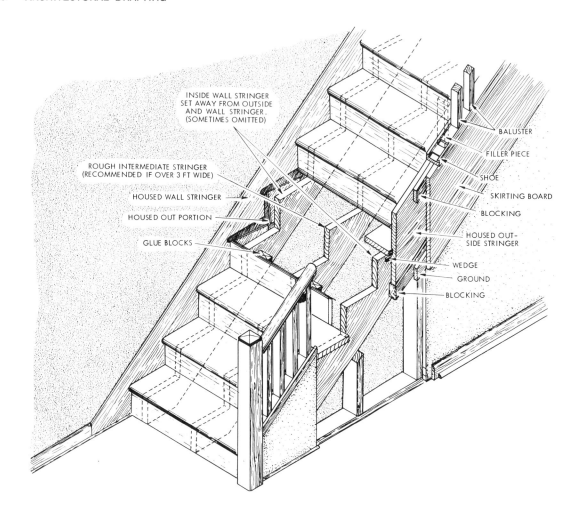

INSIDE WALL STRINGER
SET AWAY FROM OUTSIDE
AND WALL STRINGER.
(SOMETIMES OMITTED)

ROUGH INTERMEDIATE STRINGER
(RECOMMENDED IF OVER 3 FT WIDE)

HOUSED WALL STRINGER

HOUSED OUT PORTION

GLUE BLOCKS

BALUSTER

FILLER PIECE

SHOE

SKIRTING BOARD

BLOCKING

HOUSED OUT-
SIDE STRINGER

WEDGE

GROUND

BLOCKING

Fig. 10-97. The closed string stair uses housed wall and outside stringers to receive the tread and riser ends. The rough intermediate stringer is only used for wide stairways.

riages) which extend from floor to floor and are fastened to the double header by nails or clips. Two inside stringers are normally used for support. If the stair is wider than 3'-0" an intermediate stringer is used. A wall stringer and an outside stringer are used to receive the tread and riser ends. When wall and outside stringers are rabbeted (grooved, usually ½" deep) to house the treads and risers, the stair is known as the *housed* or *closed string stair.* See Fig. 10-97. Note in Fig. 10-97 the use of wedges to insure a tight fit between the upper face of the tread and housed stringer. Note also the use of glue blocks.

In an *open string stair,* the outside stringer is cut to the profile of the stair and is *mitered* (cut and fit at an angle) against

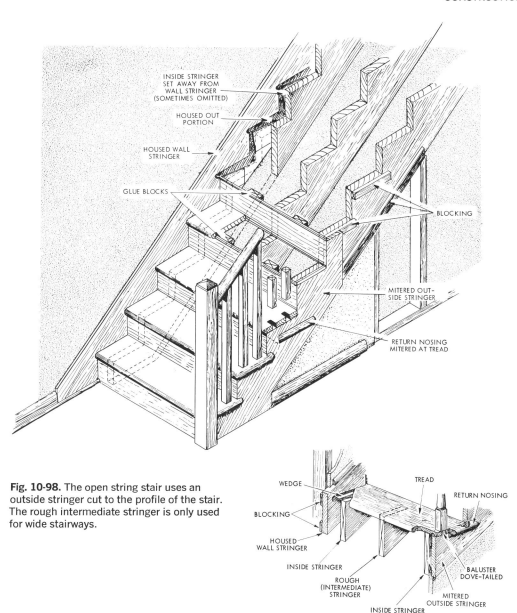

INSIDE STRINGER
SET AWAY FROM
WALL STRINGER
(SOMETIMES OMITTED)

HOUSED OUT
PORTION

HOUSED WALL
STRINGER

GLUE BLOCKS

BLOCKING

MITERED OUT-
SIDE STRINGER

RETURN NOSING
MITERED AT TREAD

WEDGE

TREAD

RETURN NOSING

BLOCKING

HOUSED
WALL STRINGER

INSIDE STRINGER

ROUGH
(INTERMEDIATE)
STRINGER

BALUSTER
DOVE-TAILED

MITERED
OUTSIDE STRINGER

INSIDE STRINGER

Fig. 10-98. The open string stair uses an outside stringer cut to the profile of the stair. The rough intermediate stringer is only used for wide stairways.

the end of the risers. Nosing is extended beyond the end of the tread by a separate solid molding. See Fig. 10-98.

Although the stair may have either closed or open strings, the open string is probably the most common type.

Stair Design

Designing stairs is a matter of ascertaining a comfortable riser height and tread depth in relation to the space allotted for the stair. If a high riser is necessary, a shallower tread should be used. Conversely, if a low riser is used, a deeper tread is necessary. The total distance of two risers and one tread should be equal to the average stride of an adult while traveling the stair. *This is approximately 25".* An uncomfortable step would result if a long tread and short riser were used. Some public buildings have long treads and short risers which are difficult to ascend or descend. Ideally a riser is 7" to 7½" high and the tread run is 10" or 10½". It is wise to follow these dimensions for stairs leading from the first to second floor and for *all* stairs in a split-level house if the required space is available. Basement or attic stairs which are usually not heavily travelled may have a slightly shorter tread and slightly higher rise. Stairs *may* be built at any angle from 20° to 50°. The *preferred* angle for safety and ease of travel is 30° to 35°.

Manufacturers commonly supply stairs in widths of 3'-0", 3'-6", and 4'-0"; treads of 10″, 10½″, or 11½″; and risers of 7″, 7½″, or 8″.

To determine the number and dimension of risers and treads required for any stair run, the following procedure is helpful:

1. Determine the total rise of the stair (the distance from finished floor to finished floor) in inches. For purposes of illustration, this distance shall be assumed as 9′-6″ or 114″.

2. Determine approximately the number of risers (of average height) this stair will require. Assuming the average riser to be 7″, divide the total rise by the *trial* riser: 114″ ÷ 7″ = 16.285 or 16²⁄₇ risers. If, as in this illustration, the result is not a whole number, go to the *nearest* whole *number* (in this example *16 risers*).

3. Determine the exact height of each riser. Divide the total rise by the number of risers (from Step #2): 114″ ÷ 16 = 7⅛″ for each riser.

4. Determine the number of treads. The total number of treads in a stair run is one less than the number of risers. The floors are not counted as treads: 16 risers − 1 = 15 treads.

5. Determine the tread depth or run. Multiply the riser (Step #3) by 2 and subtract from 25″ (the stride of an adult's foot on a stair is approximately 25″, or 2 risers and 1 tread): 7⅛″ × 2 = 14¼″; 25″ − 14¼″ = 10¾″ for each tread.

6. Determine the total run of the stair. Multiply the number of treads by

the tread width: 15 × 10¾″ = 161¼″ or 13′-5¼″.

If the total run cannot be fitted into the *allotted* total run, increase the riser height (by eliminating one riser) and recalculate starting from Step #2. These six simple steps may be used to compute any type of stair — from the basement to first floor, first floor to second floor, between levels in a split level, etc.

Step-by-Step Drawing Procedure: Stairs

The step-by-step procedure for developing the stair detail is shown in Fig. 10-99. An additional illustration developing a U-type stair is depicted in Fig. 10-100.

Questions and Problems

1. Based on the pitch triangle give the amount of rise in inches of the following fractional pitches:

   a. ¼   d. ⅐
   b. ⁵⁄₁₂   e. ⅙
   c. ⅓   f. ⅛

2. If a pitch triangle has a rise of 3½″ and a 12″ run, what is the fractional pitch?

3. A house has a floor plan with basic dimensions of 28′ × 48′, the long dimension faces the street which is on the north side of the house. A 22′ × 24′ garage is on the east side flush with the back of the house. A one-story projection of 4′-0″ × 16′-0″ is on the rear of the house toward the west and flush with the west wall.

   a. Draw a hip roof plan for a one-story building using this plan.
   b. Draw a gable roof plan for a two-story building.
   c. Draw a hip roof for a split-level house.

   Draw a gable roof with dormers for a one-and-a-half-story house.

4. In your own words, define the terms: *pitch, span,* and *run.*

5. Detail the following cornices using a scale of 1″ = 1′-0″, 1½″ = 1′-0″, or 3″ = 1′-0″. Call out all materials and sizes.

   A. An open cornice for a contemporary style home: The roof (built-up tar and gravel) has a rise of 1½″ in 12″ of run and overhangs the frame-backed brick veneer wall by 2′-6″. The interior finish is ½″ dry wall and the outside of the stud wall is covered with fabricated fiberboard. The ceiling joists are 2″ × 6″.

   B. A box cornice for a Cape Cod house: The roof overhangs the clapboard frame wall 3″, and has ⅓ pitch. The ceiling joist is a 2″ × 6″. The interior finish is plaster and the outside of the stud wall is covered with fabricated fiberboard. Three inch batts are used for insulation. Use a 6″ half-round hanging gutter.

   C. A box cornice for a 4″ rise in 12″

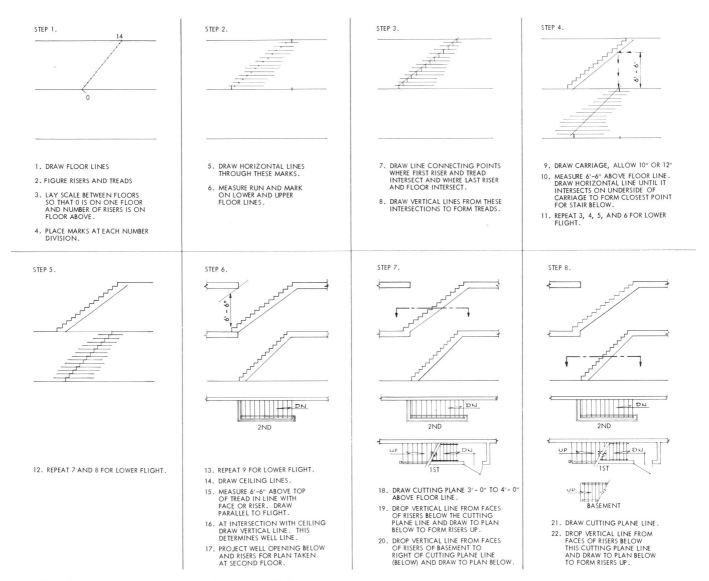

STEP 1.

1. DRAW FLOOR LINES
2. FIGURE RISERS AND TREADS
3. LAY SCALE BETWEEN FLOORS SO THAT 0 IS ON ONE FLOOR AND NUMBER OF RISERS IS ON FLOOR ABOVE.
4. PLACE MARKS AT EACH NUMBER DIVISION.

STEP 2.

5. DRAW HORIZONTAL LINES THROUGH THESE MARKS.
6. MEASURE RUN AND MARK ON LOWER AND UPPER FLOOR LINES.

STEP 3.

7. DRAW LINE CONNECTING POINTS WHERE FIRST RISER AND TREAD INTERSECT AND WHERE LAST RISER AND FLOOR INTERSECT.
8. DRAW VERTICAL LINES FROM THESE INTERSECTIONS TO FORM TREADS.

STEP 4.

9. DRAW CARRIAGE, ALLOW 10" OR 12"
10. MEASURE 6'-6" ABOVE FLOOR LINE. DRAW HORIZONTAL LINE UNTIL IT INTERSECTS ON UNDERSIDE OF CARRIAGE TO FORM CLOSEST POINT FOR STAIR BELOW.
11. REPEAT 3, 4, 5, AND 6 FOR LOWER FLIGHT.

STEP 5.

12. REPEAT 7 AND 8 FOR LOWER FLIGHT.

STEP 6.

13. REPEAT 9 FOR LOWER FLIGHT.
14. DRAW CEILING LINES.
15. MEASURE 6'-6" ABOVE TOP OF TREAD IN LINE WITH FACE OR RISER. DRAW PARALLEL TO FLIGHT.
16. AT INTERSECTION WITH CEILING DRAW VERTICAL LINE. THIS DETERMINES WELL LINE.
17. PROJECT WELL OPENING BELOW AND RISERS FOR PLAN TAKEN AT SECOND FLOOR.

STEP 7.

18. DRAW CUTTING PLANE 3'-0" TO 4'-0" ABOVE FLOOR LINE.
19. DROP VERTICAL LINE FROM FACES OF RISERS BELOW THE CUTTING PLANE LINE AND DRAW TO PLAN BELOW TO FORM RISERS UP.
20. DROP VERTICAL LINE FROM FACES OF RISERS OF BASEMENT TO RIGHT OF CUTTING PLANE LINE (BELOW) AND DRAW TO PLAN BELOW.

STEP 8.

21. DRAW CUTTING PLANE LINE.
22. DROP VERTICAL LINE FROM FACES OF RISERS BELOW THIS CUTTING PLANE LINE AND DRAW TO PLAN BELOW TO FORM RISERS UP.

Fig. 10-99. Follow this step-by-step procedure in drawing the straight run stair.

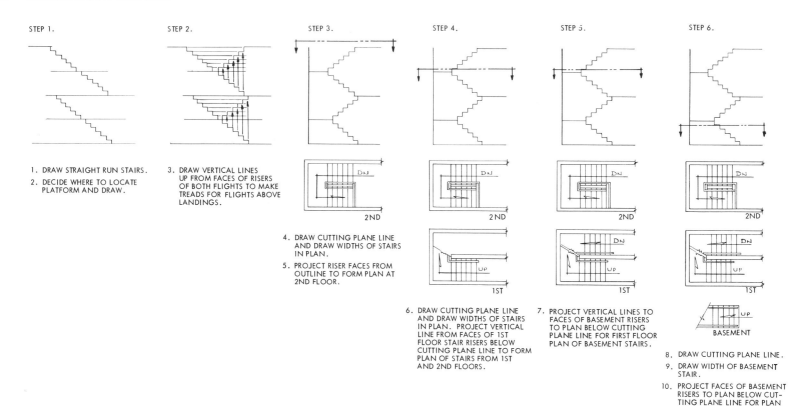

STEP 1.

1. DRAW STRAIGHT RUN STAIRS.
2. DECIDE WHERE TO LOCATE PLATFORM AND DRAW.

STEP 2.

3. DRAW VERTICAL LINES UP FROM FACES OF RISERS OF BOTH FLIGHTS TO MAKE TREADS FOR FLIGHTS ABOVE LANDINGS.

STEP 3.

2ND

4. DRAW CUTTING PLANE LINE AND DRAW WIDTHS OF STAIRS IN PLAN.
5. PROJECT RISER FACES FROM OUTLINE TO FORM PLAN AT 2ND FLOOR.

STEP 4.

2ND

1ST

6. DRAW CUTTING PLANE LINE AND DRAW WIDTHS OF STAIRS IN PLAN. PROJECT VERTICAL LINE FROM FACES OF 1ST FLOOR STAIR RISERS BELOW CUTTING PLANE LINE TO FORM PLAN OF STAIRS FROM 1ST AND 2ND FLOORS.

STEP 5.

2ND

1ST

7. PROJECT VERTICAL LINES TO FACES OF BASEMENT RISERS TO PLAN BELOW CUTTING PLANE LINE FOR FIRST FLOOR PLAN OF BASEMENT STAIRS.

STEP 6.

2ND

1ST

BASEMENT

8. DRAW CUTTING PLANE LINE.
9. DRAW WIDTH OF BASEMENT STAIR.
10. PROJECT FACES OF BASEMENT RISERS TO PLAN BELOW CUTTING PLANE LINE FOR PLAN OF BASEMENT STAIRS AT THE BASEMENT.

Fig. 10-100. Follow this step-by-step procedure in drawing the U-stair.

run: A veneer wall with a concrete block backing of 16″ is used. Plaster is applied directly to the concrete block. A 2″ × 8″ plate is secured to the back-up units by a ¾″ × 16″ anchor bolt. Use a 2″ × 2″ lookout to carry the plancier level to the wall. Use a 5″ metal box gutter.

6. Select a standard size leader for a roof having the following specifications:

   a. Gable roof (⅛ pitch) on a rectangular plan, 36′ × 24′, having a leader at each corner.
   b. Hip roof (⅙ pitch all sides) on a rectangular plan, 50′ × 26′, having a leader at each corner.

7. Why is it necessary to place the gutter below the roof line?
8. What type of materials may be used for flashing:
   a. Around a chimney projecting through a roof?
   b. Around a window?
   c. At the base of a masonry veneer wall?

9. What is the purpose of flashing?

10. What are the purposes of vents in a frame wall and weep holes in masonry veneer wall?

11. How may the decision to use trussed rafters rather than conventional framing affect:
    a. The room arrangement?
    b. The basic philosophy of planning?

12. What methods may be used for fabricating trussed rafters? What are the advantages and disadvantages of each method?

13. Compare the sizes of framing members necessary for a conventionally framed roof (include ceiling joist) with the sizes used for a trussed rafter. The roof has a $\frac{1}{6}$ pitch and a clear span of 28'. Assume a partition is placed midway in the 28' span.

14. Why is it necessary to have adequate ventilation in the attic?

15. What method(s) of venting the attic seem to be most advantageous?

16. Explain the causes for ice dams forming in the gutter. What are possible remedies?

17. Calculate the net free area for a roof having a ceiling area of:
    a. 975 sq. ft. with gable end louvers.
    b. 1,200 sq. ft. with continuous soffit vent.
    c. 1,000 sq. ft. with roof louvers.
    d. 1,175 sq. ft. with continuous ridge vent.
    e. 1,450 sq. ft. with continuous ridge and soffit vent.

Specify from a manufacturer's brochure the necessary sizes of venting devices needed to satisfy the calculated requirements.

18. What methods are used to specify and indicate the sizes of windows on a set of drawings?

19. What type of window provides the *least* amount of draft when open?

20. What type of window may be opened during a thunder shower without the probability of having rain enter?

21. Using a scale of $1\frac{1}{2}'' = 1'\text{-}0''$ draw a:
    a. Section on the vertical centerline of a window.
    b. One-half exterior elevation and one-half interior elevation of a window.
    c. One-half plan on the exterior elevation of a double-hung 2 light 24/20 window with double strength glass.
    Indicate all materials and notes.

22. Why would it be advisable to use a louvered door on a closet?

23. A designer must select doors for a closet having an opening of 7'-0". The room is occupied by two sisters; both frequently dress at the same time. What type of doors (kind, style, and action) would be best in this situation?

24. Select an opening size for a conventional, single-opening fireplace and sketch three different elevations using different materials.

25. Why should the chimney be carried above the highest point of the roof?

26. What purpose does the smoke shelf and damper serve in a well functioning fireplace?

27. What relation exists between the size of the fireplace opening and the flue?

28. Why are the sides of a single-opening fireplace angled?

29. Select a fireplace (single, projecting, double-opening, etc.), use the recommended proportional dimensions, and make several sketched preliminary studies of the exterior treatment. Have the instructor criticize the studies. Change as per his suggestions. Make a set of detail drawings, complete with dimensions, at a scale of $1\frac{1}{2}'' = 1'\text{-}0''$. Show an elevation from the finished floor to flue tile or appropriate point above. Take a vertical section through the fire chamber. Extend the vertical section up to flue tile and down to the ash pit and footing.

30. Calculate the height and number of risers and the depth and number of treads for a stair that will extend between the first and second floor (8'-8"). What is the length of the stairwell opening if the headroom is 6'-8"?

31. Make a sectional drawing of the stair calculated in problem 30 above. Show the floor framing tie-ins, headers, etc. Completely dimension and call out all materials and sizes. Scale: $1'' = 1'\text{-}0''$.

32. If space is limited for a stair run what type of stair could be designed to use a minimal amount of space?

Support Members and Floor Plans 11

As mentioned earlier, a floor plan is a two dimensional drawing (length and width) which represents a specific floor or level of a building. The floor is represented, with its roof or ceiling removed, as it would appear when viewed from above. Fig. 11-1 illustrates this concept. The name given to a specific plan refers to the particular floor or level of the building, e.g., first floor, second floor, ground level, upper level, etc. Detailed floor plans are drawn to a small scale using various standardized symbols and conventions. Prior to actually drawing the detailed floor plan, however, it is necessary to compute the structural members which support a particular floor. Structural members (joists, girders, columns, etc.) are directly related to the function and size of the rooms which they will support.

This chapter discusses the computing and design of support members and the planning and drafting of floor plans.

Fig. 11-1. Each plan view represents a horizontal section through a structure.

Computing Support Members

Support members are those structural parts which carry the load of any structure. The size and layout of the structural mem-bers are usually shown on floor plans. Before drawing the floor plans, however, the loads must be determined, and the structural members must be computed. When the load on a particular support member is known, the size, depending upon the material, may be calculated using standard tables. Tables are issued by the Federal Housing Administration and by various manufacturing, research companies and lumber associations, giving sizes, lengths, strengths, and loading capacities of building materials and products.

Most cities and communities have building codes which specify the minimum strength of structural members. For safety, the architect or designer must *never* fall short of the legal minimum.

Loads imposed upon structural members are classified as *live loads* and *dead loads*. Live loads are those static or moving weights, not part of the original structure, which the building is designed to support. Examples of such weights are the occupants, furniture, equipment, snow, wind, etc. *Dead loads* are those static or fixed weights of the *material* of the structure itself. Examples of dead loads are the weights of the lumber, drywall, flooring, roofing, etc. Dead load weight may be calculated using the size and established weights of the various building materials.

Structures are designed to support predetermined loads. The following sections cover lumber, stresses, and loads of various support members.

Stress Grading of Lumber

Each species of lumber is graded to determine the ultimate load it will withstand. There are two methods of assigning stress values: (1) visual, and (2) machine-rated.

The stress rating assigned by visual means takes into account the species, geographic area of growth, and physical characteristics of annular rings, knots, etc. Machine stress-rated lumber is evaluated by mechanical stress rating equipment. Each piece is non-destructively tested and marked to indicate the fiber stress and the modulus of elasticity. Basically the main use of machine stress rated lumber is in trussed rafters, floor and ceiling joists, and rafters, where strength capacities are major considerations. The indication of the grade, either broad classification such as SEL-STR (select-straight), CONST (construction), etc., or by mechanical means such as 1500 f (1500 psi fiber stress) and 1.4E (1,400,000 psi modulus of elasticity) are stamped on each piece of lumber.

Different factors must be taken into account when working stresses are determined for lumber. Since the characteristics of lumber vary widely, the resulting strength attributes are in direct relation to these characteristics. Through research and testing, technically trained personnel have determined the effects of different characteristics

a log may possess in relation to its ultimate strength. Since it is not feasible to test each piece of lumber for strength (other than those which are to be used in critical design situations) four steps are followed for each species from a particular geographic region: (1) testing of straight grained specimens; (2) adjusting test values of clear wood to basic working stress levels; (3) evaluating the effect of growth characteristics on clear wood strengths; and (4) translating data into grading rules for grading rules.

Kinds of Stresses

Any structural member has four types of stresses that may act *upon* or *within* the member. These four stresses are *compression, tension, shear* and *bending*. Fig. 11-2 shows a graphic illustration of each of these types of stresses.

Compression. A member is in compression whenever the forces acting on it tend to compress or squeeze it together, thus making it shorter. A post or column is in *compression* as it supports a girder or beam.

Tension. Forces which tend to pull apart

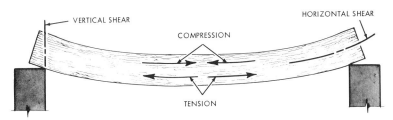

Fig. 11-2. Stresses in a simple structural member.

or stretch a member and make it longer are said to be tensile stresses. A vertical member supporting a suspended ceiling has *tensile* stresses acting upon it.

Shear. A shearing stress is the result of two forces in parallel adjacent planes sliding in opposite directions. A girder resting on a block wall is in *shear* as the stresses tend to *cut off* the end of the girder. The total load on the girder is one force and the resistance of the block wall acting in the opposite direction is the other. These forces are perpendicular to the grain of the wood. Shearing stresses may also be *parallel* to the grain of the wood. This occurs when the forces cause a member to split *lengthwise*.

Bending. Forces causing a member to deflect or bend can originate from external or internal stresses. A girder or beam may *bend* because of the distance between supports (its own weight) or it may *bend* due to the load(s) imposed upon the member.

Working Stresses

Unit stresses are determined in different types of materials (species of wood from different geographical areas, plywood, concrete mixtures) and shapes of structural members (I-beams, angles, tees, etc.) by testing machines. These machines are calibrated to indicate the point at which materials and shapes will fail under different stresses. By knowing the characteristics of any material and applying a proper factor of safety, the architect or engineer can safely design a structure. Through various and repeated testing procedures the unit stresses (the point of failure) for each types of material can be determined.

No engineer would design a building with structural members stressed to their ultimate point. If he were to do this the building would be at the point of breaking. An architect designs a building so the stresses are well below the ultimate strengths of each load bearing member used in the design. In addition to selecting the proper size member he must also anticipate the loads which may be imposed in the far distant future as the uses of the structure may change. For this reason the stresses the architect expects to be developed in the structure are always less than the ultimate strength of the material and shape he selects. The stresses which are expected to develop in the building due to wind, snow, dead and live loading are called the *working stress*. These are the stresses which the architect or structural engineer uses in his calculations.

As was just pointed out, the architect will not design a member so that it just reaches the unit stress. He will "over-design" a member by including in his calculation a safety factor. The safety factor is usually assumed to be equal to the unit stress (ultimate strength) divided by the working stress. The basic formula for the safety factor is expressed:

$$\text{Factor of Safety} = \frac{\text{Ultimate Strength}}{\text{Working Stress}}$$

The designer must be familiar with the characteristics of the materials used in the structural design. By making the correct allowances for the factor of safety and the material, he can select the correct sized member from a table giving the unit stress.

Building codes indicate stresses for varying materials. Table 11-1 illustrates a stress table taken from a building code of a large city. Each figure in this table is the maximum allowable unit stress in pounds per square inch for wood members used in that area governed by the code. It will be noted that the value for each type of stress is indicated following the material.

The values shown for *extreme fiber stress* indicate the resistance in pounds per square inch to shortening and lengthening of the fibers when the member tends to bend under a load. Fibers that slide lengthwise past each other and bend under an imposed load are said to be in *horizontal shear*. For example, the horizontal shear of Douglas Fir is 100 pounds per square inch. *Compression across the grain* is the resistance to compression at right angles to the axis of the structural member measured in pounds per square inch. *Compression parallel to the grain* is similar to the previous only that the compression is parallel to the axis. When a structural member is loaded, it will elongate at a uniform rate until it reaches its elastic limit, after which it will not return to its original length. The relationship of unit stress to unit elongation is called the *modulus of elasticity* and is expressed in pounds per square inch. The modulus of elasticity for Douglas Fir, for example, is 1,600,000 pounds per square inch.

TABLE 11-1
MAXIMUM ALLOWABLE UNIT STRESSES (POUNDS PER SQUARE INCH)

SPECIES AND COMMERCIAL GRADE	EXTREME FIBER STRESS AND TENSION PARALLEL TO GRAIN	HORIZONTAL SHEAR	COMPRESSION ACROSS GRAIN	COMPRESSION PARALLEL TO GRAIN	MODULUS OF ELASTICITY
CYPRESS	1300	120	300	900	1,200,000
DOUGLAS FIR	1300	100	325	1200	1,600,000
PLYWOOD (FIR) BUILT UP SECTION	1500	100	400	1500	1,600,000
LAMINATED TIMBER	1100	75	400	1500	1,600,000
HEMLOCK	1000	90	350	1100	1,400,000
OAK	1300	120	600	1000	1,500,000
REDWOOD	1100	75	300	1000	1,200,000
SOUTHERN PINE LONGLEAF	1300	120	450	1000	1,600,000
SHORTLEAF	1100	120	400	900	1,600,000
SPRUCE SITKA OR EASTERN	1000	75	300	800	1,200,000

TABLE 11-2
SNOW LOADS

AREA UNITED STATES	ROOF ANGLE	
	FLAT OR SLIGHT ANGLE 0°-25°	STEEP ANGLE 25°-45°
NORTHWEST NORTHEAST	45 lbs/Sq. Ft.	15 lbs/Sq. Ft.
CENTRAL WESTERN	35 lbs/Sq. Ft.	10 lbs/Sq. Ft.
SOUTH PACIFIC COAST	10 lbs/Sq. Ft.	0 lbs/Sq. Ft.

Roof Loads

Roofs must be designed to withstand the live loads imposed by snow and wind.

The additional load imposed on a roof by snow will vary. The variance is dependent upon two factors: (1) the pitch of the roof and (2) the geographic area. A roof with a slight slope will have a greater tendency to retain the snow than a roof with a steep pitch. Generally a roof with a steep slope will impose a smaller load since the snow will slide or be blown off. Depending on the nature of the snow, it may cling to even a fairly steep sloped roof. Wet snow, for example, has a high coefficient of friction and will not slide and usually will not be blown from a roof because the flakes become easily intertwined with a considerable cohesive force. Because of the slope of a roof, the weight of the snow acts in two directions: (1) one force acts parallel to the roof; and (2) one force acts perpendicular to the roof. Since the weight of the snow on a steep pitched roof can be analyzed with the two components just mentioned, the force on the roof is less than its weight. Table 11-2 gives loads in pounds per square foot for various roof angles.

Wind loads work exactly opposite to snow loads. The greater the slope of the roof the greater the wind pressure. Loads vary from 15 to 35 lbs. per sq. ft. for roofs with slopes from ⅛ to ½ pitch (15 to 45 degrees). Wind loads are not considered for flat or nearly flat roofs.

Building codes usually specify what loads are to be used. Normally, the snow and wind loads are usually taken as 30 lbs. per sq. ft. for all locations. In extreme situations, 40 lbs. per sq. ft. is considered adequate.

Sonic Booms. As we advance further into the age of jet transportation *sonic booms* become an increasingly significant factor in building construction. A sonic boom is a strong pressure wave created by an aircraft travelling at or exceeding the speed of sound. The swift movement of the aircraft compresses the air resulting in a pressure or sound wave. The shape of the sound wave is conical with the apex of the cone near the aircraft and the base trailing on the ground. The impact of the wave will impose a live load anywhere within the elliptical base of the cone.

A sonic boom is measured in pounds per square foot above the normal atmospheric pressure. The higher the aircraft, the smaller the boom and the smaller the load. Loads imposed by sonic booms are not prolonged, such as snow loads, but, rather, cause a momentary shock or impact. A load as much as 5 lbs. per sq. ft. may be exerted (in addition to atmospheric pressure) by a plane exceeding the speed of sound at 20,000 ft. or below. Large plate glass windows may be damaged by 3 to 5 lbs. per sq. ft. Ordinary residential windows may also be damaged by planes flying at the speed of sound between 20,000 and 30,000 ft. In the future, residential construction should take these added loads into consideration.

Spans

The architectural designer must be able to use the correct tables which indicate the minimum allowable spans. Depending upon where the lumber was harvested and the species, each will have a different maximum span.

Table 11-3 shows a sample of maximum spans for a selected species of lumber. A complete tabulation of spans for most kinds of lumber used in residential building construction may be found in the latest edition of *Minimum Property Standards for One*

and Two Living Units. (Washington, D.C.: U.S. Department of Housing and Urban Development, Federal Housing Administration.)

All lumber grades are based on ultimate strength (unit strength) and are grouped by extreme fiber stress. Table 11-3 shows the maximum allowable spans for Coastal Region Douglas Fir. As an example, Select Structural J & P (joist and plank) has an extreme fiber stress of 1950 f (pounds per square inch) where Construction J & P has an extreme fiber stress of 1450 f.

Each of the above-mentioned tables gives the maximum allowable spans for floor, ceiling and roof joists and roof rafters. To select the proper table, the designer must be acquainted with the specie of lumber commonly used in his area for different framing members. Once this is known, the proper table can be selected and the structural members correctly sized. The size of wood

structural members is based on S4S (surfaced four sides) lumber. The sizes given in the table are nominal sizes—meaning size before surfacing.

Rafters

Support for the roof sheathing and roofing materials is provided by rafters. Rafters must be sufficiently strong to support the protective covering (roof boards, plywood decking, and roofing material) without deflection.

The selection of the correct rafter size is based on the following step-by-step procedure:

Step 1. *Determine rafter pitch.* If no pitch angle has been computed, scale the amount of rise for each foot of run from the elevation showing the roof slope. The roof in Fig. 11-3 has a slope

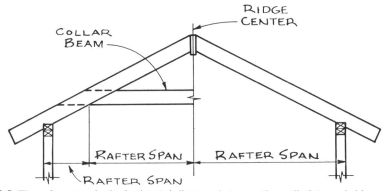

Fig. 11-3. The rafter span is the horizontal distance between the wall plate and ridge center, wall plate and collar beam, or collar beam and ridge center.

TABLE 11-3
DOUGLAS FIR, COAST REGION

Nominal size (inches)	Spacing (inches o.c.)	Select Structural J & P 1950 f		Dense Construction J & P 1700 f		Construction J & P 1450 f		Standard J & P 1200 f		Utility J & P (¹)		Select Structural J & P 1950 f		Dense Construction J & P 1700 f		Construction J & P 1450 f		Standard J & P 1200 f		Utility J & P (¹)	
		FLOOR JOISTS																			
		30 LB. LIVE LOAD										**40 LB. LIVE LOAD**									
		Ft.	In.	Ft.	In.	Ft.	In.	Ft.	In.	Ft.	In.	Ft.	In.	Ft.	In.	Ft.	In.	Ft.	In.	Ft.	In.
2 x 6	12	11	4	11	4	11	4	11	4	8	4	10	6	10	6	10	6	10	6	7	4
	16	10	4	10	4	10	4	10	4	7	2	9	8	9	8	9	8	9	8	6	4
	24	9	0	9	0	9	0	9	0	5	10	8	4	8	4	8	4	8	2	5	2
2 x 8	12	15	4	15	4	15	4	15	4	12	4	14	4	14	4	14	4	14	4	11	0
	16	14	0	14	0	14	0	14	0	10	8	13	0	13	0	13	0	13	0	9	6
	24	12	4	12	4	12	4	12	4	8	8	11	6	11	6	11	6	11	0	7	10
2 x 10	12	18	4	18	4	18	4	18	4	16	10	17	4	17	4	17	4	17	4	15	2
	16	17	0	17	0	17	0	17	0	14	8	16	2	16	2	16	2	16	2	13	0
	24	15	6	15	6	15	6	15	6	12	0	14	6	14	6	14	6	14	0	10	8
2 x 12	12	21	2	21	2	21	2	21	2	19	8	20	0	20	0	20	0	20	0	17	8
	16	19	8	19	8	19	8	19	8	17	0	18	8	18	8	18	8	18	8	15	4
	24	17	10	17	10	17	10	17	10	14	0	16	10	16	10	16	10	16	10	12	6
		CEILING JOISTS																			
		NO ATTIC STORAGE										**LIMITED ATTIC STORAGE**									
2 x 4 ²	12	11	10	--	--	11	8	8	10	--	--	9	6	--	--	8	2	6	4	--	--
	16	10	10	--	--	10	0	7	8	--	--	8	6	--	--	7	2	5	6	--	--
	24	9	6	--	--	8	2	6	4	--	--	7	6	--	--	5	10	4	6	--	--
2 x 6	12	17	2	17	2	17	2	17	2	13	6	14	4	14	4	14	4	14	4	9	6
	16	16	0	16	0	16	0	16	0	11	8	13	0	13	0	13	0	12	10	8	4
	24	14	4	14	4	14	4	14	4	9	6	11	4	11	4	11	4	10	6	6	8
2 x 8	12	21	8	21	8	21	8	21	8	20	2	18	4	18	4	18	4	18	4	14	4
	16	20	2	20	2	20	2	20	2	17	6	17	0	17	0	17	0	17	0	12	4
	24	18	4	18	4	18	4	18	4	14	4	15	4	15	4	15	4	14	4	10	0
2 x 10	12	24	0	24	0	24	0	24	0	24	0	21	10	21	10	21	10	21	10	19	6
	16	24	0	24	0	24	0	24	0	22	6	20	4	20	4	20	4	20	4	16	10
	24	21	10	21	10	21	10	21	10	19	6	18	4	18	4	18	4	18	0	13	10

¹ Denotes grade is not a stress grade.
² Denotes light framing grade. (Not Industrial Light Framing)
Notes:
(a) Spans may be increased 5 percent from those shown for rough lumber or lumber surfaced two edges (S2E).

(b) Spans shall be decreased 5 percent from those shown for lumber more than 2 percent but not more than 5 percent scant from American Lumber Standards sizes measured at a moisture content of 19 percent or less. Lumber scant more than 5 percent will not be acceptable.

TABLE 11-3
DOUGLAS FIR, COAST REGION (CONTINUED)

Nominal size (inches)	Spacing (inches o. c.)	Select Structural J & P (1950 f)		Dense Construction J & P (1700 f)		Construction J & P (1450 f)		Standard J & P (1200 f)		Utility J & P (1)		Select Structural J & P (1950 f)		Dense Construction J & P (1700 f)		Construction J & P (1450 f)		Standard J & P (1200 f)		Utility J & P (1)	
		Ft.	In.	Ft.	In.	Ft	In.	Ft.	In.	Ft.	In.	Ft.	In.	Ft.	In.	Ft.	In.	Ft.	In.	Ft.	In.

LOW SLOPE ROOF JOISTS
(Roof slope 3 in 12 or less)

		NOT SUPPORTING FINISHED CEILING										SUPPORTING FINISHED CEILING									
2 x 6	12	14	4	14	4	14	4	14	4	9	6	13	8	13	8	13	8	13	8	8	10
	16	13	0	13	0	13	0	12	10	8	4	12	4	12	4	12	4	11	10	7	8
	24	11	4	11	4	11	4	10	6	6	8	10	10	10	10	10	8	9	8	6	2
2 x 8	12	18	4	18	4	18	4	18	4	14	4	17	8	17	8	17	8	17	8	13	2
	16	17	0	17	0	17	0	17	0	12	4	16	4	16	4	16	4	16	2	11	6
	24	15	4	15	4	15	4	14	4	10	0	14	8	14	8	14	6	13	2	9	4
2 x 10	12	21	10	21	10	21	10	21	10	19	6	21	0	21	0	21	0	21	0	18	0
	16	20	4	20	4	20	4	20	4	16	10	19	6	19	6	19	6	19	6	15	8
	24	18	4	18	4	18	4	18	0	13	10	17	8	17	8	17	8	16	8	12	10
2 x 12	12	24	0	24	0	24	0	24	0	22	8	24	0	24	0	24	0	24	0	21	0
	16	23	6	23	6	23	6	23	6	19	8	22	6	22	6	22	6	22	6	18	2
	24	21	2	21	2	21	2	21	2	16	2	20	4	20	4	20	4	20	2	14	10

RAFTERS
(Roof slope over 3 in 12)

		LIGHT ROOFING										HEAVY ROOFING									
2 x 4 [2]	12	11	6	--	--	9	6	7	4	--	--	10	4	--	--	8	2	6	4	--	--
	16	10	6	--	--	8	4	6	4	--	--	9	6	--	--	7	2	5	6	--	--
	24	9	2	--	--	6	10	5	2	--	--	8	4	--	--	5	10	4	6	--	--
2 x 6	12	16	10	16	10	16	10	16	10	11	2	15	6	15	6	15	6	14	10	9	6
	16	15	8	15	8	15	8	15	0	9	8	14	4	14	4	14	0	12	10	8	4
	24	13	10	13	10	13	6	12	2	7	10	12	6	12	6	11	6	10	6	6	8
2 x 8	12	21	2	21	2	21	2	21	2	16	8	19	8	19	8	19	8	19	8	14	4
	16	19	10	19	10	19	10	19	10	14	4	18	4	18	4	18	4	17	6	12	4
	24	17	10	17	10	17	10	16	8	11	10	16	6	16	6	15	8	14	4	10	0
2 x 10	12	24	0	24	0	24	0	24	0	22	10	23	6	23	6	23	6	23	6	19	6
	16	23	8	23	8	23	8	23	8	19	8	21	10	21	10	21	10	21	10	16	10
	24	21	4	21	4	21	4	21	0	16	2	19	8	19	8	19	8	18	0	13	10

[1] Denotes grade is not a stress grade.
[2] Denotes light framing grade. (Not Industrial Light Framing)
Notes:
(a) Spans may be increased 5 percent from those shown for rough lumber or lumber surfaced two edges (S2E).

(b) Spans shall be decreased 5 percent from those shown for lumber more than 2 percent but not more than 5 percent scant from American Lumber Standards sizes measured at a moisture content of 19 percent or less. Lumber scant more than 5 percent will not be acceptable.

angle of 26°-33°. This slope is properly referred to as a ¼ *pitch* roof, which has 6″ rise in 12″ run.

Step 2. *Determine the span of the rafter.* This may be obtained by scaling the elevation. The span is measured horizontally from outside of the stud face to a centerline dropped from the ridge, as shown in Fig. 11-3. If a collar beam is used, the rafter span is divided (See Fig. 11-3). In calculating the rafter size when a collar beam is used, size the rafter according to the larger of these two spans. A collar beam prevents the rafter from spreading and serves to prevent deflection.

Step 3. *Determine the rafter size.* If the pitch of the roof is greater than 3″ rise in 12″ run, use the portion of the Table 11-3 entitled "Rafters (Roof slope over 3 in 12)." In order to select the correct table, check the type of lumber generally used for rafters. If the roof has less than 3″ rise in 12″ run, use the portion of any of the tables headed "Low Slope Roof Joists (Roof slope 3 in 12 or less)." If Douglas Fir, Construction Grade were used for rafters in the general locality where the building is to be built, Table 11-3 would be used. Sup-

posing the clear span of the rafter were 12′-6″ and the roofing were less than 4 lbs. per square foot, the "Light Roofing" portion of Table 11-3 would be used. Using the span of 12′-6″ and the correct grade of lumber, a designer would space 2″ × 6″ rafters 24″ O.C. Read down the column to the *nearest* next largest clear span, in this case 13′-6″, and then read left. The column headed "Nominal Size" will indicate the proper size rafter; the column headed "Spacing (inches, O.C.)" will give the distance rafters are spaced (O.C.).

Roof Framing Plan

Some designers draw a framing plan of the roof for a residence. A roof framing plan is mandatory in commercial and industrial architectural practice. Once the sizing of the members is determined, the details of the rafter run may be given. Notes referring to the size of the roof framing members are usually called out with a leader. If the notes are extensive the information on sizing may be keyed in a series of notes on the drawing. On the other hand, if the notes relative to sizing and spacing are not as prevalent, they are called out with a leader. Many of the dimentions for the roof framing plans may be taken from the elevation and related details.

Trusses

The conventionally framed roof in contemporary residential construction is slowly being replaced in many instances by the trussed roof. Regardless of the style of roof, the principle of the truss may be employed. A detailed discussion of trusses is given in Chapter 9. The student may refer to this earlier chapter for detailed background information. Probably the most widely used truss in light frame house construction is the W truss (Fig. 11-4). This is not to say, however, that other truss designs are not also used. Table 11-4 gives sizing for the W truss (spaced 2′ O.C.) dependent upon the slope and span. (The dimensions and letters in Table 11-4 refer to Fig. 11-4.)

To determine the correct sizes of chords and webs for a W truss using Table 11-4 follow the steps outlined below.

Step 1. *Select the desired pitch and span.* Assume a truss having a 4/12 rise and run with a 28′-0″ span is desired. Reading from left to right in the table, the top chord section (A) has a length of 7′-4⁹⁄₁₆″. The longer of the two webs (B) has a length of 6′-6¹³⁄₁₆″. The short web (C) is 3′-3¼″ long. One-third of the bottom chord (D) is 9′-4″ in length.

Step 2. *Determine the size dimension of the lumber.* Refer to the lumber heading of the table and obtain the size dimensions for the com-

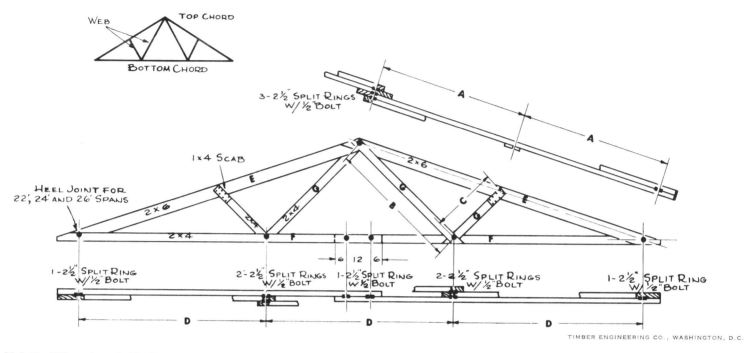

Fig. 11-4. The W truss is probably the most common design used in residential construction.

ponent members. For this example continue reading across the row for a 4/12 rise and run, 28'-0" span. The top chord will be a 2" × 8", the bottom chord will be a 2" × 6", and the webs will be 2" × 4". The lumber lengths needed are also given.

Joists

The structural members which support

the floor at each house level, including the attic, are called joists. These horizontal heavy members are laid edgewise and parallel with each other to form the floor support. Designing and selecting these joists depends entirely upon the loads which they are expected to support and their material strength.

The following step-by-step procedure illustrates the fundamental design criteria for selecting the proper joists for a particular application.

Step 1. *Determine use and expected joist load.* Again the designer must select the species of lumber which is normally used in his area for joists. In this example, suppose Coastal Region Douglas Fir is used for floor and ceiling joists, he would then use Table 11-3. In most areas, building codes provide limitations and recommendations for joist loading. For example, if

TABLE 11-4
W TRUSS SIZING WITH DRYWALL CEILING

SLOPE	LENGTH OF SPAN	DIMENSIONS				LUMBER SIZE (TWO LENGTHS NEEDED)		
		A	B	C	D	2 x 8	2 x 6	2 x 4
4 / 12	20	5'-3 1/4"	4'-8 3/16"	2'-3 13/16"	6'-8"		E (12'-0")	F (12'-0") G (8'-0")
	22	5'-9 9/16"	5'-1 7/8"	2'-6 3/4"	7'-4"		E (14'-0")	F (14'-0") G (10'-0")
	24	6'-3 7/8"	5'-7 1/2"	2'-9 9/16"	8'-0"		E (14'-0")	F (14'-0") G (10'-0")
	26	6'-10 3/16"	6'-1 3/16"	3'-0 7/16"	8'-8"		E (16'-0")	F (16'-0") G (10'-0")
	28	7'-4 9/16"	6'-6 13/16"	3'-3 1/4"	9'-4"	E (16'-0")	F * (16'-0")	F (16'-0") G (12'-0")
	30	7'-10 7/8"	7'-0 1/2"	3'-6 1/16"	10'-0"	E (18'-0")	F * (18'-0")	F (18'-0") G (12'-0")
	32	8'-5 3/16"	7'-6 3/16"	3'-8 7/8"	10'-8"	E (18'-0")	F * (18'-0")	F (18'-0") G (12'-0")
5 / 12	20	5'-5"	5'-3 5/8"	2'-7 5/8"	6'-8"		E (12'-0")	F (12'-0") G (10'-0")
	22	5'-11 1/2"	5'-10 1/16"	2'-10 13/16"	7'-4"		E (14'-0")	F (14'-0") G (10'-0")
	24	6'-6"	6'-4 7/16"	3'-2"	8'-0"		E (14'-0")	F (14'-0") G (12'-0")
	26	7'-0 1/2"	6'-10 7/8"	3'-5 1/4"	8'-8"		E (16'-0")	F (16'-0") G (12'-0")
	28	7'-7"	7'-5 1/4"	3'-8 7/16"	9'-4"		E, F * (16'-0")	F (16'-0") G (12'-0")
	30	8'-1 1/2"	7'-11 11/16"	3'-11 5/8"	10'-0"		E, F * (18'-0")	F (18'-0") G (14'-0")
	32	8'-8"	8'-6 1/16"	4'-2 13/16"	10'-8"		E (20'-0") F * (18'-0")	F (18'-0") G (14'-0")
6 / 12	20	5'-7 1/16"	5'-11 11/16"	2'-11 5/8"	6'-8"		E (12'-0")	F (12'-0") G (10'-0")
	22	6'-1 13/16"	6'-6 7/8"	3' -3 1/4"	7'-4"		E (14'-0")	F (14'-0") G (12'-0")
	24	6'-8 1/2"	7'-2 1/8"	3'-6 7/8"	8'-0"		E (16'-0")	F (14'-0") G (12'-0")
	26	7'-3 3/16"	7'-9 5/16"	3'-10 7/16"	8'-8"		E (16'-0")	F (16'-0") G (12'-0")
	28	7'-9 15/16"	8'-4 9/16"	4'-2 1/16"	9'-4"		E (18'-0') F * (16'-0")	F (16'-0") G (14'-0")
	30	8'-4 5/8"	8'-11 3/4"	4'-5 11/16"	10'-0"		E, F * (18'-0")	F (18'-0") G (16'-0")
	32	8'-11 5/16"	9'-6 13/16"	4'-9 1/4"	10'-8"		E (20'-0") F * (18'-0")	F (18'-0") G (16'-0")
7 / 12	20	5'-9 7/16"	6'-8 3/16"	3'-3 7/8"	6'-8"		E (14'-0")	F, G (12'-0")
	22	6'-4 7/16"	7'-4 1/4"	3'-7 15/16"	7'-4"		E (14'-0")	F (14'-0") G (12'-0')
	24	6'-11 5/8"	8'-0 5/16"	3'- 11 15/16"	8'-0"		E (16'-0")	F, G (14'-0")
	26	7'-6 5/16"	8'-8 5/16"	4'-4"	8'-8"		E (16'-0")	F (16'-0") G (14'-0")
	28	8'-1 1/4"	9'-4 7/16"	4'-8"	9'-4"		E (18'-0") F* (16'-0")	F, G (16'-0")
	30	8'-8 3/16"	10'-0 1/2"	5'-0 1/16"	10'-0"		E (20'-0") F* (18'-0")	F (18'-0") G (16'-0")
	32	9'-3 1/8"	10'-8 9/16"	5'-4 1/16"	10'-8"		E (20'-0") F* (18'-0")	F, G (18'-0")

*BOTTOM CHORD SIZES FOR PLASTER CEILING
LIVE LOAD, 35 LBS PER SQUARE FT; DEAD CEILING LOAD, 10 LBS PER SQUARE FT; SPACED 2'-0" OC

TIMBER ENGINEERING CO., WASHINGTON, D.C.

the joists are selected for supporting a floor area used for living, the recommended loading allowance would be 40 lbs. per sq. ft. for live loads and 10 lbs. per sq. ft. for dead loads. If the joists are to be used to support an attic floor which is not expected to carry any live loads (i.e., an attic floor having no storage space), the loading allowance would be only 10 lbs.

per sq. ft. (dead load) the "Ceiling Joists — No Attic Storage" portion of Table 11-3 would be used. If the attic is to be converted, at a later date, to a living area, the ceiling joists must be sized as floor joists having a 40 lb. live load.

Step 2. *Determine the joist span.* Measure the length of joist span from support to support (See Fig. 11-5) and find the *maximum* span for each floor (the bearing surface, 3″ to 6″ at each end, is not counted). The maximum span is used so the joist sizes will be equal.

Fig. 11-6 shows a medium sized ranch type home, with a maximum load of 50 lbs. The girder is located in a central position below the wall separating the bedroom from the hall, and the dining room and kitchen from the living room (see figure). The clear span of the joists in the

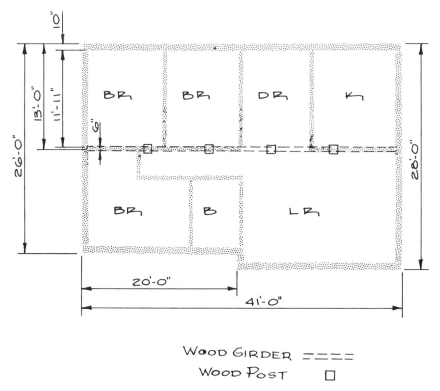

Fig. 11-6. This floor plan for a single-story, ranch-type home shows the placement of the girder posts. The roof is framed in a conventional manner, thereby requiring a bearing partition. The roof has a ¼ pitch. No provision has been made for attic storage. The basement ceiling is finished with acoustical tile.

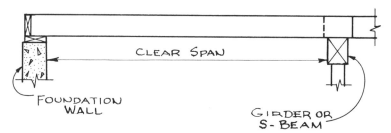

Fig. 11-5. The clear span length is measured from the inside of supports.

rear half of the house is 11′-11″; in the front half, 13′-11″. The joist span used in further calculations will be 13′-11″, since this is the greater of the two spans.

Step 3. *Determine the joist size.*

A. *Floor joists.* Table 11-3 gives the maximum spans for

floor joists. Assume the normal load imposed on the floor joists is 50 lbs. (average for a one story house, 40 lbs. live and 10 lbs. dead). Choose the proper portion of the table and read down the column headed Construction J & P to the *next largest* clear span length. Read across this row to the column headed "Nominal Size" and "Spacing (inches O.C.)." This figure represents the correct size of floor joist for the imposed load. Considering the type of lumber and span (See Step #2, 13'-11"), the nearest clear length is 14'-6", therefore, the resultant joist size is 2" × 10" spaced 24" O.C.

B. *Ceiling Joists.* Table 11-3 gives the maximum spans for ceiling joists. Since many houses have low pitched roofs, the attic is virtually non-existent. A dead load of 10 lbs. per square foot may be assumed to be adequate. Thus the "No Attic Storage" portion of the table would be used. (If the attic floor is used for *light storage,* however, a live load of 20 lbs. per sq. ft. is necessary.

Therefore, the "Limited Attic Storage" part of the table would be selected. If however, there is a possibility of converting to finished rooms, a live load of 40 lbs. per sq. ft. is recommended. Normally the same type of lumber is used for both the floor and ceiling joists. Select the type of lumber, read down the column to the desired span, then across the row to the "Lumber Size." The resultant figure represents the correct size ceiling joist. With a 13'-11" clear span, the size would be 2" × 6" Construction Grade Douglas Fir spaced 16" O.C. If the attic were to be used for limited attic storage 2" × 6" Construction Grade Douglas Fir spaced 12" O.C. would be selected.

Bearing Walls

Bearing walls or partitions carry loads imposed by floor and/or ceiling joists above. Each stud in the wall acts as a small post or column. Since the stud is a 2" × 4", and the unsupported length must be reduced to prevent lateral flexure, it must be bridged near the center with horizontal solid bridging. See Chapter 9, 9-48.

Girders

In residential construction, the girder is a structural member that supports either a wall or joists. The inner ends of the joists usually rest on the girder. The outer ends of the joists rest on the foundation wall (or are supported by masonry, a sill, ribbon, or girt). Since most homes are wider than 14' or 15' it is desirable to plan the girder near the center of the structure to prevent flexure and to prevent the necessity of using extra heavy floor joists to cover a long span. The girder replaces an interior wall in the basement (which would be used to support the joists) and provides an open area.

Because of the nature of some plans, a load bearing concrete block or 2" × 6" (horizontally bridged) stud wall replaces the need for a girder. An L-shaped or large rectangular shaped plan can use this feature to a distinct advantage. Girders may be S, M, or W shaped steel beams,[1] solid wood or built up or laminated from individual pieces of lumber.

The following explains the procedure used in selecting the proper girder size.

Step 1. *Determine the best location for the girder.* Locate the girder in a central position and under a partition if possible. The joist span should not exceed 15'-0". If the joist span is greater the

---

1. S, M, and W shapes refer to the *new names* given to I-beams (S), Light Wide Flange or Junior Beams (M) and Wide Flange (W).

size of joist will be appreciably increased. The girder in Fig. 11-7 has been placed off center to coincide with the partition.

Step 2. *Compute the girder half width.* A girder will support one-half of the joist span on each side of the girder. See Figs. 11-7 and 11-8. To find half width, add the joist spans on each side of the girder and divide by 2. In the example in Fig. 11-6, the half width in the kitchen, living and dining areas is 12'-11" (13'-11" + 11'-11" = 25'-10"; 25'-10" ÷ 2 + 12'-11") and the half width in the bed room area is 11'-11" (11'-11" + 11'-11" = 23'-10"; 23'-10" ÷ 2 = 11'-11".)

Step 3. *Locate posts or columns.* As the distance between posts or columns is increased, the imposed load concentrated on each column becomes greater. It is advisable to space wood posts approximately 8' apart and steel pipe or S-beam columns approximately 10' to 12' apart. Referring to Fig. 11-6, it can be seen that the length of the house is 41'-0". For purposes of illustration, wood posts have been selected to support the girder. Since the wood posts are spaced approximately 8' apart, divide the length by the spacing (41' ÷ 8' = 5⅛). It is impos-

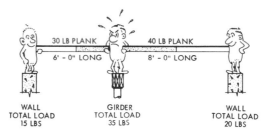

Fig. 11-7. The girder supports one half of the load on either side (girder half width).

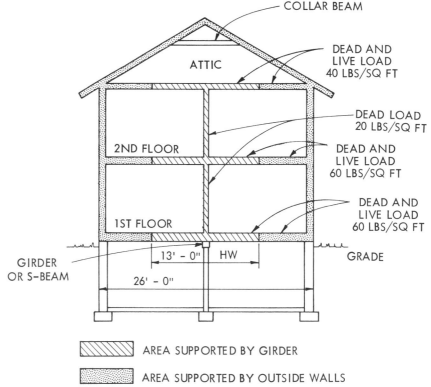

Fig. 11-8. This cross section shows the areas supported by the girders and outside walls.

TABLE 11-5

LOADS PER SQUARE FOOT OF FLOOR AREA USED IN CALCULATING GIRDER SIZE

BUILDING HEIGHT	COMPONENTS	TOTAL LOAD PER SQ FT
1 STORY*	Attic storage, bearing partition, plaster on basement ceiling.	100 lbs
	Attic storage, bearing partition, no plaster on basement ceiling.	90 lbs
	No attic storage, bearing partition, plaster on basement ceiling.	80 lbs
	No attic storage, bearing partition, no plaster on basement ceiling.	70 lbs
	No bearing partition, plaster on basement ceiling.	50 lbs
	No bearing partition, no plaster on basement ceiling.	40 lbs
1 1/2 or 2 STORY*	Attic storage, bearing partition supporting 2nd floor, plaster on basement ceiling.	150 lbs
	Attic storage, bearing partition supporting 2nd floor, no plaster on basement ceiling.	140 lbs
	No attic storage, bearing partition supporting 2nd floor, plaster on basement ceiling.	130 lbs
	No attic storage, bearing partition supporting 2nd floor, no plaster on basement ceiling.	120 lbs
2 1/2 or 3 STORY*	Attic storage, bearing partitions supporting 3rd floor, plaster on basement ceiling.	210 lbs
	Attic storage, bearing partitions supporting 3rd floor, no plaster on basement ceiling.	200 lbs
	No attic storage, bearing partitions supporting 3rd floor, no plaster on basement ceiling.	180 lbs

*If roof is framed so part of its weight is borne by bearing partitions; with composition shingled roof (light), add 20 lbs; with light slate or asbestos (medium), add 30 lbs; or with heavy slate or tile, add 40 lbs to the appropriate total load per square foot.

sible to have 5⅛ equal post spaces; therefore, drop the fraction (⅛) and divide the girder length by the whole number (41 ÷ 5 = 8.2' or 8'-2⅜"). *Four posts are required, spaced 8'-2⅜" O.C. (See Fig. 11-6.)

Step 4. *Determine the total load per square foot.* From Table 11-5 select the proper total load per square foot. If, for example, the house shown in Fig. 11-6 is single story with provisions for attic storage, and has a bearing partition and a finished basement with acoustical tile ceiling, the total load per square foot is 90 lbs.

Step 5. *Calculate the lineal foot load.* To find the lineal foot load, multiply the girder half width (Step #2) by the square foot load (Step #4). From the example (Fig. 11-6), the girder half width load was found to be 12'-11" and the total load was 90 lbs. per sq. ft. (For convenience use the decimal value 12.92' rather than 12'-11".) The lineal foot load is 1,163 lbs. (12.92 × 90 = 1,162.8 or 1,163 lbs.).

Step 6. *Calculate the total load on the girder.* Multiply the lineal foot load (Step #5) by the span or spacing of the posts or columns (Step #3). The lineal foot load was found to be 1,163 lbs. and the wood posts were spaced 8'-2⅜" (8.2') O.C. The total load on the girder is 9,537 lbs. (1,163 × 8.2 = 9,536.6 lbs. or 9,537 lbs.).

Step 7. *Determine the girder size.*
A. *Wood.* Refer to Table 11-6 and locate the span of the girder (Step #3), read down this column to the total load (Step #6) and across this row to the size of the girder required to carry this load. The span of the girder was 8'-2⅜". (Use column

TABLE 11-6

SAFE LOAD FOR SOLID WOOD GIRDERS*

*Loads given in 1,000 Lbs

No. 1 common Douglas Fir and Southern Yellow Pine

NOMINAL SIZE	ACTUAL SIZE	LENGTH OF SPAN OF WOOD GIRDER											
		4'-0" 5'-0" 6'-0"	7'-0"	8'-0"	9'-0"	10'-0"	11'-0"	12'-0"	13'-0"	14'-0"	15'-0"
6 × 8	5½ × 7½	7.26	7.26	6.78	6.0	5.38	4.87	4.44	4.08	3.76	3.49
8 × 8	7½ × 7½	9.88	9.88	9.24	8.19	7.34	6.64	6.06	5.56	5.13	4.76
6 × 10	5½ × 9½	9.16	9.16	9.16	9.16	8.68	7.86	7.17	6.59	6.10	5.66
8 × 10	7½ × 9½	12.5	12.5	12.5	12.5	11.83	10.72	9.79	9.0	8.31	7.72
10 × 10	9½ × 9½	15.8	15.8	15.8	15.8	14.99	13.58	12.4	11.39	10.53	9.78
8 × 12	7½ × 11½	15.05	15.05	15.05	15.05	15.05	15.05	14.4	13.25	12.26	11.39
10 × 12	9½ × 11½	19.08	19.08	19.08	19.08	19.08	19.08	18.24	16.79	15.52	14.43
12 × 12	11½ × 11½	23.13	23.13	23.13	23.13	23.13	23.13	22.09	20.32	18.79	17.47
8 × 14	7½ × 13½	17.63	17.63	17.63	17.63	17.63	17.63	17.63	17.63	16.96	15.78
10 × 14	9½ × 13½	22.33	22.33	22.33	22.33	22.33	22.33	22.33	22.33	21.48	19.98
12 × 14	11½ × 13½	27.04	27.04	27.04	27.04	27.04	27.04	27.04	27.04	26.01	24.19
14 × 14	13½ × 13½	31.76	31.76	31.76	31.76	31.76	31.76	31.76	31.76	30.51	28.39

NOTE (1). Built up girders of dressed lumber will carry somewhat smaller loads than
solid girders. It is, therefore, necessary to multiply the above loads for
solid girders by the following:

0.887 when a 6" girder is made up of three 2" pieces
0.867 when a 8" girder is made up of four 2" pieces
0.856 when a 10" girder is made up of five 2" pieces

NOTE (2). If the load on a span is between two load figures, go to the nearest load.

headed 8'-0" since the span is less than 8'-6".) The total load was calculated at 9,-537 lbs. A 8" × 8" solid wood girder will amply carry the imposed load. If, however, the girder were to be laminated from four 2" × 8" dressed members, the load (9.24) must be multiplied by .867 (see footnote in table) since built-up or laminated girders carry a smaller load than do solid girders. Multiplying 9.24 (safe load for a solid 8" × 8" with a span of 8" O.C.) by .867 (correction factor for 8" built-up girder) gives 8.01. This is too low. Therefore, it is then necessary to go to the next largest wood girder in load carrying capacity which is an 8" × 10". The corrected load capacity of a laminated 8" × 10" is 10,830 (12.5 × .867

TABLE 11-7
SAFE UNIFORM LOADS FOR S, W, AND M BEAMS (K 36 STEEL) IN KIPS (1000 LBS)

DEPTH	DESIGNATION	FLANGE WIDTH	WEIGHT PER FOOT (POUNDS)	SPAN LENGTH OF BEAM												
				6	7	8	9	10	11	12	13	14	15	16	17
4^1	S 4 x 7.7	2 5/8	7.7	8.1	6.9	6.1	5.4	-	-	-	-	-	-	-	-
4^1	S 4 x 9.5	2 3/4	9.5	9.0	7.7	6.8	6.0	-	-	-	-	-	-	-	-
5^1	S 5 x 10	3	10.0	13.1	11.2	9.8	8.7	7.9	7.2	-	-	-	-	-	-
5^1	S 5 x 14.8	3 1/4	14.8	16.2	13.9	12.2	10.8	9.7	8.9	-	-	-	-	-	-
6^2	M 6 x 4.4	1 7/8	4.4	6.4	5.5	4.8	4.3	3.8	3.5	3.2	3.0	-	-	-	-
6^1·	S 6 x 12.5	3 5/8	12.5	19.7	16.8	14.7	13.1	11.8	10.7	9.8	9.1	-	-	-	-
6^3	W 6 x 16.0	4	16.0	27.2	23.3	20.4	18.1	16.3	14.8	13.6	12.6	-	-	-	-
7^2	M 7 x 5.5	2 1/8	5.5	9.2	7.9	6.9	6.1	5.5	5.0	4.6	4.2	3.9	3.7	-	-
7^1	S 7 x 15.3	3 5/8	15.3	28.0	24.0	21.0	18.7	16.8	15.3	14.0	12.9	12.0	11.2	-	-
7^1	S 7 x 20	3 7/8	20.0	32.3	27.7	24.2	21.5	19.4	17.6	16.1	14.9	13.8	12.9	-	-
8^2	M 8 x 6.5	2 1/4	6.5	12.3	10.6	9.2	8.2	7.4	6.7	6.2	5.7	5.3	4.9	4.6	4.3
8^1	S 8 x 18.4	4	18.4	38.4	32.9	28.8	25.6	23.0	20.9	19.2	17.7	16.5	15.4	14.4	13.6
8^3	W 8 x 20	5 1/4	20.0	45.3	38.9	34.0	30.2	27.2	24.7	22.7	20.9	19.4	18.1	17.0	16.0
8^3	W 8 x 24	6 1/2	24.0	55.5	47.5	41.6	37.0	33.3	30.3	27.7	25.6	23.8	22.7	20.8	19.6
10^2	M 10 x 9	2 3/4	9.0	20.7	17.7	15.5	13.8	12.4	11.3	10.3	9.6	8.9	8.3	7.8	7.3
10^3	W 10 x 15	4	15.0	36.8	31.5	27.6	24.5	22.1	20.1	18.4	17.0	15.8	14.7	13.8	13.0
10^3	W 10 x 21	5 3/4	21.0	57.3	49.1	43.0	38.2	34.4	31.3	28.7	26.5	24.6	22.9	21.5	20.2
10^1	S 10 x 25.4	4 5/8	25.4	65.9	56.5	49.4	43.9	39.5	35.9	32.9	30.4	28.2	26.3	24.7	23.2

[1] S shape beam was formerly referred to as I-beam.

[2] M shape beam was formerly referred to as light wide flange beam or junior beam depending on size and weight.

[3] W shape beam was formerly referred to as light wide flange or wide flange beam depending on size and weight.

= 10.83). This is ample to carry the imposed load.

B. *Steel.* Refer to Table 11-7 and locate the span of the steel beam. The same as Step #3, but use a 10'-3" span. Posts for a steel beam may be spaced 10' to 12' apart; therefore, 41' ÷ 4 = 10.25' or 10'-3". Simply read down the 10' span column to the nearest total load (Step #), and then read left across the row to the column headed "Depth." This value (5" depth, 14.8 lbs. per ft.) represents the size of beam which will adequately carry the imposed load. The size of the beam would be designated on the detail, and floor joist framing plan as 5S 14.8. Remember the depth of a beam

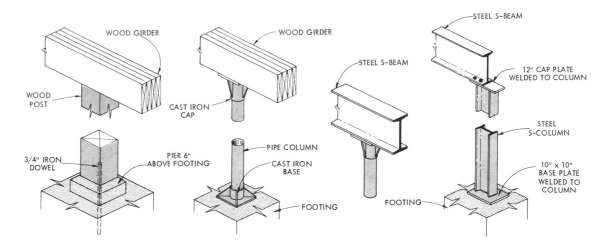

Fig. 11-9. Various posts or columns may be used to support the girder.

is the distance from flange to flange, and the width of the flange is the distance across the flange. This beam has a flange width of 3¼″. There are two 5″ beams, each with a different load per foot.

Posts or Columns

A bearing post or column is used to support the girder and may be of wood, steel, iron pipe, or lally column (iron pipe filled with concrete). Fig. 11-9 illustrates the various posts or columns which may be used. Table 11-8 shows safe loads for standard heavy weight Lally columns and Table 11-9 shows safe loads for light weight Lally columns for residential use only. Adjust-able columns called jack posts may be used in place of wood posts or steel columns. Fig. 11-10 shows two adjustable columns. These columns have the advantage of being adjustable so that their height may be altered to compensate for shrinkage of wood girders or joists.

The foundation supports a portion of

TABLE 11-8
SAFE LOADS(1000 LBS) FOR STANDARD HEAVY WEIGHT LALLY COLUMNS

OUTER DIAMETER COLUMN	AREA STEEL SQ. IN.	AREA CONCRETE SQ. IN.	WEIGHT PER FOOT	UNSUPPORTED HEIGHT OF COLUMN								
				6	7	8	9	10	11	12	13	14
3 1/2	2.23	7.39	15	45	42	40	36	33	29	26	-	-
4	2.68	9.89	20	58	55	53	50	47	42	39	34	30
4 1/2	3.17	12.73	24	72	69	67	64	61	57	54	50	45
5	3.69	15.96	29	87	84	82	79	76	72	69	65	61
5 1/2	4.30	20.01	36	105	103	101	98	95	91	88	85	80
6 5/8	5.58	28.89	49	144	142	140	137	134	131	128	124	120
8 5/8	8.40	50.03	81	232	230	228	225	223	220	217	213	209

TABLE 11-9
SAFE LOADS(1000 LBS) FOR LIGHT WEIGHT LALLY COLUMNS FOR RESIDENTIAL USE ONLY

OUTER DIAMETER COLUMN	AREA STEEL SQ. IN.	AREA CONCRETE SQ. IN.	WEIGHT PER FOOT	UNSUPPORTED HEIGHT OF COLUMN			
				6	7	8	9
LW 3 1/2	1.01	8.61	12	23	21	19	17
LW 4	1.17	11.40	15	30	28	26	24

STOCK LENGTHS: 6'-0", 7'-0", 8'-0", 9'-0", AND 6'-6", 7'-6", 8'-6"

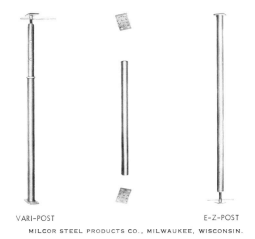

VARI-POST   E-Z-POST

MILCOR STEEL PRODUCTS CO., MILWAUKEE, WISCONSIN.

Fig. 11-10. Adjustable columns, sometimes called "jack posts," are used in place of fixed-length posts or columns.

the load carried by the girder. Between the opposite foundation walls, however, posts or columns must carry the load.

The following step-by-step procedure illustrates the method used for calculating the correct size for posts or columns.

Step 1. *Determine the total post or col-*

umn load. A post or column will carry the *girder load* to the mid-point of the span on both sides of the girder, see Fig. 11-11. The sum of the total load on the post or column is equal to one-half the load on one side of the post or column plus one-half the load on the other side of the column. (The same re-

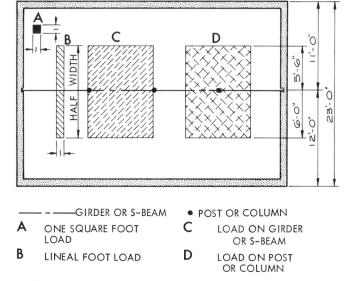

——— - ——GIRDER OR S-BEAM		• POST OR COLUMN
A	ONE SQUARE FOOT LOAD	**C** LOAD ON GIRDER OR S-BEAM
B	LINEAL FOOT LOAD	**D** LOAD ON POST OR COLUMN

Fig. 11-11. This plan illustrates the lineal foot load, girder load, and post load.

sult may be obtained if the total loads on both sides of the column were added and divided by 2.) The total load on the girder (see Step #6 from the preceding section) was found to be 9,537 lbs. 9,537 + 9,537 = 19,074 lbs.; 19,074 ÷ 2 = 9,537 lbs. The post load, though covering a different area, is the same as the girder load.

Step 2. *Determine the post or column height.* Decide on the amount of clear space you want under the girder. Make allowance for a 4″ concrete floor. See Figs. 11-8 and 11-9.

If wood posts are used, *subtract* 6″ (allowance for the 4″ basement floor plus a 2″ rise above). If steel columns (pipe or S-beam) are used, no allowance is necessary because these rest directly on the footing. See Fig. 11-9.

Using Fig. 11-6 as an example, assume that the distance from the under side of a girder to the top of the concrete footing is 7′-2″. Again, assume that a wood post is used to support an 8″ × 8″ solid wood girder. In this case 6″ must be subtracted for the pier above the footing: 7′-2″ − 6″ = 6′-8″ post height. If steel columns are used, the height would be 7′-2″.

TABLE 11-10
SAFE LOADS FOR WOOD COLUMNS OR POSTS*

*LOADS GIVEN IN 1,000 LBS   NO. 1 COMMON DOUGLAS FIR AND SOUTHERN YELLOW PINE

NOMINAL SIZE	ACTUAL SIZE	HEIGHT OF COLUMN OR POST					
		5'-0"	6'-0"	7'-0"	8'-0"	9'-0"	10'-0"
4 × 4	3 5/8 × 3 5/8	12.4	11.6	10.4	8.3	6.5	—
4 × 6	3 5/8 × 5 5/8	19.2	17.9	15.5	12.9	10.1	—
6 × 6	5 1/2 × 5 1/2	30.0	29.5	29.0	28.1	26.8	24.6
6 × 8	5 1/2 × 7 1/2	41.0	40.2	39.6	38.3	36.6	33.0
8 × 8	7 1/2 × 7 1/2	56.2	56.2	55.6	53.0	54.3	53.4

NOTE: IF THE LOAD ON A COLUMN IS BETWEEN TWO TOTAL FIGURES, GO TO THE NEAREST LOAD.

Step 3. *Determine the size of the post or column.*

A. *Wood.* Refer to Table 11-10, "Safe Loads for Wood Columns or Posts." Locate the column headed by the height nearest the measurement calculated in Step #2 above, then down the column to the total load calculated in Step #1 and then across to the specified wood post size. In the example being used (Fig. 11-6), the height of the post was 6′-8″. The column headed 7′-0″ would be correct since 6′-8″ is closer in height to 7′-0″ than 6′-0″. The total load was calculated to be 9,537 lbs. This load is under 10,400 lbs. It can be assumed that a 4″ × 4″ post is adequate

to carry the imposed load on girder.

B. *Steel Pipe.* Use Table 11-11, "Safe Loads for Standard Steel Pipe Columns." Locate the column headed with the nearest size to that found in Step #2 (7′-2″). Read down the correct height of the "Unsupported Height" column to the nearest load as found in Step #1 (9,537) and then across to the corresponding pipe diameter (3″). This pipe column would be designated on the details and floor joist framing plan as PIPE 3 STD.

C. *S-beam.* Refer to Table 11-12, "Safe Loads for S & W Shape Columns." Locate the proper column under

TABLE 11-11
SAFE LOADS FOR STANDARD STEEL PIPE COLUMNS
(K36 STEEL) IN KIPS (1000 LBS.)

NOMINAL DIAMETER	DESIGNATION	WALL THICKNESS	WEIGHT PER FOOT	UNSUPPORTED HEIGHT OF COLUMNS								
				6	7	8	9	10	11	12	13	14
3	PIPE 3 STD	.216	7.58	38	36	34	31	28	25	22	19	16
3 1/2	PIPE 3 1/2 STD	.226	9.11	48	46	44	41	38	35	32	29	25
4	PIPE 4 STD	.237	10.79	59	57	54	52	49	46	43	40	36
5	PIPE 5 STD	.258	14.62	83	81	78	76	73	71	68	65	61
6	PIPE 6 STD	.280	18.97	110	108	106	103	101	98	95	97	89
8	PIPE 8 STD	.322	28.55	171	168	166	163	161	158	155	152	149

TABLE 11-12
SAFE LOADS FOR S AND W SHAPE COLUMNS (K 36 STEEL) IN KIPS (1000 LBS)

DEPTH × WIDTH	DESIGNATION	WEIGHT PER FOOT	UNSUPPORTED HEIGHT OF COLUMN									
			3	4	5	6	7	8	9	10	11	12
3 × 2 3/8	S 3 × 7.5	7.5	36	31	24	17	12	10	-	-	-	-
3 × 2 3/8	S 3 × 5.7	5.7	28	23	18	13	10	7	-	-	-	-
4 × 2 5/8	S 4 × 7.7	7.7	39	34	28	22	16	12	10	-	-	-
4 × 2 5/8	S 4 × 9.5	9.5	48	41	34	26	19	15	12	-	-	-
4 × 4	W 4 × 13	13.0	74	71	66	62	57	51	45	39	32	27
5 × 3	S 5 × 10	10.0	52	47	41	34	26	20	16	13	-	-
5 × 3	S 5 × 14.8	14.8	76	68	58	47	35	27	21	17	-	-
5 × 5	W 5 × 16	16.0	94	91	87	83	79	74	69	64	58	52
6 × 4	W 6 × 12	12.0	68	64	60	55	50	44	38	31	26	21
6 × 6	W 6 × 20	20.0	120	117	113	109	105	100	96	91	85	80
8 × 5 1/4	W 8 × 17	17.0	100	96	92	88	83	78	72	66	60	53
8 × 6 1/2	W 8 × 24	24.0	144	141	137	133	128	123	118	113	107	101
8 × 8	W 8 × 35	35.0	-	-	-	201	197	191	186	180	174	168
10 × 8	W 10 × 39	39.0	-	-	-	224	218	213	206	200	193	186

"Unsupported Height of Column" to correspond with height established in Step #2 (7'-2"). Then read down to the load ascertained in Step #1 (9,537) and across to the left to obtain the depth (3") and weight per foot (5.7 lbs.) of the structural shape necessary to support girder.

This shape member would be called out as S3 × 5.7 on the structural details and the floor joist framing plan.

Post and Column Footings

The footings which support the posts or columns must be sufficiently strong to carry the concentrated imposed load. If the footing is not capable of supporting the load, settlement will eventually occur.

The following steps illustrate the procedure used in determining the correct post or column footing.

Step 1. *Determine the total load on the footing.* The total load imposed on the footing is the same as the total load on the post or column as found in the preceding section, "Posts and Columns," Step #1.

Step 2. *Determine the bearing power of the soil.* By visual inspection, determine the type of soil at the building site. Refer then to

TABLE 11-13
BEARING POWER OF SOILS IN TONS PER SQUARE FOOT*

MATERIAL	BEARING TONS PER SQUARE FOOT †
Crystalline bed rock — granite, gneiss, trap rock	100
Foliated rock — bedded limestone, schist, slate	40
Sedimentary rock — hard shale, siltstone, sandstone, soft limestone	15
Hard pan, gravel, sand, highly compacted	10
Gravel, sand and gravel mixture, compact	6
Gravel, loose, coarse sand, compact	4
Firm stiff clay	4
Coarse sand, loose; sand and gravel mixture, loose; fine sand compact; coarse sand, wet, confined	3
Sand clay mixed	3
Fine sand, loose; fine sand, wet, confined	2
Medium stiff clay	2 to 2.5
Soft clay	1 to 1.5

*If local building code specifies bearing capacity of soil, use those figures.

† Short ton = 2,000 lbs.

Table 11-13, "Bearing Power of Soils," to find the tons per square foot that particular type of soil will support. In some instances the local building code may specify the bearing capacity of the soil. Follow local codes if they are available. Assuming the soil at a site is medium stiff clay, it would support a load of 2 tons per square foot.

Step 3. *Determine the area of the footing.* Divide the total load on the footing (Step #1) by the bearing power of the soil (Step #2). In the assumed case: 9,537 ÷ 4,000 = 2.384 sq. ft. or 2.4 sq. ft. In other words it requires 2.4 sq. ft. of footing to support 9,537 lbs.

Step 4. *Determine the size of the footing.* Extract the square root of the area of the footing in Step 3 to obtain the length of the side of the footing:

$$\sqrt{2.4'} = 1.55' \text{ or } 1'\text{-}6\tfrac{1}{2}''$$

Step 5. *Determine the depth of the footing.* Adequate footing depth is equal to one-half the width of the footing, Step #4, plus 2" or 3". (Rarely less than 1'-0".) 1'-6½" ÷ 2 = 9¼"; 9¼" + 3" = 1'-0¼". This is rounded off to 1'-0".

Size of the concrete footing then is 1'-6½" × 1'-6½" × 1'-0".

Wall Footings and Foundations

Footings and the foundation wall must be sufficiently strong to withstand the weight of the building. Regardless of how carefully a house may be framed or built, an inadequately designed footing and foundation wall may result in uneven settlement, cracked plaster or drywall, ill-fitting windows and doors, and other difficulties.

Footings and foundation walls for residential construction are usually specified by local building codes. Building codes may specify the footing width to be twice the width of the foundation wall and its depth equal to the width of the footing projection. Some local building codes require the depth to be equal to the wall thickness *plus* 3". Figs. 9-2 and 9-3 in Chapter 9 illustrate methods for calculating residential wall footing proportions.

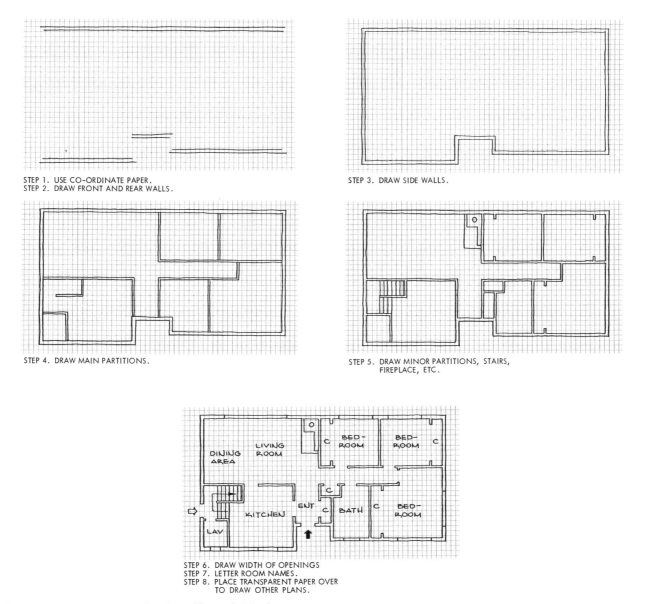

STEP 1. USE CO-ORDINATE PAPER.
STEP 2. DRAW FRONT AND REAR WALLS.

STEP 3. DRAW SIDE WALLS.

STEP 4. DRAW MAIN PARTITIONS.

STEP 5. DRAW MINOR PARTITIONS, STAIRS,
         FIREPLACE, ETC.

STEP 6. DRAW WIDTH OF OPENINGS
STEP 7. LETTER ROOM NAMES.
STEP 8. PLACE TRANSPARENT PAPER OVER
         TO DRAW OTHER PLANS.

Fig. 11-12. Follow this step-by-step procedure in making a sketch plan.

Foundation wall thickness, just as with footing proportions, are usually specified in the local building code. Table 9-2, "Concrete Foundation Thickness," in Chapter 9 gives the accepted wall thicknesses for various types of residences.

Sketch Planning

To produce the final floor plan on the first or second attempt is a rarity. Experienced builders and designers still haven't designed the ideal, moderately priced home. Each builder and designer always has ways in which the next house can be improved.

After the development of several preliminary plans (see Chapter 7 for detail), the layout may be expanded further by sketching the plan on ⅛ " co-ordinate paper (each square then represents 1'-0"). The small scale forces the designer to consider only the main functions of the house. With this type of study one may determine, before drawing the quarter scale plan, if the floor plan is feasible. It is advisable to make several sketch plan studies on co-ordinate paper prior to any final decision. It may be helpful to draw the preliminary lines very lightly, then, as corrections are made and the final shapes are decided, the lines can be darkened.

Variations of an original plan may be quickly constructed by placing a piece of vellum or tracing paper over the original sketch and *tracing off* portions that remain unchanged. New areas may then be added.

For convenience, draw the thickness of an inside partition ½ square; an outside wall, ½ square; and an outside solid masonry wall, 1 square. The step-by-step procedure for making a sketch plan is shown in Fig. 11-12.

Modular Planning

The need for a co-ordinated system of modular dimensioning becomes more significant when one observes the amount of cutting, piecing, and splicing during house construction. The total amount of time, money, and materials involved in a single construction is sizeable. The building industry has made considerable progress in attempting to eliminate this loss by designing products based upon a predetermined module.

Modular planning, in essence, is keyed so that the dimensions of the structure are co-ordinated with standard sized building materials. This greatly reduces the need for alterations on the building site. The use of the modular method results in greater economy and efficiency in home construction.

The module is an established standard unit of measurement. The most commonly used and accepted unit is 4". Studs are spaced 16" (4 modules) apart; plywood is marketed in standard size sheets, 4' × 8' (12 × 24 modules).

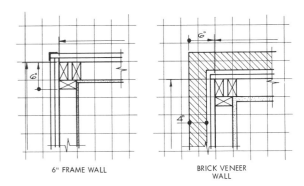

6" FRAME WALL   BRICK VENEER WALL

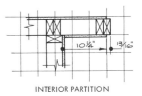

INTERIOR PARTITION

Fig. 11-13. In the modular system of planning, all measurements are based on a 4" multiple.

Materials such as brick, tile, glass block, concrete block, wood and metal windows, cabinets, plywood, etc., are some of the items available in modular sizes. Not all manufacturers, however, produce building products based on the 4″ module.

The co-ordinated system of modular planning employs building materials fitted to a grid based on the 4″ module.

Modular drafting or planning is based on five fundamental principles.

1. *Design modules* must be in *multiples of 4″*.

2. All *details begin with the grid lines*. Any dimensions to surfaces of the detail, centerlines, etc., must be dimensioned to the grid line, not to other points on the building. A modular detail requires fewer small fractional dimensions than a detail dimensioned in the regular method. See Fig. 11-13.

3. *Grid* dimensions are given in plans, sections, and elevations. On the small scale drawings (¾″ = 1′-0″, ½″ = 1′-0″, or ¼″ = 1′-0″) the 4″ grid lines usually do not appear—but they exist nevertheless. Often these lines are multiples of 4″: that is, 16″, 24″, or 48″. Small scale drawings should show nominal (rough size before finish) surfaces: nominal walls and partitions, nominal finished floor, etc. Usually the lines which indicate such surfaces will coincide with the grid lines.

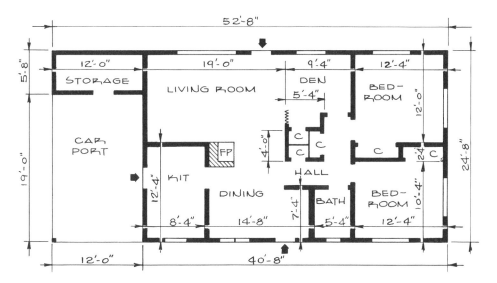

Fig. 11-14. Even though the grid does not appear, all dimensions on this small scale drawing are grid dimensions. Note the single arrow used for dimensioning.

When working with modular planning, the walls and partitions should be laid out using one side of the rough members for dimensioning. A *single arrow* method is shown in Fig. 11-14 to illustrate the point.

4. Floor levels are located on the grid lines. In wood frame construction, the top of the sub-floor or top of the finished concrete slab (with finish floor on the slab) coincides with the grid line. (The top of the slab floor is located ⅛″ below the grid line—the ⅛″ allows for tiling.)

5. As mentioned, dimensions *to* a grid line (module size) are indicated by an *arrow*. Dimensions which terminate *off* the grid line (non-module size) are signified with a *dot*. Fig. 11-15 illustrates this usage.

Modular measure makes possible an orderly and systematic dimensioning of the entire house. Vertical and horizontal reference planes, mutually perpendicular, grid the entire volume (length, depth, and height) of the building. See Fig. 11-16.

Uniform Components. Another modular system called the *Unicom Method of House*

Construction is also used. The Unicom method uses multiples of 16″ and 24″. Component house panels are made using these dimensions.

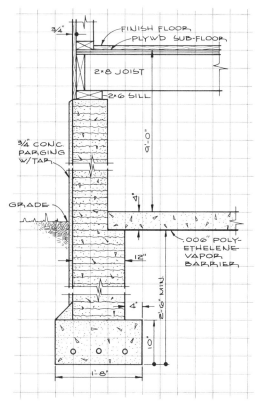

Fig. 11-15. Dimensions taken to a grid line are indicated by an arrow; those off the grid are indicated by a dot. Note the application of these principles in this foundation section.

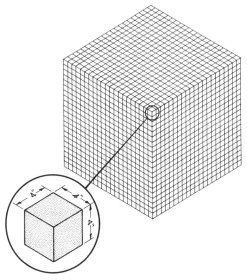

Fig. 11-16. The height, length, and width of a building may be laid out in modular grids.

Floor Plans

The floor plan, regardless whether the first floor, second floor, or basement, must clearly and accurately describe the size and shape of the house at each level. The following details should be shown on the floor plan: wall thickness and materials, placement of partitions and walls; location and sizes of doors and windows; location, size and detail of stairs and fireplace; location of built-in cabinets, range, oven, dish washer, etc.; location of plumbing fixtures; and the *approximate location* of electrical outlets, fixtures, and switches. In addition, notes are used to give any further information relating to joist size and direction, girder size and location, floor materials, etc.

Floor plans are usually drawn on a scale of ¼″ = 1′-0″. For larger buildings, however, a scale of ⅛″ = 1′-0″ is used.

Residential Planning Grid

One method of laying out the floor plan once the basic areas and their sizes have been determined is by using a planning grid. The method described in this section is one that is used by developers of tract homes, designers of panelized, pre-cut homes, and custom designers. Its basic purpose is to save time in *effective* placement of structural members and ultimately in costs to the client.

By using the grid a number of advantages may be obtained. Some of these are that it will aid in: (1) locating interior walls directly over joists, (2) placing one of the bathroom walls so the stack and plumbing are *not* over a joist, (3) determining the length of the structure so that all joists will be spaced 16″ on center, (4) spacing and locating windows in the exterior wall to save on studs, (5) locating off-sets in the building to coincide with the masonry foundation and save on joist placement, (6) placing the stairwell, fireplace, chimney, and clothes chute openings between or adjacent to joists, (7) utilizing building materials more efficiently and (8) visualizing floor joist and girder spans for structural purposes.

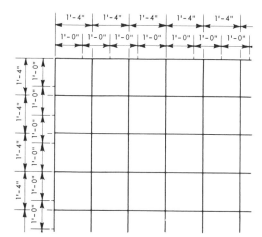

Fig. 11-17. Lightly lay out grid lines on the reverse side of a sheet of vellum.

Fig. 11-18. Calibrate every grid ruling and tic mark from one corner of the grid.

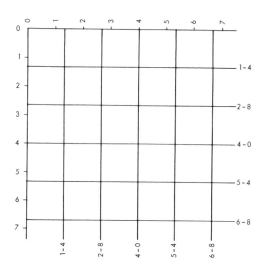

Procedure in Laying Out the Floor Plan with the Grid

The following step-by-step procedure explains how the planning grid may be used most efficiently and effectively.

1. Lay out the coordinate grid on the reverse side of a vellum sheet as shown in Fig. 11-17. Draw the grid lines in lightly and space them 1'-4" (16") apart in both directions.
2. Place consecutive tic marks at 1'-0" intervals along two adjacent sides of the grid. See Fig. 11-17. The 1'-0" divisions are used for joists spaced on 12" or 24" centers.
3. Turn the vellum sheet over and begin at one of the corners, preferably at the opposite end of the structure

Fig. 11-19. Graduations in 1'-4" increments for planning grid.

1-4	34-8	68-0
2-8	36-0	69-4
4-0	37-4	70-8
5-4	38-8	72-0
6-8	40-0	73-4
8-0	41-4	74-8
9-4	42-8	76-0
10-8	44-0	77-4
12-0	45-4	78-8
13-4	46-8	80-0
14-8	48-0	81-4
16-0	49-4	82-8
17-4	40-8	84-0
18-8	52-0	85-4
20-0	53-4	86-8
21-4	54-8	88-0
22-8	56-0	89-4
24-0	57-4	90-8
25-4	58-5	82-0
26-8	60-0	92-0
28-0	61-4	93-4
29-4	62-8	94-8
30-8	64-0	96-0
32-0	65-4	97-4
33-4	66-8	98-8
		100-0

from the garage, and calibrate (as in Fig. 11-18) each of the grid rulings and tic marks. Fig. 11-19 gives the multiples of 1'-4".

4. Select the rear corner of the structure, and begin to lay out the structure. Place the outer stud wall superstructure ½" or ¾" in from the

grid line. This ½″ or ¾″ allowance is for the sheathing. The thickness of the outer covering material, such as drop siding, plywood, brick veneer—including air space, will be *outside* the grid line. Figs. 11-20 and 11-21 illustrate the location of the exterior covering material on the wall.

5. Lay out the length of the exterior wall. Extend the wall length to the *nearest* grid line of the original dimensions. If any off-set(s) occur in the wall, adjust the off-set so it occurs on the grid line. See Fig. 11-22.

6. Locate the adjacent exterior wall that is parallel to joists in this case, and at the opposite end from the garage. As in Step 5, if any off-sets occur, adjust the off-set so it will occur on the grid line.

7. Locate the main interior partition walls *on the grid line*. A slight adjustment of the room size may be required. It is not necessary to locate closet walls on a grid line.

8. Locate interior partition walls in the opposite direction.

9. Lay out one wall of the hallway on

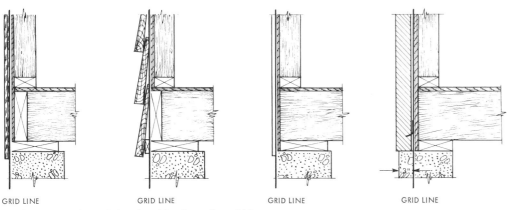

GRID LINE   GRID LINE   GRID LINE   GRID LINE

Fig 11-20. The face of the sheathing is on the grid line.

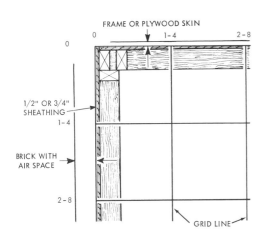

Fig. 11-21. The outer face of the stud wall is placed ¾″ in from the grid line.

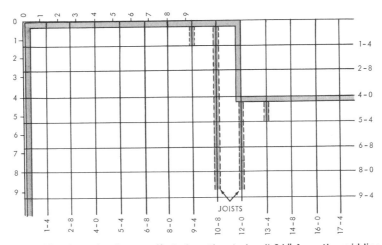

Fig. 11-22. When planning an offset, draw the stud wall ¾″ from the grid line to eliminate an extra joint.

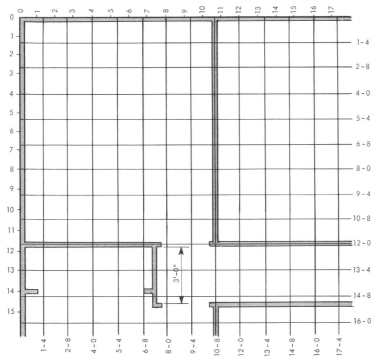

Fig. 11-23. One wall of the hallway will fall on the grid line. The other wall will fall off the grid.

the *stud opening dimension* of the window from a grid line. This can save up to 2 studs per window.

14. Add in all other necessary features. Dimensioning the plan is now an easy matter because the dimensions can be taken directly from the grid lines. The basement foundation wall lengths can be read directly from the grid lines. For the over-all foundation length of a brick veneer building, add 6″ to the grid dimension because the foundation projects 3″ beyond the grid line.

Step-by-Step Planning Procedure: First Floor or Level

The following steps enumerate the correct procedure in drawing the first floor plan. Fig. 11-24 illustrates the step-by-step procedure which is covered in detail below.

Step 1. Draw the outside wall lines to scale (based on the preliminary sketch) using the correct wall widths. See Table 11-14 for thicknesses of common types of walls.

Step 2. Locate and draw the main interior partitions, dividing the area into the main rooms.

Step 3. Locate and draw chimney flues and fireplace: allow 4″ around flues.

Design and locate stairs: first to second floor and first floor to basement.

Draw, on a separate sheet, a side view of the stairs showing head-

the grid line by adjusting the location. Locate the opposite wall of the hall 3′-0″ apart (stud face to stud face). This wall then will not be centered on the grid line. See Fig. 11-23.

10. Locate the bathroom plumbing wall slightly off the grid line to allow for the soil stack.

11. Locate remaining exterior walls

(front and right side) on the grid lines to allow for a maximum space for heat ducts.

12. Locate all features requiring openings in the floor such as fireplaces, stairwells, chimneys, clothes chute, etc., beginning adjacent to a grid line.

13. Place windows in the exterior walls by locating the window *one-half* of

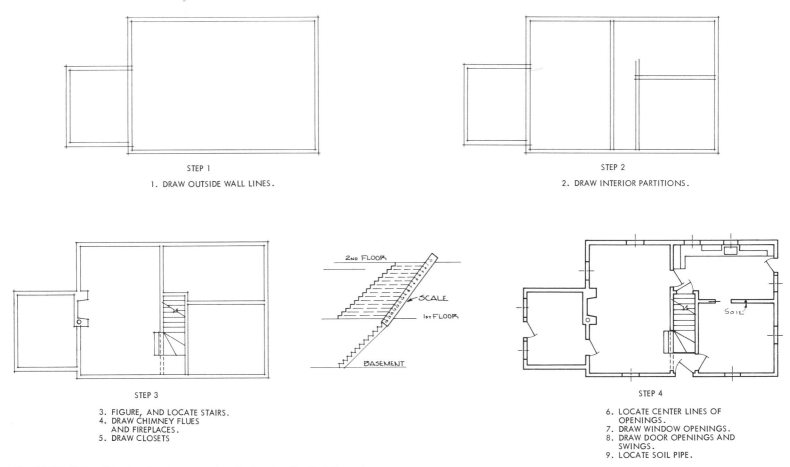

STEP 1
1. DRAW OUTSIDE WALL LINES.

STEP 2
2. DRAW INTERIOR PARTITIONS.

STEP 3
3. FIGURE, AND LOCATE STAIRS.
4. DRAW CHIMNEY FLUES
   AND FIREPLACES.
5. DRAW CLOSETS

STEP 4
6. LOCATE CENTER LINES OF
   OPENINGS.
7. DRAW WINDOW OPENINGS.
8. DRAW DOOR OPENINGS AND
   SWINGS.
9. LOCATE SOIL PIPE.

Fig. 11-24. Follow this step-by-step procedure in drawing the first floor plan.

room. Transfer plan to proper location on drawing.
Locate and draw closets.
Locate and draw the plumbing fixtures.

Step 4. Locate center lines of all openings.
Draw windows, doors (indicating swings), and archways. See Table 11-15, door openings.

Locate and draw soil pipe and necessary vents.
Locate and draw electrical fixtures, outlets and switches.
Locate and draw in girder.

TABLE 11-14

ACTUAL AND NOMINAL THICKNESSES OF COMMON TYPES OF WALLS

	TYPE OF WALL	COMPONENT MEMBERS	ACTUAL DIMENSION	NOMINAL DIMENSION
EXTERIOR	FRAME	Siding, sheathing, studs, interior finish (lath and plaster or dry wall material)	5-3/4" or 6"	7"
	CONCRETE BLOCK, STONE, BRICK, TILE OR COMBINATION	Masonry units, furring, plaster	9-1/2" or 13-3/4"	10" or 14"
	BRICK AND STONE VENEER	Masonry units, air space, sheathing studs, interior finish (lath and plaster or dry wall material)	9-3/4" or 10"	11"
	ROLOK AND ROLOK BACK	Masonry units (8" or 12"), furring, plaster	9-1/8" or 13-1/8"	10" or 14"
	SCR BRICK	Masonry unit, furring, interior finish (lath and plaster or dry wall material)	7-5/8"* or 7-7/8"†	8"
INTERIOR	REGULAR PARTITIONS	Studs, interior finish (lath and plaster or dry wall material)	4-5/8"* or 5-1/8"†	5"* or 6"†
	NON-LOAD BEARING (Between closets)	Studs, interior finish (lath and plaster or dry wall material)	3-5/8"* or 4-1/8"†	4"* or 5"†
	STACK	Stud, stack, interior finish (lath and plaster or dry wall material)	6-5/8"† or 7-1/8"†	7"* or 8"†
BASEMENT	FOUNDATION	The foundation for a frame structure will be 8" or larger. This, however, will vary depending on the local building code requirements for different types of walls (above and below grade), depth of wall and location of the building.	8", 10" or 12"	8", 10", or 12"
	PARTITION	Studs, interior finish (lath and plaster or dry wall material.)	3-5/8"* or 4-1/8"†	4"* or 5"†

*Thickness based on dry wall.
† Thickness based on lath and plaster.

TABLE 11-15
COMMON DOOR OPENINGS

USE	SIZE									
	16'-0"	15'-0"	9'-0"	8'-0"	3'-0"	2'-8"	2'-6"	2'-4"	2'-2"	2'-0"
Main Entry way					X	X*	X			
Service					X	X				
Closet †					X	X	X	X	X	X
Bath and Lavatory								X		X
Bedroom and Other						X	X			
Garage 1-car			X	X						
Garage 2-car	X	X								

*May be used in pairs.

† Closet door widths vary depending upon type of door used: sliding, bi-fold, accordion, etc. Openings for closets may be larger than 3'-0".

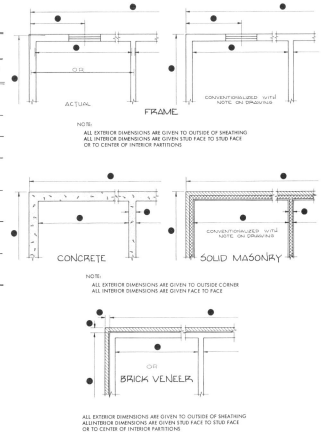

Fig. 11-25. Dimensioning practices vary with different wall types.

Note direction of second floor ceiling joists with an arrow. (Give size and distance O.C.) Dimension plan: See Fig. 11-25. Letter names of rooms and room sizes below name of room.

Step-by-Step Planning Procedure: Second Floor or Level

The second floor plan is drawn next. See Fig. 11-26. Place a piece of vellum over the first floor plan and follow the step-by-step procedure given below.

Step 1. Trace outside wall lines.

Step 2. Trace stairs and draw stair well opening.

Trace chimney. (Note: The chimney changes shape between the first and second floors as the furnace flue and the fireplace flue are placed close to one another.)

Locate interior partition and the closets.

Step 3. Trace soil pipe and vents.

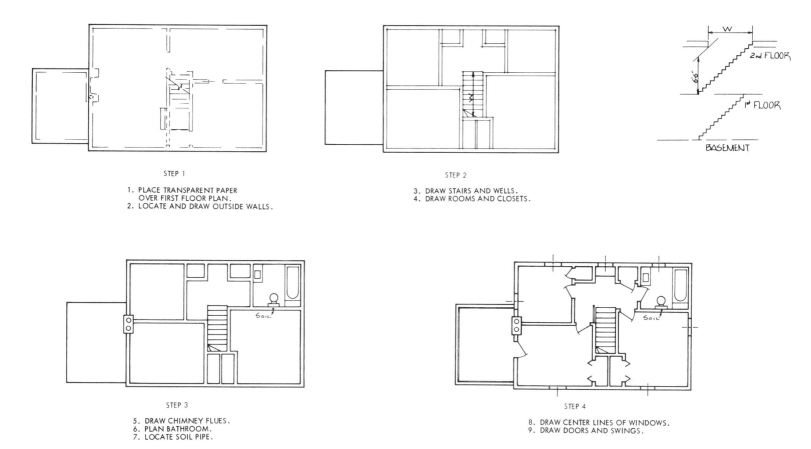

STEP 1

1. PLACE TRANSPARENT PAPER
   OVER FIRST FLOOR PLAN.
2. LOCATE AND DRAW OUTSIDE WALLS.

STEP 2

3. DRAW STAIRS AND WELLS.
4. DRAW ROOMS AND CLOSETS.

STEP 3

5. DRAW CHIMNEY FLUES.
6. PLAN BATHROOM.
7. LOCATE SOIL PIPE.

STEP 4

8. DRAW CENTER LINES OF WINDOWS.
9. DRAW DOORS AND SWINGS.

Fig. 11-26. Follow this step-by-step procedure for drawng the second-floor plan.

Locate and draw the bathroom fixtures.

Step 4. Locate and draw centerlines for windows and doors.

Draw doors (indicating swings).

Locate and draw electrical fixtures, outlets, and switches.

Note direction of attic joists with an arrow. (Give size and distance O.C.)

Draw roofs in plan if needed.

Dimension plan: See Fig. 11-25 for dimensioning practices.

Letter names of rooms and room sizes below name of room.

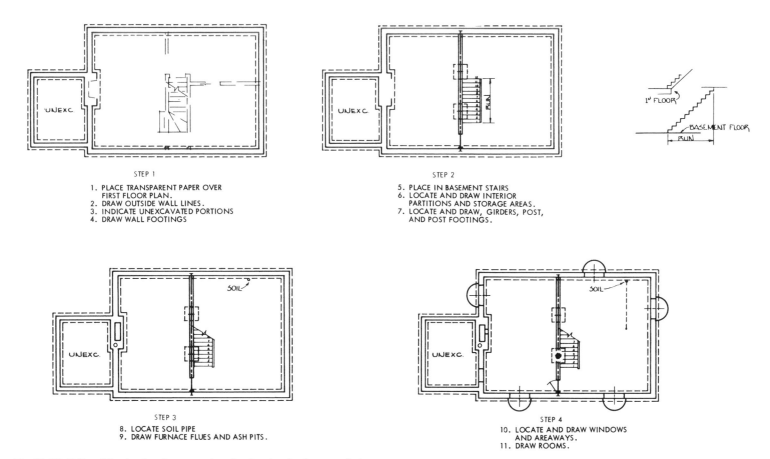

STEP 1

1. PLACE TRANSPARENT PAPER OVER
   FIRST FLOOR PLAN.
2. DRAW OUTSIDE WALL LINES.
3. INDICATE UNEXCAVATED PORTIONS
4. DRAW WALL FOOTINGS

STEP 2

5. PLACE IN BASEMENT STAIRS
6. LOCATE AND DRAW INTERIOR
   PARTITIONS AND STORAGE AREAS.
7. LOCATE AND DRAW, GIRDERS, POST,
   AND POST FOOTINGS.

STEP 3

8. LOCATE SOIL PIPE
9. DRAW FURNACE FLUES AND ASH PITS.

STEP 4

10. LOCATE AND DRAW WINDOWS
    AND AREAWAYS.
11. DRAW ROOMS.

Fig. 11-27. Follow this step-by-step procedure for drawing the basement plan.

Step-by-Step Planning Procedure: Basement

The basement or foundation plan is drawn third. See Fig. 11-27. Place a piece of vellum over the first floor plan and follow the step-by-step procedure given below.

Step 1. Locate and draw outside wall lines. If the building is masonry or masonry veneer, the wall will be flush. If the building is frame, the foundation will be placed inside the line traced from the first floor plan enough to compensate for the siding thickness.

If slab construction is used, locate and draw wall footings for bearing walls (if conventional roof framing is used).
Indicate any unexcavated areas and crawl spaces.
Draw wall footings.

Step 2. Trace basement stairs and draw stair well opening.
Locate and draw interior partitions and closets. Following the computations, locate and draw girders, posts or columns, and footing.

Step 3. Trace soil pipe.
Trace chimney.
Locate and draw fireplace, flue, ashpit, space heater, water heater, furnace or boiler, etc.

Step 4. Locate and draw centerlines for windows and doors.
Draw doors (indicating swings).
Draw windows and areaways.
Locate and draw the plumbing fixtures.
Locate and draw symbols for electrical fixtures, switches, and outlets.
Note size and location of girder, posts or columns, and footings.
Dimension plan: See Fig. 11-25.
Letter names of rooms and room sizes below name of room if applicable.

Check List

After completing the floor plans, each plan should be thoroughly checked. The points listed below will aid in the checking procedure.

1. *Closet sizes.* Are the closets sufficient in number; do they have good location, adequate depth, etc.?

2. *Door locations and sizes.* Are doors located so as to receive the maximum use? Does door swing conflict with other doors, walls, etc.? Can furniture be arranged without sacrificing too much floor space? Is 4″ allowed for each door jamb? Do the doors swing in the proper direction? Are the pockets for sliding doors free from framing obstructions?

3. *Room sizes.* Are room sizes similar to the room cutouts and the sketch plan? Will standard size rugs fit the rooms? Do the room sizes fit the joist spans (maximum 16 feet)?

4. *Girder location.* Is the girder located mid-way between the foundation walls or beneath a partition?

5. *Chimney size and location.* Is the flue the correct size for the fireplace opening? Is there proper clearance around the chimney to prevent fire?

6. *Clearances.* Is there adequate space for good traffic circulation? Be sure to check clearances for furniture, bathroom fixtures, doors, etc.

Questions and Problems

1. Sketch 4 floor plans for each of the 4 corners of an intersection of two streets running north to south and east to west. Two of these floor plans should be basementless, each having 3 bedrooms, 1½ baths, family room, living room, dining room or ell, kitchen, utility room, and 1½ or 2 car garage. The other two houses should contain 3 bedrooms, living room, dining area in kitchen, family room, 1½ baths, basement, breezeway or patio, and 1½ or 2 car garage. The lot sizes are 100′ × 300′. Develop floor plans for one of these houses.

2. Fig. 11-28 shows the floor plan and a pictorial rendering of a contemporary home. From the information given on the plan, following the procedures used for computing the structural members, answer these questions:

   a. At what location should the girder be placed? What type of girder will be used?

   b. What is the longest joist span over the basement? Considering the joist must carry a 50 lb. load what size joists must be specified if they are placed 16″ O.C.?

   c. What is the half width length?

   d. What is the total load per square foot?

   e. What is the lineal foot load?

   f. Depending upon the type of posts

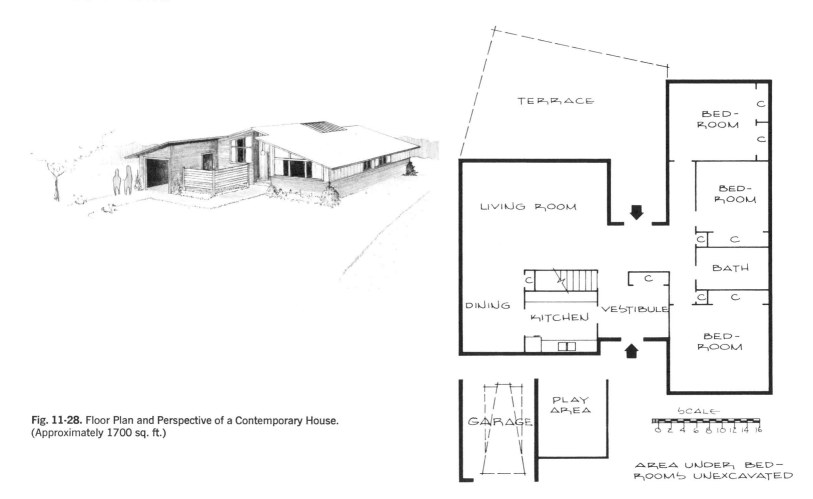

Fig. 11-28. Floor Plan and Perspective of a Contemporary House. (Approximately 1700 sq. ft.)

or columns selected, how many and how far apart will they be spaced?

g. What will be the total load imposed on the girder?

h. Depending on the type of girder selected, what will be its size?

i. If the height from the basement floor to the under side of the girder is 7'-2", what would be the height of a wood post? a steel I-beam?

j. What size wood post and I-beam would be necessary to support the girder?

k. If the house was built on hard clay, what size post or column footing would be necessary?

Lighting and Wiring 12

With increasing affluence the home owner's demand for labor-saving devices is rising. Many items that were once considered luxuries are now accepted as household necessities.

The number of appliances in common use has multiplied at an almost fantastic rate. For example, in the early 1900's the electric fan and flat iron were the only electric appliances available. This number slowly increased so that in 1930, 19 appliances were in common use in the average American household. By 1940 the number had increased to 36. Ten years later in 1950, 43 appliances were in common use. In 1970 well over 65 appliances were found in many average homes. To meet the demands of the "applianced" family, wiring must be up-to-date. It has been estimated that 3 out of 5 residences in existence today are inadequately wired. In many homes this has resulted in an octupus-like maze of appliances and lamps growing from an extension cord. Frequently this results in blown fuses or tripped circuit breakers. Extensive overloading may result in fires.

Many new homes now being constructed are inadequately wired because provisions for future electrical needs have been completely neglected. It is estimated that the electrical needs of the home will increase approximately 10 per cent every year. The circuit design and wiring layout must meet this increase of wattage requirements.

Electrical Needs

Since electricity plays an important role in our lives, all of its contributing features must be considered. As electrical power distribution is being planned in the house, an assessment must be made of the various types of portable and fixed electrical equipment that will be operated in each room. Attention must also be directed to the number of convenience outlets, switches, and lighting fixtures needed for each room.

Convenience outlets (receptacles which appliances plug into) are provided for the many different appliances used in the home: refrigerators, clocks, lamps, toasters, razors, fans, etc., etc. Convenience outlets are 115 to 120 volts. These outlets may have either single, double, or triple (triplex) receptacles. See Fig. 12-1. Each area should be ana-

Fig. 12-1. 115 v. convenience outlets may be single, duplex, or triplex.

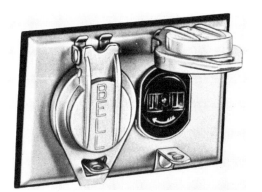

Fig. 12-2. Weatherproof convenience outlets may be either single or duplex.

lyzed to determine the intended appliance use. Allowance must also be made for future growth in use and number. A minimum of three outlets should be provided for each living area or room. Any outlet that is placed on the outside of the structure must be protected from the weather. Fig. 12-2 shows a single and duplex weatherproof outlet.

Special-purpose outlets, such as the polarized receptacle (and plug) shown in Fig. 12-3, are used for high voltage appliances or low voltage equipment which requires grounding. Polarized outlets are 220 to 240 volts. These outlets are designed so that two contacts carry the current and the third is grounded. This eliminates the possibility of serious electric shock. Appliances and

SIERRA ELECTRIC CORP., GARDENA, CALIFORNIA.

Fig. 12-4. A switch may be used to control lights, equipment and outlets from one, two, three, or four locations.

SEARS, ROEBUCK AND CO., CHICAGO, ILLINOIS.

Fig. 12-3. Polarized receptacles and plugs are used for 220 v. appliances.

equipment commonly found in the home which require special-purpose outlets are as follows: air conditioner, range, washer, dryer, water heater, power tools, water pump, sump pump, and freezer.

A check list should be made listing the appliances and equipment to be used for each room in the house. From this list the number and type of outlets may be computed. In addition, jacks must be provided for such things as the TV antenna, telephone, thermostat, door chimes, and intercom system.

Switches are required to operate lights,

appliances and equipment, and convenience and special outlets. See Fig. 12-4. A list should be made for each room of the number of lights, etc., needed. This will give a rough estimate of the number of switches needed. Traffic paths must also be taken into consideration — convenience is an important factor.

If an outlet is controlled from only *one* switch, it is referred to as a single-pole switch (S). A three-way switch (S_3) is used to control an outlet from *two* locations, as in the case of a light on the stairwell. It may be switched on or off from either the bottom or top of the stair. Four- and three-way switches (S_3 and S_4) are used to control the current from *three* and *four* different locations. (See p. 000 for a complete discussion of multiple switching arrangements).

Any switch that is placed on the outside of the building must be weatherproof. Fig. 12-5 shows a weatherproof switch.

Lighting. The following general requirements are recommended by the American Home Lighting Institute:

TABLE 12-1

FIXTURE LIGHTING REQUIREMENTS

| ROOM SIZE | CEILING FIXTURES | | CORNICE, COVER, OR VALANCE LIGHTING |
	MIN SIZE OF SHIELD	MIN WATTAGE	(LENGTH OF LIGHT SOURCE IN CORNICE, COVER OR VALANCE)
VERY SMALL (UP TO 125 SQ FT)	12" – 15"	ONE 100 W OR THREE 40 W	6 FEET
AVERAGE (125-225 SQ FT)	15" –17"	ONE 150 W OR FIVE 40 W	8-12 FEET*
LARGE (OVER 225 SQ FT)			16-20 FEET*

From: American Home Lighting Institute, FIXTURE LIGHTING GUIDE.

*Preferred in major living areas, such as living room, recreation room, etc. Recesses fixtures are acceptable for general lighting only when one 9"-12" box (100-150 w) is provided for each 40—50 sq ft of floor area. A combination of fixtures and wall lighting is desirable for added flexibility of lighting, especially in recreation or family room.

Fig. 12-5. Any switch placed on the outside of a building must be weatherproof.

1. All incandescent bulbs (ordinary bulbs) and fluorescent tubes shall be shielded in a manner which will minimize glare (except in closet and storage areas). Flashed opal and ceramic enameled glass and diffusing plastic materials are satisfactory for shielding incandescent bulbs. Materials having less diffusion (frosted or configurated glass) are satisfactory for shielding fluorescent tubes.

Low wattage (25w or less) lamps should be used in chandelier type fixtures that are equipped with clear or frosted glass shades for decorative effect. This type of fixture should be supplemented with indirect lighting.

2. A minimum of one fixture shall be controlled by a wall switch at the entrance of each room. Where ceiling fixtures are not installed, a minimum of one wall bracket, valance, cove, or cornice lighting unit must be wall switched at the room entrance.

3. Where traffic pattern into a room is from two directions and more than ten feet apart, two-way control on general lighting is desirable.

The size of the room or area to be lighted determines the lighting requirement. In Table 12-1, two alternate lighting methods are given for each room size.

Several varieties of lighting fixtures are shown in Fig. 12-6. The function of each fixture determines its shape and ultimate appearance.

SEARS, ROEBUCK AND CO., CHICAGO, ILLINOIS.

SEARS, ROEBUCK AND CO., CHICAGO, ILLINOIS.

MC PHILBAN LIGHTING, EMERSON ELECTRIC CO., INC.,
MELVILLE, NEW YORK.

A. W. PISTOL, INC., NEW ROCHELLE, NEW YORK.

ARTCREST PRODUCTS CO., INC., CHICAGO, ILLINOIS.

ARTCREST PRODUCTS CO., INC., CHICAGO, ILLINOIS.

Fig. 12-6. Lighting fixtures basically serve a functional purpose of providing light. Fixtures may also enhance a decor either by appearance or illumination.

Residential Wiring Recommendations

As with other phases of home construction, residential wiring must follow standards. The National Electrical Code establishes minimum safety standards. The recommendations given below are designed to supplement the National Electrical Code (NEC).

The design standards given in the following paragraphs are from the *American Standard Requirements for Residential Wiring*. (Wiring symbols are illustrated in Fig. 3-5, Chapter 3.)

Exterior Entrances — (Fig. 12-7)

A. *Lighting Provisions.* One or more lighting outlets, as architecture dictates, wall-switch controlled, at front and service entrances.

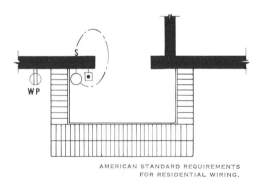

AMERICAN STANDARD REQUIREMENTS FOR RESIDENTIAL WIRING.

Fig. 12-7. One or more lighting sources are required for the entrance. The broken line represents the connection between switch and lighting outlet. Note also the weatherproof outlet.

Where a single wall outlet is desired, location on the latch side of the door is preferable.

It is recommended that lighting outlets, wall-switch controlled, be installed at the other entrances.

The principal lighting requirements at entrances are the illumination of steps leading to the entrance and of faces of people at the door. Outlets in addition to those at the door are often desirable for post lights to illuminate terraced or broken flights of steps or long approach walks. These outlets should be wall-switch controlled inside the house entrance.

B. *Convenience Outlets.* It is recommended that this (Fig. 12-7) outlet be controlled by a wall switch inside the entrance for convenient operation of outdoor decorative lighting. Additional outlets along the exterior of the house are recommended to serve decorative garden treatments and for the use of appliances or electric garden tools, such as lawn mowers and hedge trimmers. Such outlets should also be wall-switch controlled.

Living Room — (Figs. 12-8 and 12-9,

A. *Lighting Provisions.* Some means of general illumination is essential. This lighting may be provided by ceiling or wall fixtures, by lighting in coves, valances, or cornices, or by portable lamps. Provide lighting outlets, wall-switch controlled, in locations appropriate to the lighting method selected.

These provisions also apply to sun rooms, enclosed porches, television rooms, libraries, dens, and similar areas.

The installation of outlets for decorative-lighting accent is recommended, such as picture illumination and bookcase lighting.

B. *Convenience Outlets.* Convenience outlets shall be placed so that no point along the floor line in any usable wall space is more than six feet from an outlet in that space. Where the installation of windows extending to the

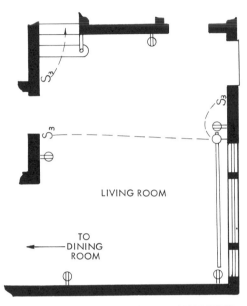

AMERICAN STANDARD REQUIREMENTS FOR RESIDENTIAL WIRING.

Fig. 12-8. Outlets should be placed so that no usable wall space is more than 6′ from an outlet. Note the fluorescent light above the window.

floor prevents meeting this requirement by the use of ordinary convenience outlets, equivalent facilities shall be installed using other appropriate means.

If, in lieu of fixed lighting, general illumination is provided from portable lamps, two convenience outlets or one plug position in two or more split-receptacle (double receptacle — one switch controlled, one independent) convenience outlets shall be wall-switch controlled.

In the case of switch-controlled convenience outlets, it is recommended that split-receptacle outlets be used in order not to limit the location of radios, television sets, clocks, etc.

It is recommended that one convenience out-

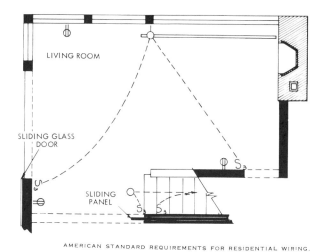

Fig. 12-9. Outlets are located for convenience.

LIVING ROOM

SLIDING GLASS DOOR

SLIDING PANEL

AMERICAN STANDARD REQUIREMENTS FOR RESIDENTIAL WIRING.

let be installed flush in mantel shelf, if construction permits.

It is recommended that, in addition, a single convenience outlet be installed in combination with the wall switch at one or more of the switch locations for the use of the vacuum cleaner or other portable appliances. Outlets for the use of clocks, radios, decorative lighting, etc., in bookcases and other suitable locations are recommended.

C. *Special Purpose Outlets.* It is recommended that one outlet for a room air conditioner be installed wherever a central air-conditioning system is not planned.

Dining Areas — (Fig. 12-10)

A. *Lighting Provisions.* Each dining room, or dining area combined with another room, or breakfast nook, shall have at least one lighting outlet, wall-switch controlled.

Such outlets are normally located over the

TO LIVING ROOM

AMERICAN STANDARD REQUIREMENTS FOR RESIDENTIAL WIRING.

Fig. 12-10. The dining room should provide split-wired convenience outlets.

probable location of the dining or breakfast table to provide direct illumination of the area.

B. *Convenience Outlets.* Convenience outlets placed so that no point along the floor line in any usable wall space is more than six feet from an outlet in that space. When dining or breakfast table is to be placed against a wall, one of these outlets shall be placed at the table location, just above table height.

Where open counter space is to be built in, an outlet shall be provided above counter height for the use of portable appliances.

Convenience outlets in dining areas should be of the split-receptacle type for connection to appliance circuits.

Bedrooms — (Fig. 12-11)

A. *Lighting Provisions.* Good general illumination is particularly essential in the bedroom. This shall be provided from a ceiling fixture or from lighting in valances, coves, or cornices. Provide outlets, wall-switch controlled, in locations appropriate to the method selected.

Light fixtures over full-length mirrors, or a light source at the ceiling located in the bedroom and directly in front of the clothes closets, may serve as general illumination.

Master-switch control in the master bedroom, as well as at other strategic points in the home, is suggested for selected interior and exterior lights.

B. *Convenience Outlets.* Outlets shall be placed so that there is a convenience outlet on each side and within six feet of the center line of each probable individual bed location. Additional outlets shall be placed so that no point along the floor line in any other usable wall space is more than six feet from an outlet in that space.

It is recommended that convenience outlets be placed only three to four feet from the center line of the probable bed locations. The popularity of bedside radios and clocks, bed

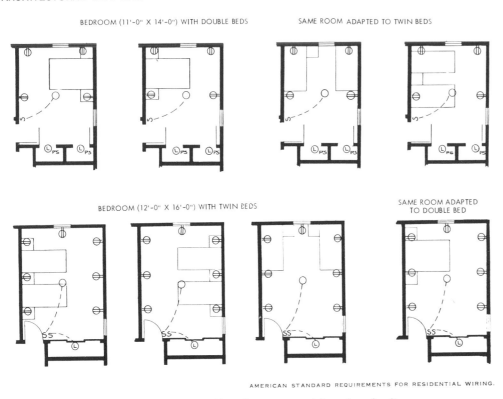

BEDROOM (11'-0" X 14'-0") WITH DOUBLE BEDS

SAME ROOM ADAPTED TO TWIN BEDS

BEDROOM (12'-0" X 16'-0") WITH TWIN BEDS

SAME ROOM ADAPTED TO DOUBLE BED

AMERICAN STANDARD REQUIREMENTS FOR RESIDENTIAL WIRING.

Fig. 12-11. Bedroom outlets should be positioned to accommodate various furniture arrangements. Note the closet lighting.

Bathrooms and Lavatories — (Fig. 12-12)

A. *Lighting Provisions*. Illumination of both sides of the face when at the mirror is essential. There are several methods that may be employed to achieve good lighting at this location and in the rest of the room. Lighting outlets shall be installed to provide for the method selected, bearing in mind that a single concentrated light source, either on the ceiling or the

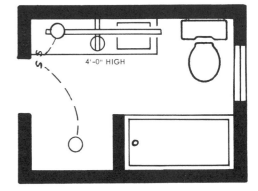

4'-0" HIGH

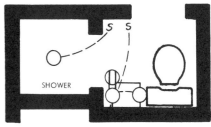

SHOWER

AMERICAN STANDARD REQUIREMENTS FOR RESIDENTIAL WIRING.

Fig. 12-12. Several light sources are needed for sufficient bathroom illumination.

lamps, and electric bed cover, makes increased plug-in positions at bed locations essential. Triplex or quadruplex convenience outlets are therefore recommended at these locations.

It is recommended that, at one of the switch locations, a receptacle outlet be provided for the use of a vacuum cleaner, floor polisher, or other portable appliances.

C. *Special Purpose Outlets*. The installation of one heavy-duty, special-purpose outlet in each bedroom for the connection of room air conditioners is recommended. Such outlets may also be used for operating portable space heaters during cool weather in climates where a small amount of local heat is sufficient.

NOTE: The illustrations in Fig. 12-11 show the application of these standards to both double- and twin-bed arrangements and also their application where more than one probable bed location is available within the room.

side wall, is not acceptable. All lighting outlets should be wall-switch controlled.

A ceiling outlet located in line with the front edge of the basin will provide improved lighting at the mirror, general room lighting, and safety lighting for combination shower and tub.

When more than one mirror location is planned, equal consideration should be given to the lighting in each case.

It is recommended that a switch-controlled night light be installed.

Where an enclosed shower stall is planned, an outlet for a vapor-proof luminaire should be installed, controlled by a wall switch outside the stall.

B. *Convenience Outlets.* One outlet near the mirror, three to five feet above the floor.

It is recommended that an outlet be installed at each separate mirror or vanity space, and also at any space that might accommodate an electric towel dryer, electric razor, etc.

A receptacle which is a part of a bathroom lighting fixture should not be considered as satisfying this requirements unless it is rated at 15 amperes and wired with at least 15-ampere rated wires.

C. *Special Purpose Outlets.* It is recommended that each bathroom be equipped with an outlet for a built-in type space heater.

Also recommended is an outlet for a built-in ventilating fan, wall-switch controlled.

Kitchen — (Figs. 12-13 and 12-14)

A. *Lighting Provisions.* Provide outlets for general illumination and for lighting at the sink. These lighting outlets shall be wall-switch controlled. Lighting design should provide for illumination of the work areas, sink, range, counters, and tables.

Undercabinet lighting fixtures within easy reach may have local-switch control. Consideration should also be given to outlets to provide inside lighting of cabinets.

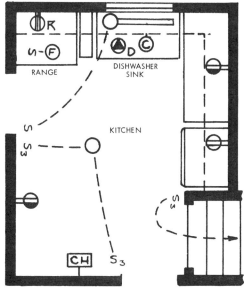

AMERICAN STANDARD REQUIREMENTS FOR RESIDENTIAL WIRING.

Fig. 12-13. Lighting design in the kitchen should provide sufficient illumination of the work area.

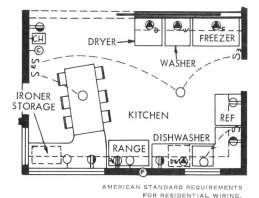

AMERICAN STANDARD REQUIREMENTS FOR RESIDENTIAL WIRING.

Fig. 12-14. Kitchen outlets should be provided near each part of the work area.

B. *Convenience Outlets.* One outlet for the refrigerator. One outlet for each four linear feet of work-surface frontage, with at least one outlet to serve each work surface. Work-surface outlets to be located approximately 44 inches above floor line.

If a planning desk is to be installed, one outlet shall be located to serve this area.

Table space to have one outlet, preferably just above table level.

An outlet is recommended at any wall space that may be used for ironing or for an electric roaster.

Convenience outlets in the kitchen, other than that for the refrigerator, should be of the split-receptacle type (one 115v and one 230v) for connection to appliance circuits.

C. *Special Purpose Outlets.* One outlet each for a range and ventilating fan.

An outlet or outlets for a dishwasher or food waste disposer, if necessary plumbing facilities are installed.

Provision shall be made for the use of an electric clock.

The clock should be located so as to be easily visible from all parts of the kitchen. Recessed receptacle with clock hanger is recommended.

It is recommended that an outlet be provided for a food freezer either in the kitchen or in some other convenient location.

Laundry and Laundry Areas — (Fig. 12-15)

A. *Lighting Provisions.* For complete laundries, lighting outlets shall be installed to provide proper illumination of work areas, such as laundry tubs, sorting table, washing, ironing, and drying centers. At least one lighting outlet in the room shall be wall-switch controlled.

For laundry trays in unfinished basement, one ceiling outlet, centered over the trays.

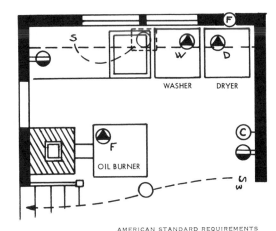

Fig. 12-15. The laundry area should have illumination over the work area.

AMERICAN STANDARD REQUIREMENTS
FOR RESIDENTIAL WIRING.

It is recommended that all laundry lighting be wall-switch controlled.

B. *Convenience Outlet.* At least one convenience outlet. In some instances, one of the special-purpose outlets, properly located, may satisfy this requirement. The convenience outlet is intended for such purposes as laundry hot plate, sewing machine, etc.

Convenience outlets in laundry area should be of the split-receptacle type for connection to appliance circuits.

C. *Special Purpose Outlets.* One outlet for each of the following pieces of equipment:

    Automatic Washer
    Hand Iron or Ironer
    Clothes Dryer

The installation of outlets for ventilating fan and clock are highly desirable. If an electric water heater is to be installed, the requirements may be obtained from the local utility.

Closets

Lighting Provisions. One outlet for each closet. Where shelving or other conditions make the installation of lights within a closet ineffective, lighting outlets should be so located in the adjoining space to provide light within the closet.

The installation of wall switches near the closet door, or door-type switches, is recommended.

Halls

A. *Lighting Provisions.* Lighting outlets, wall-switch controlled, shall be installed for proper illumination of the entire area. Particular attention should be paid to irregularly shaped areas.

These provisions apply to passage halls, reception halls, vestibules, entries, foyers, and similar areas.

It is recommended that a switch-controlled night light be installed in any hall giving access to bedrooms.

B. *Convenience Outlets.* One outlet for each 15 linear feet of hallway, measured along center line. Each hall over 25 square feet in floor area shall have at least one outlet.

In reception halls and foyers, convenience outlets shall be placed so that no point along the floor line in any usable wall space is more than ten feet from an outlet in that space.

It is recommended that at one of the switch outlets a convenience receptacle be provided for connection of vacuum cleaner, floor polisher, etc.

Stairways

A. *Lighting Provisions.* Wall or ceiling outlets shall be installed to provide adequate illumination of each stair flight. Outlets shall have multiple-switch control at the head and foot of the stairway, so arranged that full illumination may be turned on from either floor, but that lights in halls furnishing access to bedrooms may be extinguished without interfering with ground-floor usage.

These provisions are intended to apply to any stairway at both ends of which are finished rooms.

Whenever possible, switches should be grouped together and never located so close to steps that a fall might result from a misstep while reaching for a switch.

B. *Convenience Outlets.* At intermediate landings of a large area, an outlet is recommended for decorative lamps, night light, vacuum cleaner, etc.

Recreation Room — (Fig. 12-16)

A. *Lighting Provisions.* Some means of general illumination is essential. This lighting may be provided by ceiling or wall fixtures, or by lighting in coves, valances, or cornices. Provide lighting outlets, wall-switch controlled, in locations appropriate to the lighting method selected.

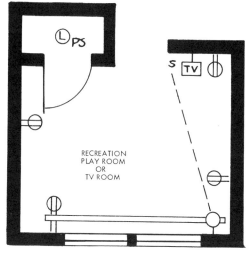

AMERICAN STANDARD REQUIREMENTS
FOR RESIDENTIAL WIRING.

Fig. 12-16. Lighting in the recreation room should take into account the major activities for which the room is planned.

Selection of lighting method for use in the recreation room should take into account the type of major activities for which the room is planned.

B. *Convenience Outlets.* Convenience outlets shall be placed so that no point along the floor line in any usable wall space is more than six feet from an outlet in that space.

It is recommended that one convenience outlet be installed flush in the mantel shelf, where construction permits. Outlets for the use of clock, radio, television, ventilating fan, motion picture projector, and the like, should be located in relation to their intended use.

Utility Room or Space — (Fig. 12-17)

A. *Lighting Provisions.* Lighting outlets placed to illuminate furnace area, and work

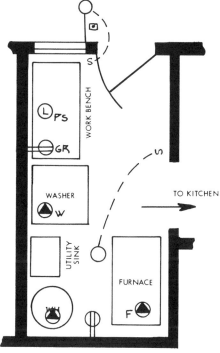

AMERICAN STANDARD REQUIREMENTS
FOR RESIDENTIAL WIRING.

Fig. 12-17. Utility room lighting should illuminate the furnace area and the work bench.

bench, if planned. At least one lighting outlet to be wall-switch controlled.

B. *Convenience Outlets.* One convenience outlet, preferably near the furnace location or near any planned work-bench location.

C. *Special Purpose Outlet.* One outlet for electrical equipment used in connection with furnace operation.

Basement — Fig. (12-18)

A. *Lighting Provisions.* Lighting outlets

shall be placed to illuminate designated work areas or equipment locations, such as at furnace, pump, work bench, etc. Additional outlets shall be installed near the foot of the stairway, in each enclosed space, and in open spaces so that each 150 square feet of open space is adequately served by a light in that area.

In unfinished basements the light at the foot of the stairs shall be wall-switch controlled near the head of the stairs. Other lights may be pull-chain controlled.

In basements with finished rooms, with garage space, or with other direct access to outdoors, the stairway lighting provisions apply.

It is recommended that for basements which will be infrequently visited a pilot light be installed in conjunction with the switch at the head of the stairs.

B. *Convenience Outlets.* At least two convenience outlets shall be provided. If a work bench is planned, one outlet shall be placed at this location.

Basement convenience outlets are useful near furnace, at play area, for basement laundries, dark rooms, hobby areas, and for appliances, such as dehumidifier, portable space heater, etc.

C. *Special Purpose Outlet.* One outlet for electrical equipment used in connection with furnace operation.

An outlet for a food freezer is recommended.

Accessible Attic

A. *Lighting Provisions.* One outlet for general illumination, wall-switch controlled from foot of stairs. When no permanent stairs are installed, this lighting outlet may be pull-chain controlled, if located over the access door. Where an unfinished attic is planned for later development into rooms, the attic-lighting out-

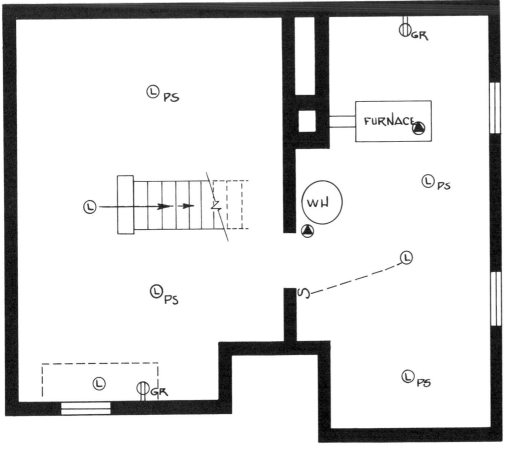

AMERICAN STANDARD REQUIREMENTS FOR RESIDENTIAL WIRING.

Fig. 12-18. Basement lighting should illuminate designated work areas and equipment locations.

B. *Convenience Outlets.* One outlet for general use. If open stairway leads to future attic rooms, provide a junction box with direct connection to the distribution panel (panelboard) for future extension to convenience outlets and lights when rooms are finished.

A convenience outlet in the attic is desirable for providing additional illumination in dark corners and also for the use of a vacuum cleaner and its accessories in cleaning.

C. *Special Purpose Outlet.* The installation of an outlet, multiple-switch controlled from desirable points throughout the house, is recommended in connection with the use of a summer cooling fan.

Porches — (See Fig. 12-19)

A. *Lighting Provisions.* Each porch, breezeway, or other similar roofed area of more than 75 square feet in floor area shall have a lighting outlet, wall-switch controlled. Large or irregularly shaped areas may require two or more lighting outlets.

Multiple-switch control shall be installed at entrances when the porch is used as a passage between the house and garage.

B. *Convenience Outlets.* One convenience outlet, weatherproof if exposed to moisture, for each 15 feet of wall bordering porch or breezeway.

It is recommended that all such outlets be controlled by a wall switch inside the door.

The split-receptacle convenience outlet shown in the illustration (Fig. 12-19) is intended to be connected to a 3-wire appliance branch circuit. This area is considered an outdoor dining area.

Terraces and Patios

A. *Lighting Provisions.* At least one ceiling an outlet on the building wall or on a post centrally located in the area is recommended

let shall be switch controlled at top and bottom of stairs.

One outlet for each enclosed space.

These provisions apply to unfinished attics. For attics with finished rooms or spaces, see appropriate room classifications for requirements.

The installation of a pilot light in conjunction with the switch controlling the attic light is recommended.

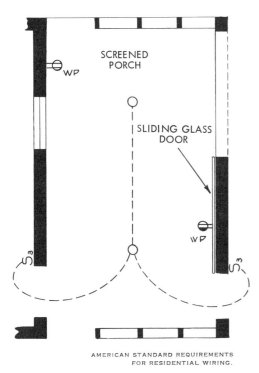

AMERICAN STANDARD REQUIREMENTS
FOR RESIDENTIAL WIRING.

Fig. 12-19. Large or irregularly shaped porch areas may need two or more lighting outlets.

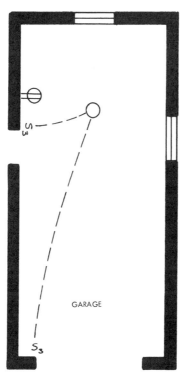

AMERICAN STANDARD REQUIREMENTS
FOR RESIDENTIAL WIRING.

Fig. 12-20. At least one ceiling light, with a switch control at each entrance, is recommended for the garage.

for the purpose of providing fixed general illumination. Such outlets should be wall-switch controlled just inside the house door opening onto the area.

B. *Convenience Outlets.* One weatherproof outlet located at least 18 inches above grade line for each 15 linear feet of house wall bordering terrace or patio.

It is recommended that these outlets be wall-switch controlled from inside the house.

Garage or Carport — (See Fig. 12-20)

A. *Lighting Provisions.* At least one ceiling outlet, wall-switch controlled, for one- or two-car storage area.

If garage has no covered access from house, provide one exterior outlet, multiple-switch controlled from garage and residence.

If garage is to be used for purposes additional to car storage, such as to include work bench, closets, laundry, attached porch, etc., rules appropriate to these uses should be employed.

An exterior outlet, wall-switch controlled, is recommended for all garages. Additional interior outlets are often desirable even if no specific additional use is planned for the garage. For long driveways, additional illumination, such as by post lighting, is recommended. These lights should be wall-switch controlled from the house.

B. *Convenience Outlets.* At least one outlet for one- or two-car storage area.

C. *Special Purpose Outlets.* If food freezer, work bench, or automatic door opener is planned for installation in the garage, outlets appropriate to these uses should be provided.

Exterior Grounds

A. *Lighting Provisions.* Lighting outlets for floodlights are often desirable for illumination of surrounding grounds. These outlets may be located on the exterior of the house or garage, or on posts or poles appropriately placed. All outlets should be switch controlled from within the house. Multiple- and master-switch control from strategic points is also desirable.

The recommendations given above provide the planner with a guide for designing home wiring plans. However, the wiring design must stay within the specification limits of the state or local building codes and the National Electrical Code. In some cases, the wiring plans must also meet requirements given by the local utility companies.

Because of the increasing need for electric power, minimum wiring requirements today may be inadequate tomorrow. When planning the electrical distribution, it is advisable to check and make sure that the wiring plan allows additional outlets to accommodate future electrical needs. The ini-

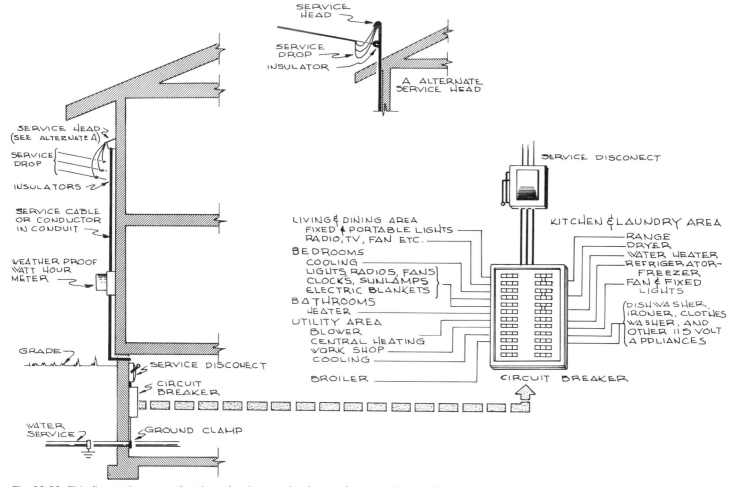

Fig. 12-21. This figure gives a section through a house, showing a schematic diagram of a typical electrical distribution system. Note the 230 v. circuit breakers for range, dryer, and water heater.

tial cost of planning and installing extra outlets is negligible when compared to the cost of addition later.

Power Control Centers

Power from the local distributor is delivered into the house through lead-in cables called a *service drop*. A *watt-hour meter*, connected between the lead-in cables and the main power switch or *service disconnect,* measures the amount of power used by the house circuits. The amount of electricity used is measured in kilowatt-hours: 1000 watts (w) equal one kilowatt (kw); one kilowatt used for an hour equals one kilowatt-hour (kwh). A main control center or *panelboard,* which contains the *fuse box* or *circuit breaker,* connects to the service disconnect and delivers current to the various outlets. Fig. 12-21 graphically describes the path of the current from the pole to service head, etc. Some communities or areas within a community have underground services that enter the house below grade. The meter is then placed outdoors. This arrangement eliminates the unsightly overhead wires strung from pole to house.

There is a marked trend in contemporary residential construction to modify the direct connection from the panelboard to the circuit outlets. This relatively new method employs a main control or panelboard to which several *branch control centers* are connected. Fig. 12-22 shows the current path in this system. The number of branch or power centers is dependent upon the number and type of circuits required. These centers are located throughout the house as close to the point of usage as possible. For the average single family dwelling it is recommended that (1) the *main control center* be limited to twelve positions: that is, there may be, for example, six single pole and three double pole circuit breakers; and that (2) the *branch control center* be restricted to eight positions (eight single poles or four

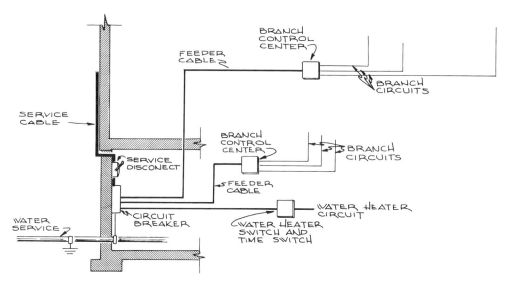

Fig. 12-22. There is a trend in residential construction to use branch control centers.

double poles). The number of branch control centers is dependent upon the needs of the home. The branch control centers may be conveniently located in the kitchen, utility room, front hall, or closet. By placing the branch control centers close to the loads, the possibility of a voltage drop is greatly reduced.

Home Wiring Design

Though each of the following terms indicates a unit of measure, each refers to a specific aspect of electrical measure. Following each definition is the common abbreviation:

Ampere. The strength of electric current. It is a unit that indicates the rate of flow of electricity through a circuit at a given time: *amp, a.*

Current. The flow of electricity through a circuit.

Ohm. A unit of electrical resistance of a conductor to the flow of current: *ohm,* Ω.

Volt. A unit of electrical force that pushes current through a wire: *V.*

Watt. A unit of electrical power. It is one volt of pressure: *w.*

Watt hour. One watt used for one hour: *watt-hr., whr, wh.*

Kilowatt. One thousand (1,000) watts: *KW, kw.*

Kilowatt hour. One thousand (1,000) watts used for one hour: *KWH, kwh, kw-h.*

Current in the house is measured in amperes (amps). Power is measured in watts. These are calculated for two voltages: 115V and 230V. Voltage may be thought of as pressure on the line. When a light bulb, for example, reads 120V/100W, this means that connected into a current source with around 120 volts of pressure (the source varies 110V-120V) the lamp will use 100 watts of power. Wattage is used to measure the electricity used by appliances. If only the amperage is known, the wattage may be found using the basic power $P = EI$ or formula:

$$\text{Watts} = \text{Volts} \times \text{Amps}$$

For example, if an electric iron was rated at 10 amps (at 115V) the wattage would be 1150W. If the wattage is known, the amps may be found using this formula:

$$\text{Amps} = \frac{\text{Watts}}{\text{Volts}}$$

For example, a 120V/110W bulb would use 0.83 amps. Amps are used in calculating the wiring size.

Loads

The load placed on the wiring system should not, of course, exceed the capacity of the wiring system. When an electrical load becomes too great for the wiring system, the efficiency of an electrical device drops. At one time or another we have experienced a momentary decrease in the size of a television picture, or a dimming of an incandescent bulb over a desk when an electrical motor was turned on or when an

iron was used. A 5 per cent voltage drop due to inadequate wiring produces a 10 per cent loss of heat in an appliance or a 17 per cent loss in illumination from an incandescent lamp. Obviously, by overloading any circuit, the maximum efficiency is not received from each appliance or light. This loss of efficiency not only causes inconvenience but also creates a possible fire hazard.

The diameter of the wire in *any* wiring system determines the amount of current which may be carried. If the appliances or equipment in a circuit require more current than the wire is designed to carry, the wire heats up. This is referred to as "overloading." The circuit should be designed for pre-determined wattage use.

Low Voltage Switching

The low voltage switching system for residential construction is gaining favor over conventional wiring arrangements in many areas of the United States. The low voltage system utilizes wall switches that control a 6-12 volt circuit. The low voltage circuit is separate from the line circuit (120 volts). The line circuit supplies current to all of the fixtures. Switch wires that would ordinarily control these fixtures have been eliminated by relays or electromagnetic switches that are controlled by the low voltage circuit. Because of the lower voltage there is no safety hazard of shock or short circuit at the switch. Several basic advantages are obtained through the use of the low voltage

system: (1) thin bell wire may be used, (2) wires do not have to be placed on conduit or in metal switch boxes; and (3) all outlets may be controlled from one central position. Due to the lower voltage some different pieces of equipment are required.

Branch Circuits

The wattage of the appliances, electrical equipment, or lights in a circuit determines the circuit size. If, for example, a lighting circuit is designed for 1500 watts, and a TV set (700W), a vacuum cleaner (500W), and five 120W bulbs were in operation, an overload would result. (The wattage use for each appliance is given by the manufacturer.) In every case the wattage being used may be determined by *adding* together the wattages of the appliances, lights, etc., which are in use. In planning the branch-circuit wiring size the projected use (with allowance for growth) is the determining factor. No. 14 wire is considered safe in a lighting circuit; however, a No. 12 wire is recommended. Special-purpose circuits usually require heavier wire. (Note: As the wire number becomes lower, the diameter becomes larger.)

Table 12-2 gives wiring sizes based on the amperage of the circuit.

Fuses or circuit breakers are calculated in amps. They should not be larger than the current capacity of the circuit they are designed to protect. Fuse or circuit breaker capacities may be calculated from Table 11-2. No. 12 wiring in conduit, for example,

TABLE 12-2

INDIVIDUAL EQUIPMENT CIRCUITS	
ITEM	CAPACITY
RANGE (UP TO 21-KW RATING)	50A-3W-115/230V*
COMBINATION WASHER-DRYER OR	40A-3W-115/230V*
AUTOMATIC WASHER	20A-2W-115V
ELECTRIC CLOTHS DRYER	30A-3W-115/230V*
FUEL-FIRED HEATING EQUIPMENT (IF INSTALLED)	15A or 20A-2W-115V
DISHWASHER AND WASTE DISPOSER (IF NECESSARY PLUMBING IS INSTALLED)	20A-3W-115/230V*
WATER HEATER (IF INSTALLED)	CONSULT LOCAL UTILITY
ATTIC FAN	20A-2W-115V (SWITCHED)
ROOM AIR CONDITIONERS OR	20A-2W-230V OR 20A-3W-115/230V*
CENTRAL AIR-CONDITIONING UNIT	40A-2W-230V
FOOD FREEZER	20A-2W-115 or 230V
WATER PUMP (WHERE USED)	20A-2W-115 or 230V
BATHROOM HEATER	20A-2W-115 or 230V
WORK SHOP OR BENCH	20A-3W-115/230V*

From: <u>American Standard Requirements for Residential Wiring</u>.

*A 115/230V circuit is a three wire (3w) circuit that terminates in an outlet with a split-wired receptacles: one 115v receptacale and one 230v receptacale.

would require a fuse or circuit breaker rated at 20 amps.

Convenience Circuits. It is recommended that two or more 20 amp (115V) circuits should be provided for the small appliance load in cooking and eating areas. This provides for 2300 watts on each circuit (20 amp × 115V).

Special-Purpose Circuits. Three wire circuits (230V), are provided for large appliances and equipment. It is recommended that heavy wattage appliances, such as the range (around 12,000W), should have an individual branch circuit. Table 12-2 gives the capacities for commonly used household appliances and equipment.

Lighting Circuits. NEC standards state that one lighting circuit should be provided for each 500 sq. ft. of house area (measured from outside walls). A 20 amp circuit is recommended. If a 15 amp circuit is used, it is recommended that no more than 375 sq. ft. be served. Lighting may also be figured as a minimum of 3 watts per sq. ft. However, these are *minimum* requirements—good design may require more lighting. The lights in any one room, for example, should be on more than one circuit. This prevents a total blackout if the fuse blows.

Two, Three, and Four-Way Switches

Single Pole Switch. Many of the outlets or fixtures in residential and commercial work are operated from one location by a single pole switch. In this arrangement the outlet(s) or fixture(s) is (are) controlled at the end of the circuit by a single switch. A single pole switch loop is shown in Fig. 12-23. By closing the switch, contact is made and current is allowed to pass through the switch and on to the outlet or fixture.

Three-Way Switch. In planning an electrical layout, frequently it is desirable to control one or more outlets from two different locations. This is frequently used where an outlet is controlled from the top and bottom of a stairwell, or a ceiling outlet switched at two separate entrys. A three-way switch (see Fig. 12-24) has 3 terminals rather than 2 as with the single pole switch.

Fig. 12-25 shows 2 three-way switches operating a single outlet or lamp. A three-

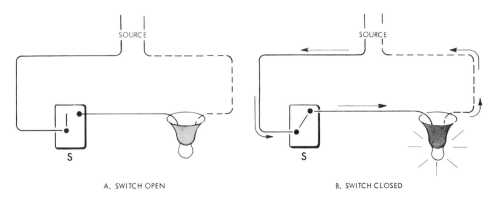

Fig. 12-23. An outlet or fixture may be controlled from a single location by a single-pole switch.

Fig. 12-24. A 3-way switch, showing the current path between the terminals.

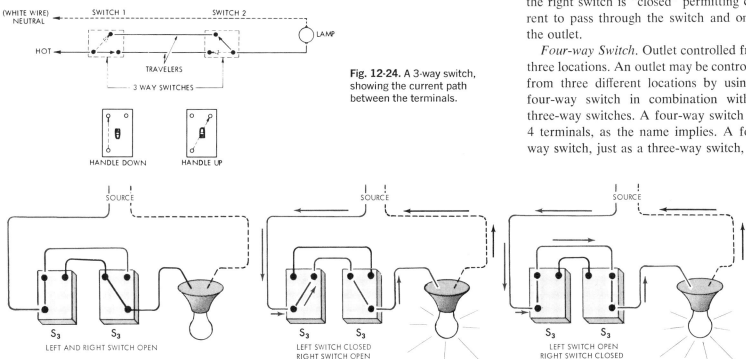

Fig. 12-25. An outlet may be controlled from two different locations by using 3-way switches.

way switch is so designed that the "hot" terminal is connected to either one of the traveler contacts as the switch is actuated: Regardless of which position the switch is turned, one or the other of the traveler terminals is made hot. The switch has no off or "open" position. In the illustration, Fig. 12-25 A, no current can reach the lamp because both of the switches are open. At B in Fig. 12-25 only the left switch is actuated allowing current to pass through the switch and on to the outlet. At C the left switch is returned to the "open position and the right switch is "closed" permitting current to pass through the switch and on to the outlet.

Four-way Switch. Outlet controlled from three locations. An outlet may be controlled from three different locations by using 1 four-way switch in combination with 2 three-way switches. A four-way switch has 4 terminals, as the name implies. A four-way switch, just as a three-way switch, has

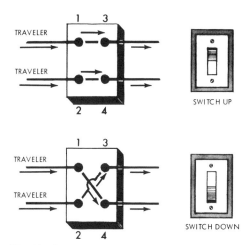

Fig. 12-26. Through-type 4-way switch, showing current path between terminals.

no "on" or "off" designation or position on the handle. The type of four-way switch illustrated in Fig. 12-26 is the through-type. The travelers on the left side of the four-way switch connect to the terminals on that side. The travelers going to the other three-way or four-way switch on the right connect to the terminals on the right side. When the switch handle is up (see Fig. 12-26) the current travels straight across from terminal 1 to 3 and 2 to 4. By moving the handle in a down position, the current travels from 1 to 4 and 2 to 3.

Fig. 12-27 shows all of the possible combinations of a single lamp controlled at three different locations. To understand how a fixture is controlled from 3 points, it will help to study the current path to the light in Fig. 12-27, A-H.

In portion A of the figure, the current is allowed to pass through all of the switches to the light. When the right switch is flipped downward, see B, the connection is broken. If the middle switch, as at C, is operated, the current is allowed to flow to the lamp. If the left switch is operated, as at H, the circuit is broken and the lamp is turned off. By actuating the middle switch, see E, the circuit is completed and the lamp will be lit.

Outlet Controlled from Four Locations. A fixture or fixtures may be controlled from 4 different locations. Usually switches at two or three different places are sufficient; however, on occasion, it may be more convenient to have switches at four locations. Such an arrangement will increase the ultimate cost of wiring. To control an outlet from four locations requires 2 three-way and 2 four-way switches to be used in conjunction with each other. Fig. 12-28 shows a typical wiring method used in controlling a fixture with three-way and the through type four-way switches.

In portion A of Fig. 12-28 the current passes through all of the switches to the lamp. If the right four-way switch is operated (see B) to a downward position, the path of the current at this point is changed; therefore the circuit is broken. By moving the handle of the left four-way switch downward, the circuit is completed and the light will be lit. Follow the path of the current at D, E, and F in Fig. 12-28 to see how a fixture may be controlled from each different location. Fig. 12-28 shows only six of many switching combinations that are possible.

Feeders

Feeder cables run from the main control center or panelboard to the branch control center. (See Fig. 12-22 for a feeder run.) In some instances the feeder cable must be of sufficient size to carry 100 per cent of the branch center load if all of the equipment is in operation at the same time. Usually the rule of thumb is to use 75 per cent of the branch load to calculate the wire size. For example, an electric range may be rated between 8,000 and 14,000 W, but it is seldom that all four surface units, broiler, and oven would draw current at the same time. Similarly, this would be true with the other appliances connected to a branch circuit. The National Electrical Code gives standards for calculating load requirements. Feeder lines to the branch centers should not have wires any smaller than No. 10.

Service Conductors

To supploy full house power, the service conductor (see Fig. 12-21) must be of ample size to assume the electrical needs of the house. As with feeder cable, service conductor sizing assumes that not all the circuits are in use at any one time. A 3-wire service entrance with a 100 amp service switch is recommended by the Adequate Wiring Bureau. In many areas, the minimum service entrance requirement on new construction is 100 amps. The 150 amp service would be necessary if, in addition to the usual equipment, the house used a range, water heater, high speed dryer, and central air condition-

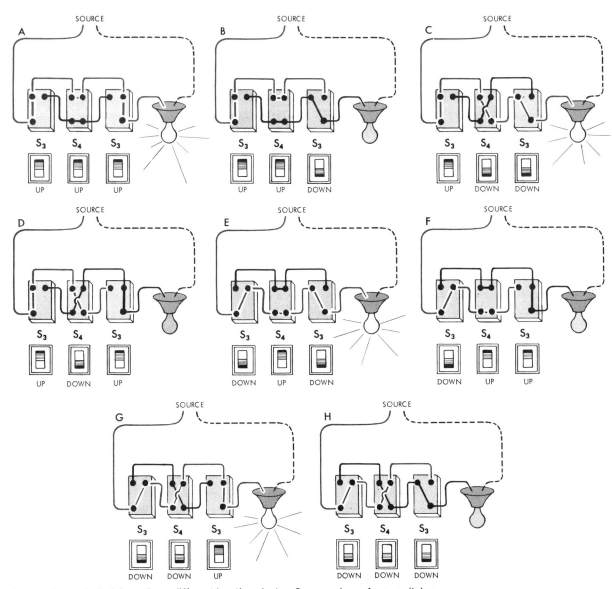

Fig. 12-27. An outlet may be controlled from three different locations by two 3-way and one 4-way switches.

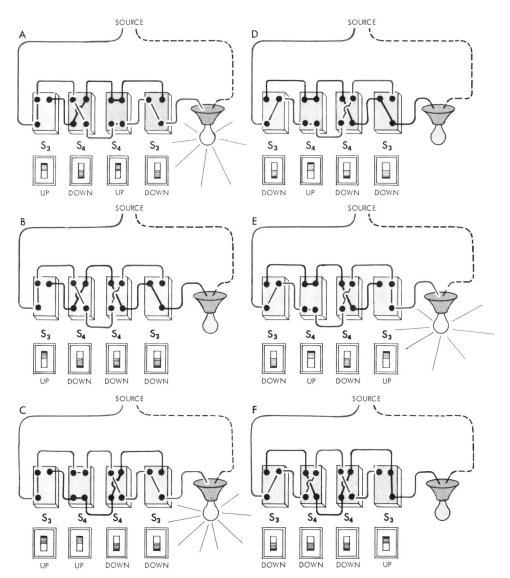

Fig. 12-28. An outlet may be controlled from 4 locations by a combination of two 3-way and two 4-way switches.

ing. If the house were heated electrically, in addition to the above mentioned items, a 200 amp service would be required.

Wiring Circuit Protection

In any house wiring circuit the cables or wires must be protected by some insulated covering. Essentially, there are four types of cable used in contemporary residential construction—each has its own particular use and special covering. See Fig. 12-29.

Rigid and Thin-wall Conduit. This type of indoor wiring is the most expensive, but it is also the safest. It provides the best protection against mechanical damage; at the same time it grounds the entire electrical system. It also provides fire protection since all wires are encased in tubing. Some building codes (for safety) require that conduit be used to protect all wires leading from the bottom of the first floor joists to the convenience outlets along the basement wall. Conduit is generally used only in new construction—since installation in old buildings is expensive and difficult. Some communities require all wiring to be conduit.

Thin-wall conduit may be used in wet or dry areas. It may also be used in masonry and concrete. Rigid conduit is made of steel which is coated with enamel or zinc. Thin-wall conduit or tubing is also of steel, but is lighter and easily cut or bent with a forming tool. No threading is required on thin-wall conduit. Black conduit has a very limited application since it is *not* permitted if it is

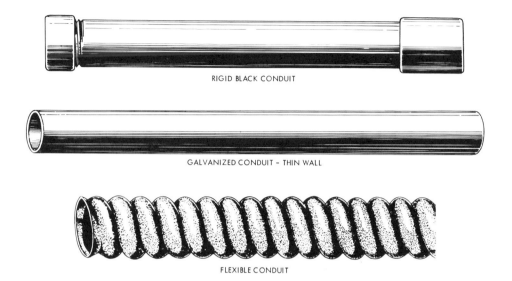

Fig. 12-29. Various types of conduit used for electrical wiring.

Fig. 12-30. Non-metallic sheathing cable.

which is highly resistant to damage by fire, rodents, acid, weather, or mechanical injury. See Fig. 12-30. An advantage of this type of cable over the non-metallic sheathed type, is that it may be buried underground. A plastic sheathed cable is flexible enough to be pulled through walls and floors, thus permitting its use in existing construction.

Working Drawings

All electrical outlets, switches, and fixtures are shown on *all* plans that contain those electrical components. The path of the switch(s) to fixtures and/or convenience outlets is shown graphically by a curved broken line. *It is not drawn freehand!* The dashed lines connecting a fixture or outlet to a switch *does not* show the intended paths of wires. The dashed line only indicates which fixture(s) or outlet(s) are controlled by a switch(s). See Fig. 12-31.

Circuit wires, conduit or cable runs are normally not indicated on residential electrical plans. Large structures such as commercial buildings, condominiums, high rise apartment complexes, or town houses, generally have the circuit wires, conduit, and

exposed to moisture or corrosion. The term "black" is derived from the black enamel coating which is applied that may chip or crack and allow oxidation.

Armored Cable. This type of indoor wiring consists of two or more insulated wires protected by a wound, galvanized steel strip cover. This metal winding forms a flexible tube. Frequently, armored cable is referred to as "B-X". Armored Cable is limited to indoor, dry locations. Because of its flexible covering, this type of cable can be used as an extension to a previously installed conduit system. Armored cable is considered acceptable by most building codes. It offers protection similar to rigid conduit. Its most common application in current building

codes is for flexible connections at motor terminals.

Non-metallic Sheathed Cable. This is a flexible cable which may be used for surface or concealed wiring in damp locations. Because of its non-metallic sheathing, this type of cable may not be used underground or in masonry work. The cable consists of two or more wires encased in a braided fabric jacket which resists fire, moisture, and acid vapors. An advantage of a sheathed cable is that it is easily "fished" through floors and walls. It can be readily attached to floor and wall surfaces.

Plastic Sheathed Cable. This type of cable is replacing the old lead sheathed cable. The wires are sheathed by a plastic material

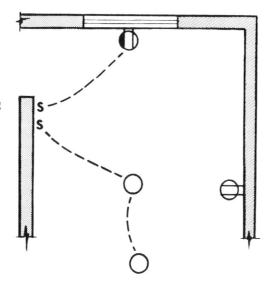

Fig. 12-31. The dashed or broken line connecting the fixture and switch does not indicate the path of the wire.

cable wires shown. Large building projects, as those previously mentioned, require the services of an electrical engineer who indicates outlets, conduit runs, panelboards and other items. As the electrical engineer does this, he writes the specifications which clearly designate in detail the standards for materials and workmanship.

The architectural designer usually does not design the circuit layout, conduit runs, wire requirements, etc. on the electrical plan. His only job is to indicate the locations of fixtures, outlets and switches. The electrical contractor in the case of residential construction, or electrical engineer in commercial applications will lay out the types of circuit, wire requirements, panel board locations, etc. The architect and de-

signer, however, must be familiar with the general electrical requirements in construction.

In residential work, specifically single family dwellings, the services of an electrical engineer are seldom, if ever, required for electrical planning. The architect or designer furnishes the home builder or contractor with an electrical plan, similar to the one shown in Fig. 12-32. An electrical plan locates fixtures, switches, etc. Occasionally the designer may not show any fixtures or switches on the electrical plan. The location of each item is determined in a meeting between the general contractor, client (homeowner), and electrical contractor.

At some point *prior* to the contractors'

wiring of the structure, the home owner must select the type of fixtures (recessed soffit lights wall bracket, ceiling outlet, etc.), and switches (touch, mercury, etc.) that are to be used. When a house is planned within a specific budget, the designer will frequently specify a given amount of money to be allotted for electrical fixtures. Any cost over the stipulated amount for fixtures is paid for by the client.

A typical electrical plan is shown in Fig. 12-32. The following is an explanation of each symbol and its use. The east and west exterior entry is lighted by flush mounted outlets (4) in the soffit of the overhang. Both of these outlets are controlled from 2 locations by a three-way switch (12). Each entry at the living room and dining room has a push button (9) that is connected to a bell or chime (10) in the dining area. One tone of the chime indicates the west entry and the other tone indicates the east push button has been used.

The deck is lit by two exterior wall brackets (7) controlled by 2 three-way switches at either entryway. Two weatherproof convenience outlets (15) are placed on the outside so appliances may be used on the deck. The east stair leading to the grade is illuminated by a wall bracket (7). This light is operated by an exterior weatherproof three-way switch (18), below the light and a three-way switch adjacent to the east entry door.

The dining area ceiling outlet (6) is controlled by a dimmer switch (17) at the west entry door. A dimmer switch controls the amount of current from zero volts to the

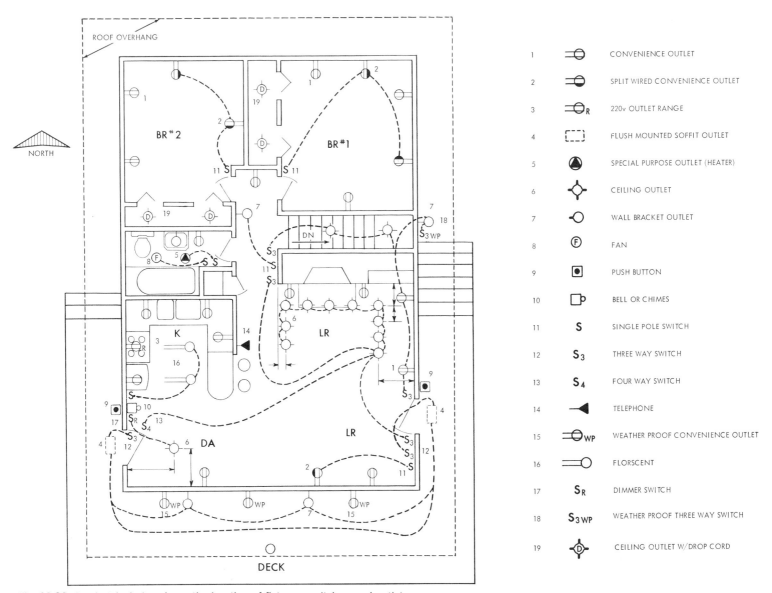

Fig. 12-32. An electrical plan shows the location of fixtures, switches, and outlets.

1		CONVENIENCE OUTLET
2		SPLIT WIRED CONVENIENCE OUTLET
3		220v OUTLET RANGE
4		FLUSH MOUNTED SOFFIT OUTLET
5		SPECIAL PURPOSE OUTLET (HEATER)
6		CEILING OUTLET
7		WALL BRACKET OUTLET
8		FAN
9		PUSH BUTTON
10		BELL OR CHIMES
11	S	SINGLE POLE SWITCH
12	S₃	THREE WAY SWITCH
13	S₄	FOUR WAY SWITCH
14		TELEPHONE
15	WP	WEATHER PROOF CONVENIENCE OUTLET
16		FLORSCENT
17	SR	DIMMER SWITCH
18	S₃WP	WEATHER PROOF THREE WAY SWITCH
19	D	CEILING OUTLET W/DROP CORD

full line 115V to the outlet. Note that dimensions are given for the location of this ceiling fixture. Normally dimensions are not given on an electrical plan unless a specific location is desired. For example, the location of a ceiling fixture or the height from the finish floor to a convenience outlet or switch.

The kitchen is lighted by two fluorescent fixtures (16) and controlled by a switch (11) next to the west entry. One convenience outlet (1) is provided for the refrigerator and three convenience outlets are placed above the counter top in the work space area. A heavy duty (220 V) outlet (3) is located in the area of the range.

In the living room ten flush mounted (6) hi-hat ceiling outlet lights are operated from three different locations. Two three-way switches and a four-way switch (13) operate these lights from the stairwell and both entryways in the dining area and living room. Four convenience outlets are planned in the living room area. Note that two of these convenience outlets are on either side of the fireplace opening.

In some cases one of the 2 outlets of a duplex convenience outlet is connected to a switch. This is called a *split wired convenience outlet* (2). A split wired outlet is shown in the living room and bed rooms #1 and #2. The purpose in split wiring an outlet is to allow a lamp or other electrical device to be controlled from some remote location.

A telephone (14) is placed adjacent to the breakfast bar in the hallway. Also in the hall, a wall bracket is controlled by a single pole switch at the stairwell. A convenience outlet at the north end of the hall is used for a vacuum cleaner or other electrically operated device.

The stairwell has two ceiling fixtures operated by 2 three-way switches at the top and bottom (not shown) of the stairwell. The bathroom has a convenience outlet wall bracket light, fan (8) and special outlet (5) for a ceiling mounted heater. Both of the latter two fixtures are actuated by individual single pole switches on the south wall of the bath.

Bedrooms #1 and #2 contain similar fixtures. Two of the convenience outlets in each of these rooms are split wired and operated by a single pole switch at the door. Each closet has two ceiling outlet fixtures with drop cords (19).

The basement plan would depict, if these items were to be included in the house, the following: convenience outlets, special purpose outlet, drop cord equipped outlet, clock outlet, single-pole switches, three-way switches, inter-connecting telephone, television outlet, and a distribution panel. Fig. 12-33 illustrates the basement wiring of a

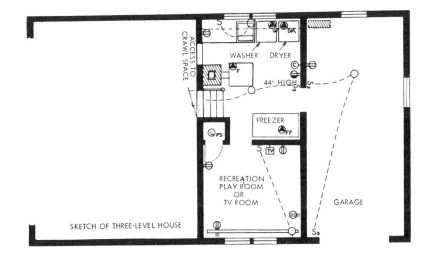

BASEMENT

AMERICAN STANDARD REQUIREMENTS FOR RESIDENTIAL WIRING.

Fig. 12-33. This plan illustrates the basement wiring for a three-level house.

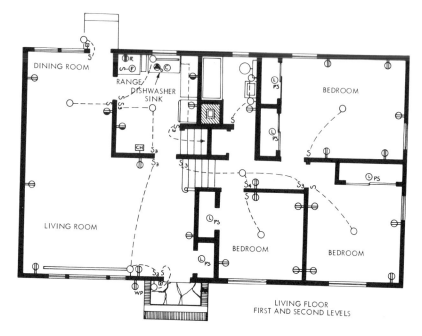

DINING ROOM

RANGE
DISHWASHER
SINK

CH

LIVING ROOM

BEDROOM

BEDROOM

BEDROOM

WP

LIVING FLOOR
FIRST AND SECOND LEVELS

AMERICAN STANDARD REQUIREMENTS FOR RESIDENTIAL WIRING.

Fig. 12-34. This figure illustrates the wiring for the first and second levels of the same three-level home.

split-level house. The wiring of the first and second levels of the same house is shown in Fig. 12-34.

The drawings are given to the electrical contractor to plan the type of wiring and to estimate the cost of services and materials. The contractor should receive the full set of plans so that he may determine the type of construction and the problems he may encounter relative to walls, floors, interior partitions, attic construction, crawl space, location of furnace and water heater, etc.

Questions and Problems

These questions and problems have been devised as a learning experience for you. Answer each carefully.

1. In your home, how many extension cords are used to supply current to small appliances?

2. How may an overloaded circuit be detected other than by a fuse failure?

3. How many electrical appliances has your family purchased in the past two years that have not been replacements for previously used appliances?

4. Study the lighting arrangement in your house. Is it adequate? How could the arrangement be improved? Draw a floor plan showing the existing (or improved) lighting.

5. Following the "Residential Wiring Recommendations" section in this chapter, plan the placement of fixtures, switches, outlets, etc., for the accepted floor plan designed in Chapter 5.

6. How many general purpose circuits will be necessary for your plan based on 15 amp rated circuits? 20 amp rated circuits?

7. What difference exists between a polarized outlet and a double convenience outlet? What purpose or advantage does the polarized outlet have?

8. Rearrange the bedroom furniture in problem 5. Sketch the new furniture arrangement. Will all of the convenience outlets be usable? What changes were necessary and why?

9. From how many locations may a 3-way switch be operated?

Conditioned Air 13

As indicated in the preceding chapter, the architect usually does not plan in detail the electrical wiring for a structure. Similarly, he does not plan the whole air conditioning system. **(Air conditioning** as used here includes both the heating and cooling systems.) Specialized contractors or consulting engineers normally do the actual detail planning. The architect or designer should, however, be able to locate the outlets and "size" the heating and cooling units. This is necessary since the contractors base their planning on the working drawings and specifications.

For utmost comfort air conditioning must perform four basic functions: (1) temperature control, (2) humidity control, (3) air circulation and ventilation control, and (4) air filtering. Fig. 13-1 illustrates the main functions of the residential air conditioning system.

Residential Heating Systems

Methods of heating have changed since the late 1940's and early 1950's. Prior to this period the stoker or hand-fired coal furnace with a gravity hot-air system was the most common type of home heating unit. Due to the price of coal and the consumer's desire for a cleaner burning fuel (plus the convenience of not having to shovel coal and remove ashes) the public has gradually moved to gas and oil. Before the mid 1950's new homes were frequently equipped with one- and two-pipe hot water and steam systems, as well as forced and gravity warm-air systems. Today, few steam, gravity hot water, or gravity warm-air systems are installed in new construction. Fig. 13-2 gives an analysis of heating systems, their outlets, and suitability.

Factors involved in selecting the type of heating facility are many. However, the basic choice is dependent upon: (1) the geographic location, relative to the availability of fuels; (2) the severity of the temperatures during the heating season; and (3) the cost and installation fee of the heating unit.

Heat Distribution

There are two basic methods by which heat may be distributed to areas: pipe and duct. Pipe requires the least amount of space

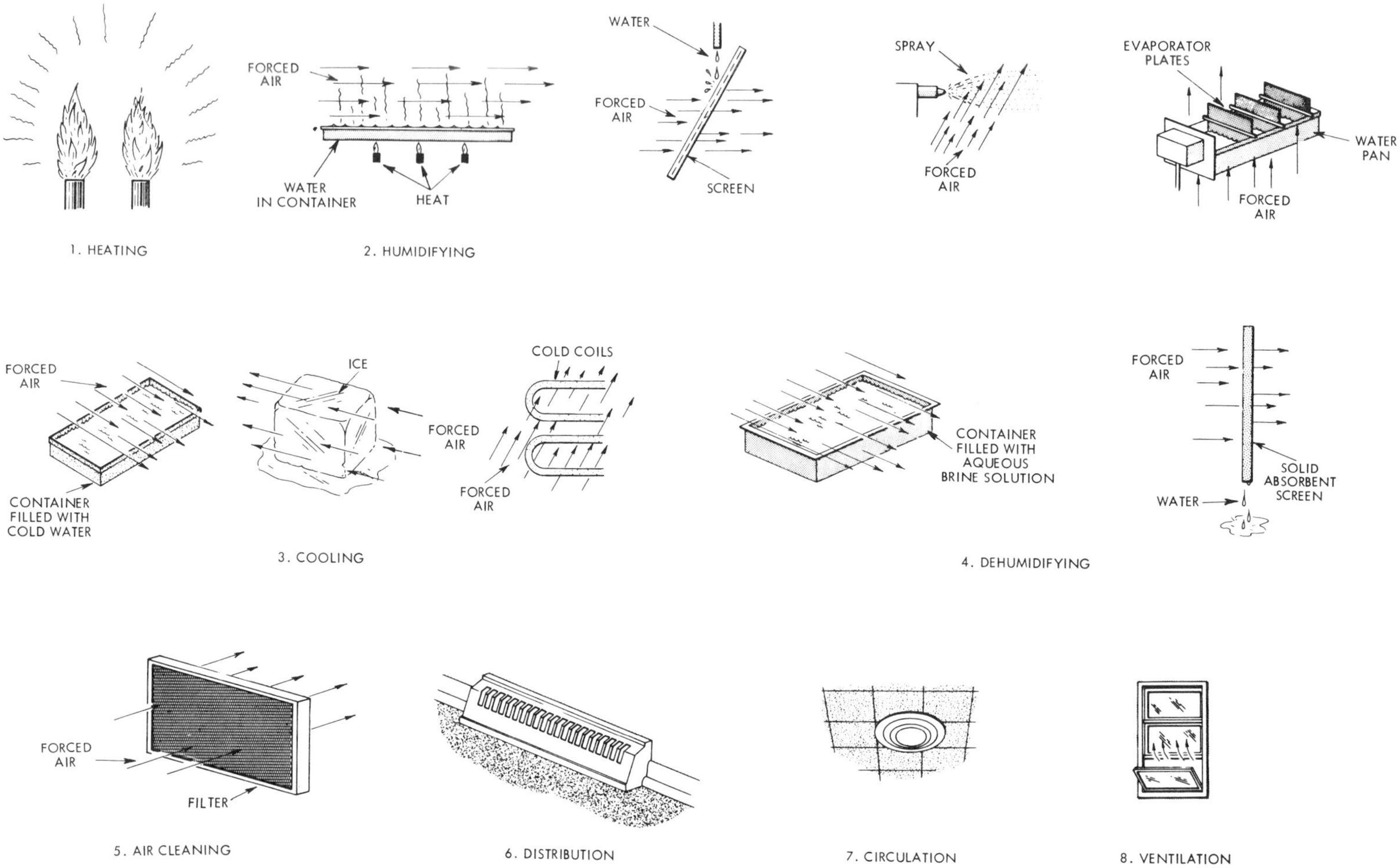

Fig. 13-1. Eight functions are performed with true year-round air conditioning.

to transmit the heat. Pipes are used to carry hot water or steam to a radiator, baseboard unit, or radiant panel located in the floor, ceiling, or wall. Ducts require more space than pipes. However, the ease with which ducts may be used for cooling and for humidification from one central location is a distinct advantage. (A pipe system may also be used for cooling if blower-equipped convector outlets are used.) Ducts are placed between floor or ceiling joists and between studs in walls.

Different methods are available to distribute heat: (1) baseboard, floor, and wall diffusers, used for warm air systems; (2) con-

TYPE OF HEAT		HEAT OUTLETS	
		TYPE	IDEALLY SUITED FOR
WARM AIR	FORCED	Register Diffuser	Houses with or without basements
	GRAVITY	Register	Rarely used in new construction or basementless houses
HOT WATER	FORCED	Baseboard unit Hollow or Finned Radiator Convector Radiant Panel	Houses with or without basements
	GRAVITY	Baseboard unit Hollow or Finned Radiator Convector	Rarely used in new construction or basementless houses
STEAM	ONE PIPE	Radiator Convector	
	TWO PIPE	Baseboard Hollow or Finned Radiator Convector	Not used in basement—less houses Rarely used in new construction

Fig. 13-2. Analysis of Heating Systems: The heating system should be suited to the house.

vectors, radiators, and baseboard (radiant and convector) type units, used for steam and hot water systems; and (3) radiant panel units, used for hot water and electrical systems. See Figs. 13-3 and 13-4.

Heating Methods

Fundamentally, there are three methods of heating the structure: (1) forced warm air, (2) hot water or steam, and (3) radiant panel.

Forced warm air is driven into the room through baseboard, floor, or side-wall diffusers or registers. The warm air rises (since it is lighter), then cools and settles. Circulation of air is aided by a blower, hence the name *forced air*. The blower returns the cool air to the furnace through a cold-air return located along the baseboard.

Hot Water or Steam. Room air, with hot water or steam heat, is warmed by hot water or steam passing through a radiator, convector, or baseboard unit. The radiator

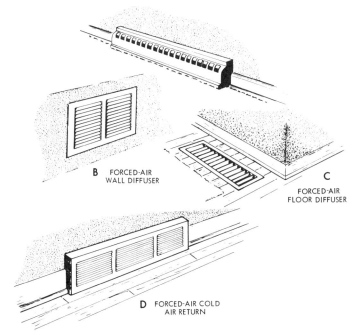

B FORCED-AIR WALL DIFFUSER

C FORCED-AIR FLOOR DIFFUSER

D FORCED-AIR COLD AIR RETURN

Fig. 13-3. Wall diffusers are used in the forced-air system.

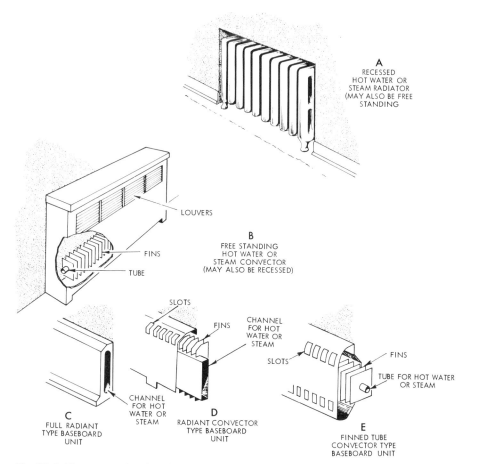

Fig. 13-4. These room heating devices are used for hot water or steam systems. (**Note:** Some convector units are equipped with fans.)

radiates a certain amount of heat, but the majority of heat is given off through convection. The convector, as its name implies, transmits heat by convection: that is, the air is heated by passing over the convector fins. Both methods of heating the room are efficient. Baseboard units may be used to heat the room in lieu of radiators or convectors.

Radiant Panel. The last method of heat-ing the house is by means of radiant panels (pipes, ducts, or electric resistance wire) installed in the floor, wall, or ceiling. The room is warmed by heat rays reflecting off various surfaces in the room. True radiant heat does not employ any radiators or baseboard diffusers.

Thermostat

All types of heating equipment installed in new construction is generally regulated by a thermostat which can be set for a desired temperature. If the temperature falls below this indicated point, the heat will automatically turn on. Most thermostats are designed to maintain a constant temperature. Some are designed to permit a low temperature for a specified length of time, and at a certain time the temperature will be raised to the desired degree. Location of the thermostat is an important feature not to be overlooked. An ideal location is on an inside wall approximately 4'-6" or 5'-0" from the floor. For the utmost efficiency the thermostat should be placed away from (1) the warm afternoon sun; (2) heat from a warm-air outlet; (3) cold air from an exterior door; and, especially, (4) the direct or reflected heat rays from the fireplace. The thermostat is usually placed in or near an area where most activity takes place.

Humidity

During the heating season it is desirable that moisture be used to condition the indoor air. Outside air during the cold season is normally much drier than inside air and when mixed they tend to lower the indoor relative humidity.

Storm windows, weatherstripping, and tighter construction has decreased the amount of infiltrating outdoor air. Although moisture is added to the indoor air by cooking, bathing, dishwashing, and laundering, it is not sufficient to raise the humidity to a desirable, healthful level. New homes with effective vapor barriers need less humidifying than normally required to maintain the desired indoor relative humidity.

Generally a relative humidity of 40 to 50 per cent is considered ideal. This amount provides the best protection against airborne infections and has a soothing effect upon the nose and throat. In addition, sufficient humidity permits woodwork and other home furnishings to retain their moisture; it also retards rapid deterioration.

When the outdoor temperature drops below 40° the relative humidity should be lowered enough to prevent excessive condensation on windows and structural components.

Forced Warm-Air Heating

Heating systems in many new homes being built use forced warm air. This system is an advancement over the gravity warm-air system. The gravity system employs large round pipes that extend octopus-like from the furnace to wall registers and cold-air returns. The forced-air system has replaced the old outlets with smaller ducts and neat, functional wall-type or base-type grilles. The forced-air or blower system insures a more direct and even circulation than the old gravity-type furnace.

All warm-air heating systems are composed of four parts: (1) a *firebox* in which the fuel (gas or oil) is burned, (2) an *air chamber* in which the air is heated, (3) a *cold air box or chamber* in which the air is returned for circulation, and (4) the *ducts* in which the heated air is carried to various rooms of the house. Humidifiers, either evaporating plate, vaporizing, or atomizer, are installed to add moisture (50 per cent relative humidity) to the air. This makes the air more comfortable to breathe. Electrostatic or fiber filters may be installed in the cold-air return of the furnace to remove dust and dirt particles prior to their entry into the heating chamber. The filter may be an easily cleaned permanent type, an inexpensive throw-away type, or an electrostatically charged type. Any of the three methods of filtering the air is satisfactory.

The forced warm-air system should provide approximately four to six air changes per hour for the average size five or six room house. The warm air leaves the air chamber at approximately 155° F and arrives at the room at approximately 140° F. Some of the heat is lost in the transmission from the furnace to the rooms.

Forced-air furnaces do not depend upon the different weights of hot and cold air to provide circulation within a room. The forced-air furnace, either gas or oil fired or heated by electric coils, is equipped with a blower that draws cool air into the air chamber and expels the heated air through the ducts to the outlets in the various rooms. Since the heated air is moving under force through the ducts, the furnace need not be placed in a central location of the house and may be above or below floor level. Outlet grilles or registers may be placed high on the walls or near the floor. Placement has been widely discussed among heating engineers and contractors. By placing the warm-air outlet high on the wall and deflecting the warm air stream downward at a 15° angle, a more uniform temperature between the floor and ceiling may be achieved. The outlet is usually placed so that its top edge is a minimum of 6″ below the ceiling line. Outlets located in this position force the warm air over the heads of the persons in the room to produce an even temperature. Heat may also be distributed by baseboard registers. This is probably the most common method. The duct is connected directly to the baseboard unit. This "register" has a narrow opening along the top edge that emits a film of warm air along the wall. In addition, the baseboard becomes warm and heats the room as a small radiant panel.

Each area must be supplied with a warm-air outlet and a cold-air return. The kitchen and bathroom, however, *do not usually* have a cold-air return. Cold-air returns are normally placed on a warm or inside wall at baseboard level to collect the downdrafts.

Forced warm-air outlets are placed so that warm air is blown against or across outside walls and/or windows. Rooms larger than 10′ × 10′ will require two or more warm-air outlets. Ducts to supply the outlets may be run in the basement or attic space or along the ceiling of the room to be heated. The structure designed with a basement or with a crawl space will usually have the ductwork between the floor joists. Base-mentless buildings may have the supply ducts placed in the ceiling or imbedded in the floor.

Warm-Air Perimeter-Loop System

Perimeter-loop heating, used almost exclusively in basementless slab houses, has a duct system which encircles the slab. Fig. 13-5 shows the general principle of the perimeter-loop system with four feeder ducts supplying the perimeter duct. The ducting may be sheet metal, concrete pipe, vitrified tile, or other precast materials. Because the perimeter-loop system is used essentially in slab homes, a downdraft furnace is necessary. (Be sure to note the differentiation in furnaces when selecting from a catalog.) Warm air is forced through the ducts and is discharged into the room through floor or baseboard diffusers. The air is returned to the furnace via air intakes either on an inside wall or in a hallway ceiling close to the furnace.

This type of system is economical to install and needs little floor space. Because the perimeter duct is imbedded in the floor and is connected to the furnace by feeder ducts, cold floors are eliminated. A humidifier and filter may be installed to eliminate dryness and dirt.

Forced Warm-Air Extended-Plenum System

Air warmed by the heating unit may also be distributed by a blower through the *plenum* and ducts to the baseboard diffusers. (A plenum system functions by placing the air under a higher *pressure*.) The blower draws the room air back to the furnace through the cold-air return and return ducts to be filtered, reheated, and humidified. After it has been heated, the air is then distributed again. Fig. 13-6 illustrates a portion of an extended-plenum installation. Note the baseboard diffuser is placed below a window and the return air intake is located along an inside wall.

In comparison to hot water and steam heating systems, the extended-plenum system has the advantage of being more economical to install. This system is well

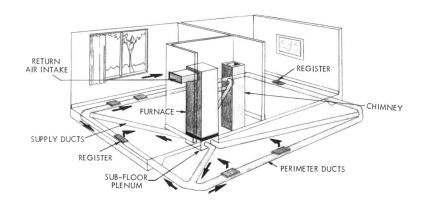

Fig. 13-5. Warm-Air Perimeter-Loop System.

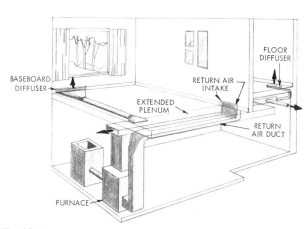

Fig. 13-6. Forced Warm-Air Extended-Plenum System.

adapted to buildings with and without basements because the blower maintains air circulation.

One-Pipe Hot Water System

The one-pipe, forced hot water system, shown in Fig. 13-7, is probably the most widely used of all *hydronic* (heating or cooling with water) systems in residential construction. Heat for this system is generated by an automatically controlled gas or oil burner that heats the water in the boiler. With the one-pipe system the boiler may be located in the basement or in the utility room on grade level. A single *main* pipe usually follows the perimeter of the building, and *branches* or *risers* connect to the radiators, convectors, or baseboard units. Special flow fittings are placed at the return of each radiator or convector so that a single pipe may be used for supply and return of the water. The flow fittings separate the cooled water from the hot water leading to the next unit. As the *main* leaves the boiler, a flow valve is placed at the first elbow. This valve opens under the flowing water pressure when the circulating pump is operating and closes when the pump is not operating. If this flow valve were not placed in the main, the water would continue to circulate, causing overheated radiators and convectors. An expansion tank permits the water to expand and contract with the changes in temperature, thereby keeping the boiler and radiator filled with water.

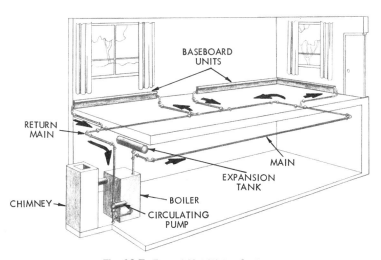

Fig. 13-7. Forced Hot Water System.

Radiant Heat Panels

One of the general laws of physics states that heat will radiate from a source of higher temperature to one of lower temperature. The same principle applies in heating individual rooms. When one is in a room and "feels" comfortable, his body is maintaining or losing a *normal* amount of heat. If the body loses a high degree of heat, one "feels" cold. For example, if the room temperature is 50° F and the body is at a normal 98.6° F, the body is losing more than the average amount of heat and "feels" cold. If the room has a temperature of 100° F one will experience a warm sensation since the body is receiving heat.

With air current heating (convection) the occupant is surrounded with circulating warm air; with radiant heating the occupant is surrounded with warm surfaces and objects. No air currents are set in motion with radiant heating since the heat rays go directly between the heated wall, ceiling, or floor to other surfaces. Almost all surfaces in the room act as reflectors, and an infinite number of reflecting, radiant rays travel in all directions. When all objects in the room have been brought to an adequate temperature, the room and its occupants will be comfortable. Comparatively little temperature difference exists between the floor and ceiling in a radiantly heated room. For example, if the heat source (hot water pipes or resistance wires) are located in the floor, a temperature difference of approximately 7° exists between the floor and ceiling.

Many basementless slab buildings, as shown in Fig. 13-8, have some form of radiant floor panel heat. If the radiant panel is heated by hot water, a serpentine coil, as in Fig. 13-9 is used. The coil is placed on a prepared base, usually concrete, and another layer of concrete is poured over the coil. The hot water is then circulated through the pipe by a pump. The amount of heat is controlled by the temperature of the water circulated through the pipe coil. Some radiant panels are heated by electric resistance wire. These, too, may be located in floors, ceilings, or walls.

Since the weight and mass of a radiant panel located in a ceiling or wall is considerably less than that of a floor panel embedded in concrete, the room temperature can be changed more rapidly. Lower night temperatures can be obtained more satisfactorily if the panel is located in the ceiling.

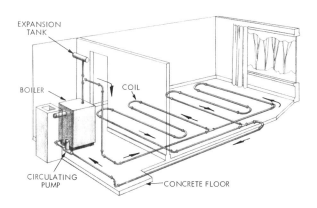

Fig. 13-8. Hot Water Panel System.

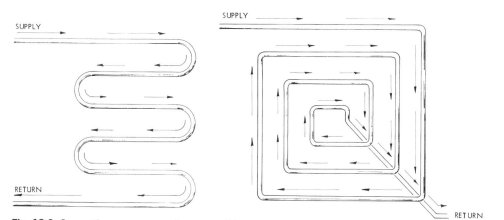

Fig. 13-9. Serpentine or square coils are used in radiant panel, floor, and ceiling heating.

Electric Heat

In some areas of the United States and in several European countries, rapid progress has been made in residential electric heating. Power companies that offer attractive kilowatt-hour rates to the consumer, as well as new and more effective types of insulative materials, have placed electric heat on a competitive basis with other fuels. However, many misconceptions exist about the function of electricity in space heating. This section will attempt to point out the various types of electric heating equipment and their basic principles.

Heating with electricity offers a number of decided advantages over the "conventional" methods previously discussed. Electric heating provides an even, draft-free warmth without periodic cooling or over-heating. Temperatures in each area may be maintained at the desired level since individual thermostats or automatic controlling devices are installed with each unit. To economically heat any structure with electricity, consideration must be given to proper insulation to reduce the heat loss. This added insulation not only serves as a sound deadener, both from the outside and from floor to floor, but also aids in reducing the inside temperature during the summer months.

With many electric heating devices, maintenance is cut or practically eliminated since the individual room control thermostat is usually the only moving part. To many, the silence of the electric heating system is a great asset. In new construction, often an electrical heating system can be installed for the same amount as the regular gas- or oil-fired systems. Since the chimney and space for fuel storage is eliminated, and in most electric heating systems duct work is nonexistent, lower building costs can be achieved. (This may be reflected in the size of a mortgage loan and may result in lower monthly payments.)

There are, however, disadvantages. In some areas, in comparison with other fuels, operating costs are higher. Some power companies, however, give very favorable rates to consumers having electric heat. Electric power failure is a disadvantage. However, no system using a blower will function without electricity. More insula-

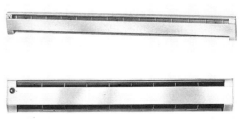

Fig. 13-10. Electric baseboards heat by radiation and convection. Some convection baseboard units are equipped with an individual thermostat.

BERKO ELECTRIC MFG. CORP.; JAMAICA, NEW YORK.

tion is required to hold the heat than with conventional heating systems. Humidity control can be a problem with resistance type radiant heaters because these do not employ moving air. To counteract the absence of humidity, a humidistat-operated ventilating fan may be necessary.

Electrical Heating Methods

Various means are available for the builder to equip the home for electric heating. Principles of operation vary. The various electrical heating units and their operation are examined in the following paragraphs.

Baseboard Electric Heating Units. Baseboard units give a uniform degree of heat over a wide area. Some of these units emit heat by both radiation and convection and are designed to replace the standard base and shoe moldings. See Fig. 13-10. These units have an opening at the bottom that allows the air to enter and pass over the resistance element. Another opening at the top allows the air to escape. Some baseboard units have attached thermostats (Fig. 13-10,

bottom) but frequently they are controlled by a wall-mounted device. A recent development in baseboard heating is the *hydronic* unit (Fig. 13-11). Each hydronic baseboard unit is filled with water and is heated by an immersion element, thus producing more evenly distributed heat since the water-filled tubes will not cool as rapidly as a resistance element.

Both the convector and hydronic units are

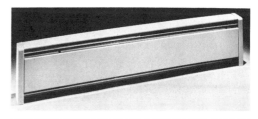

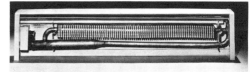

INTERNATIONAL OIL BURNER CO., ST. LOUIS, MISSOURI.

13-11. Hydronic baseboard heaters are a relatively new innovation in electric heating. Each unit is self contained.

used to heat entire buildings. They are also used to heat individual rooms that have been added to an existing dwelling.

Ceiling and Wall Electric Heating Units. Electric ceiling units or electric wall units warm the occupants of a room with radiant heat rays. The most common type of ceiling or wall unit is the resistance heater that radiates heat through a protective metal grille or screen. Fig. 13-12 shows a ceiling-type resistance radiant heater. Some architects and designers are specifying wall insert heaters in newly constructed motels, vacation homes, structural additions, etc. These heating units are so designed that they will

HUNTER DIVISION, MYERS & ROBBINS, INC., MEMPHIS, TENNESSEE.

Fig. 13-13. Some electric heaters are designed to fit between normal stud placement as this wall insert heater.

MARKEL ELECTRIC PRODUCTS, INC., BUFFALO, NEW YORK.

Fig. 13-12. Electric ceiling heaters, such as this resistance type, are used in bathrooms to provide warmth after leaving the bath. Some units are equipped with a quiet fan.

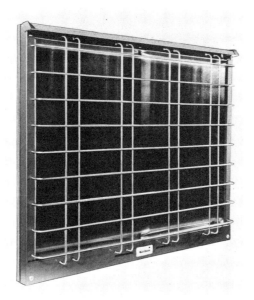

SUN-HEAT INC., ELECTRIC HEAT DIVISION OF INSTO-GAS CORP., DETROIT, MICHIGAN.

Fig. 13-14. Radiant glass panels are used in the ceiling or wall to provide spot heating. In some instances a series of panels are used to heat rooms.

fit between normally placed studs or in a concrete block wall. Fig. 13-13 shows a wall insert heater. Radiant glass panels (Fig. 13-14) are similar to the resistance heater with the exception that the resistance element is covered or imbedded in glass. Since the glass becomes hot, the panel is covered with a grille. Some wall and ceiling heaters may be equipped with a thermostat and/or fan to promote heat circulation. Frequently, rather than installing a resistance heater, an infrared unit may be desired for the wall or ceiling (Fig. 13-15.)

Wall and ceiling heaters are used in bathrooms where additional heat is required for short periods of time. Occasionally these are placed in kitchens, recreation areas, family rooms, or enclosed porches. Series of radiant glass panels may be used to heat an entire house. Infrared units are used mostly in bathrooms.

Where additions have been placed on commercial or industrial buildings original heating equipment generally is not sufficient to accommodate the increased area. Unit resistance blowers, see Fig. 13-16, may be suspended from the ceiling or mounted on the wall and easily solve this problem. These heaters are used, as well, in all-new construction.

Electric Cable Units. Electric wire used as a radiant cable converts electrical energy to heat energy. This works in the same way as the common resistance unit. Cable units (see Fig. 13-17) placed in plastered ceilings or walls are commonly covered with plastic or a non-flammable vinyl plastic material.

HUNTER DIVISION, MYERS & ROBBINS, INC., MEMPHIS, TENNESSEE.

Fig. 13-16. Electric resistance heaters are wall or ceiling mounted and installed with a minimum amount of labor and materials.

The electric cable is installed before the dry wall, plaster ceiling, or wall surface is applied. The whole wall or ceiling then radi-

Fig. 13-15. Quartz tube heaters provide infrared rays for heating.

HUNTER DIVISION, MYERS & ROBBINS, INC., MEMPHIS, TENNESSEE.

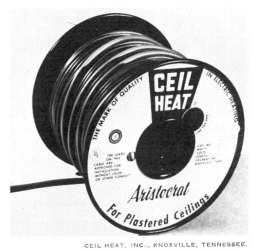

CEIL HEAT, INC., KNOXVILLE, TENNESSEE.

Fig. 13-17. Various types of radiant cable are available for heating ceilings, walls, and exterior areas of the house.

ates heat to the room. Several large manufacturers of drywall produce drywall with electric resistance wires embedded in the gypsum. The sets of wires are spliced together and connected to a thermostat to regulate the amount of current, thus controlling the temperature. This form of equipment is inexpensive, but it does not respond as well as other types of heating devices.

Cable may be used to heat one room or

Fig. 13-18. The electric duct heater is inserted directly into the ductwork.

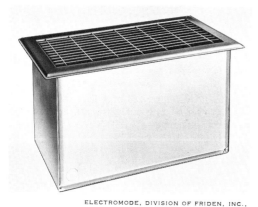

Fig. 13-19. Floor insert heaters are particularly suited for installation below floor to ceiling windows or sliding glass doors.

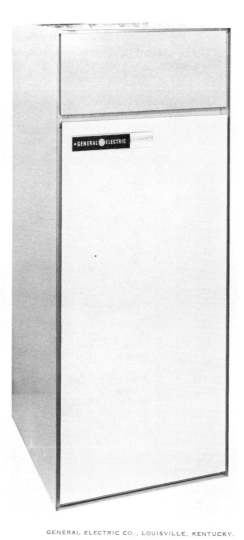

Fig. 13-20. The exterior of many furnaces are tastefully designed.

the entire home. It may also be placed in concrete floors, driveways, sidewalks, steps, downspouts, gutters, or roof edges to melt snow and ice. Cable is a temporary measure that may be used to eliminate ice dams that cause damage to gutters and shingles.

Duct and Floor Insert Heaters. Electric duct heaters (Fig. 13-18) are placed in forced-air ducts. The duct heater, in essence a resistance heater, is controlled by an integral or wall-located thermostat. The floor insert heater, shown in Fig. 13-19, is similar to the duct unit and it is placed in the floor. This unit is thermostatically controlled. These heaters are used to give additional heat or to provide complete heating requirements. The floor heater is ideally suited for installation below ceiling to floor windows and sliding glass patio doors.

Electric Furnaces. The exterior of many electric furnaces, as shown in Fig. 13-20, is well designed and pleasing in appearance. Electric furnaces heat *only* by convection. The resistance heating elements (Fig. 13-21) are arranged in a series and operate only as heat is needed. The motor driven blower propels the air over the heating elements, through the ducts, and into the rooms. Electric furnaces are not limited to forced-air heating; they may also be used with a boiler to supply hot water for radiators, convectors, and radiant panel heaters in both residential and commercial applications.

Some electric furnaces for residential heating are small enough to be placed in a closet or suspended from the basement ceiling. These are used to heat an entire house.

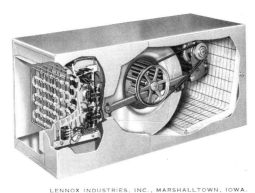

LENNOX INDUSTRIES, INC., MARSHALLTOWN, IOWA.

Fig. 13-21. This view shows the interior of an electrical furnace. Note the resistance elements, blower, and filter (Many electric furnaces are small enough to be concealed in a closet.)

WORTHINGTON AIR CONDITIONING CO.

Fig. 13-22. Heat pumps may draw heat from air, earth, or water. This is an air-cooled heat pump. Ductwork is required.

Electric Heat Pumps. One of the most recent developments in home heating has been the heat pump (Fig. 13-22). The natural heat from the outside air may be utilized with either a hot water or a forced warm-air system. Earth and water may also be used as a source of natural heat. The basic principle of the heat pump is similar to reverse refrigeration. In the summer months the heat pump acts as a cooling unit. The processes of heating and cooling are controlled by one or more thermostats located in the building.

For example, if water is the source of heat, the water will be pumped through a pipe coil buried below the frost line. As the water circulates through the coils of the heat pump, the heat is removed, thereby lowering the water temperature. The chilled water is then returned to the underground coil. The heat that has been removed is concentrated and distributed. When outside temperatures are low, 20° F or lower, heat pumps using the outside air or earth as a source of heat operate at a materially reduced level of efficiency. This requires a supplemental heat source. Some heat pump manufacturers employ an outdoor temperature control that disconnects the unit when the temperature drops below 20° F; the entire heating load is shunted to supplemental heaters. In areas where temperatures dip low, the size of the heat pump is determined by the summer cooling load. The additional heat that is required during the winter months is obtained from resistance heaters located in the duct work. (See Fig. 13-16.)

Installation costs of a heat pump are naturally higher than a resistance installation. However, the costs are comparable to separate heating and cooling systems. Reports indicate that operating costs of heat pumps are lower than the operating costs of resistance type units.

Insulation

The conveniences of electric heat can pay dividends *only if the structure is properly insulated.* Proper insulation will mean greater comfort, heating efficiency, and economy. Common insulating materials used in electrically heated buildings are: (1) loose fill (blown or poured) cellulose fiber, mineral wool, perlite, or expanded vermiculite; (2) blankets and batts of mineral wool or cellulose fiber; (3) roof deck panels, blocks, and slabs; (4) exterior fiber sheathing; (5) perimeter slabs, and block for concrete floor perimeters; (6) reflective insulation; and (7) interior panels, blocks, and tiles.

The Insulation Manufacturers' Association has adopted a uniform method of rating the effectiveness of all types of insulation when installed according to instructions. The purpose of any insulative material is to *resist* heat flow; the "resistance" of a specific thickness and type of insulation is indicated by an "R" value. This number designates the amount of resistance the material has to heat passage. For example, a piece of insulative material of a given thickness may have a R value of 12 (this is written as R-12). The insulation just specified, having a value of R-12, would offer only ¾ as much resistance as one having a value of R-16. *The higher the R value, the higher the resistance.* The following quantities of insulation are recommended for electrically heated residences.

Ceilings: 8″ or equivalent to R-28
Side walls: 4″ or equivalent to R-13
Floors: 4″ or equivalent to R-14

Additional information on insulation can be found in Chapter 9, "Construction Details: Foundations and Main Structures."

Zoned Heat Control

Zone control of the heating system is becoming more important because of the changing habits of the home owner, as well as the contemporary methods of construction and architectural styles. One thermostat located in a central position cannot satisfy the heating requirements for an entire house. This is particularly true in large homes, split-level or rambling ranch-type homes, office and commercial buildings. For some dwellings several control devices may be necessary to provide the desired heat ranges throughout the structure.

Prior to modern advances in heating it was customary to wear heavy clothing indoors throughout the winter. This provided a definite control of the loss of body heat. Room to room temperatures could vary since the clothing afforded the necessary protection.

The architectural trends toward large windows and glass areas, rambling and less compact buildings, and multi-level dwellings have complicated the problem of temperature control. Frequently, one section of the building may be sheltered, while another section may be exposed to a hard driving winter wind. One section may be exposed to the warm afternoon sun, while another may be shaded. Each section of the building has its own requirements according to its orientation and the desires of the occupants.

To accommodate these differences in heating requirements, the distribution of heat may be *zoned*. A zone is an area in which the temperature is controlled separately from another area of the building. A dwelling may be zoned by rooms, groups of rooms, or by levels. The size, orientation, protection surrounding the structure, and the activities of the occupants will determine the number of zones required.

Zoned heat is based on the premise that the piping, air ducts, or radiant panels are arranged so that heat to each area can be controlled with automatic valves, circulating pumps, or dampers. Hydronic systems probably offer more advantages than other systems because of their obvious adaptability to zone control. Overheating the entire house to increase the heat in one area is eliminated with multiple controls. The cost of zoning, of course, is greater because additional equipment is necessary. Over the years, however, the extra investment will be returned in added comfort and lower fuel costs.

Planning Points

The following set of items should be considered in planning the heating system and in planning the house. These criteria are by no means definitive, but they do provide a framework which may be used as a guide.

1. Modern space heaters are compactly and attractively designed and may function as furniture. Heating units placed in the basement or recreation area may serve as a source of direct heat without detracting from the appearance of the room.

2. Second floor partitions should be placed directly over the first floor partitions so ducts may run directly between floors. Ducts that cut partition caps weaken the building frame. However if this is necessary, the caps should be reinforced with steel plates. (Floor plans drawn on tracing paper are laid over each other to follow vertical duct runs.)

3. Floor joists should line up with wall studs if ducts are to be run horizontally.

4. Warm-air ducts should be located in interior partitions. If they are run in outside walls, they must be insulated to prevent heat loss.

5. For efficiency, duct runs should be as short as possible with a minimum number of turns and offsets.

6. If possible, registers and grilles should be located between studs and joists.

7. Forced warm-air outlets should be placed so warm air is blown against or across colder outside walls and/or windows.

8. Cold-air returns should be located low on a warm or inside wall to collect the downdrafts.
9. Radiators should be placed below windows or near cold walls. This allows cold air to be warmed before circulating in the room.
10. Baseboard heating units should be located around colder, outside walls. (They should blow upwards to counter downdrafts from windows.)
11. Radiant baseboard, floor insert heaters, or forced warm-air outlets may be used under picture windows.

Heat Loss and the Structure

Heat Loss

No material used in construction is a perfect insulator. As heat passes through the building materials, either by radiation or conduction, a significant amount of heat will be lost due to the lack of insulative qualities of the materials. Heat within the structure is also "lost" due to the air which infiltrates through the cracks around and in the frames of windows and doors. The combination of these factors is called *heat loss* and is measured in Btu's (British thermal units).

The Btu is the amount of heat required to raise the temperature of one pound of water through one degree Fahrenheit. If we raise the temperature of one pound of water from 96° F to 97° F, for example, the amount of heat (regardless of its nature)

used to increase the temperature one degree is equal to one Btu. Conversely, the amount of heat loss required to *reduce* the temperature of one pound of water one degree is also one Btu. All heat losses are expressed in terms of Btu's per hour or *Btuh*. This is the rate or amount of heat transferred or lost as expressed in British thermal units per hour.

Variations in construction, as well as the amount of insulation and ventilation, will control the amount of heat a structure may lose. *It is at this point in planning* that the architect or designer may utilize his knowledge of heating to specify those materials which will be most advantageous in retarding the flow of heat from the structure. As mentioned earlier, one of the basic principles of science is that heat is readily transferred to colder objects. In other words, it travels from a high temperature source to one of a lower source. Walls, floors, windows, and other structural elements in a dwelling act as transmission agents. Heat is transferred from the higher temperature source on the inside to the cooler temperature on the outside. This is called *heat loss.* (The reverse situation is called *heat gain.* Here the high temperature on the outside is transmitted to the cooler temperature on the inside. Heat gain is covered in the latter part of this chapter.)

Heat loss (or gain) will always occur as long as there is a temperature difference. To determine the amount of heat that is lost, each component material that forms the exterior wall, floor, or roof must be identified

as to the amount of insulative value it has. This quality of retarding heat flow is called a *transmission coefficient,* and is referred to as the *U-factor.* In addition, the difference between the outside and inside temperature will affect the *rate* at which the heat is lost. Clarifying this further, *the amount of heat loss* for a given area is dependent upon: (1) the type of construction, (2) the amount and type of insulation, (3) the temperature differential between the inside and outside, and (4) the amount of air infiltrating into the structure.

Calculating Heat Loss

To determine the amount of heat a structure will lose, it is necessary to calculate or locate in a prepared heat loss table the following:

1. Structural area
2. U values of
   a. type of exterior wall
   b. windows and doors in the wall
   c. ceiling
   d. floor
3. Temperature difference between inside and outside
4. Amount of air infiltrating into the room or structure

The formula for finding the heat loss is basically concerned, for the moment at least, with items 1, 2, and 3.

Heat loss = structural area × construction effectiveness × temperature difference.

Structural area refers to the area which is exposed to a different temperature than

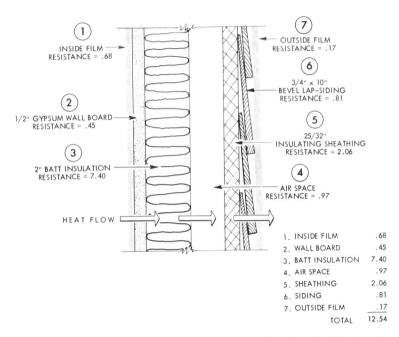

① INSIDE FILM RESISTANCE = .68

② 1/2" GYPSUM WALL BOARD RESISTANCE = .45

③ 2" BATT INSULATION RESISTANCE = 7.40

HEAT FLOW

⑦ OUTSIDE FILM RESISTANCE = .17

⑥ 3/4" x 10" BEVEL LAP-SIDING RESISTANCE = .81

⑤ 25/32" INSULATING SHEATHING RESISTANCE = 2.06

④ AIR SPACE RESISTANCE = .97

1. INSIDE FILM	.68
2. WALL BOARD	.45
3. BATT INSULATION	7.40
4. AIR SPACE	.97
5. SHEATHING	2.06
6. SIDING	.81
7. OUTSIDE FILM	.17
TOTAL	12.54

Fig. 13-23. Thermal resistance of a frame wall. To determine the U factor, all of the components must be added together (12.54) and the reciprocal calculated: 1 ÷ 12.54 = .0797. The **U factor** or **heat transmission factor** is .080. **Note:** This same wall **without insulation** would have a U factor of 0.195.

that in the room. This area may be the walls, ceiling, floor, or windows. The standard abbreviation for area is "A."

Construction effectiveness refers to the type of construction (that is, solid masonry, brick veneer, siding, stucco etc.) and the amount of insulation included in the wall. Every kind of wall has a specific ability to transfer heat. Each type of building material has been tested and assigned a *U-factor* (sometimes called a Btu Constant). The U-factor gives the number of Btu units trans-

mitted per square foot per hour per degree difference of inside and outside temperatures. This is abbreviated "U". Fig. 13-23 shows an example of one type of frame wall and the *thermal resistance* of each component and the resulting *U-factor*. It is interesting to note that by removing the mineral insulation from this wall the U-factor will increase, indicating that the wall will permit a greater heat loss. *The lower the U-factor the greater the insulative value of that structural member.* In other words, a smaller

amount of Btu's are lost through the material per square foot. Table 13-1 gives the U values for some of the common types of residential construction.

Temperature differential is a necessary factor that must be considered in correctly determining the size of the heating system. As the name implies, it is the difference between the colder outside temperature and the warmer inside temperature (see Fig. 13-24). This difference is abbreviated "T". The question arises — "What temperature do I choose—the coldest winter temperature?" No. A *design temperature* is used to

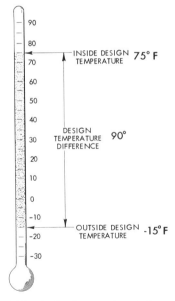

INSIDE DESIGN TEMPERATURE 75° F

DESIGN TEMPERATURE DIFFERENCE 90°

OUTSIDE DESIGN TEMPERATURE -15° F

Fig. 13-24. The design temperature is based on the difference between the inside and outside design temperatures.

TABLE 13-1

U-FACTORS FOR COMMON TYPES OF RESIDENTIAL CONSTRUCTION AND BUILDING COMPONENTS

STRUCTURAL COMPONENT	NOT INSULATED U	INSULATED U
1. EXTERIOR WALLS		
Frame Superstructure		
a. Interior finish, insulation board sheathing (25/32") and wood siding or shingles.	.21	.10
b. Interior finish, insulation board sheathing (25/32") and cement asbestos siding or shingles.	.24	.10
c. Interior finish, insulation board sheathing (25/32") and 1" stucco.	.24	.10
d. Interior finish, insulation board sheathing (25/32") and insulating siding (1/2") or wood shingles over insulating backing board (5/16")	.18	.10
e. Interior finish, insulation board sheathing (25/32") and face brick veneer (4") or stone (4").	.22	.10
Solid Masonry		
a. Interior finish, and 8" face or common brick.	.31	.10
b. Interior finish, and 12" face or common brick.	.25	.10
c. Interior finish, gravel aggregate concrete block (4") and face brick (4") or stone (4").	.32	.10
d. Interior finish, gravel aggregate concrete block (8") and face brick (4") or stone (4").	.28	.10
e. Interior finish, cinder aggregate concrete block (4") and face brick (4") or stone (4").	.28	.10
f. Interior finish, cinder aggregate concrete block (8"), and face brick (4") or stone (4").	.24	.10
Masonry Cavity		
a. Interior finish, gravel aggregate concrete block (4") and face brick (4") or stone (4").	.25	.10
b. Interior finish, gravel aggregrate concrete block (4") and common brick (4").	.21	.10
c. Interior finish, and SCR brick (5 1/2").		
Glass Block (4" nominal thickness)		
a. 5 3/4" x 5 3/4" x 3 7/8"	.60	
b. 7 3/4" x 7 3/4" x 3 7/8"	.56	
c. 11 3/4" x 11 3/4" x 3 7/8"	.52	
d. 7 3/4" x 7 3/4" x 3 7/8" with glass fiber screen dividing the cavity	.48	
e. Corrugated structural glass	1.36	
2. INTERIOR PARTITIONS		
Frame Superstructure		
a. Interior finish (3/4" plaster) one side.	.67	.12

TABLE 13-1 (Continued)

STRUCTURAL COMPONENT	NOT INSULATED U	INSULATED U
b. Interior finish (3/4" plaster) both sides.	.39	.11
c. Interior finish (3/8" dry wall) one side.	.60	.11
d. Interior finish (3/8" dry wall) both sides.	.34	.10
Masonry—Concrete block		
a. No interior finish, concrete aggregate block (4")	.49	
b. Interior finish (3/4" plaster) one side, concrete aggregate block (4")	.32	
c. Interior finish (3/4" plaster) both sides, concrete aggregate block (4")	.28	
3. WINDOWS		
a. Single glazed	1.13	
b. Double glazed (welded insulating glass)	.61	
c. Wood storm sash—permanent	.47	
d. Metal storm sash—permanent	.59	
e. Wood storm sash—installed and removed annually	.75	
4. DOORS		
a. All doors are calculated the same as though they were windows		
5. CEILING		
a. Interior finished (3/8" dry wall), no floor above.	.65	.13
b. Interior finish (3/8" dry wall) sub-floor above.	.30	.11
6. FLOOR		
Unheated below		
a. Exposed joist, sub-floor, building paper and finish floor (25/32")	.28	.13
b. Dry wall (3/8"), sub-floor, building paper, and finish floor	.21	.09
c. Concrete floor (4")	.10	
7. ROOF		
Frame		
a. Ceiling part of roof—Asphalt shingles, building paper, and plywood sheathing (5/16"), no ceiling as such	.57	
b. Ceiling part of roof—Asphalt shingles, building paper, plywood sheathing (5/16") and dry wall ceiling (3/8")		
1) Unvented	.34	.12
2) Vented	.54	

TABLE 13 – 1 (Continued)

STRUCTURAL COMPONENT	NOT INSULATED U	INSULATED U
c. Flat roof, built-up, roofing, concrete slab, and dry wall ceiling (3/8") or lath (3/8") and plaster (1/2")	.38	.19
8. SKYLIGHTS		
a. Single glass	1.40	
b. Double glass, 1/4" air space	.94	
9. BASEMENT WALL AND CRAWL SPACE		
Above Grade		
a. Poured concrete (6")	.75	
1) Rigid insulation (1")		.24
2) Rigid insulation (2")		.16
b. Poured concrete (8")	.67	
1) Rigid insulation (1")		.23
2) Rigid insulation (2")		.16
c. Concrete block (8")	.52	
1) Rigid insulation (1")		.21
2) Rigid insulation (2")		.15
d. Concrete block (10")	.50	
e. Concrete block (12")	.47	
1) Rigid insulation (1")		.20
2) Rigid insulation (2")		.14
Below Grade		
a. Poured Concrete (6", 8", or 10")	.06	
b. Concrete Block (8", 10", or 12")	.06	

calculate the temperature differential. Design temperatures are *not* the coldest temperatures recorded for a specific locality. They are the coldest *likely* to occur during an average heating season. A list of design temperatures for many cities in the United States and Canada is given in Table 13-2. As an example, the lowest temperature recorded in Kalamazoo, Michigan over a 100 year period was −25° F. The reasonable *minimum* winter temperature in Kalamazoo, according to the Table 13-2, is recorded as

−5° F. It would be senseless to design a heating facility in Kalamazoo to accommodate the −25° F temperature since this temperature was reached only for a short period of time and is not common during the heating season. The design temperature difference will vary with the location within the hemisphere. For a specific locality, however, it will be constant.

Values usually used for the inside design temperature are 70° or 75° F. In some instances the local building code will specify

which temperature is to be used in a multi-family type dwelling. Some heating codes specify that the heating system must be adequate to heat the structure to at least 70° F. However, the number of home owners who request an inside design temperature of 75° F is increasing. Many contractors building speculative homes are designing on the basis of a 75° F inside temperature.

With a 75° F inside temperature, and a −5° F outside temperature, for example, the temperature differential (T) would be 80° F.

Heat Loss Formula. By taking the heat loss formula and substituting the accepted symbols, we have:

Heat loss $= A \times U \times T$

The U-factors (given in Table 13-1) times the temperature differentials (refer to Table 13-2), times the square footage gives the total heat loss per hour. For instance, the winter outside design temperature in Cedar Rapids, Iowa is −15° F. The prospective builder may decide the inside temperature in the living area of the home will be 75° F. The design temperature difference (T) is 90° F. If the heat loss were to be calculated for 150 sq. ft. of brick veneer wall, with insulation, the heat loss formula would be:

Btuh $= 160 \times .10 \times 90 = 1,440$

Infiltration. As mentioned earlier, heat is lost not only through walls, but also through infiltration. Infiltration is caused by the air leaking through cracks around and in windows and doors, and through the walls and floor.

TABLE 13-2   OUTSIDE DESIGN CONDITIONS FOR UNITED STATES AND CANADA

State & City	Winter DB	Summer DB	Daily Range	Latitude Deg.
ALABAMA				
Anniston	10	95	M	35
Birmingham	10	95	M	35
Gadsden	10	95	M	35
Mobile	20	90	L	30
Montgomery	20	95	M	30
Tuscaloosa	10	95	M	35
ALASKA				
Anchorage	-24	70	M	60
Barrow	-48	—	—	70
Bethel	-43	—	—	60
Cordova	-13	—	—	60
Fairbanks	-57	80	M	65
Juneau	-5	—	—	60
Ketchikan	4	—	—	55
Kodiak	4	—	—	55
Kotzebue	-46	—	—	65
Nome	-36	—	—	60
Seward	-4	—	—	60
Sitka	2	—	—	60
ARIZONA				
Bisbee	30	100	H	30
Flagstaff	-5	85	H	35
Globe	30	105	H	35
Nogales	30	105	H	30
Phoenix	35	105	H	30
Tucson	30	100	H	30
Winslow	-5	95	H	35
Yuma	40	110	H	35
ARKANSAS				
Bentonville	0	95	M	35
Fort Smith	5	95	M	35
Hot Springs	10	95	M	35
Little Rock	10	95	M	35
Pine Bluff	10	95	M	35
Texarkana	10	100	M	35
CALIFORNIA				
Bakersfield	30	105	H	35
El Centro	35	110	H	35
Eureka	30	90	M	40
Fresno	30	105	H	35
Long Beach	35	90	M	35
Los Angeles	40	90	M	35
Montague	15	95	H	40
Needles	25	115	H	35
Oakland	30	80	M	40
Pasadena	40	95	M	35
Red Bluff	15	100	H	40
Sacramento	30	95	H	40
San Bernardino	30	105	H	35
San Diego	45	80	L	35
San Francisco	35	80	M	40
San Jose	40	90	M	35
COLORADO				
Boulder	-15	95	M	40
Colorado Springs	-10	95	H	40
Denver	-10	95	H	40
Durango	-5	95	H	35
Fort Collins	-15	95	M	40
Grand Junction	-5	95	H	40
Leadville	-10	95	M	40
Pueblo	-15	95	H	40
CONNECTICUT				
Bridgeport	0	85	L	40
Hartford	0	90	M	40
New Haven	0	85	L	40
New London	5	85	L	40
Norwalk	0	85	L	40
Torrington	0	90	M	40
Waterbury	0	90	M	40
DELAWARE				
Dover	10	90	M	40
Milford	10	90	M	40
Wilmington	5	90	M	40
DIST. OF COLUMBIA				
Washington	10	90	M	40
FLORIDA				
Apalachicola	25	95	L	30
Fort Myers	40	95	M	25
Gainesville	30	95	M	30
Jacksonville	30	95	M	30
Key West	55	100	L	25
Miami	45	90	L	25
Orlando	35	90	M	30
Pensacola	25	95	L	30
Tallahassee	25	95	M	30
Tampa	35	95	M	30
GEORGIA				
Athens	10	95	M	35
Atlanta	10	95	M	35
Augusta	20	100	M	35
Brunswick	25	95	L	30
Columbus	20	100	M	35
Macon	20	95	M	35
Rome	10	95	M	35
Savannah	25	95	M	30
Way Cross	25	95	M	30
IDAHO				
Boise	-10	95	H	45
Idaho Falls	-15	90	H	45
Lewiston	-10	95	H	45
Pocatello	-15	90	H	45
Twin Falls	-15	95	H	40
ILLINOIS				
Aurora	-10	95	M	40
Bloomington	-10	95	M	40
Cairo	0	100	M	35
Champaign	-10	95	M	40
Chicago	-10	95	M	40
Danville	-10	95	M	40
Decatur	-10	95	M	40
Elgin	-15	95	M	40
Joliet	-10	95	M	40
Moline	-10	95	M	40
Peoria	-15	95	M	40
Rockford	-15	95	M	40
Rock Island	-10	95	M	40
Springfield	-10	95	M	40
Urbana	-10	95	M	40
INDIANA				
Elkhart	-10	95	M	40
Evansville	-5	95	M	40
Fort Wayne	-5	95	M	40
Indianapolis	-10	95	M	40
Lafayette	-10	95	M	40
South Bend	-10	95	M	40
IOWA				
Burlington	-10	95	M	40
Cedar Rapids	-15	95	M	40
Charles City	-20	95	M	45
Clinton	-15	95	M	40
Council Bluffs	-15	100	M	40
Davenport	-10	95	M	40
Des Moines	-15	95	M	40
Dubuque	-15	95	M	40
Fort Dodge	-15	95	M	40
Keokuk	-15	95	M	40
Marshalltown	-15	95	M	40
Sioux City	-15	95	M	40
Waterloo	-15	95	M	40
KANSAS				
Atchison	-10	100	M	40
Concordia	-10	95	M	40
Dodge City	-10	95	H	40
Iola	-5	100	M	40
Leavenworth	-10	100	M	40
Salina	-10	100	M	40
Topeka	-10	95	M	40
Wichita	-5	100	M	40
KENTUCKY				
Bowling Green	0	95	M	35
Frankfort	0	95	M	40
Hopkinsville	0	95	M	35
Lexington	0	95	M	40
Louisville	0	95	M	40
Owensboro	0	95	M	40
Shelbyville	0	95	M	40
LOUISIANA				
Alexandria	20	95	M	30
Baton Rouge	20	95	M	30
New Orleans	25	95	L	30
Shreveport	15	95	M	30
MAINE				
Augusta	-15	85	L	45
Bangor	-20	85	L	45
Bar Harbor	-10	85	L	45
Belfast	-10	85	L	45
Eastport	-10	85	L	45
Lewiston	-10	85	L	45
Millinocket	-15	85	M	45
Orono	-20	85	M	45
Portland	-10	85	M	45
Presque Isle	-20	85	L	45
Rumford	-15	85	L	45
MARYLAND				
Annapolis	10	90	M	40
Baltimore	10	90	M	40
Cambridge	10	90	L	40
Cumberland	0	90	M	40
Frederick	5	90	M	40
Frostburg	-5	90	M	40
Salisbury	10	90	M	40
MASSACHUSETTS				
Amherst	-5	90	M	40
Boston	0	85	M	40
Fall River	0	85	L	40
Fitchburg	-5	90	M	45
Framingham	-5	85	L	40
Lawrence	-5	85	M	40
Lowell	-5	85	M	45
Nantucket	0	85	L	40
New Bedford	0	85	L	40
Pittsfield	-10	90	M	40
Plymouth	0	85	L	40
Springfield	-5	90	M	40
Worcester	-5	90	M	40
MICHIGAN				
Alpena	-10	90	M	45
Ann Arbor	-5	90	M	40
Big Rapids	-5	90	M	45
Cadillac	-10	90	M	45
Calumet	-20	80	M	45
Detroit	-5	90	M	40
Escanaba	-20	85	M	45
Flint	-10	90	M	40
Grand Haven	-5	90	M	45
Grand Rapids	-5	90	M	45
Houghton	-20	80	M	45
Kalamazoo	-5	90	M	40
Lansing	-10	90	M	45
Ludington	-5	90	M	45
Marquette	-15	80	M	45
Muskegon	-5	90	M	45
Port Huron	-10	90	M	45
Saginaw	-10	90	M	45
Sault Ste. Marie	-20	80	M	45
MINNESOTA				
Alexandria	-25	85	M	45
Duluth	-25	80	M	45
Minneapolis	-25	90	M	45
Moorhead	-30	95	M	45
St. Cloud	-25	90	M	45
St. Paul	-25	90	M	45
MISSISSIPPI				
Biloxi	25	90	L	30
Columbus	10	95	M	35
Corinth	5	95	M	35
Hattiesburg	20	95	M	30
Jackson	15	95	M	30
Meridian	15	95	M	30
Natchez	15	95	L	30
Vicksburg	15	95	L	30
MISSOURI				
Columbia	-10	100	M	40
Hannibal	-10	95	M	40
Kansas City	-10	100	M	40
Kirksville	-10	95	M	40
St. Joseph	-10	100	M	40
St. Louis	-5	95	M	40
Springfield	-5	100	M	40

TABLE 13 - 2 (continued)

State & City	Winter DB	Summer DB	Daily Range	Latitude Deg.
MONTANA				
Anaconda	-30	85	H	45
Billings	-30	90	H	45
Butte	-30	85	H	45
Great Falls	-40	90	H	50
Havre	-40	95	H	50
Helena	-40	90	H	45
Kalispell	-30	90	H	50
Miles City	-35	95	H	45
Missoula	-30	90	H	45
NEBRASKA				
Grand Island	-15	95	H	40
Hastings	-15	95	M	40
Lincoln	-15	95	M	40
Norfolk	-15	95	M	40
North Platte	-15	100	H	40
Omaha	-15	100	M	40
Valentine	-20	95	M	45
York	-15	95	M	40
NEVADA				
Elko	-10	95	H	40
Las Vegas	10	110	H	35
Reno	5	95	H	40
Tonopah	5	90	M	40
Winnemucca	-10	95	H	40
NEW HAMPSHIRE				
Berlin	-15	85	H	45
Claremont	-15	85	M	45
Concord	-10	85	H	45
Franklin	-15	85	M	45
Hanover	-15	85	M	45
Keene	-10	85	M	45
Manchester	-10	85	M	45
Nashua	-10	85	L	45
Portsmouth	-5	85	L	45
NEW JERSEY				
Asbury Park	5	90	L	40
Atlantic City	10	90	L	40
Bayonne	0	90	L	40
Belvidere	0	90	M	40
Bloomfield	0	90	L	40
Bridgeton	5	90	L	40
Camden	5	90	L	40
East Orange	0	90	L	40
Elizabeth	0	90	L	40
Jersey City	0	90	L	40
Newark	5	90	M	40
New Brunswick	5	90	L	40
Paterson	0	90	L	40
Phillipsburg	0	90	M	40
Trenton	0	90	L	40
NEW MEXICO				
Albuquerque	10	95	M	35
El Morro	0	85	H	35
Raton	-5	95	H	35
Roswell	5	100	H	35
Santa Fe	5	90	H	35
Tucumcari	5	95	H	35

State & City	Winter DB	Summer DB	Daily Range	Latitude Deg.
NEW YORK				
Albany	-10	90	M	45
Auburn	-10	90	M	45
Binghamton	-5	90	M	40
Buffalo	-5	85	M	45
Canton	-20	85	M	45
Cortland	-10	90	M	45
Elmira	-5	90	M	40
Glens Falls	-15	90	M	40
Ithaca	-5	90	M	40
Jamestown	-5	90	M	40
Lake Placid	-15	90	M	45
New York	5	90	M	45
Niagara Falls	-5	85	M	45
Ogdensburg	-20	85	M	45
Oneonta	-10	90	M	45
Oswego	-5	90	M	45
Port Jervis	0	90	L	40
Rochester	-5	90	M	45
Schenectady	-10	90	M	45
Syracuse	-10	90	M	45
Watertown	-15	85	M	45
NORTH CAROLINA				
Asheville	5	90	M	35
Charlotte	15	95	M	35
Greensboro	10	90	M	35
Hatteras	20	90	L	35
New Bern	20	95	L	35
Raleigh	15	95	M	35
Salisbury	10	90	M	35
Wilmington	20	90	M	35
Winston-Salem	10	90	M	35
NORTH DAKOTA				
Bismarck	-30	95	H	45
Devils Lake	-30	90	M	50
Dickinson	-30	95	H	45
Fargo	-30	95	M	45
Grand Forks	-30	90	M	50
Jamestown	-30	95	M	45
Minot	-35	90	M	50
Pembina	-35	90	M	50
Williston	-35	90	M	50
OHIO				
Akron	-5	90	M	40
Cincinnati	-5	95	M	40
Cleveland	-5	90	M	40
Columbus	-5	90	M	40
Dayton	-5	90	M	40
Lima	-5	90	M	40
Marion	-5	90	M	40
Sandusky	-5	90	M	40
Toledo	-5	90	M	40
Warren	-5	90	M	40
Youngstown	-5	90	M	40
OKLAHOMA				
Ardmore	5	100	M	35
Bartlesville	-5	100	M	35
Guthrie	0	100	M	35
Muskogee	0	95	M	35
Oklahoma City	0	100	M	35
Tulsa	0	100	M	35
Waynoka	-5	105	M	35

State & City	Winter DB	Summer DB	Daily Range	Latitude Deg.
OREGON				
Arlington	5	95	M	45
Baker	-15	90	M	45
Eugene	15	90	H	45
Medford	20	95	H	40
Pendleton	-10	95	M	45
Portland	10	85	M	45
Roseburg	20	90	H	45
Salem	15	90	H	45
Wamic	0	90	H	45
PENNSYLVANIA				
Altoona	-5	90	M	40
Bethlehem	0	90	M	40
Coatesville	5	90	M	40
Erie	-5	85	M	40
Harrisburg	5	90	M	40
New Castle	-5	90	M	40
Oil City	-5	90	M	40
Philadelphia	5	90	M	40
Pittsburgh	-5	90	M	40
Reading	5	90	M	40
Scranton	0	90	M	40
Warren	-5	90	M	40
Williamsport	-5	90	M	40
York	5	90	M	40
RHODE ISLAND				
Block Island	5	85	L	40
Bristol	0	90	L	40
Kingston	0	85	L	40
Pawtucket	0	90	M	40
Providence	0	90	M	40
SOUTH CAROLINA				
Charleston	20	90	L	35
Columbia	20	95	M	35
Florence	20	95	M	35
Greenville	10	95	M	35
Spartanburg	10	95	M	35
SOUTH DAKOTA				
Aberdeen	-25	95	M	45
Huron	-20	100	H	45
Pierre	-20	95	M	45
Rapid City	-20	95	H	45
Sioux Falls	-20	95	H	45
Watertown	-25	95	M	45
TENNESSEE				
Chattanooga	10	95	M	35
Jackson	5	95	M	35
Johnson City	0	95	M	35
Knoxville	5	95	M	35
Memphis	5	95	M	35
Nashville	5	95	M	35
TEXAS				
Abilene	5	95	M	30
Amarillo	0	95	H	35
Austin	15	100	M	30
Brownsville	30	95	M	25
Corpus Christi	25	95	M	30
Dallas	10	100	M	35
Del Rio	20	100	H	30
El Paso	20	100	M	30
Fort Worth	10	100	M	35
Galveston	25	95	L	30
Houston	20	95	M	30
Palestine	10	100	M	30
Port Arthur	20	95	M	30
San Antonio	20	100	M	30
Waco	10	100	M	30

State & City	Winter DB	Summer DB	Daily Range	Latitude Deg.
UTAH				
Logan	-10	95	H	40
Milford	-5	95	H	40
Ogden	-5	90	H	40
Salt Lake City	0	95	H	40
VERMONT				
Bennington	-10	90	M	45
Burlington	-15	90	M	45
Montpelier	-20	90	M	45
Newport	-20	85	M	45
Northfield	-20	90	M	45
Rutland	-15	90	M	45
VIRGINIA				
Cape Henry	15	90	L	35
Charlottesville	10	90	M	40
Danville	10	90	M	35
Lynchburg	10	90	M	35
Norfolk	15	90	L	35
Petersburg	10	90	M	35
Richmond	10	90	M	35
Roanoke	5	90	M	35
Wytheville	5	90	M	35
WASHINGTON				
Aberdeen	20	85	L	45
Bellingham	10	80	L	50
Everett	15	80	L	50
North Head	20	80	L	50
Olympia	15	80	H	45
Seattle	15	80	M	50
Spokane	-15	90	H	50
Tacoma	15	80	M	50
Tatoosh Island	20	80	L	50
Walla Walla	-10	95	M	45
Wenatchee	-10	90	M	50
Yakima	-5	90	H	45
WEST VIRGINIA				
Bluefield	0	95	M	35
Charleston	0	90	M	40
Elkins	-5	90	M	40
Fairmont	0	90	M	40
Huntington	0	90	M	40
Martinsburg	0	90	M	40
Parkersburg	0	90	M	40
Wheeling	-5	90	M	40
WISCONSIN				
Ashland	-25	80	M	45
Beloit	-15	95	M	45
Eau Claire	-20	90	M	45
Green Bay	-20	90	M	45
La Crosse	-20	95	M	45
Madison	-20	90	M	45
Milwaukee	-15	90	M	45
Oshkosh	-20	90	M	45
Sheboygan	-20	90	M	45
WYOMING				
Casper	-25	90	H	45
Cheyenne	-20	90	H	40
Lander	-30	90	H	45
Sheridan	-30	90	H	45
Yellowstone Park	-35	85	H	45

TABLE 13-2 (continued)

Province & City	Winter DB	Summer DB	Daily Range	Latitude Deg.
ALBERTA				
Banff	-30	—	H	50
Camrose	-35	—	H	55
Calgary	-30	90	H	50
Cardston	-30	—	H	50
Edmonton	-35	90	H	55
Grande Prairie	-40	—	H	55
Hanna	-35	—	H	50
Jasper	-30	—	H	55
Lethbridge	-30	—	H	50
Lloydminster	-40	—	H	55
McMurray	-40	—	H	55
Medicine Hat	-35	90	H	50
Red Deer	-35	—	H	50
Taber	-35	—	H	50
Wetaskiwin	-35	—	H	55
BRITISH COLUMBIA				
Chilliwack	5	—	M	50
Courtenay	10	—	M	50
Dawson Creek	-40	—	H	55
Estevan Point	15	—	M	50
Fort Nelson	-40	—	H	60
Hope	0	—	M	50
Kamloops	-20	—	H	50
Kimberly	-25	—	H	50
Lytton	-5	—	H	50
Nanaimo	10	—	M	50
Nelson	-10	—	H	50
Penticton	-5	—	H	50
Port Alberni	10	—	M	50
Prince George	-30	—	H	55
Prince Rupert	10	—	L	55
Princeton	-15	—	H	50
Revelstoke	-25	—	H	50
Trail	-10	—	H	50
Vancouver	10	80	L	50
Vernon	-15	—	H	50
Victoria	15	—	L	50
Westview	10	—	M	50
LABRADOR				
Goose Bay	-25	—	L	55
MANITOBA				
Boissevain	-35	—	H	50
Brandon	-30	—	H	50
Churchill	-40	—	L	60
Dauphin	-35	—	M	50
Flin Flon	-40	—	M	55
Minnedosa	-35	—	H	50
Neepawa	-35	—	H	50
La Prairie	-30	—	M	50
Swan River	-35	—	M	55
The Pas	-40	—	M	55
Winnipeg	-30	90	M	50
NEW BRUNSWICK				
Bathurst	-10	—	L	45
Campbellton	-10	—	L	45
Chatham	-10	—	M	45
Edmunston	-15	—	M	45
Fredericton	-5	90	L	45
Moncton	-10	—	M	45
Saint John	-5	80	L	45
Woodstock	-15	—	M	45
NEWFOUNDLAND				
Corner Brook	0	—	L	50
Gander	-5	—	L	50
Grand Falls	-5	—	M	50
St. John's	0	—	L	50

Province & City	Winter DB	Summer DB	Daily Range	Latitude Deg.
NORTHWEST TERRITORIES				
Aklavik	-45	—	L	70
Fort Norman	-40	—	M	65
Frobisher	-50	—	L	—
Resolute	-40	—	L	—
Yellowknife	-50	—	L	60
NOVA SCOTIA				
Bridgewater	0	—	L	45
Dartmouth	0	—	L	45
*Halifax C	5	80	L	45
*Halifax A	0	80	L	45
Kentville	0	—	L	45
New Glasgow	0	—	L	45
Spring Hill	-5	—	M	45
Sydney	0	85	L	45
Truro	0	—	L	45
Yarmouth	5	—	L	45
ONTARIO				
Bancroft	-20	—	M	45
Barrie	-5	—	M	45
Belleville	-10	—	M	45
Brampton	-5	—	M	45
Brantford	-5	—	M	45
Brockville	-15	—	M	45
Chatham	0	—	M	45
Cobourg	-10	—	M	45
Collingwood	0	—	M	45
Cornwall	-15	—	M	45
Ear Falls	-35	—	M	50
Fort Frances	-30	—	M	50
Fort William	-25	85	M	50
Galt	-5	—	M	45
Geraldton	-35	—	M	50
Goderich	0	—	M	45
Guelph	-5	—	M	45
Hamilton	0	—	M	45
Haileybury	-25	—	M	50
Hanover	-5	—	M	45
Huntsville	-15	—	M	45
Kapuskasing	-30	—	M	50
Kenora	-35	—	M	50
Kingston	-10	—	M	45
Kirkland Lake	-25	—	M	50
Kitchener	-5	—	M	45
Lindsay	-15	—	M	45
London	0	—	M	45
Moonsonee	-35	—	M	50
Newmarket	-5	—	M	45
Niagara Falls	0	—	M	45
North Bay	-20	85	M	45
Orillia	-10	—	M	45
Oshawa	-5	—	M	45
Ottawa	-15	90	M	45
Owen Sound	0	—	M	45
Parry Sound	-15	—	M	45
Pembroke	-20	—	M	45
Peterborough	-10	—	M	45
Port Arthur	-25	—	M	50
Port Colborne	0	—	M	45
Renfrew	-20	—	M	45
St. Catharines	0	—	M	45
St. Thomas	0	—	M	45
Sarnia	0	—	M	45
Sault Ste. Marie	-10	85	M	45
Simcoe	0	—	M	45
Sioux Lookout	-35	—	M	50
Smith Falls	-15	—	M	45
Stratford	-5	—	M	45
Sudbury	-20	—	M	45

Province & City	Winter DB	Summer DB	Daily Range	Latitude Deg.
ONTARIO				
Timmins	-25	—	M	50
*Toronto C	0	90	M	45
*Toronto A	-5	90	M	45
Trenton	-10	—	M	45
Walkerton	-5	—	M	45
Welland	0	—	M	45
Windsor	0	95	M	40
Woodstock	-5	—	M	45
PRINCE EDWARD ISLAND				
Charlottetown	-5	80	L	45
Summerside	-5	—	L	45
QUEBEC				
Amos	-25	—	—	—
Arvida	-20	—	M	45
Asbestos	-15	—	M	45
Chibougamau	-30	—	—	—
Chicoutimi	-20	—	M	45
Dorval	-10	—	M	45
Drummondville	-15	—	M	45
Fort Chimo	-40	—	M	60
Gaspe	-10	—	L	50
Granby	-15	—	M	45
Harrington Harbour	-15	—	—	—
Joliette	-15	—	M	45
Knob Lake	-40	—	—	55
Lac Megantic	-15	—	M	45
La Tuque	-25	—	M	45
Magog	-15	—	M	45
Mont Joli	-10	—	L	50
Mount Laurier	-20	—	M	45
*Montreal C	-10	90	M	45
*Montreal A	-10	90	M	45
Noranda	-25	—	—	—
Port Harrison	-40	—	L	60
Quebec	-15	85	M	45
Rimouski	-15	—	L	50
Riviere Du Loup	-10	—	L	45
Rouyn	-25	—	—	—
Ste. Agathe	-15	—	M	45
St. Hyacinthe	-15	—	M	45
St. Jerome	-15	—	M	45
St. Johns	-15	—	M	50
Seven Islands	-20	—	L	50
Shawinigan Falls	-15	—	M	45
Sherbrooke	-15	85	M	45
Sorel	-15	—	M	45
Thetford Mines	-15	—	M	45
Three Rivers	-15	—	M	45
Val D'Or	-25	—	—	—
Valley Field	-15	—	M	45
Victoriaville	-15	—	M	45
SASKATCHEWAN				
Biggar	-35	—	H	55
Estevau	-35	—	H	50
Humbot	-40	—	H	55
Moose Jaw	-35	—	H	50
Moosomin	-35	—	H	50
Nipawin	-40	—	H	55
North Battleford	-35	—	H	55
Prince Albert	-40	—	H	55

Province & City	Winter DB	Summer DB	Daily Range	Latitude Deg.
SASKATCHEWAN				
Regina	-35	90	H	50
Saskatoon	-40	90	H	55
Shaunavon	-35	—	H	50
Swift Current	-35	—	H	50
Uranium City	-45	—	—	—
Weyburn	-35	—	H	50
Yorkton	-35	—	H	50
YUKON TERRITORY				
Dawson	-55	—	H	65
Whitehorse	-45	—	M	60

*C—City

*A—Airport

From: National Warm Air Conditioning Association, Cleveland, Ohio; LOAD CALCULATIONS MANUAL J. SECOND EDITION

TABLE 13-3

INFILTRATION HEAT LOSS COEFFICIENTS BASED ON PER
CENT OF GLASS OF WALL AREA

TYPE OF WINDOW	PER CENT OF GLASS WALL AREA	COEFFICIENT
DOUBLE HUNG a. no weatherstripping	under 25% 25% to 50% 50% and over	.020 .025 .035
b. weatherstripping or storm sash	under 25% 25% to 50% 50% and over	.015 .020 .030
CASEMENT	under 25% 25% to 50% 50% and over	.030 .035 .045

Heat loss calculations must also include the infiltration factor since every cubic foot of cooler outside air which leaks into the room will create a greater load on the heating system. Tight-fitting windows and doors, storm windows and doors, and weather stripping and calking around all door and window frames will appreciably reduce the amount of air leakage.

To compensate for heat lost by infiltration, simply multiply the volume of each room (V) by the *infiltration coefficient* (C), and then by the design temperature difference (T). Table 13-3 gives the infiltration co-efficients. (Doors are figured as if they were double-hung windows without weather stripping.) The formula is:

Infiltration Btuh $= V \times C \times T$

The product is then added to the total Btuh calculated for the heat lost for each room.

Heat Loss Record Sheet

As with any mathematical calculation, the best results are usually obtained when all operations within the problem are set down in a logical, orderly manner. Fig. 13-25 shows a heat loss calculation sheet based on a step-by-step arrival at the heat losses for all areas within a home. Each calculation area has a space provided for the width and depth of that particular room, the square footage or volume, the design temperature difference, the U-factor, and the Btuh. The advantage of the heat loss being calculated as shown in Fig. 13-25 is that all steps used in arriving at the total heat loss are logically figured and recorded, thereby allowing all computations to be easily checked. Questions such as "Where did this figure come from?" or "How did I arrive at this answer?" or "What does this number refer to?" will be eliminated.

Fig. 13-26 gives the plan of a two-story home with basement. The calculations necessary to determine the total heat loss for the living room are shown in Fig. 13-25. First the gross exposed wall area must be calculated (8′ × 42.5′ = 340 sq. ft.). Next, the heat loss must be computed for the windows (as shown in Fig. 13-26). A picture window (double-hung sections) is used in the living room. From the chart accompanying this figure, the glass size of this window is 116″ × 48″. This is recorded on the calculation sheet as 9.7′ × 4′ = 38.7 sq. ft. Employing the heat loss formula: 38.7 (A) × 80 (T) × .61 (U) = 1,888 Btuh. By subtracting the total square feet of windows from the gross wall square footage, we then arrive at the net wall square footage. Calculating the total heat loss of the net wall, we would have 301.3 × 80 × .10 = 2,410.

Since the plan shown in Fig. 13-26 is a two story, there will be no appreciable heat loss because the second level is heated. The same is true of the floor as the basement would also be heated. Therefore, there would be no heat loss calculation in this case for the floor or ceiling. Infiltration is calculated for the living room by figuring the volume 8′ × 20.5′ × 22′ = 3,608 cu. ft.), multiplying it by the design temperature difference (80), and then by the infiltration heat loss coefficient (.015); this gives 4,330 Btuh. The total heat loss (8,628 Btuh) is the total of lines, 2, 3, and 6 in Fig. 13-25.

Various formulas exist for computing heat loss and infiltration. Each method results in the approximate same answer. More

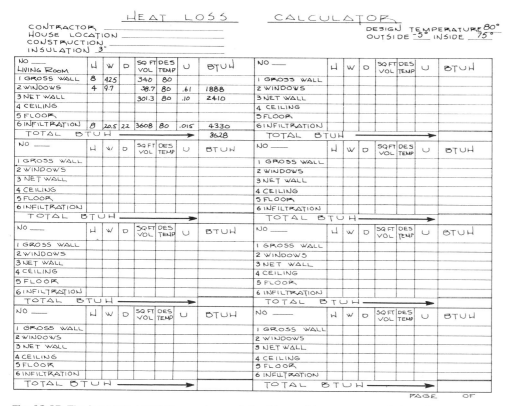

HEAT LOSS CALCULATOR

CONTRACTOR _____
HOUSE LOCATION _____
CONSTRUCTION _____
INSULATION _3"_

DESIGN TEMPERATURE 80°
OUTSIDE -5° INSIDE 75°

NO —— LIVING ROOM	H	W	D	SQ FT VOL	DES TEMP	U	BTUH
1 GROSS WALL	8	425		340	80		
2 WINDOWS	4	9.7		38.7	80	.61	1888
3 NET WALL				301.3	80	.10	2410
4 CEILING							
5 FLOOR							
6 INFILTRATION	8	20.5	22	3608	80	.015	4330
TOTAL BTUH ⟶							8628

NO ——	H	W	D	SQ FT VOL	DES TEMP	U	BTUH
1 GROSS WALL							
2 WINDOWS							
3 NET WALL							
4 CEILING							
5 FLOOR							
6 INFILTRATION							
TOTAL BTUH ⟶							

(The form continues as a blank template grid with the same NO / H / W / D / SQ FT VOL / DES TEMP / U / BTUH columns and GROSS WALL, WINDOWS, NET WALL, CEILING, FLOOR, INFILTRATION, TOTAL BTUH rows repeated in multiple panels.)

PAGE ___ OF ___

Fig. 13-25. The heat loss calculation and record sheet is used to assure an orderly and exact presentation. Partial calculations for a two-story house are shown.

exact methods are used by heating and ventilating engineers or heating contractors. For the architect's or designer's purpose, the approximate method will be sufficient.

Sizing

All home heating units are "sized." Sizing is based on the total heat loss calculated for a particular residence, *and* the total amount of Btu's the furnace can produce per hour. This later figure is stated as an **AGA** (American Gas Association) guaranteed figure. For instance, the Bryant-395 gas-fired, forced-air, upflow type (model 80-395) has an AGA output rating of 64,000 Btu's per hour. The size of the furnace must be based on the *total heat loss* calculated for the house.

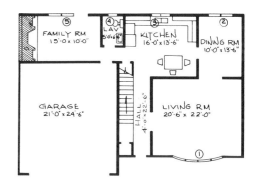

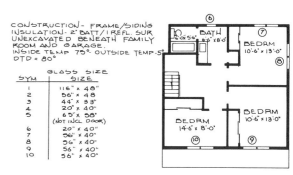

CONSTRUCTION - FRAME/SIDING
INSULATION - 2" BATT/1 REFL. SUR
UNEXCAVATED BENEATH FAMILY
ROOM AND GARAGE.
INSIDE TEMP 75° OUTSIDE TEMP -5°
DTD = 80°

SYM	GLASS SIZE
1	116" x 48"
2	56" x 48
3	44" x 33"
4	20" x 40"
5	65" x 58" (NOT INCL DOOR)
6	20" x 40"
7	56" x 40"
8	56" x 40"
9	56" x 40"
10	56" x 40"

Fig. 13-26. This plan of a two-story house with basement is used in calculating heat loss. (See Heat Loss Calculator Sheet, Fig. 13-25.)

ALL EXTERIOR DOORS 3'-0" x 6'-8"

Cooling

Although the small air cooling unit was developed at the start of the 1930's, it did not gain significantly in popularity until the late 1940's and early 1950's. It's wide acceptance as a means of providing occupants of all structures with relief from the summer heat and humidity has overshadowed the original reason for air cooling—to serve the production phase of industry.

Today, there is an increasing growth in the use of residential, commercial and industrial cooling units. Both individual room units and compact, centrally located cooling systems may be used. A central air cooling system may either have its own ducts or it may use the existing heating ducts or pipes. If a central air cooling system is used, it may be combined with the heating system into a single, central air conditioning unit. This combined unit gives year-round conditioned air.

Cooling Plant

The cooling plant should be able to reduce the building to a comfortable temperature with little or no variation between floor and ceiling. Varying factors must be considered when determining the size of the cooling unit. Some of the more pertinent factors are *heat gain* through: (1) infiltration, (2) heat conducted by windows, walls, etc., (3) heat radiated by occupants, and (4) heat produced by household activities and appliances.

During the periods when cooling is required, the indoor temperature can more easily be maintained if the sun's rays are prevented from striking the walls, glass areas, and roof. Sun screens, roof overhangs, and plantings can protect a structure from the direct rays of the sun. Insulating materials with a high R value and building materials with a low U-factor will reduce the heat conducted into a building.

The cooling part of an air conditioning system usually removes moisture from the air. (The heating system, as mentioned earlier, adds moisture.) The ability of outdoor air to hold moisture increases as the temperature increases. Moist outdoor air infiltrating will increase the indoor relative humidity. When the moist infiltrating air is added to the humidity produced by normal activities, the moisture may rise to an uncomfortably high level.

In general the relative humidity should not exceed 60 per cent when the temperature is 76°. Most cooling equipment is designed to maintain a relative humidity within comfortable limits.

The cooling system should also provide some means of cleaning the air either by a simple mesh filter or by the highly effective electrostatic precipitate filters. The latter cleaner protects the health of the occupants by trapping air-borne dust and pollens.

Distribution

The distribution system should deliver its required share of cooling to each room. In a *forced-air system*, this is accomplished with the air ducts. Conditioned air is discharged into each room through diffusers. A return system is required to send the warmed air back through the cooling plant. In a *liquid-cooling system* chilled water is piped to blower-equipped convector units in each room. (Convector units are equipped with small blowers that circulate the room air over the chilled coils. In the winter these blower-equipped convector units may be used with steam or hot water heat.)

Constant air motion is desirable to maintain uniform temperature and humidity. Care must be exercised in the selection and installation of the cooling unit because the maximum allowable air velocity (in a zone between 4′ and 5′ above floor level) is approximately 50′ per minute. The distribution system may be considered satisfactory if the temperature varies 3° or less throughout the room.

Ventilation

Some degree of ventilation is essential in the air conditioned building because there are physical and chemical changes that occur to the air as a result of human occupancy. The air will become "stale" when there is a reduction in oxygen, an increase in carbon dioxide, or an unpleasant amount of cooking and household odors.

Fortunately, some degree of ventilation is obtained by infiltration through doors and windows. If infiltration does not provide enough ventilation, an exhaust fan in the kitchen and/or bath may be used. The forced-air cooling system may require a duct to bring in outside air.

Cooling Load Calculations

The size of the cooling system required to provide comfort in the home is based primarily on the summer outside design temperature. These temperatures are shown in Table 13-2. As in the case of the winter temperatures previously discussed, the summer temperatures are not the highest temperatures recorded. It will also be noted that Table 13-2 lists the daily temperature ranges for each city. The range refers to the average maximum and minimum temperature son. For convenience these are expressed as H (high), M (medium), and L (low) ranges. (These ranges are used in later calculations.)

Generally, the most comfortable inside temperature is 75° F. If an inside design temperature lower than 75° F is specified by the home owner, the heat gain factors for a higher outside design temperature should be used.

Heat gain must be calculated for *all rooms and areas* that are to be cooled. When determining the amount of heat gain for a room, all surfaces that are exposed to the outside must be considered. Heat gain that is transmitted from floors over a basement, enclosed crawl space, or a concrete slab on the ground is so negligible that it is not calculated. Similarly, walls that are below grade are not calculated. However, the exposed portion of a basement wall, as in the case of a house designed with a walk-out basement, must be calculated.

During the summer months, sunlight through windows will constitute a large portion of the heat gain. The intensity of the sun's rays varies with the orientation of the various rooms.

The position of the sun, location of the structure relative to latitude, and the amount of overhang determine the heat gain through a window. The amount of overhang is perhaps the most significant of these factors. Glass that is protected by a permanent shading device, such as a roof overhang or awning, is considered as a northward facing window, even though the window does not face north. That portion of glass that is not screened from the sun's rays is referred to as *sunlit* glass. The line that divides the shaded from the unshaded portion is called the *shade line*. Fig. 13-27 shows the shade

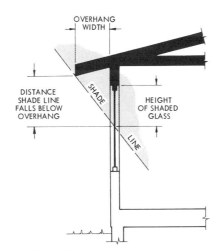

Fig. 13-27. The shade line is based on the latitude, width of overhang, and location of window.

line caused by the sun. The sunlit areas as well as shaded area must be calculated separately for each window.

As was indicated in the first portion of this chapter, heat is lost within the structure by infiltration. A similar situation also exists when cooling the structure—warm, exterior air will enter the house and an equivalent amount of cooled air will exit. To simplify infiltration calculations, the area of the exposed wall is employed to determine the amount of infiltration in each room.

The occupants of the building should not be overlooked since the human body produces heat. This adds to the heat gain within the structure. During the summer a room will be considerably "warmer" with eight occupants, for example, than with two. Of course, humidity is a contributing factor. For heat gain, 300 Btuh (British Thermal Units Per Hour) per person is considered average. If the number of occupants is not known, simply multiply the number of bedrooms by 2. This factor of 300 Btuh per person is calculated only once for the living area. (It is recommended that a *minimum* of 1,000 Btuh be used for the living area of the home.) A constant figure of 1,200 Btuh must also be added to the kitchen to compensate for the increased temperature created by cooking.

To obtain a correctly sized cooling unit for the residence, the *sensible heat gain* must be computed. The sensible heat gain is the total of all heat gains for each room plus the halls. The *final* heat gain used in "sizing" is arrived at by multiplying the sensible heat

HEAT GAIN CALCULATOR

CONTRACTOR _____
HOUSE LOCATION 914 Sixth Street
Eau Claire, Wisconsin
CONSTRUCTION Brick Veneer
INSULATION
 WALLS 3" TYPE Batt
 CEILINGS 4+" TYPE Blown
 FLOORS ____ TYPE ____

LATITUDE: N45°
TEMPERATURE RANGE: M
OUTSIDE DESIGN TEMPERATURE: 90°
INSIDE TEMPERATURE: 75°
OVERHANG: 1'-6" Uniform

	NO Living Room — SIZE 23x17			NO Bed Room — SIZE 10x11, 2@9			NO Kitchen — SIZE 18x8, 3x6			NO — SIZE			NO. — SIZE		
	AREA LIN FT	HTM	BTUH	AREA LIN FT	HTM	BTUH	AREA LIN FT	HTM	BTUH	AREA LIN FT	HTM	BTUH	AREA LIN FT	HTM	BTUH
LINEAL FEET EXPOSED WALL	23+4+23			10			18+10								
CEILING HEIGHT	8			8			8								
GROSS EXPOSED WALL	400			80			224								
DIRECTION	(A)W 6	14	84	(B)W 3	14	42	(D)E 3	14	42						
DIRECTION	(C)E 3	14	42												
DIRECTION															
DIRECTION	(A)W 54	44	2376	(B)W 12	44	528	(D)E 18	44	792						
DIRECTION	(C)E 29	44	1276												
DIRECTION															
NET EXPOSED WALL	308	1.5	462	65	1.5	98	203	1.5	305						
WARM PARTITION	104	1.4	146				120	3.4	408						
CEILING	391	1.6	626	120	1.6	192	162	1.6	259						
FLOORS															
INFILTRATION	400	1.1	440	80	1.1	88	224	1.1	246						
PEOPLE @ 300 BTUH	6		1800												
APPLIANCES @ 1200 BTUH									1200						
SENSIBLE - HEAT GAIN			7252			948			3252						
x 1.3															
TOTAL HEAT GAIN (SHG x 1.3)			9428	TOTAL		1232	TOTAL		4228	TOTAL			TOTAL		

Fig. 13-28. The heat gain calculation sheet is used to figure the loads in sizing cooling units. Partial calculations for a single-story house are shown.

gain by the figure 1.3. This factor (1.3) is the performance expectancy used in sizing cooling equipment and will result in a total heat gain adequate for most regions. The product of the sensible heat gain multiplied by 1.3 will equal the required size of the unit.

Heat Gain Record Sheet

To facilitate calculating the total heat gain for any structure, the best results are obtained when a logical method is used. Fig. 13-28 shows a heat gain calculation sheet that may be used for all rooms and areas in the home. Each portion of the record sheet has space for room, dimensions, factors,

sunlit glass windows, exposed walls, infiltration, etc.

The necessary calculations to arrive at the heat gain for a bedroom, kitchen, and living room are illustrated on Fig. 13-28 in color. These calculations refer to the partial plan of a single-story, ranch-type house with a basement shown in Fig. 13-29. This illustration is used in the sample calculations given below.

Preliminary to making any calculations, the upper portion of the heat gain calculation sheet should be completed; i.e., location, construction, latitude, outside temperature, temperature range, etc. Part of this information is obtained from Table 13-2. For purpose of example Eau Claire, Wis-

consin is used. The calculations given below are for the living room shown in Fig. 13-29.

First, the lineal footage of exposed wall (in this case: 23' + 4' + 23') and the ceiling height (8') for the living room are recorded on the heat gain calculator sheet. From this the gross exposed wall is calculated.

Next the Btuh heat gain for the windows must be computed. When figuring the heat gain for windows, the direction and the area of sunlit and shaded glass must be taken into account. Window A is 12'-0" long by 5'-0" high and faces west. Table 13-4 lists the shaded glass areas based on window width per foot of overhang. Since Window A is 12' long and the maximum length of

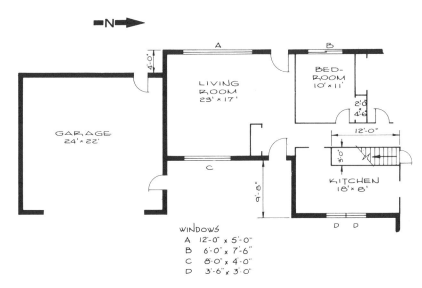

Fig. 13-29. Use this plan for calculating heat gain. (See Heat Gain Calculator Sheet, Fig. 13-28.) This is a portion of a single story, three bedroom ranch-type house with a basement, located in Eau Claire, Wisconsin. The roof overhangs the house a uniform 1'-8". All exterior walls are brick veneer with 3" batt insulation. The roof, over a naturally vented attic, is covered with black asphalt shingles. The ceiling of the house, excluding the garage, is insulated with 4" + of blown insulation. The windows in the living room and bedrooms are welded insulating glass (double glazed), while the kitchen windows are equipped with storm and screens. The kitchen windows have venetian blinds and the living and bedroom windows are draped. All windows are set at 6'-8" head height.

the window shown in the table is 6'-0", simply consider Window A to be two 6'-0" windows. To obtain the shaded area, locate the window width and compass direction (west) and read down vertically to the row indicating the closest latitude (45°). The square foot area of shaded glass per foot of overhang is 2 sq. ft. The roof overhangs the window 1'-6" (or a factor of 1.5). Therefore, 2 sq. ft. × 1.5 = 3 sq. ft. Since there are two windows, 2 × 3 sq. ft. = 6 sq. ft. This is the amount of shaded glass area. Window C faces east and is 8'-0" × 4'-0". Since the window is more than 6' it will have to be broken into two 4' windows. Locate the width in the proper column (4.0') under compass direction (east) and read downward to the 45° latitude row. The square

foot area of shaded glass per foot overhang is 1 sq. ft. Multiply the shaded glass by the overhang factor. 1 sq. ft. × 1.5 = 1.5 sq. ft.; 1.5 sq. ft. × 2 = 3 sq. ft. These are recorded, indicating the direction and area, as: W-6 and E-3.

Any *shaded portion* of a window is considered as a *northward facing window,* regardless of its direction. Table 13-5 lists the glass *heat transfer multiplier* (HTM) for windows based on type of glazing and outside design temperature. Both living room windows are double glazed. The outside design temperature in Eau Claire, Wisconsin is 90°. (See Table 13-2.) Locate the proper section marked "Regular Double Glass" and the column labeled "90°". Both Windows A and C are draped. Read down that column

to the correct HTM (14). Record the figure 14 in the HTM column of the calculator. To obtain the Btuh gain, multiply the shaded area by the HTM: 6 × 14 = 84 Btuh and 3 × 14 = 42 Btuh.

Now the Btuh gain for the sunlit glass must be calculated. To determine the area of sunlit glass for each window, subtract the shaded glass area from the window area. Window A has 60 sq. ft. of area and the shaded portion occupies 6 sq. ft.; therefore, 60 − 6 = 54 sq. ft. Window C has an area 32 sq. ft. with 3 sq. ft. being shaded. The sunlit portion is 29 sq. ft. These are recorded on the calculator with an indication of the compass direction, W-54 and E-29.

To obtain the Btuh heat gain for the windows, refer again to Table 13-5. Locate the

TABLE 13-4

SHADED GLASS AREAS

WINDOW WIDTH, FT	LESS THAN 2.0			2.0 TO 2.5			2.6 TO 3.0			3.1 TO 3.5			3.6 TO 4.0			4.1 TO 4.5			4.6 TO 5.0			5.1 TO 5.5			5.6 TO 6.0		
DIRECTION WINDOW FACES	E W	SE SW	S	E W	SE SW	S	E W	SE SW	S	E W	SE SW	S	E W	SE SW	S	E W	SE SW	S	E W	SE SW	S	E W	SE SW	S	E W	SE SW	S
LATITUDE, DEGREES	AREA OF SHADED GLASS PER FOOT OVERHANG, SQ FT																										
25	0	2	17	1	3	22	1	4	26	1	5	31	1	5	36	1	6	41	1	7	46	2	7	50	2	8	55
30	0	2	9	1	2	11	1	3	14	1	4	16	1	4	18	1	5	21	1	5	23	2	6	26	2	6	28
35	0	2	5	1	2	7	1	2	9	1	3	10	1	3	12	1	4	13	1	4	15	2	5	16	2	5	18
40	0	1	4	1	2	5	1	2	6	1	3	7	1	3	8	1	3	9	1	4	10	2	4	11	2	5	12
45	0	1	3	1	1	3	1	2	4	1	2	5	1	2	6	1	3	6	1	3	7	2	3	8	2	3	9
50	0	1	2	1	1	3	1	1	3	1	2	4	1	2	5	1	2	5	1	2	6	2	3	6	2	3	7
55	0	1	2	1	1	2	1	1	2	1	1	3	1	2	3	1	2	4	1	2	4	2	2	5	2	2	5

NOTE: If top of window is more than 1 ft below edge of overhang the wall area between top of window and overhang must be subtracted from shaded area obtained from Table 12-4. Shades areas are not calculated for NE, N, or NW windows. Use glass heat transfer multiplier indicated in Table 12-5 for entire glass area of window facing these directions.

[1]From: National Warm Air Heating & Air Conditioning Association, Cleveland, Ohio; LOAD CALCULATIONS: MANUAL J, SECOND EDITION.

type of glazing and outside design temperature "Regular Double Glass"—"90°." Read downward to the row marked "Draperies or Venetian Blinds" and "East and West." The HTM is 44. Multiply the sunlit portion of each window by the HTM. Window A = 54 sq. ft. × 44 = 2,376 Btuh; and Window C = 29 sq. ft. × 44 = 1,276 Btuh.

The next heat gain component to be calculated is the *net amount* of exposed wall (the gross wall area minus window area.) The net exposed wall area = 308 sq. ft. (23' + 4' + 23' = 50'; 50 × 8' = 400 sq. ft. gross wall; 400 sq. ft. −92 sq. ft. = 308 sq. ft. net wall). The net exposed wall area is multiplied by the HTM given in Table

13-6. This table lists the HTM per sq. ft. of various types of walls, partitions, ceilings, floors, and infiltration. Locate the daily temperature range and outside design temperature columns marked "Medium" and "90°" (obtained from Table 13-2) and read downward to the specified type of exterior wall construction—"Veneer on Frame—More

TABLE 13-5
GLASS HEAT TRANSFER MULTIPLIER   (COOLING)
Cooling load due to transmitted and absorbed solar energy and air-to-air temperature difference

OUTSIDE DESIGN TEMP	REGULAR SINGLE GLASS					REGULAR DOUBLE GLASS					HEAT ABSORBING DOUBLE GLASS				
	90	95	100	105	110	90	95	100	105	110	90	95	100	105	110
DIRECTION WINDOW FACES	NO AWNINGS OR INSIDE SHADING														
NORTH (OR SHADED)	27	31	35	38	44	21	24	26	28	30	14	17	19	21	23
NE AND NW	60	64	68	71	77	48	51	53	55	57	29	32	34	36	38
EAST AND WEST	85	89	93	96	102	70	73	75	77	79	44	47	49	51	53
SE AND SW	74	78	82	85	91	61	64	66	68	70	37	40	42	44	46
SOUTH	44	48	52	55	61	35	38	40	42	44	21	24	26	28	30
	DRAPERIES OR VENETIAN BLINDS														
NORTH (OR SHADED)	19	23	27	30	36	14	17	19	21	23	11	14	16	18	20
NE AND NW	36	40	44	47	53	29	32	34	36	38	22	25	27	29	31
EAST AND WEST	52	56	60	63	69	44	47	49	51	53	32	35	37	39	41
SE AND SW	44	48	52	55	61	37	40	42	44	46	26	29	31	33	35
SOUTH	27	31	35	38	44	22	25	27	29	31	17	20	22	24	26
	ROLLER SHADES HALF-DRAWN														
NORTH (OR SHADED)	22	26	30	33	39	17	20	22	24	26	12	15	17	19	21
NE AND NW	44	48	52	55	61	40	43	45	47	49	26	29	31	33	35
EAST AND WEST	65	69	73	76	82	56	59	61	63	65	37	40	42	44	46
SE AND SW	56	60	64	67	73	48	51	53	55	57	32	35	37	39	41
SOUTH	33	37	41	44	50	29	32	34	36	38	20	23	25	27	29
	AWNINGS														
NORTH (OR SHADED)	24	28	32	35	41	15	18	20	22	24	12	15	17	19	21
NE AND NW	25	29	33	36	42	16	19	21	23	25	13	16	18	20	22
EAST AND WEST	26	30	34	37	43	16	19	21	23	25	14	17	19	21	23
SE AND SW	25	29	33	36	42	16	19	21	23	25	13	16	18	20	22
SOUTH	24	28	32	35	41	15	18	20	22	24	13	16	18	20	22

NOTE: Factors in this table are based on data for 30 degrees and 40 degrees north latitude
and are expressed in Btu per hr per sq ft.

From: National Warm Air Heating and Air Conditioning Association, Cleveland, Ohio; LOAD CALCULATIONS MANUAL J.   SECOND EDITION

TABLE 13-6
HEAT TRANSFER MULTIPLIER (COOLING)

Daily Temperature Range	Low		Medium				High			
Outside Design Temperature, F	90	95	90	95	100	105	95	100	105	110

WINDOWS

No. 1 through No. 5—Obtain factors from Table 12-5										

DOORS

No. 6 Wood doors. (Consider glass area of doors as a window)	11.4	14.0	9.4	12.0	14.0	17.0	9.4	12.0	14.0	17.0

WALLS

No. 7 Frame and Veneer-on-frame

(a) No insulation	6.0	7.2	4.8	6.0	7.5	8.7	4.8	6.0	7.5	8.7
(b) Less than 1-in. insulation, or one reflective air space	4.3	5.1	3.5	4.5	5.4	6.3	3.5	4.5	5.4	6.3
(c) 1-in. to 2-in. insulation, or two reflective air spaces	2.9	3.6	2.4	3.1	3.7	4.4	2.4	3.1	3.7	4.4
(d) More than 2-in. insulation, or three reflective air spaces	1.8	2.2	1.5	1.9	2.3	2.7	1.5	1.9	2.3	2.7

No. 8 Masonry walls, 8-in. block or brick

(a) Plastered or plain	7.2	9.7	5.4	7.9	10.4	12.5	5.4	7.9	10.4	12.5
(b) Furred, no insulation	4.6	6.0	3.4	4.9	6.3	7.9	3.4	4.9	6.3	7.9
(c) Furred, with less than 1-in. insulation, or one reflective air space	3.1	4.1	2.3	3.3	4.3	5.4	2.3	3.3	4.3	5.4
(d) Furred, with 1-in. to 2-in. insulation, or two reflective air spaces	2.1	2.8	1.6	2.3	3.0	3.7	1.6	2.3	3.0	3.7
(e) Furred, with more than 2-in. insulation or three reflective air spaces	1.4	1.8	1.0	1.5	1.9	2.4	1.0	1.5	1.9	2.4

No. 9 Partitions

(a) Frame, finished one side only, no insulation	8.5	11.4	6.0	9.1	12.0	15.0	6.0	9.1	12.0	15.0
(b) Frame, finished both sides, no insulation	4.8	6.6	3.4	5.1	6.9	8.5	3.4	5.1	6.9	8.5
(c) Frame, finished both sides, more than 1-in. insulation, or two reflective air spaces	2.0	2.7	1.4	2.1	2.8	3.5	1.4	2.1	2.8	3.5
(d) Masonry, plastered one side, no insulation	2.6	4.4	1.2	3.0	4.7	6.6	1.2	3.0	4.7	6.6

TABLE 13-6 (continued)

Daily Temperature Range		Low		Medium				High			
Outside Design Temperature, F		90	95	90	95	100	105	95	100	105	110

CEILINGS AND ROOFS

No. 10 Ceilings under naturally vented attic or vented flat roof

(a) Uninsulation (attic must be vented for cooling)	—dark	10.0	11.0	9.1	10.0	11.4	12.5	9.1	10.0	11.4	12.5
	—light	8.2	9.1	7.2	8.2	9.4	10.4	7.2	8.2	9.4	10.4
(b) Less than 2-in. insulation, or one reflective air space	—dark	4.3	4.8	3.9	4.4	4.9	5.4	3.9	4.4	4.9	5.4
	—light	3.5	4.1	3.1	3.6	4.1	4.6	3.1	3.6	4.1	4.6
(c) 2-in. to 4-in. insulation, or two reflective air spaces	—dark	2.6	2.9	2.3	2.6	2.9	3.2	2.3	2.6	2.9	3.2
	—light	2.1	2.4	1.9	2.2	2.5	2.8	1.9	2.2	2.5	2.8
(d) More than 4-in. insulation, or three or more reflective air spaces	—dark	1.8	1.9	1.6	1.8	2.0	2.2	1.6	1.8	2.0	2.2
	—light	1.4	1.6	1.2	1.4	1.6	1.8	1.2	1.4	1.6	1.8

No. 11 Built-up roof, no ceiling

(a) Uninsulated	—dark	17.0	19.0	16.0	18.0	20.0	22.0	16.0	18.0	20.0	22.0
	—light	14.2	16.4	12.5	14.0	16.0	18.0	12.5	14.0	16.0	18.0
(b) 2-in. roof insulation	—dark	8.5	9.7	7.9	8.7	9.7	11.0	7.9	8.7	9.7	11.0
	—light	6.9	7.9	6.3	7.2	8.2	9.1	6.3	7.2	8.2	9.1
(c) 3-in. roof insulation	—dark	6.0	6.6	5.4	6.3	6.9	7.5	5.4	6.3	6.9	7.5
	—light	4.9	5.6	4.3	5.1	5.6	6.3	4.3	5.1	5.6	6.3

No. 12 Ceilings under unconditioned rooms		2.7	3.6	1.9	2.9	3.8	4.8	1.9	2.9	3.8	4.8

FLOORS

No. 13 Over unconditioned rooms		3.4	4.6	2.4	3.6	4.8	6.0	2.4	3.6	4.8	6.0
No. 14 through No. 18 Over basement, enclosed crawl space, concrete slab on ground, basement or crawl space floor		0	0	0	0	0	0	0	0	0	0
No. 19 Over open or vented space		4.8	6.6	3.4	5.1	6.9	8.5	3.4	5.1	6.9	8.5

INFILTRATION AND VENTILATION

No. 20 Infiltration, Btuh per sq ft of gross exposed wall area		1.1	1.5	1.1	1.5	1.9	2.2	1.6	1.9	2.2	2.6
No. 21 Mechanical ventilation, Btuh per cfm		16.0	22.0	16.0	22.0	27.0	32.0	22.0	27.0	32.0	38.0

[1]From: National Warm-Air Heating & Air Conditioning Association, Cleveland, Ohio; LOAD CALCULATIONS: Manual J. Second Edition.

than 2 in. insulation." The HTM for this type of construction in the medium temperature range for 90° is 1.5. Multiply the net exposed wall area by the HTM. 308 × 1.5 = 462 Btuh.

Any partitions that are not conditioned, such as the 13′ length of wall separating the living room from the garage, must be calculated. Locate the same column as above in Table 13-6 and read downward to the row labeled "Frame, finished both sides more than 1 in. insulation." Multiply this HTM by the area of the warm wall: 104 sq. ft. × 1.4 = 146 Btuh.

The area above the ceilings in this single story house is not air conditioned so this must also be computed when figuring total heat gain. Multiply the area of the ceiling (23′ × 17′) by the HTM found in Table 13-6: 391 sq. ft. × 1.6 = 626 Btuh.

If the floor of the room to be conditioned is over a basement, enclosed crawl space, concrete slab on the ground, etc., there will be no heat gain. However, if the floor is over an unconditioned room or over an open or vented space, the heat gain must then be calculated and entered on the calculator.

Heat gain due to infiltration must be calculated next (use Table 13-6) by multiplying the gross exposed wall area by the infiltration HTM: 400 sq. ft. × 1.1 = 440 Btuh.

Also figured in the heat gain are the number of occupants. This home has 3 bedrooms. As stated previously, multiply the number of bedrooms by 2. Each person is calculated to emit 300 Btuh: 6 × 300 Btuh = 1,800 Btuh. This figure is listed only once on the calculator because the heat gain, 1,800 Btuh, is averaged over all the living areas.

The *sensible heat gain* is a summation of all heat gains: 84 + 42 + 2,376 + 1,276 + 462 + 626 + 440 + 1,800 = 7,252 Btuh.

To obtain the *total heat gain* for the room, the sensible heat gain is multiplied by a constant 1.3, as discussed previously: 7,252 × 1.3 = 9,428 Btuh. This is the number of British Thermal Units that must be removed per hour to achieve an inside temperature of 75°F under the stated conditions. (This heat gain applies to the living rooms shown in Fig. 13-29.)

When calculating the kitchen, a heat gain of 1,200 Btuh must be added for the appliances.

Each room, hall, and/or other area is calculated in the same manner as the living room. The total heat gain for the entire house would then be the *sum* of all heat gains and would be a guide for selecting the proper size cooling unit. Manufacturers give the Btuh removal rate of cooling units. Cooling units are also rated in tons. A ton is the amount of refrigeration that will be produced by a ton of ice melting over a twenty-four hour period (this has a heat absorption of 288,000 Btu's). A ton is equivalent to removing 12,000 Btuh.

Working Drawings

The air conditioning system is sometimes included in the set of working drawings. The Federal Housing Administration's *Minimum Property Standards* (FHA No. 300) requires that the following be included in the working drawings:

Heating system, on separate drawing or as part of floor or basement plan showing:
a. Layout of system.
b. Location and size of ducts, piping, registers, radiators, etc.
c. Location of heating unit and room thermostat.
d. Total calculated heat loss of dwelling including heat loss through all vertical surfaces, ceiling, and floor. When a duct or piped distribution system is used, calculated heat loss of each heated space.

Cooling system, on separate drawings or as part of heating plan, floor or basement plan showing:
a. Layout of system.
b. Location and size of ducts, registers, compressors, coils, etc.
c. Heat gain calculations, including estimated heat gain for each space conditioned.
d. Model number and Btuh capacity of equipment or units in accordance with applicable ARI (Air Conditioning and Refrigeration Institute) or ASRE (American Society of Refrigerating Engineers) Standard.

e. Btuh capacity and total KW input at stated local design conditions.

f. If room or zone conditioners are used, provide location, size and installation details.

Questions and Problems

1. Based on the community in which you live, what system of heating would you choose for heating a:
   a. split-level house having 1,300 sq. ft.?
   b. ranch house having 1,100 sq. ft.?
   c. two-story house having 1,100 sq. ft.?

2. Have your instructor assign a class member to contact the local electric company concerning the rate for an electrically heated home. Are these rates based on a specific amount of electricity consumed? Is this a favorable rate? Is the rate competitive with other types of fuel?

3. What advantages and disadvantages does a hydronic system have in comparison with a warm-air system?

4. What logical reason could be stated for placing a warm-air diffuser or register on a cold wall particularly below a window?

5. Would it be sound economy to install some form of electric heating in an enclosed porch that has been added on to an existing dwelling? What factors would be considered as important in arriving at a decision?

6. What is a coefficient of transmission? Does an insulating material that has a high U-factor indicate that it is better than one having a low factor?

7. Shortly after a new snowfall, can you identify from the street, those dwellings that do not have insulation in attic floor? What signs tell you that the home does not have insulation? What causes this occurrence?

8. Using the house plan and related information shown in Fig. 13-24, which of the following furnaces with guaranteed Btuh ratings (at sea level) would most adequately heat the structure:
   a. 90,000 Btuh at the bonnet
   b. 100,000 Btuh at the bonnet
   c. 120,000 Btuh at the bonnet
   d. None of the above

9. Using the house plan shown in Fig. 13-26, sketch a warm-air heating system. Sketch a basement plan and show the arrangement. What would be the best way to provide for summer air conditioning?

10. List the basic functions of air conditioning.

11. When sizing a cooling unit, what gain factors must be considered when detailing the heat gain?

12. What is the ideal relative humidity level during the summer months?

13. What maximum temperature variation is considered satisfactory in an air conditioned room?

14. What reasons may be given for the necessity of requiring constant air motion in home cooling?

15. It is understood that ventilation is necessary in the air conditioned home. What factors contribute to stale air? How may each of these be remedied?

16. What building components (material, structural members, etc.) cause the greatest amount of heat gain?

17. What kinds of devices may be used to reduce the amount of heat gain on an exterior wall?

18. Calculate the heat gain for your bedroom at home.

19. Sketch the plan of your house or apartment. Using the tables provided in this chapter, calculate the total heat gain. Be sure to specify the type of construction, insulation, overhang, compass direction, window sizes, window protection, etc. Record your calculations in a manner similar to that illustrated by heat gain calculator or set down your results in a logical, understandable order.

Plumbing 14

The plumbing system is one of the least understood, yet most essential of our modern living conveniences. Perhaps this is true because most plumbing, like electric wiring, is hidden within the walls and floors. It is necessary, however, for the architect to have a competent understanding of the general plumbing layout and to co-ordinate the plumbing with the over-all house plan. Detail planning is usually done by the plumbing contractor.

Plumbing System

A plumbing system is designed to carry water to the various outlets in the building and to remove waste water and materials to the sanitary sewer or septic tank. Also included under plumbing is the piping for gas.

Plumbing pipes are installed after the structure has been "roughed in" (exterior shell with sheathing and interior partition walls, but with no plaster or drywall). Pipes are placed in the walls, ceilings, and floors, and are carried to the points where the fixtures will be attached. The fixtures are added after the drywall or plaster has been applied. Meters for water and gas must also be located and connected.

Today, much of the piping for supply and drainage is copper. Heretofore lead or steel pipe was used. Copper pipe has an advantage over steel pipe in that the junction between a run of pipe and a fitting (tee, elbow, ell, etc.) is soldered rather than threaded. Most plumbing jobs will allow copper piping one size smaller than steel for the same flow rate. Copper tubing is available in either flexible or rigid form. The drainage system carrying the waste water and material to the house drain may be copper, cast iron, or steel.

Many state plumbing codes now permit the use of PVC (polyvinyl chloride) plastic pipe in some phases of new plumbing installations where steel or copper have been previously used. The main advantage of plastic pipe over steel or copper is its ease of installation. Plastic pipe is easily cut and joined.

Almost all plumbing installations are governed by a code. Because a state code, such as a plumbing code, approves a particular material or procedure does not indicate that

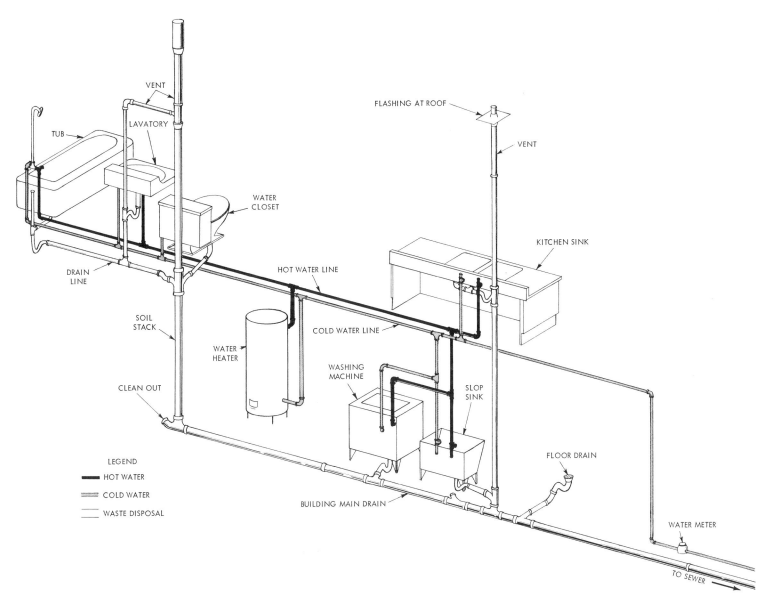

Fig. 14-1. House Plumbing System: Hot and Cold Water Supply and Waste Disposal Line.

every local code will allow that material or practice. Any state code is considered as a minimum. Each code adopted by a city, for example, may follow the state code, or it may modify it by making it more stringent.

Almost all plumbing installations are governed by some type of building code. In a few areas, however, the installation of the plumbing is left to the judgment of the plumber with no specific code to guard the home owner. If a code exists, the designer should follow it in laying out the plumbing system.

Water Supply

Plumbing supply systems, regardless of size or capacity, all have the same basic features. A water supply pipe brings the water into the structure from either a city water main (under pressure) or a private well. If a well is used, pumping will be required. Smaller pipes distribute the cold water directly to the outlets at the tub, shower, lavatories, toilet flush boxes, heating plant, hose bibs, etc. A branch line feeds the hot water heater. A main pipe with branches leads from the heater to faucets located at the fixtures. Cold and hot water pipes that run vertically are called *risers*. A simple plumbing installation showing water lines, risers, vents, etc. is shown in Fig. 14-1.

Fixture Branches

Each plumbing fixture is connected to a soil or waste stack by the means of a fixture branch. (These branches are horizontal with a slope of ¼" per foot.) Branch runs must of necessity be kept as short as possible, especially if they are laid between joists with flooring above and ceiling material below.

In areas where temperatures drop below freezing, precautions must be taken to provide adequate insulation for pipes placed in outside walls. Some plumbing fixtures, notably cast iron and vitrified clay, are often heavy and the floor joists supporting these loads must be reinforced by doubling, or by placing the joists closer together. The only area where this is usually applicable is under the bathroom. In some instances it may be necessary to run a pipe *through* a joist; provisions should be made to strengthen this opening by means of a block, see Fig. 14-2. Of necessity this cut must be placed near the top of the joist to retain the maximum load bearing quality of the joist.

Water and Waste Removal

Water that has been used for washing or

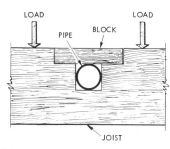

Fig. 14-2. A pipe that passes through a joist must be placed at the top and blocked to prevent appreciable weakening of that member.

as a vehicle for disposing of waste matter must have an escape to the sanitary sewer or septic tank. To serve this end a companion pipe system, carefully isolated from supply pipes, is required to guard the health of the occupants. This is probably the most important and most complicated feature in the plumbing system.

Between the fixtures and the soil and waste stacks, a water seal is necessary. Normally a P-trap is used. Fig. 14-3 illustrates a typical sewage disposal system for a residential dwelling. Note the trap.

Soil and Waste Stacks receive the waste water and materials from the various plumbing fixtures, such as lavatories, sinks, washers, dishwashers, water closets, etc. These stacks connect to the house drain. From an economic standpoint, plumbing should be grouped to require as few stacks as possible, both on a single floor and on a multi-level dwelling. The whole layout of the building must be taken into consideration in laying out the soil and waste stacks. To achieve the shortest and most practical route it is advisable to consult with the plumbing contractor. Due to the size of the soil and waste stacks (minimum 3", usually 4" in residential housing), partitions (with 2" × 6" studs) are commonly located after the pipe run has been planned. Copper pipe is fast replacing cast iron pipe since a 3" copper pipe will fit in a normal stud wall. The soil and waste stacks are extended through the highest part of the roof for ventilation.

Building Drain. Vertical soil and waste

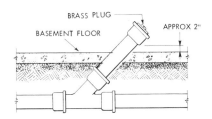

Fig. 14-4. The cleanout is located at the end of the last vertical stack and at each change in direction of the building drain.

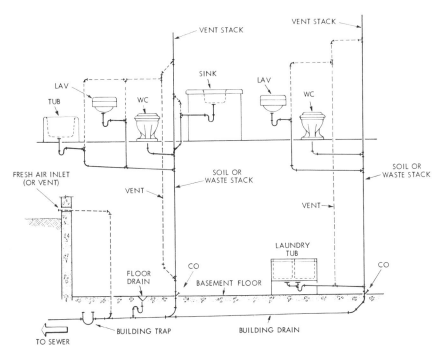

Fig. 14-3. This figure illustrates a typical sewage disposal and venting system for a residential dwelling.

stacks empty into the building drain. The drain is usually located immediately beneath the basement floor provided the city sanitary sewer is below this elevation. If the city sewer is higher in elevation, then the building drain is fastened along the inside of the foundation wall or hung from the ceiling. The drain should, if possible, have a pitch of ¼″ per foot. A 4″ inside diameter for cast iron pipe and a 6″ inside diameter for vitrified clay pipe is usually adequate for a small residential dwelling. However, local plumb-

ing codes should be consulted to determine the exact sizing and material.

In areas adjacent to the footings where excessive water is present drain tile (usually 3″) may also be laid around the inside and outside of the footing. Sometimes the seepage from this is carried by the building drain. However, the local building code must be consulted since this practice is not permitted in all cities.

Cleanouts (CO) should be provided at the end of the last vertical stack and at

each change in direction of the house drain. Fig. 14-4 illustrates a cleanout.

Building Trap. The purpose of this trap is to prevent sanitary sewer gases from entering into the plumbing. The trap is located immediately on the inside of the foundation wall and has the same diameter as the building drain. Usually a U-shaped trap is used. To facilitate cleaning, cleanouts are provided at one or both of the "horns" or "outlets" placed at the top of the U. Local plumbing codes should be checked to see if there is any restriction on the use of a building trap.

Building Sewer. This sewer connects the building trap and drain at the foundation wall to the main sanitary sewer located in the street or to the septic tank. This is usually the first part of the plumbing system to be installed.

Either cast-iron or vitrified clay pipe may be used in the building sewer, depending upon local or state plumbing codes. Cast-iron pipe should have at least a 4″ inside diameter. Vitrified clap pipe should have at least a 6″ inside diameter. Cast-iron is recommended if there are any trees in the vicinity or if the soil is unstable. Tree roots might enter between the vitrified clap pipe joints and clog the system. If vitrified clap pipe is used in unstable soil, some support must be provided.

The slope of the building sewer depends upon the difference between the depth of the drain outlet and the depth of the street sewer. The difference is distributed over the total length of the house sewer run. Usually the slope of the building sewer is at least ¼″ per foot.

If the basement is below the level of the sanitary sewer or septic tank a sump pit with a pump must be employed to pump the waste water up to the building sewer. The sump pit is a covered, cylindrical recess in the basement floor into which the waste water from the basement plumbing fixtures is drained. When the water reaches a particular level the sump pump automatically draws up the water to the level of the sewer. Fig. 14-5 illustrates the use of a sump pump.

Storm Drain. Outside drain pipes (leaders) should *not* be connected to the building drain or sewer. Water run-off in some cities may be connected into a storm drain system. If there is no storm drain, a natural drainage basin or dry well may be used. The water from the footing drain tile is sometimes carried into the storm drain. In all cases, consult the local plumbing or building code.

Venting

Venting is needed to equalize pressure within a drainage system. Equalization of pressure prevents trap seal loss, back pressure and retardation of flow. Venting also serves to remove gas and unpleasant odors from the system. Fig. 14-3 illustrates a venting system.

Vent Stacks. The vent stack is a continuation of the soil and waste stack *above* the highest branch intersection with the waste stack. Its sole purpose is to permit air to enter and circulate in the soil and waste lines. The vent stack should extend

at least 8″ above the roof. This dimension may vary depending upon the local code. The *main vent* begins at the base of the soil and waste stack, its purpose is to relieve any back pressure in the system. It joins the vent stack at least 3′ above the highest installed fixture branch. The diameter of the vent stack is usually one-half the diameter of the soil and waste stack.

Branch Vents. Each fixture branch must be vented by a branch vent. This serves in a capacity similar to the large vent stack. Waste matter flowing through the fixture branches must not be allowed to clog the branch vents. This may be prevented by attaching the vent as shown in Figs. 14-3 and 14-6. The inside diameter of the branch vent should not be less than 1¼″.

Fresh Air Inlet. Since the building trap acts as a seal preventing the back-up of sewer gases from the street, it also pre-

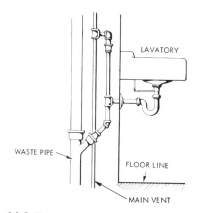

Fig. 14-6. Fixture venting is necessary to prevent the loss of the water seal.

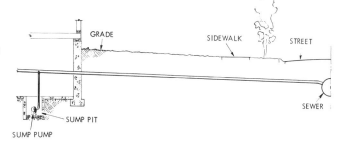

Fig. 14-5. A sump pump may be used to raise the waste water up to the building sewer.

vents the outlet of air or gases. A fresh air inlet or pipe is placed adjacent to the trap to serve as an escape and avoid the compression of gases. This inlet also allows air to enter the system if necessary. The inside diameter of the fresh air inlet should not be less than 2″. A 4″ pipe is recommended.

Sewage Disposal

In most cities sewer service is provided. Frequently, however, in newly developed areas the city sewer lines have not kept up with the unusual growth. In city locations and in country and suburban areas where sewers are not available, house sewerage is disposed by means of a cesspool or septic tank.

Leaching Cesspool. The leaching cesspool is essentially a cylindrical hole in the ground lined around the outer surface with bricks, stones, or concrete blocks with unfilled joints. The diameter of the cesspool is between 6′-0″ to 8′-0″; it is approximately 10′-0″ deep. The top of the cesspool should be close to the surface of the grade. Sewage is drained into the cesspool and is allowed to gradually seep into the surrounding soil. The solid matter is retained. If the cesspool is located too far below the grade or in hard earth, the drainage is inhibited. One of the problems with this method of sewage disposal is that the immediate area surrounding the cesspool may become contaminated, thereby polluting wells in the area. The leaching cesspool should only be used in loose or sandy soil. It should *not* be used in coarse gravel or fissured rock as contamination may extend for great distances. Many municipal plumbing codes prohibit the installation of leaching cesspools.

Watertight Cesspool. This particular type of cesspool has a distinct advantage over the leaching cesspool in that the waste material is retained in the watertight compartment. Often a watertight cesspool is connected with a dry well. See Fig. 14-7. The watertight cell may be poured concrete, or brick or block parged on the interior with waterproof cement. A metal prefabricated tank may also be used. Sewage drains into the waterproof cell and fills until the liquid reaches the overflow pipe. The overflow liquid then runs into the dry well. The material that accumulates in the watertight unit need not be cleaned so frequently. (Caution must be exercised in cleaning a watertight cesspool as there will be little free oxygen, also the gases formed may be both explosive and poisonous.)

Rain run-off from roofs should not be permitted to flow into the cesspool since this may cause excessive overflow. All cesspools must be vented with a 4″ pipe to prevent the build-up of gas pressure. The watertight cesspool (by itself) can be placed as close as 30 ft. to a well or water-tight cistern.

Septic Tank. The septic tank serves four basic functions: (1) it holds the sewage, (2) effects decomposition of waste matter, (3) retains any solids that have not been dissolved, and (4) permits the liquid overflow to drain into a distribution (purification) field. Disintegration in the septic tank itself takes place by the action of anaerobic bacteria on the waste. This chemical action takes place only in the absence of oxygen. After this initial purification, the liquid flows into the distribution system for further purification. In the purification field, chemical action takes place as the liquid overflow comes in contact with the air contained in the upper layers of soil. The

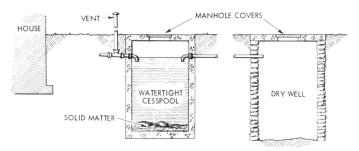

Fig. 14-7. The watertight cesspool has a distinct advantage over the leaching type in that the solid matter is not allowed to pass into the surrounding earth.

oxygen and aerobic bacteria work together to transform waste material into harmless chemical compounds.

The advantage of the septic tank over the cesspool is that it does not permit polluted waste to enter the soil. The septic tank holds the sewage (see Fig. 14-8) for a sufficient time to allow the solid waste material to become diluted. Any solids that do not completely dissolve are retained as sludge. The overflow liquid then drains into a distribution system, located 12″ below grade. This consists of 4″ field tile laid with loose joints. To prevent each joint from becoming clogged with dirt, a strip of tar paper is placed over each joint. Each joint allows the liquid to be drained into the soil and filtered. The purification and leaching field should consist of 150′ to 200′ of tile for adequate dispersion. On flat land the tile has a slope of 1″ per 20′. Fig. 14-9 shows typical distribution fields associated

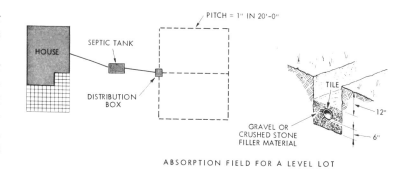

ABSORPTION FIELD FOR A LEVEL LOT

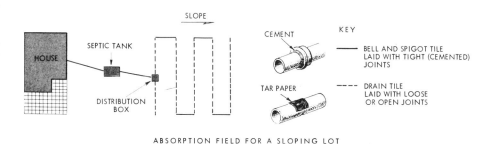

ABSORPTION FIELD FOR A SLOPING LOT

Fig. 14-9. This figure illustrates septic tank disposal systems for sites having level and sloping topography.

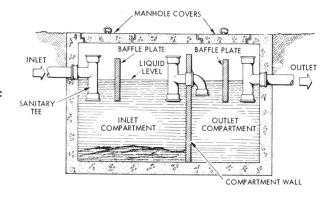

Fig. 14-8. Double Compartment Septic Tank. This system prevents pollution.

with a septic tank. Perforated fiber or clay tile may be used in place of drain tile laid with open joints.

The local plumbing codes or governing health department should be consulted for the correct size of a septic tank drainage field. The size of the drainage field is dependent upon the size of the septic tank and type of soil. Based on these facts the total lineal footage of tile to adequately disperse the liquid can be computed.

The capacity of the septic tank is usu-

TABLE 14-1

MINIMUM SEPTIC TANK CAPACITIES

NUMBER OF BEDROOMS	LIQUID CAPACITY BELOW OUTLET
2 OR LESS	750 GAL.
3	900 GAL.
4	1000 GAL.
EACH ADDITIONAL BEDROOM, ADD	250 GAL.

ally based on the number of bedrooms in the dwelling. Minimum capacities for septic tanks are given in Table 14-1. The capacities shown in this table are sufficient to accommodate fixtures and appliances including automatic washers, garbage disposers, and dishwashers. These tanks are normally prefabricated. They may be either concrete or metal.

Planning Points

In laying out a plumbing system, the practical considerations listed below should be taken into account. The designer should *always* follow the local plumbing code. What is standard in one section of the country may be restricted or forbidden in another section.

1. Water supply piping should be as direct as possible (with few offsets) to avoid friction which may cause "hammering" and retard the flow.
2. Hot and cold water pipes should be at least ½ ft. apart to prevent heat

transfer. If they are closer than ½ ft., insulation is necessary.
3. Usually, as a rough rule, one set of *stacks* (one soil and one vent) is required for each set of *risers* (hot and cold water pipes).
4. Use $2'' \times 6''$ studs in the partitions which house the soil pipe.
5. The hot water heater should be as close as possible to the area of main usage (usually the kitchen). Keep hot water pipe runs as short as possible to avoid excessive heat loss.
6. A cleanout (CO) should be located at each change in direction of the drainage system.
7. Underground piping should be below the frost line to avoid freezing. If the piping is above the frost line, insulation may be necessary.

Plumbing and Working Drawings

The location of *all* plumbing fixtures is shown on *all* floor plans that contain those fixtures. The *basement plan* would show (if

these items were to be included in the house) the water heater, exterior hose bibs, stationary tubs, bibs for automatic washer, lavatory, water closet, sump pump, and floor drains. The *first floor plan* would show the kitchen sink, dishwasher, water closet(s), lavatories, tub, shower, and frost-proof hose bibs. The *garage area,* if attached, would show a bib for automatic washer, and the floor drain. The *second floor* would show the lavatories, water closet, tub, and shower. Location of fixtures is usually all that is necessary since the plumbing contractor knows the local plumbing code and can install the piping and fixtures correctly.

In some instances the plan will show the runs of hot, cold and soft water pipes and, if used, the gas lines. These will be shown by coded single or broken lines representing each pipe run. Pipe sizes should be called out. Occasionally a section is taken through a specific portion of the house to show a particular plumbing installation (for example, pipes, valves, or elevation of fixtures). This, however, is not a common practice. A plumbing diagram, such as that shown in Fig. 14-10, is sometimes included in the working drawings.

If a septic tank or cesspool is the means of sewage disposal, a single line representation of the disposal system is included in the working drawings. The lot line, house, septic tank, drainage field, or cesspool are shown in outline only. The only dimensions that are necessary are the location dimension of the septic tank or cesspool, the outline dimensions of the

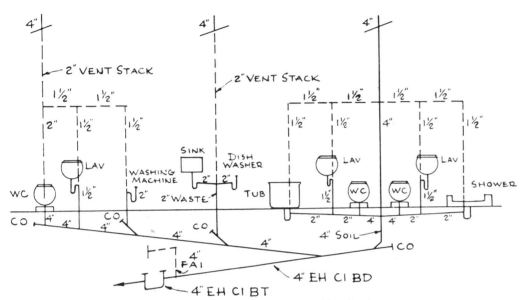

Fig. 14-10. A plumbing diagram is sometimes included in the working drawings.

drainage field, and the capacity of the septic tank. The septic tank or cesspool is also sometimes shown on the plot plan. If a lawn sprinkler system is installed, this may also be shown on the plot plan.

Questions and Problems

1. What are the disadvantages of selecting a rocky site in regard to problems of non-public sewage disposal?
2. Why must the sewer and building drain be pitched? What pitches must be maintained for each of these?
3. Is it necessary to prepare a piping diagram for the water supply or sewage disposal system for the average single family dwelling?
4. What purpose does the water seal serve in the house trap and in the traps below plumbing fixtures?
5. How many advantages could you specify for selecting a septic tank for a lot that is not served by municipal sewage disposal in comparison with a leaching type cesspool?
6. Why must tar paper, or other suitable material be placed over the loose joints of field tile in the leaching system?
7. Why is the building trap the same diameter as the building drain?
8. Why should sanitary or water pipes not be placed on an outside wall?
9. Could a soil or waste stack be placed in a "horizontal" position?
10. Why should the designer be aware of the probable placement of vent stacks?
11. Draw a plot plan showing the septic system for a two-story, three bedroom home with two baths and a basement. Draw a basement plan showing the drainage system.
12. Draw a plumbing diagram for the two-story home laid out in the problem above (Problem 11).

Perspective 15

Perspective drawings serve many purposes for the architectural designer. They may be used: (1) to illustrate alternate design principles, (2) to illustrate the proposed structure for a client, and (3) as a basic foundation in sketching. Within the broad field of graphics the area of perspective drawing offers perhaps the most varied means for arriving at the desired end. Through the years many books have been authored on the science of perspective. Each author has developed a slightly different innovation which has led to a host of methods. This examination attempts to present a practical application of perspective as it is useful to the drafting student. (Texts which give a more exhaustive study of the theory and physiological principles of perspective are listed in Appendix B at the end of the book.)

In this chapter, the three types of perspective drawing are discussed: parallel or one-point, angular or two-point, and oblique or three-point. Common drawing methods for parallel and angular perspective are discussed in detail with step-by-step drawing guides. The latter portion of this chapter is devoted to rendering, that is, "dressing the perspective."

What Perspective Is

The study and observation of the phenomena of perspective dates back far into history. The *science* of perspective (and it is a science) as we know and understand it today, goes back 250 years. Some of the laws of perspective were realized even a century earlier. Prior to this time, man groped, most often in an unrealistic manner, to achieve a natural appearance in his drawings. Evidence of this is shown in the two-dimensional art forms that remain from the Greco-Roman period. Man's earliest attempts to communicate graphically are represented by the engravings found on bones

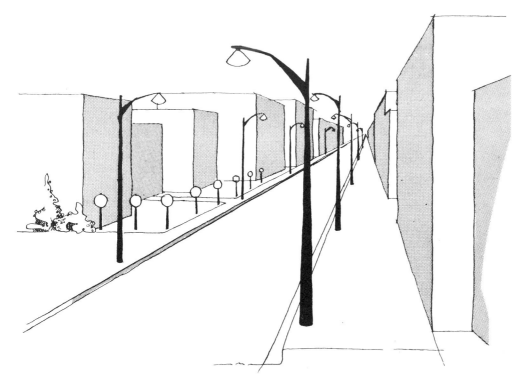

Fig. 15-1. The simplest form of perspective is the one-point or parellel perspective. All lines parallel with the observer's line of sight converge at a single point.

and by the drawings and paintings found on cave walls of the Late or Upper Paleolithic period (35,000 to 15,000 years ago). These "Ice Age" paintings and drawings are the earliest known examples of perspective realism. At this time, of course, no systematic knowledge existed of the laws of perspective.

Perhaps the desire to draw a three dimensional shape in its approximate true representation is as old as man himself.

Perspective drawings give the most natural appearance of any type of graphic description. If a photograph and a perspective

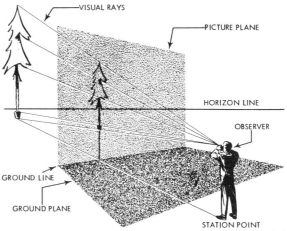

Fig. 15-2. This figure illustrates the basic concepts and terminology used in perspective.

drawing are made (from the same position and angle) of the same object and compared, the photo and drawing will be essentially the same. A correctly constructed perspective drawing will represent a true "picture" of the object.

If you stand on the sidewalk (as in Fig. 15-1) and look into the distance, the street lamps, sidewalk, street, and curb converge at a single point. This example illustrates the basic theory of perspective: all parallel lines which extend away from the observer will converge at a common distant point. This simple type of perspective drawing is called a one-point or *parallel perspective*. Before we can go any further, however, some terminology universal to all forms of perspective must be understood.

In perspective drawing, the observer assumes he is viewing all objects through a transparent *picture plane* (an imaginary plane) upon which the object is projected. (See Fig. 15-2 for an illustration of this concept and others given below.) The point from which the observer views is called the *station point* and the plane on which he stands (and on which the object rests) is the *ground plane*. The intersection of the picture plane and the ground plane is called the *ground line*. The intersection of the picture the viewer's eye to the object are the *visual rays* or *lines of sight*. Each perspective drawing contains a *horizon line:* this is a real or an imaginary line in the distance at *the eye level of the viewer*. The *vanishing points* are the points on the horizon line where the lines of the object meet. A per-

spective drawing gives a view as seen from only *one* station point.

The following abbreviations are commonly used in discussing perspective:

Station Point	(SP)
Ground Plane	(GP)
Ground Line	(GL)
Picture Plane	(PP)
Horizon Line	(HL)
Vanishing Point	(VP)
Vanishing Point Left	(VPL)
Vanishing Point Right	(VPR)

Perspective Types

Perspective drawings may be classified into three categories: (1) *parallel* or one-point, (2) *angular* or two-point, and (3) *oblique* or three-point. Each type may be used to a particular advantage.

Parallel Perspective

Fig. 15-3 (top) illustrates parallel or one-point perspective. As its name implies, it has only one vanishing point. To achieve this characteristic, *two* of the principal axes of the object must be parallel to the picture plane, while the third is perpendicular to the picture plane. The principal axes of an object are *width* (horizontal), *height* (vertical), and *depth* (receding). Another way of describing parallel perspective is to say that the picture plane is parallel to one of the *faces* of the object. One-point perspectives are particularly suited for interiors showing

three walls, the ceiling, and/or the floor (depending where the eye level is located).

Angular Perspective

Angular or two-point perspective has two vanishing points (Fig. 15-3, center). Note that only *one* axis (vertical) is parallel to the picture plane. The other two axes are at an angle to the picture plane. The angular perspective is highly adaptive to any type of object for any situation. Architecturally, the angular perspective may be used to describe exteriors and interiors of structures, as well as any detail for a presentation or display drawing. Depending on the nature of the object (solid or open) and the position of the horizon line, either two or three faces of the object may be visible.

Oblique Perspective

Oblique or three-point perspective (Fig. 15-3, bottom) has, as its name implies, three vanishing points. *No* principal axis is parallel to the picture plane: all three principal axes are at an angle. Theoretically this is the most correct type of perspective when the object is *placed above* or *below* the horizon line. As we view any object that is placed below or above our eye level (horizon line), either the top or the bottom of the object is closer to the eye. It should, therefore, be larger.

Three point perspective can best be illustrated by standing on the top of a high building and viewing an adjacent, lower building. The top of that building will ap-

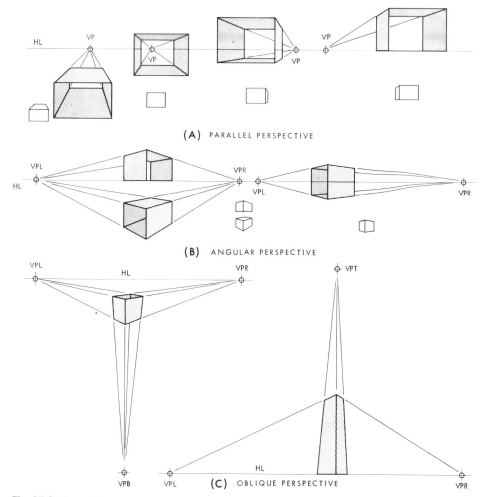

(A) PARALLEL PERSPECTIVE

(B) ANGULAR PERSPECTIVE

(C) OBLIQUE PERSPECTIVE

Fig. 15-3. These three categories of perspective show how the object lines converge at the vanishing point(s).

pear to vanish to a point at the right and a point to the left. Also the vertical sides of the building will appear to converge to a point below. The same phenomena will be evident in reverse if the same tall building is viewed from the sidewalk. The use of three-point perspective is *usually* limited to aerial views of buildings. It is seldom used in residential renderings.

Picture Plane and Station Point

The general shape of the object drawn in perspective can be changed by moving the picture plane and changing the station point. In most instances for the sake of convenience, the designer, draftsman, or illustrator will place the picture plane between the object and the station point. (The object or objects may be placed in front of the picture plane but this poses additional manipulation of the visual rays.) When the object is in its usual position (immediately behind the picture plane), the perspective drawing is smaller than its actual size in the plan and elevation views. As the picture plane is moved farther away from the object, i.e., closer to the station point, the perspective becomes smaller. This is easily illustrated by forming a frame with the index fingers and thumbs (Fig. 15-4). Simply move the hands closer to and farther away from any object. You will observe that the object appears larger within the rectangle as the rectangle is moved closer to the object. Conversely, it appears smaller as the rectangle is farther away from the object.

To achieve the least amount of distortion in a perspective, the station point should be located at such a distance from the object that the visual rays will *include* the object and form an angle *not greater* than 30°.

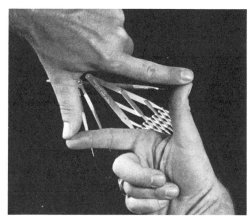

Fig. 15-4. The principle of the picture plans may be simply demonstrated by forming a frame with the hands and moving it closer to and further away from the object.

This angle (frequently caller the *clear angle of vision*) will insure the elimination of distortion. Some delineators use an angle of clear vision ranging from 30° to 45°; most, however, use a 30° angle.

Fig. 15-5 shows the same object drawn from three different station points. The station point has been kept at the same elevation and in the same line with the object. However, its distance from the object has been varied. As the station point has been moved closer to the object (as in position 1) the perspective drawing appears to be distorted. By taking a 30°-60° triangle and placing the 30° angle at the station point, note that the object is *not completely included* by the hypotenuse and adjacent side of the triangle. In position 2 the station

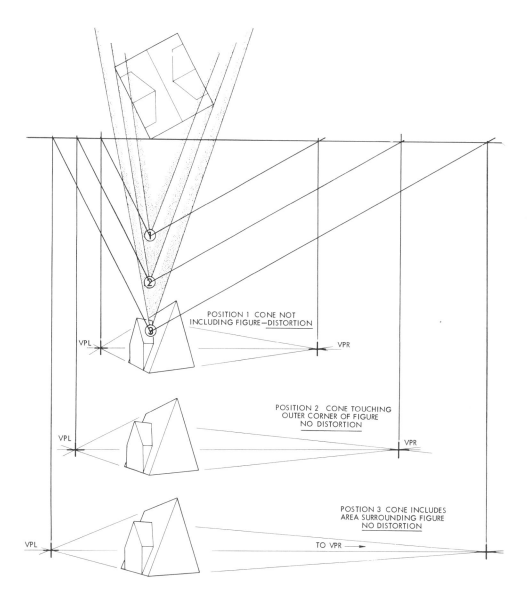

Fig. 15-5. This comparison of three perspectives shows the effects of the cone of vision.

point is located properly so that the sides of the triangle just touch the extreme corners of the object. From this vantage point the distortion has been eliminated. Position 3 shows the cone of vision including *more* than the object. Here again, there is no distortion.

By placing the station point nearer to the picture plane the vanishing points are forced closer together and thus contribute to increased distortion. Placing the station point at the minimum distance, so the object is included by the 30° angle, will prove the best rule of thumb. There are occasions when the station point may be moved closer to purposely change or draw attention to a particular feature. A more complete discussion of this matter is presented in Morgan's *Architectural Drawing: Perspective, Light and Shadow, Rendering.*[1]

The station point may be moved to the left or right or up or down to achieve emphasis on a particular face or faces. Fig. 15-6 illustrates the effect of different station points. Observe the different effects that can be achieved.

Perspective Drawing

Each of the following types of perspective drawings are explained in a step-by-step procedure. Where plans and elevations are needed for drawing perspectives, it is sug-

1. Sherley W. Morgan, *Architectural Drawing: Perspective, Light, and Shadow, Rendering* (New York: McGraw-Hill Book Company, Inc., 1950).

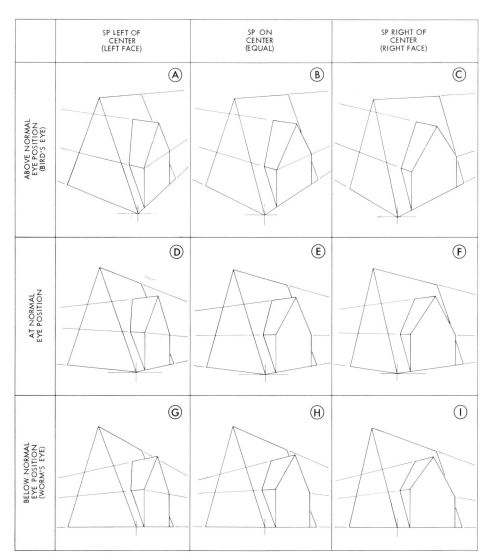

Fig. 15-6. By moving both the station point and horizon line the emphasis on the faces of an object is changed.

gested that a print of the plan and elevation be made so that a redrawing of these views is eliminated.

Parallel Perspective: Plan View Method

The *plan view method* of drawing a par-allel perspective is one of several procedures currently used. In the architectural field the plan view method has proved the most successful for the beginning student. The following step-by-step procedure illustrates, along with Fig. 15-7, the plan view method of drawing a one-point perspective.

Step   1.   Draw the top edge view of the picture plane (PP) near the top of sheet of detail paper. Cut out the plan and elevation views from a print. Tape the plan view along the horizontal PP line. The front edge of the object does not have to touch the PP. However, by placing it so that it does touch, it will reduce the number of points that must be carried to the station point (SP).

Step   2.   Draw the horizon line (HL) below the plan view. The location of the HL is determined by the vantage point of the observer. If the object is to be viewed *below* the eye level, place the HL immediately be-

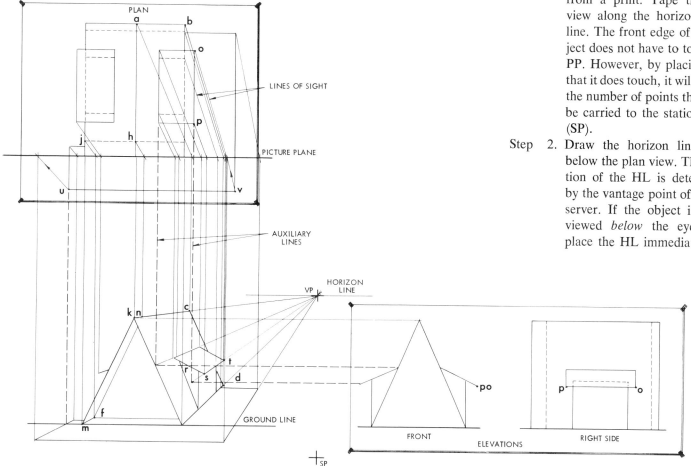

Fig. 15-7. The plan view method of drawing a parallel perspective is one of the most common.

low the plan view. If the object is *above* eye level, move the HL farther down.

Step 3. Draw the horizontal ground line (GL). The position of the ground line depends upon how far above or below the horizon line the object will be placed. Since all plans are in scale (¼″ = 1′-0″, for example) the distance between the HL and GL will be in the same scale. Tape the elevation view to one side of the perspective. Locate the elevation base *on* the GL.

Step 4. Locate the SP. To eliminate as much distortion as possible, *place the SP not closer than two times the width (length) of the object from the nearest point on the plan view.* The SP may be located at any position directly in center front, left or right. Unless some particular condition exists, it is perhaps most advisable to place the SP either to the left or right of center. Remember: the visual cone must include the object and the angle must not be *greater* than 30°.

Step 5. Locate the vanishing point (VP). Draw a vertical line from the SP to the HL. This intersection with the HL forms the VP.

Step 6. Project the width of the ob-

ject from the plan view to the ground line.

Step 7. Draw the front face of the object. This will be true size and shape since the front is touching the PP.

Step 8. Project perspective depth of the object. Carry all visible edges from the front face to the VP. From the SP draw lines to the rear corners of the object in the plan view, points *a* and *b*. (See Fig. 15-7.) The points that are formed by the intersection of the lines of sight and the PP are the perspective *depths* of each feature viewed from that particular vantage point. Draw projectors from these points of intersection to the lines carried to the VP. The intersection of these lines form points *c* and *d*—the perspective length of these two visible edges.

Step 9. Draw recessed face. The only visible portion of the recessed front face is along the left and bottom. To locate this portion, as in Step #8, draw lines of sight from *h* and *j* to the SP. Where these intersect with the PP, drop projectors to the *k* VP and *m* VP respectively, thus forming points *n* and *f*.

Step 10. Locate those features that do not touch the PP, such as line

po. To find the correct perspective of *po*, extend this line to the PP and drop an auxiliary line to the perspective. Project *po* from the *elevation* to the projection of *po* dropped from the PP, forming point *r*. Connect *r* to VP. Drop projectors from the intersection of the lines of sight (to *p* and *o*) and the PP to the *r* VP, forming points *s* and *t*.

Step 11. Add in remaining detail behind PP.

Step 12. Locate and draw any detail in front of the PP. Since points *u* and *v* appear in front of the PP, extend a line of sight from the SP through the points to the PP. Drop a projector from this intersection (on the PP) down to the perspective and locate the points as in the previous steps.

Angular Perspective: Office Method

Perhaps the best "teacher" of angular perspective is the *office method*. The following step-by-step procedure illustrates, along with Fig. 15-8, the office method of drawing a two two-point perspective.

Step 1. Draw the edge view of the PP near the top of the paper.

Step 2. Orient the print of the plan view along the PP. Determine which face (s) of the object needs to

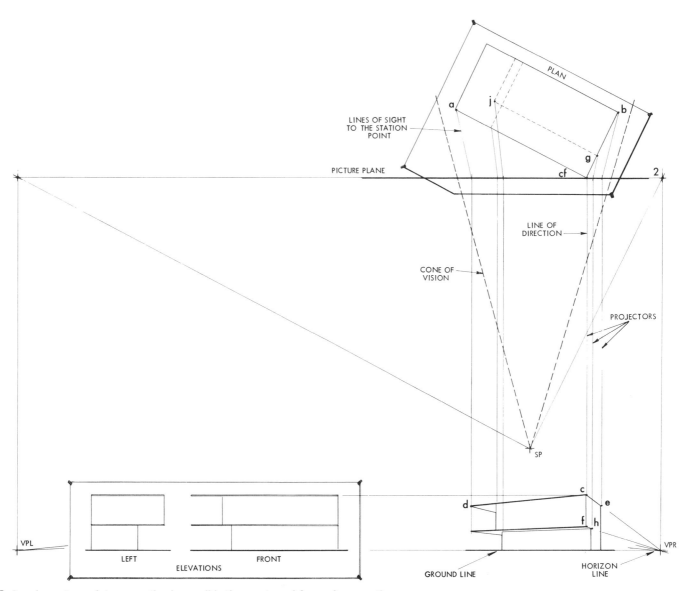

Fig. 15-8. Angular or two-point perspective is possibly the most used form of perspective.

be emphasized. Tape the print in this position. For drafting ease, allow a corner of the object to touch the PP.

Step 3. Locate the SP. The SP may be located at any position to the left, right, or "on" a line projected from the corner of the object. This is called the *line of direction* or *line of measure*. In this case (Fig. 15-8) the SP has been located to the left of the corner. Remember: the distance from the SP to the PP is the viewing distance (in scale) and the extreme corners (points *a* and *b*) of the object must be contained by the 30° cone of clear vision.

Step 4. Draw lines from the SP to the PP parallel to the sides of the object on the plan view. This forms the vanishing points in the PP (points 1 and 2).

Step 5. Draw the GL. It may be located below the SP (as illustrated) or midway between the SP and PP.

Step 6. Locate the HL or eye level line at the desired distance above the GL. (Fig. 15-6 shows the results of the movement of the eye level above and below the normal position.) The distance between these two lines must be the same scale as the plan and elevation. Normal viewing would place the HL 5'-6" above the GL. In this illustration the HL is coincident with the ground line, thus resulting in a worm's eye view.

Step 7. Tape the elevation prints on the GL. These may be located on either side of where the perspective will be drawn. The various heights will be projected to the perspective.

Step 8. Locate the vanishing point left (VPL) and the vanishing point right (VPR). Drop verticals from points 1 and 2 to the HL. This gives VPL and VPR.

Step 9. Draw lines of sight from SP to exterior corners *a* and *b* in the plan view. Where the lines of sight pierce the PP, drop verticals to the ground line. This determines the width of the perspective view.

Step 10. Project height of object from elevation view to the line of direction, forming point *c*.

Step 11. Draw in basic box shape of object. From point *c* draw lines to VPR and VPL. The basic "box shape" is formed at points *d* and *e* where these lines have intersected with the first two projectors (from *a* and *b* in the plan view) that were drawn. These lines now represent the correct length *in perspective* of these edges.

Step 12. Add in basic detail. The undercut that appears along the front edge of the object may be added in next. Project height of undercut to the front corner of the object in perspective, point *f*. Draw a line from *f* to VPR. Next determine the depth of the undercut by drawing a line from the SP to *g* in the plan view. Where the line from SP to *g* intersects the PP, drop a projector to *f* VPR. This gives the depth (point *h*) in perspective of the undercut. Because the undercut is visible, draw a line from *h* to VPL. The length of this line is obtained in the same way as line *fg*. Draw a line of sight from SP to *j*. Where this pierces the PP, drop a projector to line *h* VPL. This gives the width (length) of the undercut.

Step 13. Add in remaining detail. For example, the underside of the plane that extends along the top of the object will be visible in the perspective. Therefore, draw a line from *d* to VPR. Similarly, the point immediately below point *d* is carried to VPR. Determining what is visible in the perspective drawing primarily is a matter of projecting and drawing the correct lines and points. However, one's ability to perceive the object as it is viewed from the SP is almost as important. This will grow as more experience is gained with perspectives.

Angular Perspective: Recessed Objects

All objects do not assume a basic, simple shape as shown in Fig. 15-8. The measurements in this perspective were derived wholly or in part from heights projected from the elevations *to the corner* (located in the picture plane and on the line of direction) and from the plan view. Any height dimension that touches the picture plane will be shown in the perspective or picture plane *fundamentally* (that is, in true size) and may be used to derive other measurements, such as lines *ce, fh, cd,* etc., in Fig. 15-8. Many objects, however, are composed of lines that do not touch the picture plane. If a perspective can be drawn of any line, then a perspective may be drawn of any object regardless of its complexity or position behind the picture plane.

As the object in Fig. 15-9 is viewed, *no* height dimensions touch the picture plane. To obtain these heights their terminal points must be *extended* to the picture plane. The following is an outline of the procedure that is used (see Fig. 15-9) for finding the spatial position of lines which do not touch the picture plane.

Step 1. Draw PP.

Step 2. Orient print of plan view and tape in place.

Step 3. Locate SP relative to the 30° cone of clear vision.

Step 4. Draw lines from SP to PP parallel to sides of plan.

Step 5. Draw GL.

Step 6. Locate and draw HL.

Step 7. Tape print of elevations on GL.

Step 8. Locate VP's on the HL.

Step 9. Draw lines of sight from SP to the exterior corners in the plan view and drop projectors from these points of intersection with the PP.

Step 10. From the corner that touches the PP, drop a vertical to the ground line, point *a*. Carry point *a* to VPL and VPR.

Step 11. Locate and draw those lines which do not touch the PP.

a. Find the piercing point of line *bc* with PP.
  1. Extend line *bc* in the plan view to the PP—forming point *d*.
  2. Drop an auxiliary line from point *d* to the perspective.
  3. Extend line *bc* from the elevations until it intersects with the auxiliary line dropped from point *d* in PP. This forms point *e*. Point *e* represents the piercing point of line *bc* as it is extended to the PP.

b. Locate the height of point *b* in the perspective.
  1. Connect piercing point *e* with VPL. This is a perspective view

of a line of infinite length containing line *bc*.
  2. Draw a line of sight from SP to *b*. Where this line intersects with the PP (at point *f*) drop a projector to line *e* VPL.
  3. The intersection of the projector from *f* and *e* VPL (point *g*), represents the terminal point *b* of line *bc* in perspective. (The usual student comment at this time is: "But the height of the object in perspective is not the same as it is in the elevations." It must be remembered that point *b* is behind the PP and not touching it; therefore, it appears smaller in height since it is farther from the SP.)

c. Find the piercing point of line *hj* with the PP.
  1. Extend line *hj* in the plan view to the PP, forming point *k*.
  2. Drop an auxiliary line from point *k* to the perspective.
  3. Extend line *hj* from the elevations until it intersects with the auxiliary line dropped from *k* in the PP; this forms point *m*. This is the piercing point of *hj* extended to PP.

d. Locate the height of point *h* in the perspective.
  1. Connect piercing point *m* with VPR. This line is the perspective view of a line containing *hj*.

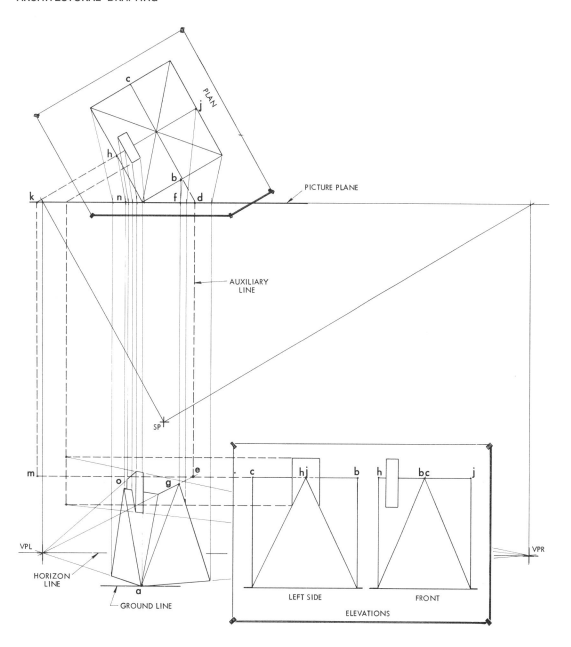

Fig. 15-9. An angular perspective of an object that has no edges touching the picture plane presents special problems.

2. Draw a line of sight from the SP to *h*. Point *n* represents the intersection of this visual ray with the PP. Drop a projector from *n* to line *m* VPR.

3. The intersection of projector *n* and line *m VPR* (point *o*) represents the end point *h* of line *hj*.

e. The height of the prismatic projection and its intersection with the inclined surface is obtained in the same manner as lines *hj* and *bc*.

Step 12. Complete the remainder of the perspective.

Fig. 15-10. A T-square perspective rendered in pencil is a quick method of producing a presentation drawing.

T-Square Perspective

The term "T-square perspective" is misleading since this type of delineation is in no sense of the word "a perspective." T-square perspectives are used on preliminary elevation studies, presentation or display drawings to give the viewer a better understanding of the structure. In essence the T-square perspective is a simple *elevation,* showing only *two* of the three principal dimensions, that has been dressed up to produce the illusion of depth—the third dimension. An example of this type of work is shown in Fig. 15-10. Obviously this delineation is quick and simple. Its basic purpose is to enable the client to visualize the building before it is constructed. Some consideration must be given to the appearance created in the foreground so that the building looks as natural as possible in the setting.

When an architect or designer presents several schemes for a structure that will be used for display or promotional purposes the T-square perspective will be more "dressed-up". Fig. 15-11 shows two excellent examples of T-square perspectives that have been used for promotional purposes. When a T-square perspective is skillfully "worked" by the delineator, it is difficult to identify at first glance if it is a true perspective or not.

The step-by-step procedure for making a T-square perspective is illustrated in Fig. 15-12. Usually a front elevation is used for this work. Sometimes, however, a rear or side view may be used if it has a particular feature which should be illustrated.

Step 1. Place a sheet of vellum over the front elevation and trace the complete elevation, using light lines.

Step 2. Locate sidewalks and driveway. Try several angles for these. The sidewalk should vanish to a point just as in a parallel perspective.

Step 3. Locate shrubs. Keep the bases of shrubs and trees away from the house by dropping their bases slightly below the grade line on the elevation. Quickly rough in the outline of the plantings.

Step 4. Outline. Draw a heavy outline around the roof(s) intersecting roofs, projecting walls, and edges of the building.

Step 5. Determine shade. Select one source of light and use this as a basis for further shading. Frequently the light comes over the observer's left shoulder and

Fig. 15-11. A T-square perspective is an elevation drawing with the addition of shadows and entourage.

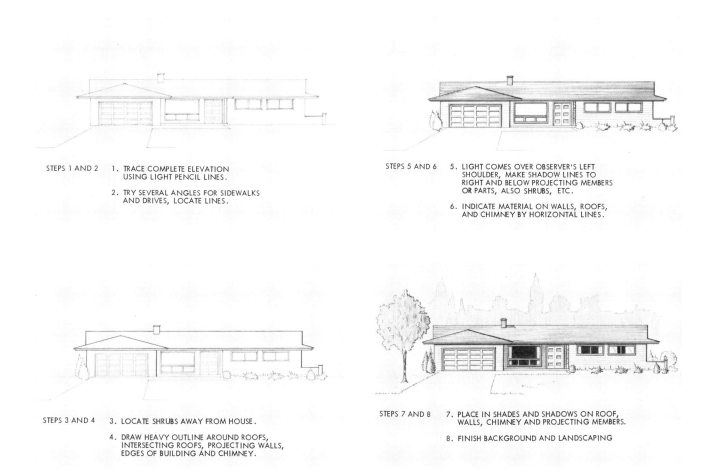

STEPS 1 AND 2   1. TRACE COMPLETE ELEVATION USING LIGHT PENCIL LINES.

2. TRY SEVERAL ANGLES FOR SIDEWALKS AND DRIVES, LOCATE LINES.

STEPS 5 AND 6   5. LIGHT COMES OVER OBSERVER'S LEFT SHOULDER, MAKE SHADOW LINES TO RIGHT AND BELOW PROJECTING MEMBERS OR PARTS, ALSO SHRUBS, ETC.

6. INDICATE MATERIAL ON WALLS, ROOFS, AND CHIMNEY BY HORIZONTAL LINES.

STEPS 3 AND 4   3. LOCATE SHRUBS AWAY FROM HOUSE.

4. DRAW HEAVY OUTLINE AROUND ROOFS, INTERSECTING ROOFS, PROJECTING WALLS, EDGES OF BUILDING AND CHIMNEY.

STEPS 7 AND 8   7. PLACE IN SHADES AND SHADOWS ON ROOF, WALLS, CHIMNEY AND PROJECTING MEMBERS.

8. FINISH BACKGROUND AND LANDSCAPING

Fig. 15-12. Follow this step-by step procedure in drawing a T-square perspective.

will be indicated on the drawing by shadows to the right and below each projecting member on the chimney cap, eaves, gutters, casings, rails, sills, stiles, etc.

Step 6. Indicate building materials.

Draw in the building materials such as siding, brick, stone, shingles, etc. Use horizontal lines spaced at the correct interval. An Ames Lettering Guide or Braddock-Rowe Lettering Tri-

angle can be used for this very readily. Note: since the roof is an inclined surface the shingles will be foreshortened. They will appear much closer together than they actually are.

Step 7. Place in shades and shadows. The exact relation of surfaces can be indicated by a pattern of shades. Properly executed shadows give the drawing life and clarity. Surrounding trees, shrubs, walls, drives, structures, etc. should be a definite complement to the house. Complete this step by placing shades and shadows on roof, walls, chimney, and under all projecting members, shrubs, fold lines in drapes or curtains, etc. Note that where nothing is behind the window, such as a drape, the glass is black. This gives a more natural appearance to the rendering.

Step 8. Add finishing touches to the background and landscape.

Success in making a T-square perspective depends almost wholly upon contrasts created by variation of lights and darks. The pencil is one of tthe most flexible rendering mediums and lends itself to these different techniques. Always express the form and texture in the *simplest* way possible. A sim-

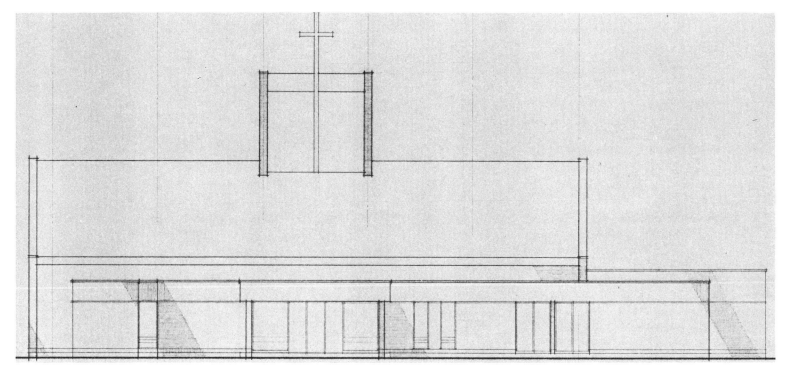

CHARLES MALTBY, DELINEATOR/ARCHITECT, ADRIAN R. NOORDHOEK AND ASSOCIATES, AIA.

Fig. 15-13. An elevation drawing may be changed from a flat projection drawing by adding shadows. This technique is used by architects in preliminary study drawings.

ple, direct drawing that immediately realizes the desired effect is preferable to one that is over rendered. When you are done—quit!

In commercial and industrial architectural practice, preliminary drawings are generally drawn of any proposed structure. These drawings show the client how the designer envisions the building. Most preliminary studies are a simplified form of T-square perspective. In these kinds of drawings shadows are emphasized to give the illusion of depth. The purpose of any T-square perspective is to quickly show how the building will appear. Of course, any elevation drawing accomplishes this end, but often it is difficult for the person who is not trained in reading a drawing to understand the configuration of the elevation.

Fig. 15-13 shows an elevation of a church before and after the shadow treatment. Shadows on elevations are easy to draw. There are 2 basic facts to be remembered: the first is that the rays of the light source (sun) are parallel because the source is at an "infinite" distance away. The second fact is that the angle of light is a compound angle, i.e., the ray makes a particular angle in the plan view and another angle in the elevation view. Fig. 15-14 shows the sun and the light rays in both plan and elevation view.

CHARLES MALTBY, DELINEATOR/ARCHITECT, ADRIAN R. NOORDHOEK AND ASSOCIATES, AIA.

Fig. 15-13 (Cont'd)

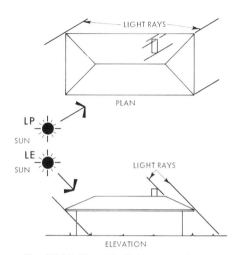

Fig. 15-14. Since the light source (sun) is considered to be at an infinite distance away, the light rays are parallel.

To demonstrate how a shadow is cast on a building, we can begin with a simple structure having no overhang. Fig. 15-15 shows a plan and elevation view of the face of a building having a series of offsets and the angle of light rays. The angle of the light rays is labeled as LP (light plane view) and LE (light elevation view). To determine the shadow on the building, follow this step-by-step procedure.

Step 1. Determine the angle of light rays and draw rays in plan view touching the corner of each projection. Carry the light ray from the corner to the surface of the building in the plan view. LP_1 is drawn through the corner, Ap, and is projected to the surface at Bp, LP_2 is drawn through Cp and carried to the surface at Dp, etc.

Step 2. Determine the angle of the light ray in the elevation view and draw it through the corner and into the recessed surface. Draw LE_1, LE_2, and LE_3 into the adjacent surfaces in the elevation.

Step 3. Draw a projection from the intersection of the light ray and the building's surface (Bp) into the elevation view. Where the pro-

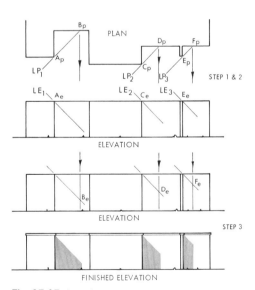

Fig. 15-15. In order to cast the shadow of an offset in the face of a building, the plan view must be used.

jector from Bp and LE_1 intersect, form the corner of the shadow on the building. The same procedure is carried out for LP_2, LE_2, LP_3, and LE_3.

Now progress a step further by considering a plain-surfaced building with a uniform overhanging flat roof. Fig. 15-16 shows a structure with a flat roof and how the shadow is projected on the surface. The following steps outline the procedure used to obtain the outline of the shadow.

Step 1. Determine the angle of the light rays in the plan view and draw through the corner of the roof overhang. The light ray LP passes through corner Ap and is carried to the surface of the wall at Bp.

Step 2. Determine the angle of light in the front view, then draw through the corner of the roof overhang and on to the surface of the wall. The light ray LE is drawn through Ae and down to the wall. The cornice of *any roof* has some thickness, so be sure to take the light ray through the lower edge of the cornice.

Step 3. Now drop a projector from the intersection of the light ray and the wall in the plan view (Bp) into the elevation view. Where this projector intersects with the light ray at Be in the elevation view, LE will form the shadow of the corner overhang on the wall.

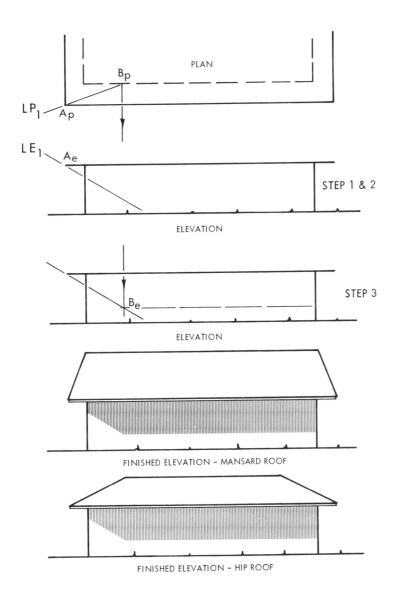

The intersection of the light ray (LE) in the elevation and the corner of the building will be the terminal point of the shadow.

The shadow cast upon the wall will be at a uniform elevation along the wall, regardless if the roof is flat, hip, gable, mansard, etc. The method used in obtaining shadows is the same.

By combining the two foregoing shadow principles, take an overhanging flat roofed building with several offsets and show the shadows. Refer to the illustration in Fig. 15-17. The step-by-step procedure given below illustrates how easily this may be accomplished.

Step 1. Determine the angle of light (LP_1 and LE_1) in the plan and elevation view and draw through corner Ap and Ae for the corner shadow cast on the recess.

Step 2. Drop a projector from the intersection (Bp) of the light ray LP_1 and the recess into the elevation to form point Be.

Step 3. Draw light ray LP_2 and LE_2 through the roof's lower corner in the plan and elevation views.

Step 4. Drop a projector from the intersection (Dp) into the elevation view. When this projector meets LE_2 it forms the corner of the shadow of the overhanging roof. This is point De.

Step 5. Draw light ray LP_3 and LE_3 through point Ep in the plan and elevation view. Point Ep is the

Fig. 15-16. The shadow of an overhang is determined by the light ray which touches the lower corner of the overhang.

extension to the edge of the over-hang from the side of the recess. Point Ep could be located any-

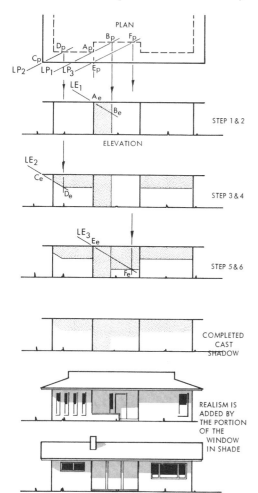

Fig. 15-17. A shadow on the surface of a building with an overhanging roof and offset face is a combination of the principles shown in Figs. 15-15 and 15-16.

where along the overhang as long as Fp would fall in the recess.

Step 6. Drop a projector from the intersection Fp into the elevation view. Where the projector meets L_3, it forms the overhanging roof's shadow in the recess. This is point Fe.

Shadows, as we have discussed, give the illusion of depth on an elevation. The same shadow principle can be used to give the effect of height on a plan view. The only occasion when height shadows are employed is on a *master plan* of a development or occasionally in a *plot plan*. It must be noted here that height shadows are not used on a floor or electrical plan.

Fig. 15-18 illustrates an architect's land use plan showing where proposed buildings are to be placed. Observe how the approximate height of each building can be determined by the length of the shadow. The same method is used in casting a building's shadow on the ground as is used in finding the shadow of a projection on the face of a structure. Once the understanding of how a shadow is cast, short cut or "fudge" methods can be used to cast a shadow. The "fudge" method is based on the amount of projection or height from a known *reference face or line*.

To illustrate the "fudge" method, assume a canopy projects from a wall 2'-0" and a portion of the wall is recessed 3'-0". Fig. 15-19 shows how a shadow may be cast, in

this case, using only the elevation view. This simple procedure is explained below:

Step 1. Assume any angle of the light. For convenience use 45° and draw through the corners of projections or recesses.

Step 2. Determine the height of each shadow by measuring along the angle of light line from the *reference face*. For each foot of projection or recess an arbitrary proportional amount of shadow is laid off. As an example 8" of shadow is used for each foot of difference from the reference face. The shadow cast by the canopy (2'-0" from the reference face) is 1'-4" or ⅔ as long as the shadow cast into the recess (3'-0" from the reference face). The length of the shadow cast into the recess is 2'-0" and is measured along the light ray line.

Step 3. Since the canopy on the left side of the structure is "in light," no shadow will appear on the visible face of this elevation.

Before using this shortcut method, be sure that the basic principles of casting shadows is understood.

The "fudge" method can be used to cast a shadow on the ground in a plan view by the same principles used for shadows in elevation views. It must be emphasized that before attempting either of the shortcuts, the student must understand how a shadow is cast.

Fig. 15-18. The illusion of height relative to the topography may be depicted by cast shadows.

SWANSON ASSOCIATES, BLOOMFIELD HILLS, MICHIGAN.

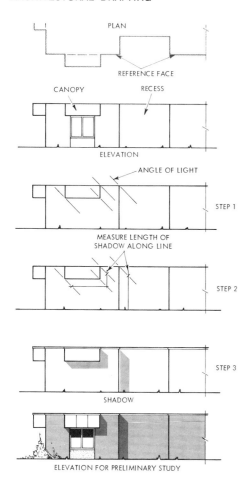

Fig. 15-19. Shadows may be "fudged" by measuring their length along the angle of light.

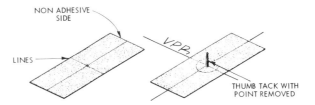

Fig. 15-20. A thumbtack attached to the board with drafting tape saves time in placing the straightedge on the vanishing points and the station point.

Mechanical Perspectives: Drawing Tips and Aids

Much time can be saved in drawing the visual rays from the station point and lines from the vanishing points by using a drafting tape and thumb tack. Draw two intersecting perpendicular lines on the non-adhesive side of a 1½″ piece of drafting tape (see Fig. 15-20) and push a thumb tack through the underside. Simply place the tape so the vertical and/or horizontal line coincides with the location of the lines forming the desired point. This will eliminate the constant repetition of placing the pencil at the vanishing point or station point to adjust the straight edge. To prevent any injury be sure to remove the tape and thumb tack and place a small piece of gum type eraser on the exposed portion of the thumb tack.

If a T-square is used as a straight edge, turn it over so the head will not interfere with the edge of the board. See Fig. 15-21.

If the perspective view is to be at the normal eye level, place the horizon line 5′-6″ to 6′-0″ above the ground line. Bird's eye views have considerable limitations, particularly when the horizon line is far above the ground line. An excessive height of the horizon line will produce added distortion. For a single story structure, the horizon line should be elevated *not more than 20 feet* above the ground line and *40 feet* for a two-story building. Station point heights greater than these will result in a perspective that shows mainly the roof. For buildings with heights greater than those just mentioned, the trial and error method is the only solution, since the building's size and plan influences this greatly.

A worm's eye view will necessitate a horizon line coincident with the ground line. If the structure is on a hill then the horizon line should be lower than the ground line.

Lay out the perspective with a hard pencil, 4H or 5H, and keep it pointed at all times. As lines are drawn rotate the pencil slightly. This will tend to keep the point conical rather than wearing it flat in one location. If a soft pencil is used it will wear

Fig. 15-21. By turning the T-square over, the head will not interfere with the working edge of the board.

quickly and have a greater tendency to smudge. Frequently, perspective layouts must be accurate. This is particularly true for plotting a curved surface or a series of offset points. A hard, well pointed pencil is good insurance for accuracy.

Radius Curves

Radius curves are used when vanishing points for the perspective fall off the sheet. Fig. 15-22 illustrates two radius curves be-ing used to draw a perspective on a short table. Radius curves are pieces of hardboard with a specific radius cut on one side. A hole is placed in the center of the curve so the curve may be accurately located on the horizon line. Radii available are 20″, 25″, 30″, 35″, and 40″. The curve selected is placed at a distance equal to the radius of the curve from the vanishing point. The radius curves are secured to the drawing board with drafting tape or push pins. When using the radius curve(s) it is necessary that the

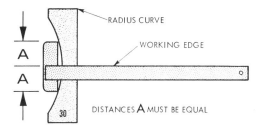

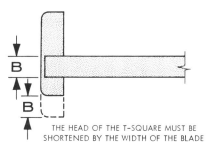

Fig. 15-23. The T-square when used with radius curves must have one end of the head shorter than the other.

T-square head be shortened so the working edge of the blade is midway between the contacting points of the T-square's head and the radius curve. Fig. 15-23 illustrates how the head is shortened. Special all-acrylic T-squares are available for use with the radius curves.

OLSON MANUFACTURING CO., AMES, IOWA.

Fig. 15-22. Radius curves are used when one or both of the vanishing points fall(s) off the sheet or board.

Perspective Sheets, Grids, and Boards

Various types of perspective sheets and grids are available for drawing parallel, angular, and oblique perspectives. Some are more complicated to use than others.

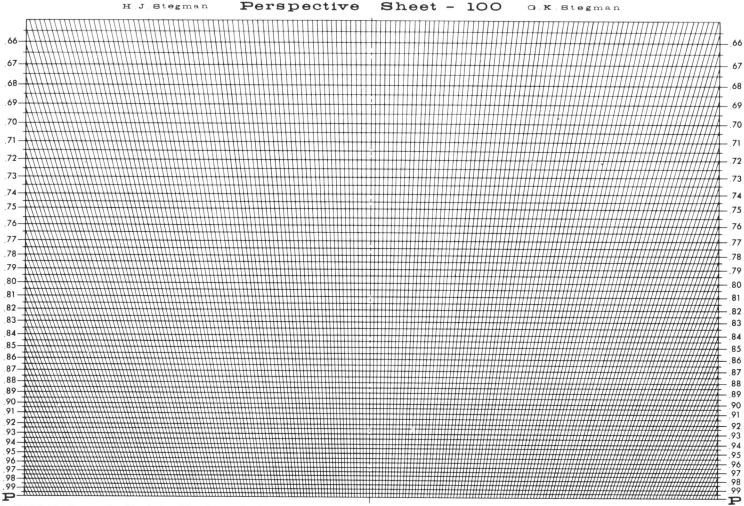

H.J.Stegman   **Perspective Sheet - 100**   G.K.Stegman

Fig. 15-24. The Perspective Sheet simplifies the mechanical perspective.

Perspective Sheets

Few grids, however, offer the advantages of the Perspective Sheet since it is both simple and flexible.

The Perspective Sheet (Fig. 15-24) first appeared, with modifications, under the name Calibron Perspective Paper. It was conceived by Theodore M. Edison and is used with his permission. The position of the object may be changed readily, thereby giving the draftsman a wider latitude of emphasis that may be placed on a particular face. The position relative to the horizon line, as well as the distance from the picture plane, is also more flexible. Perhaps the greatest asset of the Perspective Sheet is that an angular perspective *may be drawn completely* in as little space as 12″ × 16″. A normal mechanical angular perspective, drawn by the office method, may require a 2′ × 4′ to establish the station point and vanishing points. Observe in Fig. 15-24 that the upper part of the Perspective Sheet is ruled with converging lines which run to a station point below. These angular lines of sight terminate at the horizontal picture plane, and are the regular visual rays on which the plan view may be placed. The series of lines parallel to the picture plane, marked with reducing decimal values .99, .98, .97, .96, .95 etc., represent the diminishing height of vertical lines at each of these stations (horizontal lines) behind the picture plane. By placing a sheet below, as shown in Fig. 15-25, the *traces* (projectors) of the intersection of the visual ray and the picture plane may be drawn for any point on the plan view. If a point does not fall on one of the visual rays, simply interpolate its path to the picture plane. Fig. 15-25 shows the Perspective Sheet with a plan and perspective. The following is an outline of the step-by-step drawing procedure.

Step 1. Align and tape the perspective

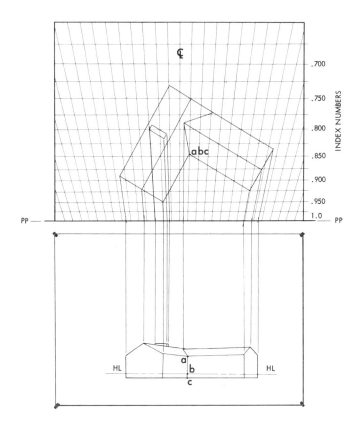

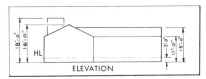

Fig. 15-25. The Perspective Sheet offers versatility and convenience when making an angular perspective.

sheet on one end of a drawing board or place on a regular drawing table.

Step 2. Orient and tape plan view of the object in any desired position (place to the left or right of the center to emphasize a particular face, etc.).

Step 3. Tape a piece of detail paper or vellum immediately below the perspective sheet.

Step 4. Draw the HL near the middle of the piece of vellum.

Step 5. Locate HL on a print of the elevation. Assume the grade line is the GL and measure from this point. All vertical distances are measured, in both perspective and elevation from the HL's.

Step 6. Locate various points on the perspective.

a. Heights are located in the perspective by multiplying the true distance or scale distance of the point above the HL by the given *index number* (numbered horizontal line) on which that point appears. Lay off the resultant value *above* the HL in the perspective on the trace of the visual ray.

b. The distance of that line below the HL is obtained in the same manner. Take the true or scale distance of the lower end of the line below the HL and multiply it by the index number. Lay off the resultant distance *below* the HL on the trace of its visual ray.

Example: To find the height in perspective of line *abc:* line *abc* falls on index line .845, therefore multiply *ab* (the portion of the line that is above HL, 9'-0") by .845; 9'-0"

× .845 = 7'-7". (The height 9'-0" is taken from the elevation.) Step this distance (7'-7") off *above* the perspective HL on the trace of this visual ray. Next multiply portion *bc* (the portion of the line that is below HL, 2'-0") by .845; 2'-0" × .845 = 1'-7". Set this distance (1'-7") off *below* the HL on the trace of the same visual ray.

Step 7. *The main outline of the object and the details are added in relation to the general mass of the object.*

Perspective Sheet Height Finder. The calculations to determine perspective heights may be eliminated by constructing a height

finder. First draw a horizontal base line with a perpendicular at the left end. Step off a series of 6" divisions (*in the same scale as the plan and elevation*) on the perpendicular. Mark off 10 equal divisions, 5/8" *(full scale)* apart, on the horizontal; erect a perpendicular at this point.

The use of 5/8" full scale divisions on the base line will permit easy sub-dividing. If a total of 20' has been set off on the left perpendicular, step off 10' on the right perpendicular. Connect the 20' and 10' graduations on the perpendiculars with a straight line and extend this angular line to the horizontal base line forming point *a*. Extend lines from each of the 6" graduations on the left perpendicular to point *a*. Mark the graduations,

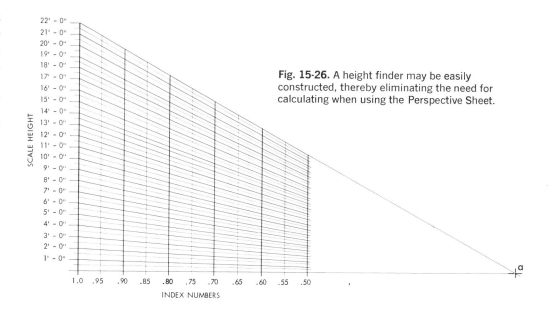

Fig. 15-26. A height finder may be easily constructed, thereby eliminating the need for calculating when using the Perspective Sheet.

beginning at the left end of the horizontal base line .95, .90, .85, .80, etc. These represent index numbers.

If it is desired, each of the ⅝″ graduations may be divided into ⅛″ graduations and the appropriate decimal value added to the existing calibrations—.99, .98, .97, .96, .95, .94, .93, .92, 91, *.90*, .89, etc. This technique will lend more accuracy to the perspective. Distances may be "picked off" by using the appropriate position on the index line and desired height. Fig. 15-26 illustrates a height finder scaled for 22′ on the left perpendicular.

Further information on the different series of Perspective Sheets and height finders may be obtained by writing to the authors.

Perspective Grids

Perspective grids differ from the perspective sheet in that most grids limit the angle

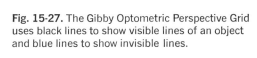

Fig. 15-27. The Gibby Optometric Perspective Grid uses black lines to show visible lines of an object and blue lines to show invisible lines.

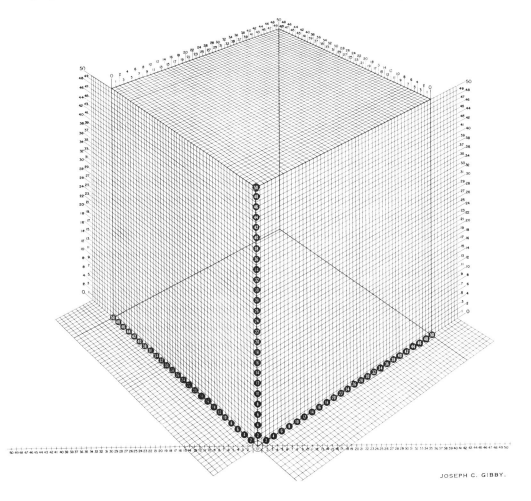

JOSEPH C. GIBBY.

of the object in relation to the picture plane. Notably, however, the *Gibby Optometric Perspective Grid* and the *Andersen Three-Point Oblique Perspective Chart* are easy to manipulate and will produce good results. (These copyrighted grids are available from The A. Lietz Co., P.O. Box 3633, San Francisco, California.) Fig. 15-27 shows the Gibby Grid and Fig. 15-28 illustrates the

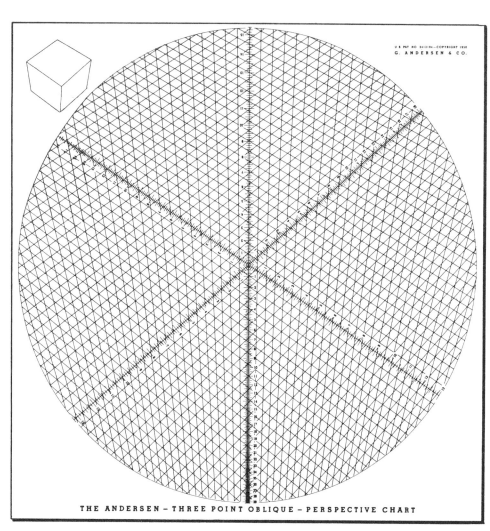

THE ANDERSEN – THREE POINT OBLIQUE – PERSPECTIVE CHART

G. ANDERSEN & CO.

Fig. 15-28. Andersen Three-Point Oblique Perspective Chart.

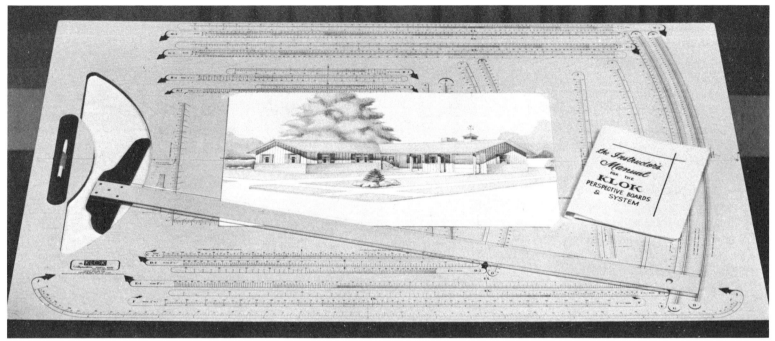

JOHN M. KLOK.

Fig. 15-29. The Klok System with Perspective Board offers many advantages in drawing parallel and angular perspective.

Anderson Three-Point grid. They may be used equally well for architectural or mechanical work.

Perspective Drawing Boards

Of all the prospective aids available to the delineator, the Klok Board is perhaps one of the most versatile perspective drawing innovations. Fig. 15-29 shows the Klok Board. The Klok Board was developed by the late Prof. John Klok who devoted much

of his life to the science of perspective. This system of perspective does not limit the draftsman to a particular distance from the station point to the picture plane, as is true with many grid systems.

Any mechanical perspective requires that plan and elevation views be used in making the drawing. With the Klok system, the designer can work directly from his original rough sketches. The Klok Board is versatile because a series of different scales appear on the Board, thus allowing the perspective

to be in scale from $\frac{1}{8}'' = 1'\text{-}0''$ to full. Five different vanishing points each are available for parallel angular and oblique perspective. The Klok system is widely used in different industries and allows anyone who has a limited knowledge of drafting to make perspectives.

Perspective Rendering

Frequently, as a student looks enviously at a finished perspective rendering, he is overheard to remark, "How much art training do I need to make a drawing like that?" The answer is three-fold. First, you do not have to be a Rembrandt or a Titian to make a good finished rendering. In fact, the student doesn't need any previous art courses. Second, it is necessary to have an interest in this type of drawing. Often a high degree of interest replaces a lack of innate ability. Each experience with a rendering can produce gratifying results. Third, and perhaps most important, the student must be willing to experiment and practice with different techniques, pencils, and papers. Each *grade of pencil,* each *point* and each type of *drafting medium* will produce different results.

Obviously, practice is important to develop any degree of skill in rendering. Many times students who have taken art courses find their results disappointing. This is frequently due to an overconfident feeling and an unwillingness to work and apply some of the basic principles that are suggested in this chapter. The student who has no previous background may well perform in an outstanding manner because of his willingness to experiment and practice.

Rendering, as in other creative endeavors, is based upon the ability to observe and experiment. This, in essence, is the basis for all learning—observation and experimentation. Notice how others have treated a particular surface or object or how they have produced a shadow effect without losing the detail. Study examples of style in rendering textures in the leading architectural and building magazines. Each illustrator ex-

DESIGNED AND DELINEATED BY DONALD BROWN.

Fig. 15-30. Heavy pencil shading may be used to create an attractive presentation drawing.

DESIGNED AND DELINEATED BY DONALD BROWN.

Fig. 15-31. Light pencil shading may also create an effective rendering.

TIIT TELMUT

Fig. 15-32. Ink techniques, combined with commercially prepared shading sheets, are often used in rendering. Shading screens are shown on the shaded areas of the house (front windows, garage doors, etc.). These are cut and applied directly to the drawing.

presses himself differently. One may give a particular treatment to limestone; another may render limestone in a different manner. Reprints of competition drawings and planning books provide good illustrations. Try copying a particular pencil style on a small sheet of paper (select a tree, window, shrub, entryway, etc.). Note critically the character of the pencil stroke and the type of pencil point used to create this effect. Figs. 15-30 through 15-32 give examples of rendering techniques.

Pencil Grade

The grade or hardness of a pencil will influence the tone of the line.

Fig. 15-33 illustrates a comparable analysis of pencil grades that are used in architectural renderings. A soft pencil will produce a granular effect when drawn on paper; by applying additional pressure the line will become deep black. A soft pencil will also give a deeper tone to a line than a medium. Sometimes this is highly desirable. As the

pencil increases in hardness, the tone created becomes lighter. Each person uses a pencil in a unique manner. This mainly depends on the amount of pressure. Some may obtain a dense, black, bright line with a 2B, while another person may find a 4B necessary to equal the same result. On the average, however, a *soft pencil* (B, 2B, 3B, 4B, 5B, 6B) will produce a black tone; a *medium pencil* (HB, F, and H) will give medium tones; and a *hard pencil* (4H, 3H, 2H) will render light tones. It is necessary to experi-

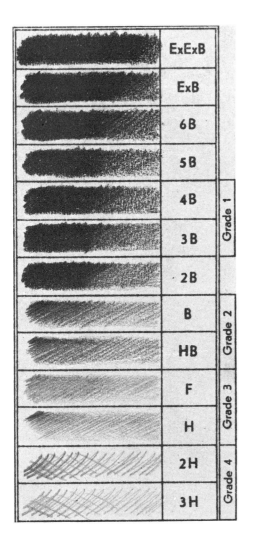

ExExB		for surfaces
ExB		for drawings and intense shadow
6B		for very light and soft drawings and for darkest shading
5B		for deep shadow
4B	Grade 1	for varieties of shading; for studies and sketching
3B		for clear outlines, especially suitable for sketches
2B		for clear and distinct hatching, down to deepest cast shadow; Superior Writing Pencil
B	Grade 2	for finer shading, soft toned drawings and plans; Popular Writing Pencil
HB		for outlines and finest shading; General Purpose Pencil
F	Grade 3	for architectural and technical plans, light cast shadow, for large lettering and heavy lines in photo-prints where edges and outlines are to be specially emphasized, also for drawings on wood and for wood engravings
H		
2H	Grade 4	
3H		for measurement indicating arrows, addressing, itemised lists, and for distinct, sharp outline drawings

J. S. STAEDTLER, INC.; MONTVILLE, NEW JERSEY.

Fig. 15-33. Each grade of pencil produces a different tonal value.

ment with different grades of pencils to obtain the "feel" of the tone it will produce.

Pencil Point

The shape of the point will determine the kind of line that will be produced. Each type of point will give a specific character to the line. The types of points commonly used (illustrated in Fig. 15-34) are described below.

Conical. The conical point is the most utilitarian since it is used for many types of general purpose work. Sharpening the pencil with a pencil sharpener or a pencil pointer will produce a fine sharp point. When this fine point breaks, however, it will "nick" the paper, thus resulting in a blemish that will be difficult to erase. With the pencil held in the normal position, simply draw the point lightly over a piece of scrap paper. This small amount of pressure will cause the fine point to break. Repoint the pencil by rotating it on the paper.

Cylindrical. The cylindrical point may be used for shading large areas with the flat face. By revolving the point 180°, a fine line may be produced. The wood casing is removed by a pocket knife or a draftsman's pencil sharpener. The exposed lead is then drawn across a file to produce a plane surface. Place the file on the table top and hold the pencil in the normal drawing position. Merely move the point along the file. The point will then be at the proper angle to produce a full broad line.

Blunt. By filing both sides of the exposed lead, yet allowing the tip to have some thickness, a broad, sharp, line may be obtained. This type of point is a time saver for drawing random bricks, shingles, lights, some types of trees, etc. Both the blunt and cylindrical point will produce a wide line. The blunt will tend to be sharper along the edges, whereas the cylindrical will be a bit fuzzy.

Chisel. The chisel point is similar to the blunt in general shape. The chisel, however, is sharpened to a fine edge. It will produce a broad crisp line similar to the blunt point, *but* it will also give a fine, thin line. In the softer leads the chisel point has a tendency to break easily. Wood cased pencils and mechanical lead holders having rectangular rather than cylindrical shaped leads are available in varying degrees of hardness. These are called "chisel-point" pencils.

Regardless of the type of point used in rendering, the point must be free of all graphite particles. Even the smallest amount of graphite will cause a smudge. To elimi-

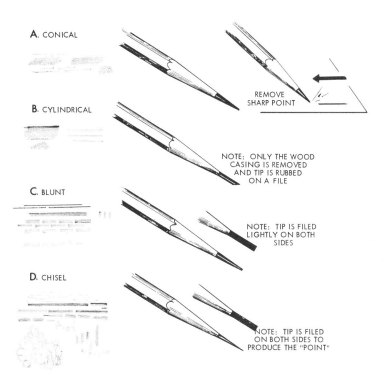

A. CONICAL

B. CYLINDRICAL

C. BLUNT

D. CHISEL

REMOVE SHARP POINT

NOTE: ONLY THE WOOD CASING IS REMOVED AND TIP IS RUBBED ON A FILE

NOTE: TIP IS FILED LIGHTLY ON BOTH SIDES

NOTE: TIP IS FILED ON BOTH SIDES TO PRODUCE THE "POINT"

Fig. 15-34. Each specific type of pencil point produces a different line.

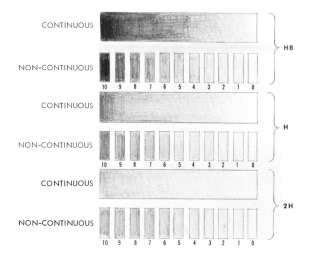

CONTINUOUS

NON-CONTINUOUS

HB

10 9 8 7 6 5 4 3 2 1 0

CONTINUOUS

NON-CONTINUOUS

H

10 9 8 7 6 5 4 3 2 1 0

CONTINUOUS

NON-CONTINUOUS

2H

10 9 8 7 6 5 4 3 2 1 0

Fig. 15-35. Building a tone scale with different pencil grades helps to develop a feeling for the limitations of each pencil.

nate graphite granules, a 4″ or 6″ mill file or ignition file is recommended rather than abrasive paper or cloth for pencil pointing. A file may be readily cleaned by tapping it on a hard surface. Abrasive paper tends to hold the graphite.

Tone Scale

One method of becoming familiar with each grade of pencil is to build a tone scale. See Fig. 15-35. Lay out several rectangles ½″ × 2½″ or 3″. Begin at one end of the rectangle with the deepest value that the pencil will produce, then progress to the right, gradually decreasing the pressure until the value of the line is light gray. Try several tone scales with different pencil grades (the grade controls the intensity and

quality of the tone). Experimentation will show that the softer pencils will produce a more granular effect than a medium or hard. Try both the continuous and non-continuous type tone scales. Since the value areas are not connected in the non-continuous tone scale, the separate areas of black and gray serve as a good comparison of the pressures required to produce a given value.

Paper

Grades and surface textures of paper have a distinct effect on pencil tones. A soft pencil on rough paper will yield a graying effect. A medium paper, however, will reduce the granular tone. For reproduction purposes, vellum is frequently used for renderings. The surface quality of vellum is considerably different from that of art papers or boards (such

as Strathmore or Bristol boards). Many vellums have a "tooth" quality. This texture readily accepts pencil and will produce dense black values with a minimum amount of pressure. Before beginning a rendering, test several grades of pencils on the medium you intend to use. Though one may be familiar with a specific type of paper used for working drawings, the *touch* that is required for renderings may be different.

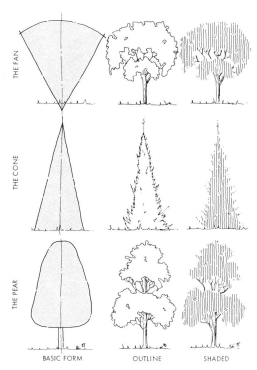

THE FAN

THE CONE

THE PEAR

BASIC FORM   OUTLINE   SHADED

Fig. 15-36. Knowing that trees generally grow in a fan, cone, or pear form helps the delineator draw the proper shape tree.

Entourage

An entourage (that is, the surroundings: shrubs, trees, people, etc.) is placed around the house to give a natural appearance. The perspective may be naturally enhanced by the addition of a simple human form on the sidewalk, driveway, or lawn. Some plantings must be placed around the structure to give it a finished, "lived-in" air. To draw a perspective of a dwelling and omit or sparsely plant the visible portions of the site would detract greatly from the building.

Trees are not difficult to draw if one remembers that they take three characteristic shapes. These are the fan, cone and pear. Fig. 15-36 illustrates these three shapes rendered in outline and shaded form. Note how the branches are irregular in appearance. Branches are usually not curved but angular.

Fig. 15-37 shows how a tree is developed. First the basic cone outline is laid out with a rough outline of foliage. Secondly, light pencil strokes are added to give the basic background for the tree's foliage. See how the pencil strokes in this second step approximate the branches as they radiate from the tree. Then, thirdly, shadowed areas are added that give the tree depth.

Delineators frequently place trees in front of a perspective or preliminary elevation study. This technique tends to eliminate the stark appearance of the structure placed on a site. Treating the rendering in this manner tends to soften the view.

Fig. 15-38 shows several trees placed between the station point (SP) and the building. When placing trees in this way, be sure the foliage is above the structure. Fig. 15-39 illustrates two trees that are ideal for this purpose.

Fig. 15-40 shows some of the many possible shapes, kinds, and styles of trees and plantings that may be used in the foreground and background of the rendering. Look closely at each illustration—study the technique that was used to form the outline. Study particularly the tonal values that give a three-dimensional effect. These add zest to a rendering.

Fig. 15-40 also gives several examples of human figures. The addition of a simple stylized figure will bring the perspective to life. Note the very simple outline that has been used to produce the human shape. If the size of the figure is too large or detailed, or is placed in a prominent position, it may detract from the purpose of the rendering. The figures should compliment the structure; they should not attract attention away from the structure.

Ink Rendering

Though the medium and technique is different for ink, the general shape of the entourage is the same. Remember that the line produced with ink is a constant value, and may not be grayed as with pencil. The illusion of grayed values is obtained by line width and spacing. As with pencil work, it is necessary to have several pens which will produce varying types of lines. Fig. 15-41 shows several examples of line techniques

Fig. 15-37. On laying out a tree, first block in its basic shape, next add background foliage, and then shadows of the foliage.

Fig. 15-38. By placing several trees between the station point and the structure, the delineator has softened the general appearance of the rendering.

Fig. 15-39. Trees that are used in front of buildings most often do not have any foliage that will hide the structure.

used to produce different tones. For those who have never sketched in ink, a Hunt #107 Hawk-quill pen is recommended. The nibs of the Hawk-quill are less flexible than the Hunt #102 or other fine nibbed pens. These nibs may be easily touched up with a hard Arkansas stone to change the line width. When testing the pen, hold it in a relaxed manner—not rigidly. Practice by making different types of strokes: horizontal side strokes made with the hand only, horizontal strokes with the arm, and vertical

Fig. 15-40. Additions of trees, shrubs, plantings, and/or human figures to the rendering give a professional touch.

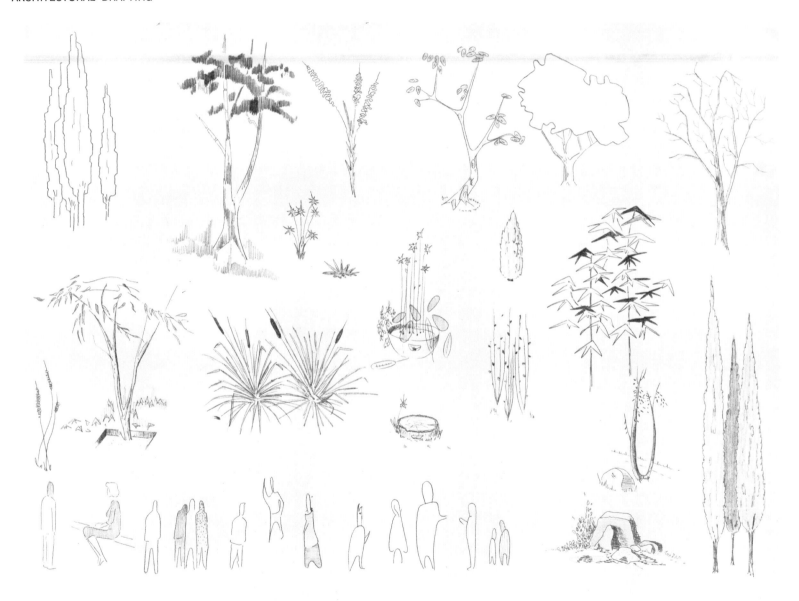

Fig. 15-40 (Cont'd)

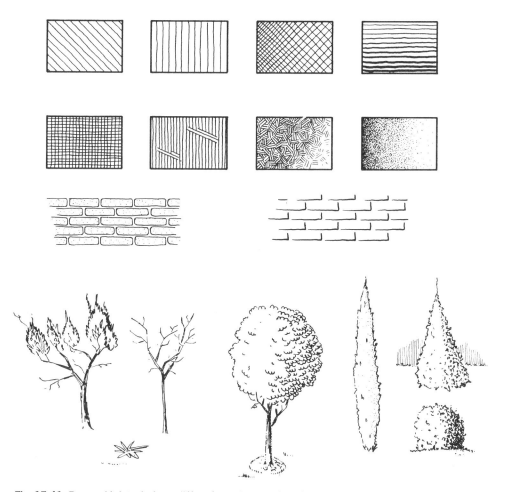

Fig. 15-41. Pen and ink technique differs from that required for pencil.

pencil line those portions that will be in shadow. Now begin to experiment with technique. For a single shrub several pens may be used to produce the appearance of foliage, light, and shadow.

Color

Pastel crayons and colored pencils are sometimes used on presentation drawings that will be displayed. The variety of effects and contrasts that may be obtained by combining pencil and color are almost limitless.

Pastel crayons offer the most promising results for the beginner since they may be easily erased if a mistake is made. Pastels may be used in two different manners.

In the first method, the crayon is rubbed on a piece of paper towel or other coarse paper to produce a crayon dust. The dust is applied to the drawing by "loading" a piece of cotton with the crayon dust and rubbing it on the paper. Several applications will intensify the value of the color. To bring the color to a line, a piece of detail or bond paper may be used as a mask, see Fig. 15-42. The cotton is moved from the mask to the drawing. This will prevent a build-up of crayon particles beneath the mask and will eliminate any smudges. Cotton wound on an orange stick or commercially prepared cotton swabs are especially handy for filling in corners, deepening color, or blending. Colors may be easily "mixed" or "grayed" by this method of application.

In the second method, which requires more experience, the crayon is applied *di-*

strokes with the fingers. Apply pressure with some strokes and ease up on others. More pressure causes the nibs of the pen to spread, an interesting effect that may be used to good advantage for some types of foliage.

Once the perspective is laid out, place a piece of vellum over the sheet. With soft pencil lines block in various trees and shrubs at the sides and along the front of the house. Do not add in detail, simply indicate with a

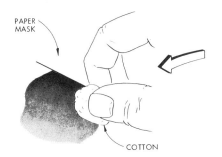

Fig. 15-42. Detail paper may be used as a mask to protect different colored areas of the rendering.

rectly to the paper and is then blended with a piece of cotton. Because the pastel is directly applied the color will be pure—that is, it will have the same value as the stick. The opportunity to obtain a delicate, realistic color is reduced when the crayon is applied directly. With the direct method of application, colors may be grayed or shaded, but care must be exercised not to apply too much black.

Colored pencils offer a convenient method of applying color to a rendering. Some brands of colored pencils are water soluble. After the desired colors have been applied, a brush dipped in clear water may be used to further blend the colors. Painting with colored pencils, as this is sometimes called, will tend to reduce the stiff appearance of the color and will give the effect of a water color. A word of caution: Thoroughly wash the brush before switching to another colored area. If water-color paper is unavailable, be sure to test the paper for its reaction to water.

Special Effects: Sepia and White

An interesting effect may be created by making a sepia print (this is sometimes referred to as an intermediate print) of a pencil or ink perspective rendered on vellum. A sepia print is made by the diazo reproduction processes. It is similar to a white print; however, rather than blue or black lines, the lines are a deep yellow-brown. Also, the sepia print is printed on a translucent paper. When a sepia print is made of a rendering, it should be run sufficiently fast to produce a slight amount of light brown background. The plain sepia print of a rendering is different and eye catching since it is a departure from the usual black on white. The monochromatic scheme of brown values from light to dark tones creates an impression of early evening. Further life may be added by "coloring in" the trees, shrubs, grass, building, etc., with colored pencils directly on the sepia print. The intensity of the light brown background may be increased to produce a later evening effect by decreasing the exposure time.

Sepia Pencils. A departure from colored pencil or pastel crayon may be achieved by rendering the perspective with a sepia pencil. As the name implies, the lead is a medium brown color. The single color produces a decidedly striking effect. The pencil is "worked" as an ordinary art pencil. Most pencil manufacturers produce the sepia pencil in only one grade with two values of brown. These pencils are used mainly on white Strathmore paper. However, a tinted paper (such as ivory, buff, light gray, light brown, or light blue) offers a new avenue for renderings.

White Pencil. An unusual and eye-catching effect is created by rendering the entire perspective in white pencil on black, brown, blue or dark green colored paper. The result appears reverse or negative to a typical black and white rendering. The same procedure is followed in laying out a perspective, only very fine light white pencil lines are used that may be easily erased. Once the layout is completed and shadow and entourage areas are blocked in, the drawing is "worked" with the white pencil just as one would do with a regular clay and graphite pencil.

Questions and Problems

1. Build a collection of pencil or pen illustrations of entourages that may be used as examples for rendering perspective.
2. Select a published drawing in an architectural, building trades, or popular home magazine and analyze it according to the tone scale in Fig. 15-35.
3. Make a white print of the front elevation of a home you have designed. Place a piece of vellum over the print and make a T-square perspective. Place the light source so it originates over your left shoulder.
4. Make a white print of the front elevation of the building you have de-

signed. Use a black, blue, or brown pencil, depending if the print is a black, blue, or brown line, and cast shadows on the face, recesses, windows, and doors of the building.

5. Use the plot plan that was drawn for your house and cast its shadows on the ground. Use the "fudge" or measured line method to create the illusion of height.

6. Make an angular perspective of a home you have designed. Carefully select the face which must be emphasized. Position the station point in relation to the face.

7. Choose one particular exterior feature of the home you have designed, such as the front entryway, sun porch, patio, etc. Make an angular perspective. Place the horizon line 10'-0" above the ground line. Render this drawing to create the effect of the sun coming over observer's left shoulder.

8. Select one of the rooms or the main entryway of one of your house plans and draw a parallel perspective with horizon line 5'-0" above the ground line.

Model Making 16

Models are a supplementary means of checking the graphical description shown on the plan, elevations, and perspective. They aid in the visualization of the finished appearance of the proposed structure and its room arrangement. Usually, models are built to a small scale and incorporate as much detail as possible to achieve a realistic effect. The realism achieved in a model sometimes may be very deceiving. Close inspection of photos of landscaped homes often reveal that they are merely a cleverly camouflaged photo of a model superimposed on a photograph of the actual site. Models frequently serve to spark a new idea in the design of a structure. Even the most accomplished designer, on occasion, has difficulty visualizing the completed project. The time and effort expended to construct a model is more than repaid if it can help to eliminate costly changes while the building is under construction. Some architects and designers employ models to study proposed changes or additions to an existing building.

Models have the distinct advantage of showing the **completed** structure from any angle. A presentation or perspective drawing, however, reveals the basic three dimensions of the building from only a single vantage point. Models are the only way the structure may be shown in the third dimension. In the eyes of the client, many mysteries hidden on the plan and elevation are solved by the model.

Architectural Models

Model making uses numerous tools and materials for purposes not originally intended. The use of matches, hat trim, bird gravel, sandpaper, marbles, sawdust — in fact anything that will result in the desired effect—is fair play in model making.

Probably one of the most important features in model making is the finish which is applied. Poor painting or staining can ruin an otherwise excellent model. The more realism that is provided in the model, the more interesting it will become. Attention must be given to all the details on the exterior of the model.

The equipment required for model making is not extensive. However, several pieces of equipment are necessary to the basic kit of tools. These are: model maker's knife or

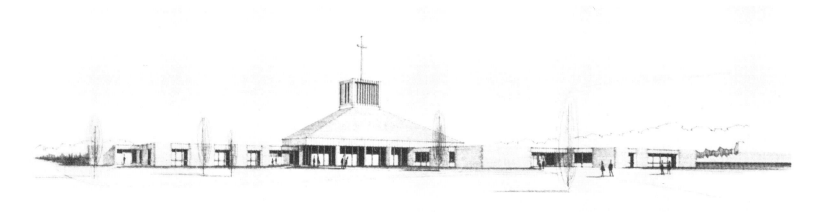

Fig. 16-1. Architects use a combination of renderings and models to help sell a design.

a single edge razor blade, 1 sheet of No. 320 abrasive paper, T-square or an old 45° or 30°-60° triangle, ½″ square × 6″ sanding block, thumb tacks, straight pins, airplane or model cement, rubber cement, and a pair of scissors.

Models are not limited only to building exteriors. Industry uses models to show various processes, flow of materials and goods, circulation patterns, production sequences, plant layout, and the spacing of equipment.

The architect many times will use a combination of photos and renderings of the model to present a proposed design to a client. Fig. 16-1 shows two photos of such a model from several vantage points. These were used together with a rendering to present a proposed design for a church. Since the model was small—12″ total length—the architect decided it would be best to present it in photographic slide form so it could be shown to a large audience for final approval. The model was placed on colored background paper and spotlighted from above. The effect created was impressive yet truthful in the design presentation.

The scale of the model is dependent upon the size of the structure. Many commercial buildings are modeled ⅛″, 1⁄16″ or 1⁄32″ to 1′-0″. Most residential models are made to the scale of ¼″ = 1′-0″. Smaller residential structures also sometimes use a scale of ⅜″ = 1′-0″.

Models fall into two classifications: Preliminary study and display. They may be constructed from either cardboard, foam core board, or balsa wood.

Fig. 16-2. The preliminary study model shows mass and form relationships. It is a simple and quick method that may be used to illustrate the general shape of the structure.

Preliminary study models are most frequently made from flat, white poster board (sometimes called show card board). No finish is added. The prime purpose of these models is to aid in the analysis of mass, space, and general form. No attempt is made to dress the model with an entourage. Fig. 16-2 shows a preliminary study model of an A-frame summer house.

Display models show the proposed structure as it will appear in its completed form. Scale figures, sidewalks, trees, shrubs, automobiles, etc., are added to give realism. By placing the model in its intended surroundings the client is better able to understand the theme the architect has planned in har-

O'DELL, HEWETT, AND LUCKENBACH, ASSOCIATES, ARCHITECTS; BIRMINGHAM, MICHIGAN.

Fig. 16-3A. This figure shows a display model of the Oakland County Courthouse, Michigan. Note the use of scale model figures and automobiles.

Fig. 16-3B. This figure shows a photo of the actual building taken from the hexagonal structure.

monizing man, nature, and materials. The quantity of entourage incorporated in the model must be carefully planned. Fig. 16-3A illustrates a large building with a discrete amount of foliage. Note the photo of the completed building (Fig. 16-3B).

Additional models of building projects are shown in Figs. 16-4 and 16-5. Each of these models has been made to show the client, in a clear concise manner, the design philosophy employed in building.

Viewing a Model

The most realistic way to view a model is to look at it through a tube or a rolled up piece of paper. See Fig. 16-6. Regardless if the model is of a single building or an entire

Fig. 16-4. Models placed in their topographic setting with scale figures give a realistic atmosphere.

Fig. 16-5. A model of an entire area that is to be developed assists the client in better understanding of general appearance and space relationships.

button thread, string, or wire may be carefully formed, painted, and cemented to the wall or structure. Small pieces of green paper may be used to represent the leaves.

Grass

Probably the most effective material that may be used to represent grass on a *flat site* is painted burlap. Other materials such as green colored felt, velvet, or blotting paper will also give the illusion of grass. Green flock or sand applied to wet shellac or paint will provide a realistic looking lawn. If green colored sand is not available, ordinary sand may be painted after it has been applied to the base coat and has had sufficient time to dry. Probably the most economical way to represent grass on the model is to use sawdust that has been dyed green with diluted food coloring. This is attached to the terrain by glue, rubber cement, or shellac.

Roads, Sidewalks, and Crushed Stone

Roads and sidewalks may be made from long strips of fine (No. 00 or 100) abrasive paper. This is cut to the proper width and length and glued in the desired location. Never cut abrasive paper or cloth on a paper cutter or with drafting shears because this will quickly dull the cutting edges. A coating of sand or bird gravel sprinkled on a coat of quick drying cement, spray adhesive, or shellac will produce the effect of crushed stone.

Water

Water may be represented by a plain or colored mirror. Patterned glass may be used for wave effects and distorted reflections. Colored cellophane or acetate cemented to the top of the mirror surface will also give the effect of waves.

Figures

Scale automobiles or human figures may be used to give the model "life." Frequently commercially made models of automobiles and figures specify the scale. If this is not indicated, measure the object to be sure it will fit with the house model. Neglect of this seemingly insignificant matter may throw the appearance out of scale. Measure carefully! Figures are also used in models of commercial structures to supply a visual scale of the approximate size. A simple, stylized figure cut from cardboard (similar to the ones shown in Fig. 15-40) may be used for this purpose. The most critical point in making the figure is to have the correct height. The average height of the individual is 5'-10" to 6'-0". Simply cut the figure from a piece of poster board, apply a coat of black paint or india ink, and cement in place on the sidewalk or on the steps of a building.

Commercially made figures, see Fig. 16-9, give life to models. These figures are available in standing, walking and running positions and in ⅛" and ¼" = 1'-0" scale. Because they are cast from a tin-lead mixture, their form may be slightly altered to

Fig. 16-9. These figures are modeled at a scale of ¼" = 1'-0" and are used on architectural models.

achieve a particular mood. Each figure is cast on a nail so they may be pushed into the model base and remain upright. Each figure is 1" to 1½" and is spray painted different colors to suit the model maker's taste.

Interior Furnishings

Some models are made with removable roofs or no roofs at all so the exterior and interior of a structure is seen. To save time several supply houses offer ⅛" and ¼" = 1'-0" scale models of dining and living room furniture and plumbing fixtures. These items are either made from a tin-lead mixture or plastic. Fig. 16-10 shows a pedestal lavatory and a watercloset that are $5/16$ high. Because of their small scale some of the castings may be rough and require reworking with a sharp knife and a file. Some

Fig. 16-10. On models where interiors are shown ready-made, $\frac{1}{4}'' - 1'\text{-}0''$ scale furnishings and plumbing fixtures save time for the model maker.

model makers will "set the table" with a complete 5-piece place setting of dinnerware and silverware. These are available only in $\frac{1}{4}'' = 1'\text{-}0''$ scale.

Building Material Details

As with the entourage, building details may use many different materials. Again, individual invention should be used to produce a realistic effect.

In addition to the hand-built details next described, a great variety of these are commercially available in definite scales, of which the 0 scale ($\frac{1}{4}'' = 1'$) and the HO scale (3.5 mm $= 1'$) are the most common.

Brick, Rock, and Stone

Often these masonry materials are simulated by grooving cardboard or balsa wood with a spent ballpoint pen or mimeograph stylus. The mortar joints may be painted in with a brush and the face of the brick or masonry material may be painted by rolling the paint on with a linoleum block brayer. (A linoleum block brayer is a 4″ or 5″ wide rubber-covered roller with a handle perpendicular to the axis of the roller. Its primary purpose is to apply ink to the face of a linoleum block for block printing.) Stone may also be made by using pieces of masking tape pre-cut to the desired shape and pressed on the wall.

Vertical or Horizontal Siding

Strips of detail or heavy paper may be cut and then cemented in place on the wall. (Remember to allow the correct amount to be laid to the weather.) When siding is made from separate strips and applied in an identical manner to regular beveled siding, the result will be strikingly realistic. If balsa wood is used for the model, the siding may be represented by using a stylus or spent ballpoint pen and making indentations in the wood to represent the joints. If board and batten siding is to be used on the model, separate pieces representing the batten strips may be fastened to the walls.

Stucco

Plaster of Paris, patching plaster, or Keene Cement mixed to a consistency of heavy cream and dipped on the wall with a No. 3 or larger sable brush, will produce a stucco effect. If it is desired that the stucco be colored, water colors or tempera paint

may be applied to the stucco after it has thoroughly dried.

Roofing

Roof shingles may be made by cutting a series of long strips of detail paper slightly wider than the width to be laid to the weather. Stack 36 or 40 of these strips and secure the ends with rubber bands or thumb tacks. To simulate shingles, make $\frac{1}{8}''$ deep cuts approximately $\frac{1}{4}''$ O.C. with a band-saw or hack saw. Fig. 16-11 illustrates this procedure. Attach each strip to the roof: begin at the eaves then stain with water color, diluted ink, or food coloring. Do not saturate the paper with the coloring agent. To prevent thin paper from wrinkling when ink or water color paint is applied, rub the brush, prior to each stroke, on a bar of soap.

Rolled roofing or tar and gravel roofing may be simulated by using sheets of abrasive paper, such as aluminum oxide (tan), garnet (red), flint (gray), or emery cloth and wet or dry abrasive paper (black). Apply these materials on roof with rubber or spray adhesive.

Wrought Iron and Metal Work

Wrought iron work may be made by using copper bell or iron stove pipe wire bent into the desired shape. This can be soldered to the supports (if these are metal) or cemented to strips of balsa wood. They then are sprayed with a flat enamel. Other metal work on the model may be formed by using nails, brads, or wire. In some

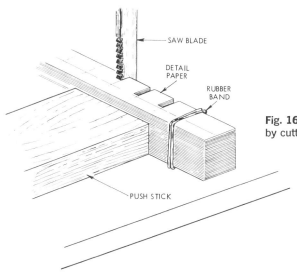

Fig. 16-11. Roof shingles may be readily made by cutting detail paper with a band saw.

MODEL BY STEVE FREDERICKSON.

Fig. 16-12. Balsa wood strips, $\frac{1}{16}$″ or $\frac{1}{8}$″ square, may be used to trim windows and doors.

instances metal work, such as muntins, may be ruled with acetate ink on a sheet of plastic.

Flashing and Sheet Metal Work

Copper tooling foil or heavy-duty kitchen aluminum foil may be used for flashing around chimneys, roof valleys, etc. Aluminum foil will be satisfactory for any other areas that require sheet metal. Always have the dull side of the aluminum foil exposed.

Windows

Many house models are spoiled by omitting window lights. Window lights may be represented by attaching sheets of acetate or plastic on the inside. To give a more realistic effect, a small piece of colored cloth may be applied to the back side of the window to serve as a curtain or drape. Do not forget to cement vertical and/or horizontal pieces of balsa wood across the window to represent the rails.

Doors

Most doors used in homes built today are flush. A plain piece of cardboard cut to the desired shape can represent a flush door. If a panel door is called for, the panels may be built up by adding additional pieces of cardboard.

Window and Door Trim

To produce an attractive model, trim must be placed around the windows and doors. The easiest method is to use a $\frac{1}{16}$″ or $\frac{1}{8}$″ square strip of balsa wood. This is cemented around the window and door openings Fig. 16-12 illustrates the use of balsa wood strips. A strip of cardboard may also be used to represent the trim. Probably the most efficient method is to use a strip of balsa wood since it is uniform in thickness and is easily molded, if this is desired, by sanding.

Prepared Materials

Classroom Model Making: For classroom model making, it is recommended that the teacher evaluate his budget first and then decide the extent to which commercially available materials will be used in conjunction with scrap-type supplies previously described.

Architectural Office Model Making: Architectural firms may use commercially available materials when building models.

Whereas these specialized materials may be too expensive for student use, their judicious use in professional work can result in significant savings, because their cost is small in comparison with the time of highly skilled personnel. Several manufacturers specialize in model building materials for architectural model makers and model railroad enthusiasts. Some items such as interior furnishings and figures have been described previously. Model supply houses have three dimensional surfaces simulating lannon stone, coursed limestone, field stone, asphalt roofing, shake roofing, cement block, brick and siding molded in plastic.

Generally the plastics used for these materials may be easily drilled, cut, sawed, and sanded. Most of these surfaces require finishing with flat or acrylic paint. In some instances they may be used in their natural color.

Many of these surfaces are also made from milled basswood. Basswood is a soft, light, fine-textured wood. Since it is harder than balsa wood, a fine-tooth model maker's saw is the best method of cutting pieces of any sizeable dimension. Because of its fine grain, basswood readily accepts imprints to give the effect of various stones, brick, block, etc.

Some model supply houses also carry different types of windows and doors. Most of these are molded in plastic and can be readily painted and cemented in place. Perhaps of all architectural features, doors and windows require the most time if they are built from scratch.

Several model supply firms have roofing, siding, brick, block and stone printed on paper. These sheets are intended to be glued on a cardboard or balsa wood wall or roof. Since these sheets are printed, they lack the realistic appearance that plastic, bass or balsa wood materials possess.

Consulting engineering firms or offices that specialize in designing chemical processing facilities frequently build complete scale models of the proposed tank and piping layout. These models are finitely detailed with purchased components down to the pipe fittings, valves, ladders, structural shapes, etc. Different types of structural shapes are available such as: S-beams, angles, tees, channels, square, rectangular and round tubing; sheet stock to represent concrete block, brick, sheet, etc.; pipe and pipe fillings such as vessel saddles, manholes, vessel heads, elbows, tees, flanges, gate valves; and miscellaneous equipment representing turbines, pumps, motors, stairs, light fixtures, etc. Most all items are molded in an appropriate color and therefore require no painting.

Some firms produce kits that may be used to construct any type of house. Kits have the advantage of being quick and easy to assemble. They do not, however, have the finished appearance because windows, doors, railings, etc., are merely printed on paper, cut from the sheet, and glued on the wall surface. Similarly roofs normally lack a fascia and have a distinctly artificial form. These kits are not normally used by professional model makers.

Sources: For up-to-date resources of model making supplies, contact a local architectural firm or a local model railroad club. Either of these will be able to give current company names and addresses and perhaps price lists, as well.

Some manufacturers of model materials furnish not only complete catalogs but also handbooks explaining the techniques of cutting, joining, painting, etc. for particular materials. This information would be a valuable addition to the library of an architectural office.

Model Construction Details

Architectural models can be constructed from balsa wood, foam core board, or cardboard.

Foam core board is an ideal material to use for preliminary study and display models. Foam core board is, as the name implies, a plastic foam core sandwiched between two sheets of paper stock. See Fig. 16-13. Because of its foam core the board is rigid and will neither buckle or bow in normal usage, and will not change with humidity conditions. It is easily cut with an X-acto type knife. Since the board is backed on both sides with paper that will readily accept black or colored ink, water color and tempera paint, as well as colored pencil, it is ideal for models that show both the exterior and interior of a project. Frequently models are fabricated from a combination of these materials. The following gives some

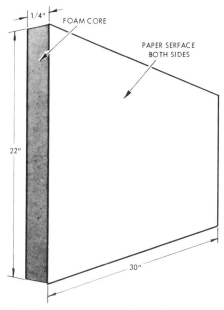

Fig. 16-13. Foam core board is an ideal material for models. Because of its foamed core it is rigid and lightweight, and the paper surface is an excellent medium for ink.

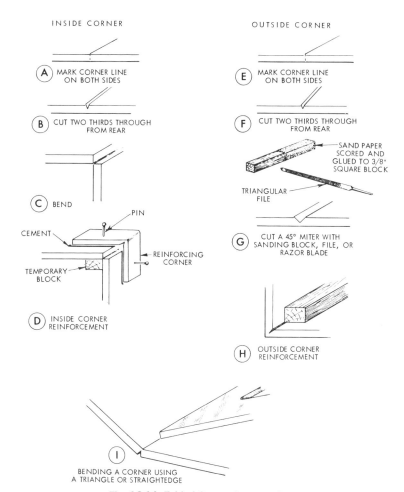

Fig. 16-14. Folded-Corner Construction.

of the methods used in constructing model details from cardboard. Poster board (show card board) is used.

Figs. 16-14 and 16-15 show the step-by-step procedure in constructing inside and outside corners. To construct either an inside or outside *folded* corner a mark is placed on both sides of the board and then a cut is made. For the inside corner (see Fig. 16-14B), a cut is made approximately ⅔ of the depth from the rear side. (When cutting, use an old magazine or a piece of hard board

to protect the work table or desk.) The piece is bent along the cut and a cardboard reinforcing corner is placed inside to give added support and rigidity. For the outside folded corner (see Fig. 16-14C) a 45° miter cut

from the rear side is made with a razor blade, triangular file, or a piece of sandpaper glued to a ⅜″ strip of soft wood. The poster board is bent along the cut so a sharp edge will result. A balsa or soft wood block is then glued on the inside of the corner for support.

Frequently the model maker will find that it is necessary to join *separate* pieces for the corner. Either a miter or a butt joint may be used. Fig. 16-15 shows methods used in making these two types of joints.

Figs. 16-14 and 16-15 also show methods of reinforcing inside and outside corners. These methods may be used for either cardboard or balsa wood. NOTE: In many cases thumb tacks or pins are shown. These are used to hold temporary blocks and to support the corner. Once the cement has dried, the pins or tacks are removed.

Fig. 16-16 (top) illustrates one method of securing a roof to the side walls. Placing the

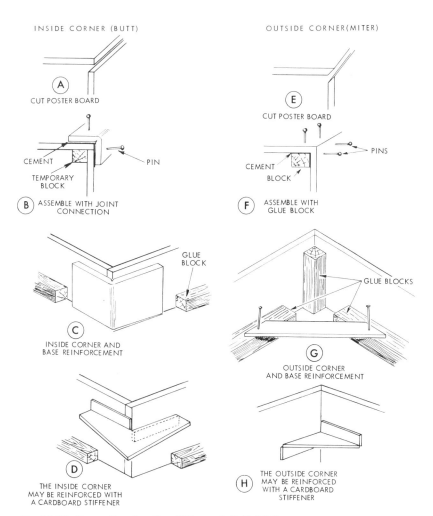

Fig. 16-15. Corner-Construction: Miter and Butt Joint.

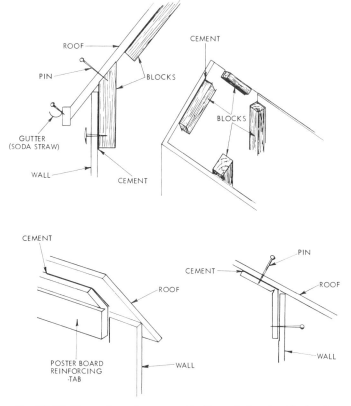

Fig. 16-16. The roof may be secured to the walls by glue blocks or cardboard reinforcing tabs.

glue blocks in this position will permit a larger bonding surface for the roof. Additional strength may be obtained by placing a frieze board at the junction of the exterior wall and the roof. Fig. 16-16 (bottom) illustrates how to secure a roof using cardboard reinforcing tabs.

The easiest method of joining two intersecting roofs that form a valley is to provide a tab on one of the members, as shown in Fig. 16-17A. The dormer may be attached by using a glue block (Fig. 16-17B). A spring clothespin may be used as a clamp to hold two pieces as the cement dries.

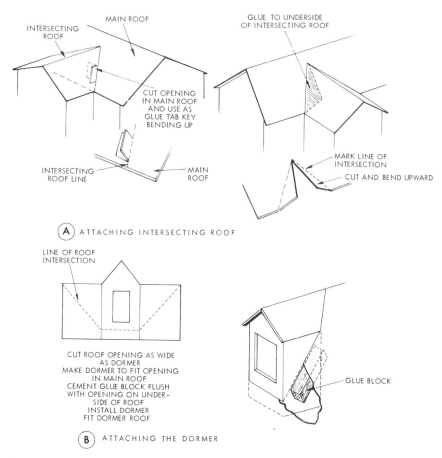

Fig. 16-17. These methods may be used for fastening intersecting roofs and dormers.

Poster Board Models

Preliminary Study Models

The purpose of a preliminary model is simply to show the relationship of the structural masses. Usually no window or door openings are shown in this type of model. The following procedure outlines the step-by-step method that is used in constructing a preliminary model.

1. Study plans and elevations for the proper layout.
2. Lay out walls, with light pencil lines, in the proper sequence on poster board. Keep the layout in line: the front elevation hinged to the right elevation, the right elevation hinged to the rear elevation, the rear elevation hinged to the left elevation. See Fig. 16-18. If the plan deviates from the rectangular or square form, any projections or offsets (such as a porch or garage) may be laid out and added separately. See Fig. 16-19.
3. Cut along the roof line.
4. Cut all corner joints ⅔'s deep.
   A. Cut inside corners from rear.
   B. Cut outside corners from rear; cut miters with the sanding block.
5. Carefully fold the walls to form the proper angles. To insure a sharp corner, place a triangle on the bend line to act as a "break."
6. Place folded walls over the plan of structure to make certain the model

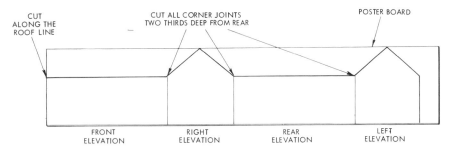

Fig. 16-18. When outlining the walls, keep the layout in the proper sequence.

will be square. To prevent movement pin walls to the plan as shown in Fig. 16-20.

7. Reinforce corners with poster board or wooden blocks.
8. Study the shape of the roof and layout in light pencil lines. NOTE: Obtain the true size of the roof from any two adjacent elevations, i.e., the front and right or rear and left elevations. This will give the eave length and slant length of the roof.
9. Cut joints for the ridges ⅔'s deep from rear, cut miters with the sanding block.

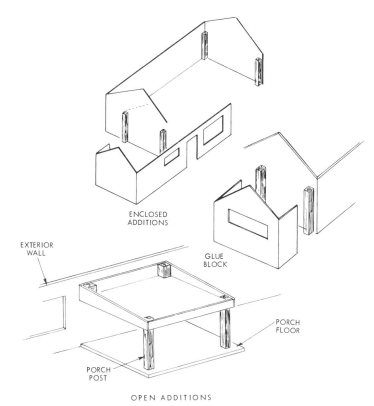

Fig. 16-19. Several methods may be used for attaching additions.

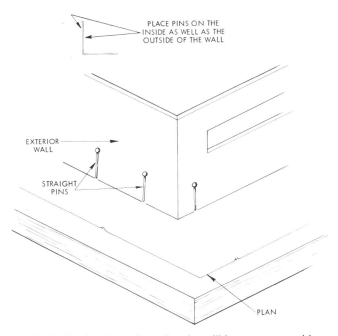

Fig. 16-20. Pinning the walls to the plan will insure a squared house.

10. Fold roof to form proper shape. Use a triangle as in step No. 5. Secure the under side of the roof with cardboard reinforcement. Some roofs because of their length will require a balsa wood strip, cemented on the underside, to act as a stiffener.
11. Place glue blocks on inside walls flush with top edge.
12. Cement roof in place.
13. Place model on a piece of felt, blotter, or dark colored material and study relation of masses and general exterior appearance.

Display Models

Many of the steps in constructing a display model are similar to those required to fabricate a preliminary study model. Of course more detail is added. The following steps outline a procedure that may be used in the construction of a poster board display model.

1. Study the plans and elevations for the proper layout.
2. Lay out the walls, doors, and window openings, with light pencil, in their proper sequence, on a sheet of poster board. Any projections will be added after the basic form of the model has been erected.
3. Cut out window and door openings.
4. Cut along the roof line.
5. Cut joints ⅔'s deep.
    A. Cut inside corners from rear.

B. Cut outside corners from rear; cut miters with the sanding block.
6. Fasten a print of the floor plan to a piece of plywood or other level surface.
7. Carefully fold the exterior walls to their proper angle and pin to plan.
8. Place reinforcement at all corners to insure square corners.
9. Place glue blocks at roof edges and along the base of the model. Keep glue blocks at least ⅛" away from window openings to prevent them from being seen.
10. Study roof for proper layout.
11. Cut out and assemble roof. If support strips are necessary, cut to length and glue in place.
12. Cut out chimney, dormers, etc.
13. Glue chimney, dormers, etc., to model.
14. Paint roof and walls or apply roofing materials and siding or brick materials to walls.
15. Add window and door trim around all openings.
16. Paint all trim.
17. Lay out window lights and fasten to the back of openings.
18. Cut out and secure curtains, draperies, etc.; cement to the rear of all windows.
19. Cut out doors and fasten to openings with tape.
20. Glue roof to model.
21. Secure model to the building site and lay out location of walks, drive, etc.

22. Apply all materials for walks and drives. Construct and fasten grass, trees, shrubs, hedges, and flowers.

Balsa Wood Display Models

Instead of using cardboard-type materials, the model may be constructed from balsa wood. Some model makers feel that balsa wood gives them more freedom and flexibility. Obviously, the walls cannot be laid out consecutively as with the cardboard-type model. Each wall is laid out and cut separately and then glued in place. (Corner reinforcement for a balsa wood model is the same as that used in cardboard models.) Otherwise, the general procedure is identical. Small bits of detail may be more readily added since balsa wood is easily shaped with a razor blade and abrasive paper. Siding materials, such as wood siding or masonry veneer and roofing materials, are applied in a manner identical to the cardboard model.

Removable Roofs

Some display models are designed so that the roof may be removed to view the interior of the model. Models of this type are usually used for commercial display purposes, such as development homes, building and loan association displays, home shows, exhibits, etc. All exterior features and appointments of the model are the same. The

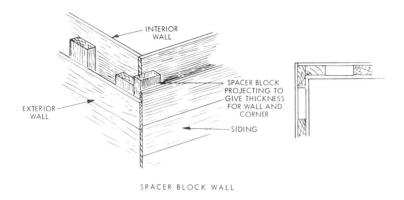

SPACER BLOCK WALL

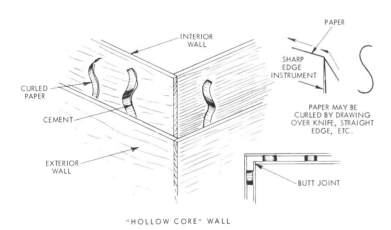

"HOLLOW CORE" WALL

Fig. 16-21. These two methods may be used when constructing walls with balsa wood.

type of model is that various color schemes may be shown in their proper relationship.

Questions and Problems

1. Construct a presentation model of one of the house plans that was designed in Chapter 7. Compare the model with the elevations. Has the impression created by the plans and elevations changed after the completion of the model?
2. What types of changes could be recommended in the plans after analyzing the mass relationships of the model?
3. How many different uses are there for a display model?

method of constructing corners will of necessity be altered. Several methods of construction are shown in Fig. 16-21.

Many of the plumbing fixtures (sink, lavatory, bath tub, water closet) and appliances (refrigerator, stove, washer, dryer, etc.) can be carved from soap. Furniture, such as sofas, chairs, or beds, may be constructed from cardboard and covered with a solid or print material. Quilted chintz material adds the illusion of padding. Tables, coffee tables, etc., can be constructed from balsa wood, veneer, or "thin wood." One of the advantages of the "open"

Building Material Sizes 17

In the process of designing and detailing, the architectural draftsman must use reference materials in the form of handbooks or catalogs to obtain sizes of specifications. This requires time away from the board, of course. As an alternative, to economize on time, some of the more frequently used information and dimensions not ordinarily found in textbooks is included in this chapter.

The subject of material sizes (which often include shapes and qualities) is exceptional in that it consists of details with little apparent relation to each other. To give these details the importance they deserve, each type of detail is listed in alphabetical order for quick reference.

Anchor Bolts

SIZES
3/8" & 1/2" x 6" to 24"
5/8" x 8" to 24"
3/4" x 8" to 24"

Anchor Joists for Masonry Walls

STYLE T	SIZES
	1/8" x 1" x 15" & 20"
	3/16" x 1" x 15" & 20"
	1 1/8" x 1 1/2" x 15" & 20"

STYLE L	
	1/8" x 1" x 15" & 20"
	3/16" x 1" x 15" & 20"
	3/16" x 1 1/2" x 15" & 20"

Area Walls — Window Wells, Metal (16 Gage Galvanized Steel)

DEPTH	WIDTH	HEIGHT
16"	38"	11 1/2"
16"	38"	17 1/2"
16"	38"	23 1/2"
16"	38"	29
16"	38"	35

Ash Dumps

SIZE
4 1/2" x 8"
5" x 8"
7" x 10"

Ash Pit — Clean Out Doors

SIZE
8" x 8"
8" x 12"
12" x 12"
18" x 24"
24" x 30"

Beams, Light Weight, Steel. (See also Discussion of "Structural Steel Shapes")

DEPTH	WEIGHT PER FOOT	WIDTH	WEB THICK.	FLANGE THICK.
6"	4.4 lbs	1 7/8"	1/8"	3/16"
7"	5.5 lbs	2 1/8"	1/8"	3/16"
8"	6.5 lbs	2 1/4"	1/8"	3/16"
10"	9.0 lbs	2 3/4"	3/16"	3/16"
12"	11.8 lbs	3"	3/16"	1/4"

*See also discussion A "Structural Steel Shapes."

Brick Sizes (Modular)*

Nominal Size of Brick in.			Number of Brick per 100 sq ft	Cubic Feet of Mortar			
				Per 100 Sq Ft		Per 1000 Brick	
t	h	l		⅜-in. Joints	½-in. Joints	⅜-in. Joints	½-in. Joints
4 x 2⅔ x 8			675	5.5	7.0	8.1	10.3
4 x 3⅕ x 8			563	4.8	6.1	8.6	10.9
4 x 4 x 8			450	4.2	5.3	9.2	11.7
4 x 5⅓ x 8			338	3.5	4.4	10.2	12.9
4 x 2 x 12			600	6.5	8.2	10.8	13.7
4 x 2⅔ x 12			450	5.1	6.5	11.3	14.4
4 x 3⅕ x 12			375	4.4	5.6	11.7	14.9
4 x 4 x 12			300	3.7	4.8	12.3	15.7
4 x 5⅓ x 12			225	3.0	3.9	13.4	17.1
6 x 2⅔ x 12			450	7.9	10.2	17.5	22.6
6 x 3⅕ x 12			375	6.8	8.8	18.1	23.4
6 x 4 x 12			300	5.6	7.4	19.1	24.7

* Modular Brick and Mortar Required for Single Wythe Walls in Running Bond (No allowances for breakage or waste)

Brick Ventilators, Cast Iron or Aluminum

Width	Length	Depth	Net Free Area
2 1/4"	8 1/8"	2 3/4"	8 1/2 sq in
2 1/2"	8"	1/2"	9 sq in
5"	8"	1/2"	19 sq in
5"	12"	1/2"	30 sq in

Concrete Blocks, Number Per Course

The standard manufactured concrete block for modular construction is a block $7⅝'' \times 7⅝'' \times 15⅝''$ — a size deliberately chosen to allow for ⅜″ joints between blocks. For practical purposes the blocks can be calculated as $8'' \times 8'' \times 16''$, which can be simplified to $⅔' \times ⅔' \times 4/3'$. One *course*, in masonry terms, means a single row of blocks. The number of courses used to build a wall will depend on the height. Disregarding openings, calculations are very simple.

First consider the length of the wall.

$N = L \times ¾$, where:

    N = number of blocks for 1 course

    L = length of wall in feet

Example: How many blocks will be required for 1 course if the wall required is 36′ in length?

$N = 36' \times ¾ = 27$. This is 27 blocks.

Next consider the height of the wall.

$C = H \times 3/2$, where:

    C = number of courses for height

    H — height of wall in feet

Example: The same wall (36′ in length) is 12′ in height.

$C = 12 \times 3/2 = 18$. This is 18 courses.

The total number of blocks required, is the number of blocks per course times the number of courses, that is:

$T = N \times C$, where:

T = total number of blocks for all courses

$T = 27 \times 18 = 486$ blocks.

In the calculation for number of blocks per course and for the number of courses, both the length and height will theoretically be ⅜″ less than calculated because the ends of both dimensions do not terminate with a ⅜″ mortar joint. This amount is negligible in comparison with the overall dimensions and is compensated for by the masons.

Courses are useful in calculating openings. For instance, the standard height for a door frame in a block wall is 7′4″ (7.33′). The total number of courses in this example would therefore be:

$$C = 7.33 \times \tfrac{3}{2} = \frac{21.99}{2} = 11$$

Doors, Folding

2'-4",	2'-10"	W × 6'-8 1/2" Ht
2'-4",	2'-10", 3'-5"	
3'-11",	4'-5", 5'0", 6'0"	W × 6'-8" Ht
7'-1"		
3'-11",	4'-5", 5'0", 6'0"	
7'-1",	8'-2", 9'-3", 10'-3"	W × 8'0" Ht

Concrete Masonry, Wall Thickness (Codes Vary: Check Requirements)

	Residence			Commercial			Cavity Wall Residence			Cavity Wall Commercial		
Story →	1	2	3	1	2	3	1	2	3	1	2	3
Foundation Basement	8"	8"	8"	8-12"	12"	12-16"	8" (SOLID) 10",	12"		10" (SOLID) 10",	10"	12"
1st Story	8"	8"	8"	8-12"	12"	12-16"	10"	10"	10-12"	10-12"	12"	12"
2nd Story		8"	8"		8-12"	12"		10"	20"		10-12"	12"
3rd Story			8"			8-12"			10"			10-12"

Doors, French

1'-6" × 6'-8" × 1 3/8"	2'-6" × 6'-8" × 1 3/4"
2'-0" × 6'-8" × 1 3/8"	2'-0" × 6'-8" × 1 3/4"
2'-6" × 6'-8" × 1 3/8"	3'-0" × 6'-8" × 1 3/4"
2'-8" × 6'-8" × 1 3/8"	3'-0" × 6'-8" × 1 3/8"

Concrete Proportions

Type	Proportion*	Aggregate Max. Size
Areaways	1 - 2 1/2 - 4	1 1/2"
Catch Basins	1 - 2 - 3	1 1/2"
Cisterns	1 - 2 - 3	1"
Curbs	1 - 2 1/2 - 4	1 1/2"
Driveways	1 - 2 - 4	1 1/2"
Floors, Reinforced	1 - 2 - 3	1"
Plain	1 - 2 1/2 - 4	1 1/2"
Foundations Mass	1 - 2 1/2 - 5	3"
Gutters	1 - 2 1/2 - 4	1 1/2"
Piers, House	1 - 2 - 3 1/2	2"
Pools, Swimming	1 - 2 - 3	1 1/2"
Retaining Walls	1 - 2 - 3 1/2	1 1/2"
Roads	1 - 2 - 3 1/2	2"
Roofs	1 - 2 - 3	1 1/2"
Sidewalks	1 - 2 1/2 - 4	1 1/2"
Steps & Stairways	1 - 2 1/2 - 4	1 1/2"
Slabs	1 - 2 - 3	1"
Septic Tanks	1 - 2 - 4	1"
Stucco	1 - 4	1/4"
Walls	1 - 2 - 4	1 1/2"
Walls Subject to Moisture	1 - 2 - 3	1 1/2"

*Proportions for concrete mixtures are usually given in the order: cement, sand, and aggregate (gravel or crushed rock).

Doors, Hollow Metal, Interior and Exterior (1⅜″ (A) and 1¾″ (B) Thick

2'-0" × 6'-8" (A, B)	3'-0" × 6'-8" (A, B)
2'-0" × 7'-0" (A, B)	3'-0" × 7'-0" (A, B)
2'-0" × 7'-2" (A, B)	3'-0" × 7'-2" (A, B)
2'-4" × 6'-8" (A, B)	3'-4" × 6'-8" (B)
2'-4" × 7'-0" (A, B)	3'-4" × 7'-0" (B)
2'-4" × 7'-2" (A, B)	3'-4" × 7'-2" (B)
2'-6" × 6'-8" (A, B)	3'-6" × 6'-8" (B)
2'-6" × 7'-0" (A, B)	3'-6" × 7'-0" (B)
2'-6" × 7'-2" (A, B)	3'-6" × 7'-2" (B)
2'-8" × 6'-8" (A, B)	3'-8" × 6'-8" (B)
2'-8" × 7'-0" (A, B)	3'-8" × 7'-0" (B)
2'-8" × 7'-2" (A, B)	3'-8" × 7'-2" (B)
	4'-0" × 6'-8" (B)
	4'-0" × 7'-0" (B)
	4'-0" × 7'-2" (B)

Doors, Louver

2'-8 1/2" × 6'-10"	2 Panel
3'-0" × 6'-10"	3 Panel

Doors, Metal, Access

Overall Dimension	Door Size	Wall Opening	Door Thickness
10" x 14"	7 1/8" x 11 1/8"	8" x 12"	1/16"
14" x 18"	11 1/8" x 15 1/8"	12" x 16"	1/16"
18" x 26"	15 1/8" x 23 1/8"	16" x 24"	12 gage
26" x 36"	25 1/8" x 31 1/8"	24" x 32"	12 gage

Doors, Outside Basement

Width	Length	Rise	Steel
3'-11"	4'-10"	2'-0"	12 gage
4'-3"	5'-4"	1'-10"	12 gage
4'-7"	6'-0"	1'-7"	12 gage

Doors, Overhead

8'-0" x 7'-0" x 1 3/8"
8'-0" x 7'-0" x 1 2/4"
8'-0" x 8'-0" x 1 3/4"
9'-0" x 7'-0" x 1 3/4"
16'-0" x 7'-0" x 1 3/4"

Doors, Wood (Interior (I) and Exterior (E)), 1⅜" and 1¾" Thick

1'-6" x 6'-6" (I)	2'-6" x 6'-0" (I)	3'-0" x 6'-8" (I, E)
1'-6" x 6'-8" (I)	2'-6" x 6'-6" (I)	3'-0" x 7'-0" (I, E)
2'-0" x 6'-0" (I)	2'-6" x 6'-8" (I, E)	3'-0" x 7'-6" (E)
2'-0" x 6'-6" (I)	2'-6" x 7'-0" (I, E)	3'-0" x 8'-0" (E)
2'-0" x 6'-8" (I)	2'-8" x 6'-0" (I)	3'-4" x 6'-8" (I, E)
2'-0" x 7'-0" (I)	2'-8" x 6'-6" (I)	3'-4" x 7'-0" (I, E)
2'-4" x 6'-0" (I)	2'-8" x 6'-8" (I, E)	3'-4" x 7'-6" (E)
2'-4" x 6'-6" (I)	2'-8" x 7'-0" (I, E)	3'-4" x 8'-0" (E)

Fireplaces, Recommended Sizes

	Location			
	Short Side		Long Side	
Room Size	W	H	W	H
10' x 14'	28"	27"	28"	27"
11' x 16'	28"	27"	32"	27"
	32"	27"	36"	27"

Fireplaces, Recommended Sizes (cont'd)

	Location			
	Short Side		Long Side	
Room Size	W	H	W	H
12' x 20'	32"	27"	36"	27"
	36"	27"	40"	27"
12' x 24'	32"	27"	36"	27"
	36"	27"	40"	29"
14' x 28'	36"	27"	40"	29"
	40"	29"	48"	29"
16' x 30'	36"	27"	40"	29"
	40"	29"	48"	29"
20' x 30'	40"	29"	48"	29"
	48"	29"	60"	32"

Flooring, Resilient

Material		Size	Thickness
Asphalt Tile		9" x 9"	1/8"
		12" x 12"	3/16"
		18" x 24"	3/16"
Rubber Tile		9" x 9"	1/8"
		6" x 6"	3/16"
		12" x 12"	3/16"
Vinyl (Plastic)		9" x 9"	1/8", 3/16"
Felt		3' Wide	1/25"
Linoleum		6' Wide	
Battleship	Reg	6' Wide	3/32"
	Hvy	6' Wide	1/8"
Embossed Inlaid	Reg	6' Wide	3/32"
	Hvy	6' Wide	1/8"
Jaspe	Std	6' Wide	3/32"
	Hvy	6' Wide	1/8"
Plain	Std	6' Wide	3/32"
	Hvy	6' Wide	1/8"
Cok Tile		6" x 6"	3/16"
		6" x 12"	3/16"
		12" x 12"	5/16"
		12" x 36"	5/16"

Flooring, Wood

Hardwood Size (Actual)	Softwood Size (Actual)
25/32" x 2 1/4"	25/32" x 2 3/8"
25/32" x 1 1/2"	25/32" x 3 1/4"
1/2" x 2"	
1/2" x 1 1/2"	
3/8" x 2"	
3/8" x 1 1/2"	

Flue Lining, Modular

Outside Diameter	Modular Dimension	Thickness*	Inside Area	Length
3 1/2" x 7 1/2"	4" x 8"	1/2"	15 sq in	2'-0"
3 1/2" x 11 1/2"	4" x 12"	5/8"	20 " "	"
3 1/2" x 15 1/2"	4" x 16"	3/4"	27 " "	"
7 1/2" x 7 1/2"	8" x 8"	5/8"	35 " "	"
7 1/2" x 11 1/2"	8" x 12"	3/4"	57 " "	"
7 1/2" x 15 1/2"	8" x 16"	7/8"	74 " "	"
11 1/2" x 11 1/2"	12" x 12"	7/8"	87 " "	"
11 1/2" x 15 1/2"	12" x 16"	1"	120 " "	"
15 1/2" x 15 1/2"	16" x 16"	1 1/8"	162 " "	"
15 1/2" x 19 1/2"	16" x 20"	1 1/4"	208 " "	"
19 1/2" x 19 1/2"	20" x 20"	1 3/8"	262 " "	"

* Minimum wall thickness

Flue Lining, Round

INSIDE DIAMETER	THICKNESS*	LENGTH	AREA INSIDE
6"	5/8"	2' 0"	26 sq. in.
7"	11/16"	2' 0"	37 " "
8"	3/4"	2' 0"	47 " "
10"	7/8"	2' 0"	74 1/2 " "
12"	1"	2' 0"	108 " "
15"	1 1/8"	2' 0"	171 " "
18"	1 1/4"	2' 0"	240 " "
20"	1 3/8"	2' 0"	298 " "

*Minimum wall thickness

Flue Lining, Standard

OUTSIDE	INSIDE	THICKNESS*	AREA INSIDE	LENGTH
4 1/2" x 8 1/2"	3 1/4" x 7 1/4"	5/8"	22 sq. in.	2'0"
4 1/2" x 13"	3 1/4" x 11 3/4"	5/8"	36 " "	"
7 1/2" x 7 1/2"	6 1/4" x 6 1/4"	5/8"	38 " "	"
8 1/2" x 8 1/2"	7 1/4" x 7 1/4"	5/8"	51 " "	"
8 1/2" x 13"	7" x 11 1/2"	3/4"	79 " "	"
8 1/2" x 18"	6 3/4" x 16 1/4"	7/8"	108 " "	"
13" x 13"	11 1/4" x 11 1/4"	7/8"	125 " "	"
13" x 18"	11 1/4" x 16 1/4"	7/8"	168 " "	"
18" x 18"	15 3/4" x 15 3/4"	1 1/8"	232 " "	"
20" x 20"	17 1/4" x 17 1/4"	1 3/8"	279 " "	"

*Minimum wall thickness

Glass Block

NOMINAL	ACTUAL
6" sq	5 3/4" sq
8" sq	7 3/4" sq
12" sq	11 3/4" sq

Gutters, Fir

SIZE	ACTUAL SIZE	LENGTHS
3" x 4"	2 1/2" x 3 1/2"	Up to 20'
3" x 5"	2 1/2" x 4 1/2"	"
4" x 4"	3 1/2" x 3 1/2"	"
4" x 5"	3 1/2" x 4 1/2"	"
4" x 6"	3 1/2" x 5 1/2"	"
5" x 7"	4 1/2" x 6 1/2"	"

Gutters, Ogee Metal Box (Galvanized)*

DEPTH	WIDTH	GAUGE
3 1/2"	3 1/2"	28-29
4 1/4"	4 3/8"	"
5"	5"	"

*10' Lengths

Gypsum Wallboard

Width	Lengths	Thickness	Joist or Stud Spacing
4'	6', 7', 8', 9', 10' 12', 14'	1/2"	16" or 24" OC
4'	6', 7', 8', 9', 10' 14'	3/8"	16" OC
4'	8', 10'	1/4"	16" OC
4'	6', 7', 8', 9', 10', 12', 14'	5/8"	16" or 24" OC

Hardboard

Material	Thickness	Size
Standard Hardboard and Tempered Hardboard	1/8", 3/16" 1/4", 5/16"	4' x 5', 6', 8', 9', 10', 12'

Insulating Board

Product	Sizes	Thickness	Edges
Building Board	4' x 7', 8', 9', 10', 12'	1/2", 3/4", 1"	Sq.
Sheathing	4' x 8', 9', 10', 12', 3' x 8'; 2' x 8'	1/2", 25/32" 1/2", 25/32"	Sq. Long edges fabricated Sq. Edge Short Ends
Thin Board	4' x 7', 8', 9', 10', 12'	1/4"	Sq.
Lath	18" x 48", 24" x 48"	1/2", 1"	Long Edge fabricated
Roof Insulation	23" x 47"	1/2", 1", 1 1/2", 2"	Sq.
Tile Board	12" x 12", 16" x 16", 12" x 24", 16" x 32"	1/2", 3/4", 1"	Fab. Edges
Plank	W 8, 10, 12, 16 x 8', 10', 12	1/2"	Fab. Long Edges

Lintels, Concrete

Span	With Wall Load One Piece Lintel		Split Lintel		
	Size	Reinforcing	Size	Reinforcing	End Bearing
T0 –7'	7-5/8" x 5-3/4" x	2 No. 3 (3/8" Dia.) bars	3-5/8" x 5-3/4"	1 No. 3 (3/8" Dia.) bar	8"
7'-8'	7-5/8" x 5-3/4"	2 No. 5 (5/8" Dia.) bars	3-5/8" x 5-3/4"	1 No. 5 (5/8" Dia.) bar	8"
7'-8'	7-5/8" x 7-5/8"	2 No. 3 (3/8" Dia.) bars	3-5/8" x 7-5/8"	1 No. 3 (3/8" Dia.) bar	8"
8'-9'	7-5/8" x 7-5/8"	2 No. 4 (1/2" Dia.) bars	3-5/8" x 7-5/8"	1 No. 4 (1/2" Dia.) bar	12"
9'-10'	7-5/8" x 7-5/8"	2 No. 5 (5/8" Dia.) bars	3-5/8" 7-5/8"	1 No. 5 (5/8" Dia.) bar	12"

Lintels, Concrete, Reinforced (With Wall and Floor Load 75 lb to 85 lb for 20′ Span)

Span	Size	Bottom Reinforcing	Top Reinforcing	Stirrups or Webs	End Bearing
3′	7 5/8″ x 7 5/8″ x	2 No. 4 (1/2″ Dia.) bars	None	None	8″
4′	7 5/8″ x 7 5/8″ x	2 No. 6 (3/4″ Dia.) bars	None	3-6 gage	8″
5′	7 5/8″ x 7 5/8″ x	2 No. 7 (7/8″ Dia.) bars	2 No. 3 (3/8″ Dia.) bars	5-6 gage	8″
6′	7 5/8″ x 7 5/8″ x	2 No. 7 (7/8″ Dia.) bars	2 No. 4 (1/2″ Dia.) bars	7-6 gage	12″
7′	7 5/8″ x 7 5/8″ x	2 No. 8 (1″ Dia.) bars	2 No. 8 (1″ Dia.) bars	9 gage	12″

Lintels, Wood (In Walls Where Roof and Floor Loads Need Not BeSupported)

ROUGH OPENING	NOMINAL SIZE STRUCTURAL MEMBERS
Up to 3′-6″	2 – 2″x 4″
3′-6″ to 5′-6″	2 – 2″x 6″
5′-6″ to 7′-6″	2 – 2″x 8″
7′-6 to 9′-6″	2 – 2″x 10″
9′-6″ to 11′-0″	1 – 1″x 12″

*In walls where roof and floor loads need not be supported.

Lintels, Steel (4″ Bearing)

MASONRY OPENINGS	ANGLE SIZE
Up to 3′-0″	3″ x 3″ x 1/2″
3′-0″ to 7′-0″	3 1/2″ x 3 1/2″ x 3/8″
7′-0″ to 8′-0″	3 1/2″ x 3 1/2″ x 1/2″
8′-0″ to 10′-0″	5″ x 3 1/2″ x 1/2″
10′-0″ to 11′-0″	4″ x 4″ x 1/2″
11′ 0″ to 15′ 0″	6″ x 4″ x 3/8″
15′ 0″ to 16′ 0″	6″ x 4″ x 1/2″

Louvers, Wall

STYLE	SIZE	SQUARE INCH OPEN AREA	SQUARE FEET FLOOR AREA
Triangular	29″ x 11″	84	168
Triangular	Adj	75	150
Triangular	36″ x 9″	70	140
Square	8″ x 8″	35	70
Rectangular	8″ x 16″	91	182
Square	12″ x 12″	99	198
Rectangular	12″ x 18″	165	330
Rectangular	18″ x 24″	330	660
Rectangular	8″ x 24″	160	320
1/4 Circle	14″ x 15″	56	112
1/2 Circle	28″ x 15″	116	232

Lumber, Standard Sizes

Type	Nominal Size Thickness	Width	Actual Size Thickness	Width
Dimension	2"	2" 4" 6" 8" 10" 12"	1 1/2"	1 1/2" 3 1/2" 5 1/2" 7 1/4" 9 1/4" 11 1/4"
Timbers 4", 6", 8"	4" 6" 8"	4" 6" 8" 10"	3 1/2"	3 1/2" 5 1/2" 7 1/2" 9 1/2"
	6"	6" 8" 10"	5 1/2"	5 1/2" 7 1/2" 9 1/2"
	8"	8" 10"	7 1/2" 7 1/2"	7 1/2" 9 1/2"
Common Boards	1"	2" 4" 6" 8" 10" 12"	3/4" or 25/32"	1 1/2" 3 1/2" 5 1/2" 7 1/4" 9 1/4" 11 1/4"
Shiplap Boards	1"	4" 6" 8" 10" 12"	3/4" or 25/32"	3 1/8" Face 5 1/8" Width 7 1/8" " 9 1/8" " 11 1/8" "
T & G Boards	1"	4" 6" 8" 10" 12"	3/4" or 25/32"	3 1/4" Face 5 1/4" Width 7 1/4" " 9 1/4" " 11 1/4" "
Bevel Siding Thin Thick	1/2" 1/2" 1/2" 1/2" 3/4" 3/4" 3/16"	4" 5" 6" 7" 8" 10" 12"	15/32" 3/16" 15/32" 3/16" 15/32" 3/16" 15/32" 3/16" 3/4" 3/16" 3/4" 3/16" 3/4" 3/16"	3 1/2" 4 1/2" 5 1/2" 6 1/2" 7 1/4" 9 1/4" 11 1/4"

Mail Receivers

WALL THICKNESS	MAIL OPENINGS
5 1/2" – 13"	6 3/4" x 2 1/4"
5 1/2" – 13"	7 1/4" x 2 1/4"
7 1/2" – 13"	3" x 7"
7 1/2" – 13"	3" x 7 1/4"

Metal Lath

TYPE	SIZE	REMARKS
Diamond Mesh Self Furring	27" x 96"	5/16" mesh
Diamond Mesh	27" x 96"	5/16" furred 3/8"
Stucco Lath	48" x 96"	1 3/8" furred 3/8"
1/8" Rib Lath	24" x 96" 27" x 96"	1/8" Rib
3/8" Rib Lath	24" x 96" 27" x 96"	3/8" Rib
3/4" Rib Lath	29" x 72" 29" x 96" 29" x 120" 29" x 144"	3/4" Rib – 3 5/8 OC " " " " " "

Molding Patterns, Stock. (See Illustrations)

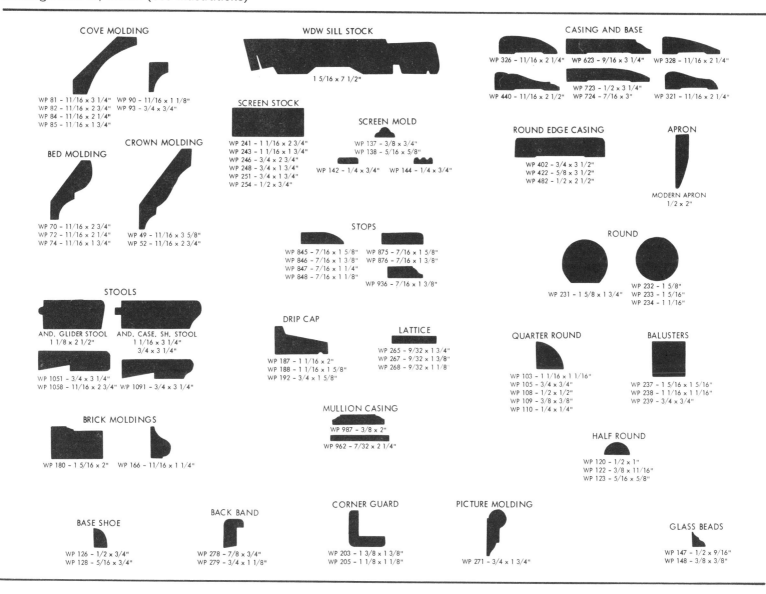

COVE MOLDING

WP 81 – 11/16 x 3 1/4"   WP 90 – 11/16 x 1 1/8"
WP 82 – 11/16 x 2 3/4"   WP 93 – 3/4 x 3/4"
WP 84 – 11/16 x 2 1/4"
WP 85 – 11/16 x 1 3/4"

BED MOLDING   CROWN MOLDING

WP 70 – 11/16 x 2 3/4"
WP 72 – 11/16 x 2 1/4"   WP 49 – 11/16 x 3 5/8"
WP 74 – 11/16 x 1 3/4"   WP 52 – 11/16 x 2 3/4"

STOOLS

AND. GLIDER STOOL   AND. CASE. SH. STOOL
1 1/8 x 2 1/2"   1 1/16 x 3 1/4"
                        3/4 x 3 1/4"

WP 1051 – 3/4 x 3 1/4"
WP 1058 – 11/16 x 2 3/4" WP 1091 – 3/4 x 3 1/4"

BRICK MOLDINGS

WP 180 – 1 5/16 x 2"   WP 166 – 11/16 x 1 1/4"

WDW SILL STOCK

1 5/16 x 7 1/2"

SCREEN STOCK

WP 241 – 1 1/16 x 2 3/4"
WP 243 – 1 1/16 x 1 3/4"
WP 246 – 3/4 x 2 3/4"
WP 248 – 3/4 x 1 3/4"
WP 251 – 3/4 x 1 3/4"
WP 254 – 1/2 x 3/4"

SCREEN MOLD

WP 137 – 3/8 x 3/4"
WP 138 – 5/16 x 5/8"

WP 142 – 1/4 x 3/4"   WP 144 – 1/4 x 3/4"

STOPS

WP 845 – 7/16 x 1 5/8"   WP 875 – 7/16 x 1 5/8"
WP 846 – 7/16 x 1 3/8"   WP 876 – 7/16 x 1 3/8"
WP 847 – 7/16 x 1 1/4"
WP 848 – 7/16 x 1 1/8"   WP 936 – 7/16 x 1 3/8"

DRIP CAP

LATTICE

WP 265 – 9/32 x 1 3/4"
WP 267 – 9/32 x 1 3/8"
WP 187 – 1 1/16 x 2"   WP 268 – 9/32 x 1 1/8"
WP 188 – 1 1/16 x 1 5/8"
WP 192 – 3/4 x 1 5/8"

MULLION CASING

WP 987 – 3/8 x 2"

WP 962 – 7/32 x 2 1/4"

CASING AND BASE

WP 326 – 11/16 x 2 1/4"   WP 623 – 9/16 x 3 1/4"   WP 328 – 11/16 x 2 1/4"

WP 440 – 11/16 x 2 1/2"   WP 723 – 1/2 x 3 1/4"   WP 321 – 11/16 x 2 1/4"
                          WP 724 – 7/16 x 3"

ROUND EDGE CASING   APRON

WP 402 – 3/4 x 3 1/2"
WP 422 – 5/8 x 3 1/2"
WP 482 – 1/2 x 2 1/2"

MODERN APRON
1/2 x 2"

ROUND

WP 231 – 1 5/8 x 1 3/4"   WP 232 – 1 5/8"
                         WP 233 – 1 5/16"
                         WP 234 – 1 1/16"

QUARTER ROUND   BALUSTERS

WP 103 – 1 1/16 x 1 1/16"
WP 105 – 3/4 x 3/4"   WP 237 – 1 5/16 x 1 5/16"
WP 108 – 1/2 x 1/2"   WP 238 – 1 1/16 x 1 1/16"
WP 109 – 3/8 x 3/8"   WP 239 – 3/4 x 3/4"
WP 110 – 1/4 x 1/4"

HALF ROUND

WP 120 – 1/2 x 1"
WP 122 – 3/8 x 11/16"
WP 123 – 5/16 x 5/8"

BASE SHOE   BACK BAND   CORNER GUARD   PICTURE MOLDING   GLASS BEADS

WP 126 – 1/2 x 3/4"   WP 278 – 7/8 x 3/4"   WP 203 – 1 3/8 x 1 3/8"   WP 147 – 1/2 x 9/16"
WP 128 – 5/16 x 3/4" WP 279 – 3/4 x 1 1/8" WP 205 – 1 1/8 x 1 1/8"   WP 271 – 3/4 x 1 3/4" WP 148 – 3/8 x 3/8"

Plywood Sizes

Exterior Widths, Ft	Length, Ft	Thickness, In
2 1/2, 3, 3 1/2, 4	5, 6, 7, 8, 9, 10, 12	3/16, 1/4, 3/8, 1/2, 3/4, 7/8, 1, 1 1/8
4	8, 9, 10, 12	5/16, 3/8, 1/2, 5/8
4	8	5/8, 3/4
Interior 2 1/2, 3, 3 1/2, 4	5, 6, 7, 8, 9, 10, 12	3/16, 1/4, 3/8, 1/2, 5/8, 3/4
4	8, 9, 10, 12	5/16, 3/8, 1/2, 5/8
4	8	1/3, 1/2, 3/16, 5/8, 3/4

Plywood Uses

Thickness	Use
1/4" or 1/2"	Interior Wall, ceiling coverings
1/4", 5/16", 3/8", 1/2"	Wall Sheathing (to be covered)
5/16", 3/8", 1/2", 5/8"	Roof Sheathing (To be covered)
1/2", 5/8"	Sub Floors
3/8", 1/2", 5/8"	Exterior Panels or Siding (Exposed to Weather)

Roofing, Built Up

Roof Slope	Description
1/4" to 4"/ft.	Gravel, Slag, Mineral – 3, 4, or 5 plies felt. Bonded with tar or asphalt and surfaced with mineral, gravel or slag.

Roofing, Wood Shingles

ROOF SLOPE			SHINGLE EXPOSURE		
Pitch	Rise	Run	16"	18"	24"
1/8	3"	12"	3 3/4"	4 1/4"	5 3/4"
1/6	4"	12"			
1/4	6"	12"			
1/3	8"	12"			
1/2	12"	12"	5"	5 1/2"	7 1/2"
5/8	15"	12"			
3/4	18"	12"			

Sound Insulation Value of Wall Panels

SOUND TRANSMISSION CLASS*						
25	30	35	42	45	48	50
Normal speech can be understood quite easily	Loud speech can be understood fairly well	Loud speech audible but not intelligible	Loud speech audible as a murmur	Must strain to hear loud speech	Some loud speech barely audible	Loud speech not audible

STC numbers have been adopted by acoustical engineers as a measure of the resistance of a building element such as a wall to the passage of sound. The higher the number, the better the sound barrier.

*Source: Insulation Board Institute

1/4" PLYWOOD

20 db

1/4" HARD-BOARD

20 db

1/8" GLASS

25 db

1/4" GLASS

30 db

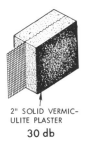

2" SOLID VERMIC-ULITE PLASTER

30 db

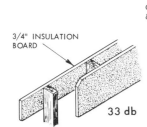

3/4" INSULATION BOARD

33 db

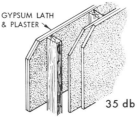

GYPSUM LATH & PLASTER

35 db

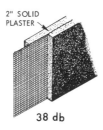

2" SOLID PLASTER

38 db

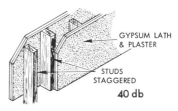

GYPSUM LATH & PLASTER

STUDS STAGGERED

40 db

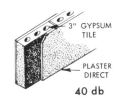

3" GYPSUM TILE

PLASTER DIRECT

40 db

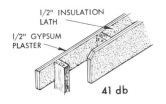

1/2" INSULATION LATH

1/2" GYPSUM PLASTER

41 db

4" CLAY TILE

PLASTER DIRECT

45 db

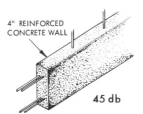

4" REINFORCED CONCRETE WALL

45 db

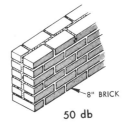

8" BRICK

50 db

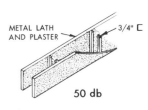

METAL LATH AND PLASTER

3/4" ⊏

50 db

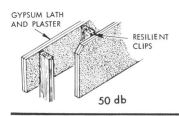

GYPSUM LATH AND PLASTER

RESILIENT CLIPS

50 db

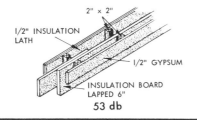

2" x 2"

1/2" INSULATION LATH

1/2" GYPSUM

INSULATION BOARD LAPPED 6"

53 db

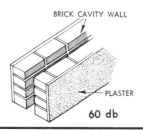

BRICK CAVITY WALL

PLASTER

60 db

The noise reduction factors given for these panels are average and conditions such as workmanship, quality of materials and other factors may raise or lower the efficiency of the panel.

They are shown primarily for comparison purposes and to illustrate how sound reduction depends on weight, thickness and air space. Those panels which have air space as an element, may have their efficiency increased by further separation of the solid surfaces.

Source: Practical Builder

Structural Steel Shapes

All designations are standard for the steel producing and fabricating industries and are used in all references to shapes when designing, detailing, and ordering.

1. Wide Flange Beams

A wide flange beam having a depth of 18″ and weighing 50 lbs./ft. is designated as:

W 18 × 50

2. Light Wide Flange Beams

A light wide flange beam weighing 18.5 lbs./ft. and having a depth of 5⅛″ is called out as:

W 5 × 18.5

3. Miscellaneous Columns

The designation for a miscellaneous column weighing 34.8 lbs./ft. and having a depth of 8″ is:

M 8 × 34.3

4. Junior Beams

The identification of a junior beam (M) having a depth of 12″ and weight of 11.8 lbs./ft. is:

M 12 × 11.8

5. Junior Channels

All junior channels are called out giving the shape designation (MC), depth and weight. Thus a junior channel weighing 10.6 lbs. and having a depth of 12″ is identified as

MC 12 × 10.6

6. American Standard Beams

All standard I beams are designated as S. A beam having a depth of 18″ and weighing 70 lbs./ft. is called out as:

S 18 × 70

7. American Standard Channels

A standard channel having a depth of 15″, flange width of 3½″ and a weight of 40 lbs./fs. is designed as:

C 15 × 40

8. Angles

All equal and unequal leg angles are designated by the symbol L followed by the length of each leg and the thickness of the leg.

Equal Leg:

L 3½ × 3½ × ½

Unequal Leg:

L 6 × 3½ × ⁵⁄₁₆

9. Structural Tees

Structural tees cut from W, M, and S sections are ginven the symbol WT, MT, and ST respectively.

Tee cut from Wide Flange Beam:
WT 5 × 10.5

Tee cut from a Column
MT 7 × 8.6

Tee cut from a Standard Beam
ST 6 × 17.5

10. Plates

The designation of a plate is by symbol PL, thickness, width and length. Thus a plate ¾″ thick, 8″ wide and 18″ long is identified as:

PL ¾″ × 8 × 18″

11. Bars

All bars (square, round, and flat) are called out by the word BAR, size and in case of square and round the symbol. Thus a:

Square

BAR 1

Round

BAR 1¼ Φ

Flat

BAR 2½ × ½

Stucco Mesh

1 1/2" x 17 gage	
1" x 18 gage	36" wide x 150' rolls
1" x 10 gage	

Ventilators, Masonry Wall

BAR TYPE SIZE	DIAGONAL TYPE SIZE
8" x 8"	8" x 8"
12" x 8"	12" x 8"
16" x 8"	16" x 8"
12" x 12"	12" x 12"
18" x 12"	18" x 12"
24" x 12"	24" x 12"

Specification Writing 18
and Fill-in Forms

One of man's greatest problems stems from his inability to communicate adequately. One of the most precise methods of conveying technical information is through a technical drawing. However, supplemental information (specifications) must frequently be added for further clarification of materials, methods, etc. In the field of architectural drawing, specifications are an integral part of planning and designing a structure.

Need for Specifications

The working drawings for a structure give only the shape and size. To be complete they must be accompanied by a set of specifications. Specifications give an explanation of the quality and kind of materials, colors, finishes, and fabrications. The quality of workmanship may also be given.

Specifications amplify and supplement the set of working drawings. They also give much of the information that cannot adequately be presented on each sheet of the set of drawings. If all the information contained in the specifications were to be placed on the drawing, it would be too scattered and difficult to find, making it an almost impossible task for the contractor and supplier to arrive at a true bid price. Directions for various aspects of the building would have to be repeated many times. Using specifications, directions are given only once.

Only information which cannot be easily placed on plans is incorporated in the specifications. This should be presented in language that is clear, simple, and concise. In addition, specifications include information such as the legal responsibilities, methods of purchasing equipment, and the insurance requirements on the building.

XYZ NURSING HOME   ENDURA/ASSOCIATES/ARCHITECTS
OUTSTATION, KANSAS   COLUMBINE, COLORADO

ARCH. PROJECT NO. 7033   MARCH 31, 1971

PRELIMINARY OUTLINE SPECIFICATION

Site Work

1. Concrete sidewalks and curbs
2. Stabilized gravel parking and roadways
3. Topsoil where required
4. Finish grading, racking and seeding by Owner

Substructure

1. Poured concrete footing with concrete block foundation walls
2. Poured reinforced concrete floor slabs

Superstructure

1. Steel open web joist on masonry bearing walls with steel lintels over
    windows and miscellaneous masonry openings
2. 1 1/2" Metal deck with 1 1/2" rigid insulation on all roof surfaces

Floors

1. Vinyl asbestos tile in all corridors, patient rooms, dining room,
    toilets, kitchen, day room, lounges, offices and activity room
2. Concrete slab with hardner in storage rooms, mechanical room,
    laundry room and janitors closets
3. Ceramic tile floors and base in tub room and shower rooms
4. Vinyl base in vinyl asbestos tile
5. Carpet in corridors

Walls

1. Exterior walls – Face brick or Aggregate finish on light–weight block
2. All interior walls to be light–weight block

Ceilings

1. Suspended exposed grid lay–in acoustical tile throughout
2. Suspended plastic covered lay–in in tub room, shower room, kitchen
    and laundry rooms
3. Exposed metal deck in storage rooms, receiving and mechanical room

Aluminum Work

1. Aluminum sliding sash throughout building on exterior
2. Aluminum gravel stops
3. Aluminum fresh air intakes

Roofing and Sheet Metal

1. Built–up 20–year bond pitch and gravel roof
2. Copper flashing where required

Miscellaneous Metals

1. Hollow metal door frames and sidelights at all doors
2. Metal sliding door tracks at closet doors
3. Hollow metal exterior doors

Preliminary Outline Specification – No. 7033
March 31, 1971
Page 2

Carpentry

1. Solid core, 1 3/4" wood doors
2. Solid core, 1 3/8" wood sliding closet doors
3. Miscellaneous shelving
4. Wood counter tops with plastic laminate covering
5. Wood corridor handrailing

Mechanical

Heating

1. All the new building will be heated with hot water

Types of Heating Units

1. Large rooms   – Unit heaters or radiation strip fin heaters
2. Corridors   – Cabinet heaters and radiation strip fin heaters
3. Storage & small rooms – Radiation or electric heaters strip fin heaters

Exhaust

1. Mechanical exhaust in required areas

Plumbing

Utilities

1. Storm   – to be spilled out at grade
2. Water   – to connect to existing and new well
3. Sanitary – connect to existing sewage lagoon (design criteria to be
               verified)

Fixtures

1. Water closets – wall hung tank type
2. Lavatories – wall hung

Miscellaneous Equipment

1. Fire extinguishers as required
2. Toilet paper holders, towel dispensers, etc.
3. Fire hose cabinet

Electrical

Service

1. Connect to existing where possible

Lighting

1. Fluorescent in general
2. Incadescent in storage and mechanical room

Telephone

1. Tie into existing

Fig. 18-1. Preliminary outline specifications assist the architect in pointing out basic features of construction to the client that might otherwise be difficult for him to understand.

Basically, the set of specifications serves three purposes. (1) It is a legal document that gives instructions for bid advertisement, bid invitations, owner-contractor agreement, and bond forms that are necessary. Before any specifications are written, the laws, building codes, the requirements of the state, and the ordinances of the local community should be consulted and used as guidelines. (2) Specifications serve as a guide for the contractor or sub-contractor who is bidding for the work. The specifications enable him to make an intelligent estimate of the costs that will be involved in the installation and/or construction. (3) Specifications also give technical descriptions and directions for fabricating and erecting the materials.

Preliminary Outline Specifications

Preliminary outline specifications are, as the name implies, specifications written to accompany the preliminary set of drawings for a building. This type of specification is normally written for most architectural designs. Preliminary *"specs,"* a commonly accepted abbreviated term, are usually not written for single family dwellings. Any type of multiple family or high-density multiple unit dwellings would require preliminary outline specifications. The basic purpose of a preliminary "spec" is to show the client exactly what is included in the design. Many persons who commission an architect to design any type of structure frequently have difficulty in completely understanding a drawing. The preliminary "specs" show exactly what is being included.

In addition, preliminary specifications are used by the contractor or the estimator to arrive at the approximate cost of the proposed building. If the client feels the estimated cost is too high, the architect can point out specific items shown in the outline specifications that may be changed in order to reduce the price.

Fig. 18-1 shows a set of preliminary outline "specs" for the XYZ Nursing Home. These specifications are divided into logical divisions of the building such as site, superstructure (footings and foundations), structure, floors, walls, roof, carpentry, heating, lighting, etc. Outline specifications do not necessarily follow the Construction Specification Institute Format.

It will be noted that some of the items are set in italicized type. The italics indicate items that were changed after conference with the contractor or estimator, architect and client. In some instances items or materials must meet municipal or state building, health or fire codes and are identified as such in the outline "specs."

Working Specifications

The specifications may be divided into several sub-divisions: scope of work, materials to be used, fabrication and erection, and guarantee. The specifications are also often divided into trade divisions, such as excavation, fill and grading, concrete, masonry, structural steel and iron, carpentry and millwork, general metal, roofing, electrical, plumbing, heating, lathing and plastering, insulation, finish hardware, painting, special equipment, landscaping, planting, and finish grading.

The specifications spell out the *scope of work* that is to be performed by the contractor. He is told precisely what work he is to do—the labor, materials, and equipment he is to furnish. The *work not included* is also spelled out. Some facets of work in the various building trades are closely related and it becomes necessary to tell the contractor what is *not* to be included in a specific area. When workmanship is specified, this tells the workmen or sub-contractor how to do the work. For example, they may state how many coats of paint and what colors are to be applied to the interior and exterior of the house. Since the specifications serve as a contract, all reference to what the contractor must do is commonly introduced by the word *"shall"*; all reference to what the owner must do is commonly introduced by the word *"will."*

Specifications can also be used in appraising a building for the purposes of loan evaluation. In some instances, lending institutions will ask for the specifications on an existing building so they may more adequately assess the value. Specifications call out the materials that have been used in the building and not merely those materials which are visible.

The architect or designer usually prepares the specifications for a set of drawings. This way there is less chance a misunderstanding will occur about the material to be used in the building. In some cases the architect will indicate that no substitutions may be made for a particular item. If, however, a substitute is permitted, the words *"or equal"* or *"or similar"* are used. Preparing specifications is becoming more involved and exacting every day. New materials and new methods of construction require close investigation by the architect or designer. It is imperative that all features of the "specs" be made clear so that there is no misunderstanding.

Specifications may have errors. Some errors to guard against are: (1) unfair and ambiguous clauses, (2) a difference between the drawings and specifications, (3) unclear specifications of materials, and (4) an omission of necessary clauses that should be included for the owner's protection.

The buyer of a new home that has been built speculatively, or the buyer who has contracted to have a house built, should ask to read the specifications. Any questions concerning the content or interpretation of the specifications should be clarified immediately. Remember, specifications are a part of a legal document and, combined with the drawings, may be used in court as binding evidence in the event of a litigation.

The CSI Format

Late in the 1960's the Construction Specification Institute, Washington, D.C., developed a uniform system for writing construction specifications. Prior to this no widespread system had been adopted. Some general guidelines, however, were followed by most architectural firms. The CSI uniform system was originated to meet the need for a consistent arrangement for specifications. Acceptance by architects and engineers of the CSI system has aided contractors and suppliers in arriving at more accurate bid figures. The term format refers to Divisions of types of work and related areas.

When using a standard format in writing specifications, the architect has a greater assurance that the specifications for a particular job are complete. A uniform specification system benefits not only the architect, but the contractor and supplier as well, because all are familiar with a standard format of specifications. Without a standard system each architect would develop his own unique method for writing specs. For example, it would be difficult to use a telephone book that was not arranged in alphabetical order, but rather based on a system unique to each community. It is obvious that difficulties would arise from a proliferation of construction specifications that do not follow a recognized or established pattern.

The Construction Specification Institute has successfully established a workable pattern for organizing and writing specifications. This system or format is based on a 16 Division framework with appropriate sections within each Division. Since the framework is uniform, specification materials can now be arranged for automated processing. Section titles in the uniform system are based on headings that are widely used and distinctly generic. Each Division and section title were selected because of their adaptability for data filing and cost accounting procedures. To save costly man hours many architectural firms now use data processing for filing and cost accounting.

The CSI format is made up of 4 major groupings for documents. These groupings are: (1) Bidding Requirements, (2) Contractor Forms, (3) General Conditions, and (4) Technical Specifications. For example, *Technical Specifications* includes 16 Divisions for specifications. These Divisions are permanent and unchanging, and are fixed in number and name. Each Division indicates the location of sections in the CSI format:

Div.
No.   Division Name
1. General Requirements
2. Site Work
3. Concrete
4. Masonry
5. Metals
6. Wood and Plastics
7. Thermal and Moisture Protection
8. Doors and Windows
9. Finishes
10. Specialties
11. Equipment
12. Furnishings
13. Special Construction

CSI FORMAT

DIVISION 1—GENERAL REQUIREMENTS
01010 SUMMARY OF WORK
01100 ALTERNATIVES
01200 PROJECT MEETINGS
01300 SUBMITTALS
01400 QUALITY CONTROL
01500 TEMPORARY FACILITIES & CONTROLS
01600 PRODUCTS
01700 PROJECT CLOSEOUT

DIVISION 2—SITE WORK
02010 SUBSURFACE EXPLORATION
02100 CLEARING
02110 DEMOLITION
02200 EARTHWORK
02250 SOIL TREATMENT
02300 PILE FOUNDATIONS
02350 CAISSONS
02400 SHORING
02500 SITE DRAINAGE
02550 SITE UTILITIES
02600 PAVING & SURFACING
02700 SITE IMPROVEMENTS
02800 LANDSCAPING
02850 RAILROAD WORK
02900 MARINE WORK
02950 TUNNELING

DIVISION 3—CONCRETE
03100 CONCRETE FORMWORK
03150 EXPANSION & CONTRACTION JOINTS
03200 CONCRETE REINFORCEMENT
03300 CAST-IN-PLACE CONCRETE
03350 SPECIALLY FINISHED CONCRETE
03360 SPECIALLY PLACED CONCRETE
03400 PRECAST CONCRETE
03500 CEMENTITIOUS DECKS

DIVISION 4—MASONRY
04100 MORTAR
04150 MASONRY ACCESSORIES
04200 UNIT MASONRY
04400 STONE
04500 MASONRY RESTORATION & CLEANING
04550 REFRACTORIES

DIVISION 5—METALS
05100 STRUCTURAL METAL FRAMING
05200 METAL JOISTS
05300 METAL DECKING
05400 LIGHTGAGE METAL FRAMING
05500 METAL FABRICATIONS
05700 ORNAMENTAL METAL
05800 EXPANSION CONTROL

DIVISION 6—WOOD & PLASTICS
06100 ROUGH CARPENTRY
06130 HEAVY TIMBER CONSTRUCTION
06150 TRESTLES
06170 PREFABRICATED STRUCTURAL WOOD
06200 FINISH CARPENTRY
06300 WOOD TREATMENT
06400 ARCHITECTURAL WOODWORK
06500 PREFABRICATED STRUCTURAL PLASTICS
06600 PLASTIC FABRICATIONS

DIVISION 7—THERMAL & MOISTURE PROTECTION
07100 WATERPROOFING
07150 DAMPPROOFING
07200 INSULATION
07300 SHINGLES & ROOFING TILES
07400 PREFORMED ROOFING & SIDING

07500 MEMBRANE ROOFING
07570 TRAFFIC TOPPING
07600 FLASHING & SHEET METAL
07800 ROOF ACCESSORIES
07900 SEALANTS

DIVISION 8—DOORS & WINDOWS
08100 METAL DOORS & FRAMES
08200 WOOD & PLASTIC DOORS
08300 SPECIAL DOORS
08400 ENTRANCES & STOREFRONTS
08500 METAL WINDOWS
08600 WOOD & PLASTIC WINDOWS
08650 SPECIAL WINDOWS
08700 HARDWARE & SPECIALTIES
08800 GLAZING
08900 WINDOW WALLS/CURTAIN WALLS

DIVISION 9—FINISHES
09100 LATH & PLASTER
09250 GYPSUM WALLBOARD
09300 TILE
09400 TERRAZZO
09500 ACOUSTICAL TREATMENT
09540 CEILING SUSPENSION SYSTEMS
09550 WOOD FLOORING
09650 RESILIENT FLOORING
09680 CARPETING
09700 SPECIAL FLOORING
09760 FLOOR TREATMENT
09800 SPECIAL COATINGS
09900 PAINTING
09950 WALL COVERING

DIVISION 10—SPECIALTIES
10100 CHALKBOARDS & TACKBOARDS
10150 COMPARTMENTS & CUBICLES
10200 LOUVERS & VENTS
10240 GRILLES & SCREENS
10260 WALL & CORNER GUARDS
10270 ACCESS FLOORING
10280 SPECIALTY MODULES
10290 PEST CONTROL
10300 FIREPLACES
10350 FLAGPOLES
10400 IDENTIFYING DEVICES
10450 PEDESTRIAN CONTROL DEVICES
10500 LOCKERS
10530 PROTECTIVE COVERS
10550 POSTAL SPECIALTIES
10600 PARTITIONS
10650 SCALES
10670 STORAGE SHELVING
10700 SUN CONTROL DEVICES (EXTERIOR)
10750 TELEPHONE ENCLOSURES
10800 TOILET & BATH ACCESSORIES
10900 WARDROBE SPECIALTIES

DIVISION 11—EQUIPMENT
11050 BUILT-IN MAINTENANCE EQUIPMENT
11100 BANK & VAULT EQUIPMENT
11150 COMMERCIAL EQUIPMENT
11170 CHECKROOM EQUIPMENT
11180 DARKROOM EQUIPMENT
11200 ECCLESIASTICAL EQUIPMENT
11300 EDUCATIONAL EQUIPMENT
11400 FOOD SERVICE EQUIPMENT
11480 VENDING EQUIPMENT
11500 ATHLETIC EQUIPMENT
11550 INDUSTRIAL EQUIPMENT
11600 LABORATORY EQUIPMENT
11630 LAUNDRY EQUIPMENT
11650 LIBRARY EQUIPMENT
11700 MEDICAL EQUIPMENT
11800 MORTUARY EQUIPMENT

11830 MUSICAL EQUIPMENT
11850 PARKING EQUIPMENT
11860 WASTE HANDLING EQUIPMENT
11870 LOADING DOCK EQUIPMENT
11880 DETENTION EQUIPMENT
11900 RESIDENTIAL EQUIPMENT
11970 THEATER & STAGE EQUIPMENT
11990 REGISTRATION EQUIPMENT

DIVISION 12—FURNISHINGS
12100 ARTWORK
12300 CABINETS & STORAGE
12500 WINDOW TREATMENT
12550 FABRICS
12600 FURNITURE
12670 RUGS & MATS
12700 SEATING
12800 FURNISHING ACCESSORIES

DIVISION 13—SPECIAL CONSTRUCTION
13010 AIR SUPPORTED STRUCTURES
13050 INTEGRATED ASSEMBLIES
13100 AUDIOMETRIC ROOM
13250 CLEAN ROOM
13350 HYPERBARIC ROOM
13400 INCINERATORS
13440 INSTRUMENTATION
13450 INSULATED ROOM
13500 INTEGRATED CEILING
13540 NUCLEAR REACTORS
13550 OBSERVATORY
13600 PREFABRICATED BUILDINGS
13700 SPECIAL PURPOSE ROOMS & BUILDINGS
13750 RADIATION PROTECTION
13770 SOUND & VIBRATION CONTROL
13800 VAULTS
13850 SWIMMING POOLS

DIVISION 14—CONVEYING SYSTEMS
14100 DUMBWAITERS
14200 ELEVATORS
14300 HOISTS & CRANES
14400 LIFTS
14500 MATERIAL HANDLING SYSTEMS
14570 TURNTABLES
14600 MOVING STAIRS & WALKS
14700 PNEUMATIC TUBE SYSTEMS
14800 POWERED SCAFFOLDING

DIVISION 15—MECHANICAL
15010 GENERAL PROVISIONS
15050 BASIC MATERIALS & METHODS
15180 INSULATION
15200 WATER SUPPLY & TREATMENT
15300 WASTE WATER DISPOSAL & TREATMENT
15400 PLUMBING
15500 FIRE PROTECTION
15600 POWER OR HEAT GENERATION
15650 REFRIGERATION
15700 LIQUID HEAT TRANSFER
15800 AIR DISTRIBUTION
15900 CONTROLS & INSTRUMENTATION

DIVISION 16—ELECTRICAL
16010 GENERAL PROVISIONS
16100 BASIC MATERIALS & METHODS
16200 POWER GENERATION
16300 POWER TRANSMISSION
16400 SERVICE & DISTRIBUTION
16500 LIGHTING
16600 SPECIAL SYSTEMS
16700 COMMUNICATIONS
16850 HEATING & COOLING
16900 CONTROLS & INSTRUMENTATION

Fig. 18-2. The CSI Format contains 16 divisions for the technical specifications grouping.

14. Conveying Systems
15. Mechanical
16. Electrical

Fig. 18-2 shows a listing of the 16 Divisions and the component sections. Each section listed denotes a basic unit of work that describes a particular material or product and its installation. The CSI format assigns a constant location for each section. This enables the specification writer to write each section independently of the other without losing continuity of the entire project.

A reference number precedes each section. For example, in *Division 3—Concrete,* Concrete Reinforcement carries a reference number of 03200. These reference numbers refer to a *uniform system* for cost accounting and play a particularly important role with the trend toward computerized accounting by contractors. Even though a Division is not used, it will be listed in the table of contents in the front of the specs. When this situation occurs, the words "not used" are placed after its listing.

The Uniform System has been devised to meet the pressing need not only for a standardized method of writing specifications, but for a better and more rapid classification of technical data. As technology increases in the building industry, the amount of information available on new products and processes progresses at an accelerated rate. Because of the rapid increase of product information, the research, storage, retrieval, and application that exists between building technology and specifications, has brought about a completely different filing system for product information.

A new filing system, based on the CSI format of 16 Divisions, is now being used in the *Sweets Architectural Catalog File.* By implementing the standard format in specifications, cataloging of information, and cost accounting, all three functions are brought under a single, congruent system.

Specification Forms

Specifications, for the most part, are similar in form and content. Materials used in the construction of a frame house will, of course, be different from the materials used in a brick veneer house with concrete block backing. However, the *form* is the same.

Residential specifications are rarely completely written from the beginning. Most

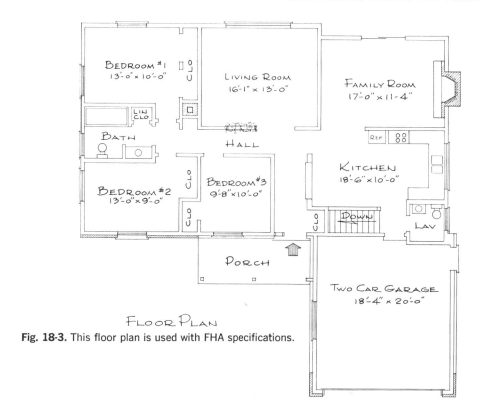

Fig. 18-3. This floor plan is used with FHA specifications.

Fig. 18-4. Use this perspective with the FHA specifications.

THE SMOKLER CO.

designers have a basic form which they use for all residential building. Fill-in forms are available in all major construction classifications. All that must be added to the fill-in or completion form is a description of the exact size, material quantity, type, or catalog number of the material. These forms are usually available from office supply houses.

The specification form shown is supplied by the U.S. Government Printing Office for builders who are seeking a FHA or GI appraisal for loan purposes. The floor plan and perspective of the one-story residence given in the specification is also shown. See Figs. 18-3 and 18-4.

VA Form VB4–1852
FHA Form 2005
Jan. 1955

For accurate register of carbon copies, form may be separated along above fold. Staple completed sheets together in original order.

Form approved.
Budget Bureau No. 63–R055.10.

Plan 329 (includes 2 car garage)

☐ Proposed Construction

☐ Under Construction

DESCRIPTION OF MATERIALS

No. ....
(To be inserted by FHA or VA)

Property address .... City .... State ....

Mortgagor or Sponsor ....
(Name)   (Address)

Contractor or Builder ....
(Name)   (Address)

INSTRUCTIONS

1. For additional information on how this form is to be submitted, number of copies, etc., see the instructions applicable to the FHA Application for Mortgage Insurance or VA Request for Determination of Reasonable Value, as the case may be.

2. Describe all materials and equipment to be used, whether or not shown on the drawings, by marking an X in each appropriate check-box and entering the information called for in each space. If space is inadequate, enter "See misc." and describe under item 27 or on an attached sheet.

3. Work not specifically described or shown will not be considered unless required, when the minimum acceptable will be assumed. Work exceeding

minimum requirements cannot be considered unless specifically described.

4. Include no alternates, "or equal" phrases, or contradictory items. (Consideration of a request for acceptance of substitute materials or equipment is not thereby precluded.)

5. Include signatures required at the end of this form.

6. The construction shall be completed in compliance with the related drawings and specifications, as amended during processing. The specifications include this Description of Materials and the applicable Minimum Construction Requirements.

1. EXCAVATION:
Bearing soil, type ...... Sand and Gravel ....

2. FOUNDATIONS:
Footings: Concrete mix ... 2500 # .... Reinforcing ....
Foundation wall: Material ... Poured Conc. 8" .... Reinforcing ....
Interior foundation wall: Material .... Party foundation wall ....
Columns: Material and size ... 3" adj. Post .... Piers: Material and reinforcing ....
Girders: Material and sizes ... I Beam 7" at 15.3 # ... Sills: Material ....
Basement entrance areaway .... Window areaways ....
Waterproofing .... Tar .... Footing drains ....
Termite protection .... Shield at Brick ....
Basementless space: Ground cover .... Insulation .... Foundation vents ....
Special foundations ....

3. CHIMNEYS:
Material ...... Face Brick .... Prefabricated (make and size) ....
Flue lining: Material ... Vitrified Clay ... Heater flue size ... 8 x 12 ... Fireplace flue size ... 12 x 12 ..
Vents (material and size): Gas or oil heater ...... 5" G. I. .... Water heater ... 3" G. I. ..

4. FIREPLACES: OPTIONAL
Type: ☒ Solid fuel; ☐ gas-burning; ☐ circulator (make and size) .... Ash dump and clean-out ... 10 ..
Fireplace: Facing ... Brick ....; lining ... Fire Brick ......; hearth ... Ceramic ......; mantel ... None ..

5. EXTERIOR WALLS:
Wood frame: Grade and species ... Cedar #2 .... ☒ Corner bracing. Building paper or felt ... 15# Felt ....
Sheathing ... Asphalt impregnated Fiberboard ...; thickness ... ½"; width ... 4 x 8; ☒ solid; ☐ spaced ...." o. c.; ☐ diagonal; ....
Siding ... Aluminum ....; grade ....; type ....; size ....; exposure ... 8"; fastening ... Nailed ....
Shingles ....; grade ....; type ....; size ....; exposure ...."; fastening ... Per Mfg. ..
Stucco ....; thickness ....". Lath ....; weight .... lb.
Masonry veneer ... Face Brick $60/M .... Sills ... Lime Stone .... Lintels ....

Masonry: Facing ....; backup .... thickness ....". Bonding ....
Door sills .... Window sills .... Lintels ....
Interior surfaces: Dampproofing, ... coats of ....; furring ....
Exterior painting: Material .....Exterior lead and oil.............................; number of coats ...3....
Gable wall construction: ☐ Same as main walls; ☐ other ...Aluminum siding in gable..................

6. FLOOR FRAMING: 2 x 10 - 16" o.c.
Joists: Wood, grade and species ..#2 Fir............; other ....; bridging ..1 x 3....; anchors ....
Concrete slab: ☒ Basement floor; ☐ first floor; ☐ ground supported; ☐ self-supporting; mix ..5 sk................; thickness ..3..";
  reinforcing ....; insulation ....; membrane ....
Fill under slab: Material .....Sand..........................; thickness ....4.....".

7. SUBFLOORING: *(Describe underflooring for special floors under item 21.)*
Material: Grade and species ..1/2" plyscore.......................; size ..4 x 8...; type ..Plyscore.....
Laid: ☒ First floor; ☐ second floor; ☐ attic .... sq. ft.; ☐ diagonal; ☐ right angles. ....Solid........

8. FINISH FLOORING: *(Wood only. Describe other finish flooring under item 21.)*

LOCATION	ROOMS	GRADE	SPECIES	THICKNESS	WIDTH	BLDG. PAPER	FINISH
First floor	Liv. Rm. Bedrooms Hall	#1	Oak	25/32	2'	Slaters Felt	Bruce
Second floor		Common	Shorts				
Attic floor	Family Rm. sq. ft.		Oak	Ranch	Plank		Prefinished

VA Form VB4—1852
FHA Form 2005   1   **DESCRIPTION OF MATERIALS**

DESCRIPTION OF MATERIALS

9. PARTITION FRAMING:
Studs: Wood, grade and species .....Cedar #2............. Size and spacing ...2 x 4 16" o.c. Other ....

10. CEILING FRAMING:
Joists: Wood, grade and species .....Trusses 24" o.c. Other .... Bridging ....

11. ROOF FRAMING: Fir 24" o.c.
Rafters: Wood, grade and species ....Trusses 24" o.c. Roof trusses (see detail): Grade and species ....

12. ROOFING:
Sheathing: Grade and species ..Fir Plyscore 3/8".........; size 4 x 8.; type ..C. D....; ☒ solid; ☐ spaced ....” o.c.
Roofing ..Asphalt shingles...................; grade ....C............; weight or thickness ..235..; size 12x36; fastening Mfg. specs.
Stain or paint .... Underlay ....
Built-up roofing ....; number of plies ....; surfacing material ....
Flashing: Material ...26 G. I................................; gage or weight ....; ☐ gravel stops; ☐ snow guards

13. GUTTERS AND DOWNSPOUTS:
Gutters: Material.......G. I................; gage or weight ...24......; size ..4"....; shape ....O. G.....
Downspouts: Material .....G. I..........; gage or weight ..24.......; size ..3"....; shape ......Rect....; number ....
Downspouts connected to: ☐ Storm sewer; ☐ sanitary sewer; ☐ dry-well. ☒ Splash blocks: Material and size ..Concrete.........
                                                                            12 x 24

14. LATH AND PLASTER:

Lath ☐ walls, ☐ ceilings: Material ....; weight or thickness .... Plaster: Coats ....; finish .... ~~Tape cement~~

Dry-wall ☒ walls, ☒ ceilings: Material Gypsum ....; thickness 1/2 .; finish Smooth ....; joint treatment ~~and sand~~
Rust-proof metal corners, back block ceiling joints ....

15. DECORATING: *(Paint, wallpaper, etc.)*

ROOMS	WALL FINISH MATERIAL AND APPLICATION	CEILING FINISH MATERIAL AND APPLICATION
Kitchen		
Bath		
All Rooms	Alkyd Resin stipple-2 coats	Same - 2 coats

16. INTERIOR DOORS AND TRIM:

Doors: Type Flush and folding ....; material Birch, Pine ....; thickness 1-3/4 & 1-3/8

Door trim: Type Casing 1-3/4 material W.P. .... Base: Type Wood ....; material W. P. ; size 2-1/4

Finish: Doors Flush-Seal and Varnish ....; trim W. P.

Other trim (*item, type and location*) ....

17. WINDOWS:

Windows: Type Dble. Hung ; make Grand Rapids ....; material W. Pine ....; sash thickness 1-3/8

Glass: Grade SS ....; ☐ sash weights; ☐ balances, type Spring ....; head flashing ....

Trim: Type Casing ....; material W. P. .... Paint Enamel ....; number coats 2

Weatherstripping: Type Friction ....; material SS ....; Storm sash, number ....

Screens: ☐ Full; ☒ half; type Alum. ....; number 9 ; screen cloth material alum.

Basement windows: Type 2-lite ....; material steel ....; ☐ screens, number 0 ; ☐ Storm sash, number 0

Special windows Wood picture - per elev.

18. ENTRANCES AND EXTERIOR DETAIL:

Main entrance door: Material W. P. ....; width 3' ; thickness 1-3/4" Frame: Material Wood ; thickness 5/4"

Other entrance doors: Material W. P. ....; width 2-8" ; thickness 1-3/4" Frame: Material W. P. ; thickness 5/4"

Head flashing Galv. .... Weatherstripping: Type Friction ....; saddles Aluminum

Screen doors: Thickness ...."; number ....; screen cloth material .... Storm doors: Thickness ...."; number ......

Combination storm and screen doors: Thickness 1 ...."; number 2 ...; screen cloth material Aluminum

Shutters: ☐ Hinged; ☒ Per Elev. fixed; Railings .... Louvers 2 - 14 x 20 metal

Exterior millwork: Grade and species 1 - W. P. .... Paint Exterior Grade ....; number coats 3

19. CABINETS AND INTERIOR DETAIL:

Kitchen cabinets, wall units: Material Birch W. P. .... Sp. ~~lineal~~ feet of shelves 25 ; shelf width 12"

Base units: Material Birch W. P. ....; counter top 16 sp. ft. ....; edging Formica ....

Back and end splash Ceramic full Back Splash Finish of cabinets Stain and Varnish ....; number coats 3

Medicine cabinets: Make Miami Carey 621 ....; model Ideal 501 ....

Other cabinets and built-in furniture 48" Formica Vanity

20. STAIRS:

STAIR	TREADS		RISERS		STRINGS		HANDRAIL		BALUSTERS	
	Material	Thickness	Material	Thickness	Material	Size	Material	Size	Material	Size
Basement	Fir	2 x 10			Fir	2 x 10	W. P.	1-3/4	Round	
Main										
Attic										

Disappearing: Make and model number ....

21. SPECIAL FLOORS AND WAINSCOT:

	LOCATION	MATERIAL, COLOR, BORDER, SIZES, GAGE, ETC.	THRESHOLD	BASE	UNDERFLOOR
FLOORS	Kitchen &	Dining area - Vinyl Tile		W.P. 2¼	5/8 Ply.
	Bath	Ceramic	Marble	Ceramic	Cement
	½ Bath	Vinyl Tile			5/8 Ply

	LOCATION	MATERIAL, COLOR, BORDER, CAP, SIZES, GAGE, ETC.	HEIGHT	HEIGHT AT TUB	HEIGHT AT SHOWER
WAINSCOT	Bath	Ceramic Tile in Mastic with bull nose			
		Tub recess only		6'	6'

Bathroom accessories: ☐ Recessed; material ....; number ......; ☒ attached; material ..Ceramic.......; number .9..

22. PLUMBING:

FIXTURE	NUMBER	LOCATION	MAKE	MFR'S FIXTURE IDENTIFICATION NO.	SIZE	COLOR
Sink	1	Kitchen	Townsend	Steel enamel Dble compartment	32 x 21	Colored
Lavatory	2	Bath	Rheem Richmond	Roundell & Richeleu	18" & 19x17	Colored
Water closet	2	Bath	Rheem Richmond	G2210		Colored
Bathtub	1	Bath	Rheem Richmond		5'	
Shower over tub*	1		Chrome pltd.Brass			
Stall shower**						
Laundry trays	1	Basement	Mustee-single	Compartment fiberglass	24 x 24	

*☒ Curtain rod   **☐ Door   ☐ Curtain rod

Water supply: ☒ Public; ☐ community system; ☐ individual (private) system. ★

Sewage disposal: ☐ Public; ☐ community system; ☒ individual (private) system. ★

★*Show and describe individual system in complete detail in separate drawings and specifications according to requirements.*

House drain (inside): ☐ Cast iron; ☐ tile; ☒ other ..copper... House sewer (outside): ☐ Cast iron; ☒ tile; ☐ other ....

Water piping: ☐ Galvanized steel; ☒ copper tubing; ☐ other .... Sill cocks, number ...2......

Domestic water heater: Type ....Automatic................; make and model ..Republic.............................

recovery ..25.2.... gph. 100° rise. Storage tank: Material ....; capacity ....40....... gallons.

Gas service: ☒ Utility company; ☐ liq. pet. gas; ☐ other .... Gas piping: ☒ Cooking; ☒ house heating.

Footing drains connected to: ☐ Storm sewer; ☐ sanitary sewer; ☐ dry well. Sump pump ....

23. HEATING:

☐ Hot water. ☐ Steam. ☐ Vapor. ☐ One-pipe system. ☐ Two-pipe system.

   ☐ Radiators. ☐ Convectors. ☐ Baseboard radiation. Make and model ....

   Radiant panel: ☐ Floor; ☐ wall; ☐ ceiling. Panel coil: Material ....

   ☐ Circulator. ☐ Return pump. Make and model ....; capacity .... gpm.

   Boiler: Make and model .... Output .... Btuh.; net rating .... Btuh.

Warm air: ☐ Gravity. ☒ Forced. Type of system .....Perimeter...

   Duct material: Supply .Sht.Metal.; return .Sht.Metal. Insulation ...., thickness .... ☐ Outside air intake.

   Furnace: Make and model ..Lennox........................ Input ..120,000.... Btuh.; output ..96,000...... Btuh.

☐ Space heater; ☐ floor furnace; ☐ wall heater. Input .... Btuh.; output .... Btuh.; number units ....

   Make, model ....

Controls: Make and types .....Minneapolis-Honeywell Automatic..

Fuel: ☐ Coal; ☐ oil; ☒ gas; ☐ liq. pet. gas; ☐ electric; ☐ other...........................; storage capacity ....

Firing equipment furnished separately: ☐ Gas burner, conversion type. Stoker: ☐ Hopper feed; ☐ bin feed.

Oil burner: ☐ Pressure atomizing; ☐ vaporizing ....

Make and model .... Control ....

Electric heating system: Type .... Input .... watts; @ .... volts; output .... Btuh.

Ventilating equipment: Attic fan, make and model .... ; capacity .... cfm.

Kitchen exhaust fan, make and model ....

Other heating, ventilating, or cooling equipment ......Rangpire Model 523 Ductless...............

24. ELECTRIC WIRING:

Service: ☒ Overhead; ☐ underground. Panel: ☒ Fuse box; ☐ circuit-breaker ..100.amp.service..... Number circuits ..7.x.1

Wiring: ☐ Conduit; ☐ armored cable; ☒ nonmetallic cable; ☐ knob and tube; ☐ other ....

Special outlets: ☐ Range; ☐ water heater; ☐ other ...Furnace-Laundry.circuit.......................................

☒ Doorbell. ☐ Chimes. Push-button locations ......Front.and.Rear.Doors.......................................

25. LIGHTING FIXTURES: 11 up

Total number of fixtures ...5.down... Total allowance for fixtures, typical installation, $..100.00....

Nontypical installation ....

3   DESCRIPTION OF MATERIALS

DESCRIPTION OF MATERIALS

26. INSULATION:

LOCATION	THICKNESS	MATERIAL, TYPE, AND METHOD OF INSTALLATION	VAPOR BARRIER
Roof			
Ceiling	3"	Blown in fiberglass	
Wall	1/2	Asphalt impregnated fiberboard & 1-1/2 fiberglass with vapor barrier	
Floor			

27. MISCELLANEOUS:

(Describe any main dwelling materials, equipment, or construction items not shown elsewhere) : ....

Birch Cabinets .... 100 Ampere Service

Brush Coat Basement .... Screens

Double Compartment Sink .... Family Rm. Paneled with Abitibi

Built-in Range and Oven .... Gun Stock

48" Formica Vanity .... Glass Doorwall

Formica Edged Countertops

Miami-Carey Sliding Mirrors

Hood and Fan

Aluminum Siding

Flush Birch Closet Doors

HARDWARE: *(Make, material, and finish)* ....Front and Rear - Quikset 400 Std.

.... Passage - Reliant 700

.... Bath Passage - Chrome 710

SPECIAL EQUIPMENT: *(State material or make and model.)*

Venetian blinds .... Number .... Automatic washer ....

Kitchen range ...... Westinghouse .... Clothes drier ....

Refrigerator .... Other ....

Dishwasher ....

Garbage disposal unit ....

PORCHES:

...Floating slabs, post hole footings on large porch elev.........................

TERRACES:

...42 x 42 on ground slab...

GARAGES:

...19 x 20 Garage, 16' Taylor Door, 42" footing-

...Brick front one side, over half, drywall sidewall, & Ceiling trusses 24 o.c., aluminum

...siding on end and rear; 12 x 19 Family Room rear of Garage

WALKS AND DRIVEWAYS: 16' at Garage, 16' at street

Driveway: Width .... Base material ..Sand.....; thickness ..4..". Surfacing material ...Concrete...........; thickness ..4..."

Front walk: Width ..3.... Material Concrete......; thickness ..4..". Service walk: Width ..2.. Material Conc.; thickness ..4..."

Steps: Material ....; treads ...."; risers ....". Cheek walls ....

OTHER ONSITE IMPROVEMENTS:

(Specify all exterior onsite improvements not described elsewhere, including items such as unusual grading, drainage structures, retaining walls, fence, railings, and accessory structures.)

...Finish grade entire lot

LANDSCAPING, PLANTING, AND FINISH GRADING:

Topsoil .....4..." thick: □ Front yard; ☒ side yards; ☒ rear yard to ..rear..of..lot..... feet behind main building.

Lawns *(seeded, sodded, or sprigged)*: ☒ Front yard ....; ☒ side yards ....; □ rear yard ....

Planting: □ As specified and shown on drawings; □ as follows:

....1...... Shade trees, deciduous, .1.1/2...." caliper.	.... Evergreen trees, ...' to ....', B & B.
.... Low flowering trees, deciduous, ...' to ....'	.... Evergreen shrubs, ...' to ....', B & B.
.... High-growing shrubs, deciduous, ...' to ....'	.... Vines, 2-year ....
.... Medium-growing shrubs, deciduous, ...' to ....'	
.... Low-growing shrubs, deciduous, ...' to ....'	

IDENTIFICATION.—This exhibit shall be identified by the signature of the builder, or sponsor, and/or the proposed mortgagor if the latter is known at the time of application.

Date .... Signature ....

Signature ....

VA Form VB4–1852
FHA Form 2005

4

Basic Specification Form

The specification shown below is referred to as a "fill-in-form."[1] This is a basic form which may be used for all residences. The architect adds the exact specifications for the particular residence. Specifications are arranged as far as possible, in the order which the various trades will work on the structure.

The specifications should spell out the responsibilities of both parties. For example, in the specification form given below the contractor is required to provide liability and workmen's compensation insurance. The owner is to provide fire and windstorm

The working drawings and the specifications function together as a whole. What is mentioned in either is considered to be in both. All items which are necessary for the completion of the structure, even though not mentioned, are considered to be included. If the specifications and the working drawings are in conflict, normally the specifications take precedence. It is the responsibility of the architect, of course, to prevent such conflict. Exactness is especially necessary since the specifications and drawings are used for making the estimate.

The specifications are binding on all parties, including the sub-contractors. Normally, modifications can only be made by mutual agreement.

1. This specification was designed by the Miller Planning Service, Kalamazoo, Michigan.

SPECIFICATIONS

The contractor shall provide all necessary labor and materials and perform all work of every nature whatsoever to be done in the erection of a residence for _____ as owner in accordance with these specifications and drawings.

The location of the residence will be as follows: _____.

GENERAL

All blank spaces in these specifications that apply to this building are to be filled in. All blank spaces that do not apply to be crossed out. The general conditions herein set forth shall apply to any contract given under these specifications and shall be binding upon every sub-contractor as well as general contractor.

The plans, elevations, sections, and detail drawings, together with these specifications, are to form the basis of the contract and are to be of equal force. Should anything be mentioned in these specifications and not shown in the drawings, or vice versa, the same shall be followed as if set forth in both, as it is the intent of these specifications and accompanying drawings to correspond and to embody every item and part necessary for the completion of the structure. In the event that items which are normally part of a complete house are omitted from both the plans and specifications, it is expected that they will still be supplied as part of the general contract. Example: area walls, bathroom towel bars, soap dishes, etc.; and similar items. The contractor shall comply with all health and building ordinances that are applicable.

EXCAVATION AND GRADING

The contractor shall do all necessary excavating and rough grading. The excavation shall be large enough to permit inspection of footings after the foundation has been completed. All excess dirt shall be hauled away by the contractor. Black surface loam to be piled where directed by the owner for use in grading and will be bulldozed into place by the general contractor. All subsoil and top soil required for fill and/or rough grading shall be paid for by the owner and bulldozed into place by the general contractor. The finish grading shall be done by the owner. Grade level shall be established by the owner, who will also furnish a survey of the lot showing the location of the building. The finish grading, seeding, sodding, and landscaping shall be done by the owner unless specified as follows: _____.

CONCRETE FOOTINGS

Footings shall be of concrete mixed in the proportion of one part Portland cement, three parts clean, coarse, sharp sand and five parts of gravel or crushed rock. Concrete shall be machine mixed with clean water to the proper consistency, and shall be placed immediately after mixing. Footings shall be thoroughly protected with hay or straw in freezing weather. All footings shall be set below the frost line and rest on firm soil and shall be flat and level on the underside. Footings shall be of sizes shown on plan.

BASEMENT WALLS

Basement walls shall be of poured concrete _____ inches thick. Poured walls shall be straight, level, and plumb,

OR

basement walls will be constructed of _____ inch concrete blocks per plan, of approved quality. Blocks shall be laid in a full bed of mortar, composed of one part of cement to three parts of sand. Mortar joints shall be filled thoroughly with cement mortar, neatly pointed on both sides.

All walls shall have uniform bearing for framing, being straight, plumb, and level. Beam fill to be placed as shown on the plans. Waterproof basement walls with two coats of waterproofing applied according to manufacturer's specifications. Mortar drippings shall be cleaned from footings, and a cement cove trowelled into place.

BASEMENT FLOOR

Basement floor shall be of _____ inch concrete, poured monolithically, with a trowelled finish. Thoroughly tamp the base concrete into place and carefully pitch to floor drains; .004" Polyethylene shall be placed under basement floors under recreation rooms, bedroom, and bathrooms, etc.

CRAWL SPACES

Crawl spaces shall have a skim coat of concrete over .004" Polyethylene. Minimum clearance between joists and slab shall be two feet.

CEMENT WALKS AND STEPS

All cement walks shall be four inches thick, of widths and in locations shown on plans and shall be poured monolithically with a trowelled finish. The steps at the front and rear entrances shall be of wood, cement, or brick construction as indicated on the plan. If rain leaders are not connected to sewer, provide concrete splash blocks for each rain leader.

CHIMNEYS

Chimneys shall be constructed of common brick with face brick top. Provide tile flue lining of size and extent shown on plans for all flues. Thimbles and cleanouts shall be built in as required. If fireplace is required, furnish and install ash dump, damper and cleanouts, fire brick for lining and hearth, facing and outer hearth of material selected by owner. Hearth to be supported on concrete slab of size shown on plan.

All flues shall be cleaned of mortar drippings, and the chimney shall be capped with a concrete cap as shown on plans -- minimum thickness at thinnest point two inches.

Concrete hearth support to be fireproof; hearth floor to be _____.

Chimneys shall be flashed and counter-flashed where they pass through the roof.

Face of fireplace opening, if masonry, shall be _____.

Mantel shelf, if masonry, shall be _____.

Incinerator, if any, shall be _____.

Damper to be _____.

BRICK WORK

All brick work, if any, shall be laid in cement and lime mortar, with all bricks well bedded and shoved into place, with both vertical and horizontal joints on straight lines. Joints to be of color selected by owner.

The price allowed for face brick is $_____ per 1,000. Any cost above that amount will be borne by the owner. Lintels to be properly placed above all openings where masonry is shown above.

TILE WORK

The contractor shall furnish and set all tile in a neat and workmanlike manner. Recessed towel bars, paper holder, and soap dish shall be furnished by tile contractor.

The following areas shall be covered with ceramic tile: (Mark "yes" or "no".)

Bathroom floors _____

Bathroom walls to a height 4 ft. above floor _____

Bathroom tub areas to a height 5 ft. above tub _____

Showers to a height 6'-6" above floor _____

Front entrance hall floor _____

Vanity cabinet tops _____

Other _____

CARPENTER WORK

The contractor shall and will provide all necessary labor and perform all carpenter work of every nature whatsoever to be done. He shall lay out all work and be responsible for all measurements and keep a competent foreman in charge. All work shall be done in a workmanlike manner, level, straight, plumb, and true and strictly in accordance with the plans and specifications.

GIRDERS AND COLUMNS

Girders or supporting beams and columns shall be as required by the size of the building and shall be of the size and location shown in the plans.

JOISTS

First floor joists 2" x ___	O. C. Grade #1 Btr. Fir - 15 to 25% #2 permitted.
Second floor joists 2" x ___	" " " "
Ceiling joists 2" x ___	" " " "
Rafters 2" x ___	" " " "
Collar ties 2" x ___	" " " "
Valley rafters 2" x ___	" " " "

Double joists under partitions and around all openings.

All dimension material covered in the above specification is Douglas Fir, as graded by the West Coast Lumber Inspection Bureau.

STUDDINGS AND PARTITIONS

Studdings shall be sized 2 x 4's, spaced 16" on centers, single plate on bottom and double plate on top of each wall or partition. 2 x 4's shall be doubled around all openings and shall be _____.

<u>BRIDGING</u>

First and second floor joists shall have one row of 1 x 3 wood or approved metal bridging for all spans of 8 to 14 feet. All spans over 14 feet shall have two rows, all fastened securely to joists at each end.

<u>ROUGH FLOORING</u>

Sub-flooring shall be _____ C-D plywood securely nailed. All joints shall be made on joists.

<u>SHEATHING</u>

Outside walls shall be covered with securely nailed _____.

Roof sheathing shall be _____.

<u>SIDING</u>

Siding, if any, to be _____.

<u>ROOFING</u>

Shingles for roof to be _____ laid _____ inches to weather, using galvanized nails.

<u>BUILT-UP ROOFS</u>

Built-up roofs shall be installed to a 15 year specification and covered with gravel, slag, or white aggregate.

<u>INSULATION AND PAPER</u>

Sidewall insulation to be _____.

Top floor ceiling to be insulated with _____.

Building paper under shingles to be _____.

Building paper over sheathing to be _____.

All exterior walls shall be covered on the inside edge of the studs from floor to plate with .004" Polyethylene. Application shall be continuous, with cutouts for windows, elec. openings, etc., being made after lath is applied.

If hot water heat is used, ceilings shall be covered as above -- application to be made to the bottom edge of the ceiling joists.

<u>OUTSIDE FINISH</u>

All lumber required for outside finish shall be _____.

All exterior siding, cornice, and miscellaneous trim shall be woodlife dipped and nailed with non-rusting nails.

<u>WINDOW AND DOOR FRAMES</u>

All window and outside door frames as shown on plans shall be of sound, clear pine, free from objectionable defects. Door sills shall be oak.

Assembled window units, if any, shall be per plan.

Assembled door units, if any, shall be _____.

<u>WINDOWS, STORM SASH, AND SCREENS</u>

All windows and sash shall be as shown on plans. Storm sash and screens shall be as required for patented units. Double-hung windows and _____ units shall have _____.

<u>FINISHED FLOORS</u>

Finished floors in living room and dining room to be _____.

Finished floors in family room to be _____.

Finished floors in bedrooms to be _____.

Finished floors in front entry to be _____.

Finished floors in kitchen to be _____.

Finished floors in bathrooms to be _____.

Finished floors in toilet to be _____.

Finished floors in _____ to be _____.

Finished floors in rear entry to be _____.

Finished floors in attic to be _____.

All hardwood floors shall be properly nailed and machine sanded to a smooth, even surface. Place 30 lb. red rosin paper between sub-floor and finish floor. Floors under linoleum shall be securely nailed with screw type or annular threaded nails.

<u>SLATE FLOORS</u>

Allow _____ per sq. ft. for slate floors in areas shown on plan.

<u>NON-RIGID FLOOR COVERINGS</u>
(not including carpeting)

Allow _____ per sq. yd. for linoleum-type floor covering where required.
Allow _____ per sq. ft. for homogenous vinyl floor covering where required.
Allow _____ per sq. ft. for vinyl asbestos floor covering where required.
Other _____.

<u>INSIDE FINISH</u>

Trim in the living room, dining room, and front entry shall be _____.

Trim in the kitchen and rear entry shall be _____.

Trim in _____ shall be _____.

Trim in the bedrooms, bathrooms, and hall shall be _____.

DOORS

All of the inside doors shall be 1 3/8" thick as follows: _____.

The front door shall be 1 3/4" thick of _____.

The remaining outside doors shall be 1 3/4" thick of _____.

Provide combination storm and screen doors for all outside doors.

Provide scuttle door to attic and plumbing access doors.

JAMBS AND CASINGS

All inside jambs shall be 3/4" thick and of kinds specified above. Casings shall be 3/4" thick of stock design.

STAIRS

Stairs leading from first to second floor shall be as shown in plans with _____ risers and _____ treads. Basement stairs shall have _____ risers and _____ treads. Three stair horses shall be provided for each stair and shall be _____ x _____. Wall stringers shall or shall not be housed. All stairs to be equipped with hand rails.

CABINET WORK

Built-in medicine cabinet in bathroom -- allow $ _____.

Size of mirrors _____.

Kitchen cabinets shall be _____ and be placed as shown on plan. Mantel and mantel shelf, if any, shall be _____. Kitchen counter tops to be _____. Splash back to be _____. Edging material to be _____. Linen cabinet to be _____. Other cabinet work, if any, shall be as follows: _____.

CLOSETS

All closets shall have one shelf and one clothes rod.

HARDWARE

The contractor shall furnish all rough hardware, such as nails. The amount to be allowed for finish hardware is $_____. Any cost in excess of that amount will be paid by the owner.

ELECTRICAL WORK

Contractor shall provide all necessary labor and material and perform all electrical work of every nature whatsoever to be done. All work to comply with local ordinances. Provide _____ openings, plus special equipment outlets as listed below, plus door bells on _____.

Provide 100 amp. service entrance facilities. All lights and switches to be placed as indicated on plans or as directed by owner. Provide special equipment outlets for

stove _____, water heater _____, washer _____, dryer _____, water pump

_____, bathroom exhaust fan _____, kitchen exhaust fan _____. Heating plant

by heating contractor. Other _____.

ELECTRIC FIXTURES

Electric light fixtures to the value of $_____ shall be furnished by contractor. Any cost in excess of this amount will be paid by the owner, and any cost lower than this amount listed is to be credited to the owner.

Allow $_____ for built-in range and oven.

LATHING, PLASTERING, AND GROUNDS

Lath all walls, ceilings, etc., with gypsum or rocklath applied strictly in accordance with manufacturer's directions. Lath all interior corners throughout with 6 inch strips of angle-shaped metal lath. Provide galvanized corner beads on all exterior corners. All plaster to be two-coat work of a standard brand of hard wall plaster mixed in accordance with manufacturer's directions and shall be straight and true. Finish for each of the several rooms shall be as called for in room finish schedule. Plastering contractor shall repair all defects and do all patching necessary to leave the work in good condition.

Finish to consist of the following: _____.

	Ceilings	Walls
Living room	_____	_____
Kitchen	_____	_____
Bedrooms	_____	_____
Halls	_____	_____
Bathrooms	_____	_____
Dining rooms	_____	_____
Front entry	_____	_____
Rear entry	_____	_____
Basement	_____	_____
Garage	_____	_____

STUCCO

If stucco is required, it shall be three-coat work applied over self-furring, galvanized, expanded metal lath weighing 3.2 lbs. per sq. yard. Final coat to be of a color selected by owner. Provide a waterproof paper on sheathing under metal lath.

PLUMBING

Contractor shall provide all labor and material and perform all plumbing work of every nature whatsoever to be done. The fixtures shall be as follows:

_____ Bath tub _____

_____ Toilet combination _____

_____ Size _____ Lavatory _____

_____ Kitchen sink _____ Size and specification _____

_____ Gallon hot water heater (gas, electric, or oil)

Two-compartment laundry tray, swing faucet _____

Dishwasher _____ Garbage disposer _____

Floor drain _____ Sill cocks _____

Towel bars _____ Soap dish _____

Paper holder _____ Shower bath _____

All of the above shall be properly installed and all connections thoroughly tested, and shall be installed according to local ordinance. Hot and cold water connections shall be made with bath tub, shower, lavatory, kitchen sink, and laundry tray. Water connections shall be made with water main in the street, sewer connection shall be made with sewer in the street, gas connections shall be made with gas main in the street, all to be paid for by the contractor. All meters will be paid for by the owner. Private sewage disposal systems, if required, shall be provided and installed in accordance with local codes.

Private water supply systems, if required, shall be provided and installed according to the owner's instructions. Allow $ _____.

HEATING

Contractor shall and will provide all necessary labor and material and perform all heating work of every nature whatsoever to be done, including the installation of _____ heating system of sufficient size to properly heat all parts of the house in coldest weather. If hot air system is to be used, it is to be installed according to the code of the National Society of Heating and Ventilation Engineers.

If hot water, steam, or any other heating system is to be used, such installation shall consist of the following: _____.

SHEET METAL WORK AND FLASHING

Contractor shall and will provide all necessary labor and materials and perform all sheet metal work of every nature whatsoever to be done, including gutters under all eaves with suitable conductors. All joints to be well soldered and securely fastened, and all work to be done in a neat and workmanlike manner. Gutters to be 26 gauge galvanized iron _____ type.

Down spouts to be _____. Proper _____ flashing shall be provided wherever necessary. Clothes chute, if shown on plan, shall be lined with _____.

INTERIOR PAINTING

All woodwork to be carefully cleaned of finger marks, stains, and other defects before any oil, filling, paint, or varnish is applied, and all rough spots to be sandpapered smooth before being filled with colored putty to match color desired. Finish to consist of the following: _____.

	Walls and ceilings	Trim
Living room	_____	_____
Dining room	_____	_____
Dinette	_____	_____
Kitchen	_____	_____
Rear entry	_____	_____
Bedroom	_____	_____
Bedroom	_____	_____
Hall	_____	_____
Front entry	_____	_____
Family room	_____	_____

All hardwood floors shall be sanded, filled, and varnished two coats, excepting _____.

EXTERIOR PAINTING

All exterior woodwork shall have _____ coats of prepared paint of colors to be selected by owner. All sash and trim to be neatly traced. All knots and other defective work to be shellacked and all nail holes to be puttied before applying last coat. All exposed sheet metal shall have one coat of red lead and two coats of finished coat paint. All paint products used on the house, both exterior and interior, shall be manufactured by a reputable firm, suitable for the surface to which they are to be applied, and shall be applied according to the manufacturer's specifications.

EXTRAS OR CREDITS

Any deviation from these specifications or plans involving an extra charge or a credit must be agreed upon in writing between the contracting parties before the change is made. The contractor shall not take advantage of any discrepancies in the drawings and specifications. If any discrepancies are found, they shall be referred to the owner or the architect and be corrected before any contract is entered into.

INSURANCE

The contractor shall provide liability insurance and workmen's compensation insurance in full until completion of the building. Fire and windstorm insurance during construction will be provided by the owner.

CLEANING UP

The contractor shall not remove all debris from the premises when the job is completed. The contractor shall not clean all window glass when job is completed.

Driveway _____.

Sidewalks _____.

Estimating and Financing 19

To approach home design and home selection on an intelligent basis, both the architect and the prospective buyer must have some knowledge of the estimated value of the home and the standard procedures used in the purchase transaction. There is a direct relationship between the financial condition of a prospective home owner and the value of the home he can afford. Given the financial condition of a prospective buyer, it is possible to determine the price range of homes he may reasonably consider. Knowing this, the architect is able to design house plans to fit within the buyer's price range. In addition to this, the architect may be expected to advise the client on financial questions.

sider operating expenses, equipment depreciation and profit.

The seemingly limitless number of items which enter into the cost of any building will vary widely with the locality, climate, labor, and market condition. It is imperative, therefore, that the prospective builder make a careful estimate in order to intelligently assess the cost of the building and the approximate number of man-hours needed to successfully complete the job.

Home Estimating

Estimating the cost of a building represents the expenditures required to cover the *entire* cost of building, or the *entire* cost of remodeling. For the contractor or builder, it represents *all* the required material and labor costs for *each* item forming the completed structure. The smallest items, such as lock sets for doors, door stops, removal of dirt from the excavation, etc., must be included in the estimate to insure an accurate cost analysis.

Besides material and labor costs, the contractor, in submitting a bid, must *also* con-

Rough Estimates

Square Footage

Probably the quickest and most simple method of computing a *rough estimate* (for purposes of comparing similarly constructed houses) is to figure the square footage. This simply involves the two principal dimensions of the house, *length* (width) and *depth*. (Note: dimensions are taken from the *outer* surfaces of the *outside* walls.)

It should be emphasized that the square footage method is of value only when comparing *similar* construction built with *similar* prices for *labor, materials,* and *design.* For example, the price per square foot of a plain frame, ranch-type house with minimal appointments *cannot* be used to estimate the cost of a two-story brick veneer colonial with above average fixtures and appointments. A multi-level dwelling will, in the long run, tend to be slightly less per square foot than a one-story, all factors being approximately equal. If the cost for a multi-level dwelling is to be estimated by the square footage method, a similar type home should be used for comparison.

Estimating the construction cost of a home may be accomplished on the square foot basis by reference to such manuals as Boeckh's *Manual of Appraisals* or Wenzlick's *Residential Appraisal Manual.* These manuals contain cost per square foot figures which must be multiplied by a factor (predicated on the location of the building in the United States) to arrive at the cost in a particular locale. The square footage method should *not* include open or closed porches, attached garages, or basements.

Take, for example, a one-story slab house, $40' \times 28'$. Using the square footage method (length times depth), the house would contain 1120 sq. ft. Let us say that similar houses in the same locality cost on the average $15.50 per sq. ft. The square footage method would give a rough estimate of $17,360 for the house (1,120 sq. ft. times $15.50). Any unusual or expensive features would, of course, cause this estimate to be too low. Conversely, using a lower grade of material or omitting common features would cause this estimate to be too high.

Cubic Footage

A more refined method (compared to the square foot method) of arriving at a *rough estimate* is by computing the *cubic footage* of the house. (Sometimes cubic footage is referred to as *cubic content.*)

This calculation takes into consideration all three principal dimensions: *length, depth,* and *height.* The cost per cubic foot is similarly dependent upon the type and quality of building materials and on the wages paid to workers. These, of course, will vary from locality to locality. Again, only *similar* houses may be compared.

The cubic content is often used before the working drawings or specifications have been completed for a cost approximation. To obtain the total cubic footage, multiply the total square footage (length $\times$ depth) in the floor plan by the height of the building. The height of the structure is measured from the floor (*underside* of concrete slab) to the plate, plus one-half the distance from plate to the ridge (outside of roof). Nonenclosed porches and attached garages may be figured at *one-half* volume; basements at

two-thirds volume. The total cubic footage is multiplied by the average cost per cubic foot for similar houses.

Take the same one story slab house ($40' \times 28'$) used in the previous section. Assume the height from *under* slab to top plate is $8'6''$. The cubic footage for the main part of the house would be 9,520 cu. ft. (1,120 sq. ft. times height $8'$-$6''$). Assume the height from top plate to the ridge (outside measurement) is $6'$, and that a symmetrical gable roof is used. The attic volume would be 3,360 cu. ft. (one-half distance from eave line to ridge, $3'$, times 1,120 sq. ft.). The total cubic footage would be 12,880 cu. ft. Assume the average cost for similar houses in the same locality is $1.45 per cu. ft. The cubic footage method would give a rough estimate of $18,670 for the house (12,880 cu. ft. times $1.45).

Exact Estimate

The most accurate method used to determine an estimate is by actually making a quantity survey of materials, labor, time, etc., needed to construct the house. All the information necessary for these calculations is taken directly from the working drawings and specifications. Information relative to the kind, quantity, and quality of materials is obtained from the written specifications. Excavation information is derived from the floor plans, details, and the plot plan. There are many forms and procedures for taking off materials from the plans and specification. However, a successful estimate depends basically upon the practical experience and knowledge gained from long familiarity with house construction.

Consulting engineers, estimators, contractors and architects fill in a cost sheet that gives a complete cost analysis of materials and labor. Cost sheets vary in their organization but all include the items listed below. Some cost analysis sheets are organized alphabetically, others may be by areas as a structure would be built, while others are organized according to the specification format — notably the Construction Specification Institute Format.

Following each item on a cost sheet, space is provided to indicate: units, size, (sq. ft., sq. yds., cu. ft., cu. yds., ft. × ft.) lineal feet, unit cost, and total cost per unit. Almost all who are responsible for estimating use a cost sheet because each cost can be readily identified and is set down in a logical and organized form.

To show how an estimating list may be used, Fig. 19-1 illustrates a home built in Seattle, Washington by Bell and Valdez Builders.[1] The floor plan, elevations, and details of this highly functional 3-bedroom basementless home are shown in Fig. 19-2. The estimating list is organized into the following categories:

1. Earth excavation and grading
2. Concrete construction and finish
3. Brick and block construction and veneer
4. Wall paving and floor paving
5. Lumber framing and construction
6. Sheet metal work
7. Wood, exterior and interior, millwork
8. Gypsum board, ceiling and wall
9. Floor and wall tiling, vinyl and ceramic
10. Metal finish hardware
11. Finish, interior and exterior paint
12. Bathroom accessories
13. Plumbing system and fixtures
14. Heating system and fixtures
15. Electrical system and fixtures

The order in which the estimating categories are presented is generally the same as that followed in the specifications. The sequence follows the order in which the various trades work on the job. Plumbing, heating, and electrical work, however, are placed at the end.

The following estimating inventory lists all of the items and considerations necessary for construction of the house shown in Figs. 19-1 and 19-2.

JOHN M. ANDERSON, AIA, ARCHITECT, BELL & VALDEZ, BUILDERS, BELLEVUE, WASHINGTON.

Fig. 19-1. This well-designed and well-planned L-ranch house has a sheltered lanai and adjoining patio with a direct access to the living room and family room.

1. "Well-planned 'L' Wins Honors in A/B Contest. *American Builder,* XXCVI.

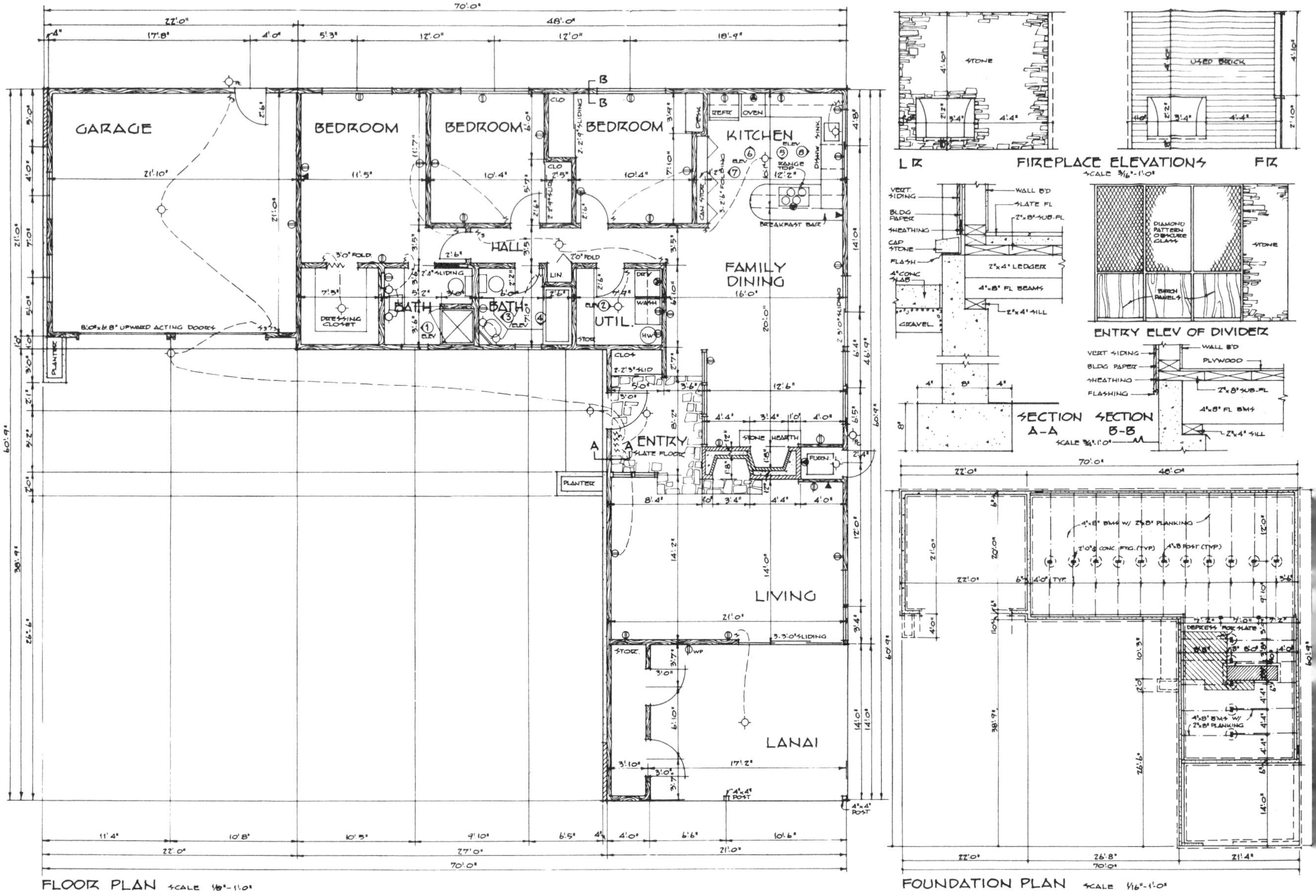

FLOOR PLAN SCALE 1/8"=1'-0"

GARAGE

BEDROOM

BEDROOM

BEDROOM

KITCHEN

HALL

BATH

BATH

UTIL

FAMILY DINING

ENTRY
SLATE FLOOR

LIVING

LANAI

PLANTER

Fig. 19-2. These working drawings show plan, elevations, and details of the L-ranch house.
(Drawing not to scale, reduced to fit page.)

FIREPLACE ELEVATIONS
SCALE 3/16"=1'-0"

STONE

USED BRICK

LR

FR

ENTRY ELEV OF DIVIDER

SECTION A-A   SECTION B-B
SCALE 3/8"=1'-0"

FOUNDATION PLAN SCALE 1/16"=1'-0"

JOHN M. ANDERSON, AIA, ARCHITECT. BELL & VALDEZ, BUILDER
BELLEVUE, WASHINGTON

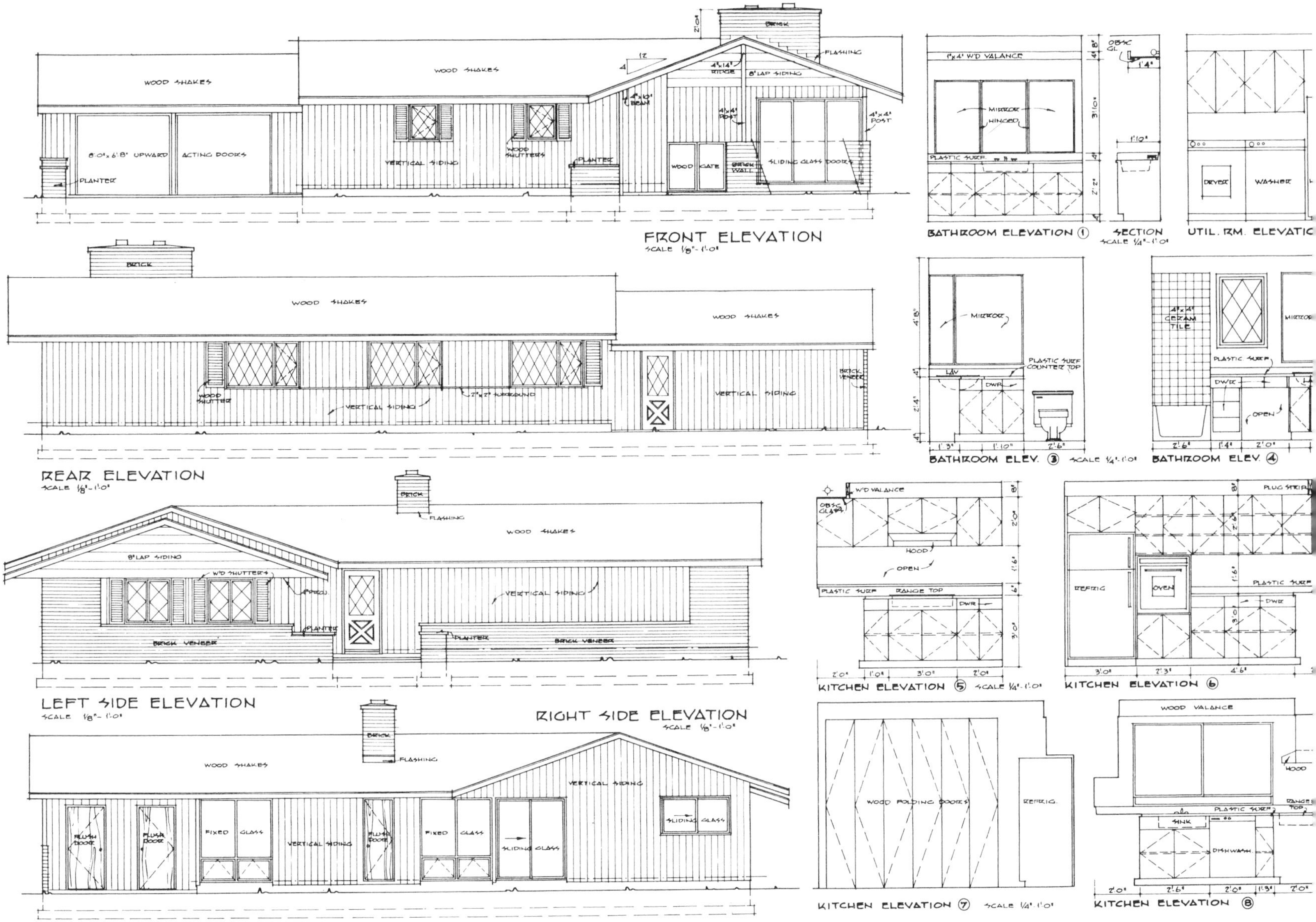
FRONT ELEVATION
SCALE 1/8"-1'-0"
REAR ELEVATION
SCALE 1/8"-1'-0"
LEFT SIDE ELEVATION
SCALE 1/8"-1'-0"
RIGHT SIDE ELEVATION
SCALE 1/8"-1'-0"
BATHROOM ELEVATION ①
SECTION
SCALE 1/4"-1'-0"
UTIL. RM. ELEVATIC
BATHROOM ELEV. ③
SCALE 1/4"-1'-0"
BATHROOM ELEV. ④
KITCHEN ELEVATION ⑤
SCALE 1/4"-1'-0"
KITCHEN ELEVATION ⑥
KITCHEN ELEVATION ⑦
SCALE 1/4"-1'-0"
KITCHEN ELEVATION ⑧
WOOD SHAKES
BRICK
FLASHING
VERTICAL SIDING
8" LAP SIDING
8'-0" x 6'-8" UPWARD ACTING DOORS
PLANTER
WOOD SHUTTERS
WOOD GATE
BRICK WALL
SLIDING GLASS DOORS
4"x4" POST
4"x14" RIDGE
BRICK VENEER
FIXED GLASS
SLIDING GLASS
FLUSH DOOR
1"x4" W'D VALANCE
MIRROR HINGED
PLASTIC SURF.
DRYER
WASHER
4"x4" CERAM TILE
OPEN
W'D VALANCE
OBSC GLASS
HOOD
RANGE TOP
DWR
PLUG STRIP
REFRIG
OVEN
WOOD FOLDING DOORS
WOOD VALANCE
SINK
DISHWASH

Fig. 19-2 (Cont'd)

House Area.

Livable floor area	1585 S[2]
Garage floor area	465 S
Lanai floor area	240 S
Lanai storage floor area	55 S

Earth Excavation & Grading.

Topsoil 6″ grade exc. & pile	7545 S
Earth floor leveling	2345 S
Earth foundation exc. & B′ fill	310 C[3]
Earth hand footing exc. & f′fill	600 C
Gravel 4″ floor sub-fill	790 S

Concrete Construction & Finish.

2500# Conc. chim. pier & wall footing	330 C
2500# Conc. chim. pier & wall footing forms	540 S
2500# Conc. foundation walls	385 C
2500# Conc. foundation wall forms	1440 S
2500# Conc. 4″ floor slab O.G.	790 S
2500# Conc. 5″ × 1″ wall cap & forms	20 L[4]
P. C. Conc. 4″ × 2½″ wall sills	40 L
P. C. Conc. 4″ chimney cap	25 S
Monolithic floor wd. float finish	790 S
Kraft paper floor wd. prot. & cure	790 S

Brick & Block Construction & Veneer.

Face brick 4″ ext. wall veneer	255 S
Face brick 4″ ext. chim. wl. veneer	90 S

Face brick 4″ planter & retain. walls	135 S
Sel. com. brick 4″ fireplace veneer	90 S
Fire brick 4″ f. p. floor paving	10 S
Fire brick 4″ f. p. wall lining	30 S
Conc. block chimney construction	215 C
Vitr. T. C. 12″ × 12″ chim. flue	25 L
Acid & mortar expose brick clean & point	610 S
Metal 12″ × 36″ F. P. dampers	2 U[5]
Metal 4″ × 8″ cleanout doors	2 U
Metal 3″ × 4″ × ¼″ F. P. lintels	8 L

Stone Wall Facing & Floor Paving.

Fieldstone 4″ f.p. wall facing	90 S
Slate 2″ hearth & floor paving	85 S
Brush & water facing & pave cleaning	175 S

Lumber Framing & Construction.

4″ × 14″ wood drs. roof ridge	15 L
4″ × 10″ wood doors roof beams	30 L
4″ × 8″ wood floor beams	370 L
4″ × 8″ wood 24″ floor beams post	18 U
4″ × 4″ wood drs. structural post	18 L
2-2″ × 10″ wood O.H. door lintel	20 L
2-2″ × 8″ wood door & wind. lintel	95 L
2″ × 8″ wood roof ridge	105 L

2″ × 8″ wood valance blocking	30 L
2″ × 8″ wood 16″ oc ceiling joists	1535 S
2″ × 8″ wood floor planks	1510 S
2″ × 6″ wood 16″ oc ceil. joists	465 S
2″ × 6″ wood 16″ oc roof rafter	3230 S
2′ × 6″ wood 16″ oc part. studs	75 S
2-2″ × 6″ wood partition sills	10 L
2″ × 6″ wood partition plates	10 L
2″ × 6″ wood o'head door bucks	30 L
2″ × 4″ wood 16″ oc part. studs	1250 S
2″ × 4″ wood 16″ oc wall studs	2165 S
2-2″ × 4″ wood studs sill	415 L
2″ × 4″ wood studs plates	415 L
2″ × 4″ wood floor ledger	45 L
2″ × 4″ found. fir. beam sills	100 L
1″ × 6″ wall lining	1760 S
1″ × 6″ roof lining	3230 S
Plyscore ½″ floor lining	1510 S
15# felt roof insulation	3230 S
15# felt wall insulation	1760 S
15# felt floor insulation	1510 S
Wood roof shakes	3230 S
Wood ext. vertical siding	1405 S
Wood ext. lap siding	100 S

Metal Sheet Work.

16 oz. copper chimney flashing	35 S
16 oz. copper wall sill flashing	40 S
16 oz. copper roof valley flashing	45 S
16 oz. copper cap & base flashing	30 S
16 oz. copper found. wall flashing	200 S

---

2. S=square feet.
3. C=cubic feet.
4. L=lineal feet.

5. U = units(s).

Wood Exterior & Interior Millwork.

Wood 8″ × 6′-8″ O'Head door
& acc. — 2 U

Wood 3′ × 6′-8″ ext. door, F&T — 2 U

Wood 2′-4″ × 7′ ext. door, F&T — 1 U

Wood & glass 3′ × 7′ ext. door,
F&T — 1 U

Wood & glass 2′-6″ × 7′ ext.
door, F&T — 1 U

Wood & glass 6′ × 7′ ext. sldg.
door, F&T — 1 U

Wood & glass 9′ × 7′ ext. sldg.
door, F&T — 1 U

Wood 2′-6″ × 6′-8″ int. door,
F&T — 4 U

Wood 2′-2″ × 6′-8″ int. door,
F&T — 1 U

Wood 2′-4″ × 6′-8″ int. sldg.
door, F&T — 1 U

Wood 2-2′ 3″ × 6′-8″ int. sldg.
door, F&T — 1 U

Wood 2- 2′ 9″ × 6′-8″ int. sldg.
door, F&T — 1 U

Wood 2′ × 6′-8″ fldg. door, F&T — 1 U

Wood 3′ × 6′-8″ fldg. door, F&T — 1 U

Wood 3-2′-6″ × 7′ fldg. door
F&T — 1 U

Wood & glass 6′ × 2′-8″ sldg.
wind. F&T — 1 U

Wood & glass 6′ × 7′ comb.
F&P wind. F&T — 2 U

Wood & glass 6′ × 3′-6″ F&Case.
wind. F&T — 3 U

Wood & glass 2′ × 2′-6″ casem.
F&T — 2 U

Wood & glass 3′-6″ × 3′-6″ fixed
wind. F&T — 2 U

Wood 1′-6″ × 3′-6″ wind.
shutters — 6 U

Wood 1′-6″ × 3′ wind. shutters — 4 U

Wood 1″ × 8″ ext. fascia — 310 L

Wood ⅜″ soffit boarding — 755 S

Wood 2″ × 2″ ext. moulding — 12 L

Wood 5′ × 4′ lanai gate & acc. — 1 U

4″ wd. & glass 8′ int. divid.
walls — 12 L

Wood 1″ × 24″ closet shelving — 15 L

Wood 1″ × 12″ storage shelving — 35 L

Wood 1″ × 18″ storage shelving — 30 L

Wood 1″ × 16″ closet shelving — 17 L

Wood 1″ × 2″ shelving cleats — 97 L

Wood 1″ d. closet poles — 32 L

Wood 1″ × 8″ wall valance — 30 L

Wood & glass 1″ × 16″ lt. fixt.
screen — 7 L

Prefin. wood 6′-6″ × 1′-8″ ×
2′-6″ van. base cab. — 1 U

Prefin. wood 7′ × 2′ × 2′-6″
van. corn. base cab. — 1 U

Prefin. wood 4′-6″ × 2′-6″ ×
1′ util. wl. cab. — 1 U

Prefin. wood 3′ × 1′-6″ × 2′-6″
desk — 1 U

Prefin. wood 2′ × 3′ kit. base
cabinet — 17 L

Prefin. wood 2′-6″ × 1′ kit. wall
cabinet — 12 L

Prefin. wood 3′ × 3′ kitchen
island base cabinet — 6 L

Prefin. wood 2′ × 1′ kit. island
wall cabinet — 8 L

Gypsum Board Ceil. & Wall Boarding.

Gypsum board ½″ T. J. ceil.
boarding — 1535 S

Gypsum board ½″ T. J. gar. ceil.
boarding — 465 S

Gypsum board ½″ T. J. wall ceil.
boarding — 3250 S

Gypsum board ½″ wall lining — 130 S

Vinyl & Ceramic Floor & Wall Tiling.

Vinyl ⅛″ floor tiling — 1425 S

Vinyl 4″ wall base — 475 L

Gypsum board ½″ wall lining — 130 S

Metal Finish Hardware.

Metal ext. cylinder locks — 5 U

Metal ext. sldg. dr. locks — 2 U

Metal int. sldg. dr. locks — 1 U

Metal int. door locks — 5 U

Metal int. fldg. dr. locks — 3 U

Metal int. door hinges — 10 U

Metal ext. door hinges — 15 U

Metal int. sldg. dr. hardware set — 2 U

Metal ext. sldg. dr. hardware set — 2 U

Metal window sldg. dr. hardware
set — 10 U

Paint Ext. & Int. Finish.

Paint ext. millwork 3 coats — 2950 S

Paint int. millwork 3 coats — 600 S

Paint wood doors 3 coats — 1525 S

Paint wood sash 3 coats — 400 S

Paint gyp. bd. ceil. 2 coats — 2000 S

Paint gyp. bd. wall 2 coats — 3250 S

Metal & Glass Toilet Room Accessories.

Metal & Glass 3′ × 7′ shower
encl. door — 1 U

Metal & glass medicine cabinet — 2 U

Chrome metal toilet paper holders — 2 U

Chrome metal soap dish & grab
bar — 1 U

Chrome metal tumbler & tooth-
brush holder — 2 U

Chrome metal 24″ towel bar   4 U

Chrome metal 5′ shower curtain
rod   1 U

Metal & glass 3′-6″ wall mirror &
acc.   12 U

Plumbing System & Fixtures.

Water service connection & piping   1 U

Sanitary service connection &
piping   1 U

Gas service connection & piping   1 U

Gas furnace connection & piping   1 U

Washer connection & piping   1 U

Dishwasher connection & piping   1 U

Dryer connection & piping   1 U

Hose bib connection & piping   2 U

Vanity sinks connection & piping   2 U

Bath tub connection & piping   1 U

Water closet connection & piping   2 U

Shower head connection & piping   1 U

Shower drain connection & piping   1 U

Kitchen sink connection & piping   1 U

Heating System & Fixtures.

Gas hot air furnace & accessories   1 U

Gas hot air temp. control equip.   1 U

Metal ducts & registers   14 U

Electrical System & Fixtures.

Electric service connection   1 U

Electric service panel & switch   1 U

Telephone service connection   1 U

Gas furnace connection & wiring   1 U

Range top connection & wiring   1 U

Built in oven connection & wiring   1 U

Dishwasher connection & wiring   1 U

Clothes washer connection &
wiring   1 U

Exhaust fan, connection & wiring   1 U

Range hood, connection & wiring   1 U

Elec. H. W. htr., connection &
wiring   1 U

Single switch, outlet & wiring   11 U

3 way Switch, outlet and wiring   7 U

Conv. recept. outlet & wiring   28 U

Telephone recpt. outlet & wiring   3 U

Conv. Recept. W. P., outlet &
wiring   1 U

Entr. P. button, outlet & wiring   2 U

Ceil. light outlet & wiring   7 U

Wall light outlet & wiring   5 U

Ext. wl. light outlet & wiring   4 U

Ceiling fixtures & bulbs   7 U

Wall fixtures & bulbs   5 U

Wall W. P. fixtures & bulbs   4 U

So that an accurate estimate may be obtained, the total man hour cost for skilled and semi skilled craftsmen and laborers must also be computed.

Many books on estimating are revised yearly to keep current with new material costs and labor rates in each general section or in major urban centers in the U.S. Since labor rates vary, even within distances of 100 miles, some books, such as the *National Construction Estimator,* give an adjustment factor to be applied to a basic wage rate or cost for each area and urban population center of the country. The estimator selects the trade or craft that will perform the work and multiplies the modification factor by the hourly wage rate. For example, an estimator in Albuquerque, N.M. preparing a bid estimate on a building that will use four 2′-2″ × 4′-0″ double hung windows would calculate the (1) contractor's price of the windows; (2) wage rate of those who install the windows; and (3) amount of time to accomplish the job. This obviously would be a time-consuming task for each item. Estimators either through experience or estimating books simplify the procedure. Using the example stated above, the total cost of windows would be calculated by finding the cost table for windows and applying the proper modification factor. This factor, for Albuquerque, N.M., is .77. As an example, Table 19-1 illustrates a section from the 20th edition of the *National Construction Estimator.*

TABLE 19-1
Double hung windows *

Size	Unit	Material	Labor	Total
1′-10″ x 48′-8″	Ea	26.00	7.86	33.86
2′-2″ x 3′-4″	Ea	22.00	7.86	29.86
2′-2″ x 4′-0″	Ea	25.00	7.86	32.86

National Construction Estimator, Los Angeles, Calif.

*Glazed S.S.B. w/screens, weather stripped,
rough opening size, two lites/unit

Since four 2'-2" × 4'-0" windows are planned, the estimator would multiply the cost per window by 4 and the labor cost by the modification factor for four windows. The total cost would be calculated as follows:

$$(4 \times \$25.00) + (4 \times \$7.86 \times .77) =$$
$$\$100.00 + \$24.21 = \$124.21$$

After all items have been estimated, a given percentage must be added for *overhead, profit,* and *supervision* to the total estimate price.

So that the person who is interested in estimating may have a basic idea of how materials and products are ordered, the following more common items are listed:

Lumber

All lumber is purchased by the *board foot* (b.f.). Price lists issued by building product suppliers list the price per thousand board feet. A board foot is one inch thick × 12" wide × 12" long. To determine the amount of board feet the following formula is used: BF =

$$\frac{W'' \times T'' \times L'}{12}$$

For example a 2" × 6" × 10' length contains 10 board feet:

$$\frac{2'' \times 6'' \times 10'}{12} = 10 \text{ board feet.}$$

Board feet can be calculated if all inch measurements are used. This, however, results in calculations involving large figures. The formula when all dimensions given in inches is:

$$\frac{W'' \times T'' \times L''}{144}$$

When large numbers are used there is a greater opportunity for error.

The width and thickness of lumber may be changed to a decimal or fraction of foot and multiplied by the total length of the lumber. This method works particularly well on an adding machine, calculator, or slide rule. The sizes are computed as follows:

- 1" × 4" —⅓ or .33 of total lineal feet
- 1" × 6" —½ or .50 of total lineal feet
- 1" × 8" —⅔ or .66 of total lineal feet
- 1" × 10"—Total lineal feet less ⅙ or .17
- 1" × 12"—Total lineal feet
- 2" × 4" —⅔ or .66 of total lineal feet
- 2" × 6" —Total lineal feet
- 2" × 8" —⅔ or .66 of double the total lineal feet
- 2" × 10"—Double the total lineal feet less ⅙ or .17
- 2" × 12"—Double the total lineal feet

Lumber is priced per thousand board feet. For example a catalog price for 2 × 6 lumber would be listed at $180/M. (M is a standard abbreviation for 1000.)

Therefore: $180.00 per 1000 board feet
$18.00 per 100 board feet
$1.80 per 10 board feet
$.18 per 1 board foot

Concrete

Concrete is ordered by the *yard and fractions (quarters and thirds) of a yard.* For example if it was calculated that an amount of concrete needed was 4.20 yard, 4¼ yard

would be ordered rather than 4⅕ yards. One cubic yard equals a cube 3' wide × 3' deep × 3' high. To determine the cubic yards, simply multiply the width in feet by the thickness in feet by the length in feet and divide by 27. The formula is expressed as:

$$\frac{W' \times T' \times L'}{27}$$

Most estimators when working with large areas change all of the dimensions to decimals or fractions of a foot. By using decimals of a foot, smaller numbers result. For example, to determine the amount of concrete required to pour a footing 10" thick × 20" wide × 120' long, first convert the inch dimensions to decimals. 10" = .83 feet and 20" = 1.67. Substituting these values in the formula, the amount of concrete required would be 6.14 yards. .83 × 1.67 × 120 = 6.14 yards. The amount of concrete that would be ordered is 6.25 yards or 6¼ yards.

Reinforcing Mesh

Wire fabric with 6" × 6", 4" × 4" spacing of wire is ordered by specifying the *wire gauge* and the number of *rolls* (5' × 150') or *sheets* (7' 10' × 12' and 5' × 10'). Determine the total square footage of concrete requiring mesh and order by the roll or sheet.

Structural Steel

Junior, S, wide flange, channel, and angles are ordered in *stock lengths of 20', 30' and 40',* or *up to 60' random.* Calculate the total lineal feet of each type of steel required and order accordingly.

Masonry

Brick. For estimating purposes, face and common brick may be considered as the same size. All brick is usually *sold and priced on the basis of 1000.* The price, for example, is listed as $85.00/M. The amount of brick in any odd-shaped area can be determined by figuring the area of brick, plus the mortar joint and dividing the square area by 144. This will give the number of bricks per square foot for a 4″ wall. For an 8″ wall, multiply by 2 and for a 12″ wall multiply by 3. The following figures can be used to determine the number of standard size brick in a running bond per square foot.

½″ Mortar Joint

1 sq. ft. of   4 in. wall =   6 bricks
1 sq. ft. of   8 in. wall = 12 bricks
1 sq. ft. of 12 in. wall = 18 bricks

¼″ Mortar Joint

1 sq. ft. of   4 in. wall =   7 bricks
1 sq. ft. of   8 in. wall = 13 bricks
1 sq. ft. of 12 in. wall = 20 bricks
1 sq. ft. of   4 in. wall = 4 Norman bricks

Concrete Block: To determine the number of 8″ × 8″ × 16″ concrete blocks in a wall, multiply the height in feet by 1.5 and the length in feet by .75. This may be easily expressed by the formula $N = (1.5N')(.75L')$. For example, to find the number of 8″ × 8″ × 16″ concrete block in a wall 58′8″ long and 9′4″ high, multiply the height (9′4″ × 1.5); 9.33′ × 1.5 = 14; and the length (58′8″ × .75); 58.66′ × .75 = 44.. Then to obtain the total number of blocks, multiply the number of blocks contained in the height by the number in the length; thus 14 × 44 = 616 blocks. In a similar manner, the number 2¾″ × 3¾″ × 8″ face or common brick by multiplying the height in feet by 5.5 and the length in feet by 1.5. The formula $N = (5.5H')(1.5L')$. Using the same size wall as in the preceding paragraph, 58′8″ in length and 9′4″ in height, substituting in the formula:

$$N = (58.66 \times 5.5)(9.33 \times 1.5)$$
$$N = (322.6)(13.9)$$

This can be rounded to (323)(14) = 4524.

Sand and Mortar. Mortar is purchased by the *bag.* Each bag weighs approximately 74 lbs. and will lay 75 blocks. Mortar is always mixed with sand and usually one yard of sand is mixed with 10 bags of mortar, using the ratio 3 sand to one mortar.

Aggregate. All *sand, gravel* and *crushed rock* is ordered by the *square yard.* Determine the number of square yards similar to concrete.

Field Tile. To determine the amount (*pieces*) of field tile for drainage purposes, use the perimeter of the foundation wall plus the length to the dry well or storm sewer and divide by 2. Field tile is usually 2′ long. Do not forget ells are required for each corner.

Building Components

Termite Shield. Termite shield is ordered by the *lineal foot.* From the plan add the length of each exterior foundation wall that is below the house and garage.

Sill Seal. Sill seal is *purchased by the roll* in 6″ and 8″ widths. Each roll contains 120 lineal feet. Calculate the total number of lineal feet of foundation wall and order the number of rolls required.

Sill. (not including boxing) Total *lineal footage* of foundation wall. Sill is usually 2″ × 6″ or 2″ × 8″.

Boxing. Boxing is placed completely around the perimeter of the foundation wall. It is an integral part of the sill and is determined by the *lineal foot.* The size of the boxing is identical to the floor joist. If a stairway is adjacent to a foundation wall, include in the calculation the length of the foundation wall that is adjacent to the stairs.

Floor Joists. Floor joists are usually placed 16″ on center. Floor joist, as with other dimension lumber, is purchased by the *board foot* and is ordered in even 20′ lengths. The number of floor joists required can be calculated by *multiplying the length of the structure by .75 and adding 1.* $N = .75l + 1$.

Bridging. Bridging may be 1″ × 2″, 1″ × 3″ or 2″ × 2″ dimension lumber. The length of the bridging is dependent upon the size and spacing of joists. This is most easily determined by drawing 2 joists at the specified on-center distance and the proper size and scaling the diagonal distance. One pair of bridging is required for each span (between foundation and girder or beam) floor joist. Determine the total length per joist spacing and multiply by number of spaces.

If *metal cross bridgings* are used, they are ordered by the *pair* in standard lengths for each span between foundation and girder or beam.

Sub-flooring. Sub-flooring and underlayment is calculated by the square foot and sold in *4' × 8' sheets*. To find the number of sheets required, calculate the number of square feet to be covered and divide by 32.

Studs. Studs in partition walls are spaced 16" on center just as joists. To allow for double studs, triple, etc., figure *one stud for every foot of exterior and interior partition wall*. This rule of thumb includes corners, backers and lap studs.

Plates. Three plates are used for each interior and exterior partition wall. A single plate is placed at the bottom and a double plate at the top of each stud wall. Determine the *total lineal feet of interior and exterior partitions and multiply by 3*.

Headers. Calculate the total number of *lineal feet* for all rough openings and *multiply by 2*.

Ceiling joists. Ceiling joists are calculated in the identical manner as floor joists; see floor joists.

Roof rafters. The number of roof rafters is determined as with floor and ceiling joists; see floor joists.

Collar beams. Collar beams are purchased to the nearest standard lineal foot length as dimension lumber. One collar beam is used on each pair of rafters. The architectural details will show collar beams if they are required and call out the placement.

Sheathing. Determine the square foot sum of all areas of the exterior walls; subtract the plywood used for bracing at each corner. Both gypsum and fiber sheathing is ordered by the *sheet* in the following sizes: 8' × 2', 8' × 4', 9' × 2' and 9' × 4'.

Roof area. To find the area of *any* roof, first determine the area from the plan view of the floor plan under roof. Then add the area of roof overhang. By using the multiplication factor given in Table 19-2 for the proper roof slope simply multiply that factor by the total square area. The result will equal the total roof area.

Roof area is used to determine the amount of roof sheathing, asphalt, shingles, cedar shingles, or built-up roofing.

Roof sheathing. Determine the number of square feet of roof area and divide by 32. This amount will be the number of *4' × 8'* sheets of plywood required to sheath the roof.

TABLE 19-2
ROOF AREAS

Pitch	Pitch Triangle (Rise–Run)		Multiplication Factor
1/8	3	12	1.03
	4	12	1.06
	5	12	1.08
1/4	6	12	1.12
	7	12	1.16
1/3	8	12	1.20
3/8	9	12	1.25
	10	12	1.30
	11	12	1.35
1/2	12	12	1.41
5/8	15	12	1.60
3/4	18	12	1.80
7/8	21	12	2.02

Roof area is used to determine the amount of roof sheathing, asphalt, cedar shingles, or built-up roofing.

Vent system. The type of vent or louver will determine how each are ordered. The following lists the major types of venting:

Ridge vent strip—8' or 10' lengths (total length of ridge)

Soffit vent strip—8' lengths (total length of soffit entering attic)

Roof vent—each (depending on ceiling area)

Gable end vent and louvers—each (each gable and opening to attic)

Gutters and downspouts. Gutters and downspouts are ordered in *10' lengths.* Determine the total lineal footage of eave requiring gutter and order the appropriate number of 10' lengths. Every 3' of gutter will require a spike and ferrule or strap hanger. Add necessary number of inside and outside corners, connectors and end caps. These are ordered as *each.*

One downspout is usually required for every 20 to 25 lineal feet of gutter. Downspouts are ordered in *10-ft. lengths.*

Felt paper. Felt paper is available in two different *weight rolls:* 15 lb. paper (144' × 3') covers about 4 square area; 30 lb. paper (36' × 3') will cover about one square area. One square covers about 100 sq. ft. Determine the number of squares in the roof area and order rolls accordingly.

Drip edge. Drip edge is sold in *10' lengths.* Total the lineal footage of the entire roof edge. Include gable ends, corners and offsets.

Rake and eave facia. Total the entire (*lineal feet*) length of rake (gable) and soffitt. Order next longest 2' length.

Shingles. Shingles are calculated by the *square* and are sold by the *bundle.* A square of shingles covers 100 square feet of roof area. Four bundles of 16" or 18" shingles or three bundles of 24" shingles equal one square. When calculating the number of squares required, add 8% for waste, caps, and valleys.

Windows. The window schedule identifies the types and size of each window. Double hung, casement, awning, etc. are ordered giving the quantity of *each* style. Multiple windows such as bow windows, "mulled" or combination fixed sash and casement (for example) are ordered as a *unit.* The window schedule identifies the type of glazing, sash, priming, etc. of each window used in the construction.

Insulation. Batt insulation is placed in side walls. Insulation placed in the ceiling can be either batt, loose fill, poured, or blown-in. To estimate the number of rolls of batt insulation required, find the sum of all the areas that are to be insulated and divide by 75 or 112. Batt insulation comes in rolls 15" × 56' that will cover a gross area of 75 sq. ft. or in rolls 23" × 56' that will cover 112 sq. ft. gross area. If the structure has finished rooms on the upper level, be sure to add insulation for the side walls. Many contractors will also insulate around storage area. For example, bulkheads above the wall-hung kitchen cabinets should be insulated.

Poured loose-fill insulation is sold by *bags* containing approximately 8⅓ cu. ft. One bag will cover 25 sq. ft., 4" thick, or 16.5 sq. ft., 6" thick. Determine the depth of insulation, 4" or 6", and calculate accordingly. Blown-in loose-fill insulation is usually let on a *contract basis* to a firm specializing in blown insulation.

Drywall. Drywall is sold in *varying size sheets.* First determine the total square footage of area that is to be covered, then calculate the size of drywall sheets. Drywall is usually available in *6', 8', 10', 12' 14', and 16' × 4'* sheets. Contractors purchase a mixture of sizes to minimize man-hour and waste material cost.

Oak flooring. In calculating the amount of oak flooring required for a given square area an allowance plus 5% for waste must be added to the area. The allowance to be added is based on the tongue and groove of each piece of flooring. The narrower the flooring the greater the allowance.

Size		Add to Total Square Feet	
$^{25}/_{32}$ × 1½"	50%	+ 5% = 55%*	
$^{25}/_{32}$ × 2"	37½%	+ 5% = 42½%*	
$^{25}/_{32}$ × 2¼"	33%	+ 5% = 38%*	
⅜ × 1½"	33%	+ 5% = 38%*	
½ × 1½"	33%	+ 5% = 38%*	
⅜ × 2"	25%	+ 5% = 30%*	
½ × 2"	25%	+ 5% = 30%*	
$^{25}/_{32}$ × 3½"	24%	+ 5% = 29%*	

*Allowance includes 5% for waste.

Doors. Interior and exterior doors quantities are taken from the door schedule. Distinction should be made between exterior and interior doors. The schedule calls out size (w × h × t) and description of each door. Both types of doors are purchased from a mill. Metal screen and storm doors are purchased complete from the mill. Each pocket door requires special pocket door hardware. One *unit* should be purchased for each door.

Door Casings. Casings and moldings are purchased by sides. Each casing *unit* consists of *2 sides and one head casing* for each door. Molding is ordered on the same basis. The quantity of casing required is obtained from the door schedule.

Door stops. One *set of stops* (2 side pieces and 1 head piece) is ordered for each door.

Stairs. Stairs are seldom made on the job site, perhaps with the exception of basement stairs. Most stairs that are designed between levels or stories are mill made or are constructed in the contractor's shop. All parts of the stairs are delivered to the site either assembled or in parts. Such stairs are listed as "Stairs, main, one flight" with necessary dimensions.

Basement stairs are usually built at the job site. Generally 2 stringers are required per stair and are either 2" × 10" or 2" × 12". The number of treads cut from 2" × 10"'s and riser board (1" × 8"'s) is dependent upon the rise and run of the stair. Disappearing stairs are ordered by *unit.*

Stair handrails. Handrails for stairs are ordered by *lineal feet* from stock patterns. If dimension lumber (2" × 4") is used the *lineal footage* is in nearest 2 foot lengths.

Stair railings. Railings for stairs depending on the design, is mill ordered in *lineal feet.* Individual balusters or pickets may be

1″ × 2″, 1″ × 3″, and 2″ × 2″, etc., or stock designs.

Siding. The amount of siding is calculated by combining the area of all surfaces requiring siding and adding a specified amount for lapping and waste.

Bevel:

1″ × 6″ with ⅞″ lap add 38% to total square feet

1″ × 8″ with 1″ lap add 33% to total square feet

1″ × 10″ with 1½″ lap add 29% to total square feet

1″ × 12″ with 1″ lap add 23% to total square feet

Shiplap:

1″ × 4″ add 28% to total square feet

1″ × 6″ add 19% to total square feet

1″ × 8″ add 16% to total square feet

D & M*:

1″ × 4″ add 23% to total square feet

1″ × 6″ add 16% to total square feet

1″ × 8″ add 14% to total square feet

* Dressed and Matched

Tile. Tile is sold in three different units: by the *square yard,* by the *square foot,* and by the *running foot* at a given width.

Base board and molding. All total *lineal footage* is figured for each room. All door openings are included because this takes care of breakage and waste.

Top set. Vinyl or rubber top set is used in place of base board or base molding over floor tile. The perimeter (including openings) of the room is calculated in lineal feet. All rooms and walls having top set are to-taled and the required *lineal footage* is ordered.

Cedar lining. Cedar closets are lined with ⅜″ thick aromatic cedar stock. Cedar lining is sold in 20 or 40 sq. ft. bundles. Each 20 sq. ft. bundle will line 16 sq. ft. and a 40 ft. bundle will line 32 sq. ft. Calculate the number of square feet in the closet and add 20% to determine the required number of *bundles.*

Shelf material. Shelves may be adjustable metal or 1″ × 8″, 1″ × 10″ or 1″ × 12″ dimension lumber ordered in its nearest *2 foot lengths.* Shelf brackets, both for wood and metal are bought by *pairs* or by the *dozen.* Some expandable metal shelves have a formed nosing that eliminates clothes hanger poles.

Clothes Poles. Poles for clothes hangers are ordered by the lineal foot to the nearest *foot lengths.* A pair of brackets are required for each pole.

Cabinets and casework. The vast majority of cabinets and cases are ordered from a mill specializing in cabinets. If the cabinets are not standard, the architect or designer will send elevation and detail to the mill. The cabinets are delivered to the job site for installation. Each piece which is listed on the take-off sheet is listed as *units, each.*

Carpet. Carpeting is normally marketed by the *square yard.* Figure the total square footage of the plan that is to be carpeted and divide by 9.

Shutters. Almost all shutters are made by millwork manufacturers. Shutters may be wood, metal or molded plastic and are made in standard stock sizes. Shutters are listed in the take-off sheets and ordered as *units.*

Wood columns. Stock wood columns are available from millwork houses in standard patterns. Columns are available in 8′, 9′, 12′, and 16′6″ lengths. Columns are ordered *each.*

Home Financing

In buying a home, no obligation should be assumed that does not take into consideration emergencies which may arise. A close relationship must exist between the mortgage payments and the family's income.

Yearly and Monthly Income

Frequently, a "rule of thumb" is used to determine roughly the amount one can afford for a house. Perhaps the most popular is 2½ times the total yearly gross income of the chief wage earner. Another "rule of thumb is to take ¼ to ⅕ of a month's salary, *or* one week's pay out of each month's salary for *housing expenses.* Housing expenses are based on the monthly payment for principal and interest to retire the loan, *plus* $\frac{1}{12}$ annual fire insurance premium (this is required), *plus* $\frac{1}{12}$ annual property tax, *plus* $\frac{1}{12}$ annual mortgage insurance premium (if desired by the home owner.) These figures give only rough estimates of how much can be devoted to housing. For some these guidelines may be followed with safety, for others it may only spell disaster. For example: a family could easily use these guidelines if they purchased a home in an established area where the schools were debt-free, the taxes low, and the house located close to the chief wage earner's employment. If, on the other hand, this same family were to purchase a home in a *new development* located some distance from the city, with no paved streets, sidewalks, etc., they would have to pay considerably more taxes, eventual assessments, and greater transportation costs. Yet, in both cases, the factors would indicate the family could afford the house.

The figures shown in Table 19-3 can be used to determine the approximate amount that can be spent for housing. These figures are based on what most families can afford to pay, namely about ⅕ of the monthly or annual income. To assess the probable cost which the family can assume, simply read across. If, for example, a family earns approximately $416.00 per month, they could adequately purchase a $12,000 house. If the family has one or two children, then take the figure in the preceding row; if there are three or more children, then two figures above. For example, if there are two children and the head of the family earns $8,-000, they can purchase a $16,000 home. A family having the same income with three or four children can afford a $14,500 home. If a family has extraordinary expenses (such as anticipated high taxes, many installment payments, large educational bills, high food costs, entertainment, travel, medicine, or doctor bills) the price of the house must be lowered. If these circumstances prevail, the house cost must be additionally lowered one figure.

Another method which can be used to determine the approximate amount that one will have to spend per month for a given house is to use 1% of the adjusted house cost. To arrive at the adjusted house cost, subtract 5% of the cost of the house and lot from the total cost. The 5% factor is the average amount of an FHA down payment for a 30-year mortgage. By taking 1% of the adjusted house cost one should arrive at the approximate *monthly* mortgage payment, insurance, taxes, heating and cooling, utilities, and upkeep.

For example, if a house costs $22,000, a 5% down payment would be $1,100, making the adjusted cost $20,900. The approximate amount one may pay per month for housing on this basis would be $209.00 (1% × 20,900). If the buyer would have more than 5% down payment or have a shorter mortgage, the monthly expense would be altered. Increasing the down payment will result in a lower monthly mortgage payment. A shorter mortgage will increase the monthly payment. Any bank or savings and loan institution will be able to identify the monthly amount on a particular mortgage.

Housing Income

A more reliable method for calculating the amount available for housing is listed by the U. S. Savings and Loan League, *What You Should Know Before You Buy a Home.*

1. List the total take-home income. This is the *spendable* income derived from the total salary or wages *minus* all deductions for income taxes, social security, hospitalization, retirement, etc. Note: The wife's income or children's income *should not* be included since this is usually temporary when compared to the life of the mortgage. Include any income derived from dividends or interest if this is permanent.
2. List *all expenses,* including money for food, clothing, medical and dental care, life insurance, education, recreation, utilities and fuel, transportation, monthly savings, contributions, dues, and installment purchases. Total these.

TABLE 19-3
APPROXIMATE HOUSE COST IN RELATION
TO INCOME

| INCOME* | | TOTAL HOUSE COST |
MONTH	YEAR	
$ 333	$ 4,000	$ 9,100
416	5,000	12,000
500	6,000	14,500
583	7,000	16,500
666	8,000	19,700
750	9,000	22,500
833	10,000	25,500
916	11,000	27,500
1,000	12,000	30,000
1,250	15,000	35,000

*Gross income or income before deductions.

3. Subtract total expenses (#2) from the total take-home income (#1). The result gives the housing income, or the amount that can be spent on housing. This determines, in part, the size of mortgage the prospective home owner can adequately carry.

Table 19-4 shows multiplying factors that can be used to determine approximate amounts that may be borrowed based on the annual budget for housing. These factors are determined by interest rate and length of mortgage.

If, for example, a prospective home owner has decided that he can afford $135 per month ($1620 annually) for housing and knows that money is available at 8% interest, he can determine the maximum loan amount. To obtain the correct factor, he must know the interest rate and length of the loan—suppose in this case 25 years. The factor would be 10.80. This factor is multiplied by the annual amount for housing: *Annual Amt. Housing × Factor = Max Loan Amt.*

$$\$1620 \times 10.80 = \$17,496$$

The maximum loan that the prospective home owner could obtain budgeting $135 per month would be $17,496. This maximum loan amount *does not* include costs for taxes and insurance. To be realistic he must estimate the amount that will have to be deducted from the budgeted amount for taxes and insurance. If the prospective home owner determines that, on the price he can afford, the taxes ($420) and insurance ($60) will be $480 annually, he must then deduct this from the yearly amount budgeted for housing: $1620 − $480 = $1140. The $1140 ($95 monthly) figure now represented the real amount that he could apply to amortizing his mortgage. Using the annual figure of $1140 and the factor of 10.80, the maximum amount he could borrow is reduced to $12,312.

$$\$1140 \times 10.80 = \$12,312$$

The $135 monthly set aside by the family does not include the costs of maintenance which must be considered and which vary with the age, size, and construction of the building. The maximum amount that can be borrowed also does not include the down payment required by all lending agencies. By adding the amount available for a down payment to $12,312, a basic figure will indicate what the family can afford.

TABLE 19-4. ANNUAL FACTORS FOR MAXIMUM LOAN AMOUNTS

	ANNUAL INTEREST RATES											
	5.75%	6.00%	6.25%	6.50%	6.75%	7.00%	7.25%	7.50%	7.75%	8.00%	8.50%	9.00%
YEARS	MULTIPLYING FACTORS											
10	7.59	7.51	7.42	7.34	7.26	7.18	7.10	7.02	6.94	6.87	6.72	6.58
15	10.04	9.87	9.72	9.57	9.42	9.27	9.13	8.99	8.50	8.72	8.46	8.22
20	11.86	11.63	11.40	11.17	10.96	10.75	10.55	10.34	10.15	9.96	9.61	9.26
25	13.25	12.94	12.63	12.35	12.06	11.92	11.53	11.27	11.04	10.80	10.35	9.93
30	14.29	13.91	13.53	13.19	12.85	12.53	12.21	11.92	11.63	11.35	10.83	10.35

Other variables may enter into the total picture and thereby affect the over-all housing cost and mortgage size. Some lending institutions consider the present income and potential income of the prospective borrower, size of the down payment, mortgage terms, present and projected taxes, utility costs, time payments on appliances, commuting costs, ability to save, number of children, and existing or potential basic improvements in the community (schools, public buildings, streets, etc.).

Home Loans

Basically, three types of home loans are currently available to the public: (1) Private conventional loans, which are assumed by a private lender, such as a bank, savings and loan association, or commercial mortgage house; (2) GI Loans, wherein the government *guarantees* the loan; and (3) FHA (Federal Housing Administration) government insured loans, wherein the money is borrowed from a private source, but the loan is *insured* by the federal government.

The conventional loan is available for financing both old and new homes. The availability of the GI and FHA loans for both new and old homes is governed by the supply of home mortgage money, demand for mortgages, level of interest rates, and other related factors. The conventional loan can easily adjust to the varying needs of the people and to changed financial conditions. The GI and FHA loan can not readily adjust because the terms are fixed by the Congress of the United States.

Conventional Loans

Private conventional loans are construed to include all loan plans in which the federal government *does not participate,* either as a *guaranteeing* or as an *insuring agent.* The loan is given by a bank, savings and loan association, insurance company, mortgage house, or by any one who wishes to lend the necessary amount. The lending institution advances its own money to the borrower, and if for some reason he is unable to repay, the lender stands the loss. The rate of interest charged on the private conventional loan is usually higher (ranging between 6 to 9 percent) and the length of time for repayment is usually shorter (10 to 20 years) than the GI or FHA loans. The down payment required for the conventional loan may be as low as 10 per cent, or may range up to 40 per cent of the purchase price. The down payment is usually less for a new home than for an old home.

GI Loans

The GI loan is for veterans only. The maximum interest rate and the terms of the loan are controlled by the federal government. The down payment is less than other types of loans and the terms are longer. The government guarantees the lending institution a greater part of the loan in case of default. Private lending institutions make the loan; *the government does not lend the money.*

FHA Loans

An FHA loan is *insured by the government* against default. As with the GI loan, a private lending agency grants the loan, but the federal government insures that the *lender* will not lose on the loan. The loan is only insured when *both* the credit standing of the borrower and the construction standards of the house are satisfactory. (The construction is checked periodically by an inspector from the FHA.) These standards enable much larger loans (higher loan to value ratio) to be granted by the lender because of the protection against loss. Thus, smaller down payments are required. The borrower pays an insurance premium of $\frac{1}{2}$ of 1 per cent computed monthly, on the outstanding principal. In addition an application fee is charged by the FHA. Both "government type" loans take much longer to obtain due to the extensive investigative measures which must be conducted.

Mortgages

The type, size, and location of a house is important. But just as important, however, is the economic status of the purchaser and his credit rating. These two features play an important role in the decision of the lending institution to grant a mortgage.

The closer the purchaser meets the borrowing standards of the lending institution, the higher (within reasonable limits) the mortgage. That is: the higher the loan will be in comparison to the value of the property. This feature is especially true when qualifying for a low interest mortgage. Usually all lending institutions will view the purchaser from the following vantage points.

His ability to pay:

1. Purchaser's income must be sufficient to support the monthly mortgage obligation. The monthly income (before deductions) should be four or five times greater than the mortgage payment.

2. Purchaser's income after deductions should be sufficient to allow for minimal size installment payments.

3. Purchaser's record of employment should be steady. One year in present position is desirable.

His willingness to pay:

1. Purchaser's credit record should be good. All lending institutions will investigate the purchaser's credit rating. It is sound business to establish a credit rating.

2. Purchaser's credit record should not contain any judgments or bankruptcies unless they can be justifiably explained.

Mortgage Contract Features

The mortgage contract may include some or all of the following features. Their inclusion makes home ownership less costly, more pleasant, and more convenient.

1. *Package Provision.* This enables the borrower to finance certain appliances and other necessary items as part of the original loan.

2. *Open End Provision.* This allows the borrower to apply for additional funds, before the mortgage is paid off, with repayment *amortized* (spread) over the term of the loan.

3. *Additional Payment Privilege.* This allows the borrower, without penalty, to make additional payments over the regular monthly payment. These additional payments apply strictly to the principal.

4. *Full Prepayment Privilege.* This permits the borrower to repay the balance of the loan prior to the maturity date. The note should be checked, since some may be prepaid in as short a period as 91 days without any service charge. With other notes, the period may range between 3 to 5 years.

5. *Loan Modification Agreement.* This permits adjusting the terms of the original mortgage in accordance with a change in the borrower's financial status.

6. *Taxes and Insurance Provision.* This allows taxes and insurance to be paid over a 12 month period.

7. *Transfer Privilege.* This allows the property to be sold with only a nominal charge for service.

8. *Mortgage Redemption Insurance.* This assures the surviving family a debt-free home in event of the home owner's death. The small amount paid for mortgage insurance is wise protection for the family.

9. *Skip-a-payment Plan.* This grants the borrower the right, in case of emergency or financial hardship, to skip one monthly payment per year. The mortgage is extended, however, and the necessary interest is added to meet the increased length of time.

Second Mortgage

The more money that can be used for the down payment, the better chance a prospective home owner has of purchasing a more costly home. And the more money that is used for a down payment, the smaller the amount that needs to be borrowed. Consequently, less total interest will be paid over the life of the loan. The greater the *equity* (the value of the property minus liens and the unpaid balance), the greater the incentive a purchaser has to achieve full ownership. However, if the buyer does not have sufficient funds for the down payment, the seller may arrange for a *second mortgage.* The risk is great.

The second mortgage may be obtained through private or conventional sources for the difference between the prospective home owners fund and the largest available first mortgage. (The first mortgage may cover only 60 to 70 per cent of the purchase price.) With a second mortgage (as with the conventional, GI, or FHA loan) the buyer retains the legal title to the property.

Monthly Payments

Most loans will be repaid on a monthly basis over a period of years. The figures shown in Table 19-5 represent the monthly amount paid to retire the mortgage for each $1,000 borrowed. These figures represent *only* principal and interest. If, for example, a loan was assumed for $17,000 at 7¾% interest for 30 years, the monthly payment, exclusive of taxes and insurance, would be $7.17 × 17 = $121.89. A more complete financial picture can be obtained by adding $3.50 per month per $1,000 borrowed to account for insurance, taxes and upkeep for the home. In this instance, an additional $59.50 would be added to the $121.89, making the total $181.39 per month. Taxes vary between towns and suburban areas just as insurance rates vary; therefore, the figure of $3.50 per $1,000 borrowed may be high or low, depending on the area.

TABLE-19-5
MONTHLY PAYMENT NECESSARY TO AMORTIZE EACH
$1,000 BORROWED FOR HOME OWNERSHIP

INTEREST RATE	LENGTH OF LOAN IN YEARS				
	10	15	20	25	30
5.75%	10.98	8.31	7.03	6.30	5.84
6.0%	11.11	8.44	7.17	6.45	6.00
6.25%	11.23	8.58	7.31	6.60	6.16
6.5%	11.36	8.72	7.46	6.76	6.33
6.75%	11.49	8.85	7.61	6.91	6.49
7.0%	11.62	8.99	7.76	7.07	6.66
7.25%	11.75	9.13	7.91	7.23	6.83
7.5%	11.88	9.28	8.06	7.39	7.00
7.75%	12.01	9.42	8.21	7.56	7.17
8.0%	12.14	9.56	8.37	7.72	7.34
8.5%	12.40	9.85	8.68	8.06	7.69
9.0%	12.67	10.15	9.00	8.40	8.05

Home Cost Considerations

Interest

Various means exist by which the cost of a house may be reduced. For example, not all lending institutions charge the same amount of interest. The interest rates of the local savings and loan association, bank, insurance company, and Veterans Administration (GI Loan) may very well differ ½ per cent. Shop for a loan — borrow the money as cheaply as possible.

Long Term Mortgage—Extra Payments

A long term mortgage (20 to 30 years) may benefit the prospective buyer more than it may appear on the surface. With this type of mortgage, thousands of dollars may be saved by making extra or additional payments. These additional payments are deducted directly from the principal, without any portion being used for interest, taxes, insurance, or escrow fund. That portion of each payment devoted to interest, particularly on a long term loan, may be used as a deductible feature on income tax. This offers a distinct advantage. The long term loan also offers lower monthly rates. It is wise to inspect the loan agreement to be sure that extra payments can be made and are deducted from the principal.

Interest Rates and Loan Length

Table 19-6 draws an interesting comparison of varying interest rates for a loan of $13,000. For example, the monthly payment, based on 7½ per cent, for 20 years is $104.73. At the same interest rate for 30 years, the monthly payment is $90.90. Compare the difference, however, in the total amount paid in the 20 year term, $25,-135.20, with the total amount on the 30 year term, $32,724.00. The lender pays $7,-588.80 for the additional 10 years use of the unpaid balance. Contrary to popular opinion the difference of ½ per cent in the interest rate does not make an appreciable difference in the monthly payment; however, on loans over 20 years the difference in total payment is significant.

Owner Construction

If the prospective owner is a "do-it-yourself man," and if the contractor or builder will permit, some work may be contracted by the owner (such as painting, landscaping, laying tile, building terraces, patios, planting grass, etc.). This type of work is frequently referred to as "sweat equity." In some instances the prospective owner is not fully aware of the enormity of his responsibility when contracting to paint the entire house inside and outside, to grade and landscape the site, or to trim the inside. For some, these contracts resolve themselves into frustrating hours, weeks, and even months of lost time.

TABLE 19-6
A COMPARISON OF INTEREST RATES AND LOAN LENGTH BASED ON A LOAN OF $13,000

INTEREST RATE	PAYMENT	LENGTH OF LOAN IN YEARS			
		15	20	25	30
5.75%	Monthly	$107.96	$91.28	$81.79	$75.87
	Total	$19,432.80	$21,907.20	$24,537.00	$27,313.20
6%	Monthly	109.71	93.14	83.76	77.95
	Total	19,747.80	22,353.60	25,128.00	28,062.00
6.25%	Monthly	111.47	95.03	85.76	80.05
	Total	20,064.60	22,807.20	25,728.00	28,818.00
6.5%	Monthly	113.25	96.93	87.78	82.17
	Total	20,385.00	23,263.20	26,344.00	29,581.20
6.75%	Monthly	115.04	98.85	89.82	84.32
	Total	20,707.20	23,724.00	26,946.00	30,355.20
7%	Monthly	116.85	100.79	91.89	86.49
	Total	21,033.00	24,189.60	27,567.00	31,136.40
7.25%	Monthly	118.68	102.75	93.97	88.69
	Total	21,362.40	24,660.00	28,191.00	31,928.40
7.5%	Monthly	120.52	104.73	96.07	90.00
	Total	21,693.60	25,135.20	28,821.00	32,724.00
7.75%	Monthly	122.37	106.73	98.20	93.14
	Total	22,026.60	25,615.20	29,460.00	33,530.40
8%	Monthly	124.24	108.74	100.34	95.39
	Total	22,363.20	26,097.60	30,102.00	34,340.40
8.5%	Monthly	128.02	112.82	104.68	99.96
	Total	23,043.60	27,076.80	31,404.00	35,985.60
9%	Monthly	131.86	116.97	109.10	104.60
	Total	23,734.80	28,072.80	32,730.00	37,656.00

Building Economy

Frequently, if the lending institution or guaranteeing agency (FHA) will permit, substitutions may be made at a savings to the purchaser. Frequently, for example, vinyl tile may be substituted for hardwood flooring, dry wall (sheet rock) for plaster, or a lavatory for an extra full bath.

Elimination of fancy and costly details obviously result in savings. Proper perspective of the funds available will aid in planning. Plan so that details may be added after the initial financial burden has passed. For example, building the garage or finishing the basement or attic can be done at a later date.

Additional Costs

A word of caution is extended at this point. Do not exhaust all savings for the sake of the down payment. Some reserve funds should be set aside for emergency use. Additional cash will be needed for:

1. Closing costs (including appraisal fees and loan charges), fees for recording the mortgage or deed, legal fees, and/or fees for title insurance or evidence of clear title to the property.
2. Repairing, decorating, and modernizing in the case of an existing home; and landscaping for a new home.
3. Drapes and fixtures, or carpeting to make the home more livable.
4. Moving costs.
5. New appliances and furnishings that may be considered necessary in purchasing a home.

Transaction Closure

Services of a competent attorney should be secured in completing the purchase of the house to insure that all statements relative to the title, deed, loan, contracts, etc., are correct. In any event, the prospective owner should be familiar with certain essentials and the terms involved in the final transaction. The architect may be expected to act as a counselor in advising and assisting the client.

Once the house plans, lot, and contractor have been selected, or the house has been selected, the usual procedure is then to make a payment of approximately 1 per cent of the purchase price to the contractor or realtor. This payment is generally referred to as *earnest money* and indicates the buyer intends to purchase the property or to build the house.

Following this, the buyer files a formal mortgage loan application with the institution who will lend the money. This loan application requires rather detailed information concerning personal income, savings, debts, credit references, property appraisal, and the amount of money to be borrowed. The information given on this form will be carefully checked and evaluated by the lending institution.

If the lender is satisfied with the qualifications of the prospective borrower and the property is a good risk, he will give the loan. The borrower then receives notification verifying the acceptance of the loan application. The terms of the mortgage will be drawn and a date set for "closing the transaction." At this date the buyer, seller (or his agent), representative of the mortgage lender, and the attorneys involved will be present.

At the loan closing the buyer presents the lender with an amount of money equal to the down payment, *plus* closing costs and *less* the earnest money previously paid. The seller will then present the deed to the property with evidence of clear title to the buyer. The seller then receives a check (from the mortgagee) for the balance of the sale price (less the seller's expenses). (The seller's expenses include: cost of abstracting, drafting of deed, payment of existing lien balances and assessments, real estate sales commission, and his share of pro-rated taxes for the current year.) The buyer then signs the mortgage.

Real Estate and Mortgage Terminology

The following lists some general terms encountered in home financing.

Real Estate

1. *Deed* is the legal instrument that transfers the title of property from one person to another.

   a. *Warranty Deed* is a guarantee by the seller that the title is flawless.

   b. *Quit Claim Deed* guarantees nothing—it merely undertakes to transfer the title. The deed has (or presumes to have) properly described the property.

2. *Title* is that which gives the right of ownership.
3. *Appraisal* is an evaluation of property in order to determine its value.
4. *Abstract* is the legal description of the property and history of previous ownerships.
5. *Certificate of Title* is the assurance that the title to the property is unmistakably in the purchaser's name.
6. *Title Search* is an investigation conducted to see that the ownership of house is free of liens.
7. *Title Insurance* insures against any defects that may exist in the title prior to the time the title is passed. These defects may come to light at a future transaction.
8. *Earnest Money* is a deposit given by a prospective buyer to the seller as evidence he is in earnest about buying the property.
9. *Purchase Agreement* contains all essential terms and conditions of the sale, and the memorandum of agreement between seller and purchaser. This is executed pending examination of the title and performance of other conditions affecting the transfer of property.
10. *Recording* of deeds with the registrar (for the county in which land is located) is the best insurance against loss of agreements affecting transfer of ownership.
11. *Escrow* is money and papers held by a third party until the conditions in the contract are fulfilled.
12. *Equity* is the increasing portion of the house the buyer owns as the mortgage is paid off.
13. *Depreciation* is the decline in value of a house from wear and age.

Mortgage

1. *Mortgage* is the pledge of property (in the case of housing) as security for payment of a debt.
2. *Straight Mortgage* comes due all at once at a specific date (that is both the interest and the principal).
3. *Amortized Mortgage* is a systematic loan reduction plan. Monthly payments are made that retire the mortgage. These payments include interest, payment on principal, taxes, assessments, and insurance premiums.
4. *Second Mortgage* is made on property where a first mortgage already exists. The risks are greater and interest rates are higher. In the case of foreclosure, the holder of the second mortgage cannot collect until the first mortgage holder has been satisfied.
5. *Mortgagee* is the one who gives the mortgage or the lender who puts up the money for the mortgage.
6. *Mortgagor* is the home buyer who has signed the mortgage. He makes out the mortgage to the mortgagee (the lender uses the mortgage as security).
7. *Lien* is in effect a mortgage. A lien may be filed by anyone who has a claim for labor or material costs against the property.
8. *Note or Bond* is a written promise to repay the money borrowed.
9. *Interest* is the *rent* paid for money borrowed.
10. *Closing Costs* are paid by the buyer as a fee charged by the lenders for making the mortgage.
11. *On Schedule* refers to payments which fall periodically on a set date.
12. *Foreclosure:* After a certain number of mortgage defaults, the mortgagee, under the terms of the contract has the right to sell the property in public auction to regain his investment.

Questions and Problems

1. Assume that the average cost for building an "L" ranch house in your area is $14.75 per sq. ft. Using the square footage method, what would be the rough estimate for the house shown in Fig. 19-2? Do not include the square footage of the garage or the lanai (exclusive of storage space). Measure from outside walls (walls are 8″ thick).
2. Using the same plan (Fig. 19-2), estimate the rough cost using the cubic footage method. Assume $1.80 per

cubic foot. Use one-half volume for the lanai and the garage.

3. A prospective home owner is able to finance a house costing $20,000. He wishes to buy an "L" ranch house. At $1.20 per cu. ft., what is the total volume he can afford? How does this knowledge aid the plan designer? How does this aid the buyer in selecting a house?

4. A prospective home owner has $3,500 for a down payment on a piece of property. This represents 25% of the purchase price. He can obtain a 6% loan over a 20 year period. How much of his income should be set aside each month to take care of housing? What is the value of the property he will own?

5. How much could be afforded for a house if the prospective buyer earned $7,000 per year, had 2 children, and had exceptional medical expenses?

6. How much could be saved on a $14,-000 loan at 5½ % interest for 15 years as compared to the same amount for 25 years?

7. A prospective owner wants to buy a piece of property for $16,000. He has $4,000 for a down payment and will borrow the rest for 15 years at 6% interest. How much must he pay per year to cover the cost of ownership? Insurance, taxes, and upkeep must be included.

8. A prospective home buyer earns $450 monthly. How much can he afford to borrow on a 6%, 20-year loan? He has $3,000 for a down payment. What would be the total home expenditure?

Light Commercial Buildings 20

There are two basic differences between light commercial and residential buildings. First, the commercial structure is planned for investment purposes. Second, the commercial plan must be concerned with the flow of materials and goods, as well as personnel. Coupled with these two main differences are numerous other features which play an important role in arriving at a workable, attractive plan. No single chapter could completely cover all of the aspects of light commercial architecture. This chapter is presented as a basis for planning and as a springboard into the multi-faceted commercial field.

Commercial Classifications and Activities

Business may be grouped together into three general classifications: *servicing, merchandising,* and *manufacturing.* A partial list representative of each group is given below. Light commercial architecture also falls into these three general groups.

1. *Servicing:* Repair, laundry, dry cleaning, insurance, brokerage, medical, dental, bookkeeping, barber, beauty, motel, gas station, branch bank, appliances, general office, garage, travel agency, etc.
2. *Merchandising:* hobby, toy, florist, dry goods, men's wear, women's wear, grocery, hardware, variety, drug, bakery, home furnishings, auto sales, res-

taurant, shoe, sporting goods, recreational vehicles, luggage, etc.
3. *Manufacturing:* sheet metal, machine shop, tent and awning, tailor, plastics, mill work, print shop, etc.

It is evident that some businesses fit poorly into any one category, or fit into more than one category. However, there are certain *activities* which are common to all types of light commercial architecture. Depending upon the building and its intended use, areas must be planned for these activities. However, not all of these may be common to any one building. The outline below gives the major activities that must be considered in planning.

1. Merchandising
   a. Sales
   b. Display
   c. Customer reception

2. Material Goods Handling
   a. Receiving
   b. Routing
   c. Storage
   d. Shipping
3. Work Areas
   a. Design/engineering
   b. Process/computer
   c. Preparation for manufacture
   d. Manufacture
   e. Fabrication
   f. Check out area
   g. Clerical
   h. Service
4. Refreshment and Sanitation Rest
   a. Customer
   b. Employees
5. Maintenance and Power

Planning Points

Using the common business activities outlined above, a series of planning points may be derived for light commercial structures.

Material Flow. All businesses must have provision for an orderly flow of materials from the *receiving dock or facility, to storage and/or dispersing area.* The flow of materials should be planned so it will not interfere with other activities of the building.

Consideration must be given to the amount and kinds of material received and the frequency of delivery. Provision must also be made for convenient and adequate storage, and for aisleways for material flow and personnel circulation. Fig. 20-1 illus-

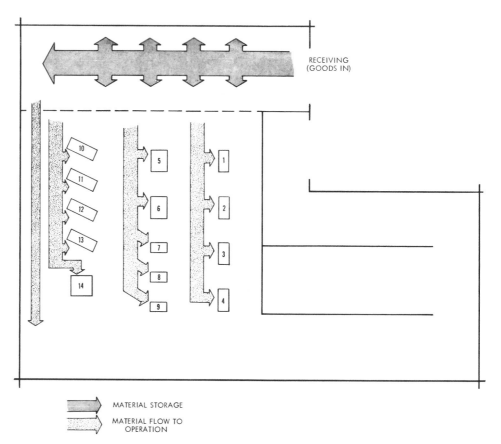

Fig. 20-1. Material Flow in a Commercial Structure.

trates typical material flow in a commercial structure.

Merchandising. Space must be set aside for *display, sales,* and *stock storage.* The type of business will determine the space devoted to merchandising. Obviously an apparel store or small super market would require much more display area than that of a light manufacturing concern. The type of merchandise offered for sale, the importance of the display location, and the area allotted for customer circulation, will frequently dictate the arrangement of the merchandising area. In the selling area, the merchandise should be separated according to the needs of the customers. For example:

1. Staple articles—those items which the customer intends to purchase.
2. Convenience articles — those goods which the "looking customer" may purchase, and which may lead to other purchases.

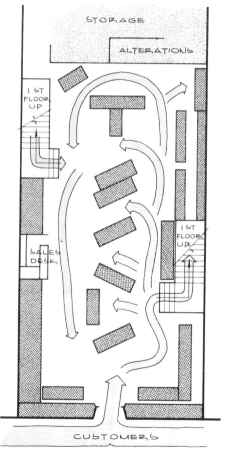

STORAGE

ALTERATIONS

1 ST FLOOR UP

SALES DESK

1 ST FLOOR UP

CUSTOMERS

Fig. 20-2. Customer Circulation in a Men's Haberdashery.

3. Luxury and "impulse buying" goods —those articles that are high profit but not necessarily high priced. These items have eye appeal that may draw customers.

Often, luxury items are placed to attract the customer's attention and to guide him to areas where he may make a purchase. Fig. 20-2 shows a customer flow pattern for a men's haberdashery. The customer flow of traffic is generally to the right and all service features should be related to this. Most businesses are designed to handle many customers. Ample space, therefore, should be provided to permit traffic flow.

Servicing. Servicing may take many forms. Depending upon the type of service offered, considerations must be given to waiting areas, eating areas, lounge areas, etc. If the business offers repair and adjustment, adequate space must be allocated for this work area. Space requirements for the necessary service equipment must be analyzed to allow for adequate movement of goods and personnel.

Manufacturing. If light manufacturing is planned, a *flow diagram* of the steps of manufacture or fabrication should be drawn. This aids in the identification of necessary work stations and personnel areas. See Fig. 20-3. (Compare this figure to the material flow in Fig. 20-1.) It may be wise to bring in consulting groups.

After the production flow has been outlined, equipment requirements (amount, size, weight, etc.) must be checked so the structure will carry the imposed live and dead loads. In addition, space must be allocated for packaging, storage, and shipping of the finished product.

Office Space. Virtually every commercial structure includes some type of provision for business transactions, conferences, etc. These areas should be away from the noise and distractions of the business itself. Many buildings include one or more offices that will provide the necessary privacy.

In some instances commercial structures are planned with a second floor or with a portion of the main level as rental office space. Frequently, contractors or developers will plan an entire building based on leased office space. Whether one portion or the entire structure is devoted to offices, the following items should be considered: (1) *reception area* (2) *waiting and display area,* (3) *main offices* (if a suite of offices is planned), (4) *subsidiary offices,* (5) *work areas for personnel,* (6) *restrooms,* (7) *custodian / janitor facility,* (8) *refreshment / snack area,* and (9) *storage facilities.* The designers must consider sound proofing and office acoustics, as well as artificial and natural lighting.

Flexibility. The interior should be planned for flexibility. This is usually accomplished by designing on a modular basis and using movable, non-load-bearing interior partition walls. Commercial buildings constructed in this flexible manner give the owner a wider possibility of meeting the potential needs of the lessee. Small businesses must consider flexibility and expansion as the business grows. The question must be

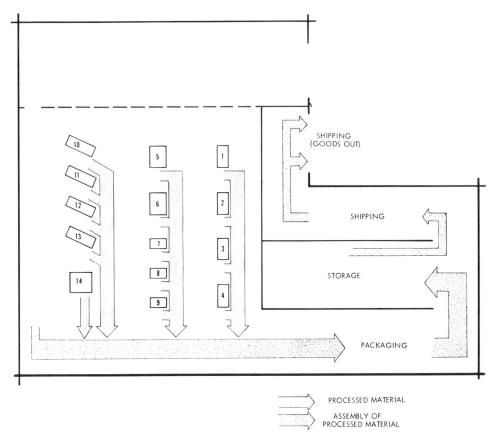

SHIPPING
(GOODS OUT)

SHIPPING

STORAGE

PACKAGING

PROCESSED MATERIAL

ASSEMBLY OF
PROCESSED MATERIAL

Fig. 20-3. Manufacturing Flow Diagram.

shops. Remember: the amount of usable floor space is an important factor in any plan (generally about 70 per cent of the gross floor area). Approximately 17 per cent of the gross area is given to stairs, elevators, toilet facilities, rest areas, shafts, etc.

With the increased use of prestressed and precast structural concrete forms, greater spans are possible than ever before. Roof trusses of steel and laminated wood beams offer a wide range of design possibilities. Manufacturers of these trusses or beams will supply technical data, and will custom manufacture their product to fit the particular design and specifications.

Ceiling Heights. All store, shop, and office ceiling heights are specified by local building codes. These should be checked before any design is begun.

Table 20-1 gives recommended light commercial store heights.

Elevators. Frequently, rental accommo-

asked "How could this plan be expanded at a later date with the least expense and disruption."

Floor Space. To be most useful, floors should be as free as possible from supporting columns. This permits greater traffic movement and utilization of space. Columns should not be spaced less than 13 ft. center

to center. If a series of stores are to be built side by side, a module for column spacing is selected based on the number of stores or shops planned. The span module selected should permit flexibility so that the stores may be enlarged or reduced as business may dictate. Once again—movable, acoustically sound partitions may be used to divide the

TABLE 20-1

RECOMMENDED FLOOR HEIGHTS FOR
LIGHT COMMERCIAL STRUCTURES

FLOOR	HEIGHT
BASEMENT	8'-0" MINIMUM
FIRST FLOOR (NO MEZZANINE)	12'-0" MINIMUM
FIRST FLOOR TO MEZZANINE	8'-0" MINIMUM
MEZZANINE TO CEILING	8'-0" MINIMUM
SECOND FLOOR	12'-0" MINIMUM

dations may be on the second floor. In this case, the builder may consider installing an elevator. In comparison to its use, the cost of an elevator for most small buildings is prohibitive. If a structure rises above two levels, and if the estimated probable traffic would be sufficient, it may be a wise investment. However, most light commercial structures do not have more than three floors. A stairway offers the most economical solution to the problem.

Entryway and Lobby. The design of an entryway and lobby will have a definite effect on the rentability of the building. The lobby and stair area should give the feeling of openness and freedom so the customer is invited to walk up to the second floor. If this is not provided, the second floor area will be difficult to rent. The lobby and stairway shown in Fig. 20-4 is an example of good design and planning. The success of a building is dependent upon the appeal it has for the customers, tenants, and employees.

Store or Office Front. Attractive fronts and display windows are means of inducing customers to enter the structure. Display windows may be opened to show the interior of the shop or closed to give the customer privacy. Location of the door and the flow of pedestrian traffic may determine the interior plan. Some means of advertising or displaying the firm's name is important in many businesses.

Site. Commercial lot frontage may be small. This will present orientation problems—particularly with regard to the glare and heat from the sun. If a northern or

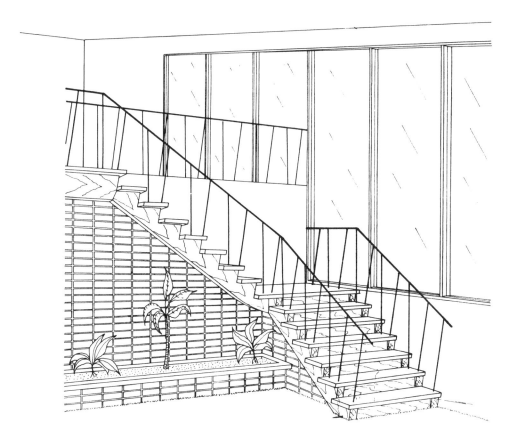

Fig. 20-4. An attractive lobby and stairway invites the customer to walk up to the second floor.

eastern exposure is impossible, double glazing, heat-resistant glass, gray or bronze tinted glass, screens, draperies, or louvered awnings must be included in the design to provide as much comfort as possible. Access must also be provided for delivery and shipment of goods without causing traffic congestion.

Parking. Communities (through zoning or code restrictions) will require a given amount of parking space per square foot of office or business space. Parking space must be provided for employees and customers. Where land values are high, the cost of parking space is increased greatly. The solution is to provide some parking facilities *in* or *under* the building. This results in pushing the building upward. Where land values are low, the shape of the building will tend to be horizontal. In this case, off-street parking should be considered.

With the increased number of cars, lack of parking spaces has spelled doom in the central city core for many small shops and office buildings. The trend is now towards decentralization away from the downtown area.

Location. As communities grow, the local businessman is faced with expansion and/or relocation. Frequently it becomes necessary to build on another location in a newly developing area of the community. Forward-looking cities have surveys conducted by professional consulting firms to determine in which direction and to what extent the community can be expected to grow in the future. The small businessman must evaluate the community's growth prior to making a large property and building investment. All property should be investigated for zoning restrictions and the future possibilities of zone changes. A light commercial establishment in a heavy industrial zone is not usually a profitable venture. For example, a millinery shop located near heavy steel industries has a poor prospect of success.

Climatic Conditioning. Air conditioning has become an accepted fact for commercial establishments. A lack of this feature may hamper the rental or sale of the property. Humidity, heat, and dust present problems for various types of products. Air conditioning, in part, can aid the control of these problems.

Planning Procedure

Prior to the preliminary layout of any light commercial structure, some basic research must be carried out on the type of business and the building in question. The extent of the research will be reflected in the final plan. Many sources are available upon which the designer may draw prior to planning.

Architectural Magazines. Architectural and building magazines periodically devote entire issues to commercial architecture. The building magazines are frequently concerned with light commercial and low rise buildings. Be sure to read the advertisements for new and existing products and materials.

Architectural Planning Books. Many fine architectural books are available that are concerned with: planning problems, construction data, examples of new construction techniques, design of specific types of construction, etc. A wealth of information awaits the reader. Investigation of books and magazines frequently leads the designer to new solutions to problems—not by copying, but by an amalgamation of ideas.

Profession or Trade Journals. Magazines or journals of a particular type of business frequently publish new material and ideas that will help the designer in producing the most efficient plan.

Financial Papers and Journals. Financial papers and journals should not be overlooked since the trends of many businesses are reported. Many feature articles on merchandizing products, consumer trends, buying habits, manufacture, etc., are published and may be of definite value to the designer.

Similar Businesses. An analysis of competing businesses, from the standpoint of layout and design, will affect the plan. This is usually carried out by observation.

Consulting Firms. Frequently the client, upon the recommendation of the designer, will bring in a consulting firm to analyze the existing business procedure. The firm's recommendations may result in a more efficient organization of the business or manufacturing procedures. This new organization will be reflected in the design of the building.

Market Analysis. Investigation into the needs, habits, and buying potential of the public in the field which the structure will serve is a must for a successful business. The designer must also determine if any changes in traffic flow are anticipated in the proximity of the proposed building site. A factor not to be overlooked is an analysis of the customer's buying habits—particularly the amount and kind of purchases.

Clients. The designer must, of course, consult with the client as to his needs and desires in the building. It is important to determine what type of products and/or services he wishes to offer his customers. Frequently the designer must diplomatically

Fig. 20-5. Tapes aid in laying out material flow in material handling.

unearth through conferences with his client, what strengths and weaknesses exist in the present business. This will allow the designer to anticipate building needs.

Once the basic concept of the building has been established, each area within the complex can be planned in depth. Meetings between the architect and client will firmly establish space requirements for processing, equipment, work stations, etc. As a part of the planning procedure for

space allocations, printed adhesive-backed tapes are frequently used to assist both the architect and client to achieve better visualization of material flow, assembly, packaging, etc. Fig. 20-5 illustrates a plan being developed for an area with tape.

Foundations

Before the foundation plan is drawn and even before a building site is purchased, an

investigation must be conducted on the bearing power of the soil. This investigation most likely will be a series of *soil borings* that will identify the nature of the underlying layers of soil composition. These soil borings, by inspecting and testing the samples, will show the load-bearing capacity of the soil and the depth of the water table. Soil borings are made by drilling into the soil with carbon steel bits attached to a drill rod to specified depths. These bits are then replaced by a sampling device forced into the bottom of the hole. The site plan, that is a part of the set of drawings, shows the locations of the soil borings. Each test site on the site plan is coded and one of the sheets within the set of drawings will show the composition and depth of each sample.

The size of the footing is dependent upon the depth of the footing and the soil bearing capacity of that stratum. Three basic types of foundations are used to carry loads imposed by the building. The three types of foundations (see Fig. 20-6) used in commercial construction are:

1. *Spread Foundations:* The imposed load is distributed over a wide area. A spread foundation may consist of an individual footing under a wall or column. Another type of spread foundation is the reinforced slab sometimes called a floating foundation. The reinforced slab distributes the load over the entire building or basement area.

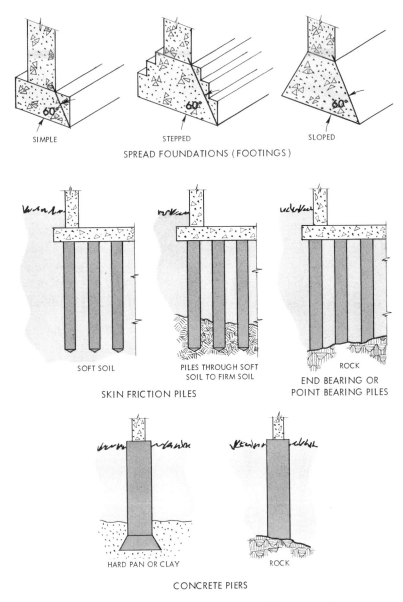

SIMPLE

STEPPED

SLOPED

SPREAD FOUNDATIONS (FOOTINGS)

SOFT SOIL

PILES THROUGH SOFT
SOIL TO FIRM SOIL

ROCK

END BEARING OR
POINT BEARING PILES

SKIN FRICTION PILES

HARD PAN OR CLAY

ROCK

CONCRETE PIERS

Fig. 20-6. Three methods of supporting foundations for commercial structures.

2. *Pile Foundations:* A pile is a thin column of steel, concrete, or timber that is driven into the ground. Pile foundations may be individual or a series of piles capped with a concrete *mat* or *raft* that will support a footing for a column or structural ends of a grade beam.

3. *Pier Foundations:* These are hollow and usually a single type of foundation element that rests on high load-bearing stratum of earth.

Due to the great loads imposed by commercial buildings, the upper strata of soil are not capable of carrying these loads. The basic reason why these upper levels of soil are unable to carry the loads is because of the shrinkage that occurs through decaying organic matter and through settling due to vibration. In sizable commercial structures perhaps the most common method of providing adequate support is by means of piling.

Since sub-strata vary, two different classifications of piles are used. See Fig. 20-6. When a pile is driven through poor load-bearing capacity soil to reach a solid stratum it is called a *point bearing* or *end bearing* pile. The second classification of pile is called a *skin friction* pile. These are used where no solid stratum is reached as the pile is driven. Skin friction piles are driven sufficiently deep so that the force required to drive the pile deeper is greater than the total load imposed by the construction. Piles may be steel taper, uniform taper, wood taper, and concrete. The choice of pilings or the construction will vary due to the type of soil.

Exterior Walls and Joining Panels

Curtain Walls

The term *curtain wall* is, as its name implies, a "curtain" or "covering". More specifically, it is a non-load-bearing shield or screen that encloses a previously erected superstructure. It provides a thermal, ac-

oustic, and protective covering from the weather. Panels that are used in curtain walls may be made from numerous materials; the most common materials are steel, aluminum, and cement asbestos concrete. Additionally, panels may be fabricated from stainless steel, bronze, plastic, glass, and pre-cast concrete.

Curtain wall construction has the advantage of being easily and quickly erected, light in weight and of possessing outstanding insulation qualities. Because of its lightweight characteristic, most curtain wall panels reduce the dead load on the superstructure members and can some-

times result in lighter structural members. The principle of curtain wall construction is applicable to one and two-story buildings as well as multi-storied office buildings. Fig. 20-7 shows a sequence of steps for erecting a curtain wall for a two-story building.

Curtain wall panels can be divided into three general classifications: (1) Stressed Skin Panels, (2) Framed Panels, and (3) Single Sheet Panels. *Stressed skin* panels are a sandwich of two surface sheets laminated to a core material. The *framed panel* has two metal surface sheets enclosed along the edges by a frame with glass fiber or mineral

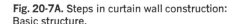

Fig. 20-7A. Steps in curtain wall construction: Basic structure.

MOBAY CHEMICAL COMPANY, PITTSBURGH, PENNSYLVANIA.

Fig. 20-7B. Steps in curtain wall construction: Steel work and masonry completed.

wool insulation between the sheets. *Single sheet* panels may be formed by mechanical means to produce an embossed design on the surface and/or they may have a rigid core backing. As the name implies, one-metal skin is used as the facing sheet.

Windows are an important element in curtain wall construction. Their inclusion in a wall unit must be considered in the over-all analysis of stresses which are created in the building *and* wall system. Manufacturers of curtain walls will recommend the use of certain types of window units.

Curtain Wall Components. With the exception of the single sheet panel without a backing skin, all panels are generally sandwich construction—an exterior covering over a core of insulative material and an interior finish skin. The exterior skin is made of anodized aluminum, porcelain-enamel on steel or aluminum, stainless steel or heat-strengthened colored glass. Porcelain-enamel, colored glass and stainless steel panels are impervious to chemicals carried in the air that would ordinarily affect any other materials. In addition, these panels are available in a variety of colors and allow the architect a wide latitude of expression. Many panels that use exterior metal covering such as aluminum or stainless steel are 3-dimensionally pat-

MOBAY CHEMICAL COMPANY, PITTSBURGH, PENNSYLVANIA.

Fig. 20-7C. Steps in curtain wall construction: Pre-cut columnar supports for panels and windows are positioned.

MOBAY CHEMICAL COMPANY, PITTSBURGH, PENNSYLVANIA.

Fig. 20-7D. Steps in curtain wall construction: Panels are installed.

terned to eliminate a wavy appearance that is unavoidable in a flat-plane sheet.

The core between the two skins must have some insulative value. Many manufactured panels use a rigid urethane foam core because it is self-bonding to the skins, fire retardant, and has the lowest rate of heat transmission of any insulating material. The panel can have a core of foam concrete, mineral wool, glass wool, or cardboard honeycomb. Regardless of the core material, some type of vapor barrier must be added to prevent transmission of moisture through the panel. The vapor barrier is placed on the warm side of the panel.

Fig. 20-7E. Steps in curtain wall construction: Panels are caulked to provide a weather seal at joints.

Fig. 20-7F. Steps in curtain wall construction: Window frames are positioned.

and panels, due to temperature and mullion movement, require that the joints in the curtain wall accommodate these changes. If the joints were tight, panel units would buckle, thereby permitting no movement. Therefore all members are designed to take this movement into account.

Though some "play" is provided between panels and mullions in the curtain wall unit, each is sealed by means of a neoprene or PVC (polyvinyl chloride) gasket, caulking, or elastomer composition material. Elastomer compositions have gained wide usage in the construction industry because of their excellent weathering and high adhesion qualities, while allowing the required degree of elasticity for movement of component parts.

MOBAY CHEMICAL COMPANY, PITTSBURGH, PENNSYLVANIA.

Fig. 20-7G. Steps in curtain wall construction: The finished building.

Panels with a skin of steel, cement, or asbestos are highly fire resistant to meet building code requirements. These latter two materials are an ideal interior finish base material in addition to being fireproof. The interior finish on the panel may be supplied by the manufacturer or applied at the building site.

Windows can be either separate units installed into the curtain wall or they may be integral parts of the panel. Mullions separating the windows and panels may be classed as either *structural* or *visual*. Structural mullions add strength and stiffness in resisting wind loads against the component panels in the system. Visual mullions have *no* structural value; their only purpose is for architectural affect.

Joining Panels. Regardless of the curtain wall panel size, some means must be made for an effective, structurally sound joint. Expansion and contraction of the mullions

Joists

Web Steel Joist

Open-web steel joists were initially developed to provide economical, rigid, fire resistant, and durable support members for floor and roof. Fig. 20-8 shows four typical applications of steel joist construction. Wood strips can be firmly attached to the top chord of the joist to provide a secure nailing ground for wood subfloors and finish floors.

Steel or wood may be used as roof decking over open-web joists. This decking is then topped with built-up roofing. Metal lath can be attached to the bottom chord

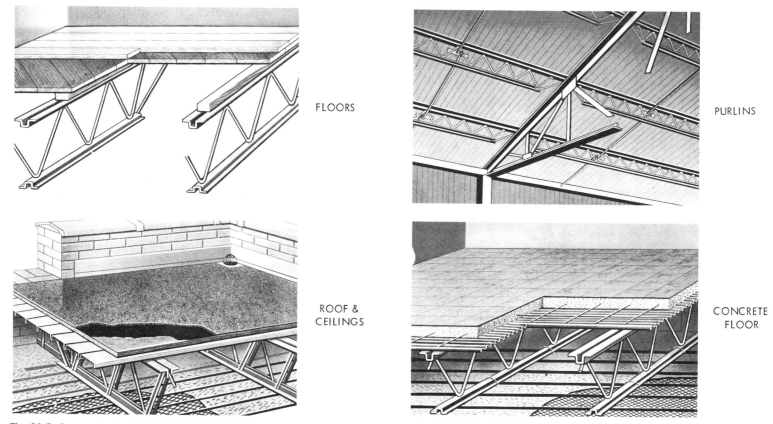

FLOORS

PURLINS

ROOF & CEILINGS

CONCRETE FLOOR

Fig. 20-8. Open web steel joists are adaptable for floors, roofs, and ceilings.

of the joist for plaster. Steel joists may also be used as purlins (horizontal members connecting each roof truss) for garages, hangars, or warehouses where large, clear spans are necessary. Open-web steel joists may also be used to support a concrete floor.

All open web joists are manufactured to standard sizes of depth, clear span and load-carrying capacities as specified by the Steel Joist Institute. These joists are simply trusses with webs welded to the chords, and supported at both ends. Joists that are designed to carry light loads are made completely of bars. Joists supporting intermediate loads are fabricated of angles and bars. Joists that are designed to carry heavy loads may be fabricated from T and angle structural shapes. The T shapes are used to form the top and bottom chords and the angles are used for the webs.

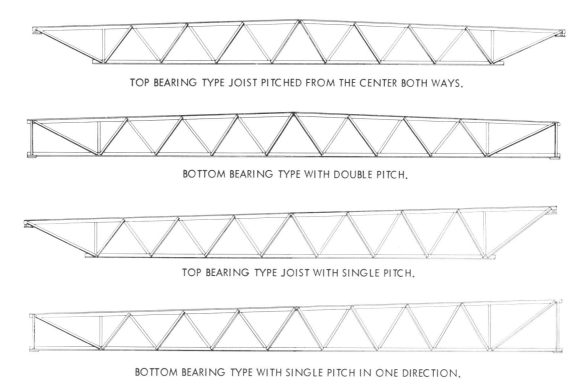

TOP BEARING TYPE JOIST PITCHED FROM THE CENTER BOTH WAYS.

BOTTOM BEARING TYPE WITH DOUBLE PITCH.

TOP BEARING TYPE JOIST WITH SINGLE PITCH.

BOTTOM BEARING TYPE WITH SINGLE PITCH IN ONE DIRECTION.

ARMCO STEEL CORPORATION, KANSAS CITY, MISSOURI

Fig. 20-9. Open web steel joists may bear on the top or bottom chord and be pitched ⅛″ in 1′-0″.

When an open web joist is to be used to support a roof, the slope of the top chord may be pitched from the center in both directions or with a single pitch in one direction. The amount of pitch is standardized at ⅛″ per foot. Depending upon the design conditions, joists are available that bear on the top (top bearing) or bottom (bottom bearing) chord. Fig. 20-9 shows how an open-web joist may be sloped and the position of the bearing plate.

Joists may be anchored to the structural member by several methods. See Fig. 20-10. If the joist bears on masonry units every third joist should be anchored with a joist wall anchor imbedded in the masonry. Joists bearing on structural steel may be welded with a 1″ weld on each side of the bearing plate or bolted with a bolt on each side of the bearing plate. Where a ceiling is to be suspended from the joists a 1″ diameter bar is welded to each end of the bottom chord.

Joist depths increase by 2″ increments from 8″ to 24″ and by 4″ increments from 24″ to 48″. A catalog of open web steel joists will show some overlapping in load-bearing capacities of joists. The load each

CEILING EXTENSION

When a ceiling is to be suspended from the bottom chord of an Armco Steel Joist, a 1"-diameter bar, as shown, can be supplied loose to be attached by others.

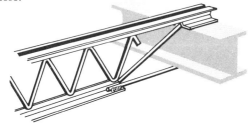

JOIST WALL ANCHOR

Steel joists require 6" bearing on masonry walls, and each end of every *third* joist in floors and *every* joist in roofs should be anchored with a joist wall anchor firmly embedded in the masonry.

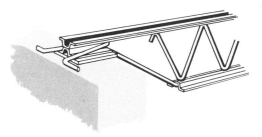

BOLTED END ANCHORAGE

If bolted connections between joists and supports are required, the bearing section of the joist is punched with slotted holes for ¹/₂" bolts. The distance between supports from center to center of slotted anchor holes must be specified. Shown below are bearing section dimensions for joists with 3¹/₂" bearing depths. For 4" and 5" bearing depths, the slotted holes are 6¹/₂" c/c.

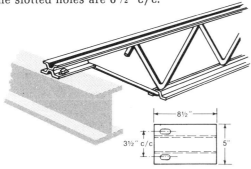

WELDED END ANCHORAGE

Armco Steel Joists bearing on structural steel may be anchored by placing a 1" long weld on each side of the bearing section. Minimum bearing on the structural steel: 4".

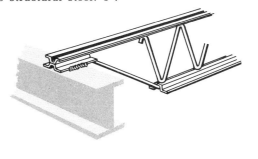

ARMCO STEEL CORPORATION, KANSAS CITY, MISSOURI

Fig. 20-10. Joists may be fastened to structural members by various methods. When a ceiling is to be suspended from joists a bar is welded to the bottom chord.

carries will depend upon the depth, weight of the component chords and webs, and the on-center space of the joists.

Joists are available in four series identified by the letters L, J, H, and LH. The L series clear spans from 25' to 96' and the J series spans from 4' to 48'. When high-strength steel is used for component chords and webs of the joist, the L series is called LH and the J series becomes the H series. Thus the same size J series joist will carry a greater load when fabricated of high-strength steel. The top chord of the J or H series joists may be cantilevered (extended) a maximum of 5'-6" beyond the bearing plate.

Doors and Windows

Door Types

Hollow metal, tubular metal and wood doors used in commercial building have a core of solid wood, asbestos fibers, or insulating material. These doors may be paneled or flush and with or without a light or lights. Special types of metal doors are used for access to plumbing or pipe runs, garages, hatchways, elevators, X-ray or radiation shielding, toilet stalls, etc.

Fire codes specify that metal doors must be used as fire stops at stairwells, between wings of buildings, or separating areas where flammable materials are stored. Fire stop doors are referred to as "label doors" because of the *label* affixed to the door—in-dicating this type of door was tested by the Fire Underwriters Laboratory Inc. The fire rating is determined by the amount and duration of heat it will withstand before collapsing. Lights placed in label doors must be wire glass to prevent breaking and the ultimate spread of flames.

Tubular steel doors have a metal channel edging around a sheet of heavy glass. Wood doors are used on closets, rooms, etc., where a fire-rated door is not necessary. Generally all wood doors are flush panel with either solid or hollow cores.

Door Swing and Traffic

Local building and state fire codes specify the swing of doors in public buildings (schools, hospitals, nursing homes, municipal buildings, etc.) Doors must open outward, i.e., in the direction of safety into a direct lane of occupant circulation. If the reverse of this rule were in effect, the door would not open in the direction of people escaping and would jeopardize human life in a rapid exit from a building.

In many public buildings doors are normally recessed from the corridor to eliminate the possibility of injury to people moving along the hall when a door is opened rapidly. Fig. 20-11 illustrates a door recessed from the corridor.

As mentioned earlier in Chapter 5, door swings should be planned to provide a maximum amount of privacy. In locker, dressing, wash, and toilet rooms that are entered from a corridor, the door should be hinged to

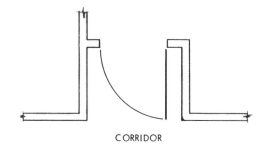

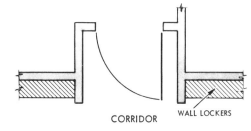

Fig. 20-11. In public buildings doors are recessed from the corridor.

block the line of sight from the hall into the room.

In some plans no alternative exists, wherein two doors must be placed so their swings conflict. If one of the doors cannot be moved, then hinge one door (A) so it will push the other door (B) closed when door (A) is opened. If two doors are hinged on the same side, their swings will obviously conflict, causing one door to block the other if it is partially opened. Fig. 20-12 illustrates doors placed on two adjacent walls.

Right and Left-Hand Hinged Doors

The designer must be able to identify the

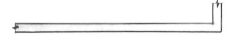

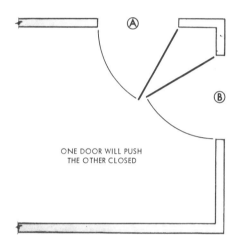

ONE DOOR WILL PUSH
THE OTHER CLOSED

Fig. 20-12. If doors must be placed in adjacent walls so their swings conflict, arrange the doors so one will push the other closed.

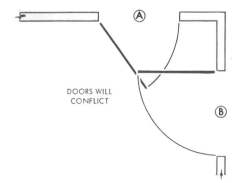

DOORS WILL
CONFLICT

"hand" and swing of a door. This seemingly minor detail is imperative in checking hardware bids for locksets and prepackaged doors, as well as in communication with the construction supervisor regarding installation problems. Fig. 20-13 shows how doors may be hinged and their correct classification. The following guidelines will be of assistance in determining the "hand" of a door:

1. Always stand on the outside of the door.
   a. Outside of an entrance door is the *street side*.
   b. Outside of a room door is the *hall side*.
   c. Outside of a door between two rooms is the side from which the

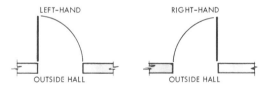

LEFT-HAND   RIGHT-HAND

OUTSIDE HALL   OUTSIDE HALL

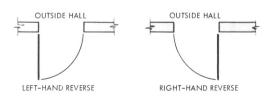

OUTSIDE HALL   OUTSIDE HALL

LEFT-HAND REVERSE   RIGHT-HAND REVERSE

Fig. 20-13. Types of hinged doors.

hinges *are not visible* when the door is closed.

d. Outside of a closet door is the *room side*.

e. Outside of a door is the key side of a lockset. (This is used when a door does not fall in any of the above categories.)

2. From the outside observe on which side the hinge is located.

a. *Right hand swing* is when the hinge is on the right side and is *not visible* from the outside when the door is closed.

b. *Right hand swing reverse* is when the hinge is on the right side and is *visible* from the outside when the door is closed.

c. *Left hand swing* is when the hinge is on the left side and is *not visible* from the outside when the door is closed.

d. *Left hand swing reverse* is when the hinge is on the left side and is visible from the outside when the door is closed.

Door Location

The main consideration in locating a door is its *convenience* in relation to the function of the room and its occupants. Two rooms of identical size, though with different functions, may have the door located in the same position; however, one door may be in a more convenient location because of equip-ment, casework, and the activities which will take place in the room.

In rooms that have walls equipped with shelving, such as a storage room, kitchen, laboratory, etc., the door is preferably positioned in the center of the wall rather than in a corner. A door located in the corner and swinging toward the adjacent wall will take up twice as much useable wall storage space as its width. If a door is to be located adjacent to a column or in a corner, adequate allowances must be made for lintel support. Allow 8″ adjacent to the jamb in a masonry wall and 4″ in frame wall construction for lintel support.

Door Frames

Hollow metal door frames that are specified by architects are usually one of the two styles illustrated in Figs. 20-14 and 20-15. Other types of hollow metal frames are produced, but the majority are like those illustrated. Metal door frames fabricated from 14 ga. or 16 ga. steel, are used for wood, glass, and metal doors. Metal wall ties or frame anchors are used to hold the frame in a masonry wall. Three ties are spaced along each jamb section of the frame and imbedded in the mortar between courses of brick or block. Fig. 20-16 shows a typical detail drawing of a section thru a hollow metal frame jamb.

For reasons of economy, most frames are shipped to the construction site pre-assembled. Some frames are delivered "knocked down." These, of course, must be assembled at the site and then installed. Metal frames may be 3⅔″, 4¼″, 5½″ or 6⅔″ wide as determined by the wall thickness.

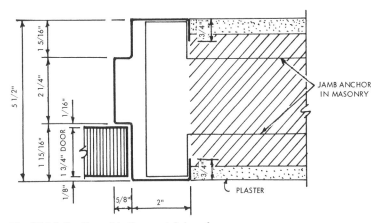

Fig. 20-14. Section of hollow metal door frame.

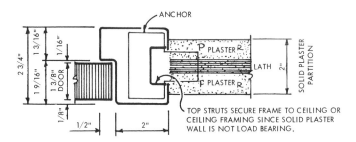

Fig. 20-15. Section of a hollow metal door frame with struts.

Windows

Steel and aluminum windows used in commercial buildings are manufactured to follow certain standards of quality, materials, thickness, and must be dimensionally coordinated with building material sizes. These standards are set by the Steel Window Institute and the Architectural Aluminum Manufacturers Association. Aluminum windows may be finished in their natural color or anodized. Anodization provides not only a protective coating against air-borne chemicals but offers attractive coloring. Steel windows are first coated with a prime coat of paint and may be pre-finished with a vinyl coating or finished in the field. The vinyl coating makes the window almost maintenance-free. Wood windows are installed in some buildings, but their combined initial cost and subsequent upkeep is greater than for metal windows. The development of vinyl-sheathed wood frames and sashes has virtually eliminated the maintenance factor where wood is specified.

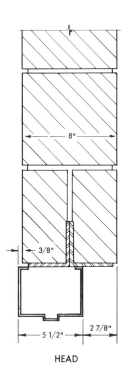

HEAD

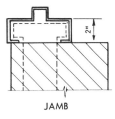

JAMB

Fig. 20-16. Typical section through hollow metal door frame and concrete block wall.

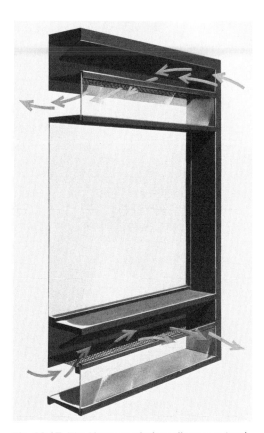

Fig. 20-17. The Ventrow window allows a natural flow of air even in a driving rain.

The type of window used depends greatly upon the allowable cost and the amount of outside air and light that is desired. The number of operable windows in commercial buildings is decreasing because of the greater number of buildings with totally conditioned air. When operable windows are

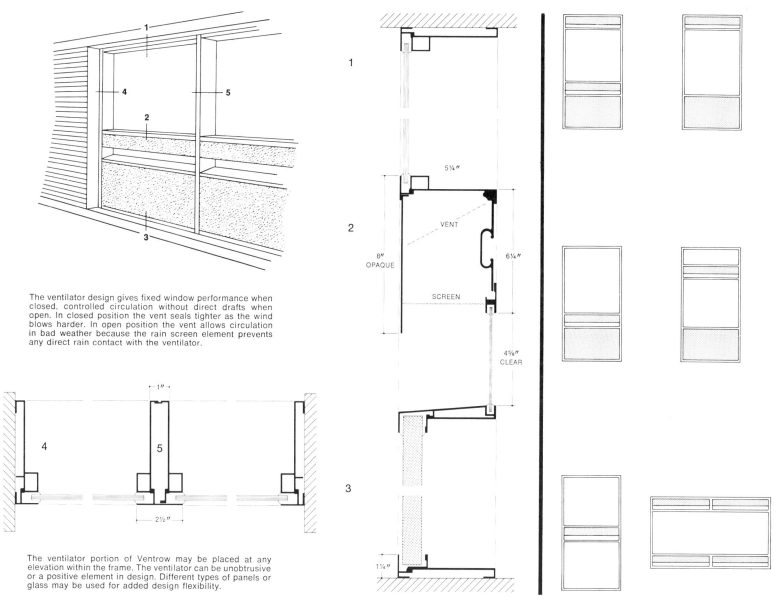

The ventilator design gives fixed window performance when closed, controlled circulation without direct drafts when open. In closed position the vent seals tighter as the wind blows harder. In open position the vent allows circulation in bad weather because the rain screen element prevents any direct rain contact with the ventilator.

The ventilator portion of Ventrow may be placed at any elevation within the frame. The ventilator can be unobtrusive or a positive element in design. Different types of panels or glass may be used for added design flexibility.

Fig. 20-18. Typical details and basic types of the Ventrow window.

desired, the standard casement, architectural projected (awning or hopper) pivoted (horizontal or vertical), sliding, or double hung are specified.

Another type of window, which fits in none of the previous categories, has the appearance of the fixed sash, but permits natural ventilation through the window as shown in Figs. 20-17 and 20-18. Because of its unique design, it is also burglarproof. Fig. 20-18 shows some of the possible locations of the vent panel(s) and a typical section through the head, jamb, sill, and mullion. Non-operable fixed sash windows, in the form of a ribbon or as single units, may be used independently or with casement, projected, slider, or double-hung. In mild, warm weather climates, jalousie windows may be used to provide 100% ventilation.

For a complete discussion of window types, see Chapter 10. Special security windows are manufactured for use in psychiatric hospitals, jails, penal institutions, and where vandal-proof and bullet-proof installations are necessary. Consult Sweets *Architectural Catalog File* for other specialty-type windows.

Window Sizes. Most metal windows in the following classifications are manufactured in standard sizes to coordinate with modular masonry unit sizes. Windows other than standard size can be ordered but at a higher cost. Steel windows are divided into two general categories: (1) *Architectural* windows, used where appearance and quality are important in installations as schools, hospitals, apartments, hotels, offices, etc.,

and (2) *Commercial/Industrial* windows, specified where plain design and suitable quality are of primary importance in factory, storage/warehouse, hangar-type buildings. Aluminum windows are classified in one of two ways: (1) *Residential,* referring to windows manufactured for residential application only, and (2) *Architectural,* indicating windows suitable for *all* commercial applications.

Steel and some aluminum window manufacturers use a 4-digit numbering system to identify the general type of window. The

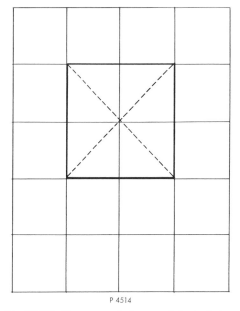

P 4514

Fig. 20-19. Many manufacturers of steel windows use a four or five digit number to identify a window in addition to the window dimensions.

first digit indicates the number of horizontal lights, the second digit, the number of vertical lights, the third digit, the number of ventilators (a ventilator is a movable vertical, horizontal, hinged, or pivoted unit); and the fourth digit, the number of lights in the ventilator. If multiple ventilators are specified in the window, the fourth digit identifies the number of lights in the lower vent unit, the fifth digit the lights in the middle vent unit, etc. For example, the window shown in Fig. 20-19 is identified as a P4514 because it is *4* lights wide, *5* lights high, *1* ventilator that contains *4* lights and is classed as a pivoted window.

Manufacturers' catalogs should be consulted for the complete range of sizes and types of windows available. Sweets' *Architectural Catalog File* gives an excellent representative sampling.

Conditioned Air

Commercial buildings can be heated and cooled by the identical principles described in Chapter 13. Many light commercial buildings are designed to distribute the conditioned air through suspended ceilings. Each tile in the system has 2 or 5 slots that may be adjusted for air flow. In the past, heated and cooled air was distributed through several diffusers placed in the ceiling, walls or other single source. Depending on their location, these single sources could cause high velocity discomfort zones. Commercial and industrial buildings are now

UNITED STATES GYPSUM CO., CHICAGO, ILLINOIS.

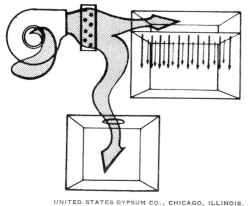

Fig. 20-20. Comparison of air distribution through the ceiling and through a single diffuser.

UNITED STATES GYPSUM CO., CHICAGO, ILLINOIS.

Fig. 20-22. Conditioned air may also be diffused through the main runners in a suspended ceiling system.

UNITED STATES GYPSUM CO., CHICAGO, ILLINOIS.

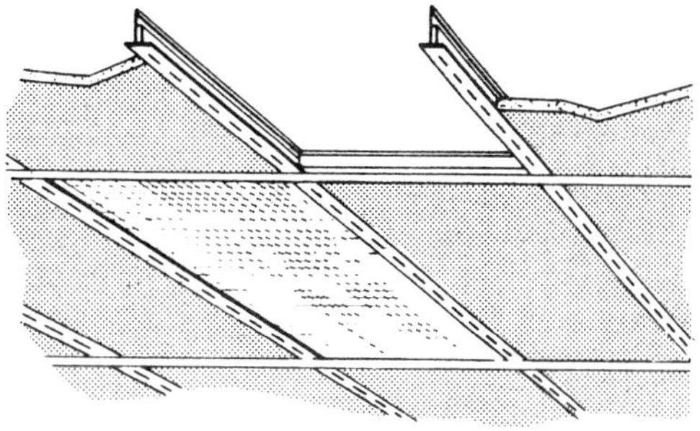

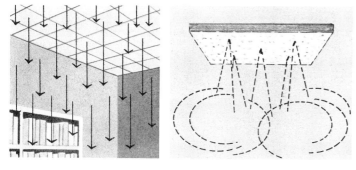

Fig. 20-21. Air flow lines are more evenly distributed through a ceiling system.

employing a distribution system where the entire ceiling acts as a diffuser.

Fig. 20-20 shows the basic comparison of air through a single diffusing source and an entire ceiling distribution system. The ceiling as a diffuser gives draft-free, wall-to-wall uniform distribution. This system not only moves the air throughout the room, but is virtually noise-free. With a conventional ducted forced-air system, noise has a direct channel from the heating or cooling source through the plenum and ducts and into the room. In the above-ceiling system, the duct work ends above the plenums, which act as sound-absorbing chambers. Fig. 20-21 shows airflow lines from an above-ceiling system as compared with a direct ceiling diffuser.

Another similar method of distributing conditioned air is through the suspended ceiling runner grid system that holds the acoustical tiles. The main runners are slotted to permit air flow. Fig. 20-22 shows a slotted runner.

Partitions, Interior Walls and Ceilings

Movable Non-Load-Bearing Partitions

Buildings are being designed and built without load-bearing interior partitions because of high-strength steels used in long span steel joists. Non-load-bearing movable walls allow more flexible use of space for the occupants. Any group or activity that offers the possibility of organizational change, resulting in different space requirements for equipment and personnel cannot be tied to fixed walls. Office or activity areas can easily be modified to meet new demands by simply moving the wall. Dependent upon the construction of the wall partition system, most have sound-proof and fire-retardant qualities, esthetic appeal and durability, plus easy installation and disassembly.

Types of partitions. Movable partitions or panels are fabricated from plywood,

Fig. 20-23A. Movable partitions can be made of many materials. There are floor to ceiling glass and hardboard.

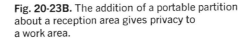

Fig. 20-24. The partitions that form this work station can be easily moved with a minimum amount of effort.

Fig. 20-23B. The addition of a portable partition about a reception area gives privacy to a work area.

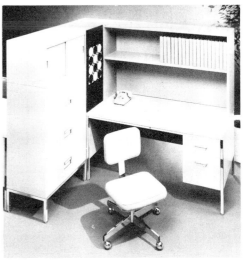

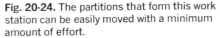

Fig. 20-25. A highly functional, esthetically appealing and private work station that can be easily moved.

hardboard, gypsum board, steel, glass and asbestos, or any combination of these. Partitions may extend completely or partially from floor to ceiling. A complete floor to ceiling partition is shown in Fig. 20-23A. Note the use of glass and hardboard panel units.

A low panel unit can offer privacy for office personnel as illustrated in Fig. 20-23B. With new acoustical qualities engineered into ceiling materials and more efficient and quiet conditioned air systems, office areas are being designed around the open plan principle. Figs. 20-24 and 20-25 picture two private work stations that are completely portable, highly functional, but yet lend a feeling of openness.

Construction of partitions. Partitions vary in thickness from ⅜″ to 3″. Most partitions are classified as sandwich construction. Depending on the manufacturer, each sets his own standard width module. Increments in width can be 5″, 6″, 10″, or 12″ up to a maximum dimension of 6′-0″. Heights of panels vary from 7′-4″ to 11′-0″ and are also available at a "railing height" of 3′-6″. See Fig. 20-23B.

A wide range of finishing materials are placed on panels, depending on their use. Some may have the front and rear surfaces covered with wood-grained vinyl, while others may have factory-applied paint. Panels may be fully glazed or partially glazed above the "railing height." This type is called a *borrowed light* panel. See Fig. 20-26. Few panels are made of wood; the majority are either metal, glass, or a combination of the two.

Every movable partition system provides units that will accommodate doors. Any type of available door such as hinged, double acting, sliding, folding, solid or hollow core wood or metal, flush, or panel can be supplied by the manufacturer. Special units are available that contain cabinets for fire hose and/or fire extinguishers, drinking fountains, book cases, etc.

Most systems secure the panel to the floor and ceiling by a channel and adjustable clamps. The panel may be easily moved by releasing the clamp and removing the ceiling floor channel. Panels are fastened together by a special locking device that is

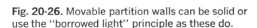
Fig. 20-26. Movable partition walls can be solid or use the "borrowed light" principle as these do.

UNITED STATES GYPSUM CO., CHICAGO, ILLINOIS.

generally unique to the manufacturer. Electrical outlets may be placed anywhere in the panel. Some systems offer "electrified" corner or meeting posts that have a series of flush-mounted convenience outlets at the bottom and at desk height. Electrical wires must run through flexible or rigid conduit in the panels as specified by the code.

Plumbing Walls

To save time and expense, architects and contractors are specifying pre-built, self-contained plumbing walls. See Fig. 20-27. As labor costs and the demand for quality increase, this new concept of "packaged plumbing" is meeting with increased favor. Each wall contains drain, waste and vent piping, all water distribution lines, brackets for wall-hung lavatories, shower-tub valve with diverter and riser, and main stack and vent stack connecting pieces. Plumbing walls can be used in high and low rise apartments, town houses, and toilet room facilities where the bathroom is backed to kitchen, back-to-back bathrooms, bathroom backed to laundry and single full bathrooms. Walls are delivered to the site, lifted into place by a lift truck or crane and secured to the floor and adjoining walls.

Suspended Ceilings

Suspended ceilings, see Fig. 20-28, offer insulative and acoustical qualities, rapid installation, minimal ceiling joist load, concealment of structural members, and economy.

CENTAUR PLUMBING SYSTEMS DIVISION, WICKLIFFE, OHIO.

Fig. 20-27. Self-contained plumbing walls may be installed rapidly and economically in all types of buildings.

Fig. 20-28. An acoustical suspended ceiling permits easy maintenance on utility services and piping.

Suspended ceilings consist of a grid-work of *main* and *cross runners* suspended from the floor or roof above by galvanized wire, light steel rods or strap hangers. All main runners are placed parallel to one dimension of the room and are the only ones that are suspended. The cross runners, placed perpendicular, rest in the main runners.

Both kinds appear as an inverted "T".

Once the runners are suspended, the ceiling tiles are lifted into place. Tiles may be vinyl faced with a ¾" to 1" cellular glass backing, acoustical to absorb sound, or slotted to act as a diffuser for heating and cooling. Openings are easily cut in the tile for light fixtures, air diffusers, speakers, etc.

Parapet Walls

A *parapet wall* is the portion of *any* wall that extends above the roof. Fig. 20-29 shows a detail of a parapet wall on the face of a building. Another example of a parapet wall is a portion of a fire wall between two

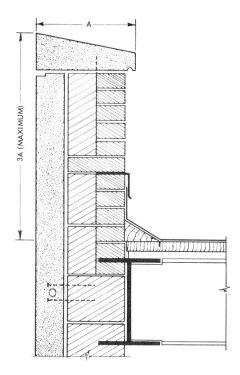

Fig. 20-29. A parapet wall extends above the roof no more than three times the thickness of the wall.

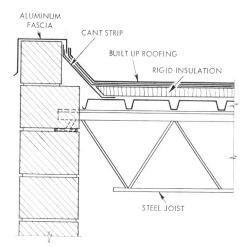

Fig. 20-30. Typical detail of concrete block wall with open web steel joist.

Fig. 20-31. Glazed tile coping protects the top courses of masonry units from the weather.

apartment units that serves as a party wall and projects above the roof. Parapet walls should be at least 8″ thick, and their height should not exceed 3 times their thickness. If the height is extended beyond 3 times the thickness, it must be reinforced to withstand possible earthquake and wind loads.

A narrow aluminum (plain or anodized) or copper fascia may be placed over the top courses of masonry units as in Fig. 20-30.

The fascia covers the top course(s) from the weather and provides a finish. A coping may be used, serving the same purpose as the aluminum or copper fascia. Coping may be made from glazed tile or cast stone. Fig. 20-31 shows a piece of glazed tile coping. Cast stone coping generally will have a kerfed drip edge along either underside.

Decking, Roofing, Fascia Panels and Gravel Stops

Decking

Rather than using a plywood roof sheathing over joists, as in residential construction, metal decking is used in commercial construction. Metal decking (see Fig. 20-32) serves as a floor deck, partition, and permanent forming for concrete floors. Most roof decks are formed from 18, 20 or 22 gauge sheet steel. When decking is used as a sub-floor, the gauge is increased. Sheets of decking are available in 12″ and 24″ widths and up to 28′-6″ in length.

Each sheet interlocks with the adjacent sheet and the ends are lapped or connected by crimping. The panels are welded to the structural member. Here a ½″ diameter plug weld or a ¾″ fillet weld is used to fasten the deck to the joist. Some manufacturers provide punched holes parallel to the edge of the decking for plug welds.

Decking is delivered to the construction site with one of the three following surface treatments: (1) shop coat of paint, (2) galvanized, or (3) chemically treated to remove all manufacturing oils and grease.

Regardless of the finish that is placed on the panel, it will be treated with hot phosphate that changes the surface into a layer of soluble phosphoric acid salts. This treatment prevents any corrosion, increases the adhesion of field-applied paint, and it will improve the bonding between any fire re-

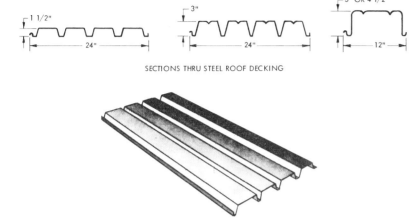

SECTIONS THRU STEEL ROOF DECKING

Fig. 20-32. Steel roof decking may be used on flat, pitched, or arched roofs. It is fastened to the supporting structure with clips or by welding.

NATIONAL GYPSUM CO., BUFFALO, NEW YORK.

Fig. 20-33. Workmen applying the first layer of a built-up roof.

tardant material (vermiculite concrete, or plaster) and the metal panel.

Roofing and Insulation

When steel decking is used as a base for roofing, it is covered with a rigid insulative material. The most common type of insulation used is 1½″ styrofoam faced on both sides with asphalt laminate kraft paper. Styrofoam is an excellent insulator, light in weight, and easy to handle and apply. Rigid insulation is available in 2′ × 4′ sheets and in thicknesses ranging from ⅞″ to 2″. (Where decreased U valves are required for lower heat transmission, multiple layers are bonded together.)

Before insulation is applied, the decking is mopped with hot bitumen to act as an adhesive between the deck and insulation. Built-up 3 or 4-ply roofing is then applied over the insulation. Fig. 20-33 shows built-up roof being applied over rigid insulation. In hot climates graveled or light-colored roof surfacings are usually used to reduce the solar heat transmission to the roof system. A metal, wood, or wood fiber *cant strip* is used where the roof joins the parapet wall. The cant strip aids in shedding the water from the wall.

Fascia Panels

Exteriors of parapet walls or any wall may be treated with one of several materials to create a particular mode of design impact. Aggregate (small to medium size) faced plywood, fiberglass or cement asbestos panels contrast well with brick or block. Several aggregate panels are shown in Fig. 20-34. These panels extend from the top of the wall down to the head of the window.

Anodized or baked-on colored enamel aluminum panels are other frequently used facing materials producing different effects. For instance, the aluminum fascia panels shown in Figs. 20-35 and 20-36 give a horizontal emphasis and color contrast to the

Fig. 20-34. Aggregate panels may be multi-colored large or small stone chips.

brick. With the resurgence of the mansard roof in commercial architectural design, aluminum mansard panels can add much to a design. See Fig. 20-37. Most fascia and mansard panels are available in heights up to 10'-0" and widths based on the O.C. spacing or multiples of the battens. If greater lengths are needed than 10', the panels can be telescoped. The same principle is used as in laying shingles to the weather. Two details of how panels may be applied are shown in Fig. 20-38 and 20-39.

Fig. 20-35. Fascia batten panels may be used to create a strong horizontal emphasis in the design of a school.

Fig. 20-36. Fascia batten panels conceal the scupper for the conductor pipe.

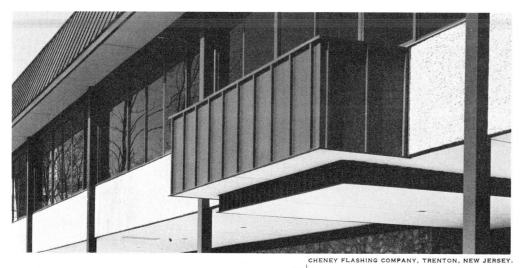

Fig. 20-37. Mansard panels and fascia batten panels contrast well with the other building materials in this structure.

CHENEY FLASHING COMPANY, TRENTON, NEW JERSEY.

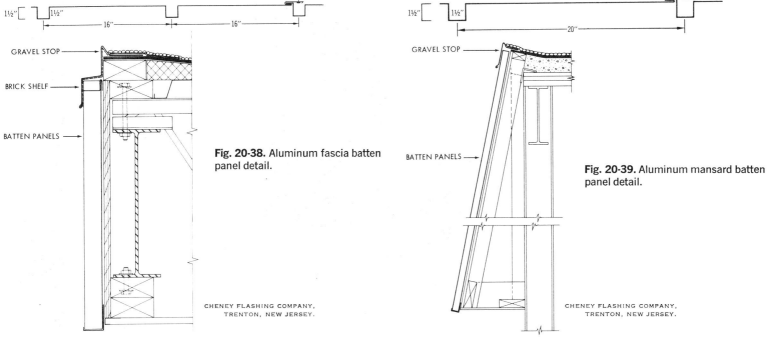

1½″   1½″
16″   16″

GRAVEL STOP

BRICK SHELF

BATTEN PANELS

Fig. 20-38. Aluminum fascia batten panel detail.

CHENEY FLASHING COMPANY, TRENTON, NEW JERSEY.

1½″   1½″
20″

GRAVEL STOP

BATTEN PANELS

Fig. 20-39. Aluminum mansard batten panel detail.

CHENEY FLASHING COMPANY, TRENTON, NEW JERSEY.

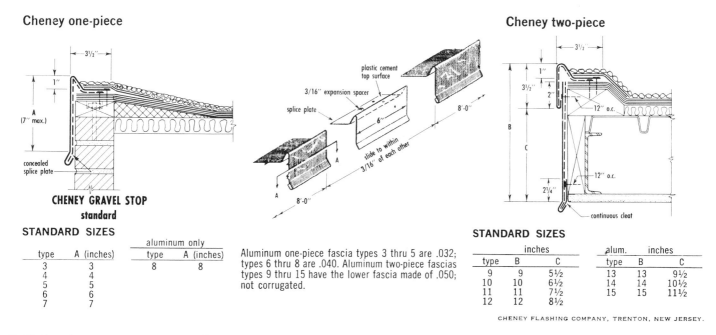

Cheney one-piece

CHENEY GRAVEL STOP
standard

STANDARD SIZES

type	A (inches)		type	A (inches)
		aluminum only		
3	3		8	8
4	4			
5	5			
6	6			
7	7			

Aluminum one-piece fascia types 3 thru 5 are .032; types 6 thru 8 are .040. Aluminum two-piece fascias types 9 thru 15 have the lower fascia made of .050; not corrugated.

Cheney two-piece

STANDARD SIZES

	inches		alum.	inches	
type	B	C	type	B	C
9	9	5½	13	13	9½
10	10	6½	14	14	10½
11	11	7½	15	15	11½
12	12	8½			

CHENEY FLASHING COMPANY, TRENTON, NEW JERSEY.

Fig. 20-40. Gravel stops serve to seal the roofs to the wall and provide a stop for the tar and aggregate.

Gravel Stops

On walls that do not extend beyond the roof level, some provision must be made to seal the built-up roof covering to the masonry wall. This is accomplished by using a metal (usually aluminum) gravel stop. The gravel stop becomes an integral part of the roof and serves as a stopping point for the tar and gravel. At the same time it makes a water-tight seal between the wall and roof. Fig. 20-40 shows two typical types of gravel stops commonly used on commercial and industrial buildings. Note in this figure how the front of the gravel stop drops below the top of the wall and is turned out to form a narrow fascia along the wall.

Shop Drawings

In architectural practice, the term "shop drawings" defines drawings that are prepared by manufacturers or fabricators who have been selected to supply various materials for the project. The drawings that are made by the supplier are based on the architectural plans and specifications. As an example, manufacturers of steel decking, framing, casework, movable partitions, etc. prepare shop drawings that would include (if applicable) plan views, necessary elevations, details of construction and details of any special conditions that may be necessary for fabrication and installation.

The general contractor then submits the shop drawings to the architect for his approval based on the quality and nature of the design. After the shop drawings have been prepared, they are submitted to the general contractor for checking and approval relative to dimensions, quantities, and details for installation. If necessary, the architect will indicate any revisions that are necessary. Upon final approval of the architect, the manufacturer will proceed to fabricate the pieces and deliver them to the job site according to the building schedule.

Questions and Problems

1. Review the special issues of *Architectural Forum, Architectural Record,* and *American Builder* that exclusively covered commercial architecture. What kind of problems did the designer encounter in designing the building and how were they solved? What kind of an alternate solution could you suggest?

2. Visit several new stores in your community and analyze the kinds of merchandise which have been placed nearest the front or main entrance, and the kinds placed farther to the rear of the store. What reasons exist for placing these goods in that particular location?

3. Borrow from the local library or a local businessman several professional, trade, or retailing journals. Search each one carefully for any new innovations in servicing, merchandising, handling of goods, etc., that might af-

fect a designer's building layout for a particular business.

4. Contact the local Chamber of Commerce or the local city government to determine if any demographic (population) surveys have been conducted in your community. Using this information or personal observation, in what direction has the population been moving? Based on this expansion, what areas have been zoned for light commercial businesses? How many commercial zoning classifications does your city have?

5. Select a site zoned for small business establishments and plan a two-story office building having a total of 15,000 sq. ft. Each floor has three suites of offices; one suite on each floor has not been rented. The owner of the building has obtained 10-year leases from the following four tenants:

A. Creative drafting service. This is a free lance drafting and illustrating firm. At present it employs three men, plus the owner.

B. Consulting marketing service. This firm is owned by two market consultants and they employ one office girl.

C. Letter and telephone answering service. A small company employing three typists, one duplicating (offset) machine operator, and two women handling the telephone answering service. In addition, plan one executive office for the owner.

D. Credit Bureau Office. This office employs three office girls, and has two men working in the field who use the office as a communications center.

Sheet Check List 21

The purpose of any check list is to aid in producing, to the greatest degree possible, an omission-free document, procedure, or plan. Essentially, the "Sheet Check List" logically groups the myriad of details that may be forgotten. The inclusion or omission of a title, symbol, note, call-out, size, etc., will represent the difference between a complete set of working drawings and those which are hastily and carelessly drawn.

Check List Use

The items listed in the "Check List" represent the chief features that are to be placed on a *complete* set of working drawings. Every effort has been made to make this list as comprehensive as possible for a structure. Each category or division of the check list may be used as an aid in determining those items that will be pertinent to the drawing at hand, such as a specific detail, elevation, plot plan, etc. The check list may be used in checking a partially completed set of plans to be sure that all features are included. Depending upon the situation, each item identified in the "Check List" may not appear in the complete set of working drawings. For example, in the case of a slab structure, plumbing features would not be shown on the basement plan.

It should be noted that the "Check List" contains a division for the lower level and main level. If an upper level or second floor is to be drawn, the items listed for the main level should be used as a guide in checking the plan. The section listed as "Elevations" should be used for *every elevation drawn*. All elevations, garage included, should be checked against the items enumerated under elevations.

Some architectural offices use prepared printed or diazo intermediate sheets for the plot plan, door, window and room finish schedules. Usually these sheets are drawn in the drafting room, reproduced and inserted in the set of drawings. For example, some offices use a standard sheet for the plot plan that has all the necessary call-outs and information. The draftsman simply fills in the necessary dimensions for each job. The same technique is used for windows, door, and room finish schedules. Offices that operate in conjunction with or that are a part of construction or development companies frequently have standard sheets that show typical details of stair, cornice, sill, footing, foundation, etc. construction.

A set of *working drawings* is included with the "Check List." They may be used as a supplementary reference.

Check List Organization

Often each section contained in the "Check List" will constitute a single sheet. Depending upon the sheet size and building size, some of these sections may be combined on a single sheet. For example, door and window schedules may be placed on the same sheet with the floor plans. Interior elevations can be drawn on the same sheet as structural details or perhaps they may be placed along with the floor plans.

Structural details might be scattered throughout the entire set of plans and placed where they seem most appropriate. Details of the footing, foundation wall and sill could be shown on the basement or lower level plan. Similarly, truss and cornice details might be placed on the roof framing plan or on the same sheet showing a typical section through the structure. Some sets of plans may show all of the elevations grouped on the same sheet (this is particularly true when a D size sheet is used), while others will show the front and rear elevations on one sheet and the right and left elevation on another. The draftsman attempts to plan all sheets so that they are completely filled and there is a sensible relationship between and among the details for each sheet.

The outline of the "Check List" presentation is as follows:

   I. Presentation Drawings
  II. Working Drawings
     A. Plot Plan
     B. Basement (Lower Level) or Foundation Plan
     C. First Floor (Main Level) Plan
     D. Elevations
     E. Interior Elevations
     F. Wall or Structural Sections and Details
     G. Fireplace Details
     H. Stair Details
     I. Schedules (Window, Door, and Room Finish)
     J. Joist Framing Plan
     K. Roof Framing Plan
     L. Electrical Plan
  III. Sheets in a Set of Working Drawings

To list all details for all types of dwellings would be impractical. If the draftsman will check each detail he believes necessary against the appropriate section, he can be fairly certain that he has included everything that will aid the contractor in estimating the cost, ordering materials, scheduling work, and constructing the building.

Some enumeration appearing in one section of the "Check List" duplicates items appearing in other sections. This is deliberate so that some key items will not be overlooked regardless of sheet organization.

The success of the plans lies in the question: "Are the plans complete enough so that this house can be built?"

Presentation Drawings

1. Pictorial view with entourage
  a. Perspective (1 or 2 point)
  b. T-square perspective
2. Pictorial view of special features
  a. Approach to entryway
  b. Patio
  c. Interior of entry hall
  d. Living room with fireplace
  e. Any other outstanding features
3. Floor plan (to scale)
  a. Basement or lower level
  b. First floor or main level
  c. Second floor or upper level, etc.
4. Proper title for each plan view
5. Proper title for each perspective
6. Room names
7. Room sizes (13'-6" × 19'-0") below name
8. Overall length and depth
9. Balanced layout of sheet
10. Indicate scale
11. Border line
12. Designer's name, draftsman's name, firm's name, etc.
13. Owner's name
14. Sheet number

Working Drawings

A. Plot Plan

1. Outline of lot—single line
2. Outline of house—single line (fill in with hatching)
3. Outline of porch—single line

4. Outline of patio—single line
5. Outline of garage—single line (fill in with hatching)
6. Outline of driveway—single line
7. Outline of public and private side walks—single line
8. Outline of other features (such as swimming pools, private wells, individual sewage systems, etc.)
9. Indicate curb line.
10. Center line of street(s) and name(s)
11. Dimensions of each lot line and bearing
12. Dimension of each feature (house, garage, patio, sidewalk, etc.) and dimension from lot lines
13. Dimension each feature from lot line
14. Call out each feature
15. Indicate and call out grade elevations at corners of house
16. Indicate and call out grade elevations at corners of lot
17. Indicate and call out grade elevations at center of street
18. Call out legal description
19. Call out house number and street.
20. Call out lot number
21. Call out block number
22. Call out subdivision name
23. Call out city, county, and state
24. Indicate north
25. Indicate title
26. Indicate scale
27. Border line
28. Draftsman's name, firm's name, etc.
29. Owner's name
30. Sheet number

B. **Basement (Lower Level) or Foundation Plan.**

1. Outline of footings—broken line
2. Outline of foundation and pilasters
3. Outline of post or column footings—broken line
4. Outline of thickened slab—broken line
5. Outline of footing for bearing wall—broken line
6. Outline of porch footings — broken line
7. Outline of porch foundation
8. Outline of planter foundation
9. Outline of stoop foundation
10. Indicate soil pipe and vents
11. Indicate drainage provision (footing, storm, sanitary)
12. Indicate floor drains and clean outs
13. Indicate sump provisions
14. Indicate heating plant
15. Indicate oil tank if applicable
16. Indicate water heater
17. Indicate water closet and lavatory
18. Indicate laundry tubs
19. Indicate hose bibs (only on exposed basement)
20. Indicate basement windows
21. Indicate window wells
22. Indicate outside entrance, if applicable, with arrow
23. Call out window and door symbols (from window and door schedules)
24. Indicate waterproof foundation wall
25. Outline of fireplace footing
26. Outline of fireplace foundation

27. Indicate fireplace cleanout
28. Outline of stairs (with directional arrow)
29. Indicate ceiling outlets
30. Indicate wall convenience outlets
31. Indicate switches and arrangements (curved dashed line from switch to outlet)
32. Indicate special appliance outlets
33. Outline any built-in features
34. Specify type and thickness of floor
35. Indicate and call out size and gage of concrete floor reinforcement
36. Dimension foundation from outside to outside
37. Dimension thickness of wall and call out type of material
38. Dimension location of post or column
39. Dimension location of door(s) and windows from outside of foundation wall to their centerlines
40. Check building code against plan
41. Indicate each room or area
42. Indicate each feature
43. Indicate where sections and details have been taken with proper symbol
44. Indicate title
45. Indicate scale
46. Border line
47. Designer's name, draftsman's name, firm's name, etc.
48. Owner's name
49. Sheet number

C. **First Floor (Main Level) Plan.**

1. Outline of outside walls — (nominal thickness)

2. Outline of partition walls — (nominal thickness)
3. Outline of patio
4. Indicate outline of roof overhang—broken line
5. Indicate window openings
6. Indicate door openings with swings
7. Outline of front porch or stoop
8. Outline of rear porch or stoop
9. Outline of fireplace and flues
10. Outline of chimney—if separate
11. Indicate stairs with number and sizes of treads and risers (show directional arrows)
12. Indicate stairwell handrail
13. Indicate kitchen
14. Indicate living room
15. Indicate dining room or area
16. Indicate family room
17. Indicate bedroom(s)
18. Indicate bathroom(s) (show fixtures; patch detail tiling)
19. Indicate lavatory(s)
20. Indicate mud room
21. Indicate laundry
22. Indicate work area
23. Indicate steps from grade or garage into house
24. Indicate closets
25. Indicate sizes of closet clothes pole and shelf
26. Indicate garage, if applicable
27. Indicate other features, such as range, refrigerator, sink, washer and dryer, water softener, cabinet, shelves, etc.
28. Indicate ceiling outlets
29. Indicate wall convenience outlets

30. Indicate bells, buzzers, TV outlets, fans, etc.
31. Indicate valance lighting
32. Indicate undercabinet lighting
33. Indicate special appliance outlets
34. Indicate quartz zone or ceiling heater for bathrooms
35. Indicate weatherproof convenience outlets
36. Indicate yard lighting
37. Indicate switches and arrangement
38. Indicate electrical service entrance
39. Indicate service disconnect, panel board, branch control centers
40. Indicate all plumbing fixtures (bathtub, lavatory, water closet, etc.)
41. Indicate soil pipe
42. Indicate hose-bibs
43. Indicate gas outlets
44. Call out window symbols (from window schedule)
45. Call out door symbols (from door schedule)
46. Indicate and call out extent or change in flooring material in each room—solid line
47. Dimension window location from outside stud face to center of window and center to center
48. Dimension door locations from outside stud face to center of door
49. Dimension overall from outside of stud face to outside of stud face
50. Dimension partition from outside of stud face to stud faces of partition or to center of partition
51. Dimension partition wall thickness

52. Dimension exterior wall thickness
53. Indicate arches and/or cased openings—broken line
54. Indicate girder or I-beam with proper symbol and call out size
55. Indicate joist size, O.C. spacing and directional arrow
56. Indicate type of floor (vinyl tile, ceramic tile, slate, carpet, etc.) below room title
57. Indicate type of wall finish (plaster, drywall, textured panel, etc.) below room title
58. Indicate type of ceiling (plaster, drywall, textured, panel, acoustical plaster, etc.) below room title
59. Indicate type of heating unit in each room if not part of the central system
60. Indicate garage drain, if applicable
61. Arrows to indicate entrances
62. Indicate where sections and details have been taken with proper symbol
63. Indicate title
64. Indicate scale
65. Border line
66. Designer's name, draftsman's name, firm's name, etc.
67. Owner's name
68. Sheet number

D. **Elevations**

1. Indicate footing (broken line)
2. Indicate foundation wall (broken line)
3. Indicate basement floor (broken line)
4. Indicate and call out grade line

5. Indicate and call out water table or drip cap
6. Indicate basement windows
7. Indicate and call out screened vents for crawl space
8. Indicate and call out finish floor(s) (heavy center line)
9. Indicate and call out finish garage floor, if applicable (heavy center line)
10. Indicate porch railings, steps, columns, or posts
11. Indicate bay — veneer materials and roofing
12. Indicate dormer — veneer materials and roofing
13. Indicate doors
14. Indicate door trim
15. Indicate windows
16. Indicate window trim
17. Indicate and call out finish ceiling (center line)
18. Indicate siding or veneer in patches
19. Call out siding or veneer on *each* elevation
20. Indicate and call out exterior lights
21. Indicate and call out weatherproof convenience outlets
22. Indicate and call out conductor pipe (leader) (size, type, and material)
23. Indicate gutter and call out type and material
24. Indicate fascia and call out size and material
25. Indicate and call out corner trim
26. Indicate flashing and call out material and gage

27. Indicate roofing material in patches and call out type
28. Indicate gravel stop and call out gage and material
29. Indicate chimney and call out material
30. Indicate pitch triangle
31. Indicate gable end louvers and call out amount of net free air (square area)
32. Indicate roof vents and call out amount of net free air (square area) for ventilation
33. Call out window symbols (from window schedule)
34. Call out door symbols (from door schedule)
35. Dimension from footing to finish grade or call out elevations
36. Dimension from finish grade to finish floor or call out elevations
37. Dimension from finish floor to finish ceiling
38. Dimension from ridge to top of chimney
39. Indicate where sections and details have been taken with proper symbol
40. Indicate title for each elevation
41. Indicate scale
42. Border line
43. Designer's name, draftsman's name, firm's name
44. Owner's name
45. Sheet number

E. Interior Elevations

1. Indicate true width of wall

2. Indicate true width of window
3. Indicate true width of doors or openings
4. Indicate door swing with broken lines
5. Indicate true width or length of stairs
6. Indicate typical section through soffit or bulkhead, wall cabinet, and base cabinet
7. Indicate cabinets with drawers
8. Indicate counter
9. Indicate shelves with broken line
10. Indicate closets with shelves and clothes pole
11. Indicate plumbing fixtures
12. Indicate towel bars
13. Indicate soap dish and grab bar
14. Indicate vanity
15. Indicate medicine cabinet
16. Indicate mirror
17. Indicate shower door
18. Indicate obscure or pattern glass
19. Indicate stove
20. Indicate range hood or counter-top unit
21. Indicate oven
22. Indicate refrigerator
23. Indicate dishwasher
24. Indicate incinerator
25. Indicate fireplace
26. Indicate bookcase
27. Indicate wall materials (tile, brick, stainless steel, wood paneling, etc.)
28. Indicate textures of surface materials
29. Indicate toe space
30. Indicate heat supply registers
31. Indicate cold air returns
32. Indicate convenience outlets

33. Indicate special outlets
34. Indicate wall switches
35. Indicate wall fixtures
36. Indicate air conditioning registers
37. Indicate direction of sliding doors and windows with arrow
38. Indicate base and shoe
39. Indicate ceiling trim, cove, or molding
40. Indicate true slope of ceiling
41. Indicate sloping ceiling
42. Indicate exposed beams
43. Dimension from finish floor to top of counter
44. Dimension from top of counter to underside of wall cabinet
45. Dimension from underside of wall cabinet to top of wall cabinet
46. Dimension over-all height from finish floor to underside of soffit
47. Dimension from finish floor to mirror
48. Dimension from finish floor to clothes pole in closet
49. Dimension from finish floor to fixed shelves in closet
50. Dimension from finish floor to top of vanity
51. Dimension from finish floor to top of wainscoting
52. Indicate where sections and details have been taken with proper symbol
53. Indicate name of each wall elevation (living room, kitchen, hall, etc.)
54. Indicate compass direction of each wall elevation
55. Indicate scale of each interior
56. Border line

57. Designer's name, draftsman's name, firm's name, etc.
58. Owner's name
59. Sheet number

F. **Wall or Structural Section and Details**

1. Indicate where section has been taken on plan(s) and elevations
2. Indicate footing with reinforcing rod
3. Indicate footing drain tile if applicable
4. Indicate foundation wall with reinforcing
5. Indicate method of waterproofing and call out material and size
6. Indicate sill construction and call out component members and sizes
7. Indicate anchor bolt and call out size and spacing O.C.
8. Indicate studs and spacing O.C.
9. Indicate wall insulation material and call out type and thickness
10. Indicate sheathing and call out type and thickness
11. Indicate siding or veneer material and call out type and size
12. Indicate perimeter insulation if applicable
13. Indicate floor joists and call out material, size, and spacing O.C.
14. Indicate sub-floor and call out material and thickness
15. Indicate finish floor and call out material and thickness
16. Indicate double plate
17. Indicate partition wall
18. Indicate blocking or horizontal bridging

19. Indicate ceiling joists and call out material, size, and spacing O.C.
20. Indicate ceiling insulation and call out thickness and type
21. Indicate finish ceiling and call out material, thickness and finish
22. Indicate typical window or sliding glass door
23. Indicate lintel over window or sliding glass door and call out material and size
24. Indicate ceiling insulation and call out thickness and type
25. Indicate finish ceiling and call out material, thickness, and finish
26. Indicate roof rafters and call out material, size, and spacing O.C.
27. Indicate collar beams and call out material, sizes, and spacing
28. Indicate roof knee braces and call out material, size, and spacing
29. Indicate roof sheathing or boards and call out size
30. Indicate roof decking and call out size and material
31. Indicate roofing and call out type and thickness
32. Indicate gravel stop and call out material and gage
33. Indicate fascia and call out material and size
34. Indicate nailing block and call out typical size
35. Indicate soffit and call out material and amount of net free air (square area) for ventilation

36. Indicate molding at underside of soffit and wall and call out type and size
37. Indicate gutter and call out material, gage, and size
38. Indicate pitch triangle and call out rise and run
39. Indicate ridge and call out material and size
40. Indicate ridge vent
41. Indicate roof vent
42. Dimension from footing to finish grade
43. Dimension from finish grade to finish floor or give elevation
44. Dimension amount siding or veneer overhangs foundation wall
45. Dimension from finish floor to finish ceiling
46. Dimension from finish floor to top of exterior wall plate
47. Dimension from finish floor to top of interior wall plate
48. Dimension rafter length
49. Dimension amount of overhang
50. Dimension head height of typical window or door
51. Indicate typical plate detail(s) with necessary call-outs and sizes
52. Indicate typical ridge detail(s) with necessary call-outs and sizes
53. Indicate typical cornice detail(s) with necessary call-outs and sizes
54. Indicate typical sill detail(s) with necessary call-outs and sizes
55. Indicate typical threshold detail(s), call out manufacturer's name, model number, and size
56. Indicate truss detail(s) with necessary call-outs and sizes
57. Indicate typical soffit or bulk head detail(s) with call-outs and sizes
58. Indicate any other details that may be necessary to clarify the drawings
59. Indicate title—each section and detail
60. Indicate scale—each section and detail
61. Border line
62. Designer's name, draftsman's name, firm's name, etc.
63. Owner's name
64. Sheet number

G. **Fireplace Details.**

1. Elevation (full or half) of fireplace
2. Plan section (full or half) of fireplace
3. Full section from basement to chimney cap
4. Indicate and call out facing material and bond, if brick
5. Indicate and call out fire brick
6. Indicate and call out outside facing material
7. Indicate flue tile and call out size
8. Indicate damper and call out manufacturer, model number, and size
9. Indicate angle iron and call out size
10. Indicate mantel and call out material and size
11. Indicate ash dump and call out manufacturer, model number, and size
12. Indicate clean-out door and call out manufacturer, model number, and size
13. Indicate molding
14. Indicate front hearth and call out material and size
15. Indicate spark arrestor and call out size
16. Indicate type of brick design over opening (jack arch, rowlock, soldier course, etc.)
17. Indicate construction over front hearth
18. Dimension width, height, and depth of fire chamber
19. Dimension angle or flare of fire chamber
20. Dimension width and depth of throat
21. Dimension angle of smoke chamber
22. Indicate smoke chamber fillet
23. Dimension length and bearing of angle iron
24. Dimension height of mantel and projection
25. Dimension overall size of front hearth
26. Dimension location of molding
27. Dimension interior facing of fireplace
28. Indicate and dimension fireplace foundation
29. Indicate and dimension fireplace footing
30. Indicate other necessary dimensions for any additional features (built-in wood box, decorations, etc.)
31. Indicate where sections and details have been taken with proper symbol
32. Indicate title (each section and detail)
33. Indicate scale (each section and detail)

34. Border line
35. Designer's name, draftsman's name, firm's name, etc.
36. Owner's name
37. Sheet number

H. Stair Details.

1. Elevation of stairs in section, including portion of floors
2. Plan of stairs
3. Indicate edge of sloping ceiling
4. Hand rail(s)
5. Typical riser and tread section
6. Call out riser material and size, if applicable
7. Call out tread material and size
8. String board
9. Shoe rail
10. Shoe fillet
11. Indicate newel post and call out material and size
12. Indicate balusters and call out material and size
13. Dimension clear head room
14. Dimension height of hand rail
15. Dimension width of stairs
16. Dimension height from finish floor to finish floor.
17. Dimension horizontal length of stair
18. Dimension tread from front face of riser to nosing
19. Dimension riser from top of tread to top of tread
20. Dimension nosing
21. Dimension hand rail and call out material

22. Indicate section through hand rail and call out pattern number
23. Indicate where sections and details have been taken with proper symbol
24. Indicate title—each section and detail
25. Indicate scale—each section and detail
26. Border line
27. Designer's name, draftsman's name, firm's name, etc.
28. Owner's name
29. Sheet number

I. Schedules.

I. Window
  1. Code Symbol—letters and number of each type of window used
  2. Quantity
  3. Sash size (W × H)
  4. Thickness
  5. Rough opening (if desired)
  6. Material (wood, aluminum, steel)
  7. Manufacturer's name
  8. Catalog number
  9. Glazing (obscure, pattern, wire, D.S., plate, etc.)
  10. Remarks (custom, pair w/mullion between)

II. Door
  1. Code symbol
  2. Quantity
  3. Size (W × H)
  4. Thickness
  5. Rough opening (if desired)

  6. Type (flush-hollow, flush-solid, panel, full louver)
  7. Material (wood-birch, mahogany, oak, metal)
  8. Manufacturer
  9. Catalog number
  10. Finish (varnish, enamel)
  11. Jamb (wood, metal, flush, etc.)
  12. Remarks (single, pair, jamb in pocket, bi-fold, by-pass, fire rating, etc.)

III. Room Finish
  1. Key to finish (natural finish, gloss enamel, semi-gloss enamel, flat paint, stain, natural finish, prefinished, exterior stain, exterior latex, exterior sash, and trim, etc.)

  2. Room
    a. Floor
      (1) Oak flooring
      (2) Carpet
      (3) Tile
      (4) Concrete
      (5) Slate

    b. Base and Shoe
      (1) Hardwood
      (2) Softwood
      (3) Tile

    c. Walls — North, South, East, West
      (1) Plaster
      (2) Gypsum board
      (3) Wood paneling
      (4) Unfinished

d. Ceiling
  (1) Plaster
  (2) Gypsum board
  (3) Acoustical tile
  (4) Unfinished
e. Cabinets and doors
f. Trim

J. Joist Framing Plan.

1. Indicate outline of foundation wall—broken line
2. Indicate sill plate and call out size
3. Indicate sill header and call out size
4. Indicate girder(s) or S-beam and call out size
5. Indicate girder posts and call out size
6. Indicate joists and call out typical size
7. Indicate cantilever framing and call out size
8. Indicate porch(s) framing
9. Location of bridging and call out
10. Indicate location of plywood subflooring panels
11. Indicate double header and trimmer around openings (chimney, fireplace, stairwell, etc.)
12. Note all structural members
13. Indicate and call out joist hangers or stirrups where necessary
14. Indicate and call out brick ridge, if applicable
15. Indicate double joists under parallel partitions
16. Indicate where sections and details have been taken with proper symbol.
17. Indicate title
18. Indicate scale
19. Border line
20. Designer's name, draftsman's name, firm's name, etc.
21. Owner's name
22. Sheet number

K. Roof Framing Plan.

1. Indicate outline of exterior walls — broken line
2. Indicate outline of bearing wall — broken line
3. Indicate outline of roof (including overhang)—solid line
4. Indicate location of supporting beams or members for roof-center line
5. Indicate posts or columns that support beams and call out size, material, and/or manufacturer and model number
6. Indicate location of breaks in roof surface (valleys, ridges, and hips) and call out size—long broken line
7. Indicate rafters with solid lines and call out material, size, and spacing O.C.
8. Indicate roof sheathing panels
9. Call out exposed rafters
10. Indicate fascia board and call out size and material
11. Indicate double header and trimmer around openings
12. Indicate and call out hangers, straps, plates, plywood gussets, rings
13. Indicate where sections and details have been taken with proper symbol

14. Indicate any additional details necessary to complete plan
15. Indicate title
16. Indicate scale
17. Border line
18. Designer's name, draftsman's name, firm's name, etc.
19. Owner's name
20. Sheet number

L. Electrical Plan.

1. Indicate outline of exterior and interior walls with all openings
2. Indicate patio, private sidewalk, and driveway
3. Indicate all vanities, counters
4. Indicate all plumbing fixtures and kitchen appliances
5. Indicate all (exclusive of central conditioned air system) air conditioners and separate heating devices
6. Indicate ceiling outlets
7. Indicate wall convenience outlets
8. Indicate wall brackets
9. Indicate bells, buzzers, TV outlets, fans, etc.
10. Indicate valance lighting
11. Indicate under cabinet lighting
12. Indicate special appliance outlets for range, air conditioner, heater, clothes dryer, etc.
13. Indicate heater and/or fan in bathroom
14. Indicate exterior weatherproof convenience outlets
15. Indicate exterior weatherproof switches

16. Indicate exterior and/or weather proof wall brackets
17. Indicate interior and exterior switching arrangements to ceiling and convenience split-wired outlets and wall brackets
18. Indicate and call out electrical service entrance
19. Indicate and call out service disconnect, power panel board, and branch control centers
20. Indicate telephone outlets
21. Number circuits and label
22. Indicate dimensions *only* for any outlets or fixtures with critical locations (ceiling outlet(s), table height convenience outlet, etc.)
23. Letter names of rooms
24. Indicate where sections and details have been taken, with proper symbol.
25. Indicate title
26. Indicate scale
27. Border line
28. Designer's name, draftsman's name, firm's name, etc.
29. Owner's name
30. Sheet number

Sheets In a Set of Working Drawings

The order of sheets in any set of drawings does not follow a hard and fast rule. Sheets are arranged in a logical progression as is indicated in the following enumeration. Departures from this order is a matter of personal taste or office standard.

In pages which follow at the end of this chapter is a typical set of working drawings numbered as follows:

1. Site plan
2. Foundation/basement plan
3. Floor plan—first floor
4. Elevations, front and rear
5. Elevations, left and right
6. Details: foundation and exterior wall, and porch construction
7. Details: interior partitions, truss details, and garage steps
8. Details: footing, back terrace, front steps, girder pocket, column footing, back steps, and garage sill
9. Details: fireplace section, first floor section, basement section, cleanout, and hearth
10. Details: stair—side elevation, stair—front elevation, handrail, and tread
11. Electrical plan—basement
12. Electrical plan—first floor
13. Floor framing plan
14. Framing details: exterior corner, wall intersection, door opening, garage door, window opening
15. Interior elevations: kitchen—north, kitchen—east, kitchen—west, and kitchen—south.
16. Window/door schedules

LOT-IO OF ELMWOOD FARMS SUBDIVISION
SECTION 25 - TOWN 2 SOUTH - RANGE 12 WEST
OSHTEMO TOWNSHIP - KALAMAZOO COUNTY - MICHIGAN

N 0° 28' 20" E 216'

SCREEN SHRUBS

4' CONC. WALK

BITUMINOUS PAVED

CONC.

8" DIA. STEEL TUBE 15' LG

N 89° 14' 55" E

POWER POLE FOR ELECTRICAL SERVICE

SCREEN SHRUBS

S 23° 20' 13" E 145'

€ POWERHORN DRIVE

€ WESTGATE DRIVE

SCALE: 1" = 20.00'

SHEET 1   **SITE PLAN**

PUBLISHER'S NOTE: THIS DRAWING WAS
ORIGINALLY DRAWN TO THE SCALE SHOWN.
THE DRAWING HAS BEEN REDUCED
AND CAN NO LONGER BE SCALED.

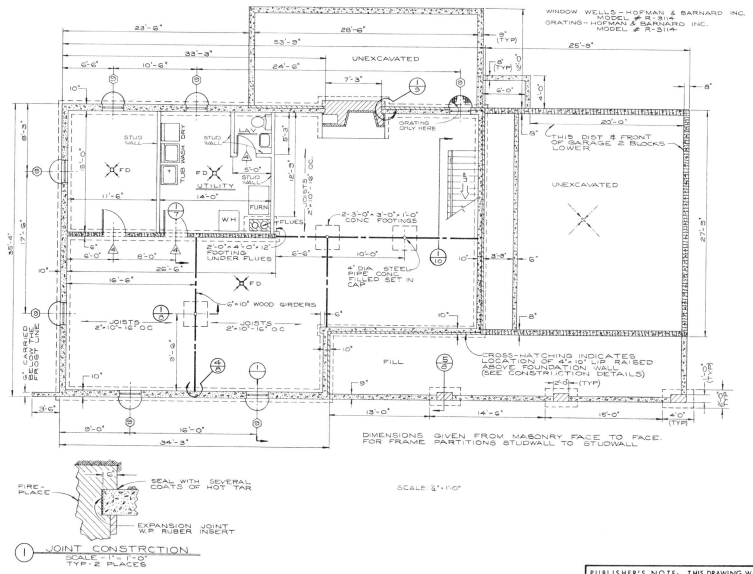

SHEET 2   FOUNDATION/BASEMENT PLAN

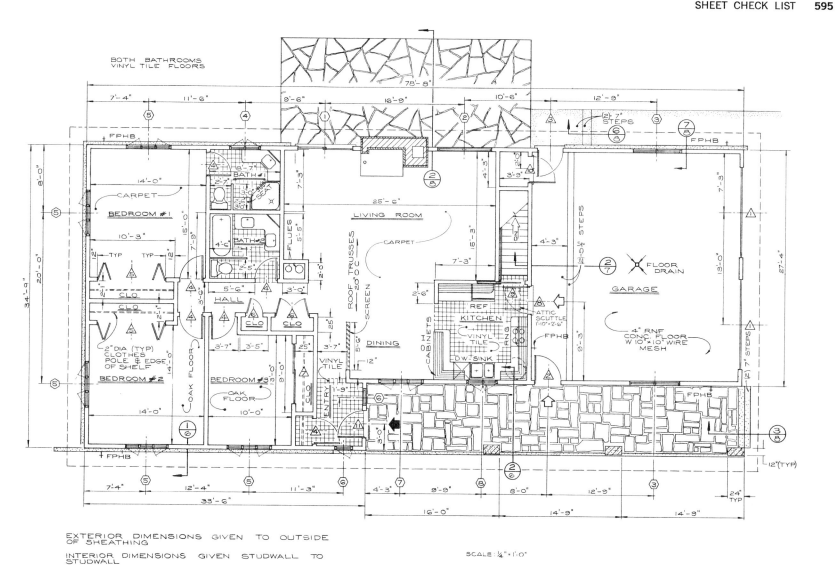

BOTH BATHROOMS
VINYL TILE FLOORS

LIVING ROOM

BEDROOM #1

CARPET

BATH

BATH-2

HALL

CLO

CLO

CLO

CLO

2" DIA (TYP) CLOTHES POLE & EDGE OF SHELF

BEDROOM #2

BEDROOM #3

OAK FLOOR

KITCHEN

VINYL TILE

REF

RNG

DW-SINK

CABINETS

DINING

ENTRY

VINYL TILE

ROOF TRUSSES 20" O.C.

SCREEN

CARPET

GARAGE

FLOOR DRAIN

4" RNF CONC. FLOOR W 10"×10" WIRE MESH

ATTIC SCUTTLE

FPHB

STEPS

SHEET 3

FLOOR PLAN

EXTERIOR DIMENSIONS GIVEN TO OUTSIDE
OF SHEATHING

INTERIOR DIMENSIONS GIVEN STUDWALL TO
STUDWALL

SCALE: ¼" = 1'-0"

PUBLISHER'S NOTE: THIS DRAWING WAS
ORIGINALLY DRAWN TO THE SCALE SHOWN.
THE DRAWING HAS BEEN REDUCED
AND CAN NO LONGER BE SCALED.

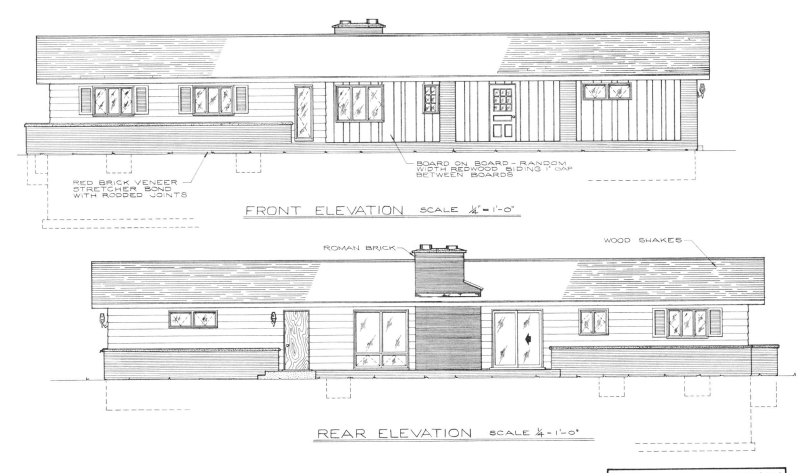

RED BRICK VENEER
STRETCHER BOND
WITH RODDED JOINTS

BOARD ON BOARD - RANDOM
WIDTH REDWOOD SIDING 1" GAP
BETWEEN BOARDS

FRONT ELEVATION SCALE ¼"=1'-0"

ROMAN BRICK

WOOD SHAKES

REAR ELEVATION SCALE ¼"=1'-0"

SHEET 4

ELEVATIONS

PUBLISHER'S NOTE: THIS DRAWING WAS
ORIGINALLY DRAWN TO THE SCALE SHOWN.
THE DRAWING HAS BEEN REDUCED
AND CAN NO LONGER BE SCALED.

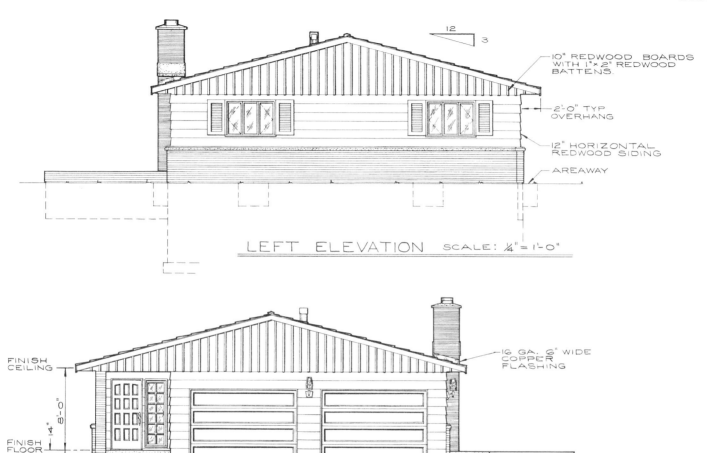

12
3

10" REDWOOD BOARDS
WITH 1"x2" REDWOOD
BATTENS.

2'-0" TYP
OVERHANG

12" HORIZONTAL
REDWOOD SIDING

AREAWAY

LEFT ELEVATION   SCALE: ¼"=1'-0"

16 GA. 6" WIDE
COPPER
FLASHING

FINISH
CEILING

8'-0"

14"

FINISH
FLOOR

GR.

8'-8"

FINISH
GRADE

FINISH
BASEMENT
FLOOR

RIGHT ELEVATION   SCALE: ¼" = 1'-0"

SHEET 5

ELEVATIONS

PUBLISHER'S NOTE: THIS DRAWING WAS
ORIGINALLY DRAWN TO THE SCALE SHOWN.
THE DRAWING HAS BEEN REDUCED
AND CAN NO LONGER BE SCALED.

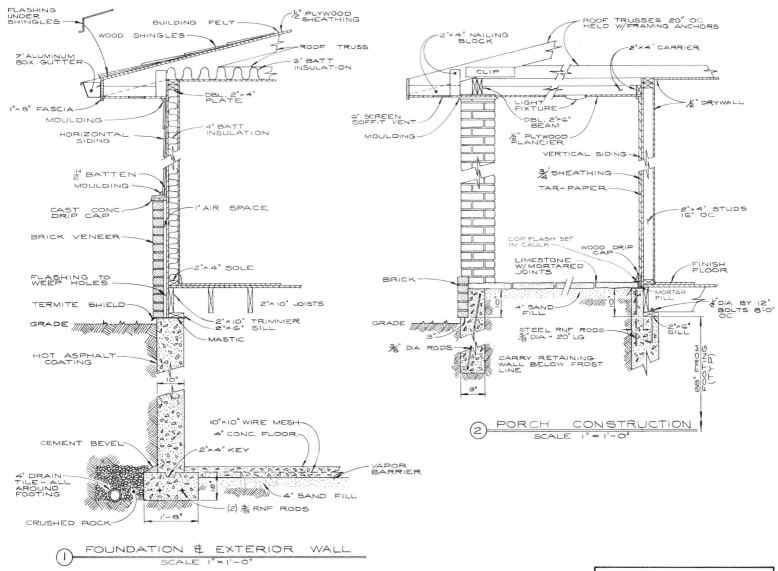

FLASHING UNDER SHINGLES
BUILDING FELT
½" PLYWOOD SHEATHING
WOOD SHINGLES
ROOF TRUSS
7" ALUMINUM BOX GUTTER
6" BATT INSULATION
1"×8" FASCIA
MOULDING
DBL. 2"×4" PLATE
HORIZONTAL SIDING
4" BATT INSULATION
½" BATTEN MOULDING
1" AIR SPACE
CAST CONC. DRIP CAP
BRICK VENEER
FLASHING TO WEEP HOLES
2"×4" SOLE
TERMITE SHIELD
2"×10" JOISTS
GRADE
2"×10" TRIMMER
2"×6" SILL
MASTIC
HOT ASPHALT COATING
10"
CEMENT BEVEL
10"×10" WIRE MESH
4" CONC. FLOOR
2"×4" KEY
VAPOR BARRIER
4" DRAIN TILE – ALL AROUND FOOTING
CRUSHED ROCK
12"
4" SAND FILL
(2) ⅜ RNF RODS
1'-8"

① FOUNDATION & EXTERIOR WALL
SCALE 1"=1'-0"

ROOF TRUSSES 20" OC HELD W/FRAMING ANCHORS
2"×4" NAILING BLOCK
2"×4" CARRIER
CLIP
½" DRYWALL
6' SCREEN SOFFIT VENT
LIGHT FIXTURE
DBL. 2"×6" BEAM
MOULDING
½" PLYWOOD PLANCIER
VERTICAL SIDING
¾" SHEATHING
TAR-PAPER
2"×4" STUDS 16" OC
COP FLASH SET IN CAULK
WOOD DRIP CAP
BRICK
LIMESTONE W/MORTARED JOINTS
FINISH FLOOR
GRADE
4" SAND FILL
MORTAR FILL
½" DIA BY 12" BOLTS 8'-0" OC
3"
⅜" DIA RODS
10"
STEEL RNF RODS ⅜ DIA × 20" LG
CARRY RETAINING WALL BELOW FROST LINE
2"×6" SILL
9"
88" FROM FOOTING (TYP)

② PORCH CONSTRUCTION
SCALE 1"=1'-0"

SHEET 6   DETAILS

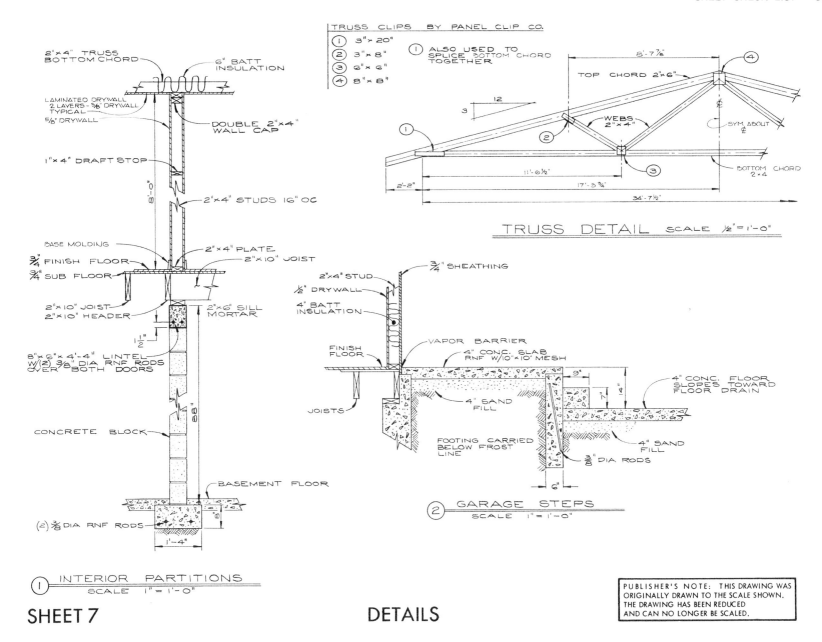

TRUSS CLIPS BY PANEL CLIP CO.
① 3"×20"
② 3"×8"
③ 6"×6"
④ 8"×8"

① ALSO USED TO SPLICE BOTTOM CHORD TOGETHER

TOP CHORD 2"×6"

WEBS 2"×4"

SYM. ABOUT ℄

BOTTOM CHORD 2×4

8'-7⅞"

11'-6½"

2'-2"

17'-3¾"

34'-7½"

12
3

TRUSS DETAIL SCALE ½"=1'-0"

2"×4" TRUSS BOTTOM CHORD

6" BATT INSULATION

LAMINATED DRYWALL 2 LAYERS-⅜" DRYWALL TYPICAL

⅝" DRYWALL

DOUBLE 2"×4" WALL CAP

1"×4" DRAFT STOP

2"×4" STUDS 16" OC

8'-0"

BASE MOLDING

2"×4" PLATE

2"×10" JOIST

¾" FINISH FLOOR

¾" SUB FLOOR

2"×10" JOIST
2"×10" HEADER

2"×6" SILL MORTAR

1½"

8"×6"×4'-4" LINTEL W/(2) ⅜" DIA RNF RODS OVER BOTH DOORS

8"

CONCRETE BLOCK

BASEMENT FLOOR

8"

(2) ⅜" DIA RNF RODS

1'-4"

① INTERIOR PARTITIONS
SCALE 1"=1'-0"

3"×4" STUD

½" DRYWALL

4" BATT INSULATION

¾" SHEATHING

VAPOR BARRIER

FINISH FLOOR

JOISTS

4" CONC. SLAB RNF W/10"×10" MESH

4" SAND FILL

FOOTING CARRIED BELOW FROST LINE

9"

4"

⅜" DIA RODS

6"

4" CONC. FLOOR SLOPES TOWARD FLOOR DRAIN

4" SAND FILL

② GARAGE STEPS
SCALE 1"=1'-0"

SHEET 7

DETAILS

PUBLISHER'S NOTE: THIS DRAWING WAS ORIGINALLY DRAWN TO THE SCALE SHOWN. THE DRAWING HAS BEEN REDUCED AND CAN NO LONGER BE SCALED.

4" ID STEEL
PIPE CONC
FILLED

WELDED
CAP

4"

(3) ½" DIA
RODS
EQUAL
SPACED

① FOOTING
SCALE 1" = 1'-0"

TERRACE GRADE FALLS
AWAY FROM HOUSE 1" PER 10'-0"

LIME STONE

FINISH
FLOOR

WOOD DRIP
CAP

6"

BRICK

4" SAND
FILL

9"

2"

MORTARED
JOINTS

⅜" DIA RODS

FINISH
GRADE

STEEL RNF.
RODS ⅜" DIA
BY 20' LG

FOOTING CARRIED
BELOW FROST
LINE

9"

② BACK TERRACE
SCALE 1" = 1'-0"

LIME STONE

MORTARED
JOINTS

8"

9"

7"

4"

4" SAND
FILL

GR

4" CONC
WALK

FOOTING
CARRIED
BELOW FROST
LINE

⅜" DIA
RODS

③ FRONT STEPS
SCALE 1" = 1'-0"

3½"

1"

9"

④ GIRDER POCKET
SCALE: 1" = 1'-0"

3"

1"

GR

FINISH FLOOR
ELEVATION

INDICATES THE
LOCATION OF
PORTCH FOOTING
& RETAINING
WALL.

2"× 4" KEY

BOTH FOOTINGS
CARRIED BELOW
FROST LINE

12"

⑤ COLUMN FOOTING
SCALE 1" = 1'-0"

4" CONC. SLAB

9"

7"

4"

4" CONC
WALK

4" SAND
FILL

⅜" DIA RODS

FOOTING
CARRIED
BELOW
FROST LINE

8"

⑥ BACK STEPS
SCALE 1" = 1'-0"

TAR-PAPER
¾" SHEATHING
2"× 4" STUDS
½"× 12" BOLTS

1" AIR SPACE

BRICK VENEER

2"× 4"
SILL

4" SAND
FILL

8" CONC. BLOCK
CARRIED BELOW
FROST LINE

⑦ GARAGE SILL
SCALE 1" = 1'-0"

SHEET 8

DETAILS

PUBLISHER'S NOTE: THIS DRAWING WAS
ORIGINALLY DRAWN TO THE SCALE SHOWN.
THE DRAWING HAS BEEN REDUCED
AND CAN NO LONGER BE SCALED.

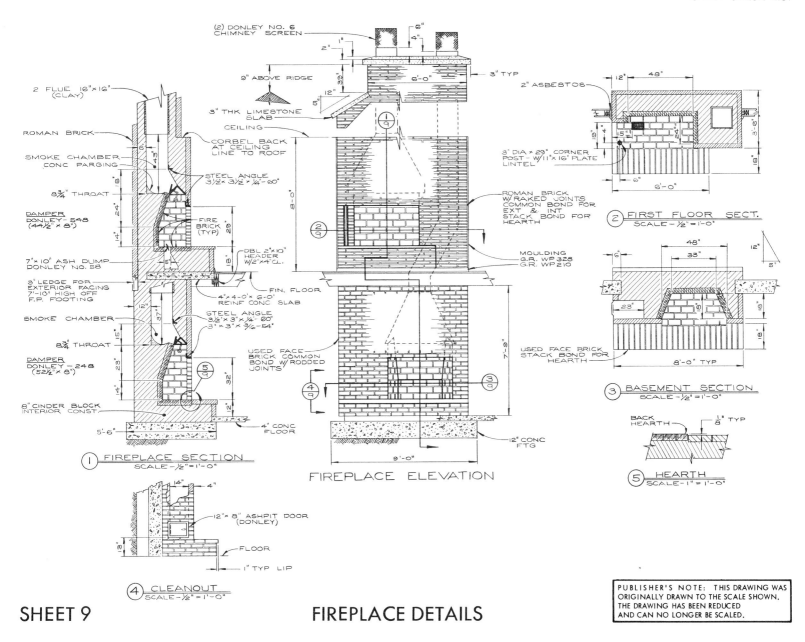

2 FLUE 16"x16" (CLAY)

(2) DONLEY NO. 6 CHIMNEY SCREEN

9" ABOVE RIDGE

3" THK LIMESTONE SLAB

CEILING

ROMAN BRICK

SMOKE CHAMBER CONC PARGING

8¾" THROAT

DAMPER DONLEY - 548 (44½" x 8")

7"x10" ASH DUMP DONLEY NO. 58

3" LEDGE FOR EXTERIOR FACING 7'-10" HIGH OFF F.P. FOOTING

SMOKE CHAMBER

8¾" THROAT

DAMPER DONLEY - 248 (52½" x 8")

8" CINDER BLOCK INTERIOR CONST.

CORBEL BACK AT CEILING LINE TO ROOF

STEEL ANGLE 3½" x 3½" x ¼" - 60"

FIRE BRICK (TYP)

DBL 2"x10" HEADER W/2"x4" CL.

FIN. FLOOR

4"x4'-0"x 6'-0" REINF CONC SLAB

STEEL ANGLE 3½" x 3" x ¼" - 60" 3" x 3" x 3/16 - 54"

USED FACE BRICK COMMON BOND W/ RODDED JOINTS

4" CONC FLOOR

5'-6"

① FIREPLACE SECTION
SCALE - ½" = 1'-0"

2" ASBESTOS

3" DIA x 29" CORNER POST - W/11"x 16" PLATE LINTEL

② FIRST FLOOR SECT.
SCALE - ½" = 1'-0"

ROMAN BRICK W/ RAKED JOINTS COMMON BOND FOR EXT & INT STACK BOND FOR HEARTH

MOULDING G.R. WP 328 G.R. WP 210

USED FACE BRICK STACK BOND FOR HEARTH

③ BASEMENT SECTION
SCALE - ½" = 1'-0"

BACK HEARTH

⑤ HEARTH
SCALE - 1" = 1'-0"

FIREPLACE ELEVATION

12"x 8" ASHPIT DOOR (DONLEY)

FLOOR

1" TYP LIP

④ CLEANOUT
SCALE - ½" = 1'-0"

12" CONC FTG

SHEET 9

FIREPLACE DETAILS

PUBLISHER'S NOTE: THIS DRAWING WAS ORIGINALLY DRAWN TO THE SCALE SHOWN. THE DRAWING HAS BEEN REDUCED AND CAN NO LONGER BE SCALED.

CARRY DRY WALL TO BOTTOM OF JOIST

ALUMINUM KICK PLATE

(2) 2"x10" TRIMMER

TREAD "A"-2"x10"x 3'-4"

2'-11"

3'-1"

3'-5"

2 STAIR- FRONT ELEVATION
SCALE - 3/4" = 1'-0"

THIS DIMENSION 4"-FOR TREAD "A"

5"

3 3/4"

4"

ALL TREADS CUT FROM 2"x10"

4 TREAD
SCALE - 1" = 1'-0"
TYP 3 PLACES

2"x4" CEILING LADDER 16" OC

(2) 2"x4" SUPPORTS

1/2 DRY WALL

GARAGE STORAGE CLOSET

SUB FLOOR

(2) 2"x10" HEADER

2"x6" NAILER

FINISH FLOOR

3'-0"

(2) 2"x10" HEADER

2"x6" CLEAT

3/10

2/10

9'-8"

8'-8"

7'-0"

2'-6"

8 1/2"

1" TYP NOSING

7 1/2" TYP RISE

(3) BALUSTER 2"x4"x4'-0" S4S DOUGLAS FIR FASTEN TO STRINGER WITH (6) 4"- 3/8 DIA BOLT DRILL BOLT HOLES AT ASSY

RAMSET- 2"x4"x 3'-6" CLEAT

10'-7"

1 STAIR - SIDE ELEVATION
SCALE - 3/4" = 1'-0"

(2) STRINGER CUT FROM 2"x12"x13'-7"

4/10

1"

1 1/8"

HANDRAIL 2"x4"x13'-6" S4S- DOUGLAS FIR

CSK FOR BOLT HEAD

FASTEN HANDRAIL TO BALUSTER WITH 3 1/2"- 3/8 DIA BOLT, WSHER, & NUT DRILL BOLT HOLES AT ASSY

3 HAND RAIL
SCALE - 1" = 2"
TYP 3 PLACES

SHEET 10

STAIR DETAILS

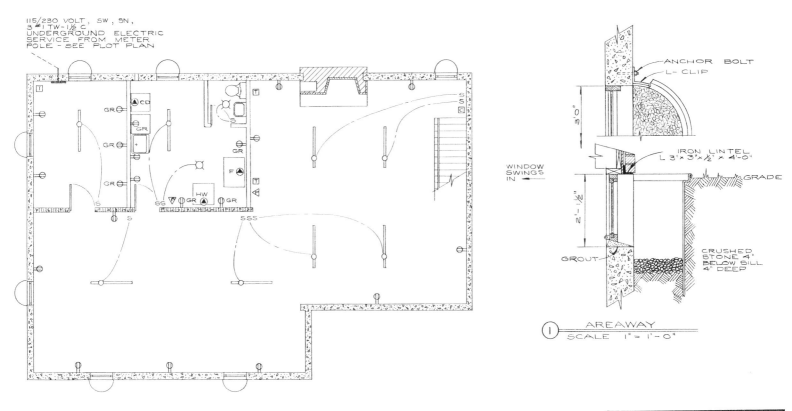

115/230 VOLT, SW, 5N,
3#1TW-1½ C
UNDERGROUND ELECTRIC
SERVICE FROM METER
POLE - SEE PLOT PLAN

WINDOW
SWINGS
IN

ANCHOR BOLT
L-CLIP
3'0"
IRON LINTEL
L 3"×3"×½"×4'-0"
GRADE
2'-1½"
CRUSHED
STONE 4"
BELOW SILL
4" DEEP
GROUT

1 AREAWAY
SCALE 1"=1'-0"

SHEET 11   **BASEMENT ELECTRICAL PLAN**

PUBLISHER'S NOTE: THIS DRAWING WAS
ORIGINALLY DRAWN TO THE SCALE SHOWN.
THE DRAWING HAS BEEN REDUCED
AND CAN NO LONGER BE SCALED.

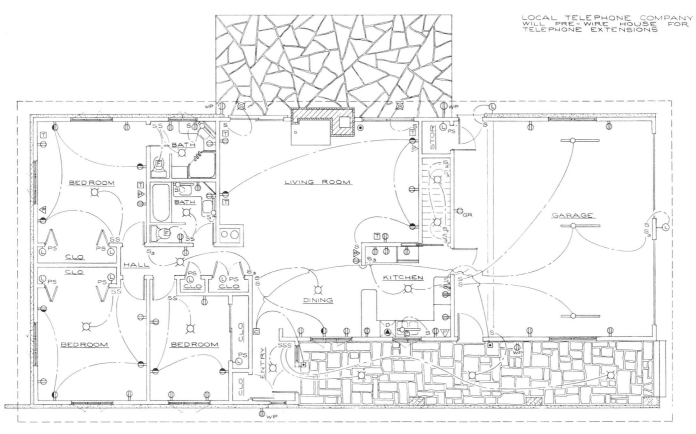

LOCAL TELEPHONE COMPANY
WILL PRE-WIRE HOUSE FOR
TELEPHONE EXTENSIONS

BEDROOM
BATH
BATH
CLO
CLO
HALL
CLO
CLO
BEDROOM
BEDROOM
CLO
ENTRY
LIVING ROOM
STOR
DINING
KITCHEN
GARAGE

GENERAL OUTLETS	CONVENIENCE OUTLETS	SWITCH OUTLETS

GENERAL OUTLETS
- CEILING FIXTURE
- F CEILING FAN
- LPS LAMP & PULL SWITCH
- SPOT LIGHT
- NEON FIXTURE

AUXILIARY OUTLETS
- PUSH BUTTON
- C CHIMES
- T TELEVISION ANTENNA
- PHONE JACK

CONVENIENCE OUTLETS
- DUPLEX
- SPLIT WIRED
- WEATHERPROOF (WP)
- 220 VOLT - RANGE
- FLOOR
- C CLOCK
- SPECIAL PURPOSE
    - D DISHWASHER
    - HW WATER HEATER
    - F FURNACE
    - CD CLOTHES DRYER

SWITCH OUTLETS
- S SINGLE POLE
- S₃ THREE WAY
- S(WP) WEATHERPROOF

SHEET 12   **1st FLOOR ELECTRICAL PLAN**

PUBLISHER'S NOTE: THIS DRAWING WAS
ORIGINALLY DRAWN TO THE SCALE SHOWN.
THE DRAWING HAS BEEN REDUCED
AND CAN NO LONGER BE SCALED.

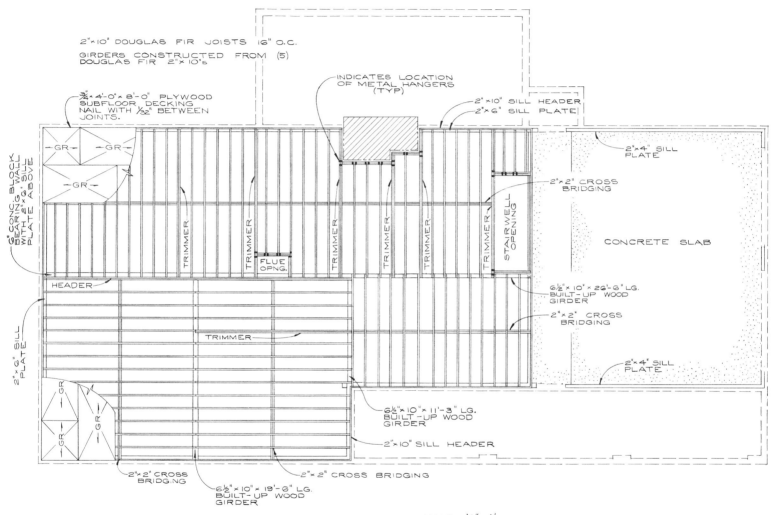

2"×10" DOUGLAS FIR JOISTS 16" O.C.

GIRDERS CONSTRUCTED FROM (5)
DOUGLAS FIR 2"×10's

INDICATES LOCATION
OF METAL HANGERS
(TYP)

3/4"×4'-0"×8'-0" PLYWOOD
SUBFLOOR DECKING
NAIL WITH 1/32" BETWEEN
JOINTS.

2"×10" SILL HEADER
2"×6" SILL PLATE

6" CONC. BLOCK
BEARING WALL
WITH 2"×6" SILL
PLATE ABOVE

2"×4" SILL
PLATE

GR   GR

GR

TRIMMER

TRIMMER

FLUE
OPNG.

TRIMMER

TRIMMER

TRIMMER

TRIMMER

STAIRWELL
OPENING

2"×2" CROSS
BRIDGING

CONCRETE   SLAB

HEADER

6½"×10"×26'-6" LG.
BUILT-UP WOOD
GIRDER

2"×2" CROSS
BRIDGING

2"×6" SILL
PLATE

TRIMMER

2"×4" SILL
PLATE

GR   GR

GR

6½"×10"×11'-3" LG.
BUILT-UP WOOD
GIRDER

2"×10" SILL HEADER

2"×2" CROSS
BRIDGING

2"×2" CROSS BRIDGING

6½"×10"×19'-6" LG.
BUILT-UP WOOD
GIRDER

SCALE: 1/4" = 1'

FRAMING MEMBERS HUNG WITH
TECO-U-GRIP TYPE A-13 HANGERS

SHEET 13   FLOOR FRAMING PLAN

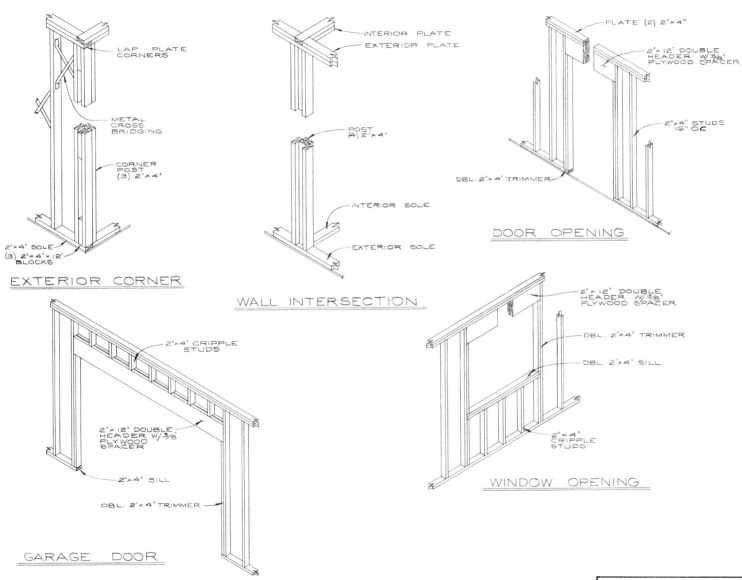

LAP PLATE CORNERS

METAL CROSS BRIDGING

CORNER POST (3) 2"x 4"

2"x 4" SOLE

(3) 2"x 4"x 12" BLOCKS

EXTERIOR CORNER

INTERIOR PLATE

EXTERIOR PLATE

POST (4) 2"x 4"

INTERIOR SOLE

EXTERIOR SOLE

WALL INTERSECTION

PLATE (2) 2"x 4"

2"x 12" DOUBLE HEADER W/ 3/8" PLYWOOD SPACER

2"x 4" STUDS 16" OC

DBL. 2"x 4" TRIMMER

DOOR OPENING

2"x 4" CRIPPLE STUDS

2"x 12" DOUBLE HEADER W/ 3/8" PLYWOOD SPACER

2"x 4" SILL

DBL. 2"x 4" TRIMMER

GARAGE DOOR

2"x 12" DOUBLE HEADER W/ 3/8" PLYWOOD SPACER

DBL. 2"x 4" TRIMMER

DBL. 2"x 4" SILL

2"x 4" CRIPPLE STUDS

WINDOW OPENING

SHEET 14

FRAMING DETAILS

PUBLISHER'S NOTE: THIS DRAWING WAS ORIGINALLY DRAWN TO THE SCALE SHOWN. THE DRAWING HAS BEEN REDUCED AND CAN NO LONGER BE SCALED.

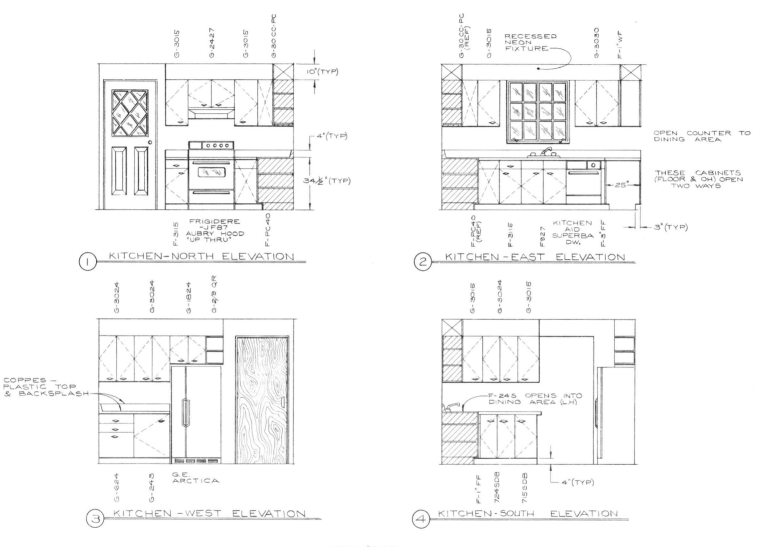

G-3015 G-2427 G-3015 G-30 CC-PC

10" (TYP)

4" (TYP)

34½" (TYP)

FRIGIDERE
-JF87
AUBRY HOOD
"UP THRU."

F-3115 F-PC40

① KITCHEN-NORTH ELEVATION

G-30CC-PC (REF) G-3015 RECESSED NEON FIXTURE G-3030 F-1" WF

OPEN COUNTER TO DINING AREA

THESE CABINETS (FLOOR & OH) OPEN TWO WAYS

25"

3" (TYP)

F-PC40 (REF) F-3115 F927 KITCHEN AID SUPERBA DW. F-3" FF

② KITCHEN-EAST ELEVATION

G-3024 G-3024 G-1824 G-2/9 QR

COPPES-
PLASTIC TOP
& BACKSPLASH

G-G24 G-243 G.E. ARCTICA

③ KITCHEN-WEST ELEVATION

G-3015 G-3024 G-3015

F-245 OPENS INTO DINING AREA (L.H)

4" (TYP)

F-1" FF 724SDB 715SDB

④ KITCHEN-SOUTH ELEVATION

SCALE: ½"=1-0"

CABINETS BY COPPES NAPANEE
THE CONTEMPORARY MODEL IN
5TO TAWNY OAK - H29-3321 PULLS

SHEET 15   INTERIOR ELEVATIONS

PUBLISHER'S NOTE: THIS DRAWING WAS
ORIGINALLY DRAWN TO THE SCALE SHOWN.
THE DRAWING HAS BEEN REDUCED
AND CAN NO LONGER BE SCALED.

WINDOW SCHEDULE

SYM	SIZE	TYPE	MANUFACTURER	CAT. NO.	GLAZING	MATERIAL	REMARKS	QUAN
①	6'-2¼" × 6'-10¾"	GLIDING DOOR	ANDERSEN	D6068-OX	TWINDOW	WOOD		1
②	6'-10½" × 7'-3⅝"	AWNING	PELLA	3616A-22	TWINDOW	WOOD		1
③	3'-½" × 2'-⅝"	AWNING	ANDERSEN	A31	TWINDOW	WOOD	2 UNITS MULLION JOINED	4
④	3'-⅛" × 3'-5¼"	CASEMENT	ANDERSEN	2N30	TWINDOW	WOOD		1
⑤	3'-6⅛" × 5'-1"	CASEMENT	ANDERSEN	3N3	TWINDOW	WOOD		5
⑥	6'-6⅞" × 2'-2"	CASEMENT	ANDERSEN	W1N6	TWINDOW	WOOD		2
⑦	4'-6¼" × 5'-2¾"	CASEMENT	ANDERSEN	3N4	TWINDOW	WOOD		1
⑧	3'-6⅛" × 3'-5¼"	CASEMENT	ANDERSEN	2N3	TWINDOW	WOOD		1
⑨	1'-11⅞" × 2'-8⅛"	BASEMENT	ANDERSEN	2820	TWINDOW	WOOD		7

DOOR SCHEDULE

SYM	SIZE	THK	TYPE	MANUFACTURER	CAT. NO.	MAT	FINISH	JAMB	REMARKS	QUAN
△1	10'-6" × 7'-0"	1¾"	OVERHEAD	FRANZ	F.P. 857	DG. FIR	STAIN	WOOD		2
△2	3'-0" × 6'-8"	1¾"	PANEL	SIMPSON	S-2570	DG. FIR	STAIN	WOOD	7" × 10¹⁵⁄₁₆" GLAZING	1
△3	3'-0" × 6'-8"	1¾"	SOLID CR.	SIMPSON	F-38	PINE	STAIN	WOOD		1
△4	2'-8" × 6'-8"	1⅜"	HOLLOW CR.	SIMPSON	F-20	PINE	STAIN	WOOD		6
△5	4'-0" × 6'-8½"	1⅛"	BI-FOLD	MORGAN	M-4FD	PINE	PAINT	WOOD	2 UNITS PER CLO.	4
△6	2'-0" × 6'-8½"	1⅛"	HOLLOW CR.	MORGAN	M-510	PINE	PAINT	WOOD		3
△7	3'-6" × 6'-8"	1⅛"	SLIDING	SEARS	64H275S	PINE	PAINT	WOOD		2
△8	3'-0" × 6'-8"	1¾"	PANEL	SIMPSON	S-2212-D	DG. FIR	STAIN	WOOD		1
△9	3'-0" × 6'-8"	1⅜	POCKET	SIMPSON	F-20-P	PINE	STAIN	WOOD		1
△10	3'-0" × 6'-8"	1⅜"	HOLLOW CR.	SEARS	64H2854	PINE	PAINT	WOOD		3
△11	3'-0" × 6'-8"	1¾"	PANEL	SIMPSON	S-2059	DG. FIR	STAIN	WOOD		1

SHEET 16   WINDOW/DOOR SCHEDULES

PUBLISHER'S NOTE: THIS DRAWING WAS ORIGINALLY DRAWN TO THE SCALE SHOWN. THE DRAWING HAS BEEN REDUCED AND CAN NO LONGER BE SCALED.

Metric Measurements In The Building Industry – Appendix A

Current controversies in the United States regarding the metric system obscure the fact that this system was recognized as early as 1875. It was then that the United States signed the Metric Convention defining metric standards for length and mass and establishing the International Bureau of Weights and Measures. Except for scientific uses the recognition was verbal rather than actual, as proved by the fact that ninety-seven years later, in 1972, the United States was the only industrialized nation in the world that had not committed itself totally to metric measure. Aside from some present engineering, scientific, and medical uses of metric measures in this country, the obvious advantages of the system have been ignored. Now, largely because of the pressures of international trade, the United States is moving gradually—but much too slowly—toward adoption of the metric system for general use. Eventually it seems certain to replace the awkward mixture of U.S. measurements which had their origin in England.

Developing Standard Measurement

When the American Colonies gained their independence from England they retained the English standard customs of weights and measures. For many years prior to the American Revolution for Independence, England had well-established standards of measurement that remained basically unchanged until 1965. Many of the units common to England and the United States had evolved through antiquity. Historically, England was the first nation to standardize weights and measures, thereby bringing together and resolving differences which previously had existed throughout various regions.

On the European continent at this time varying units of weights and measures were used between towns, countries, and even in some cases between different crafts and guilds within the same community. The confusion ultimately caused by the great multiplicity of units led the French government to support and assist in the development of the metric system.

The French Academy officially decreed a meter was to be one ten millionth of the distance from the North Pole to the Equator along a meridian running close to Dunkirk, Paris, and Barcelona. The new metric system was well accepted by the general populace of 19th century continental Europe. Because England had long before established her own standards of weights and measures she refused to align herself with the new metric system.

Gradually from the initial establishment of the metric system in Europe, nations throughout the world have adopted this system of measurement. By 1965 England, Canada, Australia and the United States were the only remaining major goods-producing countries that did not use metric measure. Realizing its lone position, England in 1965 began a 10-year *metrication* program to convert to the metric system. Shortly thereafter Canada and Australia elected to change because of their ties with England.

During the 1960's there seemed to be no necessity for the United States to convert to the metric system. Following the second world war the United States became the prime producer of goods and materials in the world. Countries purchasing goods from the United States had to learn to use the English system of measure. In the 1970's, however, the United States no longer had England as the other major nation producing goods based on the English system of measure. Many professional, manufacturing, and trade associations in the United States have stated that if the United States is to remain competitive in the world market place, she must switch to the metric system. Perhaps the big stumbling block in the changeover to a metric system is the general public's lack of knowledge of metrics despite the simplicity of the system.

Metric Calculations Are Easy

The metric system is based on the number 10. All units of weight, lineal measure, and volume are based on the number 10. The basic unit of length is the meter. The meter is similar to the yard, but it is just a bit longer. Rather than dividing by three to obtain the number of feet or by 36 to obtain the number of inches, one divides by the power of 10. For example, a *meter* has 1000 *milli*meters, 100 *centi*meters, and 10 *deci*meters. 10 meters equals a *decka*meter, 100 meters is a *hecto*meter and 1000 meters is equivalent to a *kilo*meter, as shown in the table.

Factor by which the unit is multiplied	Prefix	Symbol
10^3	kilo	k
10^2	hecto	h
10	deca	da
10^{-1}	deci	d
10^{-2}	centi	c
10^{-3}	milli	m

These prefixes are common in all units of measure in the metric system. Conversions from one unit to another are made by moving the decimal point either to the right or to the left to increase or decrease the amount.

Metric Measurements in the British Building Industry

The change to metric gave the British building industry the opportunity to modularly coordinate building design and construction practices. This has permitted greater standardized dimensional building products. For example, structural openings are 600 mm (1' 11⅝"), 700 mm (2'3⁹/₁₆"), 800 mm (2'7½"), 900 mm (2'11⁷/₁₆"), 1000 mm (3'3⅜") wide and 2100 mm (6'10¹¹/₁₆") high. It is evident from the preceding figures the modular opening widths are in 100 mm increments. Mills and door manufacturers are producing door sets, i.e., doors, frame, and casing to fit these standard openings. Similarly windows are available to fit standard 100 mm increment modules. Fig. A-1 shows a section from an English window manufacturer's catalog. It will be noted that widths are given in the module. Other building products, such as concrete block (regular and lightweight), brick, glass block, panelings, etc., have all been converted to metric sizes. Some products have changed slightly in size, not only to conform to stack or coursing dimensions of varying products but also to meet with the new modular practice.

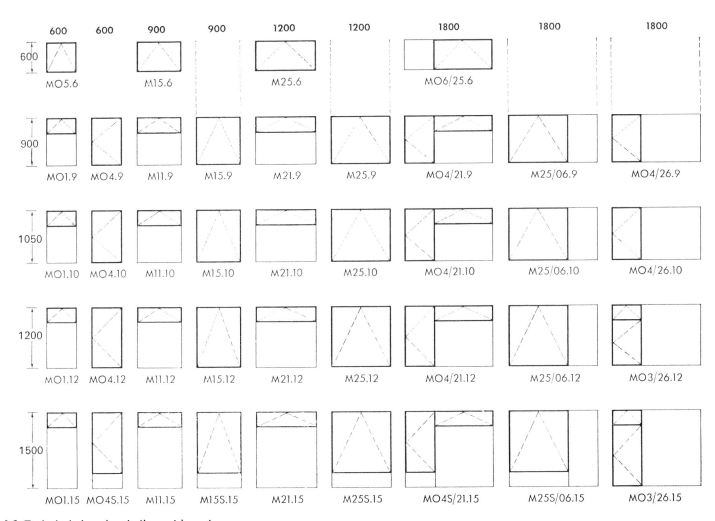

Fig. A-1. Typical window sizes in the metric system.

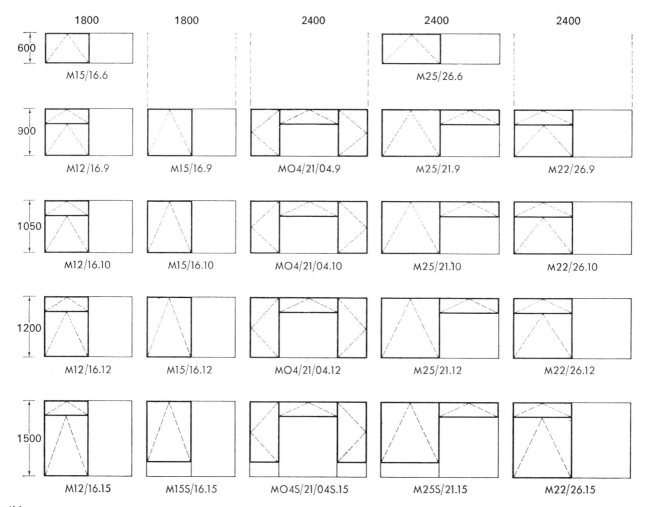

Fig. A-1. Cont'd

Cost Advantages of Metric System Realized in United Kingdom

Many advantages await the building industry by converting to the metric system. In doing so the United Kingdom now has a simple universal method of measuring which also has led to a system for dimensional and modular coordination as well as standardized component sizes. As Britain moved fully to the metric system, greater economy was realized as more standardized units were used.

A minimum amount of effort was required as architects and engineers reoriented themselves in the metric system. Costs for converting to the metric system by the building designer have been relatively small. However, the advantages ultimately obtained have benefited the architect in substantial time savings, in services rendered to the client, and in significant reduction of the final building cost.

New Metric Sizes for Building Materials and Components

Table A-1 shows the various metric sizes of dimensional softwood used for structural components and trim members. All softwood in England is sold by the *lineal meter* (*m*) rather than a lineal foot. The cross sectional size is given in *millimeters* (*mm*) instead of inches. Plywood, particle board, hard board, and underlayment are sold in units of *10 square meters* (10 m² or 10 sq. m), in sheet sizes in millimeters (mm) and by its thickness in millimeters (mm). All lengths of soft wood are sold in standard increments of *300 millimeters,* beginning at 1.8 meters, 1.8, 2.1, 2.4, 2.7 etc.

These new metric lengths are shorter than former foot lengths. Table A-2 shows the new metric lengths of wood and their equiva-

TABLE A-2

STANDARD METRIC LENGTHS OF SOFTWOOD ARE AVAILABLE FROM 1.8 M, INCREASING BY INCREMENTS OF 300 MM.

Metric Lengths	Equivalent in Feet and Inches
1.8 m	5' – 10 7/8"
2.1 m	6' – 10 5/8"
2.4 m	7' – 10 1/2"
2.7 m	8' – 10 1/4"
3.0 m	9' – 10 1/8"
3.3 m	10' – 9 7/8"
3.6 m	11' – 9 3/4"
3.9 m	12' – 9 1/2"
4.2 m	13' – 9 3/8"
4.5 m	14' – 9 1/8"
4.8 m	15' – 9"
5.1 m	16' – 8 3/4"
5.4 m	17' – 8 5/8"
5.7 m	18' – 8 3/8"
6.0 m	19' – 8 1/8"
6.3 m	20' – 8"

Timber Research and Development Association, Huhendon Valley, High Wycome, Buckinghamshire, England

TABLE A-1
METRIC SIZES OF SAWN SOFTWOOD

Thickness in mm	75	100	125	150	175	200	225	250	300
16	x	x	x	x					
19	x	x	x	x					
22	x	x	x	x					
25	x	x	x	x	x	x	x	x	x
32	x	x	x	x	x	x	x	x	x
38	x	x	x	x	x	x	x		
44	x	x	x	x	x	x	x	x	x
50	x	x	x	x	x	x	x	x	x
63		x	x	x	x	x	x		
75		x	x	x	x	x	x	x	x
100		x		x		x		x	x
150				x		x			x
200						x			
250								x	
300									x

Timber Research and Development Association, Huhenden Valley, High Wycome, Buckinghamshire, England.

lents in feet and inches. The new mm thickness sizes are close to the standard inch measure of lumber that had been used previously in Britain. A graphic comparison is shown in Fig. A-2 between the standard British millimeter increment sizes and the old Imperial inch measurements.

A standard set of dimensions, 300 mm and 100 mm, were developed to assist manufacturers in redesigning building component products. A 300 mm or 500 mm increment is used on planning grids for all types of

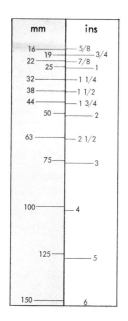

mm	ins
16	5/8
19	3/4
22	7/8
25	1
32	1 1/4
38	1 1/2
44	1 3/4
50	2
63	2 1/2
75	3
100	4
125	5
150	6

Fig. A-2. Most metric sizes for softwood are slightly smaller than standard inch measure sizes.

building. The 100 mm value is a vertical increment for elevations. To assist designers, many now use 300 mm or 500 mm coordinate paper. This minimizes the necessity of calculating and placing many dimensions.

Figs. A-3A and A-3B show buildings planned on 500 millimeter grids. Basically this method establishes a series of control lines (indicated by small circles at the extremities of the lines) which always fall on an increment of the preferred dimension. The exact position of the face of a wall or partition is then found by reference to the

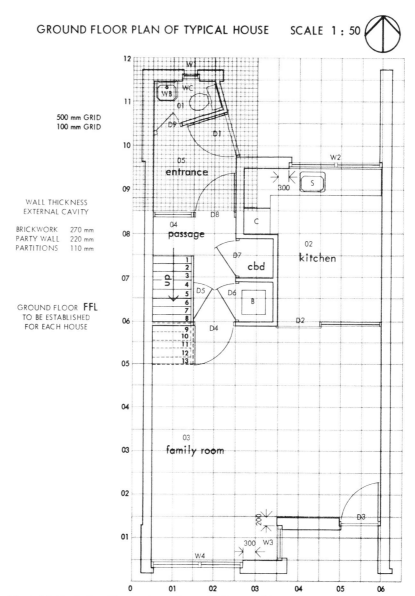

GROUND FLOOR PLAN OF TYPICAL HOUSE   SCALE 1 : 50

500 mm GRID
100 mm GRID

WALL THICKNESS
EXTERNAL CAVITY

BRICKWORK   270 mm
PARTY WALL   220 mm
PARTITIONS   110 mm

GROUND FLOOR **FFL**
TO BE ESTABLISHED
FOR EACH HOUSE

Fig. A-3A. Typical residence planned on a 500 mm grid.

GROUND FLOOR PLAN OF TYPICAL HOUSE   SCALE 1 : 50

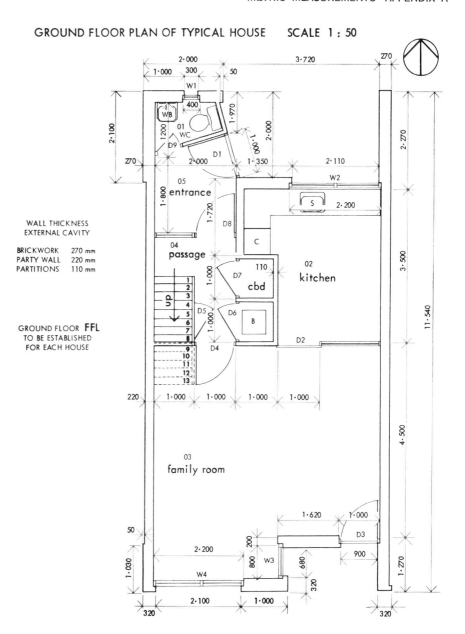

Fig. A-3B. Another typical residence planned on a 500 mm grid.

WALL THICKNESS
EXTERNAL CAVITY

BRICKWORK	270 mm
PARTY WALL	220 mm
PARTITIONS	110 mm

GROUND FLOOR **FFL**
TO BE ESTABLISHED
FOR EACH HOUSE

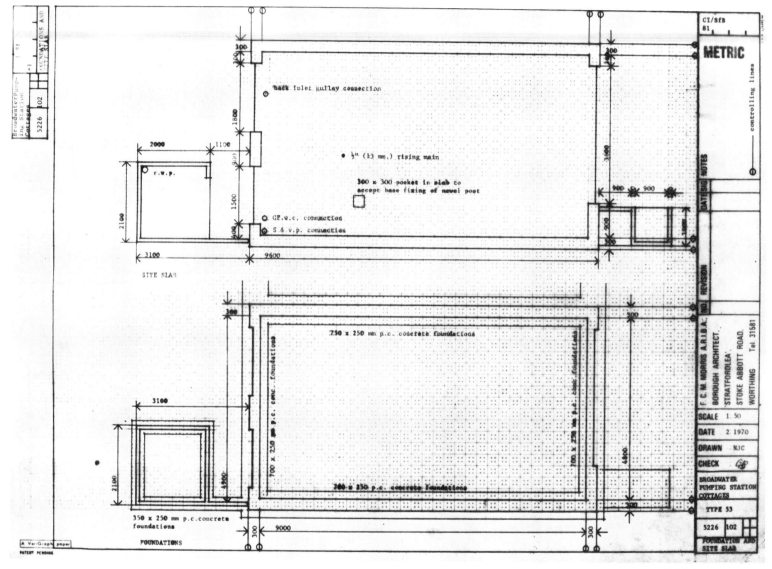

Fig. A-4. This foundation and site slab have been drawn on a 300 mm grid.

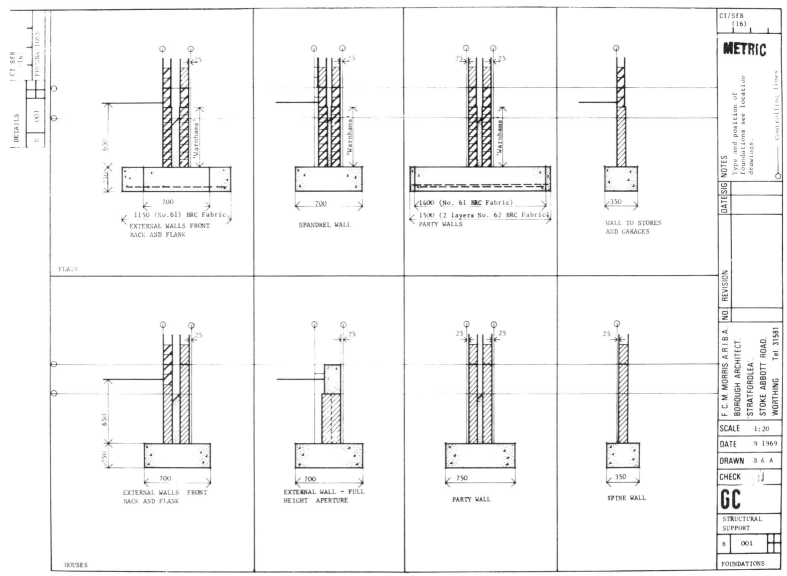

F.C.M. MORRIS, A.R.I.B.A.

Fig. A-5. Each structural detail shows its placement in the building by a set of control lines. These lines are identified by circles at the extremities of the lines.

appropriate detail. The detail illustrates the control line and sufficient dimensions to enable the builder to accordingly locate that particular feature. To illustrate this practice Fig. A-4 shows the plan views of a foundation and site slab drawn on a 300 mm grid. Several of the details for the foundation are shown in Fig. A-5. Note that in each of these details the control lines are identified by circles and how relatively few dimensions appear on the details.

This system may seem rather cumbersome by United States building practice; however, many architects and contractors report little difficulty on the part of the tradesman in making the change to this new system. Two of a number of buildings designed on the modular coordinated system by F.C.M. Morris, A.R.I.B.A., at the Broadwater Pumping Station at Worthing-Sussex, England are shown in Fig. A-6. This type of housing is typical of the style currently being designed in much larger housing developments throughout the United Kingdom. Fig. A-7 shows two details of the plans for the building shown in Fig. A-6. It will be noted that the method of dimensioning is similar to that shown previously.

Making Metric Conversions

In changing from one system to another there is an awkward period caused by the fact that the units in one are not evenly divisible by those of the other, and this awkwardness continues until one can think entirely in terms of the new system. For example, the 300 mm module (corresponding to 11.81 in.) is nearly the same as 1 ft. and serves essentially the same purpose. It is an inconvenient number only while it still has to be *translated*. When once the metric units become familiar they have their own reality and avoid the complications of calculating with common fractions. For the awkward period of changeover perhaps the easiest and most certain way is to use conversion tables such as those in Table A-3, designed for converting fractional inches, inches, and feet into millimeters. The method of using this table is shown in the example of converting $293'5^{47}/_{64}''$ into millimeters. The 89,452.053 mm result for general purposes would be stated as 89,452 mm to the nearest millimeter. This is, of course, the same as 89.452 meters, which you may prefer to think of as about 89½ meters.

Another method, particularly useful where desk calculators or slide rules can be used, is to multiply by constant factors to

Fig. A-6. Metric modular coordinated building design and construction offers a saving to the owner.

F.C.M. MORRIS, A.R.I.B.A.

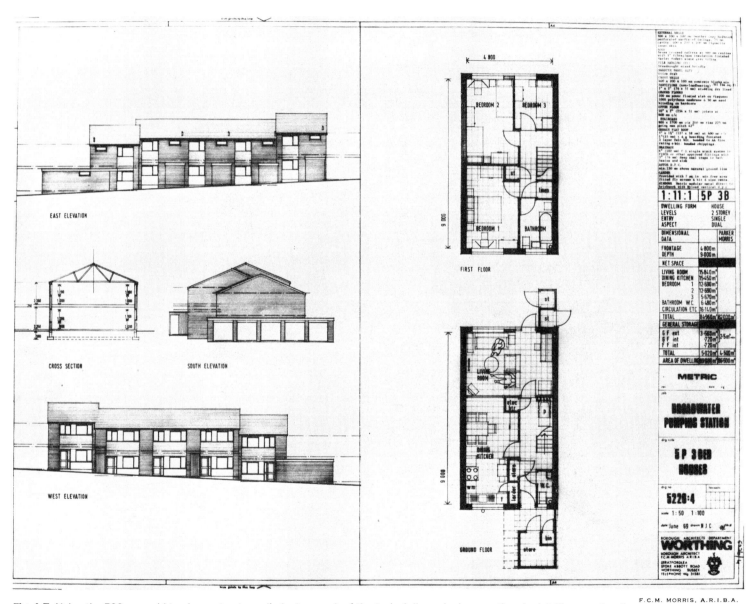

Fig. A-7. Using the 500 mm grid to plan a structure eliminates much of the typical dimensioning practices in detailing construction.

F.C.M. MORRIS, A.R.I.B.A.

TABLE A-3
Fractional Inch—Millimeter and Foot—Millimeter Conversion Tables
(Based on 1 inch = 25.4 millimeters, exactly)*

FRACTIONAL INCH TO MILLIMETERS

In.	Mm.	In.	Mm.	In.	Mm.	In.	Mm.
$\frac{1}{64}$	0.397	$\frac{17}{64}$	6.747	$\frac{33}{64}$	13.097	$\frac{49}{64}$	19.447
$\frac{1}{32}$	0.794	$\frac{9}{32}$	7.144	$\frac{17}{32}$	13.494	$\frac{25}{32}$	19.844
$\frac{3}{64}$	1.191	$\frac{19}{64}$	7.541	$\frac{35}{64}$	13.891	$\frac{51}{64}$	20.241
$\frac{1}{16}$	1.588	$\frac{5}{16}$	7.938	$\frac{9}{16}$	14.288	$\frac{13}{16}$	20.638
$\frac{5}{64}$	1.984	$\frac{21}{64}$	8.334	$\frac{37}{64}$	14.684	$\frac{53}{64}$	21.034
$\frac{3}{32}$	2.381	$\frac{11}{32}$	8.731	$\frac{19}{32}$	15.081	$\frac{27}{32}$	21.431
$\frac{7}{64}$	2.778	$\frac{23}{64}$	9.128	$\frac{39}{64}$	15.478	$\frac{55}{64}$	21.828
$\frac{1}{8}$	3.175	$\frac{3}{8}$	9.525	$\frac{5}{8}$	15.875	$\frac{7}{8}$	22.225
$\frac{9}{64}$	3.572	$\frac{25}{64}$	9.922	$\frac{41}{64}$	16.272	$\frac{57}{64}$	22.622
$\frac{5}{32}$	3.969	$\frac{13}{32}$	10.319	$\frac{21}{32}$	16.669	$\frac{29}{32}$	23.019
$\frac{11}{64}$	4.366	$\frac{27}{64}$	10.716	$\frac{43}{64}$	17.066	$\frac{59}{64}$	23.416
$\frac{3}{16}$	4.762	$\frac{7}{16}$	11.112	$\frac{11}{16}$	17.462	$\frac{15}{16}$	23.812
$\frac{13}{64}$	5.159	$\frac{29}{64}$	11.509	$\frac{45}{64}$	17.859	$\frac{61}{64}$	24.209
$\frac{7}{32}$	5.556	$\frac{15}{32}$	11.906	$\frac{23}{32}$	18.256	$\frac{31}{32}$	24.606
$\frac{15}{64}$	5.953	$\frac{31}{64}$	12.303	$\frac{47}{64}$	18.653	$\frac{63}{64}$	25.003
$\frac{1}{4}$	6.350	$\frac{1}{2}$	12.700	$\frac{3}{4}$	19.050	1	25.400

INCHES TO MILLIMETERS

In.	Mm.	In.	Mm.	In.	Mm.	In.	Mm.	In.	Mm.	In.	Mm.
1	25.4	3	76.2	5	127.0	7	177.8	9	228.6	11	279.4
2	50.8	4	101.6	6	152.4	8	203.2	10	254.0	12	304.8

FEET TO MILLIMETERS

Ft.	Mm.	Ft.	Mm.	Ft.	Mm.	Ft.	Mm.	Ft.	Mm.
100	30,480	10	3,048	1	304.8	0.1	30.48	0.01	3.048
200	60,960	20	6,096	2	609.6	0.2	60.96	0.02	6.096
300	91,440	30	9,144	3	914.4	0.3	91.44	0.03	9.144
400	121,920	40	12,192	4	1,219.2	0.4	121.92	0.04	12.192
500	152,400	50	15,240	5	1,524.0	0.5	152.40	0.05	15.240
600	182,880	60	18,288	6	1,828.8	0.6	182.88	0.06	18.288
700	213,360	70	21,336	7	2,133.6	0.7	213.36	0.07	21.336
800	243,840	80	24,384	8	2,438.4	0.8	243.84	0.08	24.384
900	274,320	90	27,432	9	2,743.2	0.9	274.32	0.09	27.432
1,000	304,800	100	30,480	10	3,048.0	1.0	304.80	0.10	30.480

* American Standard Practice for Industrial Use (ANSI B48.1)

Example 1: Find millimeter equivalent of 293 feet, $5\frac{47}{64}$ inches.

200 ft	= 60,960.	mm
90 ft	= 27,432.	mm
3 ft	= 914.4	mm
5 in.	= 127.0	mm
$\frac{47}{64}$ in.	= 18.653	mm
293 ft, $5\frac{47}{64}$ in.	= 89,452.053	mm

Example 2: Find millimeter equivalent of 71.86 feet.

70. ft	= 21,336.	mm
1. ft	= 304.8	mm
.80 ft	= 243.84	mm
.06 ft	= 18.288	mm
71.86 ft	= 21,902.928	mm

MACHINERY'S HANDBOOK, 19TH EDITION, INDUSTRIAL PRESS, NEW YORK, N.Y.

TABLE A-4
CONVERSION FACTORS FOR LENGTHS AND AREAS, IN U.S. AND METRIC MEASUREMENTS

To Convert	Multiply By
Inches to Feet	.0833
Inches to Yards	.0278
Inches to Centimeters	2.54
Inches to Meters	.0254
Inches to Millimeters	25.4
Feet to Inches	12
Feet to Yards	.33
Feet to Miles	.000189
Feet to Centimeters	30.48
Feet to Kilometers	.0003048
Feet to Meters	.3048
Feet to Millimeters	304.8
Sq. Ft. to Sq. In.	144
Sq. Ft. to Sq. Yds.	.111
Sq. Ft. to Acres	.00002296
Sq. Ft. to Sq. Miles	.00000003587
Sq. Ft. to Sq. Meters	.8361
Sq. Yds. to Sq. Ft.	9
Sq. Yds. to Acres	.0002066
Sq. Yds. to Sq. Miles	.0000003228
Sq. Yds. to Sq. Meters	.8361
Sq. Miles to Sq. Ft.	27,878,400
Sq. Miles to Sq. Yds.	3,097,600
Sq. Miles to Acres	640
Sq. Miles to Sq. Meters	2,589,600
Sq. Miles to Sq. Kms.	2.590

To reverse the process, such as finding the number of inches corresponding to 250 mm, divide the number of millimeters by the same factor. Thus, 250 mm = 250 ÷ 25.4 = 9.8425".

change from U.S. to metric measurements or divide by the same factors to change from metric to U.S. measurements. Table A-4 lists the most common of these factors for lineal and square measurements. For instance, 1 yard (36 in.) = 2.54 × 36 = 91.24 cm, whereas 91.24 cm ÷ 2.54 = 36 in. Engineering and architectural handbooks usually contain numerous tables for making all types of metric conversions for cubic inches, cubic feet, cubic yards, weights, etc.

Dimensional Values on Drawings

All dimensions are given in millimeters. A five figure mm dimension, for example, 1,540, is written 1·540 (period in middle rather than comma) or 1 540 (space rather than comma). The comma is used in place of a decimal point to denote the difference between whole and decimal values.

All metric dimensions are placed on drawings in either the aligned or unidirectional system.

Dual Dimensioning Practice

When English and metric dimensions are both used on a drawing the identification of each is by position. Identification is attained by placing the equivalent dimension in a bracket [ ] or a rectangle. If the design is based on the English system, the English dimensions should precede or be placed above its metric equivalent. If the drawing is designed in metric, the metric value is placed above or to the left of its English counterpart. Fig. A-7 shows how dual dimensions are lettered on the drawing. In all cases each sheet in a set of drawings that has dual dimensions, carries the following note *adjacent* or in the *file strip:*

DIM in [ ] are millimeters

or

DIM in [ ] are inches

If a rectangle is used for the equivalent rather than a bracket, a rectangle would, of course, replace the bracket in the note.

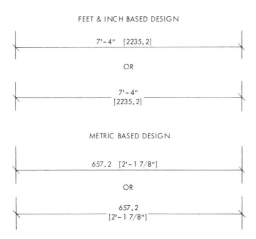

FEET & INCH BASED DESIGN

7'-4" [2235.2]

OR

7'-4"
[2235.2]

METRIC BASED DESIGN

657.2 [2'-1 7/8"]

OR

657.2
[2'-1 7/8"]

Fig. A-8. Drawings that have dual dimensions in English and metric are dimensioned as shown.

References – Appendix B

The following list of books will provide additional information on varying topics that the student may wish to pursue at greater length. The authors have found these books to be extremely useful in their classes. It will be noted that following each entry is a general classification of each book, i.e., perspective, construction, etc.

It would be an impossible task to list all of the catalogs and pamphlets from manufacturers of building supplies and materials, as well as associations and numerous pieces of advertising. It is hoped that this list will aid the student and teacher alike.

Anderson, L. O., and Heyer, O. C. *Wood Frame House Construction*. Washington, D.C.: U.S. Department of Agriculture, 1955. (Building construction — residential)

Badzinski, Stanley, Jr. *Stair Layout*. Chicago: American Technical Society, 1971. (Comprehensive study of stair layout for residential and commercial design)

Baer, Barbara. *How to Improve Your Home by Landscaping*. New York: H. S. Stuttman Co., 1958. (Landscaping)

Book of Successful Fireplaces . . . How to Build Them. Cleveland: The Donley Brothers Company, 1960. (Fireplaces)

Burke, Arthur E., Dalzell, J. Ralph, and Townsend, Gilbert. *Architectural and Building Trades Dictionary*. Chicago: American Technical Society, 1955. (Dictionary)

Carpentry and Building Construction. Washington: Department of the Army, 1960. (Building construction-residential)

Dalzell, J. Ralph, and Townsend, Gilbert. *Masonry Simplified Vol. 2; Practical Construction*. Chicago: American Technical Society, 1957. (Masonry construction)

Doblin, Jay. *Perspective*. New York: Whitney Library of Design. 1956. (Simplified approach to perspective)

Doty, Walter L., and Johnson, Paul C. *Landscaping for Modern Living*. Menlo Park, California: Lane Book Company, 1958. (Landscaping)

Durbahn, Walter E., and Sundberg, Elmer W. *Fundamentals of Carpentry, Vol. 2: Practical Construction. 4th Ed*. Chicago: American Technical Society, 1970. (Building construction-residential)

Faulkner, Ray, and Faulkner, Sarah. *Inside Today's Home*. 3rd Ed., New York: Holt, Rinehart and Winston, Inc., 1968.

Design, construction, furnishing, and function of homes)

Giachino, J. W., and Beukema, Henry J. *Engineering Technical Drafting and Graphics.* 3rd Ed. Chicago: American Technical Society, 1972. (Engineering drawing)

Godfrey, Robert Sturgis (Ed.) *Building Construction Cost Data 1965.* Duxbury, Mass.: Robert Snow Mean Co. (current year). (Estimating—commercial and residetial)

Goodban, William T., and Hayslett, Jack J. *Architectural Drawing and Planning.* New York: McGraw-Hill Book Company, 1965. (Architectural drawing)

Guptill, Arthur L. *Pencil Drawing Step by Step.* New York: Reinhold Publishing Corporation, 1959. (Pencil rendering techniques)

Halse, Albert O. *Architectural Rendering.* New York: McGraw-Hill Book Company, Inc., 1960. (Architectural rendering)

Harris, Charles O. *Elementary Structural Design.* Chicago: American Technical Society, 1951. (Strength of materials and design)

Hepler, Donald E., and Wallach, Paul I. *Architectural Drafting and Design,* 2nd Ed. New York: McGraw-Hill Book Company, 1971. (Architectural drawing)

How to Build Patio Roofs. Menlo Park, Calif.: Lane Book Company, 1956. (Patio roofs—contemporary)

Huntington, Whitney Clark. *Building Con-struction.* New York: John Wiley & Sons, Inc., 1963. (Technical aspects of build-ing construction—commercial)

Jones, Richard A. *Household Storage Study.* Urbana, Illinois: University of Illinois—Small Homes Council, 1963. (Storage spaces—residential)

Kaufmann, Edgar, and Raeburn, Ben. *Frank Lloyd Wright: Writings and Build-ings.* New York: Meridian Books, Inc., 1960. (Foundations of contemporary ar-chitecture)

Light Frame House Construction. Washing-ton, D.C.: U.S. Department of Health, Education, and Welfare. (Building con-struction—residential)

Load Calculation for Residential Winter and Summer Air Conditioning. Cleve-land, Ohio: National Warm Air Heating & Air Conditioning Association, 1964. (Air conditioning)

Lockard, William Kirby. *Drawing as a Means to Architecture.* New York: Rein-hold Book Corporation. 1968. (Drawing as part of the architectural design proc-ess)

Marshall, Robert A. *Before You Buy a House.* Washington, D.C.: Kiplinger Washington Editors, Inc., 1964. (Financ-ing the home)

Martin, C. Leslie. *Architectural Graphics.* New York: The Macmillan Co., 1970. (Perspective) 2nd Ed.

Minimum Property Standards for One and Two Family Living Units. Washing-ton, D.C.: Federal Housing Administra-tion, 1973. (U.S. Government property requirements for FHA and GI loans)

Mix, Floyd M., and Cirou, Ernest H. (Eds.). *Practical Carpentry.* Homewood, Ill.: (Goodheart-Wilcox Co., Inc., 1969. (Building construction—residential)

Morgan, Sherley W. *Architectural Drawing: Perspective, Light, and Shadow Render-ing.* New York: McGraw-Hill Book Co., 1950. (Perspective and rendering)

Moselle, Gary (Ed.) *National Construction Estimator.* Los Angeles: Craftsman Book Company (current year). (Estimating—commercial and residential)

Parker, Harry. *Simplified Engineering for Architects and Builders.* 4th Ed. New York: John Wiley & Sons, Inc., 1967. (Understandable explanations for the de-sign of structural members)

Parker, Harry, and MacGuire, John W. *Simplified Site Engineering for Architects and Builders.* New York: John Wiley & Sons, Inc., 1954. (Analysis and prepara-tion of site plans)

Ramsey, Charles G., and Sleeper, Harold R. *Architectural Graphic Standards.* Jo-seph N. Boaz, Editor. New York: John Wiley & Sons, Inc., 1970. (Standard ref-erence)

Smali Homes Council. *Kitchen Planning Guide.* Urbana, Ill.: University of Illinois —Small Homes Council, 1965. (Kitchen planning)

Small Homes Council, Urbana, Ill.: Univer-sity of Illinois.

A 1.3 *Financing the Home.*

A 2.0 *Business Dealings with the Architect and the Contractor.*
B 1.1 *Selecting Livable Neighborhoods.*
B 2.1 *A Guide to Selecting the Home Site.*
B 3.0 *Fundamentals of Land Design.*
C 1.1 *Hazard-Free Houses for All.*
C 2.1 *Designing the House.*
C 2.5 *Split Level Houses.*
C 3.2 *Solar Orientation.*
C 5.1 *Household Storage Units.*
C 5.3 *Planning the Kitchen.*
C 5.31 *Cabinet Space for the Kitchen.*
C 5.32 *Kitchen Planning Standards.*
C 5.33 *Separate Ovens.*
C 5.4 *Laundry Areas.*
C 5.9 *Garages and Carports.*
D 7.0 *Selecting Lumber.*
D 7.2 *Plywood.*
D 9.0 *Plastics as Building Materials.*
E 2.1 *Construction Methods.*
F 2.0 *Basements.*
F 2.5 *Termite Control.*
F 3.0 *Wood Framing.*
F 4.3 *Concrete Floors.*
F 4.4 *Crawl-Space Houses.*
F 4.6 *Flooring Materials.*
F 6.0 *Insulation in the Home.*
F 6.2 *Moisture Condensation.*
F 7.0 *Chimney and Fireplaces.*
F 9.1 *Counter Surfaces.*
F 11.0 *Window Planning Principles.*
F 11.1 *Selecting Windows.*
F 11.2 *Insulating Windows and Screens.*
F 12.3 *Roofing Materials.*
F 15.0 *Hardware.*

F 17.2 *Brick and Concrete Masonry.*
G 3.1 *Heating the Home.*
G 3.2 *Controls for Central Heating Systems.*
G 3.5 *Fuels and Burners.*
G 4.0 *Plans for Electricity.*
G 4.2 *Electrical Wiring.*
G 5.0 *Plumbing.*
G 5.5 *Septic-Tank Systems.*
G 6.0 *Summer Comfort.*
H 1.0 *Interior Design.*

Smith, R. C. *Materials of Construction.* New York: McGraw-Hill Book Company, 1966. (Complete range of residential and commercial building materials)

Smith, Ronald C. *Principles and Practices of Light Construction.* Englewood Cliffs, N.J.: Prentice-Hall, Inc., 1963. (Building construction—residential)

Steinberg, Joseph, Stempel, Martin. *Estimating for the Building Trades.* Chicago: American Technical Society, 1973. (Estimating)

Sundberg, Elmer. *Building Trades Blueprint Reading: Part 1 Fundamentals,* 5th Edition, Chicago: American Technical Society, 1972. (Blueprint reading)

Sundberg, Elmer, Battenberg, Rex, and Paul, W. Rahy. *Building Trades Blueprint Reading: Part 2.* Chicago: American Technical Society, 1959. (Print reading)

Sundberg, Elmer. *Building Trades Blueprint Reading: Part 3, General Construction.* Chicago: American Technical Society, 1973. (Print reading)

Sweet's Catalog Service. *Architectural Catalog File.* New York: F. W. Dodge Corporation (most current year). (Reference)

Sweet's Catalog Service. *Light Construction Catalog File.* New York: F. W. Dodge Corporation (most current year). (Reference)

Time-Saver Standards. New York: F. W. Dodge Corp. (Reference)

Townsend, Gilbert, Dalzell, J. Ralph, and Battenberg, Rex. *How to Plan a House.* Chicago: American Technical Society, 1958. (Home planning)

Watson, Ernest, and Watson, Aldren. *The Watson Drawing Book.* New York: Reinhold Publishing Corporation, 1962. (Rendering techniques—different media)

Williams, Henry Lionel, and Williams, Ottalie K. *A Guide to Old American Houses, 1700-1900.* New York: A. S. Barnes and Company, Inc., 1962. (American architecture)

Wright, Frank Lloyd. *The Natural House.* New York: Horizon Press, Inc., 1954. (A portion of Wright's philosophy)

Index